Modern Chinese Literary Thought

WRITINGS ON LITERATURE
1893–1945

Modern Chinese Literary Thought

WRITINGS ON LITERATURE

1893–1945

EDITED BY

Kirk A. Denton

Stanford University Press
Stanford, California 1996

Stanford University Press
Stanford, California

© 1996 by the Board of Trustees of the
Leland Stanford Junior University

Published with the assistance of the
National Endowment for the Humanities

Printed in the United States of America

CIP data appear at the end of the book

Stanford University Press publications are distributed
exclusively by Stanford University Press within the
United States, Canada, Mexico, and Central America;
they are distributed exclusively by Cambridge University
Press throughout the rest of the world.

For Bi Zhiwei and Yangyang

Preface

The selection of texts for a compilation such as this inevitably implicates issues of canonicity and literary history and the political and ideological motivations behind their formation. In China after 1949, the cultural wing of
the Chinese Communist Party intervened through institutions under its
control into the academic construction of a modern literary history. This
history was portrayed as an ineluctable march toward the telos of class-
based literature of political utility enshrined in Mao Zedong's "Yan'an
Talks" of 1942. Writers, works, and literary thought that did not fit this
schema were criticized and/or excluded. Compendiums of literary criticism and literary polemics gave prominence to leftist critics and those who
espoused a revolutionary role for literature; aesthetic, humanist, classicist,
and popular views of literature were included as addenda (as documents
for criticism) or excluded altogether. Although I intend with this collection
to move well beyond the narrow parameters of this Maoist interpretation,
in the selection of texts I nonetheless maintain something of its basic structure and continue to accord an important place to revolutionary views of
literature. Not to do so would be to misrepresent the fact that the idea of a
political role for literature was shared, to greater and lesser degrees, by a

broad base of writers who felt compelled, as much by a personal sense of national crisis as by threats from political leaders, to adopt "progressive," engaged views of writing. To disregard such views or play down their significance is to fail to come to terms with a reality of modern Chinese literature, however distasteful some might find that reality. In other words, the Maoist construction of modern literary history was not simply a fabrication by a handful of ideologues motivated solely by political interest; it reflects ideas central to the literary experience of many writers and theorists. At the same time, however, *Modern Chinese Literary Thought* recognizes that the political ideology generating this history of modern Chinese literature silenced, until the liberalization of the 1980's, many views of literature that held an attraction for writers and literary figures when they were first disseminated. This compilation includes a range of these marginalized views and thus reflects more fully, less as a mythic Marxist monolith, the development of modern Chinese literary thought. Further, the juxtaposition of "canonical" texts with the "marginal" should contribute to an understanding of how canon has been shaped in modern China and show us that this canon, like all canons, constantly evolves through a dialectical interplay with the marginal.

I have chosen the essays, then, based on their relative importance as examples of canonical and marginal voices in modern Chinese views of literature. "Canonical" status has been determined by (1) appearance in Chinese compilations on modern literary debates (from both before and after 1949); (2) impact on contemporary literary circles; (3) high frequency of citation in Chinese and Western scholarship on modern Chinese literature; (4) and my own personal assessment of their value. Important "marginal" texts were more difficult to determine, of course, because of their marginality. Some were chosen because they have become meaningful to a new generation of literary critics in the liberalization of the post-Mao era. I have included "aesthetic" critics (Wen Yiduo, Shen Congwen, Zhu Guangqian), modernists (Dai Wangshu, Li Jinfa), humanists (Liang Shiqiu, Su Wen), and what might be called subjectivists (Hu Feng) for this reason. Included also are essays expressing the literary values of certain marginalized groups, in particular women writers (Lu Yin, Zhang Ailing, Bing Xin, Ding Ling) and popular writers (Wang Dungen, Zhou Shoujuan).

This volume differs from standard interpretations of literary development in terms of periodization by beginning with texts from the late Qing period (1895–1911). Although 1917 has conventionally been designated as the inception of modern Chinese literature, I view the late Qing period as instrumental in the breakdown of traditional literary values, a process that led naturally to the reversal of linguistic and generic hierarchies in the May

Fourth period and the emergence of "modern" literature. Within the writings of important late Qing writers (Liang Qichao, Wang Guowei, Lu Xun, Liu Shipei, Lin Shu) can be found the roots of many of the literary views expressed by May Fourth writers. The remainder of the collection conforms somewhat more closely to the structure of literary debate conventionally presented in PRC literary histories. These essays are organized in a loose chronological order and divided into sections defined by either a recognizable cultural-historical period (i.e., the May Fourth) or by the context of a specific literary issue or debate. The essays are taken from both sides of most of the major literary debates of the Republican period and deal with a variety of broad literary issues including language and literary form, the role of the writer in politics, the relationship between the text and the external world, the effect of literary works on readers, and the role of the writer in literary creation.

Although I want to stress their varied and multiple quality, I also view (see the General Introduction) these writings as working within certain parameters and assumptions determined by cultural tradition and historical imperatives. Because they direct attention to the limits of Chinese literary modernity, especially as determined by ties to traditional literary and philosophical values, the views that I express in the introduction may be perceived as essentialist. It is my purpose, however, to counter the prevailing tendency of accepting uncritically the claims to radical anti-traditionalism within the discourse of Chinese modernity. When reacting against one negative tendency in scholarship, one inevitably risks the dangers of another. Of course, I do not hold the relativist's position of absolute (essential) differences between Chinese and Western literary values. In reaching out to non-Chinese literary values, the writers represented in this compilation were acting very much outside of their tradition. Yet, I want to avoid the smug Western assumption that the reception of Western literary values resulted in an exact copy of the original, for to assume this would be to deny the continuing force of tradition, to whitewash the historical context, and to silence the creative voices of these interpreters of the West. The dangers of this form of Orientalism are, to my mind, far worse than that which points to differences.

By presenting the Western reader with a Chinese discourse (in the more traditional sense of this word) about literature, I hope to help that reader construct a cultural context surrounding the production of the texts of modern Chinese literature. What these translations offer, in short, is a kind of cultural-historical intentionality, or motivation, without which the Western reader sometimes labors to understand its literary texts. Why did modern Chinese writers write? What goals did they have in mind? How did they think about literature and its relation to the world and its audience? To listen to responses to these questions is to deepen our understanding of Chinese literature and the experience of modernity at its root.

This compilation is offered in the spirit of contributing Third World, non-Western voices to the cultural discourses in Western academia in order to invigorate and enliven those discussions and open Western eyes to non-Western ways of looking at literature. I hope also that these texts prove useful to scholars less interest in specific literary issues and more in the general nature of modernity in China. These writings express and reflect some of the tensions and contradictions at the heart of Chinese modernity; they are sites for the contending discourses that constitute the complexity of that modernity. In this respect, they should be invaluable sources for historians of China, as well as those engaged in cross-cultural studies of the experience of modernity, especially in Third World countries.

I would like to extend a word of gratitude to the many people who helped realize this project which was long in coming. First, to all the translators, who worked selflessly and without remuneration, my deepest respect and thanks. The work of the translator is sorrily unappreciated in academia, and I hope this project makes some contribution toward rectifying that situation. My sincere gratitude to Nick Kaldis for his painstaking and careful work in editing this volume. I want to thank Theodore Huters, Minru Li, and Eugene Ouyang for their careful readings of the text and their most helpful suggestions for revision. John Ziemer's meticulous editorial scrutiny was invaluable. A personal note of thanks to Lao Yan–shuan and Timothy Wong for their many insights into thorny problems of translation. Xiaomei Chen's spirit of friendship and collegiality lent great support to my work. Howard Goldblatt offered valuable advice. Thanks also to Milena Doleželová-Velingerová for her intellectual guidance, particularly in the area of May Fourth studies. Words cannot express my feelings of gratitude to Bi Zhiwei for her love and care.

The Ohio State University College of Humanities Seed Grant and Grant-in-Aid helped to make this book possible, as did generous leave support from the Department of East Languages and Literatures. Support for publication also came from the National Endowment for the Humanities.

K.D.
Columbus, Ohio

Contents

PART III: REVOLUTIONARY LITERATURE, 1923–1930

PART IV: THE DEBATE ON LITERARY FREEDOM, 1932–1935

Modern Chinese Literary Thought

WRITINGS ON LITERATURE
1893–1945

General Introduction

Kirk A. Denton

The essays on modern Chinese literary thought compiled in this collection were written in a period of profound turmoil brought on by the combined effects of internal political and social erosion and the external threat of Western and Japanese imperialism. They are the product of the historical crisis that developed as China's long cultural heritage, faced with the technological and military superiority of the West and Japan, appeared increasingly obsolete and incapable of self-regeneration. Intellectuals, the stewards of this elite cultural tradition, were compelled to confront fundamental questions about the origins of this cultural collapse and the sources of China's future rejuvenation.[1] This process of intellectual exploration and the move toward modernity was embodied in, among other things, writings about literature, which stands at the very heart of this cultural tradition.

---

1. For a discussion of the modern category of intellectual, *zhishi fenzi* 知識分子 (literally "knowledgeable elements"), see Schwarcz 1986: 9–10; and Link 1992: 14. The English term "literati" is often used to designate the traditional Chinese scholar who, in the common view, lacked the kind of autonomy we associate with the term "intellectual."

The translations of writings about literature in this volume give voice to a difficult and complex experience with modernity.

Much of the literary thought contained in these essays is couched in terms of a break with tradition through an appropriation of radically alien Western literary values. Modernity and Westernization, though not exactly synonymous, were seen to move hand in hand. This introduction will not attempt to describe modern Chinese literary thought in terms of a Western influence exerted on it. Tagore (1967), Bonnie McDougall (1971) and Marián Gálik (1969; 1980) have contributed greatly to our understanding of the scope and depth of Western literary values in the development of modern Chinese literary criticism. Nor is it intended to be a comprehensive survey of critical writings of the modern period, or even a detailed analysis of the essays included in this volume.[2] In drawing out from these essays as a whole underlying literary orientations and discussing these orientations in relation to the tradition they ostensibly reacted against and the Western literary discourse in which they were formulated, I wish instead to direct attention away from the effects of Western influence and refocus it on that of continuity with the past.[3] In so doing, I do not mean to underemphasize the critical role of Western literary values in the development of Chinese literary modernity. The literary thought contained in these essays is clearly conceived within a distinctly Western discourse that would appear to have little obvious relation to tradition. Yet to read this discourse as an exact facsimile of the Western model is to silence the creative agency of the Chinese intellectuals who appropriated it to fulfill certain needs determined by their cultural tradition and the historical crisis that seemed to threaten their nation's existence. It would assume, moreover, the universality of Western literary values and the possibility of their being grafted seamlessly onto another cultural context without undergoing substantial metamorphosis. In presenting these essays to a Western audience, I want instead to draw attention to the historical and cultural intention behind modern Chinese literature both as a way of restoring to it its distinct otherness and as a means of challenging assumptions about the universality of Western literary val-

---

2. For analytical descriptions of important critical writings, see Gálik 1980. For the reader's convenience, each of the five sections of the present volume begins with a brief introduction contextualizing the essays included in that section.

3. Few critics in the West or China have bothered to look at modern Chinese views of literature as in any way connected to those of tradition. James J. Y. Liu concludes *Chinese Theories of Literature* with Wang Guowei (1877–1927). Marián Gálik makes insightful remarks connecting modern Chinese criticism to traditional literary values, but they are rather incidental and not central to his study. The exception is Pollard's (1973) helpful study of the relation between Zhou Zuoren's literary philosophy and traditional views of literature.

ues.[4] Modern Chinese literary discourse and the discourse of modernity were not, in other words, empty imitations unaltered from the Western cultural-historical context. As Lydia Liu has suggested, the discourse of modernity was "deployed" by Chinese intellectuals and "reinvented" in its new context.[5] Naturally, tradition exerted an influence in this process of re-invention.

The construction of Chinese literary modernity as a radical rupture with tradition, a perception that has only recently come under critical scrutiny in the sinological community, is an inheritance of the polemical iconoclasm of the May Fourth generation[6] and their Marxist descendants, who essent-ialized and absolutized a complex and multifarious tradition in order to distance themselves from it and more easily reject it. Grounded in the fun-damental assumptions of this May Fourth iconoclastic paradigm, scholar-ship has tended to stress the determining role of Western literary values in Chinese literary modernity without reflecting critically on how tradition shaped those values.[7] Those like Yü-sheng Lin (1989), who maintain a via-ble role for tradition in the "creative transformation" of Chinese society, have led the way in questioning the May Fourth paradigm's reification of tradition. Chang Hao (1989a) has challenged the homogeneity of the May Fourth's own discourse of iconoclasm and national liberation by exposing

4. Gregory Jusdanis, in *Belated Modernity and Aesthetic Culture: Inventing National Literature*, nicely expresses this project: "By focusing on what was practiced prior to literature, by examining how literature was institutionalized in another culture, we can come to understand that the 'methods, channels, and means' of present literary knowledge are not timeless and shared by all humanity but are the products of Western European culture of the last two hundred years. If we restore to the institutions of literature and criticism their history and otherness, we can realize that our apparently individual reactions to universally-recognized literary works are more than innocent responses to self-evident truths" (1991: xvii).

5. Lydia Liu (1993: 161) writes: "My emphasis on the act of deployment is intended to shift the critique of the post-Enlightenment European concept of the subject to the site where meaning does not belong to European philosophical traditions alone (even though the concept itself might have 'originated' there), but 'travels' and gets reinvented in the constant flux of historical practices, not the least of which is the encounter between languages through translation and translingual practice."

6. I take the May Fourth to be the pivotal period in the formation of Chinese modernity. My understanding of the May Fourth movement includes both the political events surrounding the May Fourth incident of 1919 (patriotic anti-imperialism and a broadening nationalist spirit) and the cultural dimension, a radical assault on tradition that began with the founding of the journal *New Youth* in 1915. For a more detailed discussion of the May Fourth period, see the introduction to Part II of this compilation.

7. In Western scholarship, C. T. Hsia (1971) and Leo Ou-fan Lee (1973) are examples of important scholars grounded in the May Fourth paradigm. Průšek (1980) in his writings at once seeks the roots of modern literature in tradition and accepts the theory of radical disjunction.

its tensions between the poles of nationalism and internationalism, rationalism and romanticism, individualism and collectivism, skepticism and reli-
giosity. Chinese modernity is much more than its "meta-narratives" would
have us believe.[8] Iconoclasm, or the discourse of liberation from tradition,
was the pivot around which a broad complex of sometimes conflicting
ideas revolved. Drawing from these and other recent revisionist views of
the May Fourth, this introduction will delve beneath the discursive surface
to explore how and why Western literary values were appropriated and the
limits placed on that appropriation by both traditional literary and philosophical values and the imperatives of China's socio-historical situation.[9]
Some understanding may then be reached about the complex formation of
China's literary modernity.

Laying emphasis on the legacy of tradition within Chinese modernity
and its cultural "difference" from the West runs the risk, of course, of
absolutizing that difference as an immutable "essence."[10] In other words, in
the process of crossing over the distinct demarcation line that has conventionally divided tradition and modernity in sinological studies, it may be
necessary at times to set China off against the West. Nevertheless, the risk
is well worth taking for what it might yield as a positive counter to views
that have too uncritically accepted the totalizing discourse of Chinese modernity's rupture with the past. I hope to move away from modernity's
claim to an absolute eradication of the past and embrace a view of tradition
and modernity as "continuous rather than separate, dialectically related
rather than diametrically opposed."[11] In viewing Chinese modernity as a

---

8. Lyotard's (1984) critique of "modernity" has been useful in helping me to think
about the Chinese experience. What is interesting is that there are areas of overlap in the
radical post-modern critique of modernity and that from the conservative sinological
camp described above.

9. Marston Anderson's study *The Limits of Realism: Chinese Fiction in the Revolutionary
Period* has been very influential in shaping the direction of my ideas.

10. Rey Chow has been most outspoken in her criticism of this "Orientalist" tendency:
"In the name of investigating 'cultural difference,' ethnic markers such as 'Chinese' easily
become a method of differentiation that precisely block criticism from its critical task by
reinscribing potentially radical notions such as 'the other' in the security of fastidiously
documented archival detail. A scholarly nativism that functions squarely within the Orientalist dynamic and that continues to imprison 'other cultures' within entirely conventional
disciplinary boundaries thus remains intact"(1993: 6). See also Longxi Zhang 1993: 86–87.

11. Jusdanis's (1991) concept of "belated modernity" has been helpful in formulating
ideas about the presence of tradition within modernity in twentieth-century China.
Jusdanis has drawn from Ian and Suzanne Rudolph's study of Indian modernity, in which
objection is made to the polarization of tradition and modernity in modernization scholarship. This polarization reduces the traditional in modernity to "residual categories" and
underestimates the "modern potentialities" within tradition.

synthetic or hybrid interaction of various cultural discourses, my approach is in spirit fundamentally opposed to the portraying of cultures as inert essences without areas of commensurability.[12]

Nationalism, Iconoclasm, and Modernity

Setting a historical context for these writings in a few paragraphs necessarily entails facile generalization and whitewashing of its complexity. (The reader should consult more detailed historical narratives of modern China for a more complete picture.)[13] In describing the historical context, it is imperative to convey at the very least the sense of urgency and crisis felt by educated Chinese as the reality of their society's disintegration conflicted with their ideals of China's cultural grandeur.

The roots of China's modern crisis extend back to the eighteenth century when a dramatic rise in population put new pressures on the limited resource of arable land, pressing an increasing number of peasants from the relative security of landownership into the economic precariousness of tenancy and landlessness. This disenfranchised class fed a series of peasant uprisings, the most extensive of which was the Taiping Rebellion (1851-64), that devastated the social fabric of traditional peasant life, forcing millions to flee the countryside for the coastal urban centers. Faced with reduced tax revenues and unable to subdue these rebellions with military forces under their own command, the Manchu leaders in the Qing court were compelled to petition the support of Chinese generals of questionable loyalty. The rebellions were eventually quelled, but in the process the power of these Chinese generals expanded, further undermining Qing central authority.

Although in previous times China had been remarkably open to and heavily influenced by foreign cultures, the Qing ruling elite was generally unreceptive to contact with the Western merchants and missionaries clamoring to gain access to the untapped financial and spiritual markets of the Chinese interior. Their staunchly conservative attitude toward Westernization only further weakened China in its response to the continued threat of Western imperialism. Through the nineteenth century, from the First Opium War (1839-42) to the Sino-Japanese War (1894-95), the European powers and Japan (which had since 1860 launched a broad reform movement based on the Western model of modernity) bent the Qing court to their will

---

12. Stephan Chan (1993) and Lydia Liu (1993), drawing from cultural studies theory, have begun to look at Chinese modernity as "sites of contending discourses." I have been influenced by their examples.

13. Jonathan Spence's *The Search for Modern China* is a good place to begin.

with their technological and military might. By the final decade of the century China had been "sliced up like a melon," as a contemporary metaphor put it, into spheres of Western influence. Although, unlike India, China was never politically colonized, it suffered from a devastating economic colonialism centered around the opium trade. The Qing court, wrapped up in internecine factionalism, proved unable to respond to the external threats to China's sovereignty, and reformist movements launched from outside the court by enterprising Chinese literati found few sympathetic ears within the government.

As destructive and violent as the nineteenth century was, the twentieth century would prove even more so. Following the anti-climactic overthrow of the two-thousand-year-old dynastic system of universal kingship in 1911 and the failure of subsequent attempts to establish parliamentary democracy, China plunged into a ten-year period of political fragmentation commonly referred to as the Warlord Era (1916–27). In response to this political disintegration and to the humiliating terms of the Treaty of Versailles (which ceded to Japan territorial rights to part of Shandong province) arose the 1919 May Fourth movement. A reformed Nationalist Party (GMD)[14] and the Chinese Communist Party (CCP), which shared anti-imperialist platforms, emerged directly from the fervent nationalism of the May Fourth period. With the advice and guidance of the Comintern, these two political parties joined forces in 1926 in a "revolutionary" movement known as the Northern Expedition aimed at subduing the regional warlords and restoring to China national unity under a central authority. This alliance was ruptured, however, in 1927, midway through the Northern Expedition, when the GMD turned against its Communist allies in a bloody coup. The remnants of the CCP were forced to seek refuge in the remote mountainous regions of southeastern China, and CCP policy gradually shifted from the urban orientation of classical Marxism to the peasant-based revolutionary movement espoused by the young Mao Zedong.

The 1930's were marked by a series of destructive military campaigns launched by the GMD on these CCP rural bases. Although not without heavy losses on its own part, the GMD was ultimately successful in uprooting the CCP, forcing it on its Long March to the northwest where it established a new base of power in the remote region around the town of Yan'an. With the imminent threat of full-scale invasion presented by the

---

14. The Nationalist Party, or Guomindang, was first established by Sun Yat-sen in 1912. It was banned by Yuan Shikai in 1913 and forced into exile in Japan, where it was renamed the Revolutionary Party (Gemingdang) in 1914. After the May Fourth movement, Sun resurrected the party's original name and a new constitution was written.

Japanese imperial army, ensconced since 1931 in the Manchurian provinces of northeastern China, these rival parties united once again in 1936 and remained so, at least officially, for the duration of what the Chinese refer to as the War of Resistance Against Japan (1937–45). The Chinese people suffered unspeakable atrocities at the hands of the Japanese military occupiers; untold numbers of civilians were raped and brutally slaughtered, and millions were forced to flee their homes for the mountainous interior provinces, which offered the insulation and protection necessary for a war of attrition. The end of the war brought a temporary respite from the horrors of occupation, but the uneasy peace quickly disintegrated, and civil war erupted once again between these long-standing political rivals. Only with the stunning Communist victory in 1949 did something like unity and social stability end this century of devastating internal warfare and imperialist humiliation.

The external threat of imperialism in the late nineteenth and early twentieth centuries and China's state of internal weakness fostered two major responses in the intellectual discourse, at once inextricably intertwined and locked in an uneasy tension: nationalism and iconoclasm. Chinese nationalism, a modern conception of national unity rooted in notions of domestic wealth and power, arose as a natural response to imperialist aggression in China.[15] The nation became a central idea with which China would resist the West. As Joseph Levenson (1965: 1: 105–8) argued, by supplanting traditional "culturalism," in which unity was derived from a set of cultural values embodied in sacred texts explicated by an intellectual elite, modern nationalism opened the way for the iconoclastic assault on tradition by offering an alternative basis for unity; this assault consequently intensified the psychological need for nationalism. Modernity in China, echoes Theodore Huters, included both the need to reject the past and the idea of national salvation from the imperialist threat (1993: 151). Interconnected and overlapping as the discourses of nation and iconoclasm were, they were also implicitly in tension. Whereas nationalism required the construction of a

---

15. I would agree with Dawa Norbu who in his *Culture and the Politics of Third World Nationalism* writes that the form nationalism takes in a particular society depends much on a sense of shared cultural tradition and transclass interests (1992: 22–30). To see nationalism in terms of a uniform response to the West is misleading and simplistic. However, it seems to me undeniable that, although the shape of its nationalism derived from cultural factors, the initial conceptualization of nationalism as a force in China had very much to do with the Western challenge. Prasenjit Duara (1993) argues against the conventional Levensonian view that modern nationalism is radically at odds with traditional culturalism. Whether or not it is continuous with certain traditional views of moral and ethnic unity, modern Chinese nationalism still marks, I believe, a changing consciousness about China's identity and its place in the world.

benign tradition on which to ground a sense of shared community, iconoclasm depicted the core of that tradition as a malignant tumor needing immediate excision. This basic tension between the two discourses is at the
root of the heterogeneity and complexity of Chinese modernity. Chinese intellectuals were caught in a difficult bind, both attracted to and repelled by
their own tradition and the Western model of modernity.

Although the late Qing period set the forces of nationalism and iconoclasm in motion, we can label this period neither wholly nationalist nor
thoroughly iconoclast.[16] The failure of the reformist movement of the 1860's
and 1870's, the humiliating defeat in the first Sino-Japanese War, and the
increasing awareness of the glaring superiority of Western technological
might led to a loss of faith in imperial institutions (including the emperor
himself) and to a collapse of their moral authority. Proposals for a Western-
style parliamentary government further eroded the legitimacy of the traditional worldview. The late Qing literatus suffered from what Hao Chang
has called a "crisis of orientational order," a breakdown of the symbolic order through which he understood the cosmos and his place in it. This crisis
led to a desperate need to "recreate a meaningful cosmos through a comprehensive worldview" (1987: 7–8). Thinkers like Kang Youwei and Liu
Shipei, drawing from a variety of indigenous and Western intellectual
sources, tried to develop philosophical systems that would restore a moral-
spiritual order to this vacuum. Kang, for example, sought to revive Confucianism by radically reinterpreting some of its canonical texts and portraying Confucius, who was conventionally glorified as a conservative longing
to restore the ideal rule of ancient sage-kings, as a progressive, utopian reformer.[17]

Other intellectuals engaged actively in introducing to their elite colleagues the ideas that had, so was their perception, buttressed the remarkable rise of the modern West: capitalism, individualism, law, and democracy. Through translations of books on a variety of subjects (i.e., Adam
Smith's *Wealth of Nations*, Thomas Huxley's *Evolution and Ethics*, John Stuart
Mill's *On Liberty*, and Montesquieu's *The Spirit of the Laws*), Yan Fu set out
to revive Chinese cultural grandeur with an infusion of the "Faustian-
Promethean" dynamism that lay at the heart, he felt, of Western wealth and
power (Schwartz 1964: 239–40). Lin Shu's free translations of over 200
Western European novels (most of them from the nineteenth century) into

---

16. For a discussion of late Qing intellectual contributions to the "collapse of scriptural
Confucianism," see Elvin 1990. For a general discussion of four major intellectual voices of
late Qing China, see Hao Chang 1987.

17. Kang's *Xinxue wei jing kao* 新學偽經考 (1891), *Kongzi gaizhi kao* 孔子改制考
(1897), and *Datong shu* 大同書 are perhaps his most important works in this regard.

classical prose were intended primarily to sustain the Ancient-Style Prose (*guwen*) and the traditional Confucian values that style was thought to embody. But by introducing Western cultural values through these translations, Lin Shu helped lay the groundwork for the iconoclasm of the May Fourth period and thus contributed to the collapse of the Confucian order he had wanted to restore (Huters 1988: 252–54).

In their writings and translations, these late Qing figures conceived a new "historical consciousness" that would mature in the May Fourth (1915–25) and post–May Fourth periods. China was thought to be in a state of crisis, tottering between tradition and modernity, on the verge of entering a new "historical age" with a new historical consciousness (Leo Ou-fan Lee 1990; Sun 1986–87). History was no longer viewed, as it had been traditionally, as the static repository of universal moral values that simply appear and reappear through its cyclical movement (Dirlik 1978: 7–8). The new historical consciousness saw China linked to the dynamic worldwide movement of history through stages progressing toward a better end.

Whereas the intent of late Qing intellectuals was the renewal of traditional values with a transfusion of Western ideas, intellectuals of the May Fourth used Western ideas (and an idea of the West) in a "totalistic" attack on tradition, which they felt was an absolute obstacle to China's modernization. As characterized by Yü-sheng Lin (1979), the May Fourth was a generation of "totalistic" iconoclasm, a radical anti-traditionalism perhaps unparalleled in world intellectual history.[18] Progressive, Western-trained intellectuals called for a sweeping elimination of the very core of the Confucian tradition, the ethics of *li*, a term that may be understood as an internalized code of behavior instilling, it was felt, an unhealthy subservience to political and parental authority. To them, Confucian ethics was at the heart of a sociopolitical system that dehumanized and oppressed the individual, and the only route to national regeneration was a radical assault on that ethics. To transform the outer world required a complete psychological and cultural reorientation.

This May Fourth idealism failed to have a discernible effect on the lives of China's poverty-ridden lower classes. Although the May Fourth ideals of enlightenment and cultural iconoclasm continued to appeal to some among the intellectual elite and were used by them in their struggle with political authority,[19] Marxism and Maoism gradually came to dominate intellectual

---

18. Hao Chang writes of the May Fourth generation: "The scope of their moral iconoclasm is perhaps unique in the modern world; no other historical civilization outside the West undergoing modern transformation has witnessed such a phoenix-like impulse to see its own cultural tradition so completely negated" (1976: 281).

19. For a discussion of the allegorical uses of the May Fourth, see Schwarcz 1986.

circles as the May Fourth ideals began to appear bankrupt in the face of horrendous social problems. Marxism appealed to Chinese intellectuals because it fulfilled at once their desires to destroy their past (anti-feudalism) and to combat the West (anti-imperialism) (Levenson 1965: 1: 134).[20] Given the absence in Republican China of the economic conditions of a developed capitalism, combined with a traditional propensity to emphasize the cultural and intellectual in social transformation, Marxism as it was received in China tended to have a highly voluntarist coloring and in that form seemed to offer a quick fix to China's predicament. Not all intellectuals were taken with Marxism, but those who were not failed to offer a viable alternative vision of China's future. Traditional and liberal-humanist voices could be heard beneath the revolutionary clamor, but the horrors of the age demanded immediate action and a comprehensive ideology that neither of these voices could generate. Liberalism and neo-traditionalism promoted gradualist approaches to social transformation that were at odds with the tenor of the times.[21]

Chinese modernity was constructed through an appropriation of Western discourses as a lever against tradition, as well as through an invention of China as a national community (for which a sense of a shared past was a necessary component). The May Fourth, the pivotal period in the formation of this modernity, sanctified an imagined West (as much a fictional construct as the West's idea of the Oriental other) and the values upon which its modernity was seen to be based, particularly science, democracy, and individualism. The literary scene was dominated, as will be discussed at length below, by the alien modes of realism and romanticism. This exalted view of the West and Western cultural values was arguably the product of Western imperialism's cultural hegemony itself: Chinese intellectuals promoted the very values of the West that were at the root of the imperialism they so fervently opposed because of a deeply felt sense of cultural inferiority provoked by that imperialism. Typical of the May Fourth valorization of the West is Hu Shi's statement that Western literature "will offer an absolutely sacred medicine to cure our lying, hypocritical, and shallow literature" (cited in Chou Min-chih 1984: 160). Yet, as Xiaomei Chen has suggested, the idea of the West was no mere passive glorification of Western values. The May Fourth generation actively appropriated Western ideas and the idea of the West as a lever from which to extricate Chinese society

---

20. Traditional organistic thinking about the unity of politics, morality, and culture may have offered a native cultural foundation upon which to receive Marxism.

21. For discussions of Chinese liberalism, see Yü-sheng Lin 1973; and Grieder 1970. For essays on traditionalism in the modern period, see Furth 1976; and Eber 1986.

from tradition. The very discourses fueling Western imperialism became in China a discourse of resistance. From the perspective of the May Fourth generation, this Chinese "Occidentalism" was a creative discourse of liberation from tradition. The idea of the West served the function of negotiating between the Chinese past and the future of a modern nation-state.[22]

Beneath the May Fourth reification of a malignant tradition, its obsession with the "new" and "modern," and the promotion of Westernization lay a profound unspoken anxiety about molding a culture without attachments to the past. To the May Fourth intellectual modernity meant the personal autonomy necessary for the iconoclastic assault on tradition, but also the sociopolitical engagement and national unity required for the anti-imperialist struggle and the building of the nation. In the iconoclastic tenor of the times, intellectuals sought to position themselves beyond the reach of political power to make their iconoclastic assault, but they also felt keenly the burden of an anti-imperialist nationalism that led them back toward political engagement and finally to a return to an intimate, if uncomfortable, relationship with political power, unwittingly resurrecting the traditional role of the Confucian scholar-bureaucrat. Cultural revolution in China has in practice seemed to restore the traditional more than it has succeeded in destroying it.

The emergence of modern Chinese literary thought was caught up in these tensions and polarities and reflects China's Janus-faced struggle with the West and with its own past. I hope to suggest in what follows that these tensions and polarities are at play in the Chinese reception of Western views of literature, specifically realism, romanticism and aestheticism. Western literary thought offered a tool to pry Chinese literature free from its traditional cosmological foundation (a propensity toward seeing the writer, reader, text, and world in terms of a harmonious unity), but it also provoked anxieties about erasing deeply rooted assumptions about the centrality of culture and the role of literature and the writer. This may not

---

22. "As a result of constantly revising and manipulating imperialistically imposed Western theories and practices, the Chinese Orient has produced a new discourse marked by a particular combination of the Western construction of China with the Chinese construction of the West, with both of these components interacting and interpenetrating each other" (Xiaomei Chen 1992: 688). Tani Barlow's concept of the "localization of sign" resonates with that of Chen. Barlow writes that signs from the West "enter and circulate within specific, autonomous, local political contexts. That is, once appropriated, signs accrue powers of their own. This happens not so much because of anything that is intrinsic or essential to the sign's initial meaning but rather because of its new role in a local sign system" (1991: 211–12). Lydia Liu's (1993) recent article on "translingual practices" similarily sees the Western "influence" in terms of an active appropriation of the alien other into a new cultural context.

seem like such a remarkable claim, but it is necessary to make it because of the power and appeal the idea of a radical break with tradition has had in the modern Chinese context and the sinological community at large.

Modern Writing on Literature: Form and Function

Form

It was the pivotally important May Fourth generation, though not without filiations to the previous generation, that consciously initiated the formation of a "modern" literary criticism in China and sought to cut itself off from traditional approaches to literature by seeking literary and critical models from the West. This process began in the late Qing when Liang Qichao and Wang Guowei became the first to reach out beyond their cultural borders for literary models unknown to their tradition, although they did so from within a set of very traditional assumptions about the role and function of literature. The May Fourth movement endeavored to establish a specialized field for writing on literature based on radically new literary orientations. They adopted the term "literary criticism,"[23] which assumed a compartmentalizing of writing about literature as an activity undertaken by a group of literary "professionals," something quite unthinkable in dynastic China where critics were always also creative writers and the amateur literary ideal reigned.[24] In traditional times, it was inconceivable that someone could write about literature without having intimate, firsthand experience in the creative process. Writing on literature was a form of creative writing (sometimes in verse) and was read and appreciated as much for its formal beauty and refined diction as for the ideas expounded. The May Fourth theorists wanted to professionalize writing on literature and to give it an objective, scientific grounding. Mao Dun, a leading member of the Literary Research Association, one of the many literary societies formed during the period, perhaps best represents this May Fourth critical ideal. At least in his early phase, Mao Dun was a "critic" whose literary activity was devoted almost solely to writing about literature.

Critics like Mao Dun who introduced this new practice of "literary criticism" wanted to disengage writing about literature, and thus literature it-

---

23. The term *wenxue piping* 文 學 批 評 entered into current use in China during the May Fourth period and was one of the many terms borrowed from a Japanese translation of a Western term, though *piping* was used in premodern writings on fiction as an alternate to *pingdian* 評點, or evaluative commentary (Rolston 1990: 5–6).

24. This professionalism was something the May Fourth strove for but failed to achieve (see below).

self, from the empty metaphysics they saw in much of traditional poetics. In his "Manifesto for the Reform of *Short Story Monthly*" (1921), Mao Dun, who had just taken over editorship of this journal of popular literature and "elevated" its editorial goals, complained of the absence of "literary criticism" in China. He argued that unlike the West, where literature and literary criticism developed together and reinforced each other, criticism had never existed in traditional China. This absence was inhibiting literature's development toward the modern and the progressive:

> Our nation has never had any real criticism. Since the standards are constantly changing, questions of evaluation are dictated by personal taste. "True literary men can only appear once we have literary critics" is a point we also resolutely affirm. But since we are not so bright, we must first introduce Western criticism to guide us. Yet we also have high regard for the importance of the spirit of free creativity, and although we strongly support criticism, we do not wish to become slaves of any ism. Nor do we wish our countrymen to blindly worship Western criticism as gospel truth, thereby putting a stranglehold on the spirit of free creativity. (1981: 1: 20–21)

What bothered Mao Dun in traditional criticism was its arbitrary application of subjective standards and its failure to "analyze" individual works and to explicate their meaning. In his "Literature and Life" (see Part II), he criticized traditional writers on literature for their inability to "come to grips with the problem of literariness" and to create for literature a realm apart from philosophy, philology, and other fields of intellectual endeavor. Hu Yuzhi, a colleague in the Literary Research Association, concurred with Mao Dun's assessment of traditional writing on literature and attributed it to a lack of a critical (scientific) spirit: "Hitherto the Chinese have lacked the spirit of criticism, so that this kind of critical literature has been completely non-existent in our country. The small degree of progress in our literary thinking is probably due to this" (cited in McDougall 1971: 220).

For Zhu Guangqian, a leading aesthetician of the 1930's and 1940's, premodern China had no "poetics," only *shihua*, "random notes, broad in subject, brief and to the point, refined and intimate, which are its good points; but its bad points are that it is chaotic and fragmentary, unsystematic; it tends toward the subjective and placing too much faith in tradition, and lacks the spirit of science and methodology." Zhu offered two explanations for this absence of poetics: (1) poets and readers alike shared the belief that the mystical nature of poetry could be understood intuitively but not adequately explained in words; to subject literature to a scientific analysis is to destroy its character; (2) Chinese psychology tended toward synthesis and not analysis; it was strong in intuition and weak in logic. Close analysis and logical induction, Zhu wrote, are the methods necessary for a poetics that should go beyond mere evaluation to determine why a poem is good or why it is not (1982: 2: 3–4).

A range of modern Chinese literary critics shared the view that traditional criticism was subjective, unsystematic, metaphysical, and above all unscientific,[25] and saw in it a fundamental methodological flaw.[26] Typical of the iconoclastic tenor of the times, tradition was denied and repressed to the point where many refused to recognize in it anything of value, or anything on which to build a modern literary criticism. The May Fourth attitude toward traditional criticism and to tradition as a whole tells us more about its own anxieties and fears of the past than it does about traditional literary criticism itself. There was, of course, a varied tradition of writing on literature that was a good deal more sophisticated than the May Fourth made it out to be. Metaphysical as much of it may have been, literary criticism did develop a technical-descriptive side on which a modern "scientific" criticism might have developed had May Fourth intellectuals been so inclined.[27] Yet, as Stephen Owen describes it, traditional writings on literature did not tend toward analytical descriptions of the literary artifact, whether the individual text or the literary system as a whole. An assumed unity between the "literary mind," language, and the external world precluded this critical orientation. Rather than the object of his representational desires, the external world served to stir in the poet's mind an emo-

---

25. Notable exceptions are Cheng Fangwu, Guo Moruo, and Zhou Zuoren, who in varying ways favored the subjective and creative involvement of the critic. But even these critics hesitated to support pure subjective criticism; see for example "Piping—xinshang—jiancha" 批 評 —欣 賞 —檢 查 (Criticism, appreciation, investigation) (Guo Moruo 1979: 271–77).

26. As Stephen Owen argues, Ye Xie's 葉 燮 (1627–1703) "Yuan shi" 原 詩 (The origins of poetry) marked perhaps the first time in the history of traditional literary criticism that a critic reviewed his predecessors and found them uniformly suffering from "conceptual disorganization" and lacking in methodological thoroughness, the same critique that May Fourth critics used against traditional criticism as a whole. As a fully developed theory, or poetics, Owen sees "The Origins of Poetry" as having much in common with Western literary theory (1992: 494). But this, Owen would agree, is the exception to the rule. Some fiction criticism arguably tended toward a structuralist-like poetics of narrative techniques (see Rolston 1990).

27. James J.Y. Liu (1975) divides traditional literary theories into the metaphysical, the pragmatic, the technical, and the expressive. The "metaphysical" theory points to literature's innate ability to embody the *Dao*, a cosmological force that is at once transcendent and immanent. The use of the term "metaphysical" in the Chinese context must be qualified, for it has nothing of the Western notion of metaphysics grounded in a fundamental disjunction of the noumenal and phenomenal, subject and object, spirit and flesh.

tional response that was then given shape through language. A poem was seen to originate not in the voluntaristic intention of the artist but in response to stimulation by the external world. Given this view of the creative process, little attention was given in critical writings to the work of art as the "product" of the artist's conscious intention and thus as an "artifact" whose techniques must be analyzed and compartmentalized into a systematic poetics, as was the case with Aristotle in the West. The centrality of poetics to Western literary criticism was inextricably tied to the view of the origins of the poem in the conscious intention of the poet's mind. China's holistic ontology, conversely, tended not to give rise to the elaboration of fully developed, all-explicating poetics of the literary artifact (Owen 1992: 21). Though technical manuals prescribing poetic form were common, more theoretically oriented poetics were not.

The focus of traditional writing on literature was the creative process, from its inception as a response to the external world to the conveyance of that response to the reader. Broadly speaking, what interested traditional Chinese critics was literature as a human communicative act that brought men together into a kind of spiritual unity with each other and with the cosmos. If we take Lu Ji's (261–303) "Essay on Literature" and Liu Xie's (ca. 465–ca. 522) *The Literary Mind and the Carving of Dragons* as typical of premodern writings on literature, this propensity toward emphasis on art as creative process is apparent.[28] Lu Ji's focus is broad; he is concerned in his relatively short essay with all aspects of literary creativity: from the self-cultivation of the writer prior to writing (through meditation and reading) to the psychology of the creative act itself. Although Lu Ji does offer a brief typology of literary genres and half of Liu Xie's book is organized around genres, the principal thrust of both is a description of the creative process. If Western criticism is text oriented, to vastly overgeneralize, then traditional Chinese criticism focuses on the author and his organic and creative interrelationship with the world and language.

This emphasis on the creative process continued in much of post-Song literary criticism in which writing is seen as an important part of one's moral and spiritual self-cultivation, an idea Richard Lynn (1975: 219) has expressed as follows: "The act of writing poetry itself was an act of self-cultivation. Poetry provided the framework or context within which the individual came to grips with himself and his environment. It not only gave him knowledge of self; it also provided him with a means to know the world outside himself—and, perhaps most important, it supplied the link

---

28. Lu Ji 陸機, *Wen fu* 文賦; tr. by Shih-hsiang Chen in Birch 1965: 1: 204–14. Liu Xie 劉勰, *Wenxin diaolong* 文心雕龍; for Chinese text and translation, see Liu Xie 1983.

between the two." Traditional criticism's relative inattention to the literary artifact derives from this emphasis on the writing process as a means for transcending the limitations of the self and joining with the other. This basic notion of the importance of art as process was reiterated by the Song philosopher Cheng Yi: "When I practice calligraphy, I am very serious (or reverent). My objective is not that the calligraphy must be good. Rather my practice is the way of moral training" (cited in de Bary 1975: 179).

Traditional writing on literature tended not to be formulated in systematic, sustained discursive arguments.[29] A Western reader might evaluate these writings in much the same way as the May Fourth did: highly subjective, impressionistic, and anecdotal views from writers presented as random, disconnected literary thoughts. China had no Aristotle who established a precedent of elaborating a comprehensive poetics. What statements on literature that do exist from the pre-Han period must be culled from Confucian and Daoist philosophical texts or from historical writings. It was not until the Han that writers first wrote essays devoted solely to the subject of literature.[30] Gradually, during the Wei-Jin period of dynastic fragmentation, a tradition of writing about literature matured along with a belletristic consciousness of literature (*wen*) as something separate from other forms of utilitarian writing (*bi*). Some of this writing is theoretical in that it examines essential issues about the origins or nature of literature, and some is comprehensive in that it treats all aspects of the literary process, but it is rarely presented in a way that would meet Western expectations for a rhetoric of literary theory. The *shihua*, or informal prose "remarks" on poetry that emerged in the Song and became perhaps the dominant form for the expression of literary thought, are a case in point. As Owen argues, it was precisely the fragmentary and spontaneous quality of these writings, taking precedence from the "recorded sayings" tradition of the *Analects*, that lent them an authenticity and a sincerity that appealed greatly to the contemporary Chinese reader (1992: 361). Apart from the *shihua* genre, there were few established forms specifically set aside for the expression of literary thought. Much of traditional literary thought was presented not in full-length expository essays but in letters and prefaces. Like poetry and prose, writing on literature was often occasional, written in response to personal requests or for specific social situations (Siu-kit Wong 1983: xxi). In short, the context and the forms in which views on literature were expressed did not lend itself to elaborate and systematic poetics.

---

29. Liu Xie's *Wenxin diaolong* may be the obvious exception to this claim.

30. Cao Pi's 曹丕 (187–226) "Lun wen" 論文 is usually seen as the first work of self-conscious literary criticism in China; see Luo n.d.: 104–5.

Modern writing on literature was formulated in reaction to a tradition the moderns were themselves in the process of reconstructing. Formally it is very different from its traditional counterpart, although I will suggest areas of resonance. Wang Guowei's essay "Incidental Remarks on Literature" (see Part I), for example, written in the transitional late Qing period, manifests obvious formal ties with traditional writings on literature. Influenced in his ideas by the aesthetic orientation of Kant and Schopenhauer, Wang's formal approach to writing on literature is nonetheless consistent with the *shihua* tradition (Bonner 1986: 123). With Liang Qichao's essays on fiction of the same period, we see the emergence of a more modern genre of criticism, although its lineage may perhaps be traced back to the "essay" (*fu*) form of writing about literature (Owen 1992: 10). In a semi-vernacular style, itself a mark of modernity, Liang's rhetoric is expository: he has a single point to make, and he argues it in a highly systematic fashion. He does make use of Buddhist terms (which he is careful to explain in detail), but Liang tends to avoid the abstruse and chameleon-like vocabulary of traditional writings on literature.[31]

May Fourth literary criticism owes much to Liang's language and expository style. Many of the writings included in this volume are literary "essays" in terms of genre and are highly systematic in terms of their presentation of ideas. With the full adoption of the vernacular, May Fourth writing on literature makes use of a medium that is, arguably, better suited to analytical description of complex ideas. The terminological problems of traditional writings on literature are avoided by widespread adoption of a critical vocabulary translated from Western languages, most often brought to China through the intermediary of the Japanese language. In adapting a Western critical vocabulary untainted by traditional metaphysics, modern literary writing seemed to establish firmer ground for a scientific approach to literature, at the same time as it served to conceal tradition behind a modern rhetorical facade.

Criticism from the May Fourth and post–May Fourth periods reflects the influence of Western discursive and stylistic practices, a more linear and architectonic argumentation, but it may still seem to some Western readers as lacking focus or a logical and forceful presentation of ideas. This may be attributed to the legacy of traditional prose writing that favored rhetorical strategies rather different from the Western tradition. The rhe-

---

31. Terminology has posed a serious problem for all modern critics of traditional literary thought. Terms are notoriously loose, and connotations depend much on context. That the term *zhi*, for example, has been variously translated as "will," "intention," "emotion," and "where the heart goes," says much about the multivalenced nature of this term and the inadequacy of English to capture it fully.

toric of one literary tradition may seem to lack argumentative power or
persuasiveness in another. The sort of rhetoric employed by Cai Yuanpei in
his essay "Replacing Religion with Aesthetic Education" (see Part II), for
example, may strike the Western reader in its repetitiveness as rather
forced and artificial, but this style derives great authority from a long prose
tradition dating back to the Confucian classics (particularly the *Mencius*).
Many of the texts may seem to be a blend of modern (Western) explicit rhetoric with the traditional propensity toward suggestiveness, evocation, and
implicitness. If some of these essays display a highly focused and organized rhetorical style, others have clearly inherited the traditional *suibi*, or
"random notes," style of seemingly fragmentary impressions that was valued precisely for its apparent spontaneousness and lack of artifice.

Expressing literary values through commentary on and evaluation of
other writers was a commonplace in traditional literary criticism. A vestige
of this tendency remains, for example, in "Class Struggle in Literature" (see
Part III) in which Yu Dafu legitimizes his own literary values by alluding to
a wide variety of Western writers, or in "On Reading *Ni Huanzhi*" (see Part
III) where Mao Dun expresses his own ideas on literature through a favorable critique of a novel of a like-minded writer. The modern critic continues
the long tradition of promoting creative imitation of past masters, although
the models of critical opprobrium are now Western. When Zhou Zuoren
writes that the salvation for Chinese fiction lies in sincere imitation of Western works,[32] one senses a transference of traditional filial admiration for
China's literary forebears onto "modern" Western literary fathers.

Like its traditional counterpart, writing on literature in the modern period tends not toward systematicity or the purely theoretical. Mao Dun's
extensive essays on literature, for example, were fragmentary and desul-
tory writings on single literary issues that he never integrated into a comprehensive theory. Mao Dun is typical of the May Fourth generation in his
expansive and eclectic literary interests. Modern writings on literature generally lack the methodological rigor that the May Fourth critics so desired
and are often highly subjective and impressionistic, poorly substantiated
with textual evidence and without solid theoretical frameworks. The essays
by Yu Dafu and Xu Zhimo included in this volume exemplify this impressionistic tendency. There is, moreover, in many of these writings a propensity toward exaggeration and hyperbole, toward making sweeping and
largely unsubstantiable claims for the powerful social role of literature.
From Lin Shu and Liang Qichao through Hu Shi and Xu Zhimo to Hu Feng

---

32. See "Riben jin sanshi nian xiaoshuo zhi fada" 日本近三十年小說之發達 (The
development of Japanese fiction over the past thirty years) (Hu Shi 1976: 2: 153–70).

and Mao Zedong, this is the case. Many of the essays were written for specific occasions, in the form of letters, prefaces, speeches, or polemical essays. Lu Xun, for example, used the preface to express some of his most important views on literature (see "Preface to *Call to Arms*" in Part II).[33] In many cases these writings were part of literary debates and, in responding to very specific literary concerns that were being argued intensely among a rather limited circle of writers, sometimes display a strong parochialness. Zhou Yang and Hu Feng, for example, both Marxist critics, engaged in the mid-1930's in a rather narrow debate about the nature of "type" and its place in realism. They were responding directly to each other's writings on the subject, and their essays suffer from the narrowness of polemical charge and countercharge. That modern writing on literature lacks scholarly rigor is also, of course, attributable to the fact that much of it was published in newspapers or popular literary journals by commercial writers trying to make a living from their prose.

Scientific criticism found it hard to bear the social and political burden placed on it and frequently slid into a mire of petty factionalism and narrow subjectivism (verifying the durability of the opening words of Cao Pi's "Discourse on Literature,": "Literary men disparage one another—it has always been that way").[34] Lu Xun complained in 1930 of the factionalism rife in critical circles:

> China has long had critics. Practically every literary group has its own set of literati. At least it has a poet, a novelist, and a critic whose function it is to proclaim the glories and achievements of the group. All these groups announce that they are out for reform and mean to storm the old strongholds; but on the way, at the foot of the old strongholds, they start squabbling among themselves till they have no energy left. Since all they do is "squabble," none of them is badly hurt—they are simply out of breath. And each as he pants imagines he is the victor and starts chanting triumphant paeans. There is no need for guards on the old stronghold—they can just stand there with folded arms, looking down on the comedy played out by these new foes. They keep silent, but they are the victors. (1980: 3: 109–10)

This literary factionalism ended up sheltering, according to Lu Xun, traditional values. To Lu Xun's regret, literary criticism had become the hand-

---

33. Lu Xun's prefaces to his many collections of writings (essays, prose poems, historical tales and fiction) tell us much about his authorial intention and offer important clues how to understand the works included in the particular collection.

34. Cao Pi in "Lun wen": "*wenren xiangqing, zigu er ran*" 文人相輕, 自古而然.

maiden of narrow political interests, the very condition modern literary criticism had sought in its inception to avoid.

The authors of these essays were, like their traditional counterparts, more often than not creative writers. Only a handful of those represented here (Zhu Guangqian, for example) were professional critics known more for their writing on literature than for their literary works. Mao Dun, who had devoted himself in the early 1920's to criticism, by 1927 began to concentrate on the writing of fiction, for which he is best known today. Many of the authors were at one time or another members of literary societies, and their ideas were often shared by a like-minded group of friends and associates. Some of the texts were written by high-ranking members of the CCP and were clearly motivated by specific political demands of the party. This is most obviously true of the essays by Qu Qiubai and those of Zhou Yang and Mao Zedong from the period of national crisis (1936–45). Zhou Yang's piece "On National Defense Literature" (see Part V), in its promotion of a united front in cultural affairs, was a direct product of the CCP decision to promote a political united front with the GMD, a policy issued ultimately from Comintern dictates (Wang-chi Wong 1991: 177–88).

It is clear from the limited circulation of the journals and literary supplements in which most appeared that the audience for these essays was a small coterie of elite, mostly Western- or Japanese-trained, male intellectuals. The average urban reader in late Qing and Republican China, more taken with the love stories and detective fiction of the popular Mandarin Ducks and Butterfly school, largely ignored works of modern literature as unappetizing and would surely have found the language and ideas of these writings on literature arcane and obscure. When Lu Xun's "On the Power of Mara Poetry" (see Part I) was first published, for example, it was read by almost no one, including members of the intellectual elite. Only with Mao Zedong's "Yan'an Talks" (see Part V) does writing on literature reach a fairly broad audience, though clearly not by popular demand.

In characterizing these modern writings on literature, it may be more appropriate to use the general and less restricted term "literary thought" rather than such culturally loaded terms as "literary theory" and "literary criticism" that may impose certain expectations that these essays cannot fulfill. In his study of modern Chinese literary criticism, Marián Gálik recognizes that writings on literature in modern China are rarely "studies of concrete works of art" and thus not consistent with the Western expectations for the generic category of literary criticism. Nor is modern literary thought particularly theoretical in orientation, although it does seek to offer generalized views on all essential aspects of the creative process, centering around the author, text, world, reader nexus. Like Owen in his study of traditional literary criticism, Gálik adopts the term "literary thought" (1980: 5) to characterize modern Chinese writings on literature. Although I will on occasion use the terms "theory" and "criticism," or "theorists" and "critics," "literary thought" better captures the nature of these writings on literature.

Function

Criticism, writes Terry Eagleton, is never a politically "innocent" discipline; it emerges at revolutionary junctures in a culture's historical development to become a crucial "ideological instrument." The aesthetic realm (of which criticism is a part) "assumes an unusual degree of dominance within the whole ideological formation" for it is "foregrounded as a privileged bearer of the themes over which that formation broods" (1990: 19–20). Literary criticism's ultimate end is to justify literature. "In a spiral of mutual reinforcements," Eagleton continues, "the literary text naturalises experience, critical practice naturalises the texts, and the theories of that practice legitimate the 'naturalness' of criticism" (1990: 18).

This ideological dimension was explicit in much of modern Chinese writing on literature; its function was to encourage and promote the development of a new "national" literature that would participate in the ideological transformation of Chinese society from tradition toward modernity. By establishing a scientific basis for literature, the May Fourth critics endeavored to assert for literature an autonomy from political power and conventional morality so that it could oversee the formation of an aesthetic realm from which to combat tradition and participate in the modernization of Chinese society. This was, of course, a fundamentally political and ideological enterprise. May Fourth critics claimed for literary criticism the important role of justifying and naturalizing, to use Eagleton's term, the new literature. One of the central paradoxes of Chinese literary criticism is that it sought at once to wrench literature from its traditional political and moral function and to infuse it with a transformative role that was inherently political, ideological, and moral. Theodore Huters suggests that the ultimate function of literary theory in the late Qing was to give authority to literature in order to provide for it "cultural significance in very difficult times" (1988: 247).

Given the violent and convulsive history of modern China, one might wonder why intellectuals felt it meaningful to write about literature at all. How could these writings appear as anything but superfluous, a meaningless intellectual exercise without immediate relevance to the palpable suffering in Chinese society? Were the cultural debates of the Republican period, as some scholars argue, symptomatic of a cowardly intellectual retreat from the dreadful and daunting abyss of real social problems? (Min-chih Chou 1984: 117). Were these intellectuals merely seeking out new discursive ground on which to reassert their very traditional roles as elite stewards of culture, morality, and social transformation?[35] Was their self-assertion through the discourse of modernity simply compensation for the loss of their traditional elite status as scholar-bureaucrats within the Confucian sociocultural hierarchy? Whatever their unconscious motivations, modern intellectuals felt a keen urgency to relate writing to the demands of this age of crisis. Although not without important exceptions, the essays collected in this volume in one way or another respond to the sociopolitical crisis; they seek out, explore, and assert ways of making the cultural sphere relevant to the transformation of Chinese society. The broad function of literary criticism was to lead writers and readers toward creating a literature that would contribute in some way to this cultural revolution.

These disparate writings share a faith that culture could play a significant role in influencing minds in the process of national renewal, an idealism summed up in Zhou Zuoren's statement that "a literature of humanity is the only thing needed in our nation today" (1972: 33).[36] This idealism permeates even the "scientist" orientation of some May Fourth writings and the explicitly Marxist essays of the post–May Fourth period. The importance placed on culture in the transformation of the material realm, as Yü-sheng Lin has argued (1979: 26–55), is a Chinese propensity grounded in the Confucian tradition itself. *Wen*, writing or culture, was rarely in premodern literary thought viewed as something extricable from politics or morality; it was seamlessly interwoven with all aspects of what it means to be human: the personal, social, moral, political, and ideological. Indeed, this traditional cultural idealism was arguably enhanced in the modern period out of historical necessity. With this traditional propensity toward a cultural-intellectual approach to social transformation, modern Chinese intellectuals "inflated," as Marston Anderson has argued, the role of criticism in the development of a modern literature: "The apparently inflated power accorded to theory in modern Chinese letters can only be understood in the context of the cultural emergency from which the new literature was born and in light of the particular kind of literary borrowing in which Chinese

---

35. This seems to be the argument of Tani Barlow (1991).

36. Based on a reading of autobiographies of several important May Fourth writers, Wendy Larson (1991) argues that this faith in the authority of writing (or textual work) was never without serious doubt. Privately, this may be true, but these very writers, some of whom were also critics, continued to write and express through that writing some kind of belief in the transformative power of writing.

intellectuals were engaged" (1990: 2). In the various editions of multi-volumed compilations of modern Chinese literature, theoretical and polemical writings on literature are always placed at the beginning, as if to point out that actual works of literature somehow grew directly out of critical writings and the theoretical vanguard.[37]

May Fourth writers in particular did not hesitate to claim for literary criticism a leading role in cultural modernization. In his "Literature and Life" (see Part II), Mao Dun sees criticism as the lever that would pry literature away from political authority, philosophy, and morality and establish for it an autonomous realm from which it could connect directly to social reality and to the reality of the sincere self. He wanted to use literary criticism to transform the social position of the writer from that of a "pawn of political power" or a mere "decoration" to that of "an important element in the process of cultural development." In breaking down traditional attitudes toward the writer and the function of writing, the critic would open the way for writers to engage directly with human life (1981: 1: 22–26). Criticism valorized and legitimized this new literature and this "new" writer cum cultural revolutionary.

Common to the broad range of functions ascribed to literary criticism by these writers was an assumption about its central importance to cultural development. Yu Dafu, a leading member of the Creation Society, saw a primary role for the "great critic" who would "use a torch to guide the masses, to allow them to see the precious treasures in the darkness of their mine shaft." The great critic, like the great writer, was a genius, and hand in hand the two would forge the new literature (1982: 5: 118). A fellow Creationist, Cheng Fangwu, wrote that the goal of the critic is to retrieve the sincerity of the writer and convey it to the reader and that the "true literary critic" is a creator "engaged in a literary activity."[38] "In an age in which we are anxiously awaiting literary creations," he wrote elsewhere, "criticism and creativity are equally important."[39] Cheng also envisioned the role of the critic as recreating aesthetic norms and standards against which literary works should be evaluated (Gálik 1980: 82). Some critics like Guo Moruo (also of the Creation Society) opposed a "scientific criticism" that described the structural properties of beauty and not the beauty itself, although he upheld a central role for the critic in determining aesthetic standards and leading the way to good creative writing. Guo also agreed with Yu Dafu's

---

37. See for example the various editions of *Zhongguo xin wenxue daxi* (Compendium of modern Chinese literature), a rich source for the study of canon formation.

38. From "Piping yu tongqing" 批 評 與 同 情 (Criticism and sympathy), *Chuangzao zhoubao* 13 (1923); cited in Gálik 1980: 65.

39. From "Jianshe de piping" 建 設 的 批 評 (Constructive criticism), *CZSZL* 1: 99.

idea of the critic as genius who guides the formation of a new literature (1979: 271–77). And Zhou Zuoren, though a member of an opposing literary group, shared Guo's distaste for a scientific criticism grounded in rational analysis and universal literary standards. For Zhou, criticism was and should be a subjective and creative engagement of the critic with the text; to remove that element from the critical process would be to render literature a lifeless relic. Critics influenced by Marxism, most notably Cheng Fangwu in his post-1925 writings, continued to maintain a central role for criticism in the transformation of Chinese society. In 1928 Cheng wrote that "first we must make the literary domain a subject of criticism, but then our criticism must pass into a criticism of the bourgeois society and ultimately to a criticism of the economic processes" (cited in Gálik 1980: 102). Criticism was a "totalistic" endeavor that would change consciousness and thus propel the revolution.

Criticism's primary charge was not exegesis. Its function was to engender the new literature, and as such its audience was first and foremost the writer, not the reader. Although practical criticism was not uncommon, it tended not to resemble New Critical "close readings" and even less Structuralist-like descriptions of the inner workings of the literary system. Writings on literature tended not to negotiate or explicate meaning for the reader.[40] Rather, like its traditional counterpart, modern criticism was concerned with the creative process. It sought to intercede into the creative process prior to the act of writing and to offer direction for writers in the formation of a modern literature.

But modern literary thought also asserted for itself the role of forging a link between author and reader and was thus the pivot around which the production and reception of the new literature would revolve. In a perceptive remark, Gálik goes so far as to suggest that modern Chinese literary criticism took the central cultural place formerly occupied by philosophy (1980: 84). In its emphasis on the spiritual, moral, and cognitive functions of literature, literary criticism was serving a philosophical (in the Chinese

---

40. This tendency may be a legacy of traditional approaches to literature. As some scholars have argued, traditional literary criticism, most obviously that inspired by the Daoist notion of the inadequacy of language, accepted the indeterminacy of meaning in literary works (Longxi Zhang 1992: 196–97). However, parallel to this "interpretive plurality" and equally influential, was a mainstream critical "intentionalism" that saw the role of the reader as one of retrieving the original intention of the historical author (133–41). As one might expect, a dogmatic hermeneutic tradition arose out of this intentionalism. But there lingered a notion that criticism which offered gratis to the reader the meaning of a literary work, that made explicit the inexplicit, would damage the reader's experience of creative communion with the text. To explicate would be to destroy the reader's experience of retrieving the authorial intention through creative interaction with the text.

sense of a moral-political philosophy) function. In the Confucian model, philosophy was a guide for self-understanding, determining proper moral comportment and one's place in society. For Cheng Fangwu, at least in his May Fourth period, literary criticism could function in a way not unlike that of traditional moral self-cultivation: "A critical work is incessant introspection in objects. Self-criticism is introspection of introspection. We may also term it re-introspection. No true criticism can exist without this re-introspection. . . . When criticizing a thing, we first distinguish whether it is good or bad, beautiful or ugly, true or false. Only thus can we elucidate truth. Our work must not stop at discriminating things, but must achieve the finding or elucidation of truth" (cited in Gálik 1980: 84–85). Cheng's ultimate goal for art was the self-transcendence of writer and reader:

> True art allows us to sink into the world of the work, to completely forget the world created by the writer and the reader and remove the boundaries between "you" and "I." . . . The goal of the artist, besides self-expression, is how to lead the reader into the world of the work and cause him to destroy all distinctions. An artist should at least be able to make us completely forget our world and be able to destroy that which prevents us from entering into everything.[41]

The goal of art, indeed of criticism, is fundamentally moral and spiritual: "to render concrete our strength of self-expression, in order that obstacles separating hearts and souls of individual people be removed" (cited in Gálik 1980: 65). Cheng Fangwu's literary thought is motivated by a desire to reconnect individuals to each other and to the external world. Gálik has observed that the basic philosophical premise at the heart of Cheng's early criticism is the Mencian notion that the universe (*wanwu* 萬物) is held within the self. The internal is thus inherently able to embody the external, and the self continues to stand at the center of the transformation of the external world.

The privileged role given to critical writings suggests anxieties about the tenuous position of literature in the late Qing and May Fourth periods, about the persistence of traditional literary values, and the irrelevance of literature in the face of the magnitude of the social and political problems of the day. Writing about literature arose in the West, claims Owen, to justify poetry after it lost its sacred authority as divine inspiration. In premodern China, poetry got its authority from claiming it was psychologically or physiologically natural, or derived from the natural world (1992:

---

41. From "Yi ye de pinglun" 一葉的評論 (A critique of *One Leaf*), *Chuangzao jikan* 2, no.1 (1923).

42–43). By modern times, however, this assumed connection with the natural world was largely seen as broken. It thus became necessary to reassert for literature some inherent bond with the external world, a function that criticism sought to fulfil. Modern writing on literature invested new concepts like the Nation, the Real, Life, the Zeitgeist, and the Masses with the cosmological force previously ascribed to the *Dao* or heaven. With the collapse of traditional cosmological assumptions about the unity of man and the divine, literature had to be given a new self-justification garnered for it from these historical forces by criticism.

The crucial role prescribed for literary criticism, however, placed on it a burden that mitigated against the iconoclastic goal of establishing for it a scientific presence. As modern writers struggled in the face of historical exigencies and the legacies of traditional literary values to forge a conception of literature as autonomous from political or ideological authority, so, too, did they struggle to create a literary criticism that was scientific and that abetted the development of a new literature invested with a crucial social purpose. In their desire to infuse literature with a social function, modern literary critics ended up repeating many of the faults they attacked in their traditional predecessors. More often than not, as the reader may discover in reading through the translations included in this volume, writing on literature in modern China was anything but what Mao Dun, Hu Yuzhi, and Zhu Guangqian intended it to be and what we in the West may presuppose it to be. Its realization hardly fits the exaggerated projections. It was perhaps inevitable, given the sociohistorical imperative of the times, that the close relationship of politics, morality, and literature existing in Confucian China would remain latent beneath efforts to forge a belletristic direction for literature and a scientific role for literary criticism.

Modern Literary Thought

"Expressing zhi" and "Conveying the Dao": Modern Constructions of Tradition

Liang Qichao, Wang Guowei, and Lu Xun may be seen as representing the starting points of three fundamental vectors in modern Chinese literary thought. Liang's conception of the role of literature is unabashedly didactic and utilitarian. Fiction, a genre publicly despised by the traditional literati as vulgar in form and immoral in message (even as they wrote and read it in private), has an inherent power to influence human behavior and should replace the difficult classics in the central cultural role of educating and shaping the minds of men, Liang believes. He asserts, as has been noted by many scholars, an absurdly optimistic role for fiction in the transformation of society (Mabel Lee 1974; C. T. Hsia 1978: 231–41). To revive a nation's morality, politics, religion, social customs, culture, and the minds of its citizens, Liang writes in "On the Relationship Between Fiction and the Government of the People" (see Part I), one need only revive fiction, for "fiction has a profound power over the Way of man [*ren Dao* 人 道]." Wang Guowei's view of literature as aesthetic "play" is radically at odds with Liang's literary "pragmatism." He deplores "bread and butter" literature that is motivated by factors beyond the literary. "Art," he wrote in 1906, "has enjoyed no independent value for a long while. It is therefore not strange that many among the successive generations of poets have relied on the principles of loyalty to one's lord, love of one's country, exhortation to goodness, and warning against evil in order to avoid (not being taken seriously by others)" (cited in Bonner 1986: 105). As Joey Bonner has remarked of Wang's aestheticism: "Works that have been produced for any reason other than the sake of beauty alone necessarily represent incomplete expressions of the play drive and, as such, cannot provide the emotional satisfaction that we seek in aesthetic contemplation" (1986: 104).

Lu Xun, in his late Qing essay "On the Power of Mara Poetry" (see Part I) negotiates between these two positions. On the one hand, he seems to rejects Liang's notion of literature's powerful utility: "Therefore in terms of utility, it falls short of histories in furthering knowledge, of maxims in warning mankind, of commerce and industry in building a fortune, and of diplomas in conferring social status." On the other hand, whereas Wang's aestheticism offers psychological consolation from a world driven by suffering, Lu Xun desires a "demonic," aggressive role for poetry. He laments the absence in China of poets who, in "singing of themselves," disturb a national psyche that wants nothing more than the peace and solace of spiritual slumber. For Lu Xun, this literature of self rarely found expression in China because it was always reined in by critical imperatives to discipline the emotions in poetry. Like Wang Guowei, Lu Xun opposed Liang Qichao's overt utilitarianism as a vulgar political appropriation of literature, but his allegiance is clearly not with any pure aestheticism in which the pursuit of beauty is art's ultimate aim. Literature was the realm of ideas and ideals and thus the perfect medium for the renewal of the national spirit. Like a swim in the recuperative swells of the vast ocean, writes Lu Xun in this essay, literature offers the reader a world in which the human imagination (*shensi* 神 思) is nurtured and rejuvenated. The writer should be a "warrior of the spirit" who in disturbing the reader will shake him out of his complacency and lead him out of the "barren homeland." The expression of self, for Lu Xun, ultimately serves the crucial social function, expressed more succinctly in his later "Preface to *Call to Arms*" (see Part II) of curing a psychologically-diseased national character.[42]

The schism in late Qing literary thought between didactic utilitarianism and self-expression has roots in traditional literary thought, at least as it was perceived and constructed by the moderns. It was commonplace in the May Fourth era to schematize traditional views of literature into two major types: *shi yan zhi* 詩言志 (poetry expresses the *zhi*) and *wen yi zai Dao* 文以載道 (literature conveys the *Dao*). Below I will discuss at some length the meaning of the two terms *zhi* and *Dao*; for now suffice it to say that the May Fourth critics understood *zhi* as emotions and *Dao* as political and moral ideology and that the two phrases came to mean something like "literature of self-expression" and "didacticism." Although not the first work to make this distinction, Zhou Zuoren's 1932 study *The Origins of Modern Chinese Literature* is perhaps the most famous.[43] Zhou's intention in this series of lectures was to "read into tradition a sanction for a departure from tradition" (Huters 1982: 16). The dominance of the "conveying *Dao*" tradition had suppressed the writer's subjective involvement in the creative process; to resurrect the "expressing *zhi*" subtradition was to empower the self against didacticism. In the contemporary context, Zhou was reacting against the insidious reemergence of a new "didacticism" among the leftist revolutionary cultural camp.

---

42. Many of the ideas expressed in Lu Xun's pre–May Fourth writings were shared by his brother, Zhou Zuoren. In a seldom cited article entitled "Lun wenzhang zhi yiyi ji qi shiming yinji Zhongguo jinshi lunwen zhi shi" 論文章之意義及其使命因及中國近時論文之失 (On the significance and mission of writing and the shortcomings of writings on literature in contemporary China), Zhou elaborates, in language less abstruse than that of his elder brother, the idealist notion that literature is the realm of the spiritual transformation of Chinese society; see *XHGM* 3: 306–30. For a comparison of the Zhou brothers' literary thought, see Qian Liqun 1984.

43. Zhou Zuoren's (1932) views China's literary tradition as an alternating movement between periods in which one or the other of these two broad conceptions of literature dominates. Whereas periods of disunity tended to favor "poetry expresses *zhi*," periods of political consolidation imposed a utilitarian function for literature, as during the Tang and Song when literati proposed the use of literature for the renewal of Confucian ethical values. For a long discussion of Zhou's thesis and informative background to the two formulations, see Pollard 1973: 1–48. Both Zhu Ziqing and Qian Zhongshu have criticized Zhou for his overly simplistic schematization of traditional literary values. Zhu seems to criticize Zhou for polarizing the two when "the original meaning of *yan zhi* was not very different from that of *zai Dao*" (1942: 4: 1116). Qian Zhongshu lightly chastizes Zhou for the same mechanical polarization, and for failing to account for these two functions being determined by genre (i.e., poetry is for self-expression and prose for moral-political purposes). For a discussion of Qian's review of Zhou's work, see Huters 1982: 13–17. Zhu Guangqian interprets *Dao* more broadly than Zhou and does not see a fundamental schism between the *yan zhi* and *zai Dao* traditions (see "Literature and Life" in Part IV).

In his earlier writings on literature, however, Zhou had denounced literature of self-expression as narrowly individualist.[44] Instead he promoted a "literature of humanity" that was at once individualist, in originating in the expression of the writer, and realist, in its orientation toward humanity beyond the self. Typical of the May Fourth generation's views of traditional literary thought, Mao Dun also frequently attacked both the "conveying Dao" and "expressing zhi" traditions. The former totally suppressed individual subjective will, he thought, and the latter degenerated into a private art, an aesthetic plaything of the elite. For Mao, the "conveying Dao" tradition posited a passive writer spouting philosophical platitudes and relinquishing his autonomy to political authority, and the "expressing zhi" tradition was associated with a kind of empty aestheticism (1981: 83–84).

The May Fourth schematization of traditional literary values and its efforts to extricate itself from those values tells us little about tradition and much about the anxieties motivating modern literary thought. This is not the place to delve into a long discussion of the accuracy of the May Fourth portrayal of these two broad traditional literary formulations. The May Fourth critics were not generally interested in objective scholarly analysis of these views; pressed by a sense of urgency and crisis, they painted a picture of traditional literary thought that was highly homogeneous and, arguably, quite mistaken in its narrow demarcation of the concepts of Dao and zhi in these two overworked slogans. The May Fourth understanding of Dao was limited to Confucianism and the ethicopolitical values it espoused and blind to the broader cosmological and metaphysical connotations of Dao that were part of both the Daoist and the Confucian philosophical traditions.

May Fourth critics also viewed zhi in a rather restricted sense. I would reinforce Pollard's implication that Zhou Zuoren imposed a Western romantic conception of literature onto the tradition of "expressing zhi" in order to better extricate it from its sometimes cozy relationship with "conveying Dao" (Pollard 1973: 12). As some have argued, Chinese individualism is markedly different from its Western romantic counterpart, which stresses the uniqueness of the self and the self's fundamental alienation from the external world (Chaves 1985: 124–26). Zhou's view of zhi corresponds roughly to a Western-romantic notion of self and differs dramatically from its more traditional understanding as a "state of mind" arising in response to the external world, explained by Owen as

\

---

44. Zhou implies a distaste for a literature of self-expression in the essay discussed in note 42 above. See *XHGM* vol. 3.

a subjective relation to some content, a relation of a certain intensity and of a certain quality. *Chih* [*zhi*] is that condition when the mind is fixed on something, a "preoccupation." *Chih* is tensional, yearning for both resolution and for external manifestation. . . . In other cases it has a broad moral frame of reference, as "goals" or "values to be realized." Ultimately the ethical and political dimensions of *chih* became so strong in the tradition that most writers on literature preferred to substitute other terms as the source of the poem in the psyche, especially *ch'ing* [*qing*], the "affections." (Owen 1992: 28)

As such, *zhi* must not be confused with "intention," which implies a Western notion of a consciously creating authorial agency.

We can see that in their traditional context both "literature conveys the *Dao*" and "poetry express *zhi*" were fluid, by no means absolutely antithetical, concepts. In a cosmological framework that posited the essential, or at least potential, unity of man with the *Dao* (an idea implicit in the neo-Confucian phrase "heaven and man are one" and manifest in much of Daoist philosophical writings) the expression of self and the conveyance of the *Dao* (with its manifold moral, political, and cosmological meanings) were not necessarily at odds. The *Dao* could include a personal subjective quality, and the *zhi*, a social and moral one. One could expresses one's *zhi* and convey the *Dao* at the same time. Indeed, this may be seen as an ideal of traditional literary thought.

May Fourth critics simplified these literary formulations and absolutized their separation in order to more easily reject the traditional literary thought they believed had irreparably sundered world, self, and literature. In an attempt to reintegrate these three fundamental fields without appearing to be traditional, modern critics sought models from the West. It is in this iconoclastic context that the reception of realism, romanticism, and aestheticism should be viewed. Beneath this iconoclastic appropriation of these modes lay deeply rooted traditional assumptions about literature and the relationship between the external and internal worlds in the creative process. A traditional desire to maintain an organic interconnection between the external and internal realms undermined any pure reception of these modes.

From its inception with the three late Qing figures discussed above, modern Chinese literary thought was marked by a fundamental tension among an outer-directed literary utilitarianism (Liang Qichao), an inner-driven literature of self-expression (Lu Xun), and an aestheticism that directed its attentions to literature itself (Wang Guowei). In the May Fourth era, the aesthetic and expressive views conjoined in the Creation Society, which held the aesthetic as the sacred realm of subjective feelings, and Liang Qichao's utilitarianism reappeared in the Literary Research Association, which espoused a socially engaged realism. This fundamental conflict between the external and the internal was reshaped once again in the post–May Fourth period around the question of the extent of the writer's active, subjective involvement in the creative process and the writer's autonomy from political power and ideology. The development of modern Chinese literary thought was thus inextricably interwoven with the problem of the role of self in the creative process. Was literature to derive from within the self or was the self to be suppressed in the creative process by an externally imposed goal or method? And, finally, what was the place of the aesthetic in this tension between the inner and outer realms? Those who upheld the utilitarian position were willing to allow the external goal to intrude on the aesthetic and subjective parts of the creative process; the aesthetic-expressive promoters maintained the primacy of the self to the creative process and, as we will see, to the transformation of the external realm. The aestheticians, who saw beauty as offering access to universal truths, deplored the encroachment of the external (most obviously the political) on the aesthetic. Although significant tensions between these positions existed throughout the modern period, we will see how traditional desires for an organic unity of literature, self, and world intervene to shape the understanding of these positions and the search for ways of integrating them.

Mimesis and Self-Expression in Traditional Criticism

A measure of consensus exists among scholars of Chinese literature that traditional Chinese literary thought lacked the well-developed conception of mimesis that has dominated Western literary values.[45] James J. Y. Liu is perhaps best known for promoting the view of the relative absence of any theory of mimesis in traditional literary criticism, though he recognizes certain similarities between the mimetic and metaphysical theories (1975: 47–53). Just as Zhou Zuoren had in the 1930's, PRC aestheticians and literary historians of the 1980's, reacting against the deadening politicization of literature in the Cultural Revolution, have begun to reexamine traditional views of literature in terms of the category of subjectivism. A distinction is

---

45. In the discussion that follows I may be guilty of generalizing about the heterogeneous literary traditions of both China and the West. I do this, on the one hand, because I find generalization a necessary tool for speaking about and highlighting differences between cultures. On the other, I am also partially reflecting Chinese modernity's perception of the radical difference between the two cultural traditions.

commonly made between the fundamentally expressive (*biaoxian* 表現) orientation of traditional Chinese views of literature and the representational (*zaixian* 再現) orientation of Western literary theory. The latter was almost wholly absent, they argue, from Chinese literary thought until its importation in the late Qing and May Fourth periods (Cao 1988; Jiu 1989; ZhouhanYang 1983).

Pauline Yu and others have suggested that these divergent views are grounded in fundamentally different ontologies.[46] Dualism, the notion that the living human is cut off from the transcendent, whether located in Platonic ideas or a Christian God, drives mimesis in the West. In his "fallen" state, the poet or artist is motivated by a desire, ontologically impossible to fulfill, to represent or imitate those realms in order to break down the distance that separates him from them. Chinese views of literature, on the other hand, arise out of a monistic cosmology, which sees the immanence of the divine or transcendental *Dao* in the real and concrete world, indeed within man himself. Yu writes that the "Great Preface" of the *Book of Songs*, a text central to traditional literary thought, assumes that

> what is internal (emotion) will naturally find some externally correlative form or action, and that poetry can spontaneously reflect, affect, and effect political and cosmic order. In other words, the seamless connection between the individual and the world enables the poem simultaneously to reveal feelings, provide an index of governmental stability, and serve as a didactic tool. Furthermore, the connections between subject and object or among objects, which the West has by and large credited to the creative ingenuity of the poet, are viewed in the Chinese tradition as already preestablished; the poet's primary achievement often lies in his ability to transcend, rather than assert, his individuality and distinctiveness from the elements of his world. (1987: 32–33)

According to this construction of traditional views of literature, China lacked not only a mimetic concept of literature but also one of pure selfexpression. The idea of a literature of self-expression is, like mimesis, predicated upon a fundamental disjunction between self and world (both social and natural). Modern individualism in the West, traceable back through romanticism's glorification of self to Descartes's ontological dualism and finally to the Judeo-Christian notion of the individual soul, posits a subject fundamentally isolated from other selves and from the world. This sense of isolation may lead to a glorification of the subject in the form of the psychological, the private, and the idiosyncratic (Bernstein 1983: 46), and to the

46. See also Yip 1976: 25–41.

expressive views of literature we associate most often with romanticism. The poet in China was not perceived as an autonomous self alienated from the social world or the divine; nor was his expression of self like Wordsworth's "spontaneous overflow of powerful feelings" that resided potentially in the uniqueness of the individual soul. Literature expressed the self, to be sure, but it also embodied at once the external world and a larger universal self with which it was innately interconnected.

Western ontological dualism leads to the idealization of either the object or the subject, and hence to mimetic or expressive views of literature. Mimesis and self-expression, realism and romanticism, are grounded in this dualism, and both are driven by a desire to mend this severing of subject and object. This ontology also produces the notion that a work of art is an *ex nihilo* creation of the writer's intention, a view of the creative act which leads in turn to a critical focus on the text in isolation from both the world and the author and, eventually, to theories of aestheticism. The Chinese holistic ontology precluded the emergence of a purely aesthetic conception of literature that would divorce the literary work from its origins in the joining of the poetic subject and the external object and its inherent seamless connection with politics and morality. Although a belletristic conception of literature did emerge after the collapse of the Han dynasty, literature was never conceived of as existing for its own sake. There was always ultimately a moral or social function to it, even if only for the moral self-cultivation of the writer.

If we accept this interpretation of traditional literary values, then modern literary thought, with its obsession with the Western modes of realism, romanticism, and aestheticism, clearly marks a radical break from this tradition. My concern here, though, is to look at these three Western categories critically and determine what happens to them when they are grafted onto a foreign cultural system. My assumption is that traditional philosophical and literary values played a role in shaping the reception of these Western literary concepts. In this process, these concepts were modified and, most important, attempts were made to integrate elements from these modes that were in the Western context perceived to be largely at odds with each other. If Chinese intellectuals suffered from an "anxiety of influence," it was, of course, directed at their own tradition, not that which characterized the successive emergence of these modes in Western literary history. There was thus no historical necessity to adhere strictly to the implications of any of these modes. Indeed, much of modern Chinese literary thought is motivated by a desire to restore a "seamless connection" among self, text, and world by synthesizing elements of realism, romanticism, and aestheticism.

Realism and Romanticism

With the beginnings of Western influence on Chinese literary thought, a division emerged in the categorization of literary modes. Both Liang Qichao and Wang Guowei distinguished realism (*xieshi* 寫 實) from idealism (*lixiang* 理 想).[47] In "On the Relationship Between Fiction and the Government of the People," Liang writes that fiction is popular because: (1) it allows the reader to enter another world and has the transformative power to mold and shape the human mind, a kind of fiction he terms "idealist"; and (2) it explains the truth or motivations hidden behind events in the world, which he calls "realist." The former seems to have the power to transform; the latter gets at the essence of something in the world. Wang Guowei made a similar distinction: "There is a creative state (*zaojing* 造 境) and there is a descriptive state (*xiejing* 寫 境). This is the basis of distinction between the idealists and realists. However, it is difficult to make a differentiation between the two because the state which the great poets create must accord with what is natural, and the state which they simply describe must approach the ideal."[48] Wang's favor is cast toward those "idealist" poets who are not inundated by sensory impressions of the material realm and who forge "worlds" in their poems through a creative interaction of subjective feeling and objective scene. These notions, though they may have been influenced by Wang's readings of Kant and Schopenhauer, derive very clearly from the early Qing critic Wang Fuzhi's dialectic of *qing* 情 (emotion/feelings) and *jing* 景 (scene) (James J. Y. Liu 1962: 84). Good literature is produced only when these two qualities are joined together into a harmonious whole.

It has been suggested that these terms, *lixiang* and *xieshi*, are the first references to romanticism and realism in the Chinese context (Anderson 1990: 28–29). In his preference for an idealist literature, Wang Guowei would

---

47. Liang may have borrowed this distinction from Tsubouchi Shōyō's 坪 內 逍 遙 *Shōsetsu shinzui* 小 說 神 髓 (The essence of the novel); for a translation of this theoretical work, see Tsubouchi 1989. This point is made in Anderson 1990: 29; and C. T. Hsia 1978: 241.

48. From Rickett 1977: 40. In her Ph.D. dissertation, Rickett glosses this passage with the following: "He has described here two approaches to writing. One is the man who, having seen and experienced much in the external world, draws on his own powers of imagination to create an ideal world which encompasses more than any one single aspect of the real world, and yet having come out of that world is a measure of reality too. The other man is bound by what he sees, by the factual, tangible world which his senses present to him. If he is a good poet he will describe what he sees accurately and vividly, but if he is a great poet he will be able to draw the reader beyond the concrete image to an idealistic realm of universality" (1967: 95–96).

seem to be the forebear of May Fourth romanticism, whereas Liang Qichao, although he does not explicitly advocate one over the other, is primarily concerned in his utilitarianism with the social effects of literature and as such may be viewed as the precursor to May Fourth realism, with its orientation toward the depiction of social life (Xu 1990: 38). Although Wang introduced such foreign concepts as tragedy into Chinese discussions of literature, he remained a fundamentally traditional critic in his emphasis on the unity among the literary text, the inner world of the poet, and the outer objective world. But Wang's repeated emphasis on this unity in literary creativity may also intimate an incipient breakdown of the traditional cosmology in which this unity was simply assumed. Liang Qichao, moreover, was so obsessed with using fiction to transform society that he paid little or no attention to how it can "reflect" or "represent" that society; as such we can hardly call his views realist. Neither critic condemned *lixiang* or *xieshi*, and there remains at the heart of their statements on the subject a sense of the fundamental unity of these two literary modes.

It is a convention we have inherited from the literary polemics of the May Fourth participants to describe that cultural period in terms of the Western models of realism and romanticism. In the early 1920's, following the initial iconoclastic zeal of the May Fourth, when writers set themselves to the task of creating a new literature, two important literary societies were founded. The Creation Society promoted an aesthetic-based literature of self-expression influenced by the Western romantic ideals of individualism, genius, creative energy, and the expression of feelings. The Literary Research Association pushed for a socially oriented literature and a "scientific" portrayal of reality through the suppression of the writer's subjectivity in the creative process.[49] The fundamental difference between these two schools of literary thought centered around the question of the role of the self in the creative process. They waged a discursive battle over whether literature should be other-directed or self-motivated. Those who referred to themselves as realists were accused by the romantics of cold objectivism, whereas the former accused the latter of subjective idealism. As we will see, however, these two groups shared fundamental assumptions about the origin and function of literature, and their battle can ulti-

---

49. Mao Dun criticized the first issue of the journal *Chuangzao jikan*, in which Yu Dafu's notorious short story "Sinking" appeared, in his "*Chuangzao gei wo de yinxiang*" 創造給我的印象 (My impressions of *Chuangzao*) (*CZSZL* 2: 921–26). For a Creationist retort, see Cheng Fangwu, "Chuangzao she yu Wenxue yanjiu hui" 創造社與文學研究會 (The Creation Society and the Literary Research Association), *Chuangzao jikan* 1, no. 4 (1923). For a general discussion of the debates between these two groups, see Chen Jingzhi 1986.

mately be seen as two different expressions of the same anxiety about the disintegration of cultural presuppositions of the self's unity with the outer world.[50]

Beneath this dogmatic effort to gain authority for their own literary views by vociferously attacking all others—what one scholar has called the "ideology of restriction" (Owen 1992: 392)—lay profound similarities between the two groups. Close analysis of the writings of "realist" and "romantic" theorists reveals shared literary orientations, as well as a profound uneasiness with the implications of the radically alien Western modes they ostensibly supported. If we accept the supposition that mimesis and radical self-expression are views of literature fundamentally at odds with the Chinese tradition, we must ask how May Fourth writers were able to embrace these very views with such apparent ease and wholeheartedness. We may conclude, on the one hand, that either the cosmological-philosophical foundation upon which traditional theories rested had withered away with the iconoclastic attacks of the May Fourth, or that the tradition contained within it elements commensurate with Western literary values, thus offering a stable foundation for their reception; or, on the other, that traditional cosmology and literary thought had a distorting influence on the reception of realism and romanticism, shaping them into something quite apart from the range of meanings they had in the original Western context. Drawing heavily from excellent scholarship already undertaken in this area, I hope to show the latter to be the case.

The Case of Realism

Some of the most virulent polemics of the May Fourth, many written by Mao Dun, Zhou Zuoren, and Ye Shengtao, were directed at popular fiction, namely, the Mandarin Ducks and Butterfly school of entertainment fiction (See the essays by Wang Dungen and Zhou Shoujuan in Part II), on the grounds of its lack of concern for social problems.[51] The May Fourth progressive critics attacked this fiction as being little more than an object of play (*youxi* 遊戲) or a literary plaything (*wanwu* 玩物). Yet the fierceness of their attack belies their fear of the powerful appeal of this urban popular fiction among the very audience they sought to influence with their own

---

50. Many critics have remarked that these two literary societies propounded ideas much less at odds than either would admit; see, for example, Leo Ou-fan Lee 1973: 21–23.

51. See Mao Dun, "Ziranzhuyi yu Zhongguo xiandai xiaoshuo" 自然主義與中國現代小說 (Naturalism and modern Chinese fiction), in Mao Dun 1981: 1: 83–99; Zhou Zuoren, "Lun heimu xiaoshuo" 論黑幕小說 (On black-screen fiction), in *ZGXDWLX* 2: 28–30; and Ye Shengtao, "On the Literary Arts" (see Part II).

writings. The battle against popular fiction was an ideological battle waged by an elite intellectual class who wished to maintain its traditional function as spokesman for culture and morality, against those who held that literature need offer nothing more than escape and consolation from a world of "unhappiness" and "grinding labor."[52] Their counter to the threat posed by entertainment fiction was realism.

Realism was thus conceived at least partly in reaction to a "purposeless" literature that lacked, May Fourth critics frequently wrote, any explicit worldview through which to filter the myriad, disconnected fragments of reality and get at the essence of the Real. It is in its attitude toward entertainment fiction that the May Fourth movement exposes its fundamental allegiance to the tradition of "literature to convey the *Dao*" (Tse-tsung Chow 1960: 285; Rey Chow 1991: 42–43). The new *Dao* for at least some May Fourth critics was the Real (the life force that moves history) or the Zeitgeist that is the essence of a historical epoch.[53] As we have seen, in defining narrowly the *Dao* that was "conveyed" in traditional literature, the May Fourth critics were trying to free writing from its subservience to political power and ideological and moral control. Investing the notion of Zeitgeist with the cosmological funtion formerly filled by the *Dao*, and bonding literature to it, gave to literature an authority and power to effect the political and moral transformation of Chinese society. Zhou Zuoren's "Humane Literature" (see Part II), for example, proposes an essentially moral role for literature indistinguishable in kind from the "conveyance of the *Dao*" tradition of a writer like Han Yu (768–824).

Marston Anderson, who opened discussion of the question of the reception of realism in the May Fourth period, believes that despite the overarching support for realism by May Fourth writers and critics, there remained at the heart of their reception of this alien mode a deep anxiety about its practice. Anderson accepts the premise of the absence of mimesis in traditional literary thought, stating that realism was a "fundamentally new model of aesthetic experience" for the Chinese (1990: 24). Although Western promoters of realism did envision for it a social function, in practice it led more to the mirror-like objectivism of Flaubert, Chekhov, James, and the early Joyce. Anderson argues that realism was adopted in China not because it meshed with cultural foundations but because it seemed to offer the greatest promise for cultural transformation. A tremendous burden was

---

52. For an excellent description of the sociological context of Mandarin Ducks and Butterfly fiction, see Link 1981.

53. For discussions of this important concept of "epoch," see Lung-kee Sun 1986–87; and Leo Ou-fan Lee 1990.

thus placed on it to transform reality, a burden it could bear only with sub-stantial modifications to its theory and practice.[54]

From the outset, May Fourth discussions of realism were couched in terms of its utility. Hu Shi and Chen Duxiu, for example, saw realism as part of the iconoclastic assault on traditional literature, the very embodi-ment of oppressive Confucian ethical values. Traditional literature was per-ceived as highly formalistic, numbingly imitative, hackneyed, allusive, and abstruse; as such, it was inherently incapable of representation of the Real, whether social reality or the sincere feelings of the individual writer. Hu's and Chen's proposals for literary reform were far less unprecedented than either would likely have been willing to admit, however. Traditional critics commonly attacked such literary abuses as formalism, parallel prose, and excessive use of allusion in order to restore to writing a purer style more ca-pable of embodying moral values.[55] Although the thrust of their orientation is clearly away from literature as the embodiment of the *Dao*, Hu and Chen are working under the traditional assumption that a reconstituted prose style would enable literature to transform the moral life of society.

One of Anderson's most important arguments is that May Fourth mi-metic theories retreated from the idea of realism as hard objectivism. The notion of a detached writer scientifically observing the world throughout the creative process was, of course, at odds with the traditional view of the origins of literature in the subjective reaction of the writer to an external scene or event. Tradition demanded that literature be rooted in a subjective experience of the world; to posit an "objective" writer would be to divorce the creative act from this experiencing self and thus remove all meaning from it. May Fourth theories of realism devised ways of reasserting the im-portance of this experiencing self into the creative process. Mao Dun, ini-tially an ardent supporter of the scientific method of naturalism, eventually shied away from this method's implicit suppression of the writer's subjec-tivity by infusing into it neo-romantic ideas (Anderson 1990: 43–44). His uneasiness with a theory of literature that finds little room for the subjec-

---

54. Stephan Chan made a similar point in a 1986 article. For the May Fourth realists, he writes, "realism could have little appeal as a period concept, or as an embodiment of the aesthetic problems of representation for that matter. Even to Mao Tun [Dun], their chief spokesman . . . realism as an ideological movement among nineteenth century European intellectuals was relatively insignificant in comparison with its strategic usefulness for the Chinese writers in developing an alternative discourse with the cultural politics of their own time" (1986: 367).

55. This is the case with the Tang Ancient-Style Prose attack on parallel prose, as well as Ouyang Xiu's attack on the imitative *Xikun* 西崑 style of poetry. Zhou Zuoren claimed that Hu Shi's proposals for literary reform could be traced directly back to the Gongan and Jingling schools of subjective literature that reacted against Ming neo-classicism (1932: 92).

tive powers of the writer is apparent in his "Literature and Life" (see Part II), in which he feels compelled to add to Hippolyte Taine's three determining categories of race, environment, and epoch, a fourth category of the "personality" (*renge* 人格) of the writer.

Ye Shengtao, a member of the Literary Research Association and another May Fourth "realist," also balked at rigid objectivism. True literature, wrote Ye, is achieved not in perfecting technique or in keenly observing the external world but in "the cultivation of the self [*ziji xiuyang* 自己修養], tempering oneself into sincerity [*cheng* 誠]" (see "On the Literary Arts," Part II). Anderson (1990: 43) is to be commended for drawing attention to this neglected concept of sincerity, one that is crucial to understanding both traditional and modern Chinese views of the creative process.[56] Sincerity is a key Confucian concept, particularly strong in the neo-Confucian revival that took place during and after the Song dynasty. According to Wei-ming Tu, sincerity is "a human reality, or a principle of subjectivity, by which a person becomes 'true' and 'sincere' to himself; in so doing, he can also form a unity with Heaven" (1989: 73). Perhaps better translated as integrity, *cheng* is the very ground on which the ideal man, or profound person, taps into the power of the divine

> and through a long and unceasing process of delving into his own ground of existence, discovers his true subjectivity not as an isolated selfhood but as a great source of creative transformation. As the inner sincerity of the profound person brings forth an unflagging supply of moral and spiritual nourishment for the people around him, the Confucian ideal of society (the fiduciary community) gradually comes into being. The continuous well-being of such a society depends upon the cultivation of the profound person in an ever-broadening net of human relations, for self-realization . . . necessarily involves a process of fulfilling the nature of others. Thus, the great foundation and the universal path of the world are both centered on the transforming influence of the profound person. (Tu 1989: 91)

---

56. David Pollard first described the importance of this traditional literary and philosophical concept to Zhou Zuoren's literary thought (1973: 64–71). "Sincerity" is also central to Cheng Fangwu's writings on literature. In a piece entitled "Piping yu tongqing" 批評與同情 (Criticism and sympathy), Cheng wrote that even "imperfect work, if the author's sincerity is manifested in it, becomes an expression of his vital force striving for immortal life. We cannot depreciate this sincerity, this will. If the critic is to fulfil his mission, he must have full sympathy for the work" (cited in Gálik 1980: 65). We might add to this list Yu Dafu whose "Yishu yu guojia" 藝術於國家 (Art and the state, 1923) (1982: 5: 149–54) also emphasizes the importance of sincerity to the literary work.

Ye Shengtao's ideas on the preparation of the writer prior to the creative act share with neo-Confucian self-cultivation a focus on the "other." Directing one's emotional energy onto the social world of the oppressed gives rise to a *tongqing* 同情 (or pity) that becomes the subjective foundation of a realist literature. Self-cultivation incorporates a "sense of self's relations to others" and builds the foundation for a unity between the outer and inner worlds. Ye was interested in writing or composition not as a technical rendering of the external world but as part of the process of the cultivation of self in its relation to the outer world. Ye's views are not exceptional in the May Fourth context, even among the promoters of "realism" in the Literary Research Association. Lu Yin's views, for example, resonate with those of Ye: "The only thing a work worthy of the name 'literary creation' cannot do without is personality (*gexing* 個性); the crystallization of art is subjectivity, the feeling of the personality" (see "My Opinions on Creativity," Part II). Zheng Zhenduo also insisted on the subjective involvement of the writer as of primary importance to the realist text.[57] Bing Xin saw the ideal literary encounter as a "spiritual contact" through which "sympathy [*tongqing*] can emerge" (see "On 'Literary Criticism,'" Part II).

May Fourth realist critics tended to see the goal of the literary text not in the "representation" of the Real but in the very embodiment of the Real. The distinction is not a trivial one. Critics such as Zhou Zuoren and Mao Dun believed that "literature equals life" (*wenxue dengyu rensheng* 文學等於 人生). To see literature as "equaling life," or embodying life, empowers it with an almost cosmological force that may then allow it to exert a transforming influence on life. As both Gálik and Anderson have argued, Mao Dun retreated from the objective and scientific implications of naturalism to embrace a "realism" that maintained a central role for the writer's personality, for it was within the mind of the writer that literature found its inherent connection to life or history. Zhou Zuoren, although associated with the realist Literary Research Association, balked at the "for life" orientation of that school's literary thought. The problem with this orientation for Zhou was that it put literature into the service of life, rather than allowing it to naturally embody that life. To place literature in this utilitarian role was to resurrect the dreaded tradition of "conveying the *Dao*." In his May Fourth writings, as we have seen, Zhou adamantly opposed the tradition of "conveying the *Dao*" (and any traces of it in modern literature), but he also hesitated before the "expressing *zhi*" literary formulation that he favored in his later writing. Similarly, while "art for art's sake" divorced literature from

---

57. See "Xie he lei de wenxue" 血和淚的文學 (Literature of blood and tears); translated in Berninghausen and Huters 1976.

life and made life an attribute of art, art for life's sake made art an attribute of life. To make art a tool in the transformation of life (and not an end in itself) is to separate art and life, and thus reduce its power to transform. "Art, I feel, is life because it is the expression of our emotional lives; how can it be separated from life? . . . Art has autonomy, but it is also of human nature; so since we must not separate it from life, nor make it serve life, let's just let it be an art of all humanity" (1984: 272). Zhou's "literature of humanity" is at once an individualist literature, a profound expression of the self, and a literature of the human collective.[58] He sought a state of organic integration of self and society, an integration motivated by a desire to maintain for the self a pivotal role in the process of social transformation.[59]

May Fourth theories of realism see the relationship between author, text, reader, and world in fundamentally traditional ways. There is in them little of the Western anxiety about representation (Anderson 1990: 27–75). Literary texts can embody the Real if they issue freely and with sincerity from the cultivated (other-oriented) mind of the writer. Although concepts like the Real, History, or Zeitgeist have replaced traditional metaphysical notions of the *Dao*, the assumption that these forces may be found within the self continues to affect modern literary thought. The Real is not something pointed to or represented in the text; rather, it is traceable back to the text's actual inception in a real historical moment in the concrete experience of a living writer. The principal focus of much modern Chinese realism is not on the aesthetic means of representing the Real, but on the writer's cultivating a personal, meaningful relationship with the external prior to the process of creation and then embodying that subjective experience in the work. May Fourth theories of realism attempt in various ways to assert for the self a crucial role in the creative process, motivated by a fear of the self being subsumed or overpowered by the external world, something that was an inherent danger in the objectivism and determinism of the realist mode itself.[60]

---

58. Zhou saw no paradox in viewing the individual as an autonomous entity organically interconnected with the whole of humanity. For the issue of tensions within Zhou's views of self, see Pollard 1973; and Leo Ou-fan Lee 1985*b*.

59. Owen's term "interior empiricism" may be used to describe this May Fourth view of the real as rooted in the self (1992: 89).

60. Jonathan Chaves's discussion of the shamanistic origins of writing in China may be helpful in elucidating the traditional view of literature that may be at play here: "The written word is not merely a symbol but is in some sense identical with the thing it denotes, just as the spoken word shares in the essence of the thing it names" (1977: 209). The ultimate source of poetry is the "primal energy of the universe itself" (207). In the creative process, the poet can tap this energy and with his writing influence and transform.

The Case of Romanticism

European romanticism, with its emphasis on literature as personal expression, would seem on the surface to have much more in common with mainstream traditional Chinese views of literature than does realism.[61] And yet, romanticism gave rise to views of the self as an isolated entity disconnected from society and history and of literature as pure self-expression that are at odds with the Chinese literary tradition. Traditional literary thought stressed the subjective origins of writing, but not as the unique expression of the isolated poet. Beneath Western romanticism lies a profound anxiety to integrate self and the natural world, an integration that was largely assumed in the Chinese context.

Romanticism offered the May Fourth a discourse through which to forge an autonomous model of self with which to launch an assault on tradition. Yet May Fourth romanticism was still at least partially grounded in desires to maintain a cosmological wholeness in which the expression of self would find deeper connections with the external world, some creative life force, society, and/or the collective. The egoism of Chinese romanticism is tempered by a strong sense of religious collectivism and anti-individualism.[62] This tension between radical egoism and a religious self-transcendence is readily apparent in the May Fourth poetry of Guo Moruo (the central figure in the Creation Society). Much of Guo's poetry employs striking imagery of self-transcendence: selves fusing with oceanic swells, bodies disintegrating into a cosmic oneness, death and rebirth into a harmonious world without distinctions between self and other. This anti-egoism is also expressed more self-consciously in Guo's critical writings. In "The Aestheticization of Life" (1924), Guo (1979: 96) consciously drew from Zhuangzi, an inspiration for much of traditional Chinese metaphysical literary thought, in developing a theory of creativity: "The spirit of art is this 'absence of self' [*wuwo* 無 我], and what I call 'the aestheticization of life' means that in our lives we must embody this spirit." This tensional view of self is expressed most clearly in Guo's "Preface to *The Sorrows of Young Werther*" (Part II), one of his most important essays on literature. What Guo admired in the figure of Werther is at once his absolute expression of self

---

61. For an excellent study of May Fourth romanticism, see Leo Ou-fan Lee 1973.

62. I draw some of my ideas in what follows from Mark Elvin 1978; Huters 1984*b*; and Hao Chang 1989*a*, 1989*b*. By "religious collectivism" I mean a religious-like willingness to submit self to collective desires, desires sometimes forged for patently ideological purposes by political authorities. This collectivism has its most obvious manifestation in the Cultural Revolution deification of Mao Zedong, but its origins can be traced back to the May Fourth impulse to worship certain idols even as they were destroying others.

and the pantheistic identifying of self with the larger forces of nature. "To complete the destruction of the ego is of the highest moral order," he wrote, "this is a truth that the tepid fellows who follow the Doctrine of the Mean cannot fully understand."

In the throes of the Creation Society's romantic period, Cheng Fangwu, the society's leading critic, unequivocally condemned romanticism and came to the support of realism:

> Only in recent times, in opposition to romantic literature and in order to be joined with life, has there appeared a realist literature that separates itself from that dream-like kingdom. This is the literature of humanity [*ren de wenxue*]: it is life in all its nakedness. This kind of literature, although it lacks the luster and variety of romanticism, takes as its material our lives, it expresses our experience; hence, it is most able to arouse our sympathy.[63]

For this so-called romantic, romanticism leads to a literature that is empty and divorced from life. In its stead he supports a literature of humanity (a term made famous by Zhou Zuoren) for its ability to depict both the world of "human affairs" and the world of feelings. According to Cheng, the process through which writers may get close to life in preparation for the act of writing is as follows: "We must pay close attention to it (reality) and discover its true face and express it in all its nakedness. Yet when we observe it, we must use all our faculties to embrace its inner life and not be entranced by external coloring. When we express it, we must reveal its entire life and let the description of a part intimate the whole, or exist interconnected with the whole." Cheng attacks the "vulgar" form of realism for capturing only surface reality: "The difference between true realism and vulgar realism is that one is expression [*biaoxian*] and the other representation [*zaixian*]. Representation has no creative conditions; only expression is as great as the sea and lofty as the sky, to allow genius its active part."[64]

Cheng's negative assessment of this kind of representation is shared by nearly all May Fourth writers.[65] The anxiety is not that the text will fail to

---

63. "Xieshizhuyi yu yongsuzhuyi" 寫實主義與庸俗主義 (Realism and vulgarism). *Chuangzao zhoubao* 5 (1923): 1–2.

64. Ibid., 2–3.

65. This is to be expected of a romantic like Guo Moruo who writes in "Lun guonei de pingtan ji wo duiyu chuangzuo shang de taidu" 論國內的評壇及我對於創作上的態度 (On our nation's critical scene and my views on creativity; 1923) that he opposes a reflective (*fanshe* 反射) literature "received purely from the sense organs . . . like a camera." Instead he promotes the role of "creativity," formed, brewed, and produced within the subjectivity of the writer; like a bee that makes honey (Guo Moruo 1979: 110). For similar critiques of literature as mere "records" of the superficial appearance of reality, see

capture reality, but that that reality in all its complexity and variety will overwhelm the author, the text, and the reader. Reality must be mediated through the self (Cheng's "expression") if it is to have any meaning. Like Zhou Zuoren, Cheng proposed an outer-directed realism that has the expression of self at its core. What links Cheng with the likes of Zhou, Mao Dun, and Ye Shengtao is his effort to integrate self and the external world through the creative process. Guo Moruo perhaps stated the issue most succinctly when he wrote: "To have results in refining objectivity lies in cultivating the subjective; a true work of art naturally is derived purely from an enriched subjectivity" (1979: 110). The self has within it an inherent connection to the objective that must be fostered through a process that resembles in kind neo-Confucian self-cultivation.

Within the creative writings and literary thought of May Fourth romantics lies a fundamental uneasiness with the kind of radical individualism implicit in the Western models they adopted. The May Fourth was a period of unparalleled individualism and subjectivism, to be sure, but these values were appropriated primarily for iconoclastic purposes. There was no all-encompassing faith in their moral rightness. Beneath the promotion of these values lay a fear of the radically autonomous self, not so much because it was perceived as Western, but because that very autonomy threatened to sever the self from the promise of social transformation inherent in the Great Learning paradigm, to which the discussion now turns.

The Self in the Creative Process

As I have argued elsewhere, profound tensions, centering around the self's role in social transformation, lay at the heart of May Fourth views of self (Denton 1992). Hu Shi's writings on the subject are a case in point. In his 1918 essay "Ibsenism," Hu favored the radical individualism exemplified by the egoistic characters in Ibsen's plays: the individual as an antagonist to society, one who will lead society out of its darkness by offering an enlightened example. Self is an independent voice from outside society able to see through the ideological obfuscation that is tradition and convention. In his "The Anti-individualist New Life" (1920), written but two years later, Hu retreated from that earlier radicalism to focus on the external social factors that shape and give meaning to the life of the individual. The latter position posits a far more passive self that changes only with the outer mate-

---

Mao Dun's "Naturalism and Modern Chinese Fiction" (1981: 84–85), Ye Shengtao, "On the Literary Arts" (see Part II) and Yu Dafu's "Xiaoshuo lun" 小說論 (Theory of fiction, 1926) (1982: 5: 15–21).

rial world.[66] Hu Shi reconciled these two views with his famous "theory of the immortality of society" in which the *dawo* 大我 (great self or society) and *xiaowo* 小我 (small self or individual) exist in a relationship of mutuality. "This small self of mine is not an autonomous entity, but is joined together through direct and indirect relations with countless other small selves; and in relations of mutual influence with the whole of society and of the world." Individuals, he wrote, at once create history and are created by it.[67]

The tension between these two selves—the one empowered, the other passive—resonates loudly with a "predicament" that Thomas Metzger sees as central to the Neo-Confucian tradition in late imperial China. The Great Learning paradigm, grounded in the cosmological assumption of a unity of heaven and man, claims that the outer world may be ordered by first cultivating the inherent goodness within the individual mind. As Metzger (1977: 134) argues, the concept of the immanence of the divine within man empowers the self to participate in social transformation, but that same immanence also gives the divine control over man; the self is both demi-god and victim. A modern paradox of self derives in part, I am suggesting, from an inheritance of the very traditional predicament of linkage. Of course, the metaphysical nature of what the self ideally strives to "link" with is concealed behind modern concepts such as Nation, History, Life, Zeitgeist, or the Masses. The tension between iconoclasm and nationalism placed the May Fourth self in a dilemma, caught between a glorified view of self as demi-god and a view of self as a passive victim of larger historical and collective forces. In his wavering between the individual's powerful role in creating history and history's role in determining the nature of the individual, Hu Shi is essentially reiterating, though in modern terms, the traditional neo-Confucian paradox of linkage. The Western model of an autonomous self required for the iconoclastic project pulled the mind away from the very source of its empowerment, History; nationalism seemed to destroy the possibility of the self's active engagement with historical development, rendering self a passive and determined entity. Either way, traditional desires for a creative role for self in social transformation seemed to be obstructed.

Modern literary thought may be understood in terms of a desire to restore this potential linkage which was fast slipping away with the disinte-

---

66. "Ibushengzhuyi" 易卜生主義, in Hu Shi 1953: 1: 629–47; translated in Eide 1987: 155–68). "Fei geren de xin shenghuo" 非個人的新生活, in Hu Shi 1953: 1: 743–54.

67. See "Bu xiu: wo de zongjiao" 不朽：我的宗教 (Immortality: my religion), in Hu Shi 1953: 1: 693–702.

gration of the Confucian worldview. The central issue of modern literary thought (the subject/object relation in the creative process) is thus part of the larger question of linkage and the role of the individual subject in transforming the objective world. The radical implications of romantic solipsism and objective realism, in unadulterated forms, would contribute to the disintegration of self's organic relation with the outer world and eliminate its role in the transformation of society, thus destroying the optimistic promise of the Great Learning paradigm. Traditional desires to maintain that connection, thus, emerged to shape the reception of these Western modes. Those who espoused romantic views of self and literature had to shy away from radical individualism and literature as pure self-expression if they were to maintain a link between self and the external world. Guo Moruo's pantheism and self-transcendence and Cheng Fangwu's fusion of the subjective and objective in the creative process should be understood in this light. Those who espoused realism could not embrace its cold objectivism if they were to maintain a role for self in embodying the external world. Hence, the importance placed on self, personality, subjectivism, and self-cultivation in the "realist" views of Ye Shengtao, Lu Yin, Zheng Zhenduo, Mao Dun, and Zhou Zuoren. Theories of literature devised ways for the individual subject to maintain a connection with the movement of history. The assertion of a fundamental unity of the subjective and the objective in May Fourth realist and romantic theories should perhaps be understood as a continuity with traditional views of individual assertion, described by Metzger (1977: 42) as follows:

> In the Confucian tradition, the value of individual assertion lies in those qualities perceived as divine, while in that prominent Western tradition associated with thinkers like J. S. Mill and the Romantic movement, the importance of the individual lies exactly in that peculiarly human condition perceived as different from divine omnipotence. One implication of this is that where the Confucians admired the individual's ability to actualize a feeling identical in all individuals, individualism in nineteenth century Europe prized his "differentness," as Arthur O. Lovejoy put it.

An assertion of self, interconnected with humanity and the external world through a shared divine nature, is necessarily an expression of the other.

Post–May Fourth Syntheses of Realism and Romanticism

It should be clear by now that the realist/romantic bifurcation of May Fourth literary thought is largely a misconstruction, although it does offer a neat frame within which to discuss the formation of literary modernity in China. Behind the polemical facade, neither the Creationists nor the members of the Literary Research Association professed the radical ideas each accused the other of promoting. Both were impelled in their writing on literature by desires to integrate self and world in order to allow for self's participation in social transformation. Nonetheless, tensions between these two groups continued to mark the Chinese cultural-intellectual scene into the late 1920's when both cultural camps began to turn to Marxism, and its anti-imperialist and anti-feudal vision, as the remedy to China's national crisis.

The Creationists had since 1925 been "converting" (publicly expressed in highly religious declarations) to Marxism, of which they generally had a superficial knowledge. Guo Moruo, one of the first to do so, denounced in 1926 his former romantic individualism, declared himself an "absolute follower of Marxism," and professed his faith in "a world in which everyone can follow their natures and develop their talents, devote themselves to truth and make their own contribution, find liberation and salvation, a most ideal and perfect world." This world was no "dreamer's utopia or an aesthete's ivory tower"; it could, Guo declared, "be realized here in our land."[68] As we have seen above, the Creationists in their romantic-individualist stage had already revealed a marked tendency toward self-transcendence and utopian collectivism that made their embracing of Marxism hardly surprising.[69] Members of the Literary Research Association, among them Ye Shengtao, caught up in the revolutionary fervor of the Northern Expedition, also began to move intellectually toward Marxist thought by the late 1920's. Mao Dun, of course, had been a founding member of the CCP in 1921.

Marxism seemed to offer the perfect theoretical framework for avoiding some of the inherent dangers that critics began to explicitly recognize in romanticism and realism. May Fourth romanticism had led to an idealist individualism that removed the intellectual from engagement with society and its problems. Realism, on the other hand, in its exposure of social ills engendered pessimism in its readers and thus contributed to social decay. Marxism posited an organic interrelationship between world and self that accorded well with traditional aspirations for such unity. It was, ironically, when the leftist movement was at its nadir, following the devastating GMD

---

68. See "Gu hong" 孤鴻 (Solitary swan; 1924). *Chuangzao yuekan* 1, no. 2 (1926).

69. In their conversion to Marxism, writes Marston Anderson, the "Creationists simply generalized their individual emotions and, overriding the obvious class distinctions, pronounced themselves spokesmen for the masses" (1989: 77).

coup of April 1927, that writers and critics in the leftist cultural camp became interested in applying Marxist theory to the Chinese literary context. As was the case after the disappointment of the 1911 Revolution, the failure to transform the material world caused intellectuals in the late 1920's to return to the cultural sphere as a field in which to change Chinese society. Culture would play an important role not only in expediting the revolutionary process by raising political consciousness but also in simply giving voice to the silent desires of the proletariat. In Marxism's inherent tension between determinism and voluntarism, the Chinese emphasis on the latter was induced by a sense of historical crisis and by a traditional cultural propensity, as we have seen, for prioritizing ideas in social transformation.

Part of the debate on "revolutionary literature" that emerged in 1928 was a rather puerile and bitter squabble between the newly radicalized members of the Creation Society and the Sun Society (a cultural organization formed in January 1928 and composed almost entirely of members of the CCP) over the provenance of the concept of "revolutionary literature." Each group, in claiming to have first raised the idea of revolutionary literature, tried to secure for itself the vanguard position in the formation of this new literature. More significant to the development of modern Chinese literary thought was the second stage in this debate in which young radical critics asserted their independence from the literary ideals of the earlier May Fourth movement. Cheng Fangwu's essay "From a Literary Revolution to Revolutionary Literature" (Part III) encapsulated this need to escape the mantle of the May Fourth and steer literary development away from the May Fourth's elite bourgeois idealism toward a new proletarian direction. Young radicals like Qian Xingcun brazenly accused Lu Xun, already something of a literary legend and totem of May Fourth realism, of being out of touch with the changing epoch in his creative works, particularly his bizarre and pessimistic prose poems collected in *Wild Grass*, but even in his earlier satiric masterpiece "The True Story of Ah Q." In failing to grasp the epoch, Lu Xun's works were holding back historical development, Qian argued. Ye Shengtao and Mao Dun (who had since 1926 begun writing fiction) were also the object of attacks by these young cultural turks. Mao Dun's "On Reading *Ni Huanzhi*" (Part III), in the guise of a retort to the radicals' criticism of Ye's novel *Ni Huanzhi*, came to a defense of May Fourth–style critical realism, though halfheartedly, because the "allegations" directed at it and Mao's own fiction "may have resonated too deeply with their own doubts to permit a spirited defense," as Anderson (1990: 51) eloquently put it.

The crux of the debate on revolutionary literature was the question of the role of the bourgeois writer in creating a proletarian literature. Most of

China's writers of the 1920's and 1930's were from gentry families, although often ones in financial decline, and there were few writers who could, even loosely, be considered of proletarian or peasant background.[70] The problem with historical materialism was that, taken literally, it seemed to force the bourgeois writer out of a role in cultural and social transformation. Broadly speaking, determinist and voluntarist positions characterized this debate. Members of the Creation Society and Sun Society held an optimistic faith in the bourgeois writer's ability to transcend ("sublate" in the Hegelian jargon current at the time) his own class consciousness so as to embrace, indeed embody, the values and interests of the lower classes. Dialectical materialism offered the theoretical justification for the possibility of this self-transcendence. The radical literary critics of both groups held wildly positive views about the role of a literature written by the bourgeoisie in a revolutionary period. In his "Revolution and Literature," the essay that inaugurated the debate, Guo Moruo went so far as to write that "literature is the vanguard of the revolution" (*GMWX* 1: 6). In subduing one's bourgeois consciousness through a process of "getting close to the workers, peasants, and masses and acquiring the proletarian spirit," the bourgeois writer could "express" and "reproduce" their ideology (*GMWX* 1: 216).

Although the Creationists seemed to abandon individualism by repressing their true selves and declaring themselves "gramophones," to use Guo Moruo's phrase,[71] for the proletariat, they were in fact manipulating Marxist dialectics in order to maintain for themselves a central role in the revolutionary process. The elitist and idealist implications are apparent, despite the rejection of the discourse of individual genius. The writer is still the exceptionally "sensitive" one of "profound feelings," and literature's role is still the conveyance of those feelings to the reader. What the sensitive writer of revolutionary literature now expresses, however, are collective feelings (*GMWX* 1: 7). The role of the revolutionary writer is, through a process of self-transcendence and self-overcoming, to embody and express the new revolutionary Zeitgeist, the force at the core of historical transformation. This offered an easy and painless way to achieve the very goal that Ye Shengtao had envisioned for literature: by incorporating the other within the self through a process of self-cultivation, the writer could produce a literature grounded in the self but oriented toward the other.

Also participating in this debate were a group of intellectuals and cultural figures from the Crescent Moon Society, whose most important criti-

---

70. Guo Moruo recognized this in his "Liusheng jiqi de huiyin" 留聲機器的回音 (Echoes from the gramophone), in *GMWX* 1: 215.

71. Ibid., 215–27.

cal voice was Liang Shiqiu. This society was composed of Anglo-American educated intellectuals who found the subjugation of literature to political purposes an egregious affront to literature's nobility. Although Liang was, as we can imagine, the object of bitter attacks by members of the Creation and Sun societies, it is striking how both sides shared a belief in the fundamentally elitist role for the writer and an idealist emphasis on culture's role in social transformation. Liang's elitist praise of genius and his belief that "revolutionary literature" actually precedes revolution is shared by the likes of Cheng Fangwu and Guo Moruo, two of his literary antagonists. Liang believed in the need for revolutionary change, but was clearly no Marxist: "Therefore, writers' creations certainly are not bound by anything extrinsic, writers' minds certainly do not hold any fixed class viewpoint, and even less do they have any preconceptions about working for the interests of a certain class" (see "Literature and Revolution," Part III). Literature is the domain not of any single group but of all humanity; it expresses human nature and universal truths.

In his famous 1927 speech "Literature in a Revolutionary Period," Lu Xun, showing the influence of the determinist theories of Plekhanov that he helped to introduce to China, rejected outright the notion that a bourgeois writer could write proletarian literature and speak for the proletariat. Yet, just a few months later, in "The Divergence of Art and Politics" (Part III), he seemed to retreat from this extreme determinist position and recognize the positive role that literature could play as a counter to politics' inherent conservatism. One senses in this essay that Lu Xun could not relinquish the May Fourth enlightenment role for literature, especially in the face of the radicals' usurpation of literature as a propaganda weapon, an act Lu Xun found potentially dangerous, both politically and aesthetically.

Marxist literary theory seemed to offer an organic conception that allowed for the kind of integration of self and world, subject and object, that motivated so much of May Fourth literary thought. In practice, however, it intensified the dangers of pessimistic determinism and idealist voluntarism already present in May Fourth realism and romanticism. The extremes of the voluntarist and the determinist positions led to a new bifurcation in the Chinese literary scene and new efforts to effect a unity of self and world (Anderson 1990: 55–56). As Paul Pickowicz points out, critics in the aftermath of the revolutionary literature debate sought to find common ground between the idealist and determinist positions (1981: 113–29). Without modification, these extremes would further sever the self from its traditional "seamless connection" with the world. Post–May Fourth literary thought thus renewed the efforts to integrate romanticism and realism that had so marked, at least as I have portrayed it, the May Fourth period.

Following the rancorous debate on revolutionary literature, the CCP, wanting to forge a more unified cultural front, convinced the various factions on the left to disband their own organizations and join an umbrella literary group, the League of Left-Wing Writers. It was in the context of the inclusive atmosphere of the League that critics began to develop theories unifying the realist and romantic, the determinist and voluntarist, positions. From Qu Qiubai to Zhou Yang to Hu Feng, critics in the progressive camp devised theories to avoid the pitfalls of the extreme positions that they perceived to have emerged when May Fourth romanticism devolved into idealistic utopianism and realism into a pessimistic determinism. In "Freedom for Literature but Not the Writer" (Part IV), Qu Qiubai (perhaps the leading literary critic of the League and a former CCP party secretary) revealed at once a strict determinism and a voluntaristic optimism about the role of literature in the revolution:

> Literary phenomena are tied in with all social phenomena. Although literature is an expression of so-called ideology (the highest level of the superstructure), and cannot determine the changes in a social system, and is by our reckoning always ruled by the conditions of the forces of production and class relations, art is still able to turn back to influence social life and, to a considerable extent, either push forward or impede the development of class struggle, or at least alter slightly the shape of this struggle by strengthening or weakening the power of a particular class.

Qu seems to want for literature an idealistic vanguard role in the revolution, yet one that can only be garnered for it through its determined relationship with the material.

Like Qu Qiubai, Hu Feng sought a synthesis of romantic idealism with the social orientation of realism. But unlike Qu, Hu Feng stressed the importance of the creative process and the role of the subjective involvement of the writer in realism. Hu glorified the May Fourth, especially its central figure Lu Xun, as the epitome of a harmonious synthesis of the positive in romantic subjectivism and realist objectivism.[72] With the politicization of literature in the late 1920's and 1930's, however, the positive subjectivism of May Fourth romanticism collapsed into an empty revolutionary idealism, a view that the bourgeois writer armed with ideology could lead the transformation of the material world. For its part, realism had slid into what Hu would later call "objectivism" (by which he meant a superficial representation of the material world void of spirit). The former tendency, which he la-

---

72. On Hu Feng's use of Lu Xun and the May Fourth, see Theodore Huters, "Hu Feng and the Critical Legacy of Lu Xun" in Leo Ou-fan Lee 1985a: 129–52.

beled "subjective formulism" (*zhuguan gongshizhuyi* 主 觀 公 式 主 義), resulted in the glorification of ideology apart from social life, whereas
objectivism (*keguanzhuyi* 客觀主義) led to the reification of the objective, social world. These views reduced the role of the individual writer to an empty vehicle for the propagation of ideology or a passive mirror to the material world, respectively. For Hu Feng, "This separation of the subject and
object, the separation of the demands of thought and the actuality of life,"
had "placed the tradition of realism in a crisis" (1984: 2: 289).

In his emphasis on the creative process and the psychological preparation of the writer prior to writing, Hu Feng accords with much of traditional literary thought. Through a process of reading and close contact with
the external world, the writer could unite with and embody in his mind the
objective. Hu praised the Soviet writer Fadeyev, who was able to:

> forget self [*wangwo* 忘 我] and sink into the midst of life, with his entire
> body and mind join in union with life, and from this union embody the
> truth of life. This is the most important period in the cultivation of the
> writer's life force and power of feeling, it is something through which the
> writer must pass before he can enter into literary activity. (1984: 1: 310)

Hu's theory of realism attempts to reintegrate self with the Real in a Marxist framework. His dialectical theory reveals some of the same equivocacy
his May Fourth predecessors expressed toward both mimesis and romantic
expressionism, and is fearful of the innate tendencies in both to remove the
writer from the creative process. But it also sees each as having value when
coupled with the other. Only dialectically can self and the external world
give meaning and transformative movement to each other.

The core of Hu's views on realism is "typicality," a concept central to
Marxist theories of realism that has had strong appeal for Chinese critics.[73]
Typicality refers to characters within realist fiction that are at once individualized (particular) and representative of a class, a Zeitgeist, or humanity
(universal). Most Chinese Marxist critics accepted the centrality of this concept to realism, but they did not always agree on how a writer should come
to create types in literary works. For Zhou Yang, one of the CCP's repre-

---

73. The "locus classicus" of the concept of type is Frederich Engels's letter to Margaret
Harkness (1888): "Realism, to my mind, implies, besides the truth of detail, the truthful reproduction of typical characters under typical circumstances" (in *Literature and Art by Karl
Marx and Frederick Engels*, 41–43). This concept receives its fullest theoretical treatment
with Georg Lukâcs. The term *dianxing* 典 型 (type or typical) was in common use in critical circles by the mid-1930's. Given the traditional cosmology of the organic interrelationship of all things, where the particular naturally represents the whole, the particular / universal tension in the Western concept of type would fit well in the Chinese context.

sentatives in the League of Left-Wing Writers, ideology was to play an important role in guiding the writer in the creation of types. Hu Feng, as we have seen, found the prioritizing of political ideology destructive to the creative process; types should be forged from an interaction of authorial subject and external object prior to the act of writing.

Efforts were undertaken under the auspices of the League to foster a literature written by the proletariat, making unnecessary theoretical writings that rationalize a place for the bourgeois writer in the creation of a proletarian literature. Given the deep-rootedness of China's tradition of intellectual elitism and the relatively small proletarian class at the time, these efforts were bound to come up short. Mao Zedong himself, in his 1942 "Talks at the Yan'an Forum on Literature and Art" (Part V), was forced to recognize a leading role for the bourgeois writer in the creation of a literature for the masses. Like the Creationists before him, Mao believed that the bourgeois writer could transcend his class interests and embrace those of the worker, peasant, and soldier. But to achieve this he had to "undergo a long and even painful process of tempering" in which his bourgeois feelings were transformed into those of the masses.

The League of Left-Wing Writers was not without serious internal discord. After a brief period of relative unity, many writers within the League began to object to the "usurpation" of literature for political purposes and the reduction of the writer to a passive "gramophone" for ideology. From within the leftist camp, Su Wen and Hu Qiuyuan balked at the strict determinism that seemed to characterize the writings of more dogmatic Marxist critics like Qu Qiubai. These two figures wanted literature to be socially engaged, but also to allow a measure of political autonomy and creative input for the writer. They abhorred the intolerance toward literary creativity and lack of concern for the asethetic dimension of literary art among the League's cultural bureaucrats. Qu Qiubai (see Part IV), presenting the CCP response to these apostates, claimed that there is no such thing as an independent or "free" stance for the writer within a Marxist theoretical frame: calls for literature's independence and the writer's creative freedom inherently glorify literature as a sacred realm of universal, unchanging truths and the writer as free from the determining forces of the material world.

The two short essays included below by the modernist writers Li Jinfa and Mu Shiying (Part IV), both sympathetic to leftist causes, express a sense of the exasperation felt by writers toward the intrusion of politics and cultural bureaucrats into their creative domain. Li Jinfa responded to critics who found his poems "difficult" by writing: "I just cannot be like others and use poetry to write about revolutionary thought, or stir people to strike out or shed blood. My poetry is a record of my own inspiration, a song sung aloud in intoxication, I cannot hope that everyone will understand it."

Modernism and the Aesthetic

Despite the predominant belief that literature should serve a moral and political function, some critics and authors stubbornly resisted this appropriation of literature. To them, the politicization of literature removed from the discussion the concept of beauty, the quality that distinguishes literature from other forms of writing. From Wang Guowei to Cheng Fangwu and Yu Dafu to Dai Wangshu and Wen Yiduo to members of the *Les contemporaines* group of modernists to the aesthetician Zhu Guangqian, Chinese critics staunchly inserted the aesthetic into the discussion of modern literary thought. Throughout the modern period aestheticism provided a realm in which those weary of the vicissitudes of politics could seek asylum. But in the context of the tradition of "literature conveying the *Dao*" and the heavy politicization of literature in China throughout the modern period, aestheticism was necessarily, in spite of itself, a political statement. Aesthetic theories of literature in China struggled to enter the mainstream.[74] Given the profundity of China's social and political problems, this aesthetic-based conception of literature had little broad appeal, although much attention has recently been given it by contemporary PRC critics in an effort to resurrect an aesthetic tradition with which to combat the extreme politicization of literature during the Cultural Revolution. Indeed, what C. T. Hsia (1971: 533–54) has called the "moral burden of modern Chinese literature," a burden that derives from an intellectual tradition of *youhuan yishi* (the mentality of anxious concern for the national state of affairs), which may ultimately grow from the Great Learning paradigm, precluded as morally irresponsible any escape into the aesthetic.[75] Few attempts were made to experiment with radical aesthetics as a from of avant-

---

74. Michelle Yeh argues that in poetry criticism the aesthetic assumed a centrally important place. Critics like Wang Duqing 王獨清 and Liang Zongdai 梁宗岱 supported "pure poetry" that would "rid itself of all objective description . . . and rely solely on those components of its form—rhythm and color—to give forth a hypnotic suggestive power in order to evoke responses in our senses and imagination. . . . It becomes a universe that is absolutely independent, absolutely free, more pure, more immortal than this reality" (cited in Yeh 1991: 17). In her admirable zeal to uncover an aesthetic-based modernism, Yeh has perhaps overemphasized the importance of these views to the whole of modern literary values. We must also recognize that different literary functions may be associated with the genre of poetry.

75. For a discussion of the concept of *youhuan yishi* 憂患意識, see Perry Link, *Evening Chats in Beijing: Probing China's Predicament* (New York: Norton, 1992).

garde critique of bourgeois ideology, as was the case in some Western modernist writing.

A belletristic conception of literature first appeared in Chinese literary history in the period of disunity following the collapse of the Han dynasty in A.D. 220. It was in this period that literary critics began to make a clear distinction between literature (*wen*) and utilitarian writing (*bi*). However, launched as a reaction against this separation of *wen* from *Dao*, the Tang Ancient-Style Prose movement sought to reunite *wen* and *Dao* in an organic whole as the initial step in restoring Confucian ethics to their former prominence, lost to the otherworldly philosophy of Buddhism and Daoist eremitism. Reinforced by Song neo-Confucian metaphysics, the unity of *wen* and *Dao* was a cultural presupposition up to the late Qing period and the beginning of Chinese literary modernity. Huters (1988) argues that the late Qing period was instrumental in leading the way to the formation of the May Fourth concept of *wenxue* (literature) as a cultural field independent of politics and morality. But the forging of this autonomous literary field was a fitful and ultimately unsuccessful process in modern China. The social imperative and the legacy of traditional literary thought constantly intruded to prevent this from occurring. Modern literary thought may be seen in some sense as a struggle to break with the traditional view of *wen* as "the human organization and elaboration of the stuff of existence, the articulation of human values and meaning captured in symbol and then transmitted from generation to generation" (Hall and Ames 1987: 45). Yet even as they tried to separate *wen* from *Dao*, modern literary critics assigned literature a role that inexorably restored to it its traditional moral-political function.

As modern realist and romantic critics retreated from the extreme positions of these literary modes, so too did exponents of aestheticism demur from the radical positions of the Western critics upon whom they based their ideas. Even as they espoused aestheticism, their writings revealed a profoundly moral character. Nowhere do aesthetic theories embrace the art for art's sake of a Walter Pater or come close to Oscar Wilde's statement that "no artist has ethical sympathies" (Ellmann 1965: 102), the inverse of which nicely encapsulates the mainstream Confucian view of the artist. Aesthetic-based theories of literature in China always took on a moral dimension that served to undermine their aesthetic position, a phenomenon Huters calls "moral esthetics" (1988: 247).

Liu Shipei, a principal member of the late Qing Wenxuan school, raised *wen* (by which he meant the parallel-prose style exemplified by the writings compiled in the sixth-century literary compendium from which his school derived its name) to a realm apart from immediate political utility. But in

wen he invests the far more historically potent role of serving as a vessel for
the conveyance of the essence of the cultural tradition, a nationalist goal
motivated by anti-Manchu and anti-imperialist sentiments. More radical
than Liu in his aestheticism, Wang Guowei found literature driven by anything other than its own internal goals distasteful. His view of literature as
aesthetic play expresses a weariness with the idea of literature's utility and
a longing for literature to give in to no external goal. Yet, as Bonner points
out, Wang also elevated literature to a "religion of the upper classes,"
through which the suffering inherent in living in the world may be allevi-
ated and people may be "prevented from succumbing to baser pastimes"
(1986: 104). The moral implications of the experience of the aesthetic are
clear. This idea of art as religion was inherited and enhanced by Cai
Yuanpei, an intellectual who in temperament and thought straddles the late
Qing and May Fourth periods. Cai's "aesthetic education" (see Part II) was
to assume religion's role of "cultivating the emotions," a process that "produces pure and lofty habits and gradually eliminates selfishness and the
concept of benefiting ourselves through harming others." Beauty is a pure
realm of universal truths, the contemplation of which will serve to bring
humanity together into a morally harmonious whole where "distinctions
between self and other" are removed and "calculations of advantage and
disadvantage, profit and loss," are eradicated.[76]

Creationist writers and critics were frequently accused of promoting art
for art's sake. Although Guo Moruo, Yu Dafu, and Cheng Fangwu often
cited Western critics who could be termed aesthetic in orientation (Wilde,
Pater, Croce, Kant), they were at pains to disassociate themselves from
aestheticism and frequently took issue with the accusations of promoting
art for art's sake. Guo Moruo, for example, refuted Wilde's claim of art's
uselessness: "There are perhaps those who might say that I am of the art for
art's school, but I do not recognize that art can be divided into the 'for art'
or 'for life' schools. Art and life are but two faces of the same crystal. Art
with no connection to life is not art; and a life with no connection to art is a
meaningless life. The question is to determine whether or not a work is art
or whether it is beneficial to man" (1979: 111). Yu Dafu's shares the sentiment: "In my view, the French literary critics who first invented those
terms ('for life' and 'for art') should have died a thousand deaths. Art is
life, and life is art, and nothing is served by making them antagonistic! Let
me ask: Is life without art worthy of the name life? In the history of the

---

76. Cai was clearly under the influence of the aestheticism of Wang Guowei (Bonner
1986: 35) whose ideas were shaped in part by Schiller's *Letters on the Aesthetic Education of
Man* (1793–95).

world has there ever been an artistic work unrelated to life?" (see Part III). Finally, in "The Mission of the New Literature" (Part II), Cheng Fangwu stated out of one side of his mouth that art should have no "particular purpose" and out of the other placed on it the moral mission of "eliminating the barriers between human hearts."

As literature became more heavily politicized in the late 1920's and 1930's, critics came to its defense. Attacking realism for its empty imitation of an imperfect nature and romanticism for its excessive concern with self, Wen Yiduo raised "form" as the true essence of literary art ("Form in Poetry"; Part III). Within the ranks of the League of Left-Wing Writers, as we have seen, writers and critics tried to extricate literature from the hands of politicians and cultural bureaucrats in order to restore its proper aesthetic dimension. In the war period (1937–45), when literature came closer than ever before to succumbing completely to political demands, voices continued to protest politics' de-aestheticization of literature. In his inimitable satiric style, Qian Zhongshu (see Part V) describes the literary world of the 1940's as infected by a rampant sickness known as "poésophobia," the fear of poetry. Like Plato (though with a manifestly ironic intent), Qian calls for the banishment of poetry from contemporary China.

Perhaps the leading voice of aestheticism in modern literary thought was Zhu Guangqian, one of the few figures included in this volume who can properly be called an academic critic.[77] Throughout his career, Zhu published numerous book-length studies, including works on tragedy, abnormal psychology, and Crocean philosophy, as well as more popular general discussions on aesthetics and literature. Zhu was a prolific writer who elaborated, more than any of the writers represented here, a systematic theory of literature. Zhu's aestheticism, however, can be traced back to views of the early Creation Society and to Wang Guowei in its clear moral and religious overtones. Zhu opposes a narrow utilitarianism, which makes literature serve some particular external cause; literature is, however, far from "useless" in his view. Indeed, literature serves a central function in human moral and spiritual development:

> Even if we determine the value of literature in real life apart from aesthetic considerations, the influence of literature and art cannot possibly be immoral; moreover, if one is properly cultivated in art and literature, the moral influence one is subject to can be much more profound and wide-ranging than that of any other experience or teaching. . . . In giving expression to feelings and thoughts, literature and art bring one's vitality to full

---

77. For an overview of Zhu Guangqian's theories, see McDougall 1975.

development, and therefore the realization of life's full potential cannot do without literature and art. (see Part IV)

The aesthetic experience of literature shapes one's moral nature. Zhu recognizes the fundamental unity of the traditional "expresses *zhi*" and "conveys *Dao*" formulations: the expression of self through literary art necessarily entails the elucidation of the *Dao*. When one's disposition has been cultivated through art, "one's life is then aestheticized, and anyone with that kind of experience can be called, I believe, a being enlightened in the *Dao*." Though Zhu's *Dao* is not the narrow *Dao* of Confucian ethics, it surely has a strong moral dimension.[78]

What joins all these "aesthetic" theories is their profoundly moral and religious character. The aesthetic is a realm through which the individual cultivates himself and humanity is bettered. This "moral astheticism" or "spiritual cleansing" (Gálik 1980: 30) is a means of moral self-cultivation (for both writer and reader), a means of aestheticizing human life and improving it through the process. For Wang Guowei and Cai Yuanpei, the religious function of art is clear. For May Fourth and post–May Fourth proponents of aestheticism, it is implicit. Guo Moruo represented this particular form of aestheticism when he wrote that literature's ultimate goal is twofold: the unification of the spirit of humanity, and the uplifting of the individual's spirit in order to make his or her life more beautiful (Gálik 1980: 30). Zhu Guangqian's central idea is that literature is the locus of community; without it individuals are disconnected from the whole and spiritually lost in their own isolation. In these aesthetic views, as well as in much of the rest of the writings included in this volume, literature is the realm through which barriers between individual selves are destroyed and a connection with humanity is made. In a world of social chaos and political fragmentation, literature offered the only place for some elites to fulfill profoundly traditional desires for collective harmony.

These critics saw literature as fundamentally a communicative act, a process through which minds connect. This longing to communicate one's intention lies at the heart of traditional Chinese views of literature that frequently appealed for a *zhiyin*, or ideal reader, and expressed anxiety about the inadequacy of language and literary technique to communicate one's intention to this reader.[79] The purpose of literature is to stir the reader to

---

78. Zhu's ideas resonate with what de Bary has called "aesthetic enlightenment," art as a creative process through which enlightenment may be achieved (1975: 179).

79. The concept of *zhiyin* 知 音 is described in a chapter of the same name in the *Wenxin diaolong* (Liu Xie 503–511). The concept is discussed in Longxi Zhang 1992: 133–41; and Owen 1992: 286–92.

feel what the writer has felt and thus to make for human communication. This traditional anxiety is expressed on numerous occasions within these modern essays. Bing Xin (Part II), for example, resents the misappropriation of her authorial intention by imperfect readers and critics motivated by personal biases. A true literary encounter for Bing Xin should not allow the reader to simply make the text his or her own; it should be an experience of radical otherness in which one is moved and transformed by contact through the text with another human being.

Conclusion

Its social, moral, political, and spiritual orientation prevented the full development of an aesthetic-based "literary modernity" in China. Leo Ou-fan Lee (1990: 123–26), borrowing from Calinescu's *Faces of Modernity*, argues that "literary modernity" in the West grew out of a discontent with the values of technological progress, science, industrialization, and capitalism. Literary modernity was locked in a struggle with the bourgeois values of historical modernity. As members of a semicolonized nation confronted with the palpable threat of the West, Chinese intellectuals were attracted to the values of Western historical modernity. But the slowness of historical modernity's arrival and the obsession among Chinese with bringing it about in order to restore to China its lost cultural grandeur precluded the emergence of an antagonistic literary modernity. Literary modernity was thus subsumed within the larger and more central goal of historical modernity. The obsessive priority placed on historical modernity caused literature to be used to promote that modernity, to aid in the process of nation building and revolution.

Twentieth-century Western literary theory, of course, grew out of literary modernism. There is a direct link between literary modernism and Russian formalism, New Criticism, and Structuralism, which in turn are the object of current post-structuralist attack. As we have seen, literary modernism struggled to find a place in China against a tradition that stressed the moral function of literature and in the face of mainstream Chinese criticism that sought for literature a part in the formation of a national or collective community. Thus, the Western and Chinese literary experiences in the twentieth century are fundamentally different. Modern Chinese intellectuals were attracted for the most part to the very ideals of science, progress, democracy, enlightenment, romanticism, and realism, that Western modernism rejected. This is arguably typical of the Third World experience of modernity. If we extend Fredric Jameson's (1986: 68–69) theory of Third World "national allegory," based largely on the example of modern Chinese literature, to the field of modern literary thought, we may see that China's experience with Western imperialism, its "life-and-death struggle with first-world cultural imperialism," determined that its critics promote a literature of national allegory.[80] The Chinese intellectual (Lu Xun is Jameson's paragon) is necessarily a cultural revolutionary in whom the personal and the collective coincide. Jameson points to Lu Xun's "Preface to *Call to Arms*" (Part II) as "one of the fundamental documents for understanding the situation of the third world artist" (1986: 75). Lu Xun's reluctant realization that writing is something he is compelled to do comes from the inextricable interrelation of private and collective goals. He recognizes the need, despite the hopelessness of China's situation, to at least attempt cultural revolution.

Jameson's observations contribute to our understanding of the difficulty in China of establishing a conception of literature autonomous from the national and collective experience, or of a modernist literature preoccupied with aesthetic experience. The Western imperialist threat that set in motion the Chinese search for modernity may be the underlying motivating factor in forming this Third World cultural revolutionary, but that threat likely deepened propensities already rooted in the tradition. The desire to retain a connection between the inner and the outer worlds is one that derives ultimately from the most basic aspects of neo-Confucian ethical thought. In the Chinese context, Jameson's Third World intellectual, the cultural revolutionary who offers a link between the private and collective, is in essence the Confucian gentleman whose mind stands potentially at the center of cultural regeneration. The fusion of the public and the private, as Ying-shih Yü has recently pointed out, was central to Song neo-Confucian attempts to make itself a state ideology (1994: 28).

As the following comment from the Tang dynasty about the most sacred of Chinese literary texts, the *Book of Songs*, will attest, the poet was long assumed to have an intimate connection with the cultural collective:

> The "one man" referred to is the writer of the poem. In writing the poem the writer is expressing one man's heart, namely his own. In essence the heart of one man so expressed is the heart of the whole country. The poet incorporates the sentiments of the whole country, hence a country's affairs devolve on this one man as spokesman. . . . hence the term "airs" (*feng*). . . . The poet encompasses the heart of the whole empire, the customs from all quarters, to form his own ideas, and sings of kingly government, hence the

---

80. Jameson's "theory" of Third World national allegory has been the object of heated attack by some Third World intellectuals who have accused him, among other things, of using a Third World "other" to satisfy his own First World desires (Ahmad 1987).

term "odes" (*ya*). (from Kong Yingda's comments on the *Great Preface*; cited in Pollard 1973: 55)

A need to hold on to this traditional ideal of the unity of self-expression and collective desires and to participate in cultural transformation under-lies the discourses, however Western their appearance, of Chinese literary modernity.

PART I

The Late Qing Period
1893–1911

Introduction

The historical period represented by the essays in this section is commonly referred to as the late Qing, beginning conventionally with the Sino-Japanese War of 1894–95 and ending with the collapse of the Manchu dynasty in 1911. The defeat of Chinese forces by the Japanese imperial army during the war over suzerainty of Korea was a tremendous psychological blow felt most keenly by the stewards of Chinese ethics and culture, the literati. Although Chinese ethnocentrism had been dealt successive blows by Western imperialist aggression since the Opium Wars (1839–40; 1856–60), this defeat at the hands of the Japanese, long the respectful students of Chinese cultural grandeur, was deeply humiliating. After the Opium Wars, the Chinese had responded to Western imperialism with halfhearted and unsystematic attempts, by a handful of reform-minded individuals, to develop industry and commerce and to modernize the military and international relations. But this transformation had left largely intact the sacrosanct spheres of politics, ethics, and culture. The defeat by the Japanese, who had fully embraced the Western model of modernity with the support and sanction of the Meiji court, shocked Chinese intellectuals into a realization of their nation's weakness and of the need for "wealth and power" to strengthen its position in the world order. Part of this process was the rejuvenation of Chinese culture, whose decline intellectuals saw as at least partially responsible for China's weakness.

Although all historical periods can be seen post hoc as transitional, the late Qing, which began on a broad scale the process of breaking down China's long-standing cultural insularity through a massive introduction of Western ideas, is manifestly so. Writings of this period by such important scholars as Yan Fu, Kang Youwei, Tan Sitong, Liang Qichao, Zhang Binglin, and others reveal at once an openness to the radical political philosophies and cultural values of the West and a desire to seek ways to hold on to tradition by reinvigorating it with Western ideas. According to Joseph Levenson (1965), late Qing intellectual figures were fooling themselves into believing that traditional ethical values could be preserved by strengthening the nation through Westernization. Yet Levenson, for whom late Qing traditionalism is but an emotional, nostalgic response to the inevitable sweep of Westernization, may have underestimated the depth of Chinese intellectuals' rational attachment to tradition. In any case, the political writings of the period reveal at once the tremendous appeal of the West (and its radical model of modernity) and a continuing allegiance to traditional values. This is true also of writings on literature.

In the two essays by Liang Qichao translated here, for example, we see a view of fiction that is at once grounded in conventional biases and seeks to break away from these biases. Liang's influential essays set in motion the process, which the May Fourth would inherit and attempt to complete, of overturning the traditional hierarchy of literary genres that placed fiction at the bottom of a strata capped by poetry and historical writings. And yet Liang's respect for fiction is a grudging one that barely conceals a disdain for this traditionally despised genre. He does not really respect fiction, but he respects its power to influence and teach and thus recognizes its utility for the all-important goal of "renewing" the nation. Liang's view of literature is fundamentally Confucian in its didacticism; his promotion of fiction as a tool for this didacticism is all that separates him from conventional views on the function of literature.

A leading figure of the Tongcheng school of writing that sought to resurrect the simple but elegant Ancient-Style Prose of the Tang and Song dynasties, Lin Shu is significant primarily as China's first and most prolific translator of Western novels and not as a literary critic per se. Working with interpreters, Lin, who knew no foreign languages, translated close to 200 novels, many of which were English and French works of the nineteenth century, into classical prose. He saw his translations as a way of rejuvenating a literary style and the traditional moral and ethical values that it conveyed. Yet by cloaking fiction in a respectable classical garb, these translations ended up promoting Western fiction and thus undermining the very literary style they were meant to invigorate (Huters 1988). With their strange and exotic heroes, they stirred the imaginations of young readers and may have encouraged a deepened interest in the Western cultural values of individualism, Faustian-Promethean dynamism (Schwartz 1964: 237–42), democracy, and human rights that were so at odds with the Confucian emphasis on social and moral harmony. Lin's translations were read avidly by most of the figures who would emerge as leaders of the May Fourth movement, and they both sowed the seeds for a modern vernacular fiction based on Western models and contributed to the anti-traditionalism of this generation. What the radicalness of promoting fiction cannot conceal is a profoundly traditional view of the social-moral function of literature. As seen in the "Preface to *Oliver Twist*," Lin Shu also shared with Liang Qichao a wildly optimistic view of the power of fiction to reform society.

Liu Shipei, a proponent of the Wenxuan parallel-prose school of writing and a founding member of the Society for the Preservation of National Learning,[1] sought to forge for literature a realm beyond mere utility, a role that the Wenxuan school granted to styles other than parallel prose, including the vernacular. Freed from any this-worldly function, the parallel-prose style advocated by Liu could simply act as the vehicle for the propagation of tradition and traditional ethical values (Huters 1988: 254–57).

Even as the Tongcheng and Wenxuan schools sought to reaffirm the centrality of traditional prose styles to cultural renovation, isolated writers had begun to develop and promote startlingly fresh literary styles more consonant with the spoken language. The semi-vernacular style in which Liang Qichao couched his ideas on fiction, as well as on a whole range of other subjects, influenced the writings of many young intellectuals and helped usher in the vernacularization movement of the early May Fourth period. As Doleželová-Velingerová has pointed out, the active promotion of the vernacular during the late Qing sits poorly with the May Fourth's self-perception of its own Promethean iconoclasm (1977: 17–35). Another such writer was Huang Zunxian, an important late Qing diplomat and a poet who wrote highly colloquial poems, drawing inspiration and language from folks songs and local dialects. His poetry and his literary motto, "I write what comes from my mouth," have been seen as important precur-

---

1. This group, founded in 1905, was at once revolutionary in advocating the overthrow of the Manchu dynasty and highly conservative in desiring to preserve and promote traditional cultural values through a rigidly structured prose style.

sors of the vernacularization movement. The preface to his collection of poems, included here, gives an idea of his view that rather than blindly imitating the ancients, literature should issue from within the self. Although
this marks a break from mainstream classicism, it is an attitude by no
means without precedent in the literary tradition, which was punctuated
by frequent reactions against rigid classicism. As with Hu Shi two decades
later, the sincere expression of self offered Huang ground on which to reject
the classical tradition.

The essays in this section also reflect the beginnings of a tension, which
continued throughout the period covered by this volume, between a utilitarian view of literature, as expressed most unmistakably by Liang Qichao,
and an aesthetic view of literature, represented here by Wang Guowei in
"Incidental Remarks on Literature."[2] Wang's analogy of literature as a kind
of play without purpose is quite at odds with Liang's overt utilitarianism
and with the mainstream tradition of didacticism, conventionally seen as
encapsulated in the maxim "Literature conveys the *Dao*." Yet, although
Wang drew inspiration from Kant, Schiller, and Schopenhauer, his admiration for poets like Qu Yuan and Tao Yuanming shows that tradition could
still offer him models for the kind of aestheticism he wished to promote.
Art for Wang was an aesthetic realm of universal transcendent beauty, offering freedom from the particularities of reality.

Finally, Lu Xun's essay "On the Power of Mara Poetry," although read
by few when it was first published in 1907, is very significant in the move
toward modernity in Chinese literature. Writing in the difficult Wenxuan
prose style and conveying a conception of literature not that different from
Liu Shipei's, Lu Xun introduced to the Chinese reader a demonic model for
the poet (based on Western Romantics like Byron and Shelley) that was essentially alien to the tradition. This ideal poet is an iconoclastic voice from
the wilderness, a solitary figure who alone speaks the truth in a world of illusion and deceit. Lu Xun felt this poet would have a liberating and rejuvenating effect on society and the nation. This essay expresses much of the romantic emphasis on individual genius that would later capture the imagination of the May Fourth generation, although Lu Xun himself by that time
had lost much of the optimism necessary to sustain a romantic vision of the
world.

---

2. Marián Gálik (1986*b*: 7–18) juxtaposes these two figures, whom he sees as literary
opposites.

Chapter 1

Preface to Poems from the Hut in the Human World

Huang Zunxian

I learned how to write poetry at the age of fifteen or sixteen.[1] I have since been occupied with work and travel that has taken me to the four corners of the world. I have had little leisure, and my poems are stacked away in the attic. However, because poetry is a longtime passion of mine, I write whenever I can. Even though I am a government official constantly travel-ing, I have never abandoned it completely.

Among my predecessors, well over a hundred can be considered mas-ters of poetry. My goal is to rid myself of their flaws and free myself from their bondage. This is a difficult task indeed. Yet, I have always believed that there is a world beyond poetry and a human subject within poetry. If the world today is different from that of old, why should the human subject be identical to that in the old days? To my mind, ideal poetry encompasses

---

1. Huang Zunxian 黄遵憲, *"Renjing lu shicao zixu"* 人境廬詩草自序, in *Renjing lu shicao jianzhu* 人境廬詩草箋注 (Draft poems from the hut in the human world: with notes and commentaries), (Hongkong: Zhonghua shuju, 1963); reprinted in *ZGJDWLX* 1: 169.

the following aspects: (1) it should revive its ancient allegorical function; (2) it should embody individual inspiration through the use of parallel prosody; (3) it should adopt the essence of Qu Yuan's "Encountering Sorrow" and the ancient Music Bureau ballads without assuming their forms; (4) it should apply the principles of classical prose of condensation and expansion, elaboration and unity. In terms of subject matter, from the Confucian classics and histories through the writings of the pre-Qin philosophers to the Han exegeses of the *Book of Songs*, any situations or references that bear a relevance to the contemporary world can be used and evoked. In terms of the presentation of subject matter, the language of official documents or dialects and colloquialisms of the modern day can all be used in writing as long as they express that which did not exist in the past and are based on true experience. In terms of the cultivation of style, from such master poets as Cao Zhi, Bao Zhao, Tao Qian, Xie Lingyun, Li Bo, Du Fu, Han Yu, and Su Shi to minor ones of recent times, I model myself after not just one poet and command more than just one style; the key is to form my own style. It is true that in so doing I may not measure up to the ancients; however, I will at least be able to establish myself as a distinct poet.

I realize that I have not succeeded in achieving my ideal. the *Book of Songs* says: "Although I cannot attain it, my heart aspires to it." I have herein expressed my ideal in the hope that someday it will be realized.

Written by the poet in the sixth month of the seventeenth year of the Guangxu reign (1891), at the Chinese Consulate in London.

—*Translated by Michelle Yeh*

Chapter 2

Foreword to the Publication of Political Novels in Translation

Liang Qichao

The genre of political novel originated in the West.[1] It is human nature to dread the solemn and to take delight in the humorous. Hence, classical music puts us to sleep, whereas songs of the States of Zheng and Wei cause us to lose ourselves in lewdness and become oblivious to our fatigue. This is indeed a characteristic trait of human nature, and even the sages could not tamper with it. A good teacher should guide his pupil in the direction that his temperament will naturally proceed. Thus, he sometimes resorts to subtle humor and sometimes uses parables to convey his meanings. Mencius, for instance, draws an analogy between King Xuan of Qi and the ancient wise men who were fond of wealth and women as banter to conceal his

---

1. Liang Qichao 梁啓超, "Yi yin zhengzhi xiaoshuo xu" 譯印政治小說序, *Qing yi bao* 清議報 1 (1898); reprinted in *ZGJDWLX* 1:155–56. This essay was a "foreword" to a projected series of political novels to be translated into Chinese and published in Liang's journal *Qing yi bao* (The China discussion).

subtle remonstrations,[2] and Qu Yuan compares the King of Chu to a beautiful lady and fragrant plants to express his loyalty to and love for the state of Chu. These two works in many ways yield a greater impact than solemn discourses and imposing argumentation; they should not be snubbed merely because they lack a satirical and tendentious edge.

Although Chinese fiction is included in the nine schools of literature and philosophy,[3] very few good works have been written since the time of Yu Chu.[4] Stories about heroes are all patterned after *The Water Margin*, whereas those about love imitate *The Dream of the Red Chamber*. Taken as a whole, Chinese novels invariably teach us either robbery or lust. Lost in a vicious circle, the novelists are unable to rise above the quagmire. For this reason, knowledgeable men often scorn the mere mention of fiction.

However, as human nature detests the solemn and finds delight in the humorous, even serious pedagogues read *The Dream of the Red Chamber* and talk about *The Water Margin* during their spare time. Works of fiction are, in the end, very difficult to ban. Instead of banning the reading of fiction, then, would it not be much better to allow people to follow their natural inclinations and guide them accordingly?

There is indeed a great deal of truth in Mr. Kang Youwei's observation that people with low levels of literacy will often stay away from the classics but cannot do without fiction. Fiction should therefore seek to teach where the Six Classics have failed to teach, to convey lessons where the official histories have failed to convey, to illuminate where the recorded sayings are unable to illuminate, and to govern where laws have failed. In the world, experienced men are few, and the ignorant are innumerable; those well-versed in literature are few, and those who can barely read legion. The Six Classics are indeed elegant, but if they are not read and understood, they are just pearls cast before swine.

---

2. *Mencius*, 1B.5. In a reply to King Xuan of Qi 齊宣王, who gives as excuses for not implementing the kingly government his weaknesses for wealth and women, Mencius cites the examples of Duke Liu 公劉, who was fond of wealth, and King Tai of Zhou 周太王, who was fond of women. Despite their weaknesses these two men could still practice kingly government. Hence Mencius admonishes King Xuan of Qi that if only he could give the people power to gratify the same feelings, there would be no difficulty in attaining the royal power.

3. According to the Bibliographic Section in *Han shu* 漢書, complied by Ban Gu 班固, there are ten schools of literature and philosophy (Confucian, Daoist, Divination, Legalist, Logician, Mohist, Politics, Miscellaneous, Agriculture, and *Xiaoshuo* 小說), although "only nine of them are worth reading" (*qi ke guanzhe jiu jia er yi* 其可觀者九家而已). Fiction, then, was not included in the nine schools.

4. According to the Bibliographic Section in *Han shu*, Yu Chu 虞初 (ca. 104 B.C.) compiled *Zhou shuo* 周說 (Tales of the Zhou dynasty), a work in the tradition of *Shan hai jing* 山海經 and *Mu tianzi zhuan* 穆天子傳. The work is no longer extant.

A story goes that Confucius once lost his horse. His disciple Zi Gong failed in retrieving the horse, whereas the man who had reared the horse succeeded in recovering it. Does this mean that Zi Gong was intellectually inferior to the horseman? Things are grouped according to their kind and men according to their class. If the giant Dragon Earl spoke in his language to the dwarf of the Kingdom of Jiaoyao, he would not be understood. Now there are few people in China who can read, and those who are well versed in literature are even rarer. In view of this, fiction could be added to increase the numerical classifications of writing from seven[5] to eight, or appended to the four bibliographic categories as a fifth component.[6]

When the Reformation was first launched in the countries of Europe, men of great learning and dedicated scholars would often use fiction as a vehicle to record their personal experiences and express their political views. Serious pedagogues would read and discuss these works during their leisure. Novels were read and discussed by soldiers, merchants, peasants, artisans, cabmen, grooms, women, and young children. A newly published book could often influence and change the views and arguments of the whole nation. Indeed, political novels should be given the highest credit for being instrumental in the steady progress made in the political sphere in America, England, Germany, France, Austria, Italy, and Japan. A celebrated scholar in England once remarked that fiction is the soul of the people. How true! How true! It is precisely for this reason that we are now specially selecting works by celebrated foreign scholars that are relevant to the current situation in China and then translating and publishing them by installment in this newspaper. In so doing, we hope to make them accessible to our compatriots.

—*Translated by Gek Nai Cheng*

---

5. *Qilüe* 七略 are the seven classifications of writing as compiled by Liu Xin 劉歆 (ca. 46 B.C.–A.D. 23) in the Han dynasty around 7 B.C. They are classics, arts, philosophy, poetry, divination and numerics, medicine, and surgery.

6. *Sibu* 四部 are the four bibliographic classifications of classics, history, philosophy, and literature, devised by Xun Xu 荀勖 (d. A.D. 289) to categorize all books.

Chapter 3

On the Relationship Between Fiction and the Government of the People

Liang Qichao

If one intends to renovate the people of a nation, one must first renovate its fiction.[1] Therefore, to renovate morality, one must renovate fiction; to renovate religion, one must renovate fiction; to renovate politics, one must renovate fiction; to renovate social customs, one must renovate fiction; to renovate learning and arts, one must renovate fiction; and to renovate even the human mind and remold its character, one must renovate fiction. Why is this so? This is because fiction has a profound power over the way of man.

Now let me pose a question. Why is it that men are generally more fond of fiction than of other types of literature? You will no doubt reply: "Because fiction is simple and easy to understand; because fiction is enjoyable and interesting." This certainly is true. However, this is not exactly the case since not all writing that is simple and easy to understand is fiction. There is indeed nothing profound and difficult in the letters of ordinary women or young children, or in official circulars and correspondence. But who

---

1. Liang Qichao 梁啓超, "Lun xiaoshuo yu qunzhi zhi guanxi" 論小說與羣治之關係, *Xin xiaoshuo* 新小說 (1902); reprinted in *ZGJDWLX* 1: 157–61.

likes to read them? Moreover, talented and erudite scholars capable of reading the most esoteric of ancient works[2] and writing commentaries on the classics[3] should have no bias against any form of writing, be it profound and archaic, or easy and straightforward. Yet why do they take particular delight in fiction? This shows that the first answer is inadequate. There are, of course, many novels that aim solely at providing pleasure and entertainment, but this kind of novel is not very highly regarded. The most popular are invariably those that are able to surprise, to startle, to make us feel sad, and to move us. Reading these works causes us to have countless nightmares and to wipe away countless tears. But if we wish to seek pleasure from something of which we are fond, why should we torture ourselves with writings that disturb our heart and soul? This shows that the second answer is inadequate.

I have been meditating hard on this question so as to understand it comprehensively. There are probably two explanations. First, human nature is such that it is often discontented with the world. The world with which we are in physical contact is spatially limited. Thus, apart from direct physical or perceptual contact with reality, we also often desire to touch and perceive things indirectly; this is the life beyond one's life, the world beyond one's world. This sort of vision is inherent in both the sharp and the dull-witted. And nothing can transcend the power of fiction in molding the human into more intelligent or duller beings. Thus, fiction often leads us to a different world and transforms the atmosphere with which we are in constant contact.

Second, man is generally unaware of the imaginings he harbors in his mind and the world he has experienced. Normally we are aware of sadness, happiness, remorse, anger, love, fear, worry, and shame, but not of their cause. We want to describe the motivations behind them, but our minds cannot understand them, our mouths cannot express them, and our pen cannot describe them. If there is someone who can give a thorough account of them, we will pound the table and cry out, "Excellent! Excellent! How true! How true!" This is exactly what happened to King Xuan of Qi

---

2. The original reads *fen dian suo qiu* 墳 典 索 丘 , abbreviated from *sanfen* 三 墳 , *wudian* 五 典 , *basuo* 八 索 and *jiuqiu* 九 丘 . In one interpretation, *sanfen* and *wudian* refer respectively to the books ascribed to the legendary three sage-kings and the five virtuous emperors of China; *basuo* refers to the Eight Diagrams devised by Fu Xi; and *jiuqiu* to the annals of the nine divisions under Yu the Great. They are used here to refer to the writings of the sages and the wise men of old.

3. The original reads *zhu chong yu cao mu* 注 蟲 魚 草 木 , "definitions of insects, fish, grasses, and trees," an allusion to the *Erya* 爾 雅 , an early Han lexicon containing commentaries on the classics, names, etc. Here it refers to those scholars devoted to philological study.

when he said to Mencius, "What you have said has deeply moved me." There is nothing more profound to move men's minds than fiction.

These two are in fact the essence of all writings and the source of the power of the pen and the tongue. If we can get to the crux of writing, we will find that any literary genre has appeal for the reader. But fiction is alone among the literary forms in giving the highest expression to both subtlety and technique. Therefore, I say, fiction is the crowning glory of literature. The first reason explains the ascendancy of the idealistic school of fiction, and the second reason that of the realistic school.[4] Although there are many types of fiction, none falls outside the parameters of these two schools.

In addition, fiction has four powers to influence the way of man. The first power is called thurification. It is like entering a cloud of smoke and being thurified by it, or like touching ink or vermillion and being tinted by it. As mentioned in the Laṅkāvatāra Sutra, the transformation of deluded knowledge to relative consciousness and of relative consciousness to absolute knowledge relies on this kind of power.[5] When reading a novel, one's perception, thinking, and sensitivity are unconsciously affected and conditioned by it. Gradually, changing day by day, it makes its effect felt. And although the effect is momentary, alternating interruptions and continuations, over the course of a long period of time the world of the novel enters the mind of the reader and takes root there like a seedling with a special quality. Later, this seedling, being daily thurified by further contact with fiction, will become more vigorous, and its influence will in turn spread to others and to the entire world. This is the cause of the cyclical transformation of all living and non-living things in the world. Thus, fiction reigns supreme because of its power to influence the masses.

The second power is known as immersion. Whereas thurification is spatial and hence its effect is proportional to the space in which it acts, immersion is temporal, and its effect varies according to the length of time it operates. Immersion refers to the process in which a reader is so engrossed in a novel that it causes him to assimilate himself with its content. When one reads a novel, very often one is unable to free oneself from its effect even long after having finished reading it. For instance, feelings of love and grief remain in the minds of those who have finished reading *The Dream of the Red Chamber*, and feelings of joy and anger in those who have finished read-

---

4. Liang uses the terms *lixiang* 理想 and *xieshi* 寫實 for idealism and realism, respectively.

5. In this article Liang makes extensive use of Buddhist ideas and terms, such as *shi* 識 (relative consciousness) and *zhi* 智 (absolute knowledge), to explain the power of fiction.

ing *The Water Margin*. Why is it so? It is because of the power of immersion. It follows that if two works are equally appealing, the one that is longer and deals with more facts will have the greater power to influence the reader. This is just like drinking wine. If one drinks for ten days, one will remain drunk for a hundred days. It was precisely because of this power of immersion that the Buddha expounded on the voluminous Avatamsaka Sutra after he had risen from under the Bodhi Tree.

The third power is that of stimulation. Whereas the effects of thurification and immersion are gradual, that of stimulation is immediate. And although the effects of thurification and immersion take place without the reader's being aware of them, that of stimulation is able to suddenly evoke in the reader strange feelings over which he has no control. For instance, before reading *The Water Margin* I am calm and peaceful. But when I read about Lin Chong's fulfilling within three days his pledge to kill a man as application for entry into Liang Mountain Marsh, or about Wu Song's creating a mighty disturbance at the Pool of the Flying Cloud, why is it that I suddenly become furious? Before reading *The Dream of the Red Chamber* I am happy, but when I read about Qingwen's leaving the Grand View Garden or Lin Daiyu's dying in the Bamboo Retreat, why do I suddenly shed tears? My emotions are under control before reading, but when I come to the scenes entitled "The Heart of the Lute" and "An Exchange of Poems" in *The Romance of the Western Chamber*, or "The Fragrant Couch" and "A Visit to the Beauty" in *Peach Blossom Fan*, why are my emotions instantly stirred up? These are instances of the effects of stimulation.

Generally speaking, the more sensitive a man is, the faster and greater will the effect of this power of stimulation be. But the effect varies in direct proportion to the stimulating power of the book. Zen Buddhism also resorts to this power of stimulation to lead men from their folly to sudden enlightenment. This power is more effective in speech than in writing. However, the effect of the spoken word is spatially and temporally limited. Because of the inherent limitations of speech, we must turn to writing. And for writing, the vernacular is a more effective medium than the classical language and the parable is a more effective form than the serious statement. Hence, nothing possesses more power of stimulation than fiction.

The fourth power is that of lifting. The first three powers work from the outside and penetrate into the mind, but the power of lifting originates from within and works outward. This in fact is the highest attainment in Buddhism. All readers of novels often feel that they have entered a state of self-transformation and that they themselves have become the principal characters once they are engrossed in them. For instance, the reader of *A Rustic's Idle Talk* invariably identifies himself with Wen Suchen, of *The*

Dream of the Red Chamber with Jia Baoyu, of *The Flower and the Moon* with Han Hesheng or Wei Chizhu, and of *The Water Margin* with Li Kui or Lu Zhishen.[6] Even if readers argue that they are not so captivated, I will not take their word for it. As one becomes transformed and enters a book during the process of reading, one is no longer one's own self but rather becomes completely cut off from this world and enters another world. This is similar to what the Avatamsaka Sutra calls "the tower of Huayan" or "the layered net of the God Indra," in which myriad lotus flowers appear in a single pore of the skin and a million kalpas are spanned in a snap of the fingers.[7] In addition, the power of writing to transform people is here carried to its limits. Therefore, if the protagonist of the novel is Washington, the reader will be transformed into an avatar of Washington; if it is Napoleon, he will feel himself an avatar of Napoleon; and if it is Buddha or Confucius, he will become an avatar of Buddha or Confucius. This is the one and only way to transcend worldly life. There is no better way than this.

These four powers are capable of shaping the world as well as establishing and nurturing the various norms of society. Religious leaders depend on these powers to establish sects or schools and politicians to organize political parties. If a man of letters can acquire just one of these powers, he will become a great writer; and if he can master all four powers, he will be a literary sage. One who possesses these four powers and uses them to promote what is good will bring benefit to millions of people. But if he uses these powers for evil, the curses they cause will last for thousands of years. It is only through fiction that these four powers most readily exert their influence. How admirable is fiction! How frightening is fiction!

Since fiction as a genre has such power to penetrate the reader's mind and move him, the universal human fondness for fiction above other kinds of writing is in fact a spontaneous psychological phenomenon beyond human control. This is true of human beings of all nationalities and not just the Chinese alone. Fiction, because of man's particular fondness for it, has become as indispensable to life as air and food—one could not dispense with it even if one wanted to. And since we are in contact with fiction everyday, its quality affects us just as the air we breathe and the food we eat; if the air is polluted or the food contaminated, all those who live in this en-

---

6. *A Rustic's Idle Talk* (*Yesou puyan* 野叟曝言) is a mid-Qing novel by Xia Jingqu 夏敬渠; *The Flower and the Moon* (*Huayue hen* 花月痕) is a late Qing novel about prostitutes by Wei Xiuren 魏秀仁.

7. For the concept of the net of the God Indra 帝網, see Garma Chang, *The Buddhist Teaching of Totality: The Philosophy of Huayen Buddhism* (University Park: Pennsylvania State University Press, 1971), 165–66; also Francis H. Cooke, *Hua-yen Buddhism: The Jewel Net of Indra* (University Park: Pennsylvania State University Press, 1977), 2.

vironment will certainly languish, fall sick, meet with tragic death, or fall into moral degeneration. If the air is not purified and food not properly selected, then even if the community is daily given precious herbs like ginseng and daily provided with medical care, eventually people will not be saved from the pains and sufferings of illness and death. Once we understand the significance of this we can point to the roots of all decadence in Chinese society.

How did the Chinese develop the idea of holding scholars successful in the official examinations and prime ministers in such high esteem? It stems from fiction. What is the origin of the Chinese obsession with beautiful ladies and talented scholars? It lies in fiction. Where does the Chinese sympathy for robbers and brigands hidden away in the river and lake areas spring from? It springs from fiction. Where does the Chinese interest in witches and fox spirits come from? It comes from fiction. Such ideas are never transmitted in a formal and serious way, as when the Buddhist master who hands over the alms bowl to his disciple. And yet, everyone, from the uneducated butchers, cooks, peddlers, messengers, old ladies, young girls and boys all the way up to those in the upper-class, including officials and men of high talents or wide learning, harbors at least one of these ideals. Although some of them may not have been directly influenced, they behave as if they have been affected by fiction. This is because there are over a hundred works of fiction whose poisonous effects have directly or indirectly affected the people. Indeed the situation has become deplorable! (There may be some who do not like to read novels; however, since this kind of fiction has already infiltrated the entire society and made its effect felt in the morals and manners of society, one has already inherited this legacy even before birth. After birth, one is again subjected to this influence, from which even the virtuous and the wise are unable to free themselves. This is what is called indirect influence.)

Nowadays our people are deluded by such superstitious practices as geomancy, physiognomy, divination, and praying to spirits to bring good fortune and to exorcise calamities. The superstitious belief in geomancy has driven people to oppose the construction of railroads and the opening of mines. Disputes over the site for a grave can embroil an entire clan in armed fighting and merciless killing. Processions and festivals intended to welcome the spirits or offer thanksgiving to the gods annually cause people to squander millions of dollars, waste their time, stir up trouble, and drain the national economy. This is all because of fiction.

Nowadays our people yearn deliriously for success in the civil service examinations and strive avariciously for rank and honor. They grovel about obsequiously with almost no feeling of modesty or shame. What they really have in mind is to turn their "ten years of study by the light of the fireflies and the snow"[8] or their secret bribes amassed in the dark of night into bragging rights before their wives and concubines and those in positions of power in their hometowns. For this kind of ephemeral satisfaction they tarnish their reputations and integrity completely. This is all because of fiction.

Nowadays our people readily forsake the virtues of honesty and righteousness and engage themselves in risky intrigues and schemes. Everyone has become harsh, cold, and crafty, and the whole nation is in great trouble. This is all because of fiction.

Nowadays our people are frivolous and immoral. They indulge in, and are obsessed with, sensual pleasures. Caught up in their emotions, they sing and weep over the spring flowers and the autumn moon, frittering away their youthful and lively spirits. Young men between fifteen and thirty years of age concern themselves only with overwhelming emotions of love, sorrow, or sickness. They are amply endowed with romantic sentiment but lack heroic spirit. In some extreme cases, they even engage in immoral acts and so poison the entire society. This is all because of fiction.

Now everywhere among our people there are heroes of the green forests. The ceremony of "swearing an oath of brotherhood in the Peach Garden" in *The Romance of the Three Kingdoms* and of "oath-taking in the Liang Mountain" as in *The Water Margin* is rampant. Dreams of having "big bowls of wine, big slices of meat, sharing gold and silver and weighing them on a scale, and putting on complete suits of clothes," as these heroes did, fill the minds of the lower classes. This has gradually led to the formation of secret societies such as the Old Brothers and the Big Swords, culminating in the Boxer Movement which was responsible for the loss of the capital and for bringing foreign troops into China. This is all because of fiction.

Alas! Fiction has entrapped and drowned the masses to such a deplorable extent! The thousands of words of the great sages and philosophers fail to instruct the masses. But one or two books by frivolous scholars and marketplace merchants are more than enough to destroy our entire society. The more fiction is discounted by elegant gentlemen as not worth mentioning, the more fully it will be controlled by frivolous scholars and marketplace merchants. As the nature and position of fiction in society are com-

---

8. "Ten years of study by the light of fireflies and snow" (*shi nian ying xue* 十年螢雪) alludes to the stories of Ju Yin 車胤 and Sun Kang 孫康, both of the fourth century A.D. Ju Yin was so poor in his early years that he studied by the light of a gauze-bag full of fireflies. He later became the president of the Board of Civil Services. Sun Kang was so poor he could not afford to buy a lamp; instead he studied in winter by the light reflected from the snow. He later rose to high officialdom.

parable to the air and food indispensable to life, frivolous scholars and marketplace merchants in fact possess the power to control the entire nation. Alas! If this situation is allowed to continue, there is no question that the future of our nation is doomed! Therefore, the reformation of the government of the people must begin with a revolution in fiction, and the renovation of the people must begin with the renovation of fiction.

—Translated by Gek Nai Cheng

Chapter 4

Preface to Oliver Twist

Lin Shu

When did histories of thieves begin to appear? *The Spirit of Dong Hu*[1] of the Song dynasty can be said to have established the precedent. About a hundred years ago, the English government was so corrupt that it was virtually no different from its Chinese counterpart. The only thing that set England apart from other nations was its imposing navy. Hence, Dickens took pains to select some long-standing defects of society present among the lower classes and dramatize them in novels, so that his government would find out about them and put them right. Each novel would raise a particular issue. This novel deals exclusively with hardened thieves, pinpointing the mismanagement of poor houses and orphanages. If an orphanage is mismanaged and only shelters children without educating them, it serves to foster talent for future thievery; as a result, the person in charge is actually a machine that manufactures thieves. People are aware that anyone who steals other people's things is a thief, but are unaware that anyone who steals the country's public funds is also a thief. Hence, the thief who steals

1. Lin Shu 林紓, "*Zeishi* xu" 賊史序, in *Zeishi* (Shanghai: Shangwu, 1908); reprinted in *ZGJDWLX* 2: 715. *The Spirit of Dong Hu* (*Gui Dong*, or *Gui Dong Hu* 鬼懂狐) is a Song collection of tales. Dong Hu was an upright historian of the Spring and Autumn Period.

funds is employed as the officer to bring the thieves to justice, and trusted by the English administrators, as if it is quite all right to permit an arch-thief to keep petty thieves under control.

If we speak of the ways of the world, whatever dazzles people's eyes with its appearance usually falls short in terms of substance. All of us feel contempt for the poor alleys where vulgar, uncouth people without any sense of propriety assemble daily. But no one seems aware that the rich and powerful living deep inside sumptuous mansions transgress the bounds of propriety and correctness a hundred times more outrageously than do the uncouth folk from poverty-stricken alleyways. By the same token, England might seem so strong and powerful that it has almost become the focus of attention from countries around the globe, and its conduct has been deemed worthy of serving as the world's model. How would anyone know that England still has thieves' dens if Dickens had not described them in his novel? And yet the reason for England's strength resides in its ability to accept good advice and reform itself accordingly. If we Chinese could also follow good advice and reform ourselves, it would also be easy for our society to change. What I regret is that there is no one like Dickens who can cite age-old malpractices and dramatize them in novels in order to inform the government of their existence. If there were, the transformation of Chinese society might be possible.

Alas, the novelist Li Baojia has already passed away. Among our novelists alive today, only Zeng Pu and Liu E are able to follow the path he took in imitating Wu Daozi's paintings of the torments suffered by wrongdoers in hell.[2] Is there any end to the benefits society could accrue from such novels? I will wipe my eyes dry to wait for their advent and bow my head in prayer for their early appearance.

Written by Lin Shu of the Spring Awakening Studio in Min County.

—Translated by Yenna Wu

---

2. See p. 170n4

Chapter 5

Preface to Part One of David Copperfield

Lin Shu

This novel stands out as the one over which Dickens took more pains in writing than any other work of his career.[1] Divided into two parts, it contains a total of over 200,000 words. In this novel his thought and power of writing reached their apogee.

In ancient times there was something called a Linked-bone Guanyin Boddhisattva, which was made by bones and joints linked together. When you lifted it up after peeling off the decayed skin, you found the whole skeleton intact, with no single scrap falling from it. Using the workmanship of the Guanyin as a comparison, this novel is obviously composed in the linked-bone style.

In general, what is stressed in a composition's opening and closing is the power of structure and the force of spirit. When giving free rein to his pen and writing about a vast amount of things, a writer often misses some details; unable to retrieve them later, he thereby enables the reader to attack

---

1. Lin Shu 林紓, "*Kuairou yusheng shu* qianbian xu" 塊肉餘生述前編序, in *Kuairou yusheng shu* (Shanghai: Shangwu, 1908); reprinted in *ZGJDWLX* 2: 713–14.

him for having left these loose ends. Although not taken as a serious flaw of an accomplished writer, this still indicates that his spirit fails to encompass the piece in its entirety. In other novels by Dickens, whenever he reaches the end of his tether, he tends to come up with an extraordinary idea that makes the reader blink in astonishment, as if espying a lone peak suddenly emerging out of nowhere. Still, those novels cannot compare with this one in its use of the device of foreshadowing,[2] which is so fine that every word embodies a deeper meaning and a remote cause is planted ahead of time for every incident. While writing, he has the characters who should be in the novel appear one by one and then exit the stage at appropriate intervals. Readers might almost have forgotten about the existence of a certain character or incident after having come across it but momentarily. Yet when they encounter it once again during the leisurely course of the author's narration, they suddenly recall it. Searching backward section by section for it, they will find that there has indeed been an account of this character or a source for that episode. In short, this resembles the technique of a skillful chess player: an apparently haphazard move on his part eventually proves to be of great significance. This is what makes him a national champion.

Shi Nai'an begins *The Water Margin* by writing at length about Shi Jin and briefly depicting several dozen other men, each of them appearing in an orderly fashion with individual characteristics. But when the author finally reaches the latter part of his novel, the characters pour out onto the scene like a pack of coyotes, no longer distinguishable from one another. This is not only because his level of interest has waned and his talent has run dry, but also because his spirit has failed to endure long enough to penetrate the entire novel. However, *The Water Margin* still thrills its readers because of its colorful anecdotes about bandits, knights-errant, deities, traitors, and arch-criminals.

In contrast, Dickens's *David Copperfield* relates the most commonplace domestic trivia of ordinary daily life. In the hands of an unskillful writer, such a novel would most likely bore its readers into a state of somnolence. But Dickens is able to transform the pedestrian into the marvelous, reassemble fragments into a whole, and gather together myriads of creatures from the five phyla, infusing all of them with liveliness. His writing is indeed superb!

Sima Qian and Ban Gu long ago recounted numerous trivial accounts of women with relish and delicacy in *Records of the Grand Historian* and *History*

---

2. Lin Shu uses the term *fumai* 伏脈 which may derive from similar terms used in traditional fiction criticism. See Rolston 1990: 183–86.

Chapter 6

Miscellaneous Notes on Literature (excerpts)

Liu Shipei

The English scholar Herbert Spencer has said that the more the world evolves, the more that writing [*wen*] devolves.[1] What he means by "devolves" is nothing more than the move from embellishment to the unadorned, from profundity to vulgarity. When we test this idea against Chinese literature, we find that in the case of works of the highest antiquity, printing had not yet been discovered and writing on bamboo and silk was cumbersome. Therefore, since writers strove to the utmost for simplicity, they valued the use of literary language [*wenyan* 文言]. By the time of the Eastern Zhou [771–221 B.C.], writing gradually became more complex, so that by the Six Dynasties [A.D. 222–589] embellished prose [*wen* 文] and plain prose [*bi* 筆] had split from one another. From the Song Dynasty [960–1279] on writing grew even more shallow, with the colloquies of the Confu-

---

1. Liu Shipei 劉師培, "Lun wen zaji" 論文雜記 ; first published in *Guocui xuebao* 國粹 學 報 (National essence journal) (1905),1–10; reprinted in *Liu Shenshu xiansheng yishu* 劉申叔先生遺書 (Posthumously collected writings of Mr. Liu Shipei), 4 vols. (Taiwan Daxin shuju, 1965).

cian scholars flourishing. Since the Yuan [1271–1368], poetic and song lyrics have flourished once again. These are all indicative of the beginning of the amalgamation of the languages of speech and writing. The growth of the novel form is part of this, and such books as *The Water Margin* and *The Romance of the Three Kingdoms* have already begun the trend of introducing the colloquial into the written language. Uneducated scholars who have not investigated this process assume that it represents an ongoing decline of writing. Within the rules of evolution, however, there is nothing that does not proceed from the simple to the complex. Why would literature alone fail to be like this? Those who discussed ancient and modern writing in the past assumed there was a difference between vulgarity and profundity, and between embellishment and lack of adornment. How could they have known that this was precisely the general principle of evolution? So from the perspective of the general principles of evolution, upon entering the contemporary period China must take the step of introducing the colloquial language into writing. In sixteenth-century Europe, the educator Datai[2] took the use of national vernaculars in literature as a way for popular education to flourish. If speech and writing become one, the literacy rate will increase. By using the vernacular to promote books and periodicals, the cause of awakening the people will be assisted by having the semiliterate all place [books and periodicals] in their homes. This indeed is a pressing task in today's China.

In no sense, however, would it be appropriate to hastily discard the old forms of writing. It would therefore be appropriate to divide contemporary forms of writing into two streams: one would be devoted to the vernacular in order to enlighten the people; the other would use ancient prose [*guwen*] to preserve the national learning. It is only through this latter form that the regulations of all the ancient worthies can be made to survive. As for boastfully indulging in the strange and the erudite and imitating Japanese models, I have never seen anything resulting from this that could be called *wen* ["embellished prose," or writing in the formal style] . . .

In China during the Three Ancient Dynasties [Xia, Shang, Zhou], cultural works were taken as *wen*, elegance was taken as *wen*, rites, music, law, etiquette, and letters were all taken as belleslettres [*wenzhang* 文 章]. From this the classics came to be called *wen*, as did writing [*wenzi* 文 字] and the spoken language [*yanci* 言 詞]. The use of *wen* in its belletristic sense began with the "Wenyan" [commentary on the *Book of Changes*] of Confucius. So

---

2. Unable to determine to whom Liu is referring, the name has been rendered in romanization of the Chinese rendering, 達泰 .

wen is to be glossed as ornament, that is to say, a beautiful and ordered display. Therefore, *wen* is the external manifestation of the *Dao* as well as the sequential ordering of events. But ornamented words also cannot fail to be called *wen*. For the ancients, since the spoken and written languages were one, they adopted the belletristic sense of *wen* to name the unified entity; for later generations, this sense became the full meaning of *wen*. As a result, the later definition of "writing" [*wenzi*] became deficient. If the gloss for "writing" is completely coterminous with the belletristic *wenzhang*, that is to force the reality to accord with the name. In fact, it is only rhyme and parallel couplets that tally with this definition of elaborated prose. Therefore, during the Han and the Six Dynasties, rhyme, parallel prose, and ballads [*xing* 行] were always taken as *wen*. When he compiled the *Wenxuan*, Zhao Ming took "profound thought" and "literary elegance" as *wen*.[3] The meaning of *wen* received its maximum illumination at this point. By the time of the Tang dynasty, however, people began to take plain prose [*bi*] as ornamented prose [*wen*], as when Han Yu said, "In composing *wenzhang*, the house is full of the books [that can be used as models]."[4]. . . They also take poetry as *wen*, as when Du Fu wrote: "Art [*wenzhang*] detests a too successful life."[5]. . . Poetry is, after all, rhymed language, and most of it is composed in couplets. So to call poetry *wen* is not completely wrong. But to consider *bi* [unadorned prose] to be *wen* is to stand contrary to the ancient definition of the word. For custom to simply rehearse this usage without looking into it is to indulge in error.

—Translated by Theodore Huters

---

3. For definitions, see David R. Knechtges, tr., *Wen xuan, or, Selections of Refined Literature*, 2 vols. (Princeton: Princeton University Press, 1982), 1: 91.

4. Han Yu 韓愈 (768–824), "Jin xue jie" 進學解, referring to the broad scope of books that can be used, not just those considered by the likes of Zhao Ming and Liu Shipei to be proper *wenzhang*, i.e., those with rhythm or metrical structure.

5. Cited in David Hawkes, *A Little Primer of Tu Fu* (Hongkong: Chinese University Press, 1990), 102.

Chapter 7

Incidental Remarks on Literature

Wang Guowei

1. The historian Sima Qian once attributed the flourishing of intellectual activities in his time, during the reign of Emperor Wu of the Han Dynasty, to the pursuit of wealth and rank.[1] I would argue, however, that all learning, except philosophy and literature, can be inspired by wealth and rank. Why? All scientific enterprises aim, directly or indirectly, for utilitarian goals. That is why they never run counter to prevailing societal and political concerns. But when a new worldview or view of human existence emerges, more often than not it conflicts with prevailing societal and political concerns. If philosophers take the concerns of government and society as their own, disregarding in the process the question of truth, what they do is no longer genuine philosophy. That is why, in taking on the task of the defense of religion, medieval European philosophy suffered such enormous indignity. That is why Schopenhauer denounced the academic philosophers of Germany. The same holds true for literature. "Bread and butter" literature can never be literature.

---

1. Wang Guowei 王國維, "Wenxue xiaoyan" 文學小言 ; reprinted in *ZGJDWLX* 2: 766–71.

2. Literature is a playful enterprise. The human energy left over from the struggle for existence develops into play. Children in their tender years, being clothed and protected by their parents, do not concern themselves with the struggle for existence. Lacking outlets for their energy, they play all sorts of games. But as the struggle for existence becomes an urgent concern, play stops. The power of the spirit, however, is singularly superior, and since the imperative of existence is not its urgent concern, it retains throughout its life its playful character. Adults, on the other hand, cannot be content with child's play. They imitate in writing, or sing about, their own feelings and the objects of their observation, in order to express the energy they have kept in reserve. Literature comes into being in a national culture, therefore, only when that culture reaches a certain level of development. As for individuals who are steeped in the struggle for existence, they lack the prerequisites to be men-of-letters.

3. Wealth, as the saying goes, begets fame. That is why ornate literature, like "bread and butter" literature, always falls short of genuine literature. Does not the enduring value of ancient literature derive from the existence of anonymous works? When literature gives rise to fame, people begin to pursue fame through literature. As a result, genuine literature must again find expression in literary forms slighted by the world. But as these forms gain currency, they become pretentious and empty of substance. Imitative literature is, therefore, the sign of ornate literature and "bread and butter" literature.

4. There are two essential qualities in literature: *jing* 景 [scene] and *qing* 情 [feeling / emotion]. The former serves the primary function of depicting nature and human affairs; the latter refers to our mental attitude toward these affairs. The former is objective; the latter subjective. The former has to do with knowledge; the latter with feeling. On the one hand, our mind must be clear of things before we can see deeply into them and experience them immediately. Which means objective knowledge and subjective feeling are inversely proportional. On the other hand, intense emotion can also be the object of direct observation and material for literature, and observing things and describing them also bring boundless joy. Literature is in essence really only the product of an interplay of knowledge and feeling. Without penetrating knowledge and profound feeling, one can never be equal to the task of literature. That is why it can only be the playful enterprise of geniuses and can never be urged upon anyone for any other reason.

5. Throughout the ages, those who have made the greatest contributions both in their endeavors and to learning invariably pass through three stages: (1) "Last night the west wind denuded the jade-green trees; / Alone I climbed the high tower / And watched the road recede to heaven's edge" [Yan Shu; tune: "Butterflies Lingering over Flowers"]; (2) "Daily the belt slackens around my waist; / Still I have no regrets. / For her I will waste myself away" [Ouyang Xiu; tune: "Butterflies Lingering over Flowers"]; (3) "For the hundredth and thousandth time, / I looked for her in the crowd. / Suddenly, as I turned, I saw her very person, / In the shadow of darkening lanterns" [Xin Qiji; tune: "Green Jade Tray"].[2] No one has ever leaped to the third stage without passing through the first and second. It is the same with literature. That is why those who are endowed with literary talents still need an enormous amount of cultivation.

6. No poet since the ancient Three Dynasties has surpassed Qu Yuan, Tao Yuanming, Du Fu, and Su Shi. These four poets would have their place in history by virtue of their character alone. There has never been a poet who, lacking nobility of character, could produce lofty and great works of literature.

7. Geniuses appear once every few decades, or once every few hundred years. But they must be nurtured with learning and aided with virtue before they can produce genuinely great literature. That is why poets like Qu Yuan, Tao Yuanming, Du Fu, and Su Shi are so rare—often they are unrecognized by their contemporaries.

8. Swallows in flight, their wings uneven.
    Swallows in flight, up and down they wing the air.[3]

Beautiful the yellow bird, melodious its song.[4]

Long ago when I left, the willows waved their farewell.[5]

The subtlety with which these poets give body to objects rivals that of the Creator. But these poems come from the mouths of a traveler, an unfilial son, and a soldier on the march. That is why we know that genuine emotion is requisite for grasping the truth of things.

---

2. These are all Song (960–1279) poets renowned for their *ci* lyrics.
3. *Shijing* 詩經 (Book of Songs), poem #28.
4. Ibid., poem #32.
5. Ibid., poem #167.

9. I drive the four stallions
   Whose necks are thick and strong.
   I look all around me
   Too little room for free rein.[6]

All that "Encountering Sorrow" and "Far-off Journey"[7] cannot do full justice to in several thousand words, these four lines cover. Are they not marvelous? But to use this as a basis to belittle Qu Yuan's literary achievement is not something a person who knows the power of the word would do.

10. Qu Yuan felt his own emotions and spoke his own words. Song Yu and Jing Cuo, who lived not long after him, felt what Qu Yuan felt and spoke what he spoke. Nevertheless, they had themselves witnessed Qu Yuan's character and what he had gone through. Hence what they said was nearly identical with what they themselves would have said. Jia Yi and Liu Xiang had more or less the same experience as Qu Yuan, but their talents were inferior. From Wang Yi onward, there have only been imitations of his style, with little feeling to sustain them. That is why no one since has written again in Qu Yuan's Chu style.

11. After Qu Yuan, Tao Yuanming must be considered the dominant figure in literature. Comparing the Song poets Wei Yingwu and Liu Changqing to Yuanming is like comparing Liu Xiang and Jia Yi to Qu Yuan. They felt what others felt and spoke what others spoke. They should of course be ranked below Li Bai and Du Fu.

12. From the Song dynasty onward, Su Shi was the only poet who could feel what he felt and speak what he spoke. Huang Tingjian can certainly be said to speak what he spoke, but not to feel what he felt. When it comes to Wang Shizhen of our own dynasty, was he doing no more than simply speaking for himself? Here is an instance of "the oriole stealing the voices of a hundred birds."

13. After the mid-Tang, poetry became merely the vehicle of goslings. That is why *shi* poetry of the Five Dynasties [907–60] and Northern Song [960–1127]—with the exception of one or two major poets—was rather lack-

---

6. Ibid., poem #191.
7. Two long poems attributed to Qu Yuan and included in the *Chuci* 楚辭. For translations, see David Hawkes, *The Songs of the South* (Harmondsworth, Eng.: Penguin Books, 1985).

luster. *Ci* poetry, on the other hand, was enjoying its season of fullest flowering. Poets like Ouyang Xiu [1007-72] and Qin Guan [1049-1100], who were at home in both *shi* and *ci* poetry, were better at *ci* than *shi*. What they wrote in the *shi* style is not as authentic as what they wrote in the *ci*. After Southern Song [1127-1279], *ci* poetry in turn became the vehicle of goslings and as a result declined. (Xin Qiji was the only exception.) Looking at it this way enables us to understand the reasons for the rise and fall of literature.

14. The above remarks all concern lyrical literature. (Qu Yuan's "On Encountering Sorrow," *shi* and *ci* poetry all belong in this category.) As for narrative literature (such as narrative poetry, epic poetry, and drama, but not prose essays), our country is still in a stage of infancy. The language of Yuan [1234-1368] drama is beautiful, but the playwrights knew nothing of characterization. As for the *Peach Blossom Fan*[8] of our dynasty, it certainly has characterization, but its song lyrics are not what they should be. In fact, they are little more than a loose sequence of tunes that have lost the essence of *ci* poetry. In this regard, China, an Eastern country with a long literary tradition, has produced nothing to rival Western Europe. It is the responsibility of future men-of-letters to redress the imbalance.

15. One does not have to be a full-time poet to write lyric poetry. But to write narratives, one must have an extended period of time and gather a wealth of materials; it is something only a talented person with plenty of leisure can do. That is why poets are so numerous, and narrative writers amount to less than 1 percent of them.

16. *The Romance of the Three Kingdoms* does not qualify as pure literature. But only a great writer could narrate Guan Yu's release of Cao Cao. The way Lu Zhishen is portrayed in *The Water Margin*, and Liu Jingting and Su Kunsheng in the *Peach Blossom Fan*, their actions certainly do not make much sense. But for this very reason, does not their total disregard for personal welfare compel our boundless interest and respect, and invite comparison with Guan Yu's heroism? Do such cases really bear out Kant's thesis that life and the cosmos are both grounded in practical reason? How much sadder would we be if we were to compare such cases to the self-serving world of the present? Thus for writers who choose to write drama and fiction, they know what to include and what to leave out.

---

8. A historical drama in operatic form written by Kong Shangren 孔尚任 (1648–1718).

17. When we call writers of drama and fiction full-time poets, we are not saying that they consider literature their profession. To consider literature a profession is to reduce it to "bread and butter" literature. Professional men of letters live on literature; full-time men of letters live for literature. The ground has today been broken for "bread and butter" literature. I would rather hear the voices of soldiers on the march and of wives longing for their husbands than demean myself and sully my ear with the clamor of such a literature.

—*Translated by Kam-ming Wong*

Chapter 8

On the Power of Mara Poetry

Lu Xun

> He who has searched out the ancient wellspring will seek the source of the future, the new wellspring. O my brothers, the works of the new life, the surge from the depths of the new source, is not far off.[1]

—Nietzsche

I

There are those who, having read the history of an ancient culture from cover to cover (through all its ages), will feel a cold shudder, as if passing from the warmth of spring to the gravity of autumn with no sign of new life, and nothing but decay ahead.[2] I have no word for this—"desolate" will do for now.

---

1. From "Von alten und neuen Tafeln"; in *Also Sprach Zarathustra*; see *The Portable Nietzsche*, tr. Walter Kaufman (Harmondsworth, Eng.: Penguin, 1983), 323.

2. Lu Xun 魯迅, "Moluo shi li shuo" 魔羅詩力說; first published in *He'nan* 河南 4, 5 (May, June 1908); reprinted in *Fen* 墳, Lu Xun 1981a 1: 63–115. The most fully annotated edition, to which the translation of this difficult text is indebted, is Zhao Ruihong 趙瑞蕻, *Lu Xun "Moluo shi li shuo"* (Tianjin: Tianjin renmin, 1982). A French translation, by Michelle Loi, may be found in Lu Xun 1981b.

Civilization's most potent legacy to later generations is the voice of the soul. The ancient imagination had access to the temple of Nature and tacit accord with all things, communed with them and spoke what could be spoken, and that was poetry. Its voice traversed millennia to enter people's souls, nor was it cleft when they went mute but spread farther than the race. When the culture declined, the fate of the race was sealed, the populace stilled, the glory dimmed; the desolate mood of those who read history flares as this record of civilization inches toward the final page. So it goes with them all, famous at the brink of history, who fashioned the dawn of culture and now are shadow nations.

The example most familiar to my countrymen is that of India. Ancient India had the four Vedas, of rare depth and beauty, renowned among the world's great works; splendid, too, are its epics, the *Mahabharata* and *Ramayana*. Later the poet Kalidasa achieved fame for his dramas and occasional lyrics; the German master Goethe revered them as art unmatched on earth or in heaven.[3] Then as the race lost its vigor and its culture shriveled, grand voices gradually ceased to issue from the minds of the nation and spread abroad like fugitives. The Hebrews are the next example: although largely concerned with faith and doctrine, the placid depth and solemnity of their writings are superb, a fountainhead of religion and art that waters the soul to the present day. Yet among the Israelites Jeremiah's is the only voice. A succession of wanton kings enraged God, Jerusalem fell, and the race lost its tongue. Wandering in strange lands, they were slow to forget their own, they held to their language and orthodoxy, and yet the "Lamentations" found no echo. Iran and Egypt are further examples, snapped in midcourse like well-ropes—ancient splendor now gone arid. If Cathay escapes this roll call, it will be the greatest blessing life can offer. The reason? The Englishman Carlyle said,

> The man born to acquire an articulate voice and grandly sing the heart's meaning is his nation's raison d'être. Disjointed Italy was united in essence, having borne Dante, having Italian. The Czar of great Russia, with soldiers, bayonets, and cannon, does a great feat in ruling a great tract of land. Why has he no voice? Something great in him perhaps, but he is a dumb greatness. . . . When soldiers, bayonets and cannon are corroded,

---

3. Goethe refers to Kalidasa's greatest play, "Sakuntala," in an untitled epigram and in an essay "Indische und chinesische Dichtung"; see *Goethes Werke* (Hamburg: Christian Wegner, 1964), 1: 206; 12: 301.

Dante's voice will be as before. With Dante, united; but the voiceless Russian remains mere fragments.[4]

Nietzsche was not hostile to primitives; his claim that they embody new forces is irrefutable. A savage wilderness incubates the coming civilization; in primitives' teeming forms the light of day is immanent. Civilization is like the flower, savagery the bud, civilization the fruit, savagery the flower; here lies progress and hope as well. Not so with the ancients of a lapsed culture: the end of development brought ruin, compounded by long basking in ancestral glory; they once had dwarfed the lands around them but then became sluggish, unknowing in their dead certainty, stale as the Dead Sea. This may be why, although they led off history sparkling, they were unknown at the end of the book.

Russian silence; then stirring sound. Russia was like a child, and not a mute; an underground stream, not an old well. Indeed, the early nineteenth century produced Gogol, who inspired his countrymen with imperceptible tear-stained grief, compared by some to England's Shakespeare, whom Carlyle praised and idolized. Look around the world, where each new contending voice has its own eloquence to inspire itself and convey the sublime to the world; only India and those other ancient lands sit motionless, plunged in silence.

Yes, the ancestral voice and written legacy are solemn and exalted indeed, yet they do not speak to the present; let the antiquarian have them to fondle and intone, but what do they hold for posterity? Aside from these, there are simply soliloquies on former glory to detract from present loneliness; they command less respect than young nations, those cultural maybes who yet have great hopes for the future. "An ancient civilization" is just a dismal name, a mockery! The scion of a fallen house babbles on that in the days of his incomparably wise and mighty ancestors, they had storied mansions, jewelry, horses, hounds, and more honor than common men. Can you blame his audience for laughing? As a nation grows, concern for the past has merit that lies in clarity, as seen in a glass brightly: the progress with a constant rear view, the advance on long highways of light with a constant image of the brilliance that was, so its new is new daily and its old does not die. To be ignorant of this and drunk with boasting is to attend the start of a long night.

---

4. This is a slightly changed and abridged version of the conclusion to Carlyle's lecture of May 12, 1840, "The Hero as Poet—Dante—Shakespeare," in *Heroes, Hero Worship, and the Heroic in History.* See *The Works of Thomas Carlyle in Thirty Volumes* (New York: AMS Press, 1969); reprint of 1896–99 ed., 5: 78–114.

Let's walk the thoroughfares of China where soldiers amble through the market squares bawling army songs that damn the servility of India and Poland; national anthemers do the same.[5] China these days would love to recount its illustrious past but has not been able to, claiming instead that this neighbor's a slave and that one's a corpse, flexing itself against conquered nations in hopes of looking superior. Regardless of who comes off worse, Cathay or the other two, if this be panegyric, if this be the voice of the nation, although people everywhere chanted it, it must be the first of its kind.

It seems a small thing when poets become extinct, till the sense of desolation hits. To praise the true greatness of your native land takes introspection and knowing others—awareness comes from careful comparison. Once awareness finds its voice, each sound strikes the soul, clear, articulate, unlike ordinary sounds. Otherwise tongues cleave to palates, the crowd's speech founders: the advent of silence redoubled. How can a soul steeped in dreams find words? Yet to be driven forward by external shocks leads not to strength but only to greater sorrow. So I say that taking a nation's spirit forward depends on how much one knows of the world.

I let the past drop here and seek new voices from abroad, an impulse provoked by concern for the past. I cannot detail each varied voice, but none has such power to inspire and language as gripping as Mara poetry. Borrowed from India, the term "Mara"—celestial demon, or "Satan" in Europe—first denoted Byron. Now I apply it to those, among all the poets, who were committed to resistance, whose purpose was action but who were little loved by their age; and I introduce their words, deeds, ideas, and the impact of their circles, from the sovereign Byron to a Magyar (Hungarian) man of letters. Each of the group had distinctive features and made his own nation's qualities splendid, but their general bent was the same: few would create conformist harmonies, but they'd bellow an audience to its feet, these iconoclasts whose spirit struck deep chords in later generations, extending to infinity. People unborn or now in nirvana might not think them worth a hearing, but people on earth who are tempest-tossed in the unshakable grip of Nature have but to listen: the voices become the height of the grand and the sublime. Yet if told to the peace-lovers, their words produce fear.

---

5. As Semanov remarks, this is an allusion to the "war song" and the "school song" of the reformer Zhang Zhidong (1837–1909), who railed against the "degradation" of the Indians and the Poles, while ignoring the servile state of his own country; see V.I. Semanov, *Lu Hsun and His Predecessors* (White Plains, N.Y.: M.E. Sharpe, 1980), 138*n*67.

II

Peace is something not to be found among men. What one contrives to call "peace" is merely cease-fire or prelude to war—undercurrents hidden by apparent calm until the time comes and the action begins. Consider Nature: woods caressed by soft breezes, everything moist with sweet rain, as though all things were meant to bless humanity; yet flames raging underneath make vents in the earth and erupt one day to destroy all things. The frequent breeze and rain are passing phenomena, not an eternal idyll as in Adam's native place. Likewise in human affairs—since food, clothing, family, nation give rise to struggles clear to see, impossible to conceal; two people sharing a room must breathe, hence a struggle for air that the stronger lungs will win. The killer instinct is born with life; "peace" is a name for what is not.

Humanity began with heroism and bravado in wars of resistance: gradually civilization brought culture and changed ways; in its new weakness, knowing the perils of charging forward, its idea was to revert to the feminine;[6] but a battle loomed from which it saw no escape, and imagination stirred, creating an ideal state set in a place as yet unattained if not in a time too distant to measure. Numerous Western philosophers have had this idea ever since Plato's *Republic*. Although there were never any signs of peace, they still craned toward the future, spirits racing toward the longed-for grace, more committed than ever, perhaps a factor in human evolution.

Our Chinese lovers of wisdom, distinct from the Western, set their minds on the distant past of the Tang and the Yu.[7] Or going straight to the origins, they made the rounds of a world of animal-human coexistence, allegedly a time before the myriad ills when life was calm, unlike this age of filth and imminent peril where none can survive. Their theory runs counter to the facts of human evolution: ancient tribes in fact spread and migrated through conflict and labor, which, if no harder, were certainly no easier than now. But that's way back and unchronicled—long gone the sweat stains and reek of blood—and so, in retrospect, a time they find worth crowing about. Were they transported to that time to share tribal hardships, they would be dismayed and then, inevitably, nostalgic for life before Pan

---

6. A Daoist concept. "Know the male, / But keep to the role of the female / And be a ravine to the empire. / If you are a ravine to the empire, / Then the constant virtue will not desert you / And you will again return to being a babe"; *Lao Tzu – Tao Te Ching*, tr. D.C. Lau (Harmondsworth, Eng.: Penguin, 1963), 85.

7. The Tang and the Yu were tribes ruled respectively by Yao and Shun, the two legendary "sage kings" invoked by Confucius as exemplars of good government.

Gu had hewed and chiseled the world from Chaos.[8] Such an idea, devoid of hope, of energy, of progress, is to Western thought as water to fire. Yet for them the alternatives are suicide to meet the ancients, or life without hope, without commitment. In front of the goal that you and I are seeking they fold their hands and sigh, as soul and body atrophy.

Further reflection on their words will show that ancient thinkers hardly found China as pleasant as some moderns proclaim; knowing how weak and incapable they were, they only wanted to slip out of their mired sandals, lured by antiquity, leaving the multitude to reptilian decline, and live out their own lives as hermits. Such were the thinkers society praised as above it all, although they themselves said "I'm a reptile, a reptile." A different sort wrote out their views to bring people back to the plain old days, notably the Laozi type. The core of Laozi's 5000-word book[9] is "Don't disturb anyone's mind," which requires one first to make deadwood of his mind and propagate inaction; acts of inaction transform society, and the world has peace. What an art!

Too bad that since the nebula condensed[10] and humanity appeared, no time, no thing, has been without the killer instinct, and although evolution were to halt, no being could revert to its original form. Obstruction of progress becomes decline and fall, examples of which fill the world, with ancient nations as solid proof. Were it possible to ease the human realm back through fauna, flora, and primeval life and on to the inanimate, then the cosmos, though vast, without the animate would be a void, the ultimate stillness. Evolution, sad to say, is like an arrow in flight that continues until it drops or strikes something, and entreating it back to the bowstring falls outside the realm of reason. Herein lies the world's sorrow and the greatness of the Mara Group. Its power enables humanity to emerge, evolve, advance, and scale the heights of the possible.

Different in intention is the ideal of China's polity: "Don't disturb." To disturb or be disturbed is forbidden by the Emperor, who intends to keep his throne and sire an infinite line of majesties—thus he must do his best, when Genius appears, to kill it. To disturb me or anyone else is forbidden, for stability's sake, by the People, who curl up, atrophy, and loathe initiative—thus they too must do their best, when Genius appears, to kill it. Plato set up his imaginary Republic, alleged that poets confuse the polity,

---

8. This refers to the Creation. Pan Gu, who was generated by the powers of *yin* and *yang*, used his chisel and axe to carve heaven and earth out of primeval chaos.

9. This refers to the *Daode jing* 道德經, a central Daoist text.

10. Refers to the Kant-Laplace theory of the formation of the solar system.

and should be exiled; states fair or foul, ideas high or low—these vary, but tactics are the same.

Poets are they who disturb people's minds. Every mind harbors poetry; the poet makes the poem, but it is not his alone, for once it is read the mind will grasp it: everyone harbors the poet's poem. If not, how could it be grasped? Harbored but unexpressed—the poet gives it words, puts pick to strings, mental chords respond, his voice pervades the soul, and all things animate raise their heads as though witness to dawn, giving scope to its beauty, force, and nobility, and it must thereby breach the stagnant peace. Breach of peace furthers all humanity. But this means that all, from su-preme god to menial slave, must change their way of life; so perhaps it is only human to want to keep the old ways by joining forces to kill him in his cradle. Old ways in perpetuity, that is an ancient nation.

Poetry cannot in fact be wiped out, so rules are devised to hold it cap-tive. Take Chinese poetry, which Shun said expresses will;[11] later worthies took the position that it manipulates human nature, that "not to stray" gives the essence of *The Three Hundred Poems*.[12] Since they express will, why say "manipulate"?[13] *Forced* not to stray is not free will. How can there be a promise of liberty under whips and halters? Later writing, try as it might, never got beyond this. No need to mention its praise and stroking of the high and mighty; even verse inspired by birds and insects, groves and springs, is largely so cramped in invisible prisons it can't unfold the world's true beauty; which leaves only grief over current events and nostal-gia for sages of yore in those dispensable works that manage to circulate. Should a work stammer onto love, gowned academics condemn it in uni-son. Imagine a strong attack on convention!

Qu Yuan[14] alone—before he died, mind cresting with the waves of the Miluo, looking back at his native hills, lamenting their lack of a goddess—composed in sorrow a rare multifoliate work.[15] Hostile to the muck of cus-

---

11. The idea *shi yan zhi* 詩 言 志 (poetry expresses will), first recorded in the *Book of History* and restated in the "Great Preface" (*Daxu* 大 序) to the *Book of Songs*, was still a commonplace in twentieth-century discussions of poetry.

12. Literally, "the three hundred," a kenning for the *Book of Songs*. The reference here is to a passage from the *Analects* (2.2) "The Master said, 'The *Odes* are three hundred in num-ber. They can be summed up in one phrase: Swerving not from the right path.' " (D. C. Lau, tr.). "Later worthies" include Liu Xie, whom Lu Xun is closely paraphrasing at this point; see Liu Xie, 60–61.

13. This refers to the verb *chi* 持 in the *Wenxin diaolong*; see Liu Xie, 60.

14. According to legend, Qu Yuan drowned himself in the Miluo River to protest his exile from court. His "Encountering Sorrow" established a new literary genre.

15. The wording of the last phrase, *yu wei qiwen* 郁 爲 奇 文 , echoes the opening of *Wenxin diaolong*, ch. 5: "After the strains of the *Odes* had ceased, nothing carried on the

tom, singer of his own rare talent, complete skeptic from antiquity's origin down to details on all things living,[16] he dared—on the shores of vastness, feeling no qualms—to give voice to what his forebears feared to say. Many were the strains of rococo pathos, but defiance was never there and the power to stir posterity was weak. Liu Xie said,

> Major talent picks up its grand style.
> Moderate skill pursues its elaborate diction.
> Reciters savor its landscapes.
> Beginners gather its fragrant herbs.[17]

They all noted appearance, not essence; the lone giant died, society was unchanged: what sorrow those four lines contain! So it's nothing new that the voice of the sublime has no resonance in our ears. People tend to dislike poets who sing of themselves.

Consider the master poets and men of letters since the advent of writing: how many were able to disseminate their magic tones and feelings to refine our natures and magnify our minds? Hardly any, search though you may. But it can't be blamed on them alone, for writ large in everyone's heart is "material gain": to get it, work; once gotten, sleep. How could any outcry disturb them? The imperturbable heart shrivels or atrophies. In it stews the thought of material gain, yet the alleged gain is too wretched to mention and tames one to cringe, scrimp, yield, and tremble; gone the earthiness of ancient tribes, instead the caustic end of an age, a trend inevitable but unforeseen by ancient philosophers. Any talk of poetry changing human nature and leading to the realm of Truth, Good, Beauty, Grandeur, Vigor, and Daring elicits incredulous sneers; after all, the impact is not visible and the result is not instant.

If conclusive counter-evidence were wanted, none could be better than the destruction of ancient nations by foreign enemies. They were flogged and fettered more easily than any beast, nor were there so much as loud cries of anguish to goad their successors toward revival. Had there been, the hearers would have been unmoved, for once the wounds' sting abated, they again hustled for a living. The game was survival, no matter how sor-

---

line; [then] a rare work multifoliate rose [*qiwen yu qi* 奇文鬱起], namely, the *Li sao*" (Liu Xie, 48).

16. Qu Yuan's poem "The Heavenly Questions" ("Tianwen" 天問) is a series of riddling cryptic questions based on fourth-century B.C. mythological accounts of the world and its history. Parts can be read as "skeptical attacks on accepted explanations or on conventional moral judgements"; see David Hawkes, *Ch'u Tz'u: The Songs of the South* (Oxford: Clarendon Press, 1959), 45–46.

17. From *Wenxin diaolong* (Liu Xie, 52).

did, and back came the foreign enemy with defeat in his wake. For war comes more often to those who will not fight than to those who like combat, and those who fear death swell the ranks of the prematurely dead more than those who defy it.

In August 1806 Napoleon crushed the Prussian army; the following July Prussia sued for peace and became a dependency. The German nation had been humiliated, and yet the glory of the ancient spirit was not destroyed. E. M. Arndt[18] now emerged to write his *Spirit of the Age* (*Geist der Zeit*), a grand and eloquent declaration of independence that sparked a blaze of hatred for the enemy; he was soon a wanted man and went to Switzerland. In 1812 Napoleon, thwarted by the freezing conflagration of Moscow, fled back to Paris, and all of Europe—a brewing storm—jostled to mass its forces of resistance. The following year Prussia's King Friedrich Wilhelm III called the nation to arms in a war for three causes: freedom, justice, and homeland; strapping young students, poets, and artists flocked to enlist. Arndt himself returned and composed two essays, "What Is the People's Army?" and "The Rhine Is a Great German River, Not Its Border," to strengthen the morale of the youth. Among the volunteers of the time was Theodor Körner,[19] who dropped his pen, resigned his post as Poet of the Vienna State Theater, parted from parents and beloved, and took up arms. To his parents he wrote:

> The Prussian eagle, being fierce and earnest, has aroused the great hope of the German people. My songs without exception are spellbound by the fatherland. I would forgo all joys and blessings to die fighting for it! Oh, the power of God has enlightened me. What sacrifice could be more worthy than one for our people's freedom and the good of humanity? Boundless energy surges through me, and I go forth![20]

---

18. The writings of Ernst Moritz Arndt (1769–1860) contributed to the German rising against Napoleon in 1812. In 1845, Arndt produced a collection with the essay "Was bedeutet Landsturm und Landwehr?" (What is the meaning of national reserves and national militia?; 1812) and "Der Rhein, Deutschlands Strom, aber nicht Deutschlands Gränze" (The Rhine, Germany's river but not Germany's border; 1813); see Arndt, *Schriften an und für seine lieben Deutschen* (Leipzig: Weidmann, 1845), 1: 289–310; 2: 1–66.

19. Theodor Körner (1791–1813), German poet and promising playwright; was appointed resident dramatist of the Hofburgtheater in Vienna in January 1813. In March 1813, he decided to join the Prussian resistance to Napoleon.

20. Cited by his biographer F. Förster; in *Theodor Körner's Werke* (Berlin: Gustav Hempel, 1879), 80–81.

His later collection, *Lyre and Sword* (*Leier und Schwert*), also resonates with this same spirit and makes the pulse race when one recites from it. In those days such a fervent awareness was not confined to Körner, for the entire German youth were the same. Körner's voice was the voice of all Germans, Körner's blood was the blood of all Germans. And so it follows that neither State, nor Emperor, nor bayonet, but the nation's people beat Napoleon. The people all had poetry and thus the poets' talents; so in the end Germany[21] did not perish. This would have been inconceivable to those who would scrap poetry in their devotion to utility, who clutch battered foreign arms in hopes of defending hearth and home.

I have, first, compared poetic power with rice and beans only to shock Mammon's disciples into seeing that gold and iron are far from enough to revive a country; and since our nation has been unable to get beyond the surface of Germany and France, I have shown their essence, which will lead, I hope, to some awareness. Yet this is not the heart of the matter.

III

From the vantage point of pure literature, the essence of all art is to rouse and delight its audience, and so it should be with literature, as one of the arts. It has nothing to do with the existence of individuals or nations. It is completely divorced from material gain, and no philosophy is to be dug out of it. Therefore in terms of utility, it falls short of histories in furthering knowledge, of maxims in warning mankind, of commerce and industry in building a fortune, and of diplomas in conferring social status. But since the advent of literature, humanity is closer to fulfillment. England's Edward Dowden once said,

> We often encounter world masterpieces of literature or art that seem to do the world no good. Yet we enjoy the encounter, as in swimming titanic waters we behold the vastness, float among waves and come forth transformed in body and soul. The ocean itself is but the heave and swell of insensible seas, nor has it once provided us a single moral sentence or a maxim, yet the swimmer's health and vigor are greatly augmented by it.[22]

---

21. After *Deguo* 德 國 for "German" (youth) and *Deren* 德 人 for "Germans" in the two preceding sentences, the appearance of *De* alone for "Germany" immediately suggests its primary meaning of "virtue." This sentence can thus also be understood as "virtue did not perish."

22. From "The Interpretation of Literature"; in *Transcripts and Studies* (London: Kegan Paul, Trench and Co., 1888), 252.

Therefore literature has at least as much utility for human life as do food, clothing, shelter, religion and morality. The reason is that in the course of their lives people must at times work hard on their own initiative, at others they will be dejected and lost; at times they have to do their best to make a living, at others they forget such things and turn to pleasure; at times they are active in the real world, at others the spirit races in the realm of ideals. If everything were channeled in one direction, the result would be unfulfilling. If chill winter is always present, the vigor of spring will never appear; the physical shell lives on, but the soul dies. Such people live on, but they have lost the meaning of life. Perhaps the use of literature's uselessness lies here. John Stuart Mill said, "There is no modern civilization that does not make science its measure, reason its criterion, and utility its goal."[23] This is the world trend, but the use of literature is more mysterious. How so? It can nurture our imagination. Nurturing the human imagination[24] is the task and the use of literature.

Among the functions of literature there is a further special use. All the great works of world literature can open one to the wonder of life and allow one to intuit the facts and laws of life, something science is unable to do. Now this "wonder" is the truth of life, a truth too delicate and profound to be found on the lips of ordinary students. It is like people in the tropics who have never seen ice: although you use physics and physiology to explain it, they still don't know that water can harden and ice is cold. Once you let them look directly at a piece of ice and touch it, even though you say nothing about the essence and potential of it, ice as an object before their very eyes will be understood instantaneously. So it is with literature. It is not as precise as science in analysis and judgment, but the truth of life lies open to intuition in its words, so that those who hear the voice are suddenly enlightened and put in touch with real life. It's like the ice that, sight unseen, tropical people vainly rack their brains to conceive, and that now is really there. Matthew Arnold's view that "Poetry is a criticism of life"[25] has precisely this meaning. Thus reading the great literary works from Homer on, one not only encounters poetry but naturally makes contact with life, becomes aware of personal merits and defects one by one, and naturally strives harder for perfection. This effect of literature has educational value, which is how it enriches life; unlike ordinary education, it shows concretely

23. The source of this quotation is unknown.
24. *Shensi* 神思, used in the *Wenxin diaolong* (Liu Xie, 298–305).
25. Matthew Arnold, "Wordsworth" (1879); in *Essays in Criticism, Second Series* (London: Macmillan, 1925), 144.

a sense of self, valor, and a drive toward progress. The decline and fall of a state has always begun with its refusal to heed such teaching.

There is yet another point of view among those who take a sociological approach to poetry: their thesis is that literature and morality are linked. The key capacity of poetry, they maintain, is soundness of concept. And what is this soundness? They say it is the identity of the poet's thought and feeling with humanity's universal concepts. How to attain soundness? Through the broadest scope of experience. A broader basis in social experience will reveal itself in the scope of a poem. "Morality" here consists of nothing but humanity's universal concepts. Thus the link between poetry and morality is inherent in Nature. Poetry, in its integration with morality, in its soundness of concept, has life and immortality. Whatever is otherwise, runs counter to social norms; in violating social norms it necessarily opposes the universal concepts of humanity and thereby fails to attain soundness of concept. Poetry that has lost this soundness must perish. So the death of poetry commonly comes from opposing morality. How then to explain the poetry that opposes morality and continues to exist? Merely temporary, they say. The doctrine of "not to stray" tallies well with this. Were there to be a Chinese literary renaissance, I'm afraid men of doctrine hacking down the new shoots would become legion. Among European critics as well, many make this doctrine the criterion of literature. . . .

[The middle portion of this essay is a long and detailed description of Lu Xun's exemplary Mara poets, including Byron, Shelley, Pushkin, Lermontov, Mickiewicz, Slowacki, and Petöfi.]

[Conclusion]

The character, words, deeds, and ideas of all these men—despite the many differences produced by the variety of nationality and background—are united in one school: each was a vigorous, unflinching defender of truth; none turned conformist to please the crowd; they spoke with strength to stir new life in their countrymen and make their country a great one.

Who on Chinese soil can compare? An advanced culture no neighbor could match, a haughty strut to enhance the distinction—this was China's posture in Asia; today, withered though it is, its fortune lies in being Western Europe's antithesis. If, rather than barring its gates for centuries, it had gone along with world trends to have constant innovation in thought and action, then conceivably it could now be standing tall on earth, not ashamed among other nations, but majestic and capable of change without panic. Therefore to gauge its standing, and ascertain what hit it, is to reveal considerable strengths and faults in Cathay as a state. As strengths, its culture is free of foreign influence and has a distinctive splendor, waning of late but still unique.[26] As faults, smug isolation and a sense of being beyond reproach, which allowed the descent to material gain; as time wore on, its spirit succumbed and, when a new force hit, melted like unresisting ice. Since the old taint is deep, all things are scrutinized with the eyes of convention, whose yeas and nays are mainly fallacies—the reason why, after two decades of reform clamor, new voices are still not raised in China, and precisely why warriors of the spirit have value.

In eighteenth-century England, when society was accustomed to deceit, and religion at ease with corruption, literature provided whitewash through imitations of antiquity, and the genuine voice of the soul could not be heard. The philosopher Locke was the first to reject the chronic abuses of politics and religion, to promote freedom of speech and thought, and to sow the seeds of change. In literature it was the peasant Burns of Scotland who put all he had into fighting society, declared universal equality, feared no authority, nor bowed to gold and silk, but poured his hot blood into his rhymes; yet this great man of ideas, not immediately the crowd's proud son, walked a rocky outcast road to early death. Then Byron and Shelley, as we know, took up the fight. With the power of a tidal wave, they smashed into the pillars of the ancien régime. The swell radiated to Russia, giving rise to Pushkin, poet of the nation; to Poland, creating Mickiewicz, poet of revenge; to Hungary, waking Petöfi, poet of patriotism; their followers are too many to name. Although Byron and Shelley acquired the Mara title, they too were simply human. Such a fellowship need not be labeled the "Mara School," for life on earth is bound to produce their kind. Might they not be the ones enlightened by the voice of sincerity, who, embracing that sincerity, share a tacit understanding? Their lives are strangely alike; most took up arms and shed their blood, like swordsmen who circle in public view, causing shudders of pleasure at the sight of mortal combat. To lack men who shed their blood in public is a disaster for the people; yet having them and ignoring them, even proceeding to kill them, is a greater disaster from which the people cannot recover.

Now survey China: where are the warriors of the spirit? Is there a genuine voice to lead us to goodness, beauty, and vigor? Is there a warm voice

---

26. Irony is unmistakable in this denial of foreign influence, since the country has just been referred to as *Zhendan* 震旦, the old Indian appellation for China (here translated as Cathay). Indian influence on Chinese culture, since the introduction of Buddhism during the Han dynasty, was well known.

to deliver us from this barren winter? Barren homeland, without a Jeremiah to compose a final lamentation as a legacy to the world. Unborn perhaps, or murdered by the public, or both—thus China has become desolate. Only for the body have great pains been taken, while the mind faded into the barrens; the onslaught of the new overwhelmed it. "Reform" said the public, a voice that confessed its habitual wrongdoing, as if to say "We repent." Along with reform came the birth of hope; as we expected, scholars introduced modern culture. But after a decade of incessant introduction, consider what they've been coming back with: nothing aside from how to manufacture cake and guard prisons. In China yet to come, perennially desolate, a second call for reform is virtually certain, given past history.

The Last Ray, a book by the Russian author Korolenko, records how an old man teaches a boy to read in Siberia: "His book talked of the cherry and the oriole, but these didn't exist in frozen Siberia. The old man explained: 'It's a bird that sits on a cherry branch and carols its fine songs.' The youth reflected."[27] Yes, amid desolation the youth heard the gloss of a man of foresight, although he had not heard the fine song itself. But the voice of foresight does not come to shatter China's desolation. This being so, is there nothing for us but reflection, simply nothing but reflection?

—*Translated by Shu-ying Tsau and Donald Holoch*

---

27. This is a condensed version of a scene from "Poslednii luch"; see V. G. Korolenko, *Sobrani sochinenii v shesti tomakh* (Moscow: Biblioteka Ogonek, 1971), 1: 377–78.

PART II

The May Fourth Period
1915–1925

the youth of China and led to a series of nationwide protests against Japanese imperialism and the Chinese warlords who had fragmented and weakened the nation to a point where it was forced to sign the treaty to appease Japanese interests. The protest movement is generally portrayed as one of the first large-scale expressions of Chinese nationalism, and leading indirectly to the founding of the Chinese Communist Party in 1921. The broader cultural dimension of this movement, for which 1919 is a pivot, may be seen as originating in 1915 with the founding of the journal *Xin qingnian* (New youth), the leading forum for a new generation of Western-trained intellectuals, and ending roughly with the May Thirtieth movement of 1925, when many intellectuals began to move decidedly toward Marxism. The break with tradition proposed by May Fourth intellectuals is perhaps unparalleled in world intellectual history in its radicalness. Writers like Chen Duxiu, Hu Shi, Wu Yu, Gao Yihan, Yi Baisha, Zhou Zuoren, and Lu Xun filled the pages of *New Youth* with calls for an end to oppressive social practices such as footbinding, concubinage, filial piety, and prescribed social ritual, as well as to the Confucian ethical system that seemed to legitimize them. Confucianism was seen as glorifying a political and familial authoritarianism that shackled the individual, thus depriving society of its principal dynamic force. With its conservative longing for a return to a lost utopian antiquity and its rigidly hierarchical social structure, the Confucian ethical system was viewed as a monolithic force that had prevented China from progressing in the manner of the Western powers.

Integral to this cultural revolution was the radical reform of the classical literary language so closely associated with Confucianism. From the perspective of young intellectuals raised on the new-style writings of Liang Qichao and the translations of Yan Fu and Lin Shu, and who had studied or were studying abroad, the Chinese literary tradition appeared moribund, deadened by a blind worship of traditional ethical values and a superficial imitation of the styles of past prose and poetic masters. In its imitativeness, its highly regulated structure, its dense allusiveness (which demanded of the reader a rigorous grounding in the philosophical classics, dynastic histories, and reams of poetry), the classical literary tradition seemed divorced from all that was real and meaningful in a time of national crisis. The classical language and the genres in which it was written (poetry, essay, history, philosophy) were unintelligible to all but the elite literati and as such were removed from the vast majority of Chinese, whom progressive intellectuals were beginning to see as indispensable to the all-important process of modernization and nation building. Western literature, which as early as the Renaissance had rejected Greek and Latin in favor of the national languages of Europe, offered these young intellectuals a vibrant example of the positive effects of an anti-classical revolution in language. China, they argued, needed such a revolution in order to displace the hegemony of the classical tradition and create a living vernacular literature that would be read by more than a small minority, would respond to modern social problems, and would aid in the transformation of society. This interrelationship of linguistic-literary reform and sociopolitical reform had long been a characteristic of cultural movements in China, as for example with the Ancient-Style Prose movement of the Tang and Song.

Of course, premodern China was not without a tradition of literature in the vernacular. Fiction, some drama, and even some poetry were written in a colloquial style remarkably close to current spoken Chinese. The high and low traditions had, moreover, a long history of mutual interaction and influence. Yet the vernacular tradition, even during its apogee with the full-length narratives of the Ming and Qing, did not strike May Fourth intellectuals as a suitably progressive model for the development of a modern literature. It was seen as mired in superstitious tales of ghosts and heroes, or fatuous narratives of amorous dalliances between talented scholars and exquisite beauties. The late Qing period, as if responding to Liang Qichao's call for a renovation of fiction, had seen an explosion in fictional writing in the vernacular, much of it political satire; this body of works was something closer to what May Fourth literary reformers sought, but it was still perceived as largely unsophisticated in linguistic and narrative technique, fundamentally Confucian in its social message, and therefore a less than perfect model. The development of a modern vernacular literature, which was seen as crucial to the renovation of Chinese society, could not then be simply a matter of building on the vernacular tradition. A modern literature would have to borrow from many sources; it would be a kind of synthesis of spoken Chinese, the traditional vernacular, and some lexical and syntactic elements from Western languages (often through the intermediary of Japanese). Only in this way, went their thinking, could Chinese literature break free from the stagnant classical and vernacular traditions.

Implicit in the essays of Hu Shi ("Some Modest Proposals for the Reform of Literature") and Chen Duxiu ("On Literary Revolution") is a recognition of the essential organic unity of literary style and cultural-ethical values. As with the Ancient-Style Prose movement and the Ming Gongan reaction to mainstream classicism,[2] the May Fourth literary revolution saw

---

2. Critics have often suggested that Hu Shi's "proposals," in their rejection of allusion, hackneyed language and cliché, were influenced by the Imagism. Liang Shiqiu (1927: 6) was the first to do so. Michelle Yeh (1991: 56–58) is right, I think, to downplay this influence. Hu Shi's distaste for allusion and parallelism resonates as loudly with the Ancient-Style Prose movement (though of course his anti-classicism is at odds with their proposal

the reform of literature as an integral part of the reform (moral, spiritual, and psychological) of the nation. The literary revolution was the necessary first step in the iconoclastic attack on Confucian morality, for the classical language was the medium that embodied and conveyed those ethical values. Although they uniformly denounced the didactic concept of "literature conveys the Dao," May Fourth literary theorists proposed to use literature in much the same way. A further irony is that these two essays were written in the very language they sought to overthrow, a compromise necessary to gain the attention of the appropriate readership.

Hu and Chen's insistence on a detailed review of the literary tradition must be understood in the context of their attack on the Tongcheng, Wenxuan, and Jiangxi literary schools,[3] which dominated the late Qing and early Republican literary scenes. All three schools promoted the imitation of the styles of earlier writers. Both Hu and Chen called for an end to imitation, allusiveness, floweriness, and pedantry in literature and promoted a new lively language closer to the spoken language. They saw the vernacular as deriving from reality itself, whether the real feelings of the writer or the actualities of everyday existence. The reader will sense what the titles of the two pieces intimate, that Chen Duxiu's call for literary revolution is more radical than Hu Shi's tamer reformist agenda. Chen Duxiu, later one of the founding members of the Chinese Communist Party, brought to the whole question of language a class understanding not present in Hu Shi's essay. The classical language is the language of the aristocracy, and the literary revolution, he implied, is part of a larger process of liberating the lower classes from oppression by the feudal aristocracy.

"Nightmare," an essay in the form of an allegorical cautionary tale by Lin Shu, expresses something of the conservative backlash to the May Fourth calls for literary revolution. This backlash was weak, short-lived, and unable to rally much broad support against the powerful tide of the literary revolution. The success of the revolution was impressive, indeed. By 1919 writers began on a fairly large scale to realize through literary practice the calls for a new vernacular literature. Through this process the modern written vernacular language began to take shape. By the mid-1920's published writings in classical Chinese were rare. A flourish of interest in reviving the classical language arose in the mid-1930's (in conjunction with the GMD's New Life movement to restore traditional values to Chinese so-

---

to return to the style and import of the classics). Zhou Zuoren saw in Hu's proposals similarities with the Gongan school of the late Ming period (1932: 42–52, 102–12).

3. For a brief discussion of the Tongcheng and Wenxuan schools, see the Introduction to Part I and the Glossary. The Southern Society (*Nanshe* 南社) followed the Jiangxi school of poetry, in particular the poetry of Huang Tingjian.

ciety), but the fact that some of its proponents were forced to use the vernacular to voice their support for the classical says much about how greatly
the linguistic situation had changed since Hu Shi and Chen Duxiu first
published their polemics.

At the same time that May Fourth intellectuals turned their sights culturally inward in their attack on Confucianism, they eagerly reached out
for knowledge and ideas beyond their own borders. Western ideas served
both as weapons in the attack on tradition and to fill the ideological vacuum left by that attack. Chen Duxiu, perhaps the most radical of all May
Fourth iconoclasts, went so far as to call for a totalistic Westernization, including the abolition of the difficult and cumbersome written language and
its replacement by a Latin script. Zhou Zuoren's "Humane Literature,"
speaking in the Western discourse of enlightenment, expresses a cosmopolitan desire for the Chinese people to join the ranks of the larger human
community. But Zhou also understood that they could not do so until they
discovered their humanity beneath the web of inhumanity that was their
tradition. Humane literature was to take the lead in this process of discovery. Like the Enlightenment in the West, the May Fourth saw itself as recovering for mankind its true humanity.

Xu Zhimo's essay "Art and Life," presented "in English with the pedantic air of an Oxford don" (Leo Ou-fan Lee 1973:156) for a Chinese audience
that had few English speakers, makes some startlingly extreme criticisms of
the Chinese national character and Chinese tradition. Xu's declaration that
traditional China had no real art because its people lacked a transcendental
spirituality inverted the conventional Chinese view that China was spiritually superior to the West, though it be materially backward. For Xu
Zhimo, the Chinese spirit first had to be cultivated, through a process of
liberating human energies and intensifying the individual's emotional experience, for art to succeed in portraying the whole of life, as he felt it did
in the West. The Chinese spirit was, in Xu's estimation, mired in lethargy,
conventionality, and petty sentiments, when it needed to unleash its inner
dynamism and fully embrace the beauty in the world. In his essay "Replacing Religion with Aesthetic Education," Cai Yuanpei, an intellectual with
strong ties to the late Qing generation but who as president of Peking University also did much to foster the liberal environment that gave rise to
May Fourth cultural iconoclasm, shares with Xu a view of the interrelationship of art and the transformation of the self. Yet Cai's aesthetic education
ultimately sought out the moral function of forging superior human beings
who seek not the satisfaction of their own selfish desires, but the spiritual
commonality of humankind. The ultimate end of an aesthetic education

was to erase distinctions between self and other in the shaping of a better moral community.

Broadest in appeal of the many Western literary modes tried out by the May Fourth generation of writers and critics were realism and romanticism, neither of which can be said to have indigenous analogues in China. Progressives like Hu Shi and Chen Duxiu perceived the literary tradition as moribund principally because it had lost a connection with the real, whether that reality lay in the external world or within the self. May Fourth realism and romanticism were motivated by the same impulse to discover the Real that was shrouded, so they saw it, in the ideological fog of traditional thought. The representation of both these inner and outer realities was seen as the only way to breathe new life into literature and thus empower it to participate in the transformation of society. Mao Dun, perhaps the most important Chinese literary critic of the 1920's, was also the leading supporter of naturalism. But Mao Dun eventually retreated from the hard objectivism of this mode of writing and came to favor a more active role for the author's subjectivity in the creative process. In "Literature and Life," he borrowed heavily from Hippolyte Taine's historical-determinist theories of literature, for they explained the poverty of China's traditional literature and offered hope for the advent of a new literature in a new historical age. But Mao Dun was uneasy with Taine's rather determinist strain and felt compelled to add a fourth category to Taine's three, that of *renge* 人格 , or personality of the writer.[4] Lu Xun's essay, "On Photography," which seems to have little to do with literature and is more in line with his earlier attacks on the Chinese national character, can be read as an allegory about the reception of mimesis in the Chinese cultural context. As the most "realist" of Western art forms, photography symbolizes the Western aesthetic of representation. As Lu Xun describes it, upon arrival in China photography is attacked as the devil's work and is used for every purpose but the representation of reality: moral instruction for the young, the consolidation of patriarchy, propagation of personal power and prestige. Finally, it runs up against and is defeated by the traditional aesthetic of Beijing opera and its gender mixing. "What a pity," Lu Xun wrote elsewhere, "that the moment foreign things reach China they change their color as if they had fallen into a vat of black dye."[5]

Like the reception of realism, the adoption of romanticism was problematic in modern China. This is readily apparent in Guo Moruo's "Preface

---

4. This is pointed out by Lung-kee Sun 1986–87: 46–47.
5. Lu Xun, "Suiganlu 43" 隨感録 (Random thought, no. 43)"; in Lu Xun 1980: 2: 39; Lu Xun 1981*a*: 1: 330–31.

to *The Sorrows of Young Werther.*" Guo's 1921 translation of Goethe's novel became something of a bible for May Fourth youth; Werther was an unconventional individual, the man of feeling par excellence, whose profound sense of self offered a model for youths in their radical attack on the constraining ethics of ritualized behavior they perceived in tradition. But what appealed to Guo Moruo in the character of Werther was at once his unbridled egoism and strong subjectivity and his "pantheistic" fusing with the divine in nature. Behind the Promethean exaltation of self in the May Fourth understanding of romanticism lies a deep anxiety with the radical autonomy of the Western self and a consequent desire for the solace of the "complete destruction of the ego."

It is precisely this religious, utopian anti-selfconsciousness that Liang Shiqiu mocked in his essay "Fusing with Nature." Liang was a classicist trained by Irving Babbitt at Harvard and thus disdainful of romantic excessiveness. His sympathies are clearly with Oscar Wilde's haughty contempt for nature and preference for the manmade artifice of literature. One may also see in Liang's writings something of the Confucian-humanist emphasis on culture as produced by men for the purpose of social cohesion. Liang was not the only figure to criticize the excesses of the May Fourth. Wen Yiduo's "Form in Poetry" (see Part III), in a similar vein, respects the formal constraints of poetic form on the poet and rejects the emotional histrionics of free verse and the romantics who promote it. Mei Guangdi, a classicist who had studied at both Northwestern University and Harvard, and likeminded scholars associated with the conservative journal *Xueheng* (Critical review) also assailed May Fourth iconoclasm. Their attack was more solidly grounded than Lin Shu's conservative reaction, for they were modern intellectuals who had studied in the West and were open to many of its cultural values. Mei's essay "A Critique of the New Culturists" opposes neither May Fourth anti-traditionalism nor Westernization but objects to the radicalness of this anti-traditionalism and the superficiality of the May Fourth understanding of Western culture. Rather than an uncritical adoption of all things Western, Mei and the writers of the *Critical Review* favored a cross-cultural synthesis between the best of Chinese and Western cultures. Like Lin Shu, Mei expresses his opposition to the vernacularization movement in the classical language.

The liberation of women was for May Fourth male writers something of a metaphor for the larger goal of the liberation of humankind from the deadening oppression of tradition. Male writers like Lu Xun and Ye Shengtao wrote sympathetically of the tragic plight of women as victims of Confucian ethics. Zhou Zuoren ("Women and Literature") was one of the leading male writers to voice support for the liberation of women as complete individuals equal to men and fully united with humanity. The development of a women's literature was for Zhou part of the larger project of creating in China a "humane literature" that sought the liberation of humankind, of which women were but a part, from tradition. It is significant how little attention Zhou actually paid in this essay on women in literature to women's literature. The idea, shared by many women writers, that the women's struggle was but part of the larger goal of the liberation of humankind, sheds some light on the relative disinclination in the Chinese context toward a "feminist" literature and suggests perhaps the inadequacy of Western feminist concepts to that context.

One of the most important trends in May Fourth literature was the emergence of women writers. Although traditional literature was certainly not without its women poets and writers, few were included in the canon and are thus unknown today. The liberation of women's voices was part of the process of throwing off the ethics of Confucianism, an ethics seen as particularly oppressive toward women. Women were active in writing poetry (Bing Xin) and fiction (Lu Yin, Feng Yuanyu, Bing Xin, Ling Shuhua), but few participated in the literary polemics of the day. The essays by Bing Xin ("On 'Literary Criticism'") and Lu Yin ("My Opinions on Creativity") are rare examples of writing about writing by women from the May Fourth period. Both tended to see literature as a communion of spirits, a transfer of "intention" between the writer and reader. Lu Yin in particular displayed a very tradition-bound anxiety that her authorial intention might be lost in the reading process. Her dark view of the age may not be consonant with the generally optimistic tenor of May Fourth writing, but her anxiety over the responsibility of the writer in influencing the youth of the day is characteristic.

Lu Xun shared Lu Yin's paradoxical dread and hopes about the psychological effects of literature on the Chinese reader. But Lu Xun ("Preface to *Call to Arms*") was perhaps more pessimistic about the dilemma of the writer; his only allowance for hope is the fact that hope cannot be said not to exist. Writing may lead to nothing but waking up the slumbering to the pain and misery of their existence, without offering a way out of the "iron house." And yet, Lu Xun was persuaded to break his silence and write in order to "encourage those fighters who are galloping on in loneliness." Beneath the fragile optimism is a deep well of fear that literature may do more harm to the reader than good. But there is little doubt, and this may be true of all the essays in this collection, about writing's power to stir the mind.

Beneath the dominant discourse of totalistic iconoclasm, resonances with tradition may be found in these essays, perhaps most obviously in Ye

Shengtao's "On the Literary Arts." In his disdain for a fiction of idle diversion, one that draws its material from the extraordinary events of the day without the subjective shaping of the artistic mind (Ye had been a writer of popular fiction prior to 1919), Ye was typical of May Fourth writers and critics who sought for fiction a moral and cultural seriousness of purpose. As Marston Anderson (1989) first pointed out, however, the centrality of the concept of "sincerity" (*cheng* 誠) to Ye Shengtao's vision of the creative process and the role of literature is profoundly Confucian. By cultivating "sincerity" through observation of and interaction with the external social world, the writer incorporates the "other" within the self; the expression of self in the literary act is thus given an inherently social dimension.[6]

Despite the May Fourth contempt for popular literature that sought but to comfort and entertain its readers, literature of this kind continued to flourish throughout the Republican period (1911–49). The May Fourth-Marxist canonical interpretation of the development of modern Chinese literature would make it seem that popular literature simply did not exist, when the fact is that fiction of the Mandarin Ducks and Butterfly school (a term coined by May Fourth literary critics to express their disdain for the superficiality of these works) succeeded, where May Fourth writers failed, in reaching the very audience that the literary revolution had sought out. Writers of Butterfly fiction were, naturally enough, not literary critics and seldom systematically defended their kind of entertainment fiction against charges of its lack of sociopolitical import; indeed, more often than not they agreed, perhaps with false modesty, that their writings were largely trivial and insignificant. Two prefaces to Butterfly journals have been included in this section to demonstrate something of the enduring appeal, both to writers and readers, of a literature that seeks little more than the temporary diversion of the reader.[7] Their playful attitude toward fiction, which was diametrically opposed to the progressive appropriation of literature for modernization and nation building, explains the May Fourth critics' virulent criticism of the Butterfly writers.

The origins of the turn toward revolutionary literature that we will see in the following section can be found, ironically enough, in the romanticism of the Creation Society. In "The Mission of the New Literature," Cheng Fangwu, a founding member of the society, reveals the unease May Fourth romantics felt with such Western notions as literature of pure self-

---

6. For an excellent discussion of the Confucian concept of *cheng*, see Wei-ming Tu (1989: 106–41).

7. This is not to say, of course, that this is all that these popular texts actually do. For a rereading of Butterfly fiction from a Western feminist-psychoanalytic perspective, see Rey Chow 1986–87; and 1991: 34–83.

expression. Cheng wanted literature to be at once purposeless (art for art's sake) and subservient to a larger mission ("the demands of the epoch"), purely aesthetic and utilitarian at the same time. There is thus a certain logic behind the irony that by 1925 members of the Creation Society converted from their early fervor for an aesthetic view of literature to an equally passionate faith that literature should serve political demands and be guided by political ideology.

As a whole, the texts included in this section reveal a May Fourth that is far more complex and paradoxical than either the May Fourth participants or their inheritors would have us believe. Beneath the radical iconoclastic surface of these texts lie profound anxieties and fears about writers' relationship with tradition and their role as cultural stewards in the forward movement of history.

Chapter 9

Some Modest Proposals for the Reform of Literature

Hu Shi

Those engaged in the present discourse on literary reform are myriad.[1] How am I, unlearned and unlettered, qualified to speak on the subject? Yet I have over the past few years, with the benefit of my friends' argumentation, pondered and studied this matter a fair degree and the results achieved are perhaps not unworthy of discussion. So I summarize the opinions I hold and list them in eight points; I have divided them in this fashion for the investigation of those interested in literary reform.

It is my belief that those wishing to discuss literary reform today should begin with eight matters, which are as follows:

1. Writing should have substance
2. Do not imitate the ancients
3. Emphasize the technique of writing

---

1. Hu Shi 胡適, "Wenxue gailiang chuyi" 文學改良芻議, *Xin qingnian* 2, no. 5 (Jan. 1917).

4. Do not moan without an illness
5. Eliminate hackneyed and formal language
6. Do not use allusions
7. Do not use parallelism
8. Do not avoid vulgar diction

I. Writing Should Have Substance

The greatest malady of letters in our nation today is language without substance.[2] All one ever hears is "If writing is without form, it will not travel far."[3] But nothing is said about language without substance, nor what function form should serve. What I mean by substance is not the "literature conveys the *Dao*" [*wen yi zai dao*] of the ancients. What I mean by substance are the two following points:

A. *Feeling.* In the "Great Preface" to the *Book of Songs* is written: "Feelings come from within and are shaped through language. If language is insufficient to express one's feelings, then one may sigh; if sighing is insufficient, then one may chant or sing; if chanting or singing is insufficient, then one may dance with one's hands and feet." This is what I mean by feeling. Feeling is the soul of literature. Literature without feeling is like a man without a soul, nothing but a wooden puppet, a walking corpse. (What people call aesthetic feeling is only one kind of feeling.)
B. *Thought.* By "thought" I mean one's views, perceptions, and ideals. Thought need not depend on literature for transmission, but literature is enriched by thought and thought is enriched by the value of literature. This is why the prose of Zhuangzi, the poetry of Tao Yuanming and Du Fu, the lyric meters of Xin Qiji, and the fictional narratives of Shi Nai'an are eternal. As the brain is to man's body, so is thought to literature. If a man cannot think, though he be attractive in appearance and capable of laughter, tears, and feelings, is this really sufficient for him? Such is the case with literature.

---

2. The expression *yan zhi you wu* 言 之 有 物 comes from the *Book of Changes* in which the gentleman is exhorted to "have substance in his words" in order to have "stability in his actions"; in *The I Ching, or Book of Changes*, trs. Wilhelm/ Baynes (Princeton: Princeton University Press, 1977), 144.

3. Citation of Confucius in the *Zuozhuan* (Zuo commentary), Duke Xiang 25: "yan zhi wu wen, xing zhi bu yuan" 言 之 無 文 , 行 之 不 遠 . The passage has been translated by Owen (1992: 29) as "If the language lacks patterning, it will not go far."

Without these two kinds of substance, literature is like a beauty without a soul or a brain; though she have a lovely and ample exterior, she is none-theless inferior.[4] The greatest reason for the deterioration of literature is that the literati have become mired in poetics and are without any kind of far-reaching thought or sincere feeling. The harm of an overly formalist lit-erature lies in this so-called language without substance. And should we wish to save it from this fault, we must save it with substance, by which I mean only feeling and thought.

II. Do Not Imitate the Ancients

Literature has changed from dynasty to dynasty, each dynasty having its own literature. The Zhou and Qin dynasties had their literatures, the Wei and Jin had theirs, as did the Tang, Song, Yuan, and Ming. This is not just a personal opinion held by me alone, but a truth of the progression of civilization. As for prose, there are the styles of the *Book of History*, the phi-losophers of the pre-Qin period, the Han historians Sima Qian and Ban Gu, the essayists Han Yu, Liu Zongyuan, Ouyang Xiu, and Su Shi, the dia-logues of Zhu Xi, and the fictional narratives of Shi Nai'an and Cao Xueqin. This is the progression of literature. To turn our attention to verse, poems such as "The Pushpin Song" and "Song of Five Sons"[5] constitute the earli-est period. Then follow the poems in the *Book of Songs*, Qu Yuan's *sao*, and Xunzi's rhyme-prose. From Su Wu and Li Ling of the Western Han to the Wei-Jin period, and the *paibi* parallel style of the Southern dynasties, to the flourishing of regulated verse in the Tang and Du Fu and Bai Juyi's "real-ism" [*xieshi* 寫實] (as in Du Fu's "Recruiting Officer of Shihao" and "Jiang Village" or Bai Juyi's "New Ballads"). The regulated verse form flourished in the Tang, but was later replaced by the lyric meter and the dramatic song (*qu*). From the Tang and Five Dynasties period to the *xiaoling* 小令 form in the beginning of the Song marks one period of the lyric meter. The lyrics of Su Shi, Liu Yong, Xin Qiji, and Jiang Kui form another period. The *zaju* and *chuanqi* dramas of the Yuan are another. All these periods have changed

---

4. Liu Kai 柳開 (b. 968), an early proponent of the Ancient-Style Prose, also uses this metaphor of woman as text: "Now it is bad if a woman's outer appearance is more culti-vated than her inner virtue, but not bad if her inner virtues are more highly cultivated than her appearance. Likewise, with writing it is bad if the words are more splendid than the reasoning, but not bad if the reasoning is more splendid that the words"; cited in Ron-ald Egan, *The Literary Works of Ou-yang Hsiu* (1007–72) (Cambridge, Eng.: Cambridge Uni-versity Press, 1984), 15–16.

5. "Jirang ge" 繫壤歌 and "Wu zi zhi ge" 五子之歌 are folk songs that may not ac-tually predate the poems of the *Book of Songs*, as Hu Shi seems to suggest. The former is preserved in a Han text called the *Gaoshi zhuan* 高士傳; the latter in the *Book of History*.

with the times, and each has its own characteristics. Our generation, look-ing back with a historical, progressive perspective, is most certainly unable to say that the literature of the ancients is superior to that of the present. The prose of the *Zuo Commentary* and *Records of the Grand Historian* is mirac-ulous indeed, but do they cede much to that of Shi Nai'an's *Water Margin*. And the rhyme-prose of the "Three Capitals" and "Two Capitals" is but dregs in comparison to the Tang regulated verse and the Song lyric meter. We see from the above that literature develops and does not stand still. Tang people should not write poems of the Shang and Zhou, and Song peo-ple should not write rhyme-prose like Sima Xiangru or Yang Xiong. Were they to do so, their results would certainly not be fine. One cannot be skill-ful if one goes against Heaven, turns one's back on one's age, and defies the footsteps of progress.

Since we now understand the principle of literary development, I can proceed to a discussion of what I mean by "not imitating the ancients." In contemporary China, in creating a literature for today, one must not imitate the Tang, Song, Zhou, or the Qin. I once saw the "Inaugural Remarks of the National Assembly" and it read: "Most glorious National Assembly, the end of penumbrous times is nigh." This is evidence that today there is a de-sire to model literature after the Three Dynasties of antiquity.[6] When we look at today's "great writers," the lesser writers model themselves after Yao Nai and Zeng Guofan of the Tongcheng School, the greater writers take the Tang-Song essayists Han Yu and Ouyang Xiu as their masters, while the greatest follow the prose of the Qin-Han or Wei-Jin periods and feel that there is no literature to speak of after the Six Dynasties. But the dif-ference between these is like the difference between one hundred steps and fifty steps; they all belittle literature. Even if it resembles the ancients in spirit, it still amounts to nothing more than adding several "realistic coun-terfeits" to a museum. Is this literature? Yesterday I saw a poem by Chen Boyan[7] that reads as follows:

> In the Garden of Waves I copied lines from Du Fu,
> Half a year passed, many brushes worn thin.
> All I have to show for myself are tears,

---

6. The language is from the *Book of Songs,* Zhou song, "Zhuo" 酌 . The phrase as it ap-pears in the original poem is used to convey the idea that one waits until one's time is right to take action, in this case military action. The sense in the "Inaugural Remarks of the National Assembly" is that the time is now ripe for this democratic institution.

7. Chen Boyan 陳伯嚴, or Chen Sanli 陳三立 (1852-1937), late Qing reformer who participated in the Hundred Days Reform of 1898. After being banished from government service, he devoted himself to old-style poetry (in the Jiangxi style) and prose writings.

Though friends passed by commenting on my "skillful creations."
The myriad souls are all silent,
The more I look up to Du Fu the higher he becomes.[8]
I turn these feelings over in my bosom
And leisurely read Qu Yuan's tragic *sao*.

This amply represents the imitative psychology of today's "poets of the first rank." The root of their sickness lies in spending "half a year passed with many brushes worn thin" in being slavish scriveners to the ancients, resulting in sighs about "the more I look up to him the higher he becomes." If we free ourselves from this kind of slavery and no longer write poems of the ancients and only write our own poems, we will not end with this sort of defeatism.

Whenever I mention contemporary literature, only vernacular fiction (Wu Woyao, Li Baojia, and Liu E) can be compared without shame to the world's literary "first rank." This is for no other reason than that they do not imitate the ancients (although they owe much to *The Scholars*, *The Water Margin*, and *The Story of the Stone*, they are not imitative works). And it is only because they faithfully write about the contemporary situation that they can become true literature. All other poets or ancient-style essayists who study this or that style have no literary value. Those today with a determination to pursue literature should understand precisely the nature of that in which they are engaged.

III. Emphasize the Technique of Writing

Many poets and essayists today neglect syntactic structure. Examples are legion and not worth raising; they are especially numerous in writings of parallel prose and regulated verse. Neglecting syntactic structure means there will be an absence of "communication." This is clear enough, and there is no need to go into further detail.

IV. Do Not Moan Without an Illness

This is not easy to discuss. Today's youth often affect a tragic view of the world. When they adopt a sobriquet it is most often something like "Cold Ashes," "Dead Ashes," or "Lifeless." In their poems and prose they write of such things as old age before a setting sun, desolation facing the

---

8. Alludes to the *Analects*, 9.10: "Yen Yuan, *in admiration of the Master's doctrines*, sighed and said, 'I looked up to them, and they *seemed to become* more high, I tried to penetrate them, and they *seemed to become more firm*' " (仰之彌高, 鑽之彌堅) (Legge 1979: 234)

autumn winds. When spring arrives, they dread its swift departure, and when flowers bloom, they fear their premature withering. These are the tragic voices of a fallen country. The old should not act thus—how much more so the young! The long-term effect of this is to foster a sense of despondency, which leads to a lack of regard for action or service to one's country, and which only knows the voice of lamentation or the literature of despair. This kind of literature will hasten writers to their grave and sap the will of its readers. This is what I mean by moaning without an illness. I am perfectly aware of the ills facing our nation today, but what effect can sobbing and tears have on a sick nation in such a perilous state? I only wish that contemporary writers become Fichtes and Mazzinis and not the likes of Jia Yi, Wang Can, Qu Yuan, or Xie Ao.[9] That they are unable to actually be like Jia Yi, Wang Can, Qu Yuan, or Xie Ao but instead write poems and essays about women, fine wine, depression, and discouragement makes them beneath contempt.

V. Eliminate Hackneyed and Formal Language

Today one is called a poet if one can summon up from memory a few literary clichés. Poetry and prose are filled with stale and hackneyed diction,[10] like "time waits for no man," "slings and arrows," "desolation," "solitary drifting," "the common man," "poor scholar," "sinking sun," "fragrant flowers," "spring boudoir," "melancholy soul," "home is where the heart is," "cry of the cuckoo," "lonely as a solitary shadow," "words formed by migrating geese," "jade pavilion," "elixir of love," "gray-eyed morn," and the like, an endlesss and most despicable gush. The long-term effect of this malady on our nation will be to give birth to poetry and prose that have the appearance of literature but really are not. Now I will demonstrate this tendency with a lyric:

> Like tiny peas, the twinkling flames of an evening lamp
> Cast a flickering shadow on a solitary figure,
> Helter-skelter and adrift.

---

9. Jia Yi 賈誼 (200–168 B.C.), politician and poet of the Western Han, banished for criticizing the government, wrote a well-known *fu* lamenting the death of Qu Yuan (343–277 B.C.), who committed suicide to protest the policies of his lord. Wang Can 王粲 (A.D. 177–217), one of the "Seven Masters of Jian'an," was an official under Cao Cao during the Three Kingdoms period and wrote poems lamenting the chaos of warfare. Xie Ao 謝翱 (1249–95) was a poet and patriot who fought with Wen Tianxiang against the Mongol invasion and wrote melancholy poems about suffering under Mongol occupation.

10. Hu uses the term chenyan 陳言, which recalls Han Yu's use of the term in his famous "Letter to Li Yi" (答李翊書); see Guo Shaoyu 1979: 2: 115–18.

Beneath his kingfisher-blue covers
Under his roof of interlocking butterfly-tile,
How can he ward off the cold of an autumn's night?
The tiny strings of the pipa murmur
Early at Dingzi Lian,[11]
Heavy frost frolicked about.
Enchanting notes lofted above
After lingering momentarily round the columns.

Glancing quickly at this piece[12] we sense that its words and lines do form a lyric, when in point of fact it is but a list of clichés. "Kingfisher-blue covers" and "butterfly-tile" may be appropriate for Bai Juyi's "Song of Eternal Sorrow," but there they refer to the emperor's covers and the tiles of the imperial palace. "Dingzi Lian" and "tiny strings" are stock phrases. This lyric was written in America, so the poet's "evening lamp" could not have "twinkled" "like little peas" and his abode had no "columns" around which the notes could linger. As for "heavy frost frolicked about," this is even more absurd. Whoever saw heavy frost "frolicking about"?

What I mean by the necessity of eliminating hackneyed and formulaic language can only be achieved through the creation of new phrases to describe and portray what people see and hear with their own eyes and ears or personally live through. It is indeed a great talent in writing to be able to mesh with reality and arrive at the goal of describing your object or conveying meaning. Those who employ hackneyed and formulaic language are indolent and unwilling to create new phrases to describe their objects.

VI. Do Not Use Allusions

Among the eight propositions that I have proffered, that which has been most singled out for attack is the one most misunderstood. My friend Jiang Kanghu[13] dispatched a letter in which he writes:

The term "allusion" has both a broad and narrow sense. Ornateness and grandiloquence have since days of yore been raised by the ancients as

---

11. Dingzi Lian 丁字簾 may here refer to a pleasure quarter in Ming dynasty Nanjing; see *Taohua shan* (Peach-blossom fan), ch. 23.

12. In later versions of this essay, Hu Shi indicates that this poem was written by "his friend" Hu Xiansu, who studied in the United States at the same time as Hu Shi and later became a member of the conservative Critical Review Group.

13. Jiang Kanghu 江亢虎 (1883–?) founded the Chinese Socialist Party in 1911. When it was banned in 1913, Jiang went into exile in the United States where he was at the time Hu Shi wrote this essay. He later returned to China to teach at Peking University.

something to be strictly prohibited. If idiomatic expressions and anecdotes are eliminated, this will not only be a loss in terms of style, but a disaster for the function of writing. The most wonderful mood that writing can evoke is through simple words with broad and varied connotations. I could not succeed in writing this present passage without allusions. Not only can poetry not be written without allusions, neither can letters nor even speeches. The letters I receive are replete with such allusions as "a second self,"[14] "broadness of mind," "fail to get to the root of the problem," "miss the forest for the trees," "calamity of nature," "make the deaf hear and the dumb speak," "join forces and forge ahead," "I'm pleased to humbly submit," "Parnassian world," "an honorable retreat of a hundred leagues," "fill the firmament," "sharp instruments of power," and "iron-clad proof." If we try to extricate them all and replace them with vulgar language and vulgar words, how will we be able to speak? Whether one uses ornate or simple diction is ultimately a trivial matter. What I fear is that if we change these allusions into other words, though we might have five times as many words, the connotations cannot in the end be as perfect. What then?

This discussion is rather to the point. According to what Mr. Jiang has written, allusion has both a broad and narrow sense, which I will discuss below.

A. Allusion in the broad sense is not what I mean by allusion. There are perhaps five kinds of allusions in this broad sense.

1. The metaphors created by the ancients and the objects from which they draw these metaphors are universal in meaning and do not lose their efficaciousness with time; we today may also employ them. If the ancients said "one has a spear, the other attacks with a shield," even an uneducated person would know how to use the metaphor of "one's own spear and shield face each other" [self-contradictory]; yet this we do not consider making an allusion. The above expressions "miss the forest for the trees," "calamity of nature," "make the deaf hear and the dumb speak," . . . are all of this sort. The important point in employing metaphors and similes is that it be done appropriately. If they are employed appropriately, then there is certainly no difference between the ancient or modern usage. Allusions like "join forces and forge ahead" and "an honorable retreat" are not

---

14. In the list of allusions that follows I have borrowed some translations from Edward Gunn (1991: 71). I will gloss only the first of these allusions as typical of the rest. "Second self," jiuyu 舊雨 (literally "old rain"), is from Du Fu's "Qiu shu" 秋述 (Autumn account). The meaning is that friends used to brave the rains to come and visit him, but now no longer do. The term has come to mean an old and dear friend, hence second self.

in common parlance; they can perhaps be employed among the literati, but it is better in the final analysis not to employ them. If you use the expression "an honorable retreat," why is it necessary to add "hundred leagues" when "miles" is much more suitable.

2. Idiomatic expressions. Idiomatic expressions bring words together to create different meanings. Some frequently used expressions have long been a part of common parlance, and they can be freely employed. And today if we desire to coin new idiomatic expressions, who is to prevent us? "Sharp instruments of power," "broadness of mind," and "miss the forest for the trees" all belong in this category. These are not allusions, but quotidian expressions.

3. Historical references. When we compare historical references to what we are discussing here, we cannot call them allusions. A Du Fu poem has the following line: "We do not hear that the Shang and the Zhou declined / because they themselves put Bao and Da to death."[15] This is not an allusion. A more recent poem reads: "Therefore, even Cao Cao / keeps the name of Han to the bitter end."[16] This is also not allusion.

4. Using the ancients metaphorically. This is also not employing allusions. Du Fu's line "Bright and fresh is Yu Xin, / Refined and easy Bao Zhao"[17] is making a parallel between contemporary and historical figures and should not be considered an allusion. "Among his equals are Yi Yin and Lu Shang, / Had he gained power, even Xiao He and Can Shen would not measure up."[18] This also is not allusion.

5. Citing the words of the ancients. Nor is this allusion. I once wrote the following lines: "I have heard the ancients speak, 'Only death is difficult.'"[19] Or: "'There have been no successful experiments since ancient times'; these words of Lu You are not necessarily true."[20] But these are simply citations and not allusions.

---

15. From Du Fu's ancient-style poem, "Beizheng" 北 征 (Journey north). "Bao" and "Da" refer to the imperial concubines Bao Si 褒 姒 and Da Ji 妲 己 , who are seen as responsible for the decline of the dynasties in which they lived.

16. I have been unable to trace the author of this line.

17. From Du Fu's poem "Chunri yi Li Bai" 春 日 憶 李 白 (Remembering Li Bai on a spring day). Yu Xin 庾 信 (513–81) and Bao Zhao 鮑 照 (414–66), literary figures of the period of disunity, are used by Du Fu to praise the literary style of his friend Li Bai.

18. From the fifth of Du Fu's series "Yong huai gu ji" 詠懷古跡 (Reciting thoughts on historical sites), in which he praises Zhuge Liang by comparing him with other historical figures who were powerful statesmen close to the emperor.

19. Hu Shi is citing his own poem "Zisha pian" 自 殺 篇 (Suicide; 1914), written after the suicide of the younger brother of his good friend Ren Shuyong (Ren Hongjun).

20. See "Changshi pian" 嘗 試 篇 (Hu Shi 1984: 4). The whole line reads: "Today I want to turn the phrase around to read: From ancient times success has been measured by the extent of experimentation." He explains this distortion of Lu You in Hu Shi 1984: 153.

(The above five categories fit into the broad definition of allusion and are not what I mean by allusion. These sorts of allusion can be used or not.)

B. I am proposing that allusions in the narrow definition of the word not be employed. What I mean by this use of allusion is when men of letters are incapable of creating their own words and expressions to write about what is before their eyes or in their hearts and instead borrow, in part or wholly inapposite, anecdotes and hackneyed language to do it for them, allowing them to muddle along. The allusions in the "broad" definition discussed above are, excluding the fifth category, all metaphors or similes. But they use one thing as a metaphor for another, not as a substitute for it. The narrow definition of allusion, on the other hand, sees allusion as substituting for language; because they are unable to directly express themselves, they can only let allusion speak for them. This is what I mean by the distinction between what is and what is not allusion. And yet we still must distinguish between the skilled use of allusion and its crude or clumsy use. Skilled use is occasionally acceptable. Crude use should be eliminated altogether.

1. The skilled use of allusion is what Mr. Jiang calls the use of simple words with broad and varied connotations. We could extract myriad examples of this from just about any writing, but let us just raise a few to prove my point.

a. Wang Jinqing[21] wrote a poem to Su Dongpo asking to examine, though his intention was to purloin, the valuable "Qiuchi stone," which Su had hidden away. Su Dongpo felt he had to lend it to him, but first he wrote him a poem in which appear the following lines: "I want to keep it, but lament the weakness of the state of Zhao. / I'd rather offer it to Qin and let them bear the burden of disgrace. / Pray not let it be passed around for all to admire. / Return it posthaste." This poem alludes to Lin Xiangru's returning of the treasured "jade of the He clan." [22] How skilled and precise!

b. Su Dongpo has another poem entitled "Zhang Zhifu sends six jugs of wine, the note arrives but not the wine": "Though his intention was to send good wine by messenger, it all came to naught."

c. Ten years ago I wrote a poem after reading *The Talisman*: "Is there one such as Yang Hu to poison a man? / Or such as King Wuling of Zhao to

---

21. Wang Shen 王詵 (1036–?), painter, calligrapher, and art collector.

22. The allusion is to a story in the *Records of the Grand Historian* in which Zhao must give up the valuable He clan jade to the stronger state of Qin (see "Lin Xiangru zhuan"). The commentator to the *Su Dongpo shiji* (1918) edition of Su Dongpo's collected poems writes positively of this poem in terms similar to Hu Shi's: "Tang and Song poetry is pure. The substance of this timeless treasure is written so clearly."

spy on the enemy? / Compared to these, what the crusaders did was really just child's play. / Only these two men are immortal."[23] These two allusions can cover the entire book. At that time we were quite smug and self-satisfied; in fact this kind of poem really should never be written.

d. In his eulogy to Chen Yingshi,[24] Jiang Kanghu, representing the overseas Chinese community, wrote: "Before the Great White imperial flag was raised / The Great Wall was destroyed.[25] / As this world is without a Chu Ni / Zhao Dun has been slain."[26] I personally find this very appealing. The use of Zhao Dun as an allusion is very skilled and precise.

e. In a historical poem by Wang Guowei is the following: "Tigers and wolves stalk the palace / Exiled among the Western barbarians how can the dynasty be restored. / China is sinking toward disaster, / For a hundred years chaos has reigned. / If you send a message to Huan Wen, / Don't blame Wang Yifu."[27] This too can be considered a skillful use of history.

The above examples all use allusion to say something that cannot be said more directly. Where they excel is in not losing in the end the original meaning of what they set out to compare; but as they were limited by the forms in which they wrote, their metaphoric use of allusion changed toward a substitutive use. The problem in using allusion is that it causes people to lose the original meaning behind the metaphor. Crude uses of allusion are when the host and guest are reversed, so to speak, and the reader becomes lost in the complexity of historical fact and allusion and ends up

---

23. After reading Lin Shu's translation of Sir Walter Scott's *Talisman* in 1909, Hu Shi wrote this poem which was included in his *Hu Shi liuxue riji* 胡適留學日記 (Diary of an overseas student). Hu seems to be expressing national pride in the superiority of Chinese heroes over those described in Scott's novel. For the entire poem, see *Hu Shi shi xuan* (Selected poems of Hu Shi), (Taibei: Pingping, 1966), 2–3.

24. Chen Yinshi 陳英士, or Chen Qimei 其美 (1876–1916), member of the Nationalist Party who waged a movement against Yuan Shikai during the Second Revolution of 1915; assassinated in 1916 by Yuan's henchmen.

25. This line refers allegorically to the fact that Yuan Shikai declared himself emperor, after Chen Yingshi had already been executed.

26. Zhao Dun 趙盾 was a minister of the state of Jin during the Spring and Autumn period. Lord Ling of Jin, upset by Zhao Dun's repeated remonstrances, sent Chu Ni 鉏麑 to assassinate him. When Chu Ni came before the noble Zhao Dun, he was unable to carry out his lord's order and committed suicide to avoid disgrace.

27. Huan Wen 桓溫 (312–73); see *Jinshu* 晋書 8/98/2568. Wang Yifu 王夷甫 (256–311), minister of the Western Jin, known as a traitor for having served the Xiongnu lord, Liu Yuan, who was planning to use the opportunity of the internal divisions of the state to take it over. Wang Guowei's poem is an allegory of Qing internal politics after the suppression of the Hundred Days Reform Movement in 1898.

forgetting the object the writer set out to compare. When the ancients wrote long poems, they only used a handful of allusions (Du Fu's "Journey North" and Bai Juyi's "Temple of Truth Realized"[28] do not make use of a single allusion). Men today cannot write long poems without using allusion. I once read a poem with eighty-four couplets which made over one hundred allusions, none of which was used skillfully.

2. Crude allusions. Crude allusions are used by indolent people who know not how to create their own language and use them simply as a tactic to conceal their lack of talent. And because they are incapable of creating their own language, they do not know how to use allusions properly. There are also, among the sum of crude allusions, several categories:

a. Metaphors used imprecisely, having several possible meanings and no basis for a set interpretation. I present Wang Shizhen's poem "Autumn Willow" as an example of what I mean:[29]

> Graceful, covered in a cool near-frost dew,[30]
> A maze of willow branches caress the Jade Pool.
> Lotus leaves in the pool as mirrors for women,
> Yellow bamboo by the riverside made into daughters' dowry chests.[31]
> In vain we long for Ban Stream to be forged into the Sui Embankment,
> Nowhere is one like the great king of Langya to be found.[32]
> Passing through the scenic spots of Loyang,
> One should ask again about the Yongfeng ward.[33]

---

28. "You Wuzhen si" 遊悟眞寺. Translated by Levy as "Frolicking to the Temple of Truth Realized"; see Howard S. Levy, *Translations from Po Chü-i's Collected Works*, 4 vols. (New York: Paragon Books, 1971), 1: 57–61.

29. Wang Shizhen 王士禎, or Wang Yuyang 王漁洋 (1634–1711), poet and literary critic. Although Hu Shi chooses not to discuss it, this poem purposefully conceals its meaning with historical allusion because it was written as an allegory in support of the Southern Ming loyalists during the early years of the Qing dynasty. The allusions all express regret at the failure of the Ming restoration.

30. This line alludes to a poem in the *Book of Songs*, and simply points to the coming of autumn.

31. A line from "Huangzhu zhi ge" 黃竹之歌 (The song of yellow bamboo), an anonymous *yuefu* folk song.

32. The first line in this couplet alludes to Emperor Yangdi of the Sui who unified the empire after a long period of disunity, built the Grand Canal, and planted willows along its Sui Embankment. The second line laments the absence of one such as Jin Yuandi (276–322), who was able to unify southern China.

33. Loyang was a northern capital during the Sui dynasty. Yongfeng ward was a section of the capital famous for its willows.

The allusions used in this poem are all open to several explanations.

b. Incomprehensibly obscure allusions. Literature is for the conveyance of meaning and the expression of feeling. Let us no longer write literary works that require one to read "five carts of books"[34] to understand them.

c. Paring down classical expressions to the point where they become ungrammatical. "To use *konghuai* for brothers, and *zeng shi* for official position"[35] are examples (from Zhang Taiyan). The contemporary expression "to prepare the dowry for another's wedding" also does not make sense.

d. Losing the original meaning of an allusion. As when someone who wants to describe a mountain being so tall that it meets heaven and writes "It meets in the West with the falling sky of Qi."[36]

e. Historical facts have a specific meaning that cannot be changed. Today they are often used carelessly to indicate common things. When the ancients "broke a willow branch at the bridge over the Ba River" as a way of sending off a friend, it originally referred to a specific custom. Yang Pass and Wei City also referred to actual places. But today's indolent writers, unable to describe the feeling of separation, say they are at the Ba River (although actually they are in the deep south); and though they have no idea what Yang Pass and Wei City were like, they still speak of "three refrains at Yang Pass" or the "parting song at Wei City." Or the expression "water roots, porridge, perch, and minced meat" used by Zhang Han when the autumn winds blew and made him long for his home in the Wu region (the only place those delicacies could be had). Now, although not from Wu and not knowing what these delicacies taste like, we still indicate our homesickness with the expression "thoughts of water roots and perch."

This reflects not only an indolence beyond salvation, but a self-deception and a deception of others.

Men of letters devote much time and energy to all these various sorts of allusions. Once you are stung with their poison, there is no recovery. This is why I have advocated not employing allusions.

---

34. From *Zhuangzi*, "Tianxia" (Under heaven), a reference to the breadth of Huizi's book learning.

35. *Kong* 孔 (very) *huai* 懷 (care) or the feelings one has for one's brother, i.e., brothers; from *Book of Songs*, Xiaoya, "Changdi" 常棣. The rendering "official position" for *zengshi* 曾是, which means something like "as such," is an extrapolation from a line in the *Book of Songs*, Daya, "Dang" 蕩, that reads "*zeng shi zai wei*" 曾是在位.

36. The allusion is to the parable of the man from Qi who is worried that the sky will fall. To Hu Shi it makes no sense to compare a majestically tall mountain to the skies of Qi.

VII. Do Not Use Parallelism

Parallelism is a characteristic of human language.[37] For this reason we find occasional parallel lines even in such ancient texts as those by Confucius and Laozi. For example:

> The way that can be spoken is not the constant way;
> The name that can be named is not the constant name.
> The nameless was the beginning of heaven and earth;
> The named was the mother of the myriad creatures.
> Let there forever be non-being so we may see their subtlety;
> Let there forever be being so we may see their outcome.[38]

Or the following parallel lines from the *Analects*:

> In food [the gentleman] does not seek satiety,
> Nor in his dwelling does he seek ease and comfort.[39]

> Poverty without sycophancy
> Wealth without arrogance.[40]

> You love his goats,
> I love his rites.[41]

Yet these are all not far from natural language, without a trace of being forced or artificially constructed, especially since rules had yet to be established as to the length of lines, tones, or diction. As for the decadent literature of subsequent generations, it was without substance and showy to such a degree that it led to the advent of parallel prose, regulated verse, and extended regulated verse. There are some excellent works written in parallel prose and in regulated verse, but these are rare in the final analysis. Why is this? Is it not because they constrict man's freedom to such an extent? (Not a single excellent work of long regulated verse can be mentioned.) Now, in our discussion of literary reform, we must "first stand fast

---

37. Hu Shi's opposition to parallelism resonates with the Ancient-Style Prose movement, as well as with the Qing Tongcheng school's reaction to the parallel style advocated by the Wenxuan school.

38. *Daode jing*, ch. 1; translation borrowed from D. C. Lau, *Lao Tzu: Tao Te Ching* (Harmondsworth, Eng.: Penguin, 1963), 57.

39. *Analects*, 1.14.

40. *Ibid.*, 1.15.

41. *Ibid.*, 3.17.

on what is of greater importance"[42] and not waste our useful talents on minute detail and subtle technique. This is why I have proposed the elimination of parallel prose and regulated verse. Even if they cannot be eliminated, we should nonetheless look upon them as mere literary tricks, not something to be undertaken with any urgency.

Today people still look down upon vernacular fiction as the lesser tradition and are not aware that Shi Nai'an, Cao Xueqin, and Wu Woyao are the truly canonical and that parallel prose and regulated verse are the lesser tradition. I know that when you hear this there will certainly be some among you who simply cannot bear it.

VIII. Do Not Avoid Vulgar Diction

Since my literary canon is composed only of Shi Nai'an, Cao Xueqin, and Wu Woyao, I have the theory of "do not avoid vulgar diction." (Refer to Section 2 above.) And yet for a long time the spoken and literary languages in our country have been turning their backs on each other. Ever since the importation of Buddhist scriptures, translators have been aware of the fact that the classical language is deficient in conveying meaning, so they have used in their translations an ordinary and simple language, whose style verged on the vernacular. Later, Buddhist lectures and catechisms mostly made use of the vernacular, which gave rise to the dialogue (*yulu* 語錄) form. When the Song neo-Confucians used the vernacular in the scholarly lectures of their dialogues, this form became the standard in scholarship. (Ming scholars later followed this style.) By this time, the vernacular had already long since entered rhymed prose, as can be seen in the vernacular poetry and lyrics of the Tang and Song. By the end of the Yuan dynasty, northern China had already been under the occupation of a foreign race for more than three hundred years (Liao, Jin, and Yuan dynasties). In these three hundred years, China developed an incipient popular literature, out of which emerged the novels *The Water Margin*, *The Journey to the West*, and *The Romance of the Three Kingdoms* and innumerable dramas (Guan Hanqing et al. each produced more than ten different dramas; no period in the history of Chinese literature exceeded this in terms of wealth of productivity). Looking back from our contemporary perspective, the Yuan should without doubt be seen as the most vigorous period of Chinese literature, producing the greatest number of immortal works. At that time, Chinese literature came closest to a union of spoken and written languages, and the vernacular itself had nearly become a literary language. If this ten-

---

42. *Mencius*, 6A.15.

dency had not been arrested, then a "living literature" might have appeared in China and the great endeavor of Dante and Luther might have developed in old Cathay. (In the Middle Ages in Europe, each country had its own vulgar spoken language and Latin was the literary language. All written works used Latin, just as the classical language was used in China. Later, in Italy appeared Dante and other literary giants who first used their own vulgar language to write. Other countries followed suit, and national languages began to replace Latin. When Luther created Protestantism, he began by translating the *Old Testament* and the *New Testament* into German, which ushered in German literature. England, France, and other countries followed this pattern. Today the most widely circulated English Bible is a translation dating from 1611, only 300 years ago. Hence, all contemporary literature in the various European nations developed from the vulgar languages of that time. The rise of literary giants began with a "living literature" replacing a dead literature in Latin. When there is a living literature, there will be a national language based on the unity of the spoken and written languages.) Unexpectedly, this tendency was suddenly arrested during the Ming. The government had already been using the "eight-legged essay" to select its civil servants, and scholars like Li Mengyang [1472–1529] and the followers of the "former seven masters" raised "archaism" [*fugu*] as the most lofty of literary goals. So the once-in-a-millennium opportunity to effect the unity of the spoken and written languages died a premature death, midway in the process. Yet, from today's perspective of historical evolution, we can say with complete certainty that vernacular literature is really the canonical and will be a useful tool for developing future literature. (My "certainty" is only my opinion, one shared by few of my contemporaries.) For this reason, I propose the appropriate use of vulgar diction in the writing of prose and poetry. It is preferable to use the living words of the twentieth century than the dead words of three millennia past (like "Most glorious National Assembly, the end of penumbrous times is nigh"); it is preferable to use the language of *The Water Margin* and *The Journey to the West*, which is known in every household, than the language of the Qin, Han, and Six Dynasties, which is limited and not universally understood.

Conclusion

The eight points related above are the result of my recent investigation and contemplation of this important question. Since I am studying in a far-off foreign land,[43] I have little leisure for reading, so I must ask my learned

---

43. Hu was studying at Cornell University when he wrote this essay.

elders back home for their scrutiny and circumspection, for there may well be places in need of severe rectification. These eight points are all fundamental to literature and merit investigation. So I have drafted this essay and hope that it elicits some response from those who care about this issue, both here and in China. I have called them "modest proposals" to underscore the sense of their incompleteness and to respectfully seek the redaction of my compatriots.

—Translated by Kirk A. Denton

Chapter 10

On Literary Revolution

Chen Duxiu

From whence arose the awesome and brilliant Europe of today?[1] I say from the legacy of revolution. In European languages, "revolution" means the elimination of the old and the changeover to the new, not at all the same as the so-called dynastic cycles of our Middle Kingdom. Since the literary renaissance, therefore, there have been a revolution in politics, a revolution in religion, and a revolution in morality and ethics. Literary art as well has not been without revolution: there is no literary art that does not renew itself and advance itself with revolution. The history of contemporary European modernization can simply be called the history of revolutions. So I say that the awesome and brilliant Europe of today is the legacy of revolution.

My oblivious and fainthearted countrymen are as fearful of revolution as they are of snakes and scorpions. So even after three political revolutions, the darkness has yet to wane. The lesser reason is that all three revolutions started with a bang and ended with a whimper, unable to wash away old perspiration with fresh blood. The greater reason is the ethics,

---

1. Chen Duxiu 陳獨秀, "Wenxue geming lun" 文學革命論, *Xin qingnian* 2, no. 6 (Feb. 1917); reprinted in *ZGXDWXCKZL* 1: 20–23.

morality, and culture, layered in darkness and mired in shameful filth, that have occupied the very core of our people's spirit and have prevented the emergence of revolutions with either bangs or whimpers. That is the reason the political revolutions have not brought about any change, have not achieved any results, in our society. The overall cause of all this is the ill-will our people bear toward revolution, not knowing that it is the cutting edge of modernization.

The problem of Confucianism has been attracting much attention in the nation: this is the first indication of the revolution in ethics and morality. Literary revolution has been fermenting for quite some time. The immediate pioneer who first raised the flag is my friend Hu Shi. I am willing to be the enemy of the nation's scholars and raise high the banner of the "Army of Literary Revolution," in vocal support of my friend. On the banner will be written large the three great ideological tenets of our revolutionary army: (1) Down with the ornate, sycophantic literature of the aristocracy; up with the plain, expressive literature of the people! (2) Down with stale, pompous classical literature; up with fresh, sincere realist literature! (3) Down with obscure, abstruse eremitic literature; up with comprehensible, popularized social literature![2]

The "Airs of the States" in the *Book of Songs* were full of the lowly speech of the streets, and the *Elegies of Chu* employed rustic expressions in abundance, but both were unfailingly elegant and remarkable. In their wake, however, writers of *fu* poetry in the Former and Later Han dynasties raised their eulogistic voices and produced ornate and sycophantic writings, dense with words but sparse in meaning. This was the beginning of the trend in classical aristocratic literature of making artifacts for the dead. The five-syllable poetry since the Wei and Jin [A.D. 220–420] was expressive and descriptive, a change from the pedantic and allusive style of the preceding period. For its time, it could have been called a great literary revolution, and indeed, it was a great literary advance. Still, it relied on high antiquity and was artless in its diction and obscure in its meaning. It did not draw from social phenomena for its source material. So ultimately it remained the stuff of the upper class and cannot be called the popularized literature of the people. After the Qi and the Liang dynasties [A.D. 479–557], prosodic parallelism was still *de rigueur*. In the Tang dynasty, it developed into regulated verse, while parallelism persisted in prose, as it has always done since the time of the *Book of History* and the *Book of Changes*. (In prose compositions, the habit of the ancients was not only antithetical parallelism,

---

2. This section of the translation borrows heavily from Marston Anderson's rendering (1990: 27–28ff).

but also the frequent employment of rhyme. For this reason, many experts in parallel prose favor the theory that parallelism is the most orthodox of Chinese prose forms. My late friend Wang Wusheng was one such person. They do not know that in ancient times it was not simple to write down compositions, and rhyme and parallelism helped to make them easier to recite and to transmit. How can later writers be so muddled about this?)

Since the Eastern Jin [A.D. 319–420], parallel prose was used even for minor reports and notices; in the Tang, it became the antithetical form. That poetry should be "regulated" and prose "parallel" was an idea that originated in the Six Dynasties and became well established in the Tang period. These genres developed further into linked verse and into "four-six" prose. At its best, this kind of ornate, sycophantic, pompous, and hollow classical literature of the aristocrats is no more than a clay doll applied with powder and rouge. Its value is hardly higher than that of "eight-legged" examination essays. It can be considered a literary dead end.

The abrupt rise of Han Yu and Liu Zongyuan wiped away the effete and redundant style of their predecessors. The drift of the times was a transition between the aristocratic classical literature of the Six Dynasties and the popularized literature of the Song and Yuan. Han Yu, Liu Zongyuan, Yuan Zhen [779–831], and Bai Juyi rose with the times and became the central figures of the new literary movement. It is commonly said that Han Yu's essays reversed the decline of the eight dynasties from the Eastern Han to the Sui. Even though this is not certain, he nevertheless is a giant for changing the literary practices of the eight dynasties and for opening the way to Song and Yuan literature. That we today are less than totally satisfied with Han Yu, however, can be traced to two points. The first is his idea that literature should follow ancient authority. Even though it is no longer classicist, his literature does not depart from the aristocratic mold. In terms of content, it is far less rich than that found in the various fictional works of the Tang. In the end, he succeeded only in creating a new kind of aristocratic literature. Second, his view of "literature to convey the Way" is erroneous. Literature was originally not designed to carry such burdens; the concept of "literature conveys the Way," which was established by Han Yu and ended with Zeng Guofan, is no more than an extremely shallow and unsubstantial subterfuge co-opted from the tradition of Confucius and Mencius. I have often said that the "literature to convey the Way" practiced by the great writers of the Tang and the Song dynasties is of a kind with the view of "speaking through the sages" in the "eight-legged" essay. From these two points, we can see that Han Yu's reversal of ancient traditions was brought about by his times. In terms of literary history, he himself was not extremely remarkable.

Brilliantly remarkable in the literature of more recent history are the plays of the Yuan and Ming dynasties and the fiction of the Ming and Qing dynasties. Regrettably, the development of these genres was blocked by fiendish forces, and they were aborted before they could emerge naturally from the womb. The result is that China's literature today is lifeless and stale, unable to stand next to that of Europe. Now who were these fiends? They are none other than the Earlier and the Later Seven Masters[3] of the Ming dynasty and those who followed Tang-Song literary thought, Gui Youguang, Fang Bao, Liu Dakui, and Yao Nai.[4] These eighteen fiends worshiped the past and despised the contemporary. They dominated the literary scene with their plodding, unspontaneous style, so that even the names of the era's real literary heroes—such as Ma Zhiyuan or Shi Nai'an or Cao Xueqin—remained almost unknown to their countrymen.[5] Poems like those of the Seven Masters are so intensely imitative of the ancients that we can consider them copies. The essays of Gui, Fang, Liu, and Yao are either elegies written for the sake of literary fame and glory, or wailings without woe, full of pedantic language. There are always back-and-forth discussions and circumlocutions—about what I don't know. These literary authors were not creative talents; there was nothing of substance in their hearts. Their only skills were in imitating the ancients and deceiving people, and they did not write a single word of lasting value. Even though they measured themselves by their writings, what they wrote had not a smidgen of relevance to the modernization or progress of contemporary society.

China's literature today has inherited the faults of previous eras. What is called the Tongcheng school is merely the amalgamation of Tang-Song style with that of the "eight-legged" essays. And the so-called "parallel

---

3. These fourteen "Masters" were well-known classicists. The Early Seven Masters, mostly northerners who were together only very briefly, were led by Li Mengyang 李夢 陽 (1475–1529), and included Wang Jiusi 王九思 (1468–1551), Bian Gong 邊貢 (1476– 1532), Kang Hai 康海 (1475–1541), Wang Tingxiang 王廷相 (1474–1544), Xu Zhenqing 徐禎卿 (1479–1511), and the outstanding poet and theorist He Jingming 何景明 (1483– 1521). The Later Seven Masters, led by Li Panlong 李攀龍 (1514–70), were southerners who developed and expounded their literary thought in the northern capital. The group also consists of Xie Zhen 謝榛 (1496–1575), Xu Zhongxing 徐中行 (1517–78), Liang Youyu 梁有譽 (1520–56), Zong Chen 宗臣 (1525–60), Wu Guolun 吳國倫 (1529–93), and the more eclectic Wang Shizhen 王世貞 (1526–90), perhaps the dominant literary figure of his time.

4. The last three figures were founders of the Qing dynasty Tongcheng school. Of these four Gui Youguang 歸有光 (1507–71), as an advocate of the prose style of the Tang-Song masters, was actually in the forefront of the opposition to the classicists. See Tongcheng School entry in Glossary.

5. Ma Zhiyuan 馬致遠 (1260–1325) is considered the outstanding Yuan dynasty writer of dramatic lyrics and plays.

prose" is merely the "four-six" prose of Zhang Zaogong and Yuan Mei,[6] just as the Xijiang [*sic*] School is the idolization of Huang Tingjian.[7] Look as one might, there are no representative literary giants who, naked and unadorned, expressed their inner feeling or described the world of their times. Not only are there none in our nation who can be considered literary giants representative of the times, the very idea of such a figure does not exist. So although our literary writings are not worth reading, our practical compositions are even more absurd. Inscriptional writings and epitaphs are so fulsome in their praise that readers definitely do not believe what they are reading even as writers must carry on pro forma. Everyday notices begin and end with all sorts of formulaic hyperbole. Someone in mourning for the dead may be living in luxury and eating well; but the funeral notice has to claim that he is "numb with grief on a mat of straw with an earthen pillow." A testimonial plaque presented to a physician will either say that "His skill surpasses that of the legendary healers Qi Bo and the Yellow Emperor" or that "Cures come with every touch." Decorative couplets on the doorways of poor, rustic, and extremely tiny out-of-the-way bean curd shops will always say that "Business flourishes throughout the four seas, / Profits proliferate to reach the three rivers." This kind of unsightliness in the practical writings of the people can all be laid at the feet of the sycophantic, empty, and pompous classical literature of the upper class.

During this time of literary change and innovation, all literature classified as aristocratic, classical, and eremitic has been the subject of criticism. What is the reason for the criticism of these three? The answer is that aristocratic literature embellishes according to traditional practice and has lost its independence and self-confidence. Classical literature is pompous and pedantic and has lost the principles of expressiveness and realistic description. Eremitic literature is highly obscure and abstruse and is self-satisfied writing that provides no benefit to the majority of its readers. In form, Chinese literature has followed old precedents; it has flesh without bones and body without soul. It is a decorative and not a practical product. In content, its vision does not go beyond kings, officials, spirits, ghosts, and the fortunes or misfortunes of individuals. As for the universe, or human life, or society—they are simply beyond its ken. Such are the common failings of these three kinds of literature.

---

6. Zhang Zaogong 章藻功 was a master of parallel prose during the Kangxi reign of the Qing Dynasty. The colorful Yuan Mei 袁枚 (1716–98) was as well known for his interest in food, ghost stories, and theatrical arts, as for his literary thought.

7. Xijiang 西江 is a misprint for Jiangxi 江西, the name of the twelfth-century school of poetry associated with Huang.

Literature of this sort, I think, has a mutual cause-and-effect relationship with our sycophantic, self-aggrandizing, hypocritical, and impractical national character. Since we now want to reform our politics, we cannot by necessity ignore the reformation of the literature that has a hold on the spiritual world of those wielding political power. The present literature has prevented us from opening our eyes to the world, to society, to literary trends, and to the Zeitgeist. We bury our heads day and night under a pile of old paper. What we train our eyes on and direct our hearts to are nothing other than kings and officials, ghosts and spirits, or the fortunes and misfortunes of single individuals. To seek reform of literature and reform of politics from this is to fight a formidable foe with hands and feet tied.

Much of European culture benefited from politics and science; it also benefited considerably from literature. If I love the France of Rousseau and Pasteur, I especially love the France of Hugo and Zola. If I love the Germany of Kant and Hegel, I especially love the Germany of Goethe and Hauptmann. And if I love the England of Bacon and Darwin, I especially love the England of Dickens and Wilde. Among the outstanding literary figures of this nation, are there those who dare consider themselves China's Hugo, Zola, Goethe, Hauptmann, Dickens, or Wilde? Are there those who, without concern for the praise or blame of pedantic scholars, would with bright eyes and stout hearts declare war on the eighteen fiends? I wish to tow out the largest cannon in the world and lead the way.

—Translated by Timothy Wong

Chapter 11

Nightmare

Lin Shu

The person who occupied the official position of Imperial Seer in the Zhou dynasty controlled the media of the Three Omens, the Three Changes, and the Three Dreams. One part of the Three Dreams is called "Dream Destiny"; another "Dream Realization"; and the third "Total Comprehension" [*xianzhi* 咸 陟].[1] (Note: "Dream Destiny" concerns the destination of the dream and is the invention of the founders of the Xia dynasty. "Realization" means acquisition and indicates what a dream brings about; the concept is the invention of the people of the Shang dynasty. *Xian* means "all" and *zhi* also means "acquisition"; the term indicates what dreams do altogether and is the invention of people in the Zhou dynasty.) This last medium is actually sufficient to divine the fortunes of the nation. For good fortune is nothing better than the common comprehension of humanist ethics, and catastrophes cannot be worse than the willingness of the nation's leaders to descend to the level of beasts. This is how the nightmare came about.

---

1. Lin Shu 林紓, "Yaomeng" 妖夢, *Xin Shenbao* 新申報, Mar. 18–21, 1919; reprinted in *Zhongguo xin wenxue daxi* 2: 435–37.

A certain Zheng Sikang, a native of Ganquan in Shaanxi, was a student of mine. He came to see me one day. "I have had an inauspicious dream," he told me quite without warning. "Do you think this means I will die?"

"What kind of dream?" I asked. "I'll interpret it for you."

"On the seventeenth day of the tenth month," said Zheng, "I had had a bit to drink and was lying down when I suddenly dreamed of a man with a long beard who invited me to visit the netherworld. 'Am I dead?' I exclaimed in surprise.

" 'There is a very strange thing in the netherworld,' said the bearded man, 'and I am simply inviting you to witness it, so that when you wake up, you can enlighten people in the world. For, you know, what living people can comprehend is also comprehensible to ghosts.'

" 'What are you talking about?' I asked.

" 'All lawbreakers, having done evil in their lives, remain unchanged after death. They gather their gangs about themselves and openly carry on their unruly ways.'

" 'What kind of people are these?' I asked.

" 'Madmen,' the bearded man replied.

"As he had already tethered two ghostly horses beside the door, he led me outside and we mounted them. Wind and sand swirled about as we sped along the way, and I could see no other travelers in the haze. We found our way into a town where the traffic was very disorderly. Then we rode together to a large square. There was a gate to an official building above which was written in large characters: Vernacular Academy. On either side of the gate was a couplet in big characters: 'The vernacular is superhuman, and *The Dream of the Red Chamber* and *Water Margin* incredible; / The classical language is disgusting, and who anyway are Ouyang Xiu and Han Yu?' When I saw that, my sweat poured out.

" 'The principal of the school is Yuan Xu,' said the bearded man. 'The dean of studies is Tian Heng, and the assistant dean is Qin Ershi. They are all highly notable among ghosts. Let's go in and meet them.'[2]

"So we handed in our name cards and asked for an interview. On entering the inner gate, we saw 'Kill Confucius Hall' written on a large placard above it. There was another couplet that read: 'Beasts are truly free, so what's the use of social ethics? / Benevolence and righteousness are extremely evil, so we should destroy them at the roots.' I became very angry

---

2. The nightmare is, of course, a thinly disguised allegorical attack on the proponents of the literary revolution and their base at Peking University or, in the nightmare, the Vernacular Academy. Yuan Xu refers to Cai Yuanpei, chancellor of Peking University during most of the May Fourth movement. Tian Heng is Chen Duxiu, and Qin Ershi is Hu Shi, leaders of the literary revolution.

and said to the bearded man, 'We have been told that King Yama exists. Where is he?'

" 'Since there is no government in the human world,' he replied, 'how can you expect the nether regions to have a King Yama?'

"In a while Yuan Xu appeared. He looked unremarkably bookish. Tian Heng, however, had eyes like an owl's, and a nose and mouth that protruded like a dog's. As for Qin Ershi, he looked like a Westerner, with deep set eyes and a high-bridged nose. The latter pair came out on either side of Yuan Xu. As we began to converse, but before we could finish introducing ourselves, Ershi said to me, 'Does your name Sikang [Thinking of Kang] indicate that you are enamored of Zheng Kangcheng [Zheng Xuan, the Han Confucianist]? Since Confucius is useless, how much more so is Zheng!'

" 'Zheng wrote in a dead language, which cannot compare at all to living language,' said Tian Heng. 'Had we not come forth and advocated living language, China would have been ruined by this stale scholar. Especially detestable are the five human relationships and the five constant virtues; they have so limited us that we have had no room even to turn around.'

" 'If the Confucian relationships and virtues are useless,' I wasted no time in asking, 'who would be our teachers?'

" 'Wu Zetian is our sacred ruler, Feng Dao our worthy prime minister, and Zhuo Wenjun our virtuous lady,' said Tian Heng. 'But for Feng Dao, the world would not have had anyone who understood power and change. And without Zhuo Wenjun, women would not have had the right to freedom.[3] Without reading *The Water Margin*, moreover, the world would have no heroes, just as families would have no happiness without reading *The Dream of the Red Chamber*. What do you think about that?'

"Boiling with anger, I got up and left. The bearded man, smiling, also came along with me. We went on for perhaps a mile when we suddenly saw a shaft of golden light coming from a long distance. Most of those on the road recoiled in fright, saying that the king of titanic demons Rahuasura has arrived. Under the glare of the light, we saw that the demon was over a hundred feet tall. His gaping mouth alone was possibly over eight feet in circumference, with a veritable forest of craggy teeth. He headed straight for the Vernacular Academy, seized the people there, and ate them

---

3. Wu Zetian was empress of China in the Tang dynasty and has been reviled for her evil and cunning; Feng Dao (882–954) was an official who served many different lords during the Five Dynasties period; Zhuo Wenjun was a widow who, in defiance of her father, eloped with the famous Han poet Sima Xiangru. All personify values scorned by the Confucian tradition; hence their supposed glorification by the anti-traditionalists.

up. After the meal, he defecated. The excrement piled up high as a hill, and the stench was forbidding. Then I woke up with a start."

"Hooray for Rahu," I said with a hearty laugh. "In a *sastra* on the great Prajna-paramita Sutra, it is said that this titanic demon was about to swallow the moon. The moon god was concerned and hurried to where the Buddha was. The Buddha issued a command, and Rahu quickly released the moon. Now, you should know that even though the moon can be spared, those beasts with no sense of human relationships cannot. It is very fitting to render them into excrement. These events have no connection with your own fortunes. But if they actually happen, the nation will then be at peace."

Old Man Calabash[4] remarks:

The three words "*si wenzi*" — dead language — did not just originate with Tian Heng. The great British author Mr. Dickens used them in discussing ancient writings in Latin and in Greek. If the resources of Dickens could not wipe out Latin, could the power of a single Tian Heng wipe out classical Chinese? Did not even their revered *Water Margin* and *Red Chamber* derive from ancient texts? The diction employed in *The Water Margin* is mostly that found in Yue Ke's *Golden Crag Collection*[5] of essays. As for *The Dream of the Red Chamber*, it was completed only after emendations by innumerable men of broad learning. We can compare the situation to jewelry on display in a store. If we want to acquire the goods, we must enter the place to examine them. If, on the other hand, we merely take the labels to be the precious jewels themselves, would anyone be satisfied with that? To write the vernacular, one must first study texts and understand the essence of the literary tradition. Only after we can express ourselves thoroughly can our writing be effective. But if we can just use the vernacular to teach the vernacular, without knowing the ins and outs of literary thought, then even rickshaw pullers in markets selling horses and asses can be said to know the vernacular. Why would we need to teach it? Those who advocate the vernacular are not convincing; so they write in a contrary manner in order to shock the masses. Those who understood what they were doing were at first not affected. The younger generation, however, has been harmed. Our elementary schools have no accomplished teachers, and our secondary

---

4. Old Man Calabash 蠡叟 is another name for Lin Shu. This final section of the essay, in the style of Sima Qian's *Records of the Grand Historian*, offers a concluding didactic commentary on the contents of the story.

5. Yue Ke 岳珂 (1183–1234) wrote *Jintuo cuibian* 金陀萃編 to restore the tarnished reputation of his grandfather, the great Song general Yue Fei.

schools lack books; both have had to carry on with what they had. So how can they be anything but delighted on hearing of the vernacular movement? Once this wind of change was fanned, no one bothered to read anymore. The movement, moreover, went on to equate the rebellion against social ethics with freedom. Who could then resist going along with the flow, hurrying down the road toward a bestial existence.

How well spoken are the words of the Western philosopher Francis Bacon: "The wise and the foolish both suffer no harm. It is only the halfway wise or halfway foolish that are most in danger." How so? Well, those we call foolish just go abroad to study. Because they do know a bit of Chinese, they are not then identified as foolish. But to consider them wise would be problematic since they know no philosophy beyond what is on the surface. With no more than a cursory knowledge of Chinese, they take themselves to be experts in both Chinese and foreign cultures. Caught up in their own rhetoric, they curse Confucius and Mencius and wag their fingers at Han Yu and Ouyang Xiu. They assume both ethics and the classical language to be harmful to the people and, moreover, detrimental to the new learning. We should realize that just as the classical language is not hurtful to science, science is of no use to the classical language. That neither one has anything to do with the other is common knowledge. It is only those lazy and uneducated youths who adopt science as a slogan. They can use it to deceive their parents, all of whom then bow their heads in approval of what they are told. There is even talk of revolutionizing the family system, for which ignorant souls happily give their thunderous support.

I regret that Mr. Zheng's dream is not reality. If there actually is a moon-swallowing King Rahu, I would invite him to begin by taking a bite out of people like these.

—*Translated by Timothy Wong*

Chapter 12

Humane Literature

Zhou Zuoren

The New Literature that we must now promote may be expressed in one simple term, "humane literature," and what we must reject is its opposite, "inhumane literature."[1]

"New" and "old" are really inadequate terms; actually, according to the principle that there is "nothing new under the sun," we can speak only of "right" and "wrong" but not of "new" and "old." If we use the term "new" as in "New Literature," then we use it to mean "newly discovered" but not "newly invented." The New Continent was discovered by Columbus in the fifteenth century, but the land had already been there from all antiquity. Electricity was discovered by Franklin in the eighteenth century, but the phenomenon had also already existed all along. Not that earlier men could not have perceived it, it only so happened that Columbus and Franklin were finally the first to discover the facts. It is the same with the discovery of a truth. Truth always exists without any limitations in time; it is only because of our ignorance, in being so late to perceive the truth, and being still

---

1. Zhou Zuoren 周作人 , "Ren de wenxue" 人的文學 , *Xin qingnian* 5, no. 6 (Dec. 1918).

near the time of its discovery, that we call it "new." Actually it is of extreme antiquity, the same as the New Continent or electricity, it was always in the world and it would be a great mistake to regard it as new as a fresh fruit, or a new dress made to the fashion of the day.

For instance, when we now speak of humane literature, does this phrase not also sound like something new-fashioned? But doing so would be ignoring the fact that as soon as human beings came into existence in this world, humaneness was born. Unfortunately, man was ignorant and persistently would not give heed to humanity's will to walk this correct path, but rather strayed along the paths of animals and ghosts, wandering about aimlessly for many years until finally achieving his emergence. He is like a man who, in bright daylight, has covered his eyes and has blindly dashed about, only to discover, when he finally opens his eyes, that there is good sunlight in this world. Actually, the sun had been enlightening the world all along like this for an immeasurable length of time.

In Europe, the truth of this humaneness was discovered for the first time in the fifteenth century, resulting in two developments: the religious revolution and the renaissance in art. A second time, it produced the great French Revolution; for a third time it will probably lead to as yet unknown future developments after the European war. The discovery of women and children, however, emerged only as late as the nineteenth century; the old traditional position of woman was merely that of man's chattel or slave. In the Middle Ages, the Church was still debating whether woman had a soul and whether woman was to be considered human!

Children, too, used to be nothing but their parents' property. A child was not recognized as a human being that had not yet fully matured, but was taken as a complete man in miniature, an attitude which resulted in innumerable domestic and educational tragedies. Only after Fröbel[2] and Mrs. Godwin[3] did the light break through; at present, research is being instituted in two great fields, the study of children and the women's question, and one can hope that results will be of the best.

In China, investigation of these questions must start right from the beginning. Here the problem of man has heretofore never been solved, not to mention the problems of women and children. If we now make our first step and begin to discuss man, if, after he has been living for over four thousand years, we still investigate the meaning of man, if we try to redis-

---

2. Friedrich Fröbel (1782–1852) was the German educational reformer who is considered the founder of the kindergarten.

3. Mrs. Mary Godwin, née Wollstonecraft (1759–97), thought of as a radical in her time because of her *Vindication of the Rights of Women* (title of her book; 1792) and also of her advanced *Thoughts on the Education of Daughters* (1787).

cover him, "clear the 'man' jungle," this has something of the ridiculous in it. However, learning in old age is always one grade better than not learning at all. It is in this sense that we hope that, starting out from literature, we will promote some of the ideas of humanitarianism.

Prior to discussing humane literature, we should first clarify the term "human." The human being that we want to deal with is not the so-called crowning piece of nature, or the "round skull, square footed" man, but rather the "human species, as it has progressively evolved from the animal kingdom." There are two points of importance here: (1) the evolution has taken place *from animal*, and (2) man has *progressed* from animal.

We acknowledge that man is a living being which, in its outward signs of life, does not differ at all from other living beings. We therefore believe that all man's vital faculties being naturally endowed are beautiful and are good, and should find their complete satisfaction. Anything contrary to human nature, unnatural customs and institutions, should be condemned and amended.

Expressed in other words, these two important aspects constitute the dual nature of man's life: the spirit and the body. Men of old thought that the two primary elements in man's nature, the spirit and the body, existed simultaneously and were in eternal conflict with each other. The bodily element is that which had come down from man's original animal nature. The spiritual was seen as the beginning of man's divine nature. The purpose of man's life was viewed as being predominantly the development of his divine nature. The method to achieve this was to sacrifice the body for the salvation of the soul. Old traditional religions, therefore, all rigorously enforce asceticism and by various strenuous efforts oppose man's natural instincts. On the other hand, there were the epicureans, who had no regard for the soul and saw the end merely as a "when I die, bury me" (i.e., "Death is the end of all"). Both these parties were extreme and cannot be said to have shown man the correct way of life. Only in modern times have people realized that the spirit and the body are basically two facets of one thing, and not two primary elements in opposition. The animal nature and the divine nature jointly constitute man's nature. The English eighteenth-century poet Blake has expressed it excellently in his *Marriage of Heaven and Hell*:

1. Man has no Body distinct from his Soul, for that called Body is a portion of Soul discernible by the five Senses.
2. Energy is the only life, and is from the Body, and Reason is the bound or outward circumference of Energy.
3. Energy is Eternal Delight.

Although his words have the flavor of mysticism, they very well express the essential idea of the unity of the spirit and the body. What we believe to be the right way of life for mankind is precisely this life of unison of spirit and body. If we refer to man as having progressively evolved from the animal, it is nothing else but indicating in other words that in this man, spirit and body are in harmonious unison.

What would be an ideal life for this kind of man? First of all, mutual relations among humanity should improve. All men constitute humanity, and each is but one unit of humanity. Therefore, man should live a life of benefiting self while also benefiting others, and of benefiting others while also benefiting himself. First, regarding the material things of life, each should exert himself to the utmost of human strength, and each should obtain adequate clothing, food, shelter, medical care, and medicine in exchange for his physical or mental labors, so that he will be able to sustain a healthy life. Second, regarding his moral life, the four elements of love, wisdom, trust, and courage shall be its basic morality; all traditional sub-human or ultra-human rules of society should be eliminated, so that every person may enjoy a free and genuinely happy life. Realization of such a humane, ideal life would actually benefit every single person on earth. Although the rich feel they would inevitably have to lose their so-called status, they would thereby obtain salvation from an "inhuman" life, to become perfect human beings; would that not be the utmost of blessings? We may really call this the Gospel of the twentieth century, and only regret that few people know of it and that immediate realization is not possible. We shall therefore promote it in the field of literature, and thereby make our humble contribution toward this idea of humanity.

However, it still has to be explained that what I call humanitarianism is not charity as referred to in such common sayings as "have pity and commiserate with the people,"[4] or "wide generosity and relief of distress among the masses."[5] It is rather an individualistic ideology of basing everything on man. The reasons are:

1. Within humanity, a man is just like one tree in a forest. If the forest thrives, the single tree in it will also thrive. But if we want the forest to thrive, we have to care for each single tree.
2. The individual loves humanity because he is one unit of it and because of its relationship to him. Mozi gave as his reason for all-embrac-

---

4. The phrase *beitian minren* 悲天憫人 is from Han Yu's (768–824) essay "Zheng chen lun" 爭臣論.
5. The phrase "*bo shi ji zhong*" 博施濟衆 is condensed from the *Analects* 6.28.

ing love the fact that "I am within humanity," which is penetratingly expressed.[6] It has the same meaning as the above-mentioned benefiting self by benefiting others, and benefiting others through benefiting oneself.

The humanitarianism that I have in mind therefore starts with man, the individual. To be able to discuss humaneness, love of humanity, one must first have acquired the qualifications of man and stand in the position of man. Jesus said: "Love your neighbor as you love yourself." If you don't love yourself, how would you know to love others "as you love yourself"? As to love without personal involvement, purely for the sake of someone else, I consider this impossible. It is conceivable that a man sacrifice himself for the person *he* loves, or the idea *he* believes in; but such acts as cutting off a piece of your flesh to feed an eagle, or perhaps giving up your body to a hungry tiger to devour, would constitute ultra-human morality, something that human beings cannot do.

Writing that applies this humanitarianism in its recordings and studies of all questions concerning human life, that is what we call humane literature, which can be again divided into two kinds:

1. the principal kind: description of the ideal life, or writings on the heights of advancement attainable by men, and
2. the secondary kind: descriptions of man's ordinary life, or his inhuman life, which can also contribute toward the purpose of the study.

The largest amount of writing is of the latter kind and it is also the more important, because it enables us to understand the true circumstances of man's life, to point out how it differs from the ideal life, and to devise methods of improvement. Within this category, descriptions of the inhuman life that some men are forced to lead are very frequently mistaken by people for "non-human" literature, but actually there is a big difference. For instance, the Frenchman Maupassant's *Une vie* is humane literature about the animal passions of man; China's *Prayer Mat of Flesh*,[7] however, is a piece of non-human literature. The Russian Kuprin's novel *Jama*[8] is literature describing the lives of prostitutes, but China's *Nine-tailed Tortoise*[9] is

---

6. "*Ai ren bu wai ji, ji zai suo ai zhi zhong*" 愛人不外己, 己在所愛之中 is from *Mozi*.
7. *Rou putuan* 肉蒲團, erotic novel by Li Yu 李漁 (1611–80).
8. Alexander Ivanovich Kubrin (1870–1938), leftist writer most famous for his novel *Yama* (The pit; 1909–15), a work about prostitutes.
9. *Jiu wei gui* 九尾龜, a Wu dialect novel about prostitutes by Zhang Chunfan 張春帆; published serially in 1906–10.

non-human literature. The difference lies merely in the different attitudes conveyed by the works, one is dignified and one is profligate, one has aspirations for human life, and therefore feels grief and anger in the face of inhuman life, whereas the other is complacent about inhuman life, and the author even seems to derive a feeling of satisfaction from it, and in many cases to deal with his material in an attitude of amusement and provocation. In one simple sentence: the difference between humane and "non-human" literature lies in the attitude that informs the writing, whether it affirms human life or inhuman life. This is the crucial point. The content or the method of writing are of no importance. For instance, stories that advocate that women be buried with their dead husbands, that is, commit suicide rather than remarry, don't they, on the surface, voice "maintenance of customs and ethics"? But forcing people to commit suicide is exactly what constitutes inhuman morality; such writings are therefore non-human literature. In the literature of China, in fact, there has been extremely little humane literature. Almost none of the writings from the Confucian or Daoist schools qualify. Let us cite examples only from the field of pure literature:

1. Profligate, pornographic books
2. Books on demons and gods (*Investiture of the Gods*,[10] *Journey to the West*, etc.)
3. Books on immortals (*Lüye xianzong*,[11] etc.),
4. Books on supernatural appearances (*Strange Tales from the Studio, The Master Speaks Not*,[12] etc.)
5. Books about slavery (group A themes: emperors, first-rank scholars, prime ministers; group B themes: sacred fathers and husbands)
6. Books on banditry (*Water Margin, Qixia wuyi, Cases of Judge Shi*,[13] etc.)
7. Books on men of talent and beautiful women (*Destiny of the Three Smiles*,[14] etc.)

---

10. *Fengshen zhuan* 封神傳, or *Fengshen yanyi* 演義, a Ming novel described by C. T. Hsia as a "historical fantasy."

11. *Lüye xianzong* 綠野仙蹤, a novel by the Qing writer Li Baichuan 李百川.

12. *Liaozhai zhiyi* 聊齋志異 is a well-known collection of classical tales by Pu Songling. *Zi bu yu* 子不語 is a collection of ghost tales by the Qing literatus Yuan Mei 袁枚. The title is a play on "Zi bu yu guai li luan shen" 子不語怪力亂神 (The Master speaks not of ghosts, feats of strength, disorder, and gods), *Analects* 7.10.

13. *Qixia wuyi* 七俠五義 is a late Qing revision of the adventure novel *Sanxia wuyi* 三俠五義. *Shi gongan* 施公案 is a detective novel from the mid-nineteenth century.

14. *Sanxiao yinyuan* 三笑姻緣. This refers to an early nineteenthth century Suzhou *tanci* 彈詞 about the Ming painter Tang Bohu 唐伯虎 and his dalliance with the maid Qiuxiang 秋香.

8. Books of low-class humor (*Tales from the Forest of Laughter*,[15] etc.)
9. Scandal literature[16]
10. The old dramas, in which we find all the above ideas crystallized in one.

All these categories of literature are a hindrance to the growth of human nature; they are things that destroy the peace and harmony of mankind; they are all to be rejected. Naturally, this type of literature is extremely valuable in the study of national psychology. Literary criticism may also find some of them admissible as literature, but from an ideological point of view, all are to be rejected. We do not object to persons of good sense and maturity reading these books. We should heartily welcome it if they would study and criticize them for this would be of great value to the world.

Humane literature must take human morality as its basis. This question of morality is very broad and cannot be dealt with in detail at once. I only want to mention here a few aspects that have a bearing on literature.

Take for instance love between the sexes: here we have two propositions: (1) equal status for both sides, men and women, and (2) marriage based on mutual love. Works of world literature that have expounded these ideas are among the most excellent pieces of humane literature. For instance Ibsen's plays *A Doll's House* and *The Lady from the Sea*, the Russian Tolstoy's novel *Anna Karenina*, the Englishman Hardy's novel *Tess*, etc., are all of this nature. The origin of love, according to the Norwegian scholar Westermarck, is "man's liking for what gives him pleasure." The Austrian Lucka then added that love became an exalted emotion because of the many years that the moral nature of man had progressively developed. True love and the life of the two sexes has therefore also this unison of the spiritual and the physical. However, due to the oppressive circumstances and powers of today's society, the emphasis has unavoidably shifted most commonly to one side. This, then, should be stated and studied on the basis of humanitarianism, but we must not extol nor propagate this one-sidedly physical life as happy or divine or sacred. I need not even mention Chinese profligate, pornographic literature, but I find equally unacceptable the asceticism of the old Christian Church.

There is also the Russian writer Dostoyevsky, a great author of humanitarian literature, who in one of his novels describes how one man loves a

---

15. *Xiaolin guangji* 笑林廣記, a version of Feng Menglong's 馮夢龍 *Guang xiaofu* 廣笑府 (Treasury of jokes), published under the pseudonym Youxi zhuren 遊戲主人.

16. *Heimu* 黑幕 fiction was particularly detested by Zhou Zuoren, who wrote several essays during the May Fourth period attacking it as the worst of popular entertainment fiction; see "Lun heimu xiaoshuo" 論黑幕小說 in *ZGXDWLX*, vol. 2.

woman, who later falls in love with another man, but in devious ways and with great effort the first man causes them [the second man and the woman] to be united. Although Dostoevsky's own words and actions are always consistent, we can never accept the fact that these various actions described in the story are compatible with human feelings and with human capabilities; we therefore should not advocate such actions.

Another case is the Indian poet Tagore, who in his novels continuously sings the praises of Eastern thought. In one story he records the life of a widow and describes her *suttee* of the heart (*suttee* is the custom of self-immolation of a widow on the funeral pyre of her husband). In another story he describes how a man forsakes his wife and remarries in England, and how his Indian wife even sells her jewelry to keep on supporting the husband.

If a person is free of body and mind, and from free choice binds himself in love to another person, and then, upon reaching the time when death parts them, will give up his own life, this might indeed be called a matter of morality. But the whole affair must spring from free determination. An act brought about under pressure of despotic traditional rules of society is an altogether different matter. The Indian human sacrifice, the *suttee*, as everybody knows, is an inhuman custom, now recently forbidden by the British. The *suttee* of the heart is merely a variant form of it. One amounts to capital punishment, one to life imprisonment. To speak in Chinese terms: one is to "die for chastity" by committing suicide rather than remarry; the other is to "maintain chastity" by remaining unmarried after the death of the husband. The Sanskrit word *suttee*, I am told, originally had the meaning "chaste woman." Because Indian women have suffered *suttee* for thousands of years, they have nurtured this perverted form of chastity. Those who expound "Easternization" may consider it a valuable national characteristic, whereas in fact it is merely the evil fruit of an unnatural custom.

The Chinese, for instance, have become accustomed to kowtowing. When they meet, they will for no particular reason salute each other by folding their hands and bowing deeply, all as if they should prostrate themselves before each other. Can we call this the admirable virtue of politeness? If we see such perverted types of so-called morality, it is like seeing a man raised in a pickle jar with a body like a carrot. We would certainly not hold him up for emulation, or voice our approbation.

Next then there is the love between parents and children. The men of old said: "Love between parents and children has its source in natural disposition." This is well said. Because it is originally indeed a natural love, there would seem to be no need for people to apply binding obligations to it, impeding its growth. If one said that parents beget children because of selfish lust, people may perhaps consider parenthood something immoral. It is therefore much more appropriate to define it as arising from "natural disposition." Considering it on the basis of biological fact, parents indeed beget children out of a natural desire. When there is sex life, there will naturally follow propagation of life and efforts to raise one's young; this is the same with all living creatures. When it comes to man, with his greater consciousness of the blending harmony of love and the continuation of one's kind in children, there is an even deeper relationship between parents and children. What intelligent people have recently said about the rights of children and the duties of parents are merely deductions from this natural principle, and as such nothing new. As to ignorant parents, who look on their children as property to be raised like cattle and horses, that are eaten or ridden at one's convenience when they will have grown big, they show a retrograde misconception. The English educationalist Gorst calls such parents "ape-like degenerates," which is truly no exaggeration.[17]

The Japanese Tsuda Sōkichi in his *Study of National Thought in Literature*,[18] volume 1, says:

> An attitude of filial piety that is not based on love of the parents for their children contravenes the common biological fact that elders exist for their offspring, and the factual conditions of human society, namely, that man labors for the future. If one were even to assume that offspring exist for their elders, such kind of morality obviously contains elements of the unnatural.

Elders exist for their offspring. It therefore stands to reason that parents should love and treasure their children, and that children should in turn love and respect their parents. This is a natural fact; it is also a natural disposition. We find literary expression of the love between parents and children most beautifully conveyed in the Greek Homer's epic, the *Iliad*, and in Euripedes' tragedy *Troiades*, in the two chapters where Hector is taken by death from his wife and children.

Recently, Ibsen's *Gengarere* (Ghosts), the German Sudermann's play *Heimat*, the Russian Turgenev's novel *Father and Sons*, etc., are all deserving of our study.

---

17. Sir John Eldon Gorst (1835–1916), was in his early yeas a politician; after retirement he turned to education and children's welfare, writing such works as *The Children of the Nation* (1906).

18. Tsuda Sōkichi 津田左右吉 (1873–1961). *Bungaku ni arawaretaru kokumin shisōno kenkyū*文學に表れたる思想の研究, 4 vols. (Tokyo, 1918–21).

As to such cruel superstitious acts as those of Guo Ju, who buried his son,[19] and of Ding Lan, who carved the wooden image,[20] we should, of course, cease to praise or propagate such. Cutting out a piece of one's flesh to feed one's parents[21] is merely a residue of a belief in witchcraft and cannibalism; it cannot of course be considered moral, and we should never again permit such themes to get into our literature.

From the above, it will have become generally clear what kind of literature we should promote and what kind we should reject. However, we must still add a few words on the matter of old versus new, Chinese versus foreign, to forestall some misunderstandings.

On literature that is opposed to our ideology, we should not, like Hu Zhitang[22] or the Qian Long emperor, write treatises to bring them down by abuse, one by one, old and new, merely following one's own personal viewpoint. If we establish our theory, it shall incorporate only this one viewpoint: the viewpoint of the age. Criticism and proposals shall be two separate things. In criticizing the writings of the old, we have to realize their time and age, to correctly evaluate them and allot them their rightful position. In propagating our own proposals we must also realize our time and age. We cannot compromise with opposite ideas. For those, we have only one way, namely, to reject them. For instance, in primeval times only primeval ideas prevailed, and witchcraft and cannibalism were then a matter of course. Songs and stories about these customs are therefore still worth studying to increase our knowledge. However, if anyone in modern society would still want to practice witchcraft or cannibalism, he would just have to be seized and confined in a mental hospital.

Next, regarding the question of Chinese versus foreign, we should also firmly embrace the viewpoint of our time and age, and not stake out other boundaries. Geographically and historically, there are indeed many differences, but communications have improved and the intellectual atmosphere spreads fast. Mankind can hope to move gradually closer together. The unit is I, the individual, the sum total is all humanity. One should not think of oneself as different from the mass of mankind, or as superior in morality, and draw up borders and spheres, because man is always related to mankind and vice-versa.

---

19. Guo Ju 郭巨, of the Later Han is one of the twenty-four models of filial piety; he killed his son in order to be better able to provide for his mother during a famine.

20. Ding Lan 丁蘭, another model of filial piety, is said to have carved a wooden image of his deceased mother in order to be able to continue his services to her.

21. Du Shishou 杜世壽 is said to have fed his starving parents with his own flesh.

22. Hu Zhitang 胡致堂 (1098–1156) was a high official involved in policy struggles during the defense of the Song dynasty against the incursions of the Jurchen.

If a Zhang and a Li are suffering, and somewhere else a Peter and John are suffering, and if I maintain that it is a matter of no concern to me, then my indifference applies to all equally. If I maintain that it is of concern to me, then I am equally concerned in all cases. In detail, this means that although the Zhangs and Lis, the Peters and Johns, may have names and nationalities different from my own, they are all in the same way units of mankind, all equally endowed with emotions and natural dispositions. What one of them feels as pain must also be painful to me. The misfortune that befalls one of them can certainly also befall me. Because mankind's fate is one and the same, the anxiety about my own fate should therefore also be anxiety about the common fate of mankind. That is why we should speak only of our time and age and not distinguish between Chinese and foreign. In our occasional creations, we naturally tend toward the Chinese, which we can understand more accurately. Beyond that we must introduce and translate foreign writings in large quantities, expand the mind of the reader, so that he can perceive humanity as a whole, and we must nurture a humane morality and achieve realization of a humane life.

—*Translated by Ernst Wolff.*
Previously published in *Chou Tso-jen* by Ernst Wolff
(Boston: Twayne, 1971), 97–105,
an imprint of Simon & Schuster Macmillan.
Reprinted with permission of Twayne Publishing.

Chapter 13

On the Literary Arts (excerpts)

Ye Shengtao

Part III

I have often heard an event described as "fascinating, extraordinary, fit to be material for a work of fiction."[1] Those who utter such things disparage fiction as something facile and superficial. Although material for fiction can indeed be drawn from the events of the world, these events in and of themselves do not necessarily constitute fiction.

There are many literary figures who adhere to the idea expressed in the above statement and who bring their works to fruition by simply drawing their material from the sea of human events and recording them on paper. When the events they would like to have happen fall short of their expectations, they indulge in fantasy and fabricate things without substance, thus compensating for any deficiency in material in their works.

---

1. Excerpts from Ye Shengtao 葉聖陶, "Wenyi tan" 文藝談, *Chenbao*; published serially from March 5 to June 25, 1921; reprinted in *Ye Shengtao lun chuangzuo* 葉聖陶論創作 (Ye Shengtao on creativity) (Shanghai: Shanghai wenyi, 1982), 3–73.

The function of this sort of literary work is only to divert or to be subject matter for idle conversation or to satisfy one's curiosity, and no further benefit may be derived from it. We can thus call it a literary plaything.

Most now acknowledge that "literature is the expression and the critique of life." The expression and critique of life is something to which real writers devote themselves, as they do to life itself. How can literature merely serve as a diversion, as subject matter for casual conversation or the satisfaction of one's curiosity? Works that do are the so-called literary playthings, which, with their limited reach, fall far short of being true works of art.

So those truly devoted to literature should not disparage fiction as something facile or superficial. To simply draw material from the common events of human life results in nothing more than a hollow record. We should recognize that these playthings are useless in the human world, and that it would be of no great consequence were more of them to be produced because they could never amount to more than a drop of water in the vast sea of literature, nor could they increase the volume of the sea of literature. We should devote our energies to true literary works.

A characteristic of a true literary work is "profound feeling." One might even say that this is the soul of literature. These feelings store up in all things and in peoples' hearts, and it is the writer who senses them deeply and whose heart is stirred in response, welling up irrepressibly until a faithful written record is made. Whether it is something encountered everyday, an ordinary person, a fleeting thought, or an eternal flight of imagination, to become material for fiction it need only have this profound feeling. It does not glean the fascinating or the strange, for it is able to express the whole of life. If a writer is able to feel the simplicity of the feelings behind the events of the human world, then anything may be suitable material for fiction.

The humanist tendency to empathize with the plight of the weak is certainly an example of this profound feeling, as of course is the depiction of darkness in the world. For there lurks in us a powerful striving for light. Even cynicism, decadence, melancholy, and sorrow are examples of profound feelings. All literary schools produce good works. Writers should not bother with schools, nor with modeling their writing after a particular school; they need only know how to feel more keenly than others and to stir their profound emotions to be able to create good and true literary works. True literary works are not for diversion, and a person's love and delight in them must far surpass that for the literary plaything, because true literary works not only recount something fascinating and satisfy one's curiosity, they stir one's empathy. Their purpose is not only to present a bunch of words, but a work full of vigor that can draw the reader in without his being aware of it. The reader feels the profound feeling seep into his spirit, and from this he can increase his own understanding, compassion, and delight. This is something that humankind needs and expects and something to which writers should devote themselves.

Part IV

I often feel that "sincerity" [*cheng*][2] is the essential condition necessary for any occupation. Sincerity occurs when our feelings pour out toward some thing or event, and we saturate our very lives in that thing or event to the point where it becomes a faith or religion.

Literary works express nothing more than the things and feelings of human life, yet the ways they achieve this are manifold because the attitudes of writers vary. The attitude of each writer is naturally unique, but broadly speaking we can draw a line and divide these attitudes into two kinds: the "sincere" and the "insincere."

For a writer to uphold a truly sincere attitude, he must firmly believe that the function of literature is to stir people's empathy, to advance their understanding, compassion, and delight. He must have a variety of very profound feelings for his epoch and his environment. When he begins to compose, not yet having this attitude or fearful of going against it, he must be particularly careful if he wishes to produce true literature with a universal quality naturally. Whether the writer uses realist techniques or infuses his writing with an air of romanticism, whether he expresses himself from a positive perspective or describes things from a negative perspective, in each case a new hue is added to the literary rainbow. Although he is just like other men, because he has at heart this true sense of sincerity and is absolutely without any intentional artifice, what he expresses in his work is the feelings and thoughts of people of his time and his environment. How can one not pause to reflect on it or be moved by it?

If a writer's attitude is not sincere and he has no real understanding of literature, when he puts pen to paper to compose his works, there will only be a kind of mocking or droll sentiment. In his insincerity, his feelings will be exposed as flat and thin. His feelings for life will be either very shallow or non-existent, and the soul of literature will be lost. And these soulless lit-

---

2. The full sense of this term is not adequately captured in the English word "sincerity." *Cheng* means integrity, commitment, dedication, and honor. It was an important concept in Confucian texts like the *Doctrine of the Mean*, where, as mentioned in the General Introduction, it was seen as the ground upon which the ideal man could tap into the power of the divine to enlarge himself.

erary works can only have superficial feelings and thought or end up being degenerate and inhuman statements. Although he may produce works by modeling them after those of others, transforming their original appearance by filling them with his own material, what is being copied are just words and not the heart of the other writer, which cannot be copied. Although a literary work is built from words alone, the soul of the writer is still everywhere present in them. But of what possible use is it to copy the physical words that can be copied? Of these sorts of literary works, the former may be called "anti-life" and the latter "without individuality." To borrow an idiom, in our evaluation it is "to lose one's will in the pursuit of petty playthings."

There are no copybooks, no shortcuts, for us to use in creating the true literary works we hope for. The only method lies in the cultivation of the self, in tempering oneself into sincerity. We should saturate our entire beings in literature, we should pour our profound feelings out onto the life that literature seeks to express.

But how many times, in our conscious lives, have we been sincerely moved or experienced a deep tenderness? Two people greet each other with the nod of a head, but their eyes do not meet; each goes his separate way, and they never see each other again; nor do they even retain a memory of the other. A letter arrives with two sheets of eight-line paper, but on them are written only the formulaic expressions of the epistle. An old woman, weak of limb, slips and falls, provoking only a clap of applause and derisive laughter. A neighbor is robbed and one person injured, and I can but selfishly take relish in the good fortune that I was not also a victim. . . . One could go on and on. In sum, this great crowd of ours is full of hypocrisy, ridicule, selfishness, coldness, barriers. . . .

This will always be a hindrance to the literary world. And yet this is not a literary problem. But I am one who likes literature and hopes that literature will mature slowly. With this token of sincerity, I wish for the transformation of my companions' lifeview.

Part XVI

Since the same natural and social world provides creative material for all writers, then excellent literary works will be produced regardless of the time and place in which they are written. Why should they be abundant in one time or place, and meager in another?

I feel that all literary works produced by writers whose talent is limited to recording the myriad things [*yiqie* 一切] that surround them will be of equal value, regardless of the time or place in which they were written.[3] The greater detail and accuracy of the record, the better naturally will be the work. But this anyone can do. The talent of the writer must never lie in this.

A writer is absolutely not a loyal servant to or stenographer for the myriad, nor is he a cold puppet-like person who just casually records what he sees and hears as a diversion. In short, he does not serve the myriad. As a writer he has the cultivation of self [*xiuyang* 修養], he has a worldview and a lifeview and an ego. He relies on these things to come into contact with the myriad, and of course he has his unique feelings and unique ideals. Applying artistic methods to all of this, he can then begin to write. What he writes about is naturally only a slice of life, a drop in the eternal flow of life; yet it is transformed, transformed into a literary work permeated by the spirit of the writer.

It makes no difference what literary school he adheres to. The so-called realist and naturalist schools have referred to their writing as "faithful description, without subjective opinion," which basically means a separation of the writer from his work. Yet is it possible to really effect such a separation? Try reading a realist work by any writer. In the places where he describes the "oppressed and abused," although he doesn't shout out his grief for their suffering and anguish, an earnest sympathy and pity always emerge from between the lines. This is still putting it in general terms. Getting to the heart of it, this feeling of sympathy for the weak is in fact a universal feeling common to all writers. If these feelings well up from a deep store, then they will emerge unselfconsciously. Even the dullard has a commiserating heart, how much more the writer with his particularly profound feelings.

Similarly, whatever the nature of the spirit of the writer, it will be reflected in his work. It waits for nothing to be expressed and cannot be concealed. So the true talent of the writer is to have his ego at the center of the myriad, serving his purposes. The myriad supplies the self with materials and stirs its emotions. Others, of course, have their individual spirits, but if those spirits are at least brought into a unity with the spirit of the Self, it will find expression in the work. Here's another analogy: the artist sees nature as the greatest beauty, and artistic talent lies in expressing nature. But this view seems to allow no room for the participation of the spirit of the artist, who only retreats to a point outside the curtain of nature in order to

---

3. Ye may be using the term *yiqie* in more than its colloquial sense of "everything." The term is used in Chinese Buddhism to refer to the total aspect of all phenomena.

faithfully copy it. But this cannot be. How is it possible to know great beauty and to express the innate life of nature, and not simply copy its external appearance, without the artist's spirit at the core? So we may say that without the spirit of the artist, despite nature's innate beauty, there can be no art.

The more advanced the writer's self-cultivation, the more complete his "ego," the clearer his work will reflect its spirit. Reading the works of all great writers, even those we pick up without knowing who authored them, we can often say immediately and unmistakably who the author is. This is true not only of literature, but also of art. The reason an appreciator of art can distinguish an authentic work from a forgery lies in this.

Two writers who have both embraced humanism and who base the composition of their works on the same events, will still each have his own distinct and unmistakable character. Why is this? Because the external events are but one dimension, whereas what the spirit of the writer attends to is multifaceted. One writer will extend his pity toward one aspect of an event, another will express his excitement toward a different aspect of the same event; the former offers words of consolation, the latter excited shouts, the two are not the same. In terms of form, each has a style that cannot be confused with the other. Those devoted to literature have a common saying: "This theme has already been treated thoroughly by other writers; there is simply nothing more that can be said about it." I say that all writers who have a real "ego" can produce fresh works out of stale themes, because what comes naturally from the spirit is not forced, it has to be fresh and creative and must not be stale or hackneyed. From this we can see that the paths of literature are many and that with a spirit served by the myriad, one's creativity will be endless. Anytime, anywhere, your spirit can fuse with it. You are the center of the myriad, its avant-garde. How proud you can be of this!

Not considering the sorts of literary playthings discussed above, there are now quite a few worthwhile literary works that strive toward truth. But there are among them some that do not move one, or that do not express themselves fully, or whose mood is flat. The reason for this is rather simple: it is only that their writer has no unique spirit; in other words, his worldview and lifeview have not yet established a foundation. But this is really not cause enough for someone with determination to lose courage, for a literature that strives toward truth has already focused on a most precise target, and all it lacks are the time and effort involved in refinement and cultivation. With strenuous effort there is no reason why it cannot reach its target.

Chapter 14

Art and Life

Xu Zhimo

One can speak neither of art nor of life without drawing, first of all, an indictment—and one can't be too vehement at it—against the prevailing social conditions to which we are all of us compelled to adapt ourselves.[1] If the materialistic West is a civilization without a heart, as we are accustomed to regard it nowadays, ours, on the other hand, is one without a soul, or at any rate with no consciousness of its ever having had one. If the Westerners are being dragged along by their own machinery of efficiency, all bustle and hustle, to nobody knows whither, my almost brutal imagery of the society we know would be a deadly stagnant pool of water, dark with mud and noisy with base insects and worms swarming over and about it; it smacks all but of decay and lifelessness. Indeed it would not require an extreme cynic to aver that here in China one finds a magnificent nation of physical weaklings, intellectual invalids, moral cowards, and withal, spiritual paupers. In a community like ours where one experiences but extremely rarely, if indeed ever, thrills of music, excitements of the in-

1. Tsemou Hsu (Xu Zhimo) 徐志摩, "Art and Life" (in English), *Chuangzao jikan* 創造季刊 2, no. 1 (1922). The editor has made numerous corrections and the occasional stylistic change in the original English. Chinese characters in the text appear in the original.

tellect, delights and sorrows of worthy love, or raptures of religious and aesthetic moments, where idealism of any kind is not only unacceptable, but doomed to be misunderstood and laughed at with scorn should ever any such appear, one possesses a body without a soul joined to it, or is, as the poet Shelley would say, spiritually dead.

Now let us look around and see what happened with our arts—music, painting, poetry, sculpture, drama, architecture, and dance. We had a great period of sculpture during the Wei [220–265], that is, some fourteen or fifteen centuries ago, but how many of us have seen and sincerely appreciated even a fragment of it, not to say the grand achievement, possibly one of the finest exhibits of sculpture in the world, at Yungang, Shanxi?[2] Music is a paradise lost to us long long ago, perhaps never to be regained, and today that divine function has sadly degenerated into the vulgar hands of the *jinghu* 京 胡 and *pipa* 琵 琶 instruments that help to animate the so-called theaters and *laozi guan* 落 子 館.[3] Painting is another sad story. A dim memory of the fact that we once have seen the vast generous sweeps of Wu Daozi 吳 道 子,[4] and the large and subtle compositions of Wang Wei 王 維, or, to name a more recent instance, the calm and sure vision of Jin Dongxin 金 冬 心,[5] revolts us to think that for many a day, we have seen but at best skillful technicians, sham imitators, and frank humbugs, totally devoid of originality and creative force. And then there are those ninth-rate followers of European methods, who are as puerile in technique as they are void in imagination, worse than the tame practitioners of traditional type in the sense that the latter generally puts you into humor and makes you smile, whereas the former frequently puts you out of humor and excites your sadist complex to distinction [*sic*]. Drama as an art is quite unspeakable, although some old-fashioned plays are admirable as a form of vulgar amusement and give a fair sense of what Mr. Dickinson calls the Chinese sense of humor.[6] "The greatness of a people," says the eminent dramatic critic Granville Barker, "the depth of a race's soul, is to be measured by the attainment it makes of tragic poetry, and drama." The essence of tragedy is

---

2. Yungang 雲 崗 , in Shanxi province, is the location of huge Buddhist statues dating from the Wei period.

3. A place where the *laozi* form of performace art is presented.

4. Eighth-century painter famous for his murals and frescoes in the temples of Chang'an and Luoyang.

5. Courtesy name for the painter and calligrapher Jin Nong 金 農 (1687–1763), one of the Eight Eccentrics of Yangzhou.

6. Goldsworthy Lowes Dickinson (1862–1932) taught political science at Cambridge where Xu studied. He was an admirer of Chinese culture and had written a series of controversial letters, in the voice of a Chinese, portraying China in utopian terms as a critique of Britain and its policy toward China (*Letters from John Chinaman*; 1901).

an artistic presentiment of spiritual crises, and we Chinese, not having developed that art, nor any adequate substitute, possess no means of fathoming our own tragic capability, or, rather, having never been aware of the reality, at once beautiful and terrible, of the soul, are proud that we have chosen, obviously wisely, a safer walk by shunning and ignoring it all. Modern architecture, again, is anything but artistic, and as far as Peking is concerned, I have discovered its hideous culmination in the monument of *Justice Prevails* 公 理 戰 勝 that inevitably grates on your nerves upon entering the Central Park. As to dance, needless to say, we are quite satisfied with the beautiful gestures of a Mei Lanfang 梅 蘭 芳 or a Qin Xuefang 琴 雪 芳 in the *Heavenly Maids Scattering Flowers* or *Chang'e* 嫦 娥 *Running to the Moon.*[7]

When we come to poetry, we can't fancy a more poverty-stricken predicament. A mere mention of the names of Fan Fanshan 樊 樊 山 and Yi Shifu 易 實 甫 [8] as our poets has something of a nauseating effect. The patriotic poets of the *kengzi* 庚 子 [9] type have wasted their tears and wailed sufficiently to make their poetry quite forgotten. Of versifiers indeed, there are as many today as there ever have been, but as for a true poet we have been rubbing our eyes for centuries to behold in vain. But then, there is the so-called new poetry, some one will interpose. Quite so, and that is about the only thing we can yet look to without despair. And yet a promising future may not induce our critical faculty to sleep and delude us into believing that really we already have true poetry. On the contrary, the experiments so far are quite unflattering and everywhere—in magazines, newspapers, school annals, love letters—one is fated to encounter what I should call preposterous applications of undigested theories. In the new verse there is, ostensibly, realism, the salient characteristic of which, however, is its fatal unreality; there is, further, naturalism, which is anything but natural; there is symbolism, which succeeds in devising symbols devoid of meaning; or, when any ism is actually achieved, nobody would venture to call it poetry. I shall omit to give examples to support my criticism here, but those of you who keep up with the movement will know that I am not indulging in extravagancy in this my unfavorable verdict.

Well! this brief survey amounts to as much as to say that we have no arts to speak of whatever. The question arises as to why this deplorable state of affairs is possible; how it has come into being. The answer, it seems

---

7. Two early twentieth century stars of the Beijing opera stage and their famous roles.

8. Fan Fanshan is Fan Zengxian 樊 增 祥 (1846–1931) and Yi Shifu is Yi Shunding 易 順 鼎 (1858–1920). Both were notoriously imitative poets who embodied everything the May Fourth literary revolution opposed.

9. This refers to patriotic poems written during the xenophobia of the Boxer Rebellion.

to me, is to be found in the simple statement that *we have no art precisely because we have no life.*

With all our virtues and qualities, we Chinese as a race have never realized and expressed ourselves completely, as the Greeks and the Romans did, through the medium of art—which is the consciousness of life. "In oriental thought," remarked the perfect critic Walter Pater, "there is a vague conception of life everywhere, but no true appreciation of life itself by the mind, no knowledge of the distinction of man's nature: in its consciousness of itself, humanity is still confused with the fantastic, indeterminate life of the animal and vegetable world."[10] He mentioned that as a contrast to Greek sculpture, where the "Lordship of the soul" is established and gives authority and divinity, as Pater beautifully puts it, to human eyes and hands and feet.

"No true appreciation of life itself by the mind, and no recognition of the distinction of noble humanity." That is the most cogent piece of criticism on our culture I have ever known. Our sages are preoccupied, like the Bolshevist leaders of today, although perhaps in a different fashion, with the not very easy task of equilibrating and harmonizing the obvious impulses that men share with their fellow beings—such as food, sex, etc.—but alas! how they forget to contemplate man as a spiritual as well as physical being, and the necessary considerations and provisions for such. Hence the Confucian system—admirable as it is—when rendered to practice after later distortions and alterations, resulted in a sort of culture resting upon a comfortable basis of mere sentimentalities, amiable perhaps, but no more than sentimentalities, leaving out, as it did, man's spirit as unworthy of attention.

And as they forget the spirit they suppress the senses. Confucius, with a superb gesture, delimited man's sensual extension and enjoyment by referring us to a standard he never defined, namely *Li* [ritual].

Laozi and Zhuangzi, with even sweeter voices, pointed our bewitched minds to the ideal monster of life completing itself, which like Shakespeare's old babe of the Seventh Age,[11] was to be sans teeth, sans eyes, sans taste, sans everything. That gentleman, Hundun, would not have preserved his vital integrity were he once given organs of the senses, which they

---

10. Walter Pater, "Winckelmann," in *The Renaissance: Studies in Art and Poetry*; from *The Works of Walter Pater in Eight Volumes* (London: Macmillan, 1900), 1: 206.

11. "All the world's a stage. / And all the men and women, merely players; / They have their exits and their entrances, / And one man in his time plays many parts, / His acts being seven ages. At first the infant, / Mewling and puking in the nurse's arms" (*As You Like It*, II.vii).

thought to be at once distractive and destructive of one's innate energy.[12] That stupid Mozi, likewise, would have been ecstatic should human beings consent to feed on grass and to find shelter in caves and renounce, of course, all forms of the delight our natural senses are likely to discover.[13]

With his soul unrecognized and senses denied, together with an ingenious device in operation by which his natal forces are directed, partly through repression, partly through sublimation, into "safe" and practical channels, the Chinese man has come to be a creature, human enough to be sure, yet capable neither of religion nor of love, nor indeed of any spiritual adventures. We are admired, as by sincere friends like G. Lowes Dickinson, and Bertrand Russell, Miss Eileen Power,[14] for our dispassionate attitude toward life, love of moderation, reasonableness, and compromising spirit and so forth, a compliment we assuredly deserve; yet I for one in accepting it can't help feeling the poignancy of the irony that is behind it. For what is a dispassionate attitude toward life but a patent negation of life by smothering the divine flame of passions almost to extinction? What is love for moderation but an amiable excuse for cowardice in thought and action, for shallowness and flatness in life activities. And what is obsequiously called the rationalistic and compromising spirit has produced nothing but a habit of laziness at large and that ridiculous monster which we are told to regard as the Chinese Republican Government! O, do not our friends know with what a price have we managed to secure an apparent, though not real, peaceful mode of life, which the extremist and turbulent West has of late come to envy and admire? "What we want today," Mr. H. G. Wells once told me, "is peace, peace and peace, but mind you, not that sort of peace which is timid, flat, breathless, easygoing and all that—that is not peace in my sense—but a peace that must be ever active, vivid, creative—the kind of peace the ancient Athens, for instance, once realized."

And since so, we have come to be, indeed, too rational and reasonable for passionate love, as for passionate religious thoughts. For love, that Divine Madness as Plato had it, is anything but reasonable, and those who are familiar with Catholic teaching will have heard that, in that creed, love is

---

12. Refers to the Daoist myth of the Emperor Hundun 混沌, who represents a return to the primal condition before entry into the civilized world of the senses, language, and a separation of subject from object. The myth of Hundun comes from Zhuangzi. For a study of chaos mythology in China, see N. J. Girardot, *Myth and Meaning in Early Taoism: The Theme of Chaos (hun-tun)* (Berkeley: University of California Press, 1983).

13. Mozi 墨子 (468–376 B.C.), in reaction to the excessive ritual associated with the Confucians, proposed a life of frugality and austerity.

14. Eileen Power (1889-1940) taught history at Girton College, Cambridge, when Xu was a student there.

exalted into a "great Sacrament" holding that, with transubstantiation—
which it resembles—it is unreasonable only because it is above reason. "Indeed," writes Coventry Patmore, "the extreme unreasonableness of this
passion which gives cause for so much blaspheming to the foolish, is one of
its surest sanctions and a main cause of its inexhaustible interest and power."[15] For who but a scientist values greatly or is greatly moved by anything
we can understand—that which can be comprehended being necessarily
less than we are ourselves? Love, therefore, like religion, which is but divine or cosmic love as the case may be, is transcendental and transfiguring,
and being transfigured through that mysterious force, one's mortal eyes
are, for once, to behold visions that belong to the spiritual realm and are
commonly denied to matter-of-fact perception, and his ears are to be overwhelmed by the grand and sublime music that comes, like mighty waves in
the sea, from the spheres. It is through that transcendental elevation of
one's spirit that the creative energy heretofore inert and latent, begins to
liberate itself and strives—by whatever medium it may happen to choose—
to realize its own volume and shape. "Love is rooted deeper in the earth
than any other passion; and for that cause its head, like that of the Holy
Tree, soars higher into Heaven. The heights demand and justify the depths,
as giving them substance and credibility." Indeed it is but a commonplace
to claim for love the most vital and potent fountain of creation. Subtract the
element of sexual passion and all that radiates from it and you will be
shocked to see the irretrievable bankruptcy of European literature and arts.
And every man or woman, without necessarily being a Freudian, will admit, or at any rate feels, that love, though the least serious, is the most significant of all things. And yet this simple truth has never been recognized
in the sickeningly long history of China, and even today my personal experience has only discovered two classes of people in China, regarding this
matter: namely, cynics who despise love, and cowards who are afraid of it.
Had the tree of knowledge been planted in the middle of the Chinese Empire, instead of the Garden of Eden, Adam and Eve would have remained
superb creatures, blind of heart as of eye and insensible to the life prompt-
ings within, and God Himself would have been spared all the indignations
and troubles consequent of the snake's heroism and Eve's curiosity.

   And another fatal consequence of our Sage's defining and planning for
us the scope of life (which is all but an unattractive series of ethical platitudes) is the barring and curbing influence upon our faculty of imagination.
You have only to look into our fiction and poetry to be convinced of how

---

15. Coventry Patmore (1823-96), English poet and essayist. The source of this citation
is unknown.

extremely narrow the role of imagination therein is. Isn't it significant that none of our poets, with the only possible exception of Li Bai, can be said to be of cosmic character? Isn't it striking that we look in vain in the scroll of our famous literary figures for even the least resemblance of a Goethe, a Shelley, a Wordsworth, not to say a Dante or a Shakespeare? And as for the other arts, who is there here to rank with the vast genius of men like Michelangelo, Leonardo da Vinci, Turner, Correggio, Velázquez, Wagner, Beethoven—to name but a few? Is it then inherent in our race's nature that, in art as in other things, we are to be always unlike the rest of the world, or is it rather due to the undergrowth and ill-nourishment of an imaginative power, since the difference is not so much of kind as of degree, that we possess an artistic heritage, essentially inferior to that of the West, in that it fails *to comprehend life as a whole*, which must be required of all great works of art? The training of our mind and eyes from a very early age to adapt to the practical details and appropriate etiquette of an unexciting life rather than opening up for them the secret and enchanting possibilities of a great life, is the greatest failure in Chinese education and is responsible for the death of true personality and endless manufacturing of excellent mediocrities.

The fount and source of life and joy, as well as the faculty of imagination, being relentlessly thwarted in its natural flow, what remains to our mortal existence is obvious and wretched indeed. *And poverty of life necessarily begets poverty of art*, as a full and beautiful life spontaneously flowers into tangible beauties that will ultimately lay claim upon our notion of immortality. As a tree that is full of vital energy cannot but yield its fertility in the form of either superb foliage or of fruits of exquisite color, so a life overflowing with self-consciousness, is certain to crystallize itself in thought, which will be art, or in action, which will be deeds worthy of remembrance. *Therefore, enrich, augment, multiply, intensify* and *above all spiritualize your life*, and *art will come of itself.*

I have said enough to explain, or rather condemn, the sluggish and superficial aspect of Chinese art and life. Now let us pause a moment to cast a cursory glance at the correspondence of art and life discoverable in Western history; and for this, as for anything else, we can do no better than turn to the ancient Greeks and Renaissance Italy for light and intelligence.

The supremest achievement of Hellenic culture, it seems to me, is not in its politics, much less its science and metaphysics, but in the discovery of the dignity and beauty of the human body. "By no people," says Winckelmann, the great German Renaissance art historian, "has beauty been so highly esteemed as by the Greeks. The priests of a youthful Jupiter at Aegae, of the Ismenian Apollo, and the priest who at Tanagra led the processions of Mercury, bearing a lamb upon his shoulders, were always youths to whom the prize of beauty had been awarded. . . . And as beauty was so longed for and prized by the Greeks, every beautiful person sought to become known to the whole people by this distinction, and above all to approve himself to the artists, because they awarded the prize; and this was for the artists an opportunity of having supreme beauty ever before their eyes. Beauty even gave a right to fame; and we find in Greek histories the most beautiful people distinguished. . . . The general esteem for beauty went so far, that the Spartan women set up in their bedchambers a Nereus, a Narcissus, or a Hyacinth, that they might bear beautiful children."[16] And in this, as in other things, nature had its responsible portion too. For the happiest readiness with which the Greeks eagerly transformed their thoughts about themselves and their relation to the world in general into objects for the senses was not accidental: they were given to beauty in bodily form, as to comprehensiveness in intellect. The delicate air nimbly and sweetly recommending itself to the senses, the finer aspects of nature, the finer lime and clay of the human form, and modeling of the dainty framework of the human countenance: these are the good fortunes of the Greek when he enters upon life. Beauty becomes a distinction, like genius, or noble places. Open an ethnological book of comparative physiology where you find the nude bodies of the various races exposed, or read that cruel description of a Japanese nude dancer by I think the Frenchman Courier—I am not sure I remember it right—and then turn to the supreme beauties of a Venus de Milo, or the Apollo Belvedere and you will have some fascinating yet uncomfortable sense of the playful unfairness of Nature in shaping for the different peoples different form and proportion, not to mention the color and smell, as in the case of a black beauty.

Yet this preoccupation with beauty does not argue that, on that account, the Greeks are therefore a nation of irresponsible aesthetes. On the contrary the Greeks are concerned with beauty only in so far as it contributes to the realization of a good life, to the blending together in a perfect harmony of the various elements of the soul. And it was only by the perfect and robust intellect of Greeks that the ultimate good was deemed conceivable and ultimately expressible only in terms of the beautiful. One of the greatest human documents—Plato's *Republic*—which is itself aesthetic through and through, deals with establishing the relation between the good and the beautiful, which leads to the identification of the ideal citizenship with the

---

16. Johann Joachim Winckelmann (1717–68), art historian known for his appreciation of the art of ancient Greece. His most famous work is *Geschichte der Kunst des Altertums* (1764). This passage is cited by Pater in his essay on Winckelmann. See note #10 above.

good life. It is unique of the Greeks that their attitude to life is the same as their attitude to art; to them, and to them alone, life and art are one. The standard by which art and life are judged are the same: in the Greek view art is truly the consciousness of life. It is significant that their word for gentleman was *kalos kagathos*, the beautiful good.

If the salient heritage the Greeks have left us with is the discovery of the human body, the gift of the Renaissance from fifteenth-century Italy is the discovery and embodiment of the human spirit. It is, like present-day China, a great age of revolt. It is a many-sided but yet united movement in which man, after a long period of oppression and repression, struggles to recover his dignity and independence, and in which the love of the things of the intellect and the imagination for their own sake, the desire for a more liberal and comely way of conceiving life, make themselves felt, urging those who experience this desire to search out first one and then another means of intellectual or imaginative enjoyment, and directing them not merely to the discovery of old and forgotten sources of this enjoyment, but to the divination of fresh sources thereof—new experiences, new subjects of poetry, new forms of art. It is an age—the age of Lorenzo may be fairly compared to that of Pericles—productive in personalities, many-sided, centralized, complete. "Here, artists and philosophers and those whom the action of the world has elevated and made keen, do not live in isolation, but breathe a common air, and catch light and heat from each other's thoughts. There is a spirit of general elevation and enlightenment in which all alike communicate. It is the unity of the spirit which gives unity to all the various products of the Renaissance and it is to this intimate alliance with mind, this participation in best thoughts which that age produced, that the art of the 15th-century Italy owes much of its grave dignity and influence."

This unity of spirit is important; it pervades art as well as life. The same force that gives birth to so many splendid personalities ministers to the efflorescence thereof in the shape of fine art of astonishing beauty filled with the warmth of life and expressive of the deepest and noblest feelings the human soul is ever capable of. It moves toward the recognition of the right of the individual to complete self-expression, which it ultimately achieved, and the recognition of the objective reality of the universe, which initiated the scientific method and led to the subsequent discoveries.

I have selected the Hellenic and the Renaissance periods to the exclusion of all other movements, in order to show that in these, more clearly than in any other, the human spirit enjoyed the happy opportunity of realizing itself in a cultural unity, in a coherent demonstration of the utmost capabilities of a life, which is full, intense, vivid, and self-conscious. If our modern China to which the name Renaissance is not wholly inapplicable has anything to learn from Western history, it is to the Hellenic culture and Renaissance spirit that we would do well to look. As for the cocksure rationalism and bald-headed materialism that originated with the eighteenth and grew rampant in the nineteenth century, they have made their charming turn and ended in contradicting themselves to disaster, leaving a few pseudo-scientists clinging in fury to their experimental tools and the sanguine-colored Bolshevists worshipping their infallible God, Karl Marx, against a general awakening of a new idealism, embracing humanity as its creed and art as its religion. And into this movement, China, if she has not yet completely exhausted her vitality and smothered her genius, will, we believe with a delighted heart and awakened soul, throw herself and ultimately prove worthy of her old inheritance. And if so, it will not be long before we shall be able to get rid of the lethargic habits and conventional trammelings that are characteristic of Chinese culture and once more, after a long interval, as the Renaissance after the Dark Ages, to behold and delight in ideal personalities—of which we must admit we have detected but little sign—and works of art that will embody and manifest what is fundamental in man in general and in our race in particular. I have always fancied that the appearance of a great musician, or rather a composer of music who will not only revivify what we have lost in the past but also give utterance to the long, long suppressed voice of our mighty nation, will probably do well to signify the now nascent spirit maturing into fruition. For music, rather than any other art, is the true type and measure of perfected art, and it also touches deeper into the fibers of the human heart as it conveys thoughts and emotions to those who have an ear for it, more convincingly, more irresistibly, more forcibly, and more ideally.

I shall sum up what I intend to convey in this paper: I have shown, very sketchily, why the Chinese arts fail, as the European arts more or less succeed, in comprehending life as a whole and interpreting it wholly through the faculty of imagination; I have argued a relative position of our life and art, taking the latter as being reflective of the former, and the former as being responsible for the latter. I have also instanced the Hellenic antiquity and Renaissance achievements as signifying a unity of spirit revealed in perfect forms of art, which is largely humanistic, as must be our own.

I have also dared to put forth the dictum: namely, mind your life and art will take care of itself. By "minding life" I mean the conscious opening up of the natural resources, so to speak, inherent in our nature and making use of every opportunity of having them turned to profitable account: in other words, we must consciously cultivate our self-consciousness, and having attained that, let our innate creative spirit do its own work. For indeed not many of us here dare say, "I have completely made my own acquaintance." And remember, seeking to express always results in self-revelation and understanding, often enough to one's own surprise. And the opening up of what is native will depend for its inspiration and efficacy on what is imbibed from without. Aesthetic appreciation will prove a potent factor in this regard, and a delicate sensibility for what is beautiful is by far more important and fruitful to life than a strong intellect or moral character. Do well to court artistic thrills and you will know beauty and the value of being alive. If you are not moved by a Hamlet or a Prometheus unbound, Shakespeare and Shelley are not to be blamed. If you do not experience ecstasies when a well-conducted Beethoven symphony is in full sway, you'd better consult an ear specialist to see if your auditory organ is in normal condition. If a *Tristan und Isolde* fail to stir you to your soul's depths—unless you dislike Wagner by taste—you ought to feel at least as much disgraced as you would when you flunk out in mathematics or gymnastics, which is not saying much. If you do not stand entranced in front of the statue of Moses in Rome or the Cologne Cathedral, if you see nothing in Turner and Whistler and Matisse but a mass of pretty color, you may safely persuade yourself that, after all, your education is not half so perfect as you might have thought it yourself. If you don't detect any secret joy when you pass the inner yard of Shunzhi men 順治門,[17] where a magnificent array of ceramic beauties is exquisitely arranged against walls of grave antiquity, you'd better give up your effort to appreciate the post-Impressionists, Cézanne for instance, and relapsing into your easy chair curse the world about you for being shabby in beautiful things. And so on. I do not propose, of course, that all of us can, without previous training or acquaintance at all, fall in love with European arts as nimbly as a professional critic; on the contrary the fundamental idea embodied in Western arts, as well as the technique, are always baffling, because unfamiliar, to a normal Oriental intelligence, and I suspect not even 1 percent of the Chinese students abroad have the least sense of the arts, beyond a shallow sort of sensual pleasure about them. But forget not that nothing worth getting is got without difficulty; after all, it is only our silly education and sluggish habits that prevent us from feeling and enjoying things as they are; remove them and you will recover your aesthetic intuition, starved perhaps, and its passionate avidity and penetrating fervor. And then life itself should be treated as a piece of art, as an artistic problem. We are given this earthly body and the mind and the heart much as an artist is given a subject or situation for painting or casting into stone. And having mastered the material, as we all hope to do, oughtn't we feel a sense of responsibility when applying our pen or knife to

---

17. This was one of the city gates of the old wall surrounding Beijing.

the limited and delicate substance that may be spoiled by a single stroke or transformed into a work of beauty? As the passionate Italian poet D'Annunzio says, we can yet, even in this world, only if we will and try, make of our life a beautiful fable. And there is no better way of attaining to the good than through being beautiful; as we are glad enough to follow the wisdom of the Greeks, our aesthetic intuition is by far a safer and surer ultimate standard than our indistinct, evasive sense of moral goodness. Life as a work of art! So prepare yourself for the final retrospect, say at the age of seventy, when every blush of youth will be turned into hideous wrinkles in the skin and sweetness of voice into harshness of aged cough, and see if then you are not well pleased with the eventful career that your own hands have been helping to shape and form. Read biographies of great men like Goethe's, or any lesser soul's, and regard it as a standard by which to judge your own, and see how the comparison comes out. For a great life like that of Goethe's cannot fail to be recognized as no less an accomplished work of art, a masterpiece, than the St. Peter's of Rome for instance is a work of art; equally full of beautiful mysteries, and mysterious beauties. But as for admonitions in & principles of a worthy and sensible life, I can do no better than to quote once more Walter Pater from his famous "Conclusion" to the studies in the Renaissance.

> The service of philosophy, of speculative culture, towards the human spirit is to rouse, to startle it into sharp and eager observation. Every moment some form grows perfect in hand or face; some tone on the hills or the sea is choicer than the rest; some mood of passion or insight or intellectual excitement is irresistibly real and attractive for us,—for that moment only. Not the fruit of experience, but experience itself, is the end. A counted number of pulses only is given to us of a variegated, dramatic life. How may we see in them all that is to be seen in them by the finest senses? How shall we pass most swiftly from point to point, and be present always at the focus where the greatest number of vital forces unite in their purest energy? To burn always with this hard, gemlike flame, to maintain this ecstasy, is success in life.

And again:

> Well! We are all *condamnés*, as Victor Hugo says: we are all under sentence of death but with a sort of indefinite reprieve. . . . we have an interval, and then our place knows us no more. Some spend this interval in listlessness, some in high passions, the wisest, at least among the "children of this world," in art and song. For our one chance lies in expanding that interval, in getting as many pulsations as possible into the given time. Great pas-

sions may give us this quickened sense of life, ecstasy and sorrow of love, the various forms of enthusiastic activity, disinterested or otherwise, which come naturally to many of us. Only be sure it is passion—that it does yield you this fruit of a quickened, multiplied consciousness. Of this wisdom, the poetic passion, the desire of beauty, the love of art for art's sake, has most; for art comes to you professing frankly to give nothing but the highest quality to your moments as they pass, and simply for those moments' sake.[18]

This essay in English is a draft of a lecture presented by Mr. Xu Zhimo at the Qinghua Literary Society. It was typed by a friend of his, and though it was revised a fair bit, it still has quite a few mistakes. When I was ready to print it, I looked it over carefully and revised quite a lot. I also revised some of the citations. The essay discusses the extremely clear relationship between art and life. He sees the reason for the lack of artistic production in the fact that we Chinese have no life of substance. He originally wanted to translate it, but then thought it over and felt it would be rather too much trouble, so in the end he didn't translate it.

---

18. Walter Pater, "Conclusion," in *The Renaissance: Studies in Art and Poetry*; from *The Works of Walter Pater in Eight Volumes* (London: Macmillan, 1900), 1: 236, 238.

Chapter 15

Replacing Religion with Aesthetic Education

Cai Yuanpei

A lecture delivered in 1917 to the Shenzhou Scholarly Society

Because I have not conducted systematic research in the scholarly world, I have no right to express my opinions before your learned society.[1] Since I accepted the obligation of lecturing to you gentlemen, however, I have no choice but to select an issue of research value to our nation, namely, the theory of "Replacing Religion with Aesthetic Education," for presentation to you.

In the various countries of Western Europe, the problem of religion is already one of the past. Scholars have resolved the nature of religion with scientific inquiry. When we visit Europe, we see that although churches dot the landscape and most people do attend them, it is a kind of custom rooted in historical practice. This is like the dress uniforms of the previous Qing

---

1. Cai Yuanpei 蔡元培, "Yi meiyu dai zongjiao" 以美育代宗教; first publshed under the name Cai Jiemin 蔡子民 in *Xin qingnian* 3, no.6 (1917); reprinted in *Cai Yuanpei xiansheng yiwen leichao* 蔡元培先生遺文類鈔 (Taibei: Fuxing shuju, 1961).

dynasty, which originally had no use in our Republican period, but since there were so many left, destroying them would be a pity; we thus designated them as uniforms of the second rank so as to continue using them, and there is nothing wrong with this. In similar manner, ceremonies for birthdays and funerals are completely worthless from a scientific point of view, but if relatives and friends receive invitations to them, they cannot but follow precedent and attend, so as to share the sentiments of the family. The European continuation of religious ceremonies is like this.

What is strange is that, lacking this particular European custom, we in China take the past reality of those countries as novel knowledge and bring it up frequently for discussion. This is because the students who study abroad see the advancement of those societies and erroneously believe what religious teachers say, that all can be attributed to religion; consequently, they wish to guide our people with Christianity. Moreover, some who continue the old thinking adopt theories of the past, with slight modifications, and see Confucius as the Jesus of China. They thus wish to organize a Confucian religion, and they run from place to place shouting about it, considering it the most important issue of the day.[2]

In my opinion, religion is invariably constructed as a response to our spiritual functions. Our spiritual functions ordinarily may be divided into three kinds: the first is knowledge; the second is will; and the third is emotion. The earliest religions usually possessed all three of these objectives.

In our prehistoric era, when our mental faculties were simple, we perceived ourselves and the things of the world as incomprehensible. From where does life come? Where do we go after death? Who is the creator? What is the art of the ruler? All of these various questions were raised by people in that time, as they sought the answers.

Thereupon, the theologians fabricated answers. Christianity found the creator to be God; Hinduism found it to be Brahma; Chinese mythology found it to be Pan Gu. They also considered the divine as the sole cause of various other phenomena. Thus were the functions of knowledge bonded to religion.

From birth, we humans have a desire to survive, but from this desire arises a kind of selfishness. At first, people thought that if something did not harm others, it could not benefit themselves. So people relied on might to maltreat the weak, and all forms of robbery and seizure by force oc-

---

2. Cai is likely referring to Kang Youwei 康有為 (1858–1927), who sought to revive Confucianism, through a series of novel textual reinterpretations of Confucian writings, and who supported establishing Confucianism as a state religion in the period from 1912 to 1916.

curred. Later, with a little more experience, people knew that those who helped others were necessary, and then theologians advocated altruism. Thus were the uses of will bonded to religion.

Savages never tired in their enjoyment of dancing and singing. They carved and painted decorations for their dwellings; from the relics of the Neolithic era we can examine their love of Beauty. This is a normal human feeling, but the theologians used it as a method of seducing people into faith. Consequently, there is no art from the precivilized era that is not related to religion. Thus were the functions of emotion bonded to religion.

The laws of evolution were carved out of chaos. Spiritual functions, in that time, were part of the primeval chaos, but then were brought together to fashion religion. Because it was unopposed by other forms of scholarship, religion possessed a special power over society. Later, society and culture gradually advanced, science developed, and scholars raised the questions that ancient man thought inconceivable, one by one explaining them through science.

The phenomena of the sun and the stars, the origins of the earth, the distribution of flora and fauna, the differences in human races, were confirmed by the sciences of physics, chemistry, biology, anthropology, archaeology, and so forth. What the theologians said was that mankind was created by God, but from the viewpoint of biological evolution, mankind's earliest ancestor was a kind of tiny organism that gradually evolved into a human. This is evidence that the function of knowledge had separated from religion and become independent.

Theologians think that the rules of the human community are divinely ordained and can never be changed. But the sophists of ancient Greece, who traveled in many lands, knew that the so-called morality of various nations was often mutually contradictory, and already doubted the existence of invariable principles. Modern scholars, who apply the laws of biology, psychology, and sociology to ethics, know that concrete morality cannot but change with time and locale. Moreover, the principles of morality can be induced from a variety of different concrete things, but the deductive methods of the theologians are completely inapplicable. This is proof that will has separated from religion and is independent.

If knowledge and will are divorced from religion, then, of the three functions with the closest relationship to religion, only the function of emotion, that is to say, aesthetic feeling, remains. All religious architecture is built in the most beautiful of settings. For example, on China's so-called famous mountains are many Buddhist temples. Within them are ancient trees and famous flora, made known to all by the brushes of the poets, who use natural beauty to move people's feelings. The temples always have towering pagodas, grand and mysterious halls, delicately worked sculptures, extraordinarily beautiful murals and somber light, as well as subtle music to add to the mood. Those who hymn must use well-known lyrics; those who orate must develop forceful eloquence. All such things are for artistic purposes, so as to engage people in their beauty. If they discarded all these facilities, I suspect they could not do battle.

The history of the evolution of art actually shows a tendency toward separation from religion. For example, in the period of the Northern and Southern dynasties, the most famous buildings were *sanghārāma* [Buddhist monasteries]; their sculptures were idols; most of their paintings were Buddha images and scenes of hell; and part of their literature was devoted to Buddhist stories. But literature after the Tang period took its subjects from scenery, human feelings, or affairs of the world. Painting, since the Song and Yuan periods, described landscapes, birds and flowers, and other kinds of natural beauty. Bronze vessels made before the Zhou period were used for ritual sacrifices. The metalwork of the Han through Tang periods and the renowned porcelains produced from the Song and Yuan periods onward, however, have been made for the sole purpose of giving pleasure. The dances of the primitive era were performed for the entertainment of the gods, but today we use them for our own enjoyment.

The most famous architecture surviving from the European middle ages is probably the cathedral. The themes of its sculpture and painting are usually taken from the Old and New Testaments; its music consists of hymns; and its dramas rehearse the stories of Jesus, similar to China's ancient drama "Mulian Rescues His Mother."[3]

After the Renaissance, all forms of art gradually separated from religion and instead valued humanism. Today, therefore, the most magnificent architecture may be found in schools, theaters, and museums, whereas newly constructed churches with aesthetic merit are almost nonexistent. Other kinds of art often take their subjects from natural phenomena or social conditions.

Thus, there are already two schools of thought in aesthetic education, one separate from religion and one joined to it. In comparing the two schools, the aesthetic education that is attached to religion often is constrained by religion; it consequently loses its function of educating and instead simply stimulates the feelings.

---

3. Mulian 目 蓮 is the Chinese name for Maudgalyayana, a disciple of Buddha who, according to legend, made trips to hell to save his mother from torture. Versions of this Buddhist miracle tale appear in the *Dunhuang bianwen* 敦 煌 變 文 (Bianwen texts from Dunhuang) (Taibei: Shijie shuju, 1973), 701ff.

There is no religion that is not based on expanding itself and attacking paganism. Islam's Mohammed held the Koran in his left hand and a sword in his right, so as to kill those who did not submit to his teachings. Christianity's conflict with Islam led to the Crusades, which lasted for a century. Within Christianity there were the Wars of Religion, which lasted for several decades.

Buddhism's accommodating nature is something that other religions cannot hope to attain. Buddhists who are constrained by the prejudices of religious doctrine, however, follow ignorant practices, such as worshipping relics and adhering to sutras and repentances; even the educated willingly do this, to the extent that in their goal of protecting the Buddhist doctrine they care little for the Republican age and will play sycophant to dictatorship. Bonds of religion that are this tight are the effects of stimulating the emotions.

If, having scrutinized the harm of exciting the emotions, we instead advocate the art of cultivating the emotions, then we will not reject religion but will transform it into pure aesthetic education. What cultivates our emotions in pure aesthetic education is that it produces pure and lofty habits and gradually eliminates selfishness and the concept of benefiting ourselves through harming others.

If beauty is universal, there cannot exist within it the consciousness of ourselves as differentiated from other people. The food that enters my mouth cannot fill the stomach of another person, and the clothing on my body cannot keep someone else warm; this is their nonuniversality. Beauty is otherwise. For example, when I travel to the West Mountains near Beijing at the same time that other people do, my presence does not harm their experience, nor does their presence harm mine. Or, separated by thousands of miles, all of us gaze at the moon, but neither I nor someone else can possess it privately. Everyone can enjoy the flowers and rocks in Central Park or the ponds and vegetation at the Agricultural Experiment Grounds. Countless people have viewed and admired the pyramids of Egypt, the temples of Greece, and the Roman coliseum, but, after so many years, their value remains undiminished.

The museums of all nations are open to the public, and even the works of private collectors are sometimes made available for all to view. The success of concerts and dramas in all countries is marked by high attendance. The pleasure of music experienced alone cannot compare to that experienced with others; the enjoyment of music experienced with the few cannot compare to that experienced with the many. Even in his stupidity, King

Xuan of Qi could recognize this.[4] We know, then, the universality of beauty. Moreover, although the evaluation of beauty differs from person to person, no one says "It is beautiful to me," but instead says, "It is beautiful." This is another proof of the universality of beauty.

Because of the universality of beauty, the distinction between myself and other people no longer exists, and there can be no relationships based on self-interest or harming others. Horses and oxen are used for the benefit of man, but one never thinks of riding the oxen painted by Dai Song or the horses painted by Han Gan.[5] Lions and tigers terrify people, but the stone lions at Marco Polo Bridge and the stone tigers at Divine Tiger Bridge never induce fear of being mauled or eaten. Although plants flower in order to produce fruit, when we enjoy flowers we never think of them making fruit for us to eat. Songbirds are never used as food. Brilliantly colored snakes are often poisonous, but if you look at them from an aesthetic point of view, they have their own value. All men love female beauty, but when we look at the unclothed statues of Greece, we don't dare feel lust. In viewing nudes painted by Raphael or Rubens, we don't entertain the thoughts aroused by Zhou Fang's painting *Secret Pleasures*.[6] Beauty's transcendence of reality is thus.

Moreover, its meaning becomes more obvious when we look beyond ordinary beauty to see special beauty. For example, there are two sorts of exalted beauty, namely the most grand and the most unyielding. Grandeur is the feeling we might have if we were in the middle of the ocean and could see only the water and the sky, which merge, seemingly without boundaries. Or, if we look up at night to count the infinite stars, we discover that each star is a world of its own without visible boundaries. We suddenly feel the minuteness of our own bodies (even the metaphor of a speck of dust is inadequate to capture this) and know that no one can possess it all.

That which is unyielding is like the gales and thunderclaps that overturn boats and topple buildings, or the floods that cover the land, or erupting volcanoes (it even has the power to uproot mountains and sweep across the earth),[7] nothing affects it no one can dominate it.

---

4. The allusion is to *Mencius*, "Liang Hui wang," pt. II.

5. Dai Song 戴嵩 and Han Gan 韓幹 were eighth-century artists; see Zhang Yanyuan, *Lidai minghuaji* 歷代名畫集, 2d ed., in *Huashi congshu* 畫史叢書 (Shanghai People's Art Press, 1982), vol. 1, *juan* 10, p. 123; *juan* 9, p. 115.

6. Zhou Fang 周昉 was a late eighth-century artist who specialized in paintings of beautiful women. See ibid., *juan* 10, p. 123. This painting is not known to be extant.

7. *Ba shan gai shi* 拔山蓋世 is a phrase used by Xiang Yu to describe his martial might in a poem recited to his beloved concubine shortly before his demise; from "Xiang Yu benji" 項羽本紀, *Shiji* (Taibei: Zhonghua shuju), 1: 333.

The grand and the unyielding are only relative terms. Since at present grandeur is not something that can be spoken of, nor is unyielding power a stable concept, when we suddenly transcend the limits of these relative terms, we find that the aforesaid concepts of grandeur or the unyielding merge into a single entity and our pleasure becomes limitless. At such a time, how could concern for advantage and harm, gain and loss, enter one's consciousness?

Other elements of aesthetic education, such as the beauty of tragedy, can eliminate our desire for good fortune. The complaint of the poems in the "Xiaoya" section of the *Book of Songs* or the grief of Qu Yuan's "Encountering Sorrow" can profoundly move one. If *The Romance of the Western Chamber* concluded with Cui Yingying and Student Zhang's marriage, it would be bland and ordinary. Only because the original ends with the dream at Grass Bridge does it stir people's thoughts. If the *Story of the Stone*, like the *Later Dream of the Red Chamber*, required that Baoyu and Daiyu get married, then there would be no point in writing the book. What moves people in the original version is precisely that one dies and the other disappears, which is completely the opposite of what we call happiness.

Comic beauty, similarly, is not based on a direct correspondence with reality. In a person's physical appearance, every part has its proper proportion. The characters in comic pictures, however, have one part too long or another too short. Or in rhymes, we might use words of unsuitable tone or play with meaning by using homophonous characters. When Dongfang Shuo sliced meat intended for court use to give to his wife, he not only failed to apologize, he instead boasted of it and made the king laugh.[8] When You Zhan exhorted the second Qin Emperor to lacquer his city walls, he did not speak of the plan's extravagant inappropiateness, but instead said the opposite, that if the vast walls were lacquered, bandits would be unable to scale them because they would slip.[9] All these examples make people laugh because they do not accord with reality.

In aesthetics, the main division is between ornamental beauty and sublime beauty (which the Japanese have translated as *yusōbi* 優 壯 美). Moreover, tragedy, which is bound to the beauty of the Sublime, and humor, which is bound to ornamental beauty, are both sufficient to remove our distinctions between self and other, and eradicate our calculations of advantage and disadvantage or profit and loss. Thus, they clearly cultivate the

---

8. Dongfang Shuo 東方朔 (159–93 B.C.) was a literary figure of the Han, noted for his broad learning and sense of humor; see "Huaji liezhuan" 滑稽列傳 (The jesters), *Shiji* (Taibei: Zhonghua shuju), 10: 3205–8.

9. You Zhan 優旃 was a dwarf jester at the Qin court, ibid. 10: 3202.

spirit, making it daily nearer to the sublime, and that is already enough. Why, then, waste words on good or evil, attacking other sects of religion to excite people's hearts, and causing them to gradually lose their pure aesthetic feeling?

—*Translated by Julia F. Andrews*

Chapter 16

Literature and Life

Mao Dun

My topic for today is literature and life.[1] The Chinese have always imagined that literature is not something needed by ordinary people. Only self-satisfied people of leisure and highbrow taste were thought of as concerning themselves with literature. To be sure, throughout its history there have been in China a great many works of literature, poetry, lyrics, fiction, etc. On the other hand, works that treated the questions of what literature is, of what kind of issues it treats, have been very few and far between: equally rare has been that type of work which instructs us how to read a piece of literature or how to critique one. Liu Xie's *Literary Mind and the Carving of Dragons* might be considered a specialized treatment of literary issues: on closer examination, however, it also falls short because Liu Xie did not come to grips with the problem of literariness, etc. He merely defined the various forms of literature by the application of subjective criteria. As for what is a regulated verse poem [*shi*], what is a prose poem [*fu*], *The Literary*

---

1. Shen Yanbing 沈雁冰 (Mao Dun 茅盾), "Wenxue yu rensheng"; originally presented as a lecture in August 1922, to the Songjiang diyici shuqi xueshu yanjianghui 松江第一次暑期學術演講會 and published in *Xueshu yanjianglu* 學術演講錄 (1923); reprinted in *Mao Dun zhuanji* 茅盾專集, 2 vols. (Fujian renmin, 1982), 1, no. 2: 1052–56.

Mind and the Carving of Dragons provides a subjective definition but fails entirely to analyze or study individual works. Nor do we find any treatment of questions such as "What does poetry convey?" in the *Twenty-four Moods of Poetry* of Sikong Tu.[2] However we look at it, the fact is that there are countless works of literature, but theoretical works about literature are very few indeed. Consequently, there has been no clear-cut demarcation in China between literature and various other fields such as philosophy or philology.

Those who have commented upon literature have done so mainly by criticizing its rhetoric and paying virtually no attention to its ideas. As for the relationship between literature and other fields of knowledge, this has not even been broached. In approaching this topic, there are almost no sources within Chinese writing to which one can refer. Thus I have little choice but to first discuss what some Westerners have written about literature and then take up the question of whether or not there has been any relationship between literature and life within China's literature.

One of the most prevalent formulations among Western experts writing about literature is "Literature is a reflection of life." How people live, their social conditions, these are all reflected by literature. For example, if we take life as a cup, literature would be the reflection of that cup in a mirror. Thus we may say, "The background of literature is society." By "background" is meant the place whence it derives. Take, for instance, a piece of fiction that describes the conditions under which a family prospers and then declines, would we not necessarily want to know during which dynasty this took place? Supposing the work had been set in the time of the Qianlong emperor of the Qing dynasty, we would then look at the writing and assess whether or not it actually achieved a convincing likeness of the Qianlong period. Only if the work met that criterion would it be deemed successful.

There is nothing extraordinary about what I have said in the last two sentences above. Even so, from these two sentences we probably can surmise what literature is, although it cannot be denied that included within literature are some works that transcend normal life and some that create idealized worlds. Literary works of this kind can be very good indeed, but all such works lack a social context. As we now consider the relationship between literature and life, it does not suffice to merely illustrate the "social

---

2. *Ershisi shipin* 二十四詩品 by Sikong Tu 司空圖 (837–908) is a series of twenty-four tetrasyllabic poems describing various poetic moods. James J. Y. Liu (1973: 35–36) sees this work as one of the leading examples of a metaphysical view of literature that stresses the poet's apprehension of the Dao.

context." We may discuss this further by subdividing it into the following four items:

1. Race [*renzhong*]. Literature and race are closely connected. Just as there are different races, so there are different modes of literary expression; each race has its own literature exactly as it has its own skin, hair, eyes, etc. Generally speaking, each race has its own distinctive quality; the Oriental races [*minzu*] have a strong mystical streak, and their literature is thus also supernatural. By the same token the character of each race and its literature are interrelated. The Teutons are tough and stoic and moreover have the quality of moderation; the same is true of their literature. Even if they write a love story, when it reaches a sorrowful ending, the emotional intensity will never be as unbridled as would a Frenchman's. In their delineation of character and description of their characters' feelings, French writers are very passionate. Suppose a character has something weighing on his mind and wants a drink, an Englishman will just quaff some beer whereas the Frenchman will necessarily go for the more potent brandy. In comparing the English with the French, this makes for a very apt metaphor. Those points of comparison in literature are equally obvious.

2. Environment. We live here and are surrounded by what? Let's suppose we are Songjiang people, then Songjiang society is my environment. What kind of family do I have, what kind of friends—that is all part of my environment. The influence of environment on literature is extremely powerful. For people in Shanghai, a literary work will invariably take up the conditions of Shanghai; for people engaged in revolution, discourse is invariably imbued with revolutionary spirit; as for someone born into a wealthy family, even though he may ardently side with the common people, there will be times when a certain air of being highborn will unexpectedly manifest itself.

Each era has its own environment and also has its own literature belonging to that era and environment. Now, environment is not strictly limited to the physical world—contemporary ideological trends, the political situation, social customs, and practices all go into the environment of a given period. The influence of his environment is constantly and stealthily at work upon any writer, it being quite impossible for him to shake loose from it or become independent of it. Even in the case of a mystic poet who is probing the mysteries of the universe and whose literary creation seems to have no connection with his environment, that is to say, never even refers to the environment, the ideas in his work will nonetheless be directly related to his overall environment. Even if a poem is directly opposed to the ideological trends of the period, it is still related to them. Thus the poet's "anti" [stance] is a response to the stimulus of the era's dominant values, not something that just pops up out of nowhere.

As for positive examples, these are beyond counting throughout the history of literature. For instance, it was France that produced George Sand and that group of important writers who witnessed the second revolution and restoration; the characters they depicted were thus all situated in the environment of France of that time. Even though adherence to revolutionary ideals forced Sand to flee abroad, the flavor of France at this time nonetheless suffuses all of this writer's works. To cite an example from right in front of our noses, here in Shanghai what we see are streetcars and automobiles and what we listen to is mainly the intelligentsia; so in the case of fiction, it is simply out of the question for us to detach ourselves from our environment and to try to write about life in the mountains or villages.

The pastoral poetry of the English [*sic*] poet Robert Burns now is widely acclaimed by people for its excellence, its beauty and serenity, whereas writers who wrote about the conditions in large cities at the end of the nineteenth century are being called degenerate by some people. This is all a consequence of environment. By the same token, there were a great many poets in Germany at the same period who were fed up with urban life and went out to write about the countryside, but the fact that they were wistfully gazing at it from afar is instantly discernible. This example is but the other side of the same coin.

It is clear that there is an extremely close connection between environment and literature: only living within a certain environment can one create that environment in writing; nor can anyone living within a certain environment jump out of it to portray a different one successfully. There are those who claim that the scope of recent Chinese fiction is too narrow, i.e., those works that deal with romantic love limit themselves to middle-school students, those that center on family life treat only the commonplace and trivial, and those of a humanitarian bent concern themselves with naught but accounts of rickshaw men hauling their passengers around, etc. Actually this is not because we Chinese lack the capability of writing better works than these; rather, it is because the writers' environment is like this. If a writer intends to write about the life of society's lower stratum and the only thing he sees is the rickshaw puller at work, how is he going to be able to write about something else?

3. Era [*shidai*]. Perhaps *shidai* is an inadequate translation. The sense of the English word, Epoch, even includes the intellectual trends of the times, the social conditions, etc. Possibly the word *shishi* [the trend of the times] would come closer. By now everyone has heard of this term, *shidai jingshen* [Zeitgeist, or spirit of the times]. The Zeitgeist governing politics, philos-

ophy, literature, art, etc., is as inseparable from them as a shadow from shape. That the writers of each era have a distinctive appearance, necessarily share a common tendency, is the result of the Zeitgeist. Naturally there are exceptions, but in general this is the case.

We have often heard it said that the Han dynasty had its own literary style just as the Wei-Jin period had its own—this is precisely because the Han had its Zeitgeist and the Wei-Jin period had its Zeitgeist. Modern Western literature is realist because science forms the spirit of the times. Because the scientific spirit emphasizes the pursuit of truth, literature also takes the pursuit of truth as its sole purpose. Just as the approach of the scientist emphasizes objective observation, that of the literary artist emphasizes objective description. In accordance with the pursuit of truth, in accordance with emphasizing objective description, it follows that whatever meets one's eye will determine what one writes. In our proper respect for individuality, it would be wrong to refuse to speak out merely for fear of being misunderstood or just because everyone else might consider something to be abnormal or bad. Our mouths should voice whatever we feel in our hearts. We need true honesty, not deception. This is an example of the modern Zeitgeist revealing itself in literature and art.

4. The writer's personality [*zuojia de renge*]. The writer's personality is of extreme importance. Revolutionaries will definitely write revolutionary literature; nature lovers will certainly suffuse their writings with nature. The resolute, unique personality of the Russian writer Tolstoy appears in his literature. The works of a major author, albeit influenced by the era and environment, will inevitably be imbued with the author's personality. In this vein it was the French writer Anatole France who claimed, "any work of literature, strictly speaking, is the autobiography of the author."

The above is Western critical thinking, and this line of thinking was not to be found previously in China. Nonetheless, Chinese literature can also serve to prove each of these four points. In the first instance, the temperament of the Chinese [race] is expressed by Chinese literature—we care not for reality, being partial rather to the mysterious and to seeking compromise in all things. Chinese fiction, no matter whether good or bad, must always conclude with a happy reunion: this is not evidence of taking things to extremes. Thus in the category of race, it may be stated that there is no contradiction here [i.e., Chinese literature conforms to Chinese cultural traits]. In the second instance, the category of environment is even more obviously confirmed. The environment of Chinese literature is, naturally, the Chinese family-centered society. In the third instance, although at first glance we might fail to detect any clear indication of the relationship between the era and Chinese literature, when we look closely, there it is. As has long been noted by those commenting on Chinese literature, the prose poem of the Han dynasty is not the same as the prose poem of the Wei and Jin dynasties. Likewise the regulated verse of the early Tang, the high Tang, and the late Tang dynasty differs each from the other. Any one of Li Shangyin's poems would never be placed among those of the four great poets from the early Tang. Whether in composition or prosody, because they derive from different eras, these works are completely distinct. The writing employed in *A New Account of Tales of the World*[3] is quite different in syntax and in tone from that of other works; the same is true of the Song *Dialogues*.[4] They, too, are different from *The Water Margin* and from the *Anecdotes from the Xuanhe Reign Period*.[5] These differences all stem from the differing atmosphere of each era. The works differ not only in ideology but in tone and prosody as well. The influence of the era is also very powerful.

As for personality, real authors (as opposed to those who will stoop to anything in the pursuit of fame) invest their works with something of their own personalities. Consequently, these four linkages between literature and life are also to be found in Chinese literature.

This, in a nutshell, explains the relationship of literature to life. From this, we should derive the following lesson: those who would study literature must at least possess a commonsense understanding of race, must at least understand the era and environment that produced this type of literary work, must at least comprehend the Zeitgeist in which it was produced, and moreover must at least understand the life and mentality of the person who created this type of literary work.

—*Translated by John Berninghausen*

---

3. *Shishuo xinyu* 世說新語, by Liu Yiqing 劉義慶 (403–444). Considered one of the most important collections of *zhiguai* 志怪 stories, arguably the earliest of Chinese fictional narratives.

4. Mao Dun uses the title *Songren yulu* 宋人語錄, which must refer to the *Er Cheng yulu* 二程語錄, the collected dialogues of the Song neo-Confucianists Cheng Yi 程頤 and Cheng Hao 程顥.

5. *Xuanhe yishi* 宣和遺事 is a semifictional Yuan work relating the events of the fall of the Northern Song dynasty. It is considered an important source for *The Water Margin*. For a translation of this work, see William O. Hennessey, *Proclaiming Harmony* (Ann Arbor: University of Michigan Center for Chinese Studies, 1981).

Chapter 17

On Photography

Lu Xun

I. Materials

During my childhood in S City—and by childhood I mean thirty years ago, which from the perspective of a progressive savant like myself seems like a century—as for S City, I am not about to divulge its true name, nor will I tell the reason why I won't reveal it—in any case, one often heard in S City men and women of all ages discussing how the foreign devils would pluck out people's eyes.[1] There was once a woman who was a servant in a foreign devil's household. After leaving their employ, it came out that her reason for quitting was that she had herself seen a jar of pickled eyes piled like carp fry, layer upon layer, right up to the edge of the jar. She fled quickly and far to avoid this peril.

It is the custom in S City that by winter's arrival families of means pickle in large jars enough cabbage to provide for the coming year's needs. Whether the cabbage is meant to be used in the same way as Sichuan pick-

---

1. Lu Xun 魯迅 , "Lun zhaoxiang zhi lei" 論 照 相 之 類 , *Yusi* 9 (Jan. 12, 1925); collected in *Fen* 墳; reprinted in Lu Xun 1981*a*: 1: 181–90.

led vegetables I know not. The use foreign devils had for pickled eyes, of course, lay elsewhere, only the preparation was influenced by S City's pickling of cabbage, which is sure proof of the saying that China has great power of assimilation over the West.[2] When people were asked what these things were that look like carp fry, their response was that they really were the eyes of the residents of S City. In the temples of S City one often finds a Boddhisatva known as Our Lady of Sight. Those with eye ailments can go to her to pray, and if they are cured, they cut a pair of eyes out of cloth or silk and place it on the statue or to its side as gratitude for her holy protection. You need only see how many eyes are hanging from a statue to know how wondrous are its powers. And these hanging eyes are tapered to a point at either end just like carps; you will look in vain for a pair of round-shaped eyeballs like those sketched in foreign biology drawings. The dialogues on medicine between the Yellow Emperor and Qi Bo belong to the mythical days of yore and deserve no mention![3] And we have no way of knowing whether drawings were made when the Han usurper Wang Mang killed Zhai Yi and had his body dissected for the inspection of his physicians (and even if they were, they are now long lost, so it is pointless to say "Antiquity is the source of all things"). The Song dynasty *Classic of Dissection*, included in the *Shuofu*[4] (which I myself have read) relates eyewitness medical reports, but they are mostly nonsense and likely spurious. When such eyewitness accounts are so confused, can we really blame the people of S City for stylizing eyes into the form of carps?

Did the foreign devils actually eat these pickled eyes in place of pickled vegetables? Surely not, although I understand they did put them to several practical uses. First, as wire. This information derived from the account of a villager, who merely stated that they *were* made into wire and did not elaborate on how this feat was achieved. He did, however, say something about the intended use of the wire: every year the foreigners would add

2. Lu Xun is humorously turning upside-down the *tiyong* 體用 formula, which states "Chinese learning for the essence, Western learning for practical use."

3. Lu Xun is referring to the Chinese medical book *Yellow Emperor's Classic of Internal Medicine (Huangdi neijing* 黃帝內經) by the names of Huangdi (the mythical Yellow Emperor) and his minister Qi Bo 岐伯, whose dialogues constitute the form of this "classic." *Shang yi* 尚矣 (long ago) is using the diction of the classics to mock this classic. The reader should be reminded of Lu Xun's virulently negative attitude toward traditional Chinese medicine as expressed in his short story "Medicine" and his "Preface to *Call to Arms*." For an English translation of the medical classic referred to here, see Ilza Veith, tr, *The Yellow Emperor's Classic of Internal Medicine* (Berkeley: University of California Press, 1972).

4. *Classic of Dissection (Zhegufen jing* 折骨分經) is erroneously ascribed by Lu Xun to the Song collection *Shuofu* 說郛. It is actually a Ming text found in the *Xu Shuofu* 續說郛, a Qing addendum to the *Shuofu*.

some to the fence they were constructing to keep the Chinese from escaping on the day the foreign soldiers arrived. Second, for photography. Here the reason is clear enough, and there is no need to elaborate, for one has only to be face to face with someone and a little photograph of oneself is bound to appear in their pupils.

The foreign devils also had a practical use for the hearts they tore out of people. I once overheard an old devoted Buddhist woman explain the rationale: after they tear them out, they boil them into oil, which they use to light lamps to search for buried treasure. Since the heart of a man is a most greedy thing, when the lamp is shone on a place where treasure is buried, the flame leaps downward. They would then quickly dig it up and take the treasure away, thus explaining why foreign devils are all so wealthy.[5]

The neo-Confucian belief that "all the myriad things are there in me" is known throughout the country, and in S City, at least, it is even known by those who can't tell B from a bull's foot. According to this belief, man is the "spirit of all things." Menstrual juices and semen can prolong one's life; hair and fingernails can thicken one's blood; excrement and urine can be used to treat myriad diseases;[6] and a piece of flesh from the forearm can keep one's parents alive.[7] But all of this is beyond the scope of this essay, so let's leave it at that for now. Since the people of S City are very concerned about face, moreover, there are many things that cannot be spoken of, and those who utter such treachery will be severely punished.

II. Forms

Photography was, in short, like witchcraft. During Emperor Wenzong's reign [1851–1861], it happened that in a certain province some peasants destroyed the property of a person who practiced photography. Yet, when I was young (thirty years ago) S City already had a photography studio and no one was particularly wary or terrified. During the Boxer Rebellion, twenty-five years ago, there were those in another province who believed that canned beef was the flesh of Chinese children killed by the foreign devils. But these are exceptions, and nothing is without exception.

In short, S City had long had a photography studio. It was a place at which I could not resist lingering in enjoyment every time I passed, although that was no more than four or five times a year. How I marveled at

---

5. In *The Water Margin*, ch. 10, the fat of human bodies is used to fuel oil lamps.

6. These uses of elements of the human body as medical curatives are recorded in Li Shizhen 李時珍, *Bencao gangmu* 本草綱目, in the "Renbu" 人部 section.

7. This is a reference to one of the twenty-four paragons of filial piety, Du Shishou 杜世壽, who is said to have cut off a piece of his own flesh to feed his starving parents.

the glass bottles of every imaginable shape and color and the smooth and prickly cacti. Hanging on the wall were framed photographs of the great Zeng Guofan, Minister Li Hongzhang, General Zuo Zongtang, and Commander Bao. A well-intentioned elder from my clan once used these photographs to offer me moral instruction. "These men," he said, "were all great officials of the day, distinguished public servants who had suppressed the Long Hair rebellion, you should follow their example." At that time I was keen to follow their example; yet I thought that for this to be possible there had better soon be another Long Hair rebellion.[8]

At the time I knew only this: the people of S City did not seem to like to have their photographs taken, and since a person's spirit could be stolen by the camera, it was especially inappropriate to have one's photograph taken when one's luck was good (the spirit was also known as the "noble light"). Only recently have I learned that there are renowned scholars who never wash themselves for fear they will lose their "vital essence," the vital essence being no doubt equivalent to the noble light. How much wiser I now am: the Chinese spirit, that vital essence and noble light, can be stolen by the camera or washed away with water.

And yet, though by no means many, there were people who did indeed patronize the photography studio. I am not that clear who they were, however—perhaps some luckless souls or reformists. Portrait photographs of the upper half of the body alone were generally taboo, for this was like being chopped in half at the waist. Naturally, the Qing court had already abandoned this style of execution, but one can still see on the stage Judge Bao's execution of his nephew Bao Mian: one slice of the knife and the body is rent in two. How horrible! And even though this is part of our glorious "national essence," I "desire it not done unto me."[9] It is indeed most unfitting to have one's picture taken in this manner. Instead, they would take pictures of the entire body; to the side would be a tea table on which would lie a hat rack, teacups, a flower vase, and below which would be a spittoon (demonstrating that the subject's bronchial tubes were full of mucus and in need of continuous clearing). The subject would be sitting or standing, with a book or scroll in his hands or a very large timepiece hanging on his chest. If we look at the photograph with a magnifying glass, we can know what time the picture was taken, and since flash bulbs were not used then, we needn't wonder about whether it was taken at night.

---

8. The Long Hairs refers to the Taipings, who wore their hair loose, thus breaking with the Manchu practice of tying the hair in a queue.

9. See *Analects* 5.11: "Zigong said, What I do not want others to do to me, I have no desire to do to others"; in Arthur Waley, trs. *The Analects of Confucius* (New York: Vintage Books, 1938), 110.

What age is without its Bohemians and dandies? Those of truly sophisticated taste had long been dissatisfied with the bland uniformity of the herd, and they would remove all their clothes and pretend to be the Jin dynasty eccentric Liu Ling or dress up in the traditional silk garb of someone from X dynasty, but there were not many of these.[10] What was rather more popular was to take two pictures of oneself, each with a different costume and expression, then put them together into a single photograph: two selves, like a guest and host, or a master and slave. This we called the "Picture of Two Selves." But a different name was used when one of the selves was seated imperiously above the other, which knelt before it depraved and pitiful: "Picture of Me Entreating Myself." After a picture was developed, it was obligatory to write some poem or lyric on it (like "Melody for the Scented Garden" or "Catching Fish")[11] and then hang it up in one's library. Because they belonged to the herd, the wealthy elite could never in a million years imagine such refined designs. But they too had their particular pose, although it was little more than a "Family Togetherness" picture: oneself seated in the middle with a multitude of sons, grandsons, great-grandsons (and so on) arranged at one's feet.

In his *Fundamental Issues of Ethics*, Th. Lipps makes the point that anyone who is a master can easily become a slave. Since the master recognizes that he is master, he naturally knows that he can become a slave; so that as soon as he tumbles from power, he devotes himself heart and soul to serving the new master. Unfortunately I do not have the book with me, and I only remember the general idea. There is, fortunately, a Chinese translation, and although it contains only excerpts of the original, this passage is probably included. The example that most clearly proves with solid fact Lipps's theory is that of Sun Hao: when he conquered the state of Wu he was an arrogant and cruel tyrant, but when he succumbed to the state of Jin he became a depraved and shameless slave. In China there is a common saying that gets right to the heart of the matter: "He who is arrogant to his inferiors will be servile to those above." But nothing surpasses the "Picture of Me Entreating Myself" in fully expressing this idea. If in China we were to print an *Illustrated Fundamental Issues of Ethics*, this would truly be a perfect illustration, one that even the world's greatest satirical artist could never imagine or draw.

---

10. From *Shishuo xinyu* 世 說 新 語 : "Liu Ling often indulged in wine and caroused. Sometimes he would take off his clothes and stand stark naked in his house. When people mocked him, he replied: 'Heaven and Earth are my house, my house is my pants. What are you doing in my pants?'" (my tr.).

11. Names of *cipai* 詞牌, tunes for lyric compositions.

But what are common now are not photographs of the depraved and pitiful on bended knee. What we see are group commemoratives or an enlarged bust of someone grand and awe-inspiring. I often want to see these as half of the "Entreating Self" photographs, but this is like the vain anxiety of the man from Qi who was obsessed with the fear that the sky was falling.

III. Without Title

The custom of photography studios selecting enlargements of one or several important men and hanging them on their doors for display is, it seems, either peculiar to Beijing or has only recently become more widespread in its popularity. The photographs I used to see of Zeng Guofan and his ilk in S City were only six or eight inches long, and it was always Zeng Guofan and his ilk who hung there, not as in Beijing where the photographs change from time to time, never the same from year to year. Perhaps after the revolution the pictures in S City were torn down, but I am not sure about this.

But I do know a little about what has been going on in Beijing over the past ten years. Those of wealth and power alone have their portraits enlarged and hung in this manner, and once they have left the halls of power, their portraits are nowhere to be found, vanished in a flash of light. If one were to search Beijing day and night for one of these variously sized, ever-alternating photographs that was not of a man of wealth and power, then, according to my humble knowledge, one would find only those of a single man: the Peking Opera star Mei Lanfang. Portraits of Mei Lanfang doing the *Celestial Maiden Scatters Flowers* or *Daiyu Buries Flowers* (acted in the style of the fairy Magu) are more elegant indeed than those of men of wealth and power, and this is sufficient to prove that the Chinese do indeed have eyes with aesthetic sensibility. If photographs of pompous men sticking out their chests and stomachs continue to be enlarged and hung out for display, this is simply because it cannot be helped.

I have read *The Dream of the Red Chamber*, but before seeing these pictures of "Daiyu Burying Flowers," I would never have imagined Daiyu's eyes to protrude so, nor her lips to be so thick. I had always thought she should have a thin, consumptive face. Now I know hers is a visage radiating health and good fortune, just like that of Magu. One need only look at photographs of the string of imitators of the Heavenly Maiden (whose faces are contorted with pain because they are tightly bundled up like little children wearing new clothes) to understand immediately Mei Lanfang's eternal appeal (his eyes and lips, of course, cannot be helped!). And this again is sufficient to prove that Chinese do indeed have eyes with aesthetic sensibility.

When the Indian saint of poetry, Tagore, visited China, he aromatized like sweet perfume several of our gentlemen of letters with his literariness and mysticism, but only Mei Lanfang earned the honor of sitting with Tagore to celebrate his birthday: their joining of hands symbolized the union of artists from the two nations. After this venerable poet changed his name to Zhu Cathay[12] and took leave of his all-but-ideal country of Cathay, the sage-poets of Cathay no longer much wore their Indian turbans, and the newspapers only very rarely reported news of Tagore. But what continued to adorn this all-but-ideal country of Cathay were those pictures of the "Celestial Maiden Scattering Flowers" and "Daiyu Burying Flowers," which hung so imposingly in the windows of the photography studios.

Only the art of this "artist" is in China eternal.

Although I have only seen a few photographs of famous foreign actors and beauties, I never saw one of a man playing the part of a woman. I have seen several of other famous people. Tolstoy, Ibsen, Rodin were all old; Nietzsche was fierce, and Schopenhauer appeared to be suffering; Oscar Wilde, decked out in his aesthete's frippery, looked rather doltish; Romain Rolland had an odd air about him, and Gorki simply looked like a hoodlum. And although I could see in all of these the traces of tragic suffering and bitter struggle, none were as manifestly "good" as the Celestial Maiden. If one thinks of the seal-carver Wu Changshi as a "sculptor" and recalls that his seals sell at the same price as some paintings, this should suffice to make him an "artist" in China, but nowhere do we see his photograph. His literary reputation is so well founded that the world does not appear keen on "bidding fond farewell" to Lin Shu.[13] Although I once saw his photograph on some literature for a pharmacy, it was printed to express the gratitude of his "concubine" for the efficacy of the pharmacy's medicine and not for the excellence of his literary oeuvre. And what of those good sirs who use the "language of cart pullers and street hawkers" to write their works. The likes of Li Boyuan and Wu Woyao are now long gone, and we

---

12. The Chinese is Zhu Zhendan 竺震旦. The surname Zhu is a classical designation for India and was often adopted as a Chinese surname by Indian monks who came to China. "Zhendan" is the Chinese rendering of the term for China in ancient Indian Buddhist texts. Tagore's adopted name, thus, symbolized the unity of the two cultures. I have rendered Zhendan as Cathay to give the sense of an obsolete designation for China.

13. The expression *shijing* 識荊, to "recognize Jing," originally from a poem by Li Bai, has come to be used as a polite literary way of bidding farewell. Jing is also the name given by Lin Shu to a character in his 1917 anti-vernacular parable, "Jingsheng" 荊生, and it may be that Lu Xun is mocking Lin Shu's conservatism. For a discussion of this piece, see Tse-tsung Chow 1960: 66–67.

can forgo mentioning them. More recently there are the good sirs of the Creation Society who have struggled valiantly and produced many literary works, but they have printed only one photograph of three of their members together, and it was but a copperplate photo.

The art that is the most noble and eternal in China is the art of men acting as women.

Generally, it is members of the opposite sex who love one another. Eunuchs cause others no anxiety, absolutely no one loves them, because they are without sex—that is, assuming that I have not committed any error in usage in this word "without." And yet, we can see that it is the "man who plays the part of a woman" who most causes anxiety and yet is most precious. This is because each of the two sexes sees this role as the opposite sex: men see a woman being acted, and women see a man acting. Therefore, this type of photograph hangs eternally in the windows of photography studios and in the minds of our citizens. Foreign countries do not have this kind of complete artist. All they can do is give free reign to the will of their rock chiselers, blenders of color, and ink masters.

The art that is the most noble, most eternal, and most universal in China is the art of men acting as women.

—Translated by Kirk A. Denton

Chapter 18

Preface to The Sorrows of Young Werther

Guo Moruo

The modern Italian philosopher Benedetto Croce has judged this book a "simple poem," *Naive Dichtung*.[1] My feelings about it are rather similar. Since it is for the most part a compilation of lyrical letters, with but a weak narrative line, we do better to call it poetry, or a collection of prose poems, than fiction.

Those constricted by conventionality invariably believe that "without rhyme it is prose, with rhyme it is poetry," and by rhyme they have in mind only end-rhyme. I cannot see why this sort of superficial view has penetrated so deeply and ineradicably the minds of men. Recently some of my countrymen have been discussing poetry; what is surprising is that the

---

1. Guo Moruo 郭沫若, "*Shaonian Weite zhi fannao xuyin*" 少年維特之煩惱序引, *Chuangzao jikan* 創造季刊 1, no. 1 (1922): 1–9. *Naive Dichtung* appears in German in the original. Guo incorrectly capitalizes the first letter of the adjective *naive*. Guo likely read Croce's view on *Werther* in his study of Goethe which was translated into German in 1920. The term "naive Dichtung" can be found in the third chapter of Croce's *Goethe* (trs. Julius Schlosse. [Zurich: Amathea-verlag, 1920]).

debate over rhyme has been especially fierce and that prose-poems have been slandered as somehow unsound. They fail to understand that the essence of a poem lies not in the end-rhyme. Some poems with end-rhymes are poetry, but poems with end-rhymes are not all necessarily poetry. Official notices and magic spells also use end-rhymes, but we would not call these poetry. True poetry may be rhymed but need not be so. When people read a lyrical essay without rhyme, they most often say that it has a luxuriant poetic quality; hence we know that the heart of a poem lies elsewhere. The ancients called prose that incorporates poetic forms rhymed-prose and poetry that incorporates prose forms they called prose-poems. This makes abundant sense.[2] A prose-poem is like a male playing the female role in opera, and rhymed-prose is like a female playing the male role. Although the costumes are ill-matched, the essence has never changed—Fine, let's not get off track here. Should anyone still not understand the definition of "prose-poem," I invite them to read *The Sorrows of Young Werther*!

The idea of translating *The Sorrows of Young Werther* came to me some three or four years ago. But it was only when I came to reside in Shanghai last July that, at the renewed urgings of some friends, I resolved to translate it. At first I had planned to complete it during the three months of the summer holiday. Later when I went to Hui Mountain to escape the heat, I caught malaria from the many mosquitoes. For a period my temperature was consistently high, then it fluctuated up and down, and although I took a fair bit of quinine, I could not in the end progress with my translation. By the middle of September I had returned to Japan, where I was pressed during the day with my courses and could only steal a little time at night to work on the translation, which accounts for the carelessness of certain parts of it. Now at last I dare to introduce it to my dear readers, for I have a certain confidence that those friends who read this translation will not be greatly disappointed.

As I translated this book, I realized that there are many areas where my thought resonates with that of Goethe. The personality of Werther, the novel's protagonist, is essentially that of the young Goethe during his Sturm und Drang period; Werther's thought is the thought of the young Goethe. Goethe was a great subjective poet, and his oeuvre is a compendium of his personal experiences and true emotions. The various areas of resonance that I have with this book are as follows.

---

2. The following line gives the rather awkward English terms "prose in poem" and "poem in prose" for the Chinese *yunwen* 韻 文 (rhymed prose) and *sanwenshi* 散 文 詩 (prose-poems), respectively. They have been omitted from the translation.

The first is his emotionalism. Goethe says: "A man is a man; whatever be the extent of his meager powers of reason, they are of little or no avail when passion overflows and bursts through the boundaries of human nature." This fact most of us have experienced, and it may be fair to say that it is a kind of basic truth requiring no further substantiation. When Count C. is favorably impressed with his intellect and talent but overlooks his feelings, Werther replies: "My feelings alone are my most precious treasure, only they are the fountainhead of everything, all power, all happiness, all misfortune." What his intellect knows, he says, may be known by anyone, only his heart is unique to him. He does not use reason to analyze or dissect the universe, but allows his heart to fuse together and to create. His feelings are able to invent a paradise from anything around him. At anytime he can find the "presence of the Almighty," the "wandering of universal selfless compassion" in the tiniest insects and plants. A world without love is a magic lantern without light. Werther's feelings are the light from this magic lantern, able instantly to project a variety of pictures against a white screen or give birth to a universe of feeling from the midst of death and destruction.

The second is his pantheism. Pantheism is atheism. All natural phenomena are but manifestations of the divine; the self, too, is but a manifestation of the divine. The self is thus divine, and all natural phenomena are expressions of the self. When man is without self and has fused with the divine, he transcends time and sees life and death as one and the same. But once man has self-consciousness, he sees only the external appearance of the universe and the ego, only the mutable and transient, giving rise to a tragic sense of life and death, being and non-being. The myriad things will live and die, life has no control over itself, nor can death prevent itself; so the man of self-consciousness only sees "heaven and earth and the energy of all living things as an ever-devouring, avaricious monster, nothing more." But this energy is the source from which all things are created, it is the will of the universe, it is the thing-in-itself, the *Ding an Sich*. If and when one joins with this energy, one will see only life and not death, only constancy and not mutability. Paradise is everywhere around oneself, the heavenly kingdom is realizable at any time, offering eternal happiness and an overflowing of spirit. "You and I are forever present before the 'infinite' and in the midst of the eternal embrace." Man's ultimate goal is but to seek out this eternal happiness. The first step in finding this eternal happiness is forgetting the self. Goethe seeks to forget himself not in quietude but in activity. With the energy of a lion assailing a rabbit, with his whole heart and soul, he seeks the fulfillment of each moment and the enlargement of his Self, with his entire spirit he seeks to devote himself to everything. Reflecting on the time he had known Charlotte, Werther says: "And since that time sun, moon, and stars may quietly pursue their course: I know not whether it is day or night; the whole world about me has ceased to be." How fully, with all his spirit, does he love! Ecstasy touches the core of his spirit, sorrow and grief consume it. Everything to the marrow, everything to the end! And so he expresses a profound sympathy for those who suffer from madness and he praises, rather than censures, the act of suicide. To complete the destruction of the ego is of the highest moral order—this is a truth that the tepid fellows who follow the Doctrine of the Mean cannot fully understand.

The third is his exaltation of nature. Goethe sees Nature as the manifestation of the one divinity. As Nature is the solemn appearance of the divine body, he never renounces it. He affirms Nature, he treats it as a benevolent mother, a friend, a lover, a teacher. "From this day forward," he says, "I will devote myself to Nature. Nature alone is boundless and able to foster the great artist. . . . All rules and conventions are sufficient to destroy the genuine feeling of nature and its true expression." He dearly loves Nature, worships it, and in return Nature bestows upon him inexhaustible affection, solace, guidance, and cultivation. So he fights against pure artistry, established morality, the class system, established religion, and all superficial learning. Books are dross, language is dead bones, and art itself verges on superfluity. He says: "I have completely lost all design and ambition in the serenity of my solitary seclusion, my art no longer fulfills any use" (Ich bin so ganz in dem Gefuehle [sic] von ruhigen Dasein versunken, dass meine Kunst darunter leidet). And: "What is poetry? painting? the pastoral? Is such affectation necessary when enjoying natural phenomena?" How true! When man loses designs and ambitions in Nature, sometimes even poetry and art can seem superfluous, how much more so scholarship, morality, religion, and class.

The fourth is his reverence for the primitive life. The life of primitive man is the purest, the simplest, and the closest to Nature. He who worships Nature and praises Nature naturally cannot but revere the primitive life. Homer and Ossian are thus the poets whom Werther enjoys. Next to the spring, he feels the floating presence of ancient spirits. The hermit's grotto, sackcloth, and a belt of brambles are the only solace for which his soul longs. He also expresses such deep sympathy for the peasant life: "They plant their own cabbage, pick it when it is ripe, and make a dish of it. When eating it, they not only appreciate the exquisite flavor, they can recapture and savor in an instant the splendid days when they planted and watered it and the fine evenings they watched it grow." The pure, unhindered enjoyment of these men, he says, he can feel in his heart, and this is a truly happy event. Only this kind of man is truly sincere, toils honorably, is fervent in his love, and can pour out his soul everywhere, living for the moment, the epitome of the life of absolute self-realization.

The fifth is respect for children. The American child psychologist Hall[3] feels that childhood is the Paradise of the race from which adult life is a fall. This sort of discussion is the vanguard of our current child protection movement. Respect for children was advocated continuously in ancient times, many centuries ago, by philosophers in both the East and the West. Laozi said: "In concentrating your breath can you become as supple as a babe?"[4] Mencius said: "The great man is he who loses not his child's heart."[5] The Hebrew prophet Isaiah said that childhood is the realization of the golden age of the prophets, where "the wolf shall dwell with the lamb, and the leopard shall lie down with the kid, and the calf and the lion and the fatling together, and a little child shall lead them" (Old Testament, Isaiah 11). Jesus said: "Children are the greatest among those in the Kingdom of God."[6] Why should children be so respected? Just pick any child for observation, and you will see that every minute and second of the day they devote their entire beings to creation, expression, and enjoyment. In the behavior of children we see the life of a genius in miniature; it is the epitome of the life of absolute self-realization. And yet we adults, past and present, East and West, uniformly mistreat, confine, whip, and scold children, not allowing them freedom of will, regarding them as slaves and prisoners. Let's listen to Goethe come to their defense: "Children are our models, they should be our teachers, but we treat them as inferiors, and do not allow them a will of their own! . . . Why is it that we privilege ourselves?"

"*The Sorrows of Young Werther* has been published!"
"A bright star has appeared in the literary firmament!"
When *The Sorrows of Young Werther* was published in 1774, youths rose up and shouted, they admired the Wertherian style and imitated his attire, the Werther-fever (*Werthersfieber*) for black frocks and yellow trousers raged for a time, there were even those suffering from amorous sorrows

---

3. Granville Stanley Hall (1844–1924) was instrumental in developing the field of psychology in the United States. He contributed to the advancement of psychoanalysis and was a pioneer in child psychology with such works as *Content of Children's Minds*. He was so influenced by Darwinian thought that he became known as the "Darwin of the mind."

4. From the *Daode jing*, 10; see D. C. Lau, tr., *Lao Tzu: Tao Te Ching* (Harmondsworth, Eng.: Penguin, 1963), 66.

5. From *Mencius*, "Lelou, II"; see D. C. Lau, tr., *Mencius* (Harmondsworth, Eng.: Penguin Books, 1970), 130.

6. Matt. 18:2–4.

who carried out their own suicides after reading this book. One could find a copy of this little book, as a burial token, in the pockets or up the sleeves of these suicides. In Weimar a princess drowned herself in the Ulm River because of a love affair; next to her breast was concealed a copy of *The Sorrows of Young Werther*. Such a variety of stories rocked an age—a twenty-four-year-old writer from Frankfurt am Main with a single leap became the object of criticism, respect, and admiration.

Goethe's reputation rose daily. The notables of the day, like the religious teacher Lavater, the educator J. B. Basedow, and even that star of the German poetry scene, Klopstock, all sooner or later hastened to pay their respects before the radiance of this new literary star.[7] The young Goethe who bore on his shoulders the suddenly rising fate of the German literary world, like the early morning sun, brilliantly lighting the roiling atmosphere, raised high his triumphant song, to follow the track laid out for him by the will of Heaven. From a Germany previously void of literature, Goethe suddenly became the favorite of eighteenth-century Europe. The great hero Napoleon on his long campaign to Egypt also carried with him *The Sorrows of Young Werther*, to accompany him as he rose and slept among the ruins of this ancient civilization, between the Pyramids and the Sphinx. The Duchess of the principality of Weimar, Anna Amalia, younger sister of Frederick the Great, sent her son August Karl to visit Goethe. Shortly after that, in 1775, Goethe became an honored guest at the Weimar palace, and the Weimar palace became the center of the German literary world.

An Intermezzo

Time: The summer of 1774.

Place: Duisburg, on the banks of the Rhine River. The dining hall of a certain inn. Several middle-aged gentlemen and a young literary man are seated around a table talking spiritedly, opening a rare and exquisite flower of literature and thought.

One of the gentlemen: (asks of the youth) Sir, are you not Herr Goethe?

Youth: (nods) . . .

Gentleman: Are you not the one who wrote the world-renowned *Sorrows of Young Werther*?

---

7. Johann Kasper Lavater (1741–1801), Swiss physiognomist who was also something of a prophet of Christ. Johann Bernard Basedow (1723–90) was a follower of Rousseau and an educational reformer, later a traveling companion of Goethe. Friedrich Gottlieb Klopstock (1724–1803), the "patriarch of German poetry," greatly admired by the young Goethe for his unconventionality, his breaking with formal strictures, and his exploration of novel themes.

Youth: I am.

Gentleman: Then, I feel it my duty to express to you my terror of this thoroughly dangerous book. I pray that God will transform your prepossessed, evil mind, for sinners encounter unexpected misfortune.

(A kind of ill-humored silence falls, all hold their breath in anticipation.)

Youth: (agreeably) From your excellency's point of view, you can only criticize me in this way. I understand you and respectfully accept your sincere admonitions. I beg you in your prayers not to forget my name.

(A joyous laughter refills the room and each is liberated from this feeling of anxious expectancy—Curtain.)

There is of course no need to say that the youth was Goethe and the middle-aged gentleman the Rector Hasenkampf, seated with them were Lavater and Basedow as well. Where there is profound love, there will also be profound hatred. Werther was both well received by people and opposed by many who saw in him the moral deterioration of the world. One of these was Hasenkampf, who recounted at the same gathering that a publisher named Christoph Friedrich Nicolai wrote his own version of the Werther story entitled *The Joys of Young Werther* to express his opposition to Goethe.[8] In this version, he said, Werther does not commit suicide, and the story ends happily in marriage. The same phenomenon occurs in our country where there is a *Suppression of Bandits*[9] adaptation of *The Water Margin*, a sequel to the *Western Chamber*, and several different sequels to *The Dream of the Red Chamber*—what is so disappointing is the superficiality of these utilitarian and indifferent writers! To lengthen a sable fur with a dog's tail is of no benefit to the world. Literature should be a kind of revolutionary manifesto against established morality and established society. To use the conventional concepts of the old morality to criticize literature is like carrying ice into a fire; unfortunately there are many who are carrying ice, and most of the fires ignited by geniuses are easily extinguished. "Why do the currents of genius so seldom appear, so seldom reach high tide and crash against the souls of those who stare on in amazement. The silent ones who live on either bank try to prevent the current's rising waters from submerging their gardens, flower beds, vegetable plots; they know how to build levies to resist the current."

---

8. This is recounted in Goethe's autobiography, *Warheit und Dichtung*, from which Guo Moruo likely took many of the details related here.

9. *Dangkou zhi* 蕩 寇 志 , an adaptation of *The Water Margin* dating from the mid-nineteenth century.

I had originally intended to recount Goethe's career, but such a brilliant eighty-three years cannot be told with much detail in the space of a short preface—Goethe was born on August 28, 1749, and died on March 22, 1832. Here I can only briefly relate the story of this book's inception for the reader's scrutiny.

In May 1772, a year after he graduated from the Law School of Strassburg University, Goethe traveled to Wetzlar am Lahn, seat of an Imperial German Court of Justice, where the young Frankfurt lawyer went to look around before beginning his career.

The German Imperial Magistrate Amtmann Heinrich Adam Buff had a daughter named Charlotte who was only nineteen years of age. (One account has it as fifteen.) When her mother died, she took her place in raising her ten younger brothers and sisters and in managing family affairs. Fairhaired, blue-eyed Charlotte was healthy and charming. On the evening of June 6, en route to a ball at Volperthausen [Garbenheim?], Goethe and a woman companion arrived to pick up Charlotte to take her with them. From this moment on the two fell in love, but Charlotte had already been betrothed. Her fiancé, Johann Christian Kestner, was a secretary in the Hanoverian embassy in Weztlar. He, too, developed a profound friendship with Goethe.

Goethe suffered from this hopeless love and frequently harbored thoughts of suicide. On September 11, 1772, he left a letter for Charlotte and took resolute leave of Wetzlar am Lahn and returned to Frankfurt. The entry for September 10 in Kestner's diary has the following account:

"Sept. 10. Today Solicitor Goethe and I drank together in the garden. When evening fell, we went to Deutsche Haus (Charlotte's home), and the three of us discussed recent events. Charlotte asked him if the dead could return to the world of the living. The three of us made a vow that the first to die would inform the others as to the situation after death. Goethe felt listless, I fear, because he was preoccupied with his departure the following day."

Shortly after returning to Frankfurt, Goethe heard about Jerusalem's suicide.

Carl Wilhelm Jerusalem was born in Wolfenbuttel in 1747 and studied with Goethe at Leipzig University.[10] In 1771 he was appointed a secretrary in the Brunswickian embassy, where he suffered from *melancholie* and began to doubt the Christian faith. He had fallen in love with the wife of his friend, the Minister Herdt, and had lost all hope. He excused himself from his duties and went traveling. He then borrowed Kestner's pistol and on

---

10. It seems that Jerusalem and Goethe were no more than casual acquaintances.

the night of October 30, 1772, clad in dark dress tails, yellow cape, yellow trousers, and high brown boots, killed himself.

With Jerusalem's death, *The Sorrows of Young Werther* was born. At first Goethe had planned to make it a drama. But in four successive weeks the novel was completed, and at the beginning of March 1774 he submitted the manuscript, which was printed immediately and became popular throughout the world.

After *Werther* was published, the rage for Werther grew daily. "Sentimental" men and women shot themselves with pistols one after the other. Especially well known among them was the double suicide of the literatus Herr von Kleist and his friend's wife. In editions after 1778, Goethe engraved on the first page of *The Sorrows of Young Werther* a prefatory poem:

> Who among young men does not fall in love?
> Who among young women does not ponder love?
> These are the great sages and saints of human nature.
> How can bitter pain encroach upon them?
>
> Dearest reader, cry for him, love him,
> Save his reputation before he is destroyed;
> Look! The eyes of his escaped soul are speaking to you:
> "Be a dignified man and do not follow in my footsteps."

Submitted Wednesday, January 22, 1922, from Fukuoka

—Translated by Kirk A. Denton

Chapter 19

Fusing with Nature

Liang Shiqiu

One day in the bustling metropolis of New York I got to talking with a friend on the subject of "fusing with Nature."[1] (Discussing the subject of fusing with Nature in the city of New York is certainly incongruous.) Just as our voices had reached a tumultuous pitch, a friend burst brazenly into our room, and before he could open his mouth, I asked him abruptly: "Have you ever fused with Nature?"

He knit his brow and said: "Fused with *what*?"

"Nature," I said.

He then asked dully: "Nature? Where is it?"

We all laughed, but in fact we shouldn't have. The question "Where is Nature" is not easily answered. The simplest answer, I think, is that Nature lies in the God-created mountains, rivers, plants, trees, clouds, lightning, wind, rain, birds, beasts, fish, and insects; from the most majestic and lofty mountain peak to the tiniest granule of sand on an ocean beach, from the pure and placid fall sky to the dazzling beauty of a butterfly's wing; every-

---

1. Liang Shiqiu 梁實秋, "Yu ziran tonghua" 與自然同化, in *Langmande yu gudiande* 浪漫的與古典的 (The romantic and the classical) (Shanghai: Shangwu, 1927), 55–61.

thing that has not been touched by the hand of man, all of this is Nature. Living in the bustle of the business district, nothing of what we hear, see, and smell has not been touched by the hand of man. True, in the city there are parks, but what do you see when you go there: the pine trees next to the path have been clipped so that they look like they have just come out of the barber shop, every needle has been touched. There are indeed many things in a park, just not Nature.

If we really want to get to know Nature, we must leave the city. It is not that Nature is to be found only in the majestic and lofty peaks or the forests and groves, you need only go as far as where you no longer hear the sound of cars. This would seem to resolve our question: to know Nature, go outside the city. But how to "fuse with Nature" is still a rather mysterious problem.

I have heard that Rousseau was the "child of Nature." Someone who has reached the stage of being a "child of Nature" has likely "fused with Nature" more than once. So we might as well seek guidance from Rousseau. We know that Rousseau in his childhood, beginning with the time when he was a sculptor's apprentice, enjoyed strolling outdoors at dusk and tasting the rural scenery. He would often be so enthralled by his experience that he would neglect to return home before the city gates closed. The next day when he returned to the shop he would be subjected to a fierce beating by his master. How many times Rousseau was beaten in this manner! But the last time Rousseau was locked out from the city, he began to think about the terrible beating he would receive; so he dared not return and fled without a trace.

Just think, although we dare not say that Rousseau would risk a beating to go out into the countryside in order to "fuse with Nature," there is still something rather extraordinary about it.

In the fourth chapter of his *Confessions*, Rousseau says:

The common man may perhaps see a plot of open plain as beautiful, but in my eyes this cannot be considered beauty. What I need are raging torrents, forests of pines, winding paths through soaring peaks and deep valleys, precipices to either side so steep they cause one to tremble with fear. When I approached Chambery, I walked to a place not far from the mountain called Pas D'Echelle, a pleasure I had previously experienced. There was a small road chiseled out of solid rock; looking down from the road one could only see a stream rushing along a chasm that had probably taken tens of thousands of years to form. On the side of the road a railing had been built to prevent mishaps. Leaning up against the railing, I could see the depth of the gorge, and I began to feel slightly dizzy and giddy. Strangely enough, the wonder of it lay in the dizziness; as long as I stood in a solid spot, I loved that dizzy sensation. I leaned against the railing for a good many hours, sticking my head out occasionally to look down at the foaming torrent of water; the roar of the water shook my eardrums, and at the same time I heard the calling of some crows and fierce birds who were flying around in some small trees on the precipice about six hundred feet below.[2]

Aha! So that's fusing with Nature. A dizzy head is a sign of fusing with Nature. At least this is Rousseau's version of fusing with Nature. The kind of mind that enjoys only dangerous scenery is abnormal, sick. Its seeking after excitement is the same as smoking opium or taking morphine, for it demands a similar dizziness, or a similar pleasure found in dizziness.

There is another who has fused with Nature, and who is even more mystical than Rousseau. There is the following story about Tieck:

It happened one day in July of 1792 when Tieck was but nineteen-years old. He was staying in an inn in Eisleben when a noisy open-air festival in front of the inn kept him from sleeping all night. When dawn broke, he left the inn and continued on his way. The sun had not yet completely arisen. It looked like a ball of fire peeping its head over the horizon. Suddenly, the morning fog broke apart and the rays of sun pierced through it to shine right on the spot where Tieck stood. He was startled, feeling the rays' brilliant light shine upon him, as though his entire body and soul had been pierced and emblazoned by the light. It was as if a curtain had been lifted from his soul and the light from his heart filled his body. . . . (Wernaer, *Romanticism and the German Romantic School*)[3]

Tieck is much more mystical than Rousseau; he can see a ray of sunlight as the incarnation of God, causing his whole body to tremble and his eyes to shed torrents of tears. But God does not often make such divine interventions, so I fear that the sort of experiences had by Tieck can only be had by the truly fortunate. The two men I have raised above are extreme examples. Modern man is forever talking about fusing with Nature, but without, I fear, the abstruseness of these men. I believe that modern man's fusing with Nature can be limited to two significances: (1) one fuses with Nature in order to escape real life; (2) one fuses with Nature to lead one to the realm of self-abnegation.

---

2. J. J. Rousseau, *Confessions* (Paris: Livre de poche, 1972), 264.
3. See Robert M. Wernaer, *Romanticism and the Romantic School in Germany* (New York: Appleton, 1910), 176.

Navalis [*sic*] said: "All unhappy and discontented people in this world should walk toward Nature and live in its otherworldly palace. In Nature can be found a benevolent heart, a friend, a hometown, God" (*Collected Works*, 3:5). This says it very clearly: fusing with Nature is to escape from real life. "Escape" is a fundamentally repugnant notion. Men who do not recognize failure or who do not wallow in despair would never seek escape. Having said this, I must mention a characteristic of our Chinese literati. Many of our Chinese poets and men of letters did their studies as youths, became officials in middle age, and led reclusive lives in their dotage. In China the life of the literati and the recluse are nearly one and the same, but there is a subtle difference between the Chinese literatus's love for Nature and that of the Western Romantic's "fusing with Nature." The Chinese love for Nature in the end still sees man as the essential element. When we talk about "singing with the wind and toying with the moon," the one singing and toying is still most certainly a man; "companions of fish and shrimp, friends of deer and antelope" refers to companions and friends of men. On this point, the Chinese spirit is really a little like the ancient Greeks. The Chinese love of Nature is not to escape from real life but to escape from society. For we fundamentally acknowledge Nature as part of reality. We don't see Nature as a divinity; we simply see it as something which gives us pleasure and enjoyment. The Chinese love of Nature has no religious feel to it, and so it is difficult for us to discuss "fusing" with Nature.

Oscar Wilde once said: "In Nature I feel myself to be exceptionally infinitesimal, and so lose my personality" (See "Decay of Lying").[4] Wilde really disliked Nature and thought that Nature and art stood in opposing positions. His hatred for Nature comes from his "megalomania," an abnormality I have a good deal of trouble condoning. And yet those who make the radical proposal of "fusing with Nature" are of yet another abnormality. That is, romantic revelry. So-called romantic revelry is the melting of the ego. When facing a great natural phenomenon, a sense of terror and awe issues from their hearts, and at that moment the concept of "self" melts away like ice and their entire body and mind transforms into a path of light and flows away. They have entered fully into the realm of self-abnegation, making the ego but a part of Nature, like a dream or a fancy.

---

4. This may be a loose rendering of the following passage of Wilde: "Out of doors one becomes abstract and impersonal. One's individuality absolutely leaves one. And then Nature is so indifferent, so unappreciative. Whenever I am walking in the park here, I always feel that I am no more to her than the cattle that browse on the slope, or the burdock that blooms in the ditch" (from "The Decay of Lying," in Stanley Weintraub, ed., *Literary Criticism of Oscar Wilde* [Lincoln: University of Nebraska Press, 1968], 166).

This is what they call "fusing with Nature." Actually, there is nothing strange about it. It is simply the effect of their emotional inhibition, a subjective illusion. This is a false religious spirit. True religious spirit is disciplined, a sort of compact and united force, not a loose and unrestrained revelry. Look, when a true believer of religion prays, he goes to his room and with intense concentration controls and purifies his thoughts, he does not wander idly through hill and dale.

Byron has a famous line of poetry "I love not man the less but Nature more." Byron clearly separates man and Nature, but after separating them there is a problem: What relationship do man and Nature have in the end? Should I humanize Nature, or naturalize man? To humanize Nature is the proposal of the classicists and humanists; to naturalize man is the proposal of the romantics and naturalists. For the former, man is the center of the universe, and the phenomena of the natural world are there for our use and enjoyment. For the latter, the unity of man and Nature makes man rank equally with the plants and trees. "Fusing with Nature" is an old trick the romantics and naturalists must play.

—*Translated by Kirk A. Denton*

Chapter 20

A Critique of the New Culturists

Mei Guangdi

It has been several decades since our fellow countrymen first discussed reform.[1] The reform began with the realization of the superiority, at least in industry and commerce, of the West over us; then there arose an admiration for Western government and law; and now education, philosophy, literature, and the fine arts of the West have also been included in the discussions. The speed of our Westernization seems astonishing, but if we look closely into the reality, results and speed are actually in inverse proportion. Industry and commerce are things visible and differ very little among nations of the world. Once we have learned the theories and techniques of such things and put them to work, the task of introduction will be accomplished. I do not mean that we have learned everything about Western industry and commerce, but comparatively speaking we have learned more about them than about other things. As for Western government and law, since they are based on the subtle and recondite nature of history and national character, we cannot understand them without delving deep into

---

1. Mei Guangdi 梅光迪, "Ping tichang xin wenhua zhe" 評提倡新文化者, *Xue heng* 1 (Jan. 1922); reprinted in *Mei Guangdi wenji* (Taipei: Zhonghua congshu weiyuanhui, 1956), 1–4.

them. Furthermore, because of the differences in history and national character between the East and the West, what suits the Westerner may not suit us; hence we cannot rely solely on imitation. As for education, philosophy, literature, and the fine arts, which are grounded even more securely in the history and national character of the remote past, they are more difficult to pry into and must be adopted with greater caution. Although we have been discussing problems of government and law for nearly twenty years, our government and law remain as rotten as before. Those self-proclaimed "New Culturists" who have expounded on education, philosophy, literature, and the fine arts had no sooner uttered a word on these subjects than numerous corrupt practices transpired and evil consequences immediately ensued, for which they have been mortified by the far-sighted. Precisely because of the complexities of these areas, an expedient and spurious solution readily presents itself and makes it possible for the shallow-pated charlatans to produce forced and obsequious interpretations, seeking to comply with the trend of the time in order to fulfill their ambitions for gain and fame. The failures of those who expound on government and law are known to everyone, and I need not make a hubbub here. Only the so-called New Culturists, by virtue of their skills in self-justification, persuasion, and making connections, still have a considerable following among the young and innocent, as well as among the common herd. I intend, therefore, to tear off their masks so as to reveal their true identity and subject them to close scrutiny, not because I am fond of making harsh criticisms but because it is something that must be done.

First, they are not thinkers but sophists. The term "sophist" came from late ancient Greece when philosophy enjoyed a heyday of free expression of thought, and the sophists became eminent, teaching rhetoric and promoting new knowledge as their profession, similar to the practices of Zou Yan, Zou Shi, Gongsun Long,[2] and the like in China during the Warring States period [475–221 B.C.]. The Greek youth followed the sophists with enthusiasm. The great sage Socrates confronted the sophists with his eloquence and refuted their teachings, very much like Mencius' opposing

---

2. In the Chinese text Zou Yan 鄒衍 (ca. 305–240 B.C.) and Zou Shi (fl. 3d c. B.C.), two leading thinkers of the Yin-Yang school, are referred to by their epithets: the former as "the talker about the heavens" (*tantian* 談天) derived from his exotic descriptions of the universe, and the latter as "the carver of dragons" (*diaolong* 雕龍) on account of his superb verbal art. And Gongsun Long 公孫龍 (ca. 320–250 B.C.), a noted member of the School of Names, is referred to by his well-known arguments of "separateness of hardness and whiteness" (as of stone) and "unification of similarity and difference" (theory of the universal).

Yang Zhu and Mozi, or Xunzi's refuting the Twelve Philosophers.[3] *The Dialogues of Plato* that we have today contains mostly Plato's teacher Socrates' debates with the sophists. The sophists aimed at pleasing the youth with novel and attractive knowledge and making judgment of things and events from their biased opinions and private intentions. These things they did for the sake of temporary expedience, without consideration of everlasting truth. Even more unworthy of mention is the discrepancy between their words and deeds that has been sneered at by enlightened thinkers. The New Culturists in our country are very much like them. They have mistakenly brought together into a single topic of discussion classical prose [*guwen*] and the eight-legged essay [*baguwen*], which have nothing to do with each other. In Chinese literature parallel prose was popular in the Han, Wei, and Southern and Northern dynasties; with the advent of the Tang and Song, classical prose enjoyed popularity; and beginning with Song and Yuan times, there were vernacular fiction and drama. The New Culturists declare that literature must change with time, and we moderns ought to stage a literary revolution to abolish the literary language and adopt the vernacular tongue. Now, what we call "revolution" means to replace the old with the new, or to substitute this for that. As for the successive rises of classical prose and vernacular writing, they were additions to literary styles, really not wholesale changes, certainly not revolution. If what they say is true, then parallel prose should not have arisen after the advent of classical prose, or classical prose should not have followed the emergence of vernacular writing. But why since the Tang and Song periods have the major writers in the mainstream of Chinese literature all specialized in either classical prose or parallel prose? How could they deny this fact of Chinese literary history so as to justify their own theory? For literary styles vary, and each has its own merit; they must not be replaced or mixed up, because they are worthy of being independent and coexistent. How can we abolish all the other styles and honor vernacular writing alone? The evolution of literature is not something easily expounded on. Famous scholars in the West such as Hazlitt, a nineteenth-century English master of prose and literary criticism, often criticized the theory of literary evolution as a mistake accepted by the common herd.[4] But our fellow countrymen

---

3. Mencius (390–305 B.C.) opposed Yang Zhu (ca. 395–335 B.C.), an early Taoist, for his egotism (*weiwo* 爲 我), and Mozi (ca. 480–420 B.C.), the founder of Mohism, for his teaching of universal love (*jian'ai* 兼 愛). The Twelve Philosophers refuted by Xunzi (313?–208 B.C.) were both Xunzi's predecessors and contemporaries, representing various schools of thought, including Confucianism, to which Xunzi himself belonged.

4. Hazlitt's anti-evolutionary view of literature is reflected in his argument that the arts, contrary to the sciences, are "nonprogressive" and "stationary or retrograde"; see P.

put blind faith in it. And they also say that modern Western literature has changed from classicism to romanticism, from romanticism to realism, and now again from realism to impressionism, to futurism, and to neo-romanticism; it seems that the later schools must have been superior to the earlier, so that as soon as the later arrived, the earlier would become extinct. But with a little study of the history of Western literature and the discourses of well-known Western scholars, one would abstain from making such absurd claims. Why should our fellow countrymen be so naive as to turn things upside down like this? Furthermore, they say that thoughts are given shape in the mind through the vernacular language, but that when put in writing these vernacular thoughts are converted, translated so to speak, into classical prose. This certainly is false and most uneconomical. But since Chinese men of letters have over the millennia never had such an experience, what else can it be if not words of deception? In the past the Greek sophist Protagoras maintained forcibly that truth is undefined, depending as it does on the opinion of the individual. To this Socrates responded: "If each man has his own truth, then there will be no distinction between the wise and the ignorant. But how is it possible for Protagoras to be a teacher who forces people to follow his own teachings?"[5] Today's promoters of literary revolution also say that the goal of literature is to express individual personality, to emphasize creativity; they feel that only if there is a "self everywhere in one's writing" can the old habits of imitation be kicked. In other words, each man has his own literature, and all the models and rules may be abolished. But why do they themselves formulate their theories and publish their books and proudly take their positions as teachers while at the same time being so hostile to classical prose writers as not to allow them also to have a self and individual personality and freedom of creation?

Second, they are not creative writers but imitators. None of their theories is more attractive than that concerning creativity. They have a near monopoly on the word "new." Everything they say and do is "new." Yan Fu once said that a technical term that has been used by the general public will lose its true sense.[6] Cautious persons are already afraid of using the word "new" for fear that it will no longer mean anything. The New Culturists make it their mission to overthrow the ancients and all the established in-

P. Howe, ed., *The Complete Works of William Hazlitt*, 21 vols. (London: J. M. Dent and Sons, 1930-34), 5: 44-45.

5. *Theaetetus*, 161d–e, in Edith Hamilton and Huntington Cairns, eds., *The Collected Dialogues of Plato* (Princeton: Princeton University Press, 1978), 867.

6. See "Yingwen Han jie: zonglun" 英文漢解總論 ; in *Yan Fu ji*, 5 vols. (Beijing: Zhonghua shuju, 1986), 2: 287.

stitutions, falsely charging that their own country has no culture and that their traditional literature is dead literature. Such are the contents of their bold and loud arguments that startle the audience and dazzle the public. But if we study the facts, we see they are imitators of the lowest grade. What they praise and show off in front of their fellow countrymen as creativity is but a part of theories popular in Europe and America; some of these were brought into being several decades ago and are now regarded as erroneous, worthless, and unwanted. John Dewey and Bertrand Russell are only two of the influential thinkers, and they worship them like gods; so it seems that there have been only these two men throughout the several millennia of European and American thought. The socialism of Marx has long been refuted by economists, but they revere it like the Bible. In discussing government they prefer the Russian model; in literature they follow the recent Decadent movement. (Impressionism, mysticism, futurism all belong to "the Decadent movement." The so-called modern vernacular Chinese poetry simply picks up the dregs of "vers libre" and American imagism of recent years. "Vers libre" and imagism are also two branches of the Decadent movement, but the advocates of modern vernacular Chinese poetry, forgetting its sources, claim it to be their own creation—that is really hoodwinking their fellow countrymen!) Zhuangzi said: "You can't discuss the ocean with a well frog—he's limited by the space he lives in."[7] Since the New Culturists have not made extensive and concentrated studies of Western culture, what they know about it is very rudimentary and what they cull from it is even absurd. To let them introduce Westernization is an insult to Westernization. It is all because their fellow countrymen do not read Western languages and have not traveled outside China, and because those they take advantage of are elementary and middle-school students, that they can liberally and arrogantly promote their heretic teachings, regarding the whole country as a no-man's-land. If a country is without true scholars and allows spurious scholars to pretend to scholarship, it casts shame on its citizens. Yet these pretenders are proud of being creative, while sneering at their fellow countrymen for being so imitative as to become slaves to their ancients. But in fact imitating Westerners and imitating the ancients are enslavement alike, only what they imitate differs. Besides, what the pretenders have copied from Westerners turns out to be nothing but junk, whereas what their fellow countrymen have written following the model of their ancients often catches the essence of their ancients' works. Moreover, the pretenders not only mimic Westerners but mimic one another as well. They

---

7. Burton Watson, tr., *Chuang Tzu: Basic Writings* (New York: Columbia University Press, 1964), 67.

had no creative genius to begin with, but on the pretext of creativity put aside books and refuse to read, thus developing an inertia and a hollowness inside. The books and journals they publish repeat one another and look almost identical, showing no individual personality or particular qualities. What difference do we find between such writings and the eight-legged essay for the civil service examination of early times? Yet they brag about their creativity without a sense of shame? Who would be deceived by them?

Third, they are not scholars but seekers after political success. A scholar seeks truth for truth's sake; he places self-confidence over recognition by the world, and self-accomplishment over reward in his lifetime. He therefore exerts himself throughout his life, guarding his knowledge, waiting, without easily revealing his learning to the world. He must be very careful in finding the most appropriate moment to speak, and his words must be well studied and perfected before they are put in book form. The great scholars of our country have always warned students against writing books carelessly. In the past scholars at Oxford University regarded it a great shame to write books in one's early years, for one's works reveal the dignity of learning and the character of a scholar. The so-called scholars today are not so, for their scholarship lacks in-depth research as well as self-confidence and self-accomplishment. It is all because they are spurred on by the thoughts of gain and fame that they use learning as a springboard to their goals. In early times of despotism the rulers and prime ministers possessed the power to determine political success, through which they had the scholars of the entire nation at their command. And the scholars in turn looked up to the taste and preference of the rulers and prime ministers as their standards of conduct. Since the founding of the republic, the power to determine political success has fallen into the hands of the masses; the less knowledge the masses possess, the greater their power. Today's elementary and middle-school students are equal to the rulers and prime ministers of the past. If this were not true, what use would modern vernacular Chinese and all the fashionable isms have for the seekers after political success? Generally speaking, the common people favor what is new and easy; this is especially true in the case of the youth. These people have no ability to judge and select the teachings that come to them; therefore, if certain knowledge is imported from Europe or America and never heard of before in this country, and if it is suitable for the proletarian majority, it will miraculously spread fast and with noticeable results. Precisely because their audience has no powers of judgment and selection and must substitute their ears for their eyes, the so-called scholars have access to advertisement to expand their market and propaganda to popularize their disciples. The louder the noise, the greater the profit. An English proverb says: "Good wine needs no bush." If it is true with wine, would it be even more so with learning? Now that they use learning simply as an instrument for success, they show no respect for learning but only want from it fashionableness and opportuneness. When Dewey and Russell were in China and were so greatly admired, all they could talk about were Dewey and Russell. When socialism and decadent literature were likewise favored by the youth, all they could talk about were socialism and decadent literature. But how many are there who really understand Dewey and Russell, socialism and decadent literature, who have profited from studying them, and know their merits and demerits? Now that learning aims at being fashionable and opportune and does not require serious study, it is very easy to pump out. As a result, those who can cover the fields of philosophy, literature, politics, and economics all at once are myriad, and youths are without exception impressed by their boundless knowledge. In America a certain scholar who published several hundred books on such diversified subjects as philosophy, mathematics, literature, science, and Confucian and Buddhist teachings was censured by critics for lacking the conscience of scholarship and denied the title of "scholar." This happened in America where the criterion for scholarship is high. This scholar was thus ridiculed by his contemporaries and prevented from practicing his broad but shallow learning. Were this to take place in China today, however, such a person would enjoy the fame of being the most erudite scholar of his time. Most of the scholars in the East and the West exert efforts for several years, or several tens of years, in preparing a book that will become an imperishable work to be handed down to posterity, whereas a so-called scholar in China today might produce five or six histories of Chinese learning, or recruit members for an organization designed to be the sole agency for socialism, or found organizations for Russian, Jewish, and Polish languages. Or he may wait, pen in hand, for each newly published book for which he is obligated to write a foreword to fulfill his leader's obligation to a young writer. Gu Yanwu has commented that the problem of the man of letters is his fondness for writing forewords for others[8]—could his remark apply here? To tell such people about the criterion and conscience of scholarship is like telling merchants about ethics, or prostitutes about chastity. Being possessed by the desire for gain and fame, they are ready to sacrifice scholarship without re-

---

8. This perhaps refers to a letter in which Gu refused to write a preface to somebody's collected works; see Gu Yanwu 顧炎武, *Gu Tinglin shiwen ji* 顧亭林詩文集 (Beijing: Zhonghua shuju, 1983), 96.

gret! What is this if not a version of the dream of political success through the traditional civil service examination system?

Fourth, they are not educators but politicians. In recent years nothing has been more infested by them than education. It is true that we cannot be disinterested bystanders and look coldly on the perils in our government and in foreign relations, the corruption in our society, and the degradation of our education. But even the worst fool would not sacrifice the learning experience and moral principle of all the youths of China, with no consideration for the future of the nation and only the slimmest hope for the slightest of temporary remedies; contrary to expectations, though, the so-called educators were the first to do precisely that. Despite the fact that educational circles have been somewhat active since the May Fourth movement, the foundation of our education has been substantially impaired. It is human nature to prefer action over quietness, or to delight in rushing into shouting crowds and engaging in frantically mad actions, and to loathe uneventful, dreary daily routines. It is even more so with youth, for they prefer organized class strikes and street demonstrations hundreds of thousands of times more than studying in a quiet classroom, with their heads buried in old books, not to mention that they are urged on by the great cause of patriotism and supported by the powerful majority. And the cleverest among them may suddenly spring to fame and become national VIPs. Now, true men of ability are prepared through a long period of cultivation and discipline, or their minds will be prone to pride and indolence to such a degree that they think everything in the world is easy, and consequently they will accomplish nothing in their lives. Within the school all kinds of new terms, such as "struggle," "students' voluntarism," and "school administration made public," have developed. There is nothing wrong with these terms, but when they are put in the simple minds of elementary and middle-school students, they will likely have a detrimental effect. A certain American scholar said: "If you teach a new thought to a person who is incapable of using his mind, disaster will follow immediately." This is why students today either are used by politicians or make trouble themselves without a cause, and the school we regard as holy ground has been turned into something close to a den of countless iniquities. What, then, is the intention of the so-called educators today? I would say: "It is to take advantage of mob psychology, the weakness of human nature, and the limited knowledge and strong emotion of the young, to make loud speeches from high above—like rainwater pouring down eaves troughs—only to fulfill their ambitions of gain and fame." Then someone may respond: "Your words are too harsh. How could they expect such a phenomenon to take place in education? Besides, they have already repented. Have you not heard of the remedial measures of 'higher standards' and 'strict discipline' that they are talking about in response to current events?" My response to this begins with a line from Yang Xiong: " 'To say something that cannot be proved is falsehood.'[9] Since they occupy high positions in education, the entire nation will respond to any words they utter. But not paying attention to right or wrong, benefit or harm, and by not calculating the future effects of their actions, they make unfounded claims at will and make the innocent youth of the entire nation specimens in their experiments; their wealth and fame is gained at the cost of the youth. If they can bring themselves to do these things, they are capable of anything.[10] They certainly are smart people who most firmly believe in the expression 'Cater to the needs of the time and circumstances.' Now the time and circumstances are different from those of a few years ago, and what they advocated a few years ago has totally failed; so they penitently turn back and, recognizing the needs of the time and circumstances of today, go for 'higher standards' and 'strict discipline.' Since they are responsible for whatever damage has already been done, how can they be free from charges? In the martial code a defeated soldier must die in combat, or he will be executed. In the West, if a ship sinks, the captain must go down with it. In the case of a speaker who speaks recklessly and does harm to others with his ideology, however, there is no law to punish him; there are only matters of public opinion and private conscience. So, in terms of public opinion and private conscience, those whose words have been proven untrue are disqualified from speaking again. It is now too late for them to be still talking shamefacedly about 'higher standards' and 'strict discipline.' "

Everyone realizes the necessity of constructing a new culture. For several millennia our country, because its geographical location is such that it is surrounded by countries with cultural levels formerly much lower than ours, has independently and without external help created a great and glorious culture. Our forefathers' intelligence and courage, efforts and achievements, indeed suffice to make us proud. Today, since communications have been built up between the East and the West to facilitate mutual visitation and observation, any cultural advancements of others may be fully utilized to compensate for our shortcomings. This is a rare chance in the history of

---

9. Yang Xiong 揚雄, *Fa yan* 法言 (*juan* 5, "Wen shen"); my tr. The author seems to be intentionally quoting Yang Xiong (53 B.C.–A.D. 18), a major figure in early Han Confucianism, to further indicate his traditionalist viewpoint.

10. "Shi ke ren, shu be ke ren" 是可忍,孰不可忍 is a quotation from a statement by Confucius criticizing the misconduct of the head of the powerful Ji family of Lu; see *Analects* 3.1. Note that the subject of the original Chinese sentence is understood as in the third person singular. I have taken the liberty of using its plural form to suit the context.

Chinese culture, something that we ought to celebrate with jubilation. Nevertheless, there must be things within our culture as it is that can be amplified and made imperishable; for we are unlike the islanders of the Philippines or Hawaii, or the black people of America, who originally did not have much of a culture and therefore had to adopt a culture from others (which is an extremely simple matter). As for Western culture, it also has a long tradition that extends from ancient Greece to the present, and there is plenty in every country and every period that offers us something to choose or adopt. But how could a twentieth-century culture embrace the entirety of Western culture? Therefore, revising our traditional culture and absorbing other people's culture first requires thorough study. This should involve the exercise of clear and correct judgment, the support of the most appropriate methodologies, and the collective efforts of hundreds of erudite scholars who are capable of synthesizing Eastern and Western learning, in order to teach and guide our fellow countrymen on this course of reform and develop it into a significant trend. Then after forty or fifty years results will be quite noticeable. But now we let the politicians, sophists, and seekers after political success launch this great enterprise with their plagiarism,[11] wrangling, and fluky experiments. They are taking advantage of a time when criteria for thought and learning have not yet been established in China and those who have received a higher education are few, in order to inflame with their false Westernization the poorly educated and immature youth. Therefore, they had no sooner begun than the signs of failure became manifest. The wiser youth may have pried into the truth about such an enterprise and found nothing in it, or they may have already become so tired of it that they will embark on a campaign of their own. That the false Westernization is doomed to a total failure has long been foreseen clearly by the wise. For "a squall lasts not a whole morning; / A rainstorm continues not a whole day."[12] Such is the way things must be under the circumstances, and there is nothing strange about it. But, after all, is the establishment of a true new culture hopeless? To this I would say: "Not so. I would, in spite of my ignorance and shallowness, make some humble suggestions in this respect. But because the space is limited here, and because a discussion of the construction of culture does not fall into the scope of this essay, I would have to ask you to wait until another day."

—*Translated by David Y. Ch'en*

---

11. In the Chinese text, the character compound *biaoxi* 標襲 is a misprint for *piaoxi* 剽襲 (plagiarism).

12. From the *Daode jing*, ch. 23, sec. 1.

Chapter 21

Women and Literature

Zhou Zuoren

It is traditionally believed that women have nothing to do with literature.[1]
Literature is a vehicle for carrying the Way, although "chanting about the
wind and the moon" is also a sophisticated pastime of the literati. Of these
two functions of literature, one is upright and grand, whereas the other is
extremely dangerous. Even to the most open-minded, women are but ancillary to men, and their activities are to be limited to the boudoir. They are
expected neither to speak for the sages nor to chant about the wind and the
moon, so as to avoid dangerous situations. "A woman's virtue lies in having no talent" sums up the traditional view. Even when this view is not ar-
ticulated explicitly, women's literature is deemed trivial. A good example is
an elderly friend of mine, who once remarked: "The only place for wom-
en's poetry in an anthology is after the Buddhist and Daoist monks, before
the courtesans."

---

1. Zhou Zuoren 周作人, "Nüzi yu wenxue" 女子與文學; speech given to the Student Council at Beijing Women's Normal College, May 30, 1920; published in *Funü zazhi*
婦女雜誌 8, no. 8 (1920).

However, concepts about women and literature have changed completely in recent times. Literature is now recognized as a form through which life is realized, not ancillary to life as a tool of edification or entertainment. Its essence lies in self-expression, its function in emotive effects on humans. The individual is its center, and humankind is its domain. As a member of humankind, a woman has an independent character and is not subservient to anyone. We admit that there are physical and mental differences in the three worlds of men, women, and children; yet they are equal as human beings. It is generally recognized that children, whose world differs from that of grown-ups, also need their own literature. Then it is only more urgent that women have the same need, because the desire to express one's own and to understand others' feelings and thoughts is a key ingredient of human society, and literature is the best way to cultivate this.

"Member of humankind" is a new term. Only Esperanto has the expression "homarano," meaning a part of the human collective. Ordinarily we think that the individual is opposed to humankind and society, that to benefit the individual we must harm society and to benefit society we must sacrifice the individual. As such, individualism and humanism are treated as opposite terms, thus creating many unnecessary arguments. Actually, humankind and society are the sum total of individuals; without individuals, they are empty concepts. Individuals can only live safely within society; without society they would find it hard to survive. Therefore, individuals without society and society without individuals are equally unimaginable. As a member of humankind, each individual has the dual instinct for self-preservation and preservation of the race. Thus, we are even more aware of the inseparability of the individual and humankind. Self-interest and altruism are one and the same thing. To love your neighbor you must love yourself first, and to love your neighbor is to love yourself. When seen from this point of view, individualism and humanism are two sides of the same coin. The new concept about literature that I advanced earlier is based on this relationship.

Without a foundation brought to it by women's self-awareness, however, this theory is just empty, ineffectual words. In recent years, Chinese women have ushered in a new atmosphere, but from my point of view they have achieved self-awareness only as citizens and not as individuals. The situation is certainly quite common and even exists to some extent among men. But if this is the only kind of self-awareness we have, then our powers of understanding will be limited to our country alone and will be unable to communicate with the people of the world. We will be even less likely to understand art, for enmity plays no part in art. In issue no.1034 of *Beijing University Daily*, there was a correspondence from Tokyo that declared:

"Art is an indispensable part of life, but the art of a shallow culture can hardly satisfy our desires. . . . Japanese painting cannot arouse noble sentiments in us; its coloring and brushwork are representative only of the mentality of an island-country and lack the grandeur of a great nation." This is an excellent example. Individual self-awareness means the awareness of being a member of humankind and seeing eye to eye with others on equal footing and without any barriers. Only in this way can we understand each other. With such self-awareness, we won't encounter difficulty in national movements. We will know that our people are only part of humankind, but since it is closer to us, to improve it is the first step toward improving the world. Thus, to understand one's national literature is the first step toward understanding world literature. To put oneself in the other's place is a most correct method. If one does not know oneself, one cannot know others; if one knows oneself, one cannot fail to know others. Therefore, individual self-awareness is of paramount importance, and it is clearly illustrated in literature and art.

The root of individual self-awareness lies in an evolutionary philosophy of life. It is not very hard for men to become aware. But women, who have inherited many negative ideas of the past, are hampered in this regard and must pay more attention. The ideas are perceptions toward the fate of women, whether they are to transcend reality or submit to reality. The first attitude is religious, which holds that women are filthy and sinful and should seek transcendence. Although there may be other reasons, I know that among my women students, many are pessimistic and prone to renouncing the world to become Buddhist nuns. The second is derived from the Confucian doctrine, which sees women as subsidiary and their duty as pleasing men and yielding their own independence. Once they accept this notion, women live contentedly and see no injustice.

Neither of these aspects, whether pessimistic or optimistic, is true to reality, for real life is not as noble as their ideals would have it, nor as ugly as in their nightmare. Of course there are many unreasonable things in real life in need of improvement, but the principle of life is that all human beings must openly affirm the necessity of the preservation of the self and the race (preservation includes both existence and development). The evolutionary philosophy of life demonstrates this attitude; it affirms life and pursues with courage a life that is complete, good, and beautiful. As J. M. Synge said, "To be a good human being one must first be a good animal." And Nietzsche urges us to be "loyal to the earth."[2] A woman of self-

2. This refers to Nietzsche's Zarathustra, who importunes others to "Be loyal to the earth," as a reaction against airy metaphysics.

awareness should adopt this attitude, resolutely affirm life in human society, get rid of the inherited prejudices against women, and participate in activities of life as a member of humankind in order to establish the so-called third motherland founded on the love of oneself and of other human beings. Once we understand this, we will not have any problem understanding the spirit of modern literature, for literature is a form of life and part of life.

Modern literature is getting more and more complicated. In order to understand it, we must have considerable training. The reason is not hard to understand, for the spiritual life of today has become more complicated. Given this situation, however, everyone has the ability and the need to understand literature in terms of its essential nature. Because the many restrictions placed on women led to their developing defects, women were not understood by others and could not really understand others. The creation and study of literature can be an effective solution to the problem. There are many women poets and novelists in the world, but few truly express their thoughts and feelings freely. John Stuart Mill said that all the books women have written about women aim to flatter men but do not portray women as they really are.[3] This is not an overstatement. From now on, women should take advantage of artistic freedom to express their true feelings and thoughts and to dispel the age-old misunderstandings and confusion about women. But this possibility is limited to the few women who have a talent for writing. Besides, under the pressure of age-old societal norms, they can hardly enjoy complete freedom of expression. This is true even for men; how much more so for women! Therefore, we have to focus our attention on the study and appreciation of literature. If creation is the expression of one's own thoughts and feelings, appreciation is to be receptive to others' thoughts and feelings. The proverb "Without stepping outside one's room, an educated person knows what is happening in the world" is applicable. When our experience is limited and we are unable to feel a variety of complex moods, writers describe fictions from their own experiences or their extraordinarily rich imaginations and allow us to see what they have seen. Say we have never been to a battlefield, but reading the novels of Tolstoy and others enables us to experience the misery of war and provokes in us antiwar thoughts. Because we do not have much contact with the unfortunate, we are often unfairly opposed to them. Literature and art depicting the dark side of life enable us to correct our misconcep-

---

3. Mill wrote something to this effect in a letter in French to August Comte, dated July 13, 1843; see *Collected Works of John Stuart Mill* (Toronto: University of Toronto Press, 1963), 13: 590.

tions. There is no need to idealize the poor as good people struck down by bad luck; a realistic portrayal of an ordinary person who has good and bad attributes the way we do and falls victim to fate is enough for us to rid ourselves of our prejudices and realize that "all men are brothers." These effects are most striking in modern literature, but classical literature may also be seen to have a similar impact if we look at it broad-mindedly. In the preface to *The Seven Who Were Hanged*, Andreyev says: "Our misfortune lies in the almost total lack of understanding of others' souls, lives, pains, habits, wishes, and hopes. As a writer, I feel what makes literature respectable is its ability to erase all boundaries and distances." This is a succinct definition of the function of literature. That appreciation of literature also brings artistic pleasure and benefits children's education is another important point, but I shall not go into education here.

—*Translated by Michelle Yeh*

Chapter 22

On *"Literary Criticism"*

Bing Xin

True literary works are filled with emotion.[1] The writer writes and the reader reads, and when their spirits come into contact all kinds of interpretations and critiques will emerge naturally.

When there is spiritual contact, sympathy [*tongqing*] can be born, but also a lack of sympathy. This "sympathy without sympathy" comes after reading through an entire work, experiencing a change in feelings from melancholy to joy, from joy to melancholy, and then showing sympathy only for the words themselves; even though there is general praise for the work, as far as the writer is concerned the original meaning and value of the work are already lost.

I feel deeply that when readers come up with various interpretations and critiques, they are not showing a bit of responsibility toward the writer. The explanation for this is that we cannot know in any detail—or not know at all—the writer's past and present, or the writer's philosophy of life. And it is even more true that we cannot know the writer's motivation at the time

---

1. Bing Xin 冰心, "Lun 'wenxue piping' " 論文學批評, *Chenbao—wenxue xunkan* 晨報—文學旬刊, (Jan. 22, 1922); reprinted in *Bing Xin lun chuangzuo* 冰心論創作 (Bing Xin on creativity) (Shanghai: Shanghai wenyi, 1982), 117–18.

of writing those words. Furthermore, when we read, we bring with us our own feelings and biases, and we hold on to these feelings and biases as we barge forward thoughtlessly in our zeal to criticize literary works. It is like putting on blue-colored glasses and seeing the world in a different hue. But I don't need to go on this way; I just pity the frustration of a writer who garners this endless sympathy!

We have no choice but to recognize fully that until we understand the writer, our evaluation of a work will be the opposite of its original meaning. The praise that comes from this "sympathy without sympathy" destroys creativity at a level that is more profound than that resulting from mere sympathetic attack. What is truly unfortunate is that in our well-intended praise we may unwittingly destroy some writers who are not so brave!

For each writer there are thousands of readers. The work that floats out from the various feelings and biases of thousands of readers can have thousands of reincarnations. The original meaning of the work long since will have disintegrated into fragments.

A writer—one not yet discouraged—who wants to avoid this danger must add thousands of footnotes at the end of the work. As for myself, I don't want to let a writer sink into footnoting and allow a lively work to become a poetic collection of allusions. This would mean the essential destruction of true "literature" in the world!

As one reader before the writers of the world, I must admit my guilt, offer an apology and, even more, make a profound promise: until I have thoroughly understood a work, I will not allow my personal reactions to unduly influence the light emitted from a literary star, the fragrance exuded from a literary flower. I will only remain silent, with reverence and perfect sincerity, as I salute this sacred literature, impenetrable and incomprehensible.

—Translated by Wendy Larson

Chapter 23

My Opinions on Creativity

Lu Yin

What is creativity?[1] Parroting street gossip, recounting past history, imitating the clichés of bygone writers, and plagiarizing a hodgepodge of famous works: these go by the name "creativity." These kinds of creative hoaxes are numerous as the "sands of the Ganges" in today's transitional China. Even people with the slightest knowledge of literature deride them.

The only thing a work worthy of being called a "literary creation" cannot do without is personality [*gexing* 個性]—the crystallization of art is subjectivity, the feelings of the personality. These sorts of feelings are decidedly not common to all people. Although "the views of the heroic are of a kind," they are only "of a kind" and never identical. Because of differences in personality, when A and B examine the same thing at the same time, the results of their examination are different, each having his own perspective. Some of their observations produce intense associations and passions that develop into some kind of literature able to arouse sympathy and excitement in the reader. This, then, is true creativity.

---

1. Lu Yin 盧隱, "Chuangzuo de wo jian" 創作的我見, *Xiaoshuo yuebao* 12, no. 7 (July 10, 1921): 18–22.

The myriad phenomena of the universe are mysterious and profound. With a light and easy touch, the creative writer can express, point by point, what the common person can hardly see or observe. Creative writers have a tremendous effect on humanity without appearing to, and their works are thus the spiritual food of humanity: herein lies the value of creative writers.

Since creative writers are so precious and their influence so enormous, their responsibility is uncommonly great. Therefore, I must say a few words regarding my opinions on creativity. . . .

Works of creative writers are all artistic expressions. However, there are two kinds of art: "art for life's sake" and "art for art's sake." There is no agreement of opinion in the numerous debates between the two. Personally, I have no preference between them. The initial emotional impulse of the creative writer is extraordinarily mysterious, but in the act of writing the writer's true essence is revealed. The rhythm and tempo of the writer's emotions result in a beautiful harmony. Although this kind of work is said to be art for art's sake, its worth is absolutely undeniable.

I will now proceed to discuss tendencies in subject matter. Although there are huge differences among the manifold phenomena in society, only two kinds are played out: tragedy and comedy. Comic portrayals are good at provoking laughter and happiness, but they leave no deep impression and are forgotten in a twinkle of an eye. Because happy events are not universal, they neither move one profoundly nor arouse one's sympathy easily. Depictions of tragedy, on the other hand, are for the most part full of sorrow and pain. People throughout the world, from aristocrat to commoner, all experience pain and misery, so this kind of work moves people very easily and can make them reflect on their lives. Moreover, natural catastrophes and human misfortunes are never-ending in the world today. Society is enshrouded in a cloud of sorrow and a fog of misery. Unable to live, many people would rather die; yet some muddle through to the end with sweet song and strong wine. Inequities of wealth severely divide the social classes. People feel bitter and depressed and are becoming more dispirited day by day. They do not know to search for the cause of their bitterness and depression, or to seek out light amid darkness. Bitterness only adds to bitterness, and life loses all pleasure. Suicidal youth become more numerous by the day! I cannot bear to speak in detail of such sorrow and misery! Creative writers should depict the tragedy in this kind of society with intense sympathy and a somber tone—both to provide the tormented with the absolute solace of profound sympathy and raise their self-consciousness so they may fight ardently to find light in the midst of darkness, thus adding to their pleasure in life. This is to take on the responsibility of the creative writer.

However, at a time when people are suffering extreme hardship and pain, although the sympathy of a tragic portrayal can console them, a work should not dwell on the path of absolute despair. Because youths frequently feel "the anguish of life," they are very easily swayed. If a literary portrayal makes them feel too fearful and despondent, it will inevitably lead them to suicide. Therefore, a new road to life must be built amid the sorrow and pain. This is my opinion on the tendencies in the subject matter of creative works.

—Translated by Paul Foster and Sherry Mou

Preface to Call to Arms

Lu Xun

When I was young I, too, had many dreams. Most of them I later forgot, but I see nothing in this to regret.[1] For although recalling the past may bring happiness, at times it cannot but bring loneliness, and what is the point of clinging in spirit to lonely bygone days? However, my trouble is that I cannot forget completely, and these stories stem from those things which I have been unable to forget.

For more than four years I frequented, almost daily, a pawnshop and pharmacy. I cannot remember how old I was at the time, but the pharmacy counter was exactly my height and that in the pawnshop twice my height. I used to hand clothes and trinkets up to the counter twice my height, then take the money given me with contempt to the counter my own height to buy medicine for my father, a chronic invalid. On my return home I had other things to keep me busy, for our physician was so eminent that he prescribed unusual drugs and adjuvants: aloe roots dug up in winter, sugarcane that had been three years exposed to frost, original pairs of crickets,

---

1. Lu Xun 魯迅, "*Nahan zixu*" 呐喊自序, *Chenbao-wenxue xunkan* 晨報-文學旬刊, Aug. 21, 1923; reprinted in *Nahan* (Beijing: Xinchao, 1923); and Lu Xun 1981*a*: 1: 415–21.

and ardisia that had seeded. . . . most of which were difficult to come by. But my father's illness went from bad to worse until finally he died.

It is my belief that those who come down in the world will probably learn in the process what society is really like. My eagerness to go to N— and study in the K— Academy[2] seems to have shown a desire to strike out for myself, escape, and find people of a different kind. My mother had no choice but to raise eight dollars for my traveling expenses and say I might do as I pleased. That she cried was only natural, for at that time the proper thing was to study the classics and take the official examinations. Anyone who studied "foreign subjects" was a social outcast regarded as someone who could find no way out and was forced to sell his soul to foreign devils. Besides, she was sorry to part with me. But in spite of all this, I went to N— and entered the K— Academy; and it was there that I learned of the existence of physics, arithmetic, geography, history, drawing and physical training. They had no physiology course, but we saw woodblock editions of such works as *A New Course on the Human Body* and *Essays on Chemistry and Hygiene.* Recalling the talk and prescriptions of physicians I had known and comparing them with what I now knew, I came to the conclusion that those physicians must be either unwitting or deliberate charlatans; and I began to feel great sympathy for the invalids and families who suffered at their hands. From translated histories I also learned that the Japanese Reformation[3] owed its rise, to a great extent, to the introduction of Western medical science to Japan.

These inklings took me to a medical college in the Japanese countryside.[4] It was my fine dream that on my return to China I would cure patients like my father who had suffered from the wrong treatment, while if war broke out I would serve as an army doctor, at the same time promoting my countrymen's faith in reform.

I have no idea what improved methods are now used to teach microbiology, but in those days we were shown lantern slides of microbes; and if the lecture ended early, the instructor might show slides of natural scenery or news to fill up the time. Since this was during the Russo-Japanese War, there were many war slides, and I had to join in the clapping and cheering in the lecture hall along with the other students. It was a long time since I had seen any compatriots, but one day I saw a newsreel slide of a number of Chinese, one of them bound and the rest standing around him. They

2. N— refers to Nanjing, and K— to the Kiangnan (Jiangnan) Naval Academy where the author studied in 1898.
3. The Meiji period (1868–1912).
4. This refers to the Sendai Medical College where Lu Xun studied from 1904 to 1906.

were all sturdy fellows but appeared completely apathetic. According to the commentary, the one with his hands bound was a spy working for the Russians who was to be beheaded by the Japanese military as a warning to others, while the Chinese beside him had come to enjoy the spectacle.

Before the term was over I had left for Tokyo, because this slide convinced me that medical science was not so important after all. The people of a weak and backward country, however strong and healthy they might be, could only serve to be made examples of or as witnesses of such futile spectacles; and it was not necessarily deplorable if many of them died of illness. The most important thing, therefore, was to change their spirit; and since at that time I felt that literature was the best means to this end, I decided to promote a literary movement. There were many Chinese students in Tokyo studying law, political science, physics and chemistry, even police work and engineering, but not one studying literature and art. However, even in this uncongenial atmosphere I was fortunate enough to find some kindred spirits. We gathered the few others we needed and after discussion our first step, of course, was to publish a magazine, the title of which denoted that this was a new birth. As we were then rather classically inclined, we called it *Vita Nova* (New Life).

When the time for publication drew near, some of our contributors dropped out and then our funds ran out, until there were only three of us left and we were penniless. Since we had started our venture at an unlucky hour, there was naturally no one to whom we could complain when we failed; but later even we three were destined to part, and our discussions of a future dream world had to cease. So ended this abortive *Vita Nova.*

Only later did I feel the futility of it all. At that time I had not a clue. Later it seemed to me that if a man's proposals met with approval, that should encourage him to advance; if they met with opposition, that should make him fight back; but the real tragedy was for him to lift up his voice among the living and meet with no response, neither approval nor opposition, just as if he were stranded in a boundless desert completely at a loss. That was when I became conscious of loneliness.

And this sense of loneliness grew from day to day, entwining itself about my soul like some huge poisonous snake.

But in spite of my groundless sadness, I felt no indignation; for this experience had made me reflect and see that I was definitely not the type of hero who could rally multitudes at his call.

However, my loneliness had to be dispelled because it was causing me agony. So I used various means to dull my senses, to immerse myself among my fellow nationals and to turn to the past. Later I experienced or witnessed even greater loneliness and sadness which I am unwilling to recall, preferring that it should perish with my mind in the dust. Still my attempt to deaden my senses was not unsuccessful—I lost the enthusiasm and fervor of my youth.

In S— Hostel was a three-roomed house with a courtyard in which grew a locust tree, and it was said that a woman had hanged herself there. Although the tree had grown so tall that its branches were now out of reach, the rooms remained deserted. For some years I stayed here, copying ancient inscriptions. I had few visitors, the inscriptions raised no political problems or issues, and so the days slipped quietly away, which was all that I desired. On summer nights, when mosquitoes swarmed, I would sit under the locust tree waving my fan and looking at specks of blue sky through chinks in the thick foliage, while belated caterpillars would fall, icy-cold, on to my neck.

The only visitor to drop in occasionally for a talk was my old friend Jin Xinyi.[5] Having put his big portfolio on the rickety table he would take off his long gown and sit down opposite me, looking as if his heart was still beating fast because he was afraid of dogs.

"What's the use of copying these?" One night, while leafing through the inscriptions I had copied, he asked me for enlightenment on this point.

"There isn't any use."

"What's the point, then, of copying them?"

"There isn't any point."

"Why don't you write something? . . . "

I understood. They were bringing out *New Youth*, but since there did not seem to have been any reaction, favorable or otherwise, no doubt they felt lonely. However I said:

"Imagine an iron house having not a single window and virtually indestructible, with all its inmates sound asleep and about to die of suffocation. Dying in their sleep, they won't feel the pain of death. Now if you raise a shout to wake a few of the lighter sleepers, making these unfortunate few suffer the agony of irrevocable death, do you really think you are doing them a good turn?"

"But if a few wake up, you can't say there is no hope of destroying the iron house."

True, in spite of my own conviction, I could not blot out hope, for hope belongs to the future. I had no negative evidence able to refute his affirmation of faith. So I finally agreed to write, and the result was my first story,

---

5. Jin Xinyi 金心異 refers to Qian Xuantong 錢玄同 (1887–1939), an editor of *New Youth*, a proponent of literary reform in the May Fourth period, and a linguist.

"A Madman's Diary." And once started I could not give up, but would write some sort of short story from time to time to humor my friends, until I had written more than a dozen of them.

As far as I am concerned, I no longer feel any great urge to express myself; yet, perhaps because I have not forgotten the grief of my past loneliness, I sometimes call out to encourage those fighters who are galloping on in loneliness, so that they do not lose heart. Whether my cry is brave or sad, repellent or ridiculous, I do not care. However, since this is a call to arms I must naturally obey my general's orders. This is why I often resort to innuendoes, as when I made a wreath appear from nowhere at the son's grave in "Medicine," while in "Tomorrow" I did not say that Fourth Shan's Wife never dreamed of her little boy. For our chiefs in those days were against pessimism. And I, for my part, did not want to infect with the loneliness which I had found so bitter those young people who were still dreaming pleasant dreams, just as I had done when young.

It is clear, then, that my stories fall far short of being works of art; hence I must at least count myself fortunate that they are still known as stories and are even being brought out in one volume. Although such good fortune makes me uneasy, it still pleases me to think that they have readers in the world of men, for the time being at any rate.

So now that these stories of mine are being reprinted in one collection, for the reasons given above I have chosen to entitle it *Call to Arms*.

Beijing, December 3, 1922

—*Translated by Yang Xianyi and Gladys Yang;*
Previously published in *Lu Xun: Selected Works,*
4 vols. (Beijing: Foreign Languages Press, 1980), 33–38.

Chapter 25

Remarks on the Publication of Saturday

Wang Dungen

Someone posed the question: "You have entitled your weekly magazine *Saturday*.[1] Why did you not name it Monday, Tuesday, Wednesday, Thursday, or Friday?"

I replied, "On Mondays, Tuesdays, Wednesdays, Thursdays, and Fridays, people are preoccupied with their work. Only on Saturdays and Sundays can they rest and enjoy their leisure to read fiction."

"Then why not name it *Sunday* rather than *Saturday*?"

I said, "On Sundays most businesses are closed. The magazines are for distribution on Saturday afternoon so that we could afford our readers earlier enjoyment."

"But there are so many other pleasures available on Saturday afternoon. Do people not want to enjoy music and songs at the theaters, to intoxicate themselves in the taverns, or to revel in the pleasure quarters? Or would

---

1. Wang Dungen 王鈍根, "*Libailiu* chuban zhuiyan" 禮拜六出版贅言, *Libailiu* 1 (June 6, 1914); reprinted in *YYHDP* 1: 7.

they rather take to joyless solitude, idling their way alone to purchase and then read your fiction?"

To which I replied, "Not so. Pleasure quarters are costly, drinking is unhealthy, and music and songs can be clamorous, unlike reading stories, which is economical and relaxing. Furthermore, the thrills derived from the former are ephemeral, incapable of lasting even until the next day. But dozens of new and fascinating stories can be acquired with only one silver dollar. When you are exhausted from a night out and return home, you can turn on the light and open the magazine, or enjoy a spirited conversation on the stories among friends, or peruse the stories with one's beloved wife sitting by one's side. And when your interest flags, the remainder can be put away for the next day. When the morning sun shines through the windows and the sweet fragrance of flowers permeates the seats, all worries will vanish with a copy of the stories in hand. Is it not happiness indeed to enjoy a day's leisure and repose in such a manner after an entire week of grinding labor? Hence, there are people who do not enjoy pleasure quarters, drinking, music, and songs, but there are none who do not love reading fiction, particularly that in *Saturday*, which is so portable and full of such interesting stories. The novelists who have contributed their best works to *Saturday* are all renowned and celebrated writers, and we are certain that the magazine will enjoy widespread popularity among our readers. Incompetent editor as I am, I will act as a mere distributor of writings for our readers."

It would be most fortunate for our readers if they did not reject these excellent writings; otherwise they would miss a great opportunity simply because of the inferiority of the distributor.

Saturday, June 6, third year of the Republic of China, 1914

—*Translated by Gilbert C. F. Fong*

Chapter 26

Congratulations to Happy Magazine

Zhou Shoujuan

When *Happy Magazine* was first published, I was asked to write a happy story.[1] I thought perhaps I really should happily write one, but I was too tied up with other things, and I could not think of anything good to write. The lesson was that even if I wanted to, I still could not be happy. So with a bellyful of unhappiness, I thought I might as well say a few words to express my best wishes to *Happy Magazine*.

It is a most unhappy world today. Both Heaven and Earth are pervaded with an air of unhappiness, and you can hardly find a happy person in sight. Well, a powerful emperor in an absolute monarchy should be happy, but his lowly subjects scream for revolution, so he is unhappy. The gods in Heaven should be the happiest, but the new generation wants to eliminate superstition, so they are also unhappy. As for the common man, needless to say, he is unhappy. Amid all this unhappiness, we should be thankful to the owner of *Happy Magazine* who has brought about such a happy publica-

---

1. Zhou Shoujuan 周瘦鵑. "*Kuaihuo* zhuci" 快活祝詞. *Kuaihuo* (Happy Magazine) 1 (1923). Reprinted in *YYHDP* I:15-16.

tion to make people happy, to help them forget the many unhappy things. With all my heart, I wish *Happy Magazine* a long life, and I also wish the happy publishers, the happy printers, the happy editors, the happy writers, and the happy readers all the happiness; I hope they will be happy every second, happy every minute, happy every quarter of an hour, happy every hour, happy every day, happy every month, happy every year, and happy for ever and ever.

—Translated by Gilbert C. F. Fong

Chapter 27

The Mission of the New Literature

Cheng Fangwu

Literary creation has always been a simple matter of expressing the demands of one's heart; it has never been necessary to have any sort of predetermined goal.[1] However, if in the midst of writing we attempt to bring all the activities of our heart into our consciousness, then it becomes easy for those thoughts to fix upon a certain objective. This is not just a likely occurrence, it is also a gratifying one.

At the mere mention of objectives in literature, we immediately sense a sort of startling paradox. There has never been a single thing on this earth that has provoked a greater diversity of views and conflicting opinions than literature. Some claim that it isn't worth so much as a penny whereas others devote their lives to it. Even in a like-minded group of avowed literary men, one can distinguish between those who believe in art for life's sake—"*l'art pour la vie*"—and those who believe in art for art's sake—"*l'art pour l'art.*" Since its value and foundation are so unstable and indetermi-

---

1. Cheng Fangwu 程仿吾, "Xin wenxue zhi shiming" 新文學之使命, *Chuangzao zhoubao* 1, no. 2 (May 20, 1922).

nate, if we try to apply art to the pursuit of a special goal or say it has a particular purpose, this is simply building castles in the sand.

Nevertheless, this sort of controversy is not absolutely unavoidable. If we take the demands of our heart and make them the impetus for all of our literary creativity, then neither art nor life will be able to impede us, nor will our literary creations become slaves to either. Furthermore, this sort of controversy knows no limits. If we thoughtlessly enter the fray, then we will never experience so much as one day of creativity, and literature without creativity is the same as having no literature at all. In light of this, it would be best for us to plant the roots of literature in a place that transcends all useless controversies. The significance of this is exactly the same as the scientist's selection of the point of "absolute rest." Having done this, we can henceforth remove all obstacles and contradictions and directly pursue the object of our study.

Since literature is one of the activities of our hearts, we had best make the natural desires of our hearts the motivating force behind literature. As for those involved in all the noisy debates about the purpose of literature, they can only be looked at as people with various forms of color-blindness putting undue faith in what they see with their own eyes, each insisting that what he sees is the total picture and what he doesn't see doesn't exist. For example, a man who is colorblind to red can only perceive its complementary color, even though both colors come from the selfsame beam of white light. If we recognize that light is white, we will realize that the reason for the misperceptions of the color-blind lies in their individual understanding being limited to only a small portion of the total picture. From each of the various arguments (presented by people with different types of color-blindness), we can also get an approximate idea of the elements that constitute white light. We can further determine our own understanding of the whole from the nature of the individual constituents. If we pursue our study in this manner, we will not only be undaunted by contradictions, we will also be able to subdue and manipulate them to our own advantage.

Since we are able to obtain a superior vantage point from which to survey these contradictions and to look among them for evidence verifying the authentic in literature, it will not be difficult for us to envision the direction the activities of our hearts should take, or to freely indulge ourselves in the pursuit of our desires.

This is what we mean when we talk about literature having an objective, a mission.

Yet the goal or mission of literature is no simple matter. Furthermore, what the average person cherishes as his literary goal is, in actuality, already a far cry from literature proper. If he's not placing too much emphasis on the times, then he's treating the literary arts too superficially. As a result, among the writers of the new literature there are already more than a few following the wrong path, wasting their energies. At this point I think it best to take my original tenet—the tenet that the primary force motivating literature should be the demands of the heart—and move into an investigation of what the mission of our new literature should be.

I think that our new literature should at least undertake the following three types of missions:

1. A mission toward the epoch.
2. A mission toward the National Language.
3. A mission toward literature itself.

I don't think it wise to covet more than these three types of missions.

We're not much more than a bubble in the tide of the present epoch, and all that we create naturally bears the mark of our epoch. But this doesn't mean we should limit ourselves to unconsciously rehearsing the script of the epoch; we must step forward and take charge of the epoch and consciously express it. Our epoch, its life, its thought—we must use the most forceful methods to express these things, thereby giving the average man a chance to reflect and pass judgment on his own life. Thus, above all, we have a mission that carries a tremendous amount of responsibility toward the present.

We need to adopt a serious attitude toward present-day life, its style and content, making accurate observations and impartial critiques. As far as unjust institutions and inherited evils are concerned, we must vigorously denounce them.

These are the heavy responsibilities of the writer. And yet some writers often fabricate laughter and tears, doing their utmost to curry favor with others. These people are not simply weaklings who incite our disgust, they are also incapable of sincere passions and are already lacking a literary life. A writer's ardent longings are much stronger than others', as is the malevolence in his heart. Literature is the conscience of an epoch, and writers should be the champions of this conscience. In our society, where conscience is diseased, writers shoulder an especially heavy burden.

Our epoch is one in which the strong prey on the defenseless, brute force predominates over principle, an epoch with a withered conscience, with no sense of shame, an epoch that grapples for material things and profit, merciless and cold-blooded. Since our social organizations are the cohorts of this epoch, and our system of education is but an empty facade, writers have a great duty and personal responsibility in this area. We want to ignite a furious blaze and incite a violent movement in this numbed, unfeeling conscience.

We should spare no effort in subjecting the hypocrisy and iniquity of our epoch to a violent barrage. We should be warriors for truth and goodness, just as we should be disciples of beauty.

Our epoch has already been saturated with hypocrisy, iniquity, and hideousness! Life is already suffocating in the midst of this foul stench! Destroying this state of affairs is the mandate of the new writer.

From the moment it burst onto the scene, our new literature movement has been a National Language movement. Yet, judging from the results of the past several years and the current state of affairs, it seems that this movement of ours has had a tendency to satisfy itself by making only cosmetic changes. For example, some writers' idea of a new literary form means nothing more than scattering around a handful of punctuation marks and updating a few archaic terms. And as far as new content goes, they think this amounts to no more than including some inordinately abstract terms of the "flower of life" and "sea of love" type. In actuality, talent for literary expression has been on the decline for some time.

Our new literature movement simply cannot be satisfied by such minimal changes. The goal of our movement is to replenish and enrich our talent for self-expression, to eliminate the barriers between human hearts. No language matches our own for weakness in expressive capacity. When a group of Chinese get together, if the conversation doesn't center around food and drink, then it's the usual moaning about current events. And this moaning about current events is their loftiest subject matter and richest form of expression. Should the conversation happen to touch upon more complex matters, they immediately sense that their own expressive powers are quite feeble.

The rich expressions we can find in foreign works of literature are lacking in our own lives and literature. Is it that our countrymen, who have been so proud of their own literary works for the past several thousand years, have entered a cyclical period of decline? Or is it that the abundant texts of the past several thousand years, in the final analysis, are just empty wordplay?

In the past our lives were so dull and dry that it caused our souls to wither up inside us, and we burned up our talents in old-style writing. These are indeed the reasons for the current impoverished state of our lives and our literature, instilling in us an ever-growing sense of the profound importance of the mission of the new literature. But what finally is this newfound literature? Within such a short period of time, we can't expect a great deal from it. But as long as we proceed systematically and don't stray from the path, we can count on our eventual success. Unfortunately, in its very first steps, our new literature has already strayed.

We know that we can't be too exacting of our literature, but if we leaf through some current publications it seems that they don't contain too many places with a sufficiently clear grammar and style (not to mention content) to prevent readers from turning away in disgust. This is terribly disappointing. The majority of our writers are students, some of whom have yet to progress beyond a middle-school level. Although this could surely serve as an explanation, the fact that they produce slipshod works and make no effort to improve leaves us no leeway in which to plead their case. People with good sense can easily discern that the literary works we see every day obviously do not represent our writers' best efforts, although the newspapers and magazines publish them with a great deal of fanfare. Since these writers are, above all, lacking in effort, the majority of them are consequently unable to distinguish between what is good and bad. The most offensive among them copy down lists of people's names or leisurely throw together a couple of sentences and pass it off as poetry—these aren't even worth discussing. There are young students who generally don't understand the real nature of things and only pride themselves on the quantity of material they have published. Inevitably, the real value of our new literature has more or less been buried by the outpourings of these inferior writers. If our writers continue to be unable to put greater effort into their work, the real builders of our new literature will probably have to be sought in a later generation.

National pride often makes us praise our monosyllabic characters and speak out in defense of our monotonous sentence structure. Conversely, our despicable penchant for imitation often makes us adopt vulgar foreign words. This is quite a contradictory and extremely laughable situation, though some actually see it as a natural thing. I am unaware of any inherent value that makes, for example, Japanese tanka-style poems[2] worth imitating, yet their promoters praise their marvels and imitators flock to them like geese. Between those writers who are unwilling to put forth any effort, on the one hand, and these mindless imitators, on the other, I really can't say at what point in the future we may actually witness the appearance of real literary works.

The two divergent paths just described are still nothing more than summaries of the two most obvious practices. Since most of those among our vanguard were ignorant in literary matters, they led us onto a wayward

---

2. *Tanka*, 短詩, 31-syllable poems in five lines, with a 5-7-5-7-7 pattern, were a dominant traditional style of poetry in Japan.

path from the very beginning. The bright among them were able to retrace their steps, whereas those who were foolish got confused and lost the way altogether. In the final analysis we have no choice but to blame our predecessors for this. Yet contemporary writers should also shoulder half the blame themselves. Furthermore, if from now on they don't start showing a greater awareness, I fear that our literature and our national language will temporarily stagnate in this current wretched condition.

We must create a new and rich expressiveness within our language! We cannot forget that an important part of the mission of the new literature lies in this area! In order not to disgrace ourselves in this part of our mission, from now on we must consciously strive to work harder in the area of expression and avoid thoughtless imitation!

I would now like to talk about the mission of literature itself.

In addition to a mission toward the external world, in any area there is always a mission toward the self. This is equally true of literature. Moreover, not a few people regard this sense of personal mission with a special seriousness. This is the case with the so-called art-for-art's-sake school. They believe that literature must possess its own intrinsic significance, that one can't always measure it on the abacus of utilitarianism. They say that regardless of whether literature's objective is the pursuit of beauty or indulgence in excessive pleasure, if we make a special effort to chase after it, we will never be made to feel regret for having wasted our efforts. . . .

What the art-for-art's-sake school advocates isn't necessarily entirely correct, still there *are* at least portions of it that contain truth. Someone who doesn't take great interest in the arts could never understand a painter's willingness to toil on in oppressive heat and bitter cold, or the willingness of a poet to meditate without food or sleep. Our inability to understand the art-for-art's sake school perhaps lies along the same lines as the inability of the average person—who has no interest in art—to understand any one particular artist.

At the least, I feel that to do away with all utilitarian intentions and to exclusively pursue literary "perfection" and "beauty" is quite possibly worth the expenditure of our entire lives. Furthermore, even if a certain type of literature of beauty has no educational value, the aesthetically pleasing feeling and comforting effect it has on our everyday lives can't be ignored.

Moreover, literature also benefits us positively in a more concrete sense. Our epoch has imposed a heavy tax on our intellect and will. Our lives have already been pushed to their arid outer limits. We thirst for a literature of beauty that will nourish our more refined sentiments and cleanse our lives. Literature is the sustenance of our spiritual lives. How much happiness we can experience through literature! What great bounds we can make through literature! We must pursue the perfection of literature! We must realize the beauty of literature!

I have now stated my general views on what the mission of the new literature ought to be. At this point, I'd like to add a few words to summarize and conclude my arguments.

Some people claim that the Chinese tend to pursue a life of ease and run away from trouble. As a result, there have been few Chinese in recent times who have tried to study the most difficult of fields, science. At the same time, larger numbers have been attracted to the relatively easier field of philosophy, and the easiest area—literature—has been completely inundated. It goes without saying that these sorts of ideas are completely absurd, yet this does reflect the psychology of most young people. I'm afraid that not only those who espouse these views and those referred to by these statements believe that such an obvious hierarchy of difficulty exists between science, philosophy, and art, but that those among our young people who now hold this misunderstanding are probably in the majority. Our new literature movement is certainly the result of our desire for self-expression, but this sort of misunderstanding will always make some sort of small contribution.

"Science is more difficult than philosophy and much more difficult than literature"—this sort of bizarre theorizing once again reminds me of the crude products of our new literary circles. Among our youthful writers, perhaps there are some who harbor such misunderstandings and really take literature to be a thoroughly simple affair; if such a group indeed exists, then who knows what sort of absurdities our new literature movement has yet to come out with.

I am prevented by space from giving a more detailed explanation of science, philosophy, and literature—which is simpler and which is more difficult—but I would like to use this opportunity to offer a few words of warning to our young writers:

Science is certainly not any more difficult than philosophy and literature, literature is certainly not any easier than science and philosophy.

If one wants to be a writer, one must first attain a thorough grounding in science and philosophy.

Literature is definitely not a game; literature is by no means a simple matter.

We must understand that countless literary works of the past represent an entire lifetime of painstaking effort on the part of their authors—no less effort than a scientist requires for his inventions or a philosopher for his tenets.

One's priority must be to gain ample training, applying oneself to the utmost.

Only in this manner will one be able to fulfill the mission of the new literature.

—*Translated by Nicholas A. Kaldis*

PART III

Revolutionary Literature
1923–1930

Introduction

With the reemergence of visible Western and Japanese imperialism in China after its relative absence during World War I, Chinese intellectuals turned in increasing numbers toward the left and to the ideology of Marxism. A handful of late Qing intellectuals had shown interest in Marx and his writings after the 1905 Russian Revolution (a small portion of *The Communist Manifesto* was first translated in 1906),[1] and the success of the 1917 Russian Revolution along with the growth of anti-imperialist nationalism had led directly to the founding of the Chinese Communist Party in 1921. But a deeper intellectual and political preoccupation with Marxist thought only began to take hold on a broad scale in intellectual circles after the May Thirtieth movement of 1925 (Dirlik 1989: 255). A series of anti-imperialist demonstrations sparked by the killing of Chinese students by British-hired Sikh police, this movement seemed to rally intellectuals out of their internecine factionalism toward a recognition of the need for political and intellec-

---

1. Translated in an appendage to an article by Zhu Zhixin 朱執信, "Deyizhi shehui gemingjia xiaozhuan" 德意志社會革命家小傳, *Minbao* 2 (Jan. 1906): 1–17. For a brief discussion of the introduction of Marxist thought in China, see Meisner 1970: 52–70.

tual unity. The subsequent success of the Northern Expedition, led by a co-
alition of the CCP and GMD to rid Chinese territory of warlord rule,
seemed to promise the national unity necessary to confront the Western imperialist powers. But when the GMD turned against its ally in a violent
coup in April 1927, the nearly decimated CCP was forced to seek haven in
the mountainous rural interior. Yet this coup, and the subsequent White
Terror of the 1930's, mobilized many intellectuals, even those who had previously shown little inclination toward political activism, against a common enemy and led directly to their further radicalization. It was, ironically, when the revolutionary movement was at its nadir that leftist intellectuals and writers sought out for literature a crucial role in the revolution.

The initial appeal of Marxism in a country lacking the advanced industrial base and large self-conscious working class essential to a Marxist revolutionary movement lay not in the notion of class struggle, but in the idea
of a national war against imperialism. As Maurice Meisner says in his
study of Li Dazhao, early Chinese Marxists put the nation in the dialectical
position of the proletariat and the imperialist nations in that of the bourgeoisie (Meisner 1970: 144–46). Marxism offered Chinese intellectuals a
ready explanation for the plight of their nation, as well as hope for a utopian future. The desire for rapid transformation of Chinese society (which
the reality of the material base precluded) and a traditional propensity for a
"cultural-intellectual approach" to social transformation predisposed the
Chinese intellectual toward a highly voluntaristic interpretation of Marx.[2]
The realm of culture, to which literature was central, would play an important role in effecting this rapid transformation. It is in this political-
ideological context that we must understand the debate on "revolutionary
literature" that emerged in the period immediately after the split between
the Nationalists and Communists in 1927.

Calls for the development of a class-based literature had appeared before this debate, particularly in the writings of Creationists like Guo Moruo,
Cheng Fangwu, and Yu Dafu, who had since the mid-1920's begun to "con-
vert" to Marxism. But these calls, represented here by Yu Dafu's "Class
Struggle in Literature" (1923), reveal a highly romantic understanding of
class literature. Yu was influenced in his views by Plekhanov's theories of
the organic unity of art and life, but his understanding of proletarian literature amounts to little more than revolutionary sloganeering. Yu is still very
much tied to the romantic ideals from which he was attempting to free
himself. His primary allegiance seems to be to literature and to the restoration of its organic connection to life through the unleashing of the literary

---

2. This point is made in Lin Yü-sheng 1979: 153–61.

energies of a proletarian class. Behind his call for proletarian literature lie the polemical wranglings between the Literary Research Association (which promoted the slogan "art for life's sake") and the Creation Society (which countered with the slogan "art for art's sake"), which had, each in their own way, sundered this connection.[3]

The emergence of the radical supporters of revolutionary literature from the ranks of the Creation Society's romantic individualists is not as ironic as first appearances might suggest. As Marston Anderson has remarked, "The 'pantheism' extolled in Guo Moruo's early poetry allows a lyric equation of the self with all who might share in the joy of creation." In their conversion to Marxism, the "Creationists simply generalized their individual emotions and, overriding the obvious class distinctions, pronounced themselves spokespersons for the masses" (1989: 77). Other, even more radical, voices in the promotion of a revolutionary literature came from the Sun Society, established in 1928 by young intellectuals who were CCP members. Before uniting in an attack on the older generation of May Fourth writers, however, members of these two literary societies squabbled over who had been first to raise the slogan of revolutionary literature and had thus gained the moral legitimacy to lead the new literary revolution.

The initial step in developing a proletarian revolutionary literature was to move out from under the mantle of the May Fourth. Qu Qiubai, one of the first Chinese intellectuals to study in the Soviet Union and to gain a solid foundation in Marxist theory, had been among the first to attack May Fourth elitism in the mid-1920's. The radicals of the Creation and Sun societies took Qu's lead a step further. May Fourth literature, they argued, was in its own Westernized and cosmopolitan way as elitist and divorced from the masses as the classical literary tradition. The title of Cheng Fangwu's "From Literary Revolution to Revolutionary Literature" became something of a slogan for the young radicals' desire to go beyond the limits of the May Fourth movement. They criticized May Fourth writers' narrow thematic preoccupation with bourgeois intellectuals, their neglect of the lower classes, and their propensity toward a dark and pessimistic view of the

---

3. The origins of the phrase "art for life's sake" (wei rensheng er yishu 爲人生而藝術) may be traced to "Wenxue yanjiu hui jianzhang" 文學研究會簡章 (Statement of principles of the Literary Research Association), *Xiaoshuo yuebao* 12, no. 1 (Jan. 1921). Although the idea is referred to in the early writings of Zhou Zuoren and Mao Dun, the slogan is something that was "more or less thrust on them by the reading public and members of other literary societies" (Tagore 1967: 51). It is less clear where the slogan "art for art's sake" (wei yishu er yishu 爲藝術而藝術) first appeared. Although there is an implicit aestheticism in the early writings of Guo Moruo, Tian Han, and Cheng Fangwu, much rhetorical energy is spent denying that literature should be a transcendent realm of the purely aesthetic. For more on this, see the General Introduction to this volume.

world. Qian Xingcun's attack on Lu Xun ("The Bygone Age of Ah Q") is typical of the young radicals' impatience with the previous generation's view of literature as exposure of social ills and depiction of the psychological backwardness of the Chinese people. His revolutionary view of the world makes no room for the profound moral uncertainty and "hesitation" so pronounced in Lu Xun's collection of prose poems, *Wild Grass*. The late 1920's was an age with "demands" very different from those of the May Fourth, requiring a new literature that was more positive and offered proletarian heroes who could be models for the revolutionary cause. The role envisioned for literature by the young radicals was one that would support and enhance the political cause of the proletarian revolution and suppress the reactionary individualism of the May Fourth. As Jiang Guangci put it: "Revolutionary literature must be an anti-individualist literature, its heroes must be the masses, not individuals; it must be directed not toward individualism, but toward collectivism. . . . The duty of revolutionary literature is to show in this life struggle the power of the masses, to instill into people collective tendencies."[4]

Mao Dun's "On Reading *Ni Huanzhi*" reflects something of the awkward position in which May Fourth intellectuals found themselves as the object of the radicals' scorn. When his *Eclipse* was attacked as a novel that portrayed only the disillusionment of young intellectuals with the revolutionary movement, Mao Dun chose to respond obliquely with a critique of *Ni Huanzhi*, a novel by Ye Shengtao that is similarly about intellectuals' disillusionment. He praised the novel and so vindicated himself against his critics' attacks. But Mao Dun's support for May Fourth–style critical realism was not unswerving; as an intellectual sympathetic to the goals of the young radicals, he recognized the changing demands that history had placed on the cultural realm.

The literary scene in this period, of course, was not monopolized by leftists or their sympathizers, although they were arguably its dominant galvanizing force during the 1930's and 1940's. There were many influential writers who attempted to carve out for literature a niche that was quite apart from utilitarian political concerns. Liang Shiqiu, the leading critical voice of the Crescent Moon Society (formed in 1923 as a loose-knit group of writers and poets concerned with aesthetic aspects of literature, principally poetry) and the frequent butt of Lu Xun's wicked satire in the debates of the late 1920's and 1930's, was what we today might call a liberal humanist. In his faith in a universal human nature, Liang felt that the leftist emphasis

---

4. From Jiang Guangci 蔣光慈, "Guanyu geming wenxue" 關於革命文學 (On revolutionary literature), *GM WX* 1: 138–146; cited in Gálik 1980: 157.

on class struggle and a literature which promoted that struggle would only divide humanity ("Literature and Revolution"). Predictably, Liang placed great value on the role of the writer as creative genius, in much the same way that Lu Xun had in his "On the Power of Mara Poetry." Liang's essay and those by Wen Yiduo (another member of the Crescent Moon Society) and Dai Wangshu (a "modernist" poet heavily influenced by French and Spanish Symbolists) express a faith in the importance of literature as craft and art, an implicitly apolitical stance that the radicals perceived as furthering the interests of the bourgeoisie.

Lu Xun's contributions to the revolutionary literature debate (here represented by "The Divergence of Art and Politics") are typically complex and ambiguous. He seems to waver between a view that literature serves little purpose in a period of revolutionary war[5] and his earlier May Fourth faith in the writer as an essential counter to political power which necessarily upholds the status quo. "The Divergence of Art and Politics," given as a speech in late 1927, dispels the myth that Lu Xun had by that time fully embraced Marxism (Leo Ou-fan Lee 1987: 134–42). Indeed, Lu Xun reveals a wariness of all political power, including that held by revolutionaries, as inherently conservative and oppressive, requiring an antagonistic role for the writer.

Implicit in the writings of the revolutionary literature debate was the important question of the role of the bourgeois writer in a period of "proletarian" revolution. It is one that haunts literary politics throughout the Republican era and into the Maoist period in the PRC. Whereas Lu Xun did not easily accept the notion that bourgeois writers can transcend their class interests to create a literature of and for the proletariat, and Mao Dun rejected outright the idea that bourgeois writers should write about subjects unfamiliar to them, the young radicals maintained a vanguard role for the writer in the revolution by devising neat, vaguely Marxist, dialectical methods for transcending their class consciousness. Through contact with the masses, by abandoning their former individualism and adopting a Marxist worldview, writers could "negate" or "deny" themselves (their bourgeois class backgrounds), thus allowing them to maintain their roles as cultural stewards and speak for the subaltern they purported to represent. The radicals of the Creation and Sun societies promoted a "collectivist" literature of the proletariat, but a literature that was to be realized by an elite group of bourgeois intellectuals. One may sense in this sort of rationalizing the dif-

---

5. Lu Xun expressed this idea very clearly in an earlier, more famous talk "Literature in a Revolutionary Era" (*Geming shidai de wenxue* 革命時代的文學); in Lu Xun 1980: 2: 334–41; 1981a: 3: 417–24.

ficulty with which a very traditional faith in the power of the self-cultivated individual to initiate the transformation of external reality is abandoned. We will see in the final section that Mao Zedong, too, believed in the possibility of intellectuals' transcending their class and speaking for the masses, but not without first passing through a difficult process of psychological remolding.

The final two essays, by Zhou Yang and Hu Feng, do not properly belong to the debate on revolutionary literature, since they were written in 1936 well after the furor aroused by the debate had subsided. (Hu's essay is a response to Zhou's and should be read after it.) Yet both deal with the important question of the relationship between political ideology and literature and can thus be seen as part of the larger discussion on the role of literature in politics. These essays focus on the important concept of "type," central to much Marxist realist literary theory. Both writers accept the view that for a character "type" to be truly realistic it should be drawn from both the particular and the universal. Where they are at odds with one another is primarily in the role they envision for ideology in guiding the writer in the creative process of making types. Hu objected to the primacy of Marxist ideology that Zhou Yang wanted for the creative act. For Hu Feng ideology can play a part in the creation of realist literature, but should not be applied in a doctrinaire fashion that divorces the writer from a creative and subjective engagement with the real.

Chapter 28

Class Struggle in Literature

Yu Dafu

I

Mount Olympus, surrounded by pure air and beautiful vistas, has been the playground of the Muse since ancient times.[1] Utopia, where simple, honest customs and enlightened politics hold sway, is a realm that has emerged from the minds of contemporary literati at home and abroad. Why have artists, ancient and modern, invented these places and chased the flowers of their dreams? Simply stated, it is only because they have no other way to vent the melancholy and anger in their hearts; all they can do is write about their discontent with reality and their fervent opposition to the society around them, whiling away their tedious days on earth and laying plans for future generations to realize. Romantics old and new, affecting a facade of transcendence, are in reality filled with the most profound abhorrence of human society. Yet they lack the power to wage a victorious struggle over the evils of society; that is why advocates of lofty political ideals like Rous-

---

1. Yu Dafu 郁達夫, "Wenxue shang de jieji douzheng" 文學上的階級鬥爭, *Chuangzao zhoubao* 創造週報 4 (May 27, 1923).

seau and Voltaire were inevitably cast aside, and preachers of the gospel of moral freedom like Verlaine and Wilde wound up in jail.

Such artists, driven to despair by the realization that their ideals have no place in real society, must escape into the Republic of Art, where they create Sphinx-like monuments for posterity to vent their grief and indignation toward contemporary society. But all for naught, since their inept successors, unable to see through to the pain and anguish of their predecessors, created instead such terms as "art for art's sake" and "art for life's sake" to calumniate them and deny them a salutary role in human history. In my view, the French literary critics who first invented those terms should have died a thousand deaths. Art is life, and life is art, and nothing is served by making them antagonistic! Let me ask: Is life without art worthy of the name life? In the history of the world has there ever been an artistic work unrelated to life?

II

Thought evolves through changing situations. The unfocused resentment and rebelliousness embraced by artists of the late eighteenth and early nineteenth centuries, when Romanticism prevailed, grew progressively concrete during the mid-nineteenth century. At first their unfocused attacks were directed at human life in general; gradually they took aim at such specific targets as national politics, the social system, or the attitudes of the defenders of evil society.

All movements produce countermovements. We don't have to look to Hegelian philosophy for proof, for history is replete with clear examples. After each fervent attack by one group of artists, another group in blind pursuit of wealth and fame will of course emerge to lead a countermovement. The history of art, like the history of social movements, involves the emergence of many mutually antagonistic classes. In this essay I shall describe and explain one aspect of class struggle in the realm of literature.

III

"The sociopolitical history of civilization is nothing more than a record of class struggle." Everyone who reads Hegelian philosophy and studies Marxism knows and acknowledges the truth of this statement. In searching for the origins of class struggle in literature, we find that it is as old as mankind. Here I shall not try to flaunt my erudition by dealing with Hebrew or Greco-Roman literature; rather, I shall briefly describe literary changes after the rise of anti-classicist Romanticism and then analyze the attitude of young people currently engaged in literary work.

Post-Renaissance neo-classical literature was the plaything of monarchs and degenerate aristocrats; the proletariat was denied any participation. The Romantic movement was an uprising against this literary tyranny. The Romantics' rebelliousness, their despair in the face of reality, and the path they trod are dealt with briefly in the first part of this essay. The melancholy and anger in their work, opposed by a group of bogus writers interested only in personal wealth and fame, were not discovered for several generations. The French Revolution, the American War of Independence, the anti-Napoleonic German federation, and the Italian unification campaign were real-life dramas acted out by many young writers, the fruits of seeds sown by earlier generations of idealists.

When their castles in the air were only half completed—the remaining half lacking a foundation—the dashing young Romantics became literary "veterans." Lethargic and dejected, they followed in the footsteps of their predecessors, turning into literary aristocrats who suppressed their young successors and embraced degeneracy. Young readers of their early works then raised the banner of rebellion against them, as they, their forebears, had done in their opposition to neo-classicism. Old and decrepit, they could mount no defense; so Romanticism, unique in so many ways, raised the white flag of surrender as the progressive class that replaced it set out on its own path.

Naturalism caught on for a while, since it seemed capable of capturing the totality of things. Its fatalism and lack of initiative, however, made it impossible for writers to freely express their individualism. By adopting an attitude of passive resistance, one group of young progressives created a movement characterized by decadence and symbolism; another group, adopting a stance of active resistance, became the vanguard of the contemporary neo-idealist, neo-heroic movement. The colors of this latter movement are brighter, the rebelliousness more ardent. It has merged with real-life movements in boldly raising the banner of the proletariat and combining life and art. Armed with their art and their lives, they have declared war against the old, conservative literati, while remnants of the Naturalist movement continue to make an empty show of strength, claiming that they want to reform an entire generation. Most of these writers grovel at the feet of the bourgeoisie and the ruling class, for whom many of them have become mere decorations. Class struggle in twentieth-century literature must therefore adopt the same tactics as that of real class struggle in society.

IV

Let us now look briefly at recent literary trends in other parts of the world to substantiate what I have written above.

In France the works of the Decadent school, following the lead of Baudelaire and Verlaine, feature most prominently a philosophy of nihilism and anarchism. Decadent writers in other countries can virtually all be called Nihilists. By denying life and self, they deny everything. Not surprisingly, their most ferocious attacks are aimed at sociopolitical absurdities and at government, law, and morality, which impede the development of individualism. On the surface the plays of Maeterlinck and the novels of Rodenbach appear not to attack the social system, but a closer look reveals a resentment toward reality in all their works, a rebellion against society in every sentence. Even more obvious and ardent a desire to destroy contemporary systems is seen in Romain Rolland, a staunch advocate of positive progress who believes that man must pursue his goals as long as there is life in his body, and in Barbusse, promoter of an enlightenment movement to consign the world's evil societies to the flames. In recent years, we are told, the venerable Anatole France has also been involved in social movements, writing in support of the proletariat. His enthusiasm commands our respect. Other works, including the mournful novels of the late C. L. Philips and the Dolorisme writings of Georges Duhamel,[2] are permeated with loathing for and opposition to contemporary society.

Germany is the birthplace of the Expressionists, whose fervent social rebelliousness is actually a zealous desire to turn contemporary society upside down. It's right there in all their works. Although old literary diehards like Hermann Bahr cling to the classics, an immutable trend is visible in the works of such young poets as Max Barthel, Franz Werfel, and Reinhard Coering. Since they are personally involved in class struggle, virtually all the materials they choose are reflections of class struggle. Georg Kaiser's play *Die Bürger von Calais* [The citizens of Calais], for instance, portrays a struggle between justice and ruthlessness. Fritz von Unruh's tragedy *Ein Geschlecht* [A generation] depicts a struggle between a mother and a son. The theme of Walter Hasenclever's masterpiece *Der Sohn* [The son], is the struggle between a father and a son. Others, such as Ernst Toller's plays *Die*

---

2. "Dolorisme" appears in English and is Yu's rendering of the Chinese term *tongku zhuyi* 痛 苦 主 義 ; it does not seem to be a term used by or commonly associated with Duhamel (1884–1966), whose writings on war (*Civilisation, 1914–1917* and *Vie des martyrs, 1914–1916*) are filled with a strong sense of human suffering and discontent with modern civilization.

Wandlung [Transfiguration] and *Maschinenstürmer* [The machine wreckers], are literary works that enthusiastically take class struggle as their content.

Class struggle in Russian literature has become a thing of the past. The proletariat is now in actuality imitating art in its flesh-and-blood human life. The inaction of Oblomov (in Goncharov's novel of the same name) and the cruelty of Artsybashev's Sanin are powerful attacks on the bourgeoisie and the ruling class. Just look, has not the grand and stately kingdom of the proletariat been created for its descendants? You magnificent Russians, don't let a momentary failure deflect your courage and your will! Remember: "Peu nous importe le succés [sic]. Il s'agit d'être grand." [the important thing for us is not success but greatness].

Works by modern Russian writers are the crystallization of the modern spirit. We need only read a stanza of "Twelve Apostles" [The twelve], by the late A. Blok, to come to an understanding of this: "Hungry dogs behind, bloody banners ahead. Oh! Oh! Violent winds, bullets penetrating rocks, indescribable pain. Soft snow beneath the feet, snowflakes like pearls. Who is avant-garde? The one in the rose-festooned white hat—Jesus Christ."

The English literary world is the most conservative and most accommodating of all. The fetid air of thousands of years continues to circulate through English literature, and the spark our youth seeks cannot be found in the works of English literary royalists. The shallow socialism of Bernard Shaw and H. G. Wells, is it an apology for the rich or a lullaby for the proletariat? If we seek a modern temperament in the English language, we must turn to the novels of the late Americans Jack London and Upton Sinclair for consolation.

Young writers in the nations of southern and northern Europe and in countries situated between Asia and Europe have without exception declared war against traditional ideologies, their strongest attacks coming against the protectors of those ideologies, the bourgeoisie and the ruling class. I am confident that the ideals of these red-blooded youths will someday be realized. I know that for us these are hard times, much like the prerevolutionary days of the Russian youth. But we must press forward. We may fail, and we may die, but our legacy will live forever. So in the spirit of Marx and Engels, let me proclaim:

Downtrodden members of the international proletariat,
Oppressed comrades in literary circles and society at large,
All writers warring against the running dogs of the bourgeoisie and ruling classes,
We must unite to

Chapter 29

From a Literary Revolution to a Revolutionary Literature

Cheng Fangwu

I. The Social Basis of the Literary Revolution

Every social phenomenon must have a social basis from which it necessarily arises.[1] So, wherein lies the social basis of our Literary Revolution of the past decade or more? According to my investigation, it should be as follows:

1. The 1911 Revolution, the failure of the democratic revolution against feudal power, along with the rapidly advancing oppression of imperialism, caused a portion of the so-called intellectual class that had already been in touch with world currents to engage wholeheartedly in the thought enlightenment movement (the so-called New Culture movement).

---

1. Cheng Fangwu 成仿吾, "Cong wenxue geming dao geming wenxue" 從文學革命到革命文學, *Chuangzao yuekan* 1, no. 9 (Feb. 1, 1928).

2. This kind of campaign for enlightened, democratic thinking necessarily demanded a new medium of expression (the Vernacular Literature movement).

However, the leisured-class intelligentsia of the time lacked both a thorough knowledge of the age and a thorough understanding of its thought. Moreover, since the majority were literary people, their achievements were limited to superficial enlightenment, and their greatest efforts were primarily in the area of the new literature. Consequently, the New Culture movement more or less became identical with the New Literature movement, and it was overshadowed by the literary movement almost to the point of disappearing without a trace. In fact, in terms of visible achievement, only a few slight and indistinct rays of light of the literature remain.

II. The Historical Significance of the Literary Revolution

Historical development invariably proceeds by the dialectical method (*dialektische Methode*). As a result of a change in the economic base, the mode of human life and all ideology change accordingly. Consequently, the old way of life and old ideology are sublated (*auf[geho]ben*) as new ones emerge.[2]

The invasion of the torrent of modern capitalism has long since destroyed the foundations of our old economic system. During the European War there sprang up in China a modernized capitalist class as well as a group of petit-bourgeois intelligentsia. The revolution in the form of ideology that is literature gradually became inevitable, and the key to the solution of it all lay in the antithetical relationship between the literary and the spoken language.

The literature of the ancient period and the spoken language of the time did not have separate and distinct principles. Later, the combined result of the refining of the written language, the stubborn adherence to tradition, and the special creation of rare and useless terms (Emperor Qin Shihuang's special term for "I, imperial we" [a pronoun that can only be used by an emperor], etc.), caused the literary and spoken languages gradually to separate and become mutually distinct. However, the elements of the spoken language and their influence outside the sphere of classical literature could not be wiped out.

Chinese translations of the Buddhist canon, largely because of their catechistic format and wide dissemination, plainly caused the colloquial

---

2. For a discussion of Cheng's use of this term, see Gálik 1980: 99.

style to constitute itself into a significant school. Later, following the development of the vernacular lyric [*ci*] and the dramatic verse [*qu*] and the flourishing of vernacular fiction, the effecting of a "qualitative change" here lacked only a slight "quantitative change." On the other hand, the classical written style, as it gradually developed to the point of exhaustion, came to shackle the expression of new content; it could but idly await the pealing bell that would announce the hour in which it, the classical written style, would be sublated forever.

Ultimately, the slight quantity needed to effect the aforementioned "qualitative change" arrived, via foreign literature and the new thought, and the shackles were broken. Newly developed content sought new forms by which to soar to freshly opened realms.

III. The Course of the Literary Revolution

It is not necessary to relate here at length the historical facts of the Literary Revolution. I will limit myself to briefly summarizing its general course, as well as comparing it with the New Culture movement. Because theoretically speaking the former is a division of the latter, they have many common tendencies.

The first task of the New Culture movement was the negation of the old thought; the second task was the introduction of the new. But neither stage produced the required results. This is because the people engaged in these two tasks were not complete in their negation of the old thought; even less did they bear the responsibility of introducing the new. We need go no further than mention the so-called National Learning movement, which emerged but a short time after the New Culture movement had been launched. Hu Shi and his ilk, having yelled out just a few shouts, fled back to their old nest as if they had exerted themselves to a state of exhaustion. Once there, they voraciously drank from the broken old wine bottle of classical learning, thinking to imbibe thereby a dose of vitality. The rest of the half-dead monsters and ghosts kept pace with their confused shouting. We need only look at half-baked translations made by Zhang Dongsun and others of the Study Clique and the Cooperative Study Society; we need but read Liang Shuming's queer work, *Eastern and Western Civilizations and Their Philosophies.*

Most unfortunate, however, is that these "famous personages" totally lacked comprehension of their times, totally lacked understanding of their readers, and totally lacked clarity as to the goods they were peddling. This is why the New Culture movement in no more than three or four years seemed to die peacefully of old age. They did not realize that the awakened youth of the period had already refused their anesthetic herbs; they really ought to have carried their medicine baskets to the stable capitalist countries and gone begging for food!

The literature movement, during its initial period, on the whole had the same tendency as the New Culture movement. Hu Shi and his set were never able to discard their old cadence; the Literary Research Association's translations pretty much matched those of the Cooperative Study Society. Standing opposite to the "National Learning movement" was the "Modern Punctuation" group; in fact, they were merely punctuating chaotically.

After 1921, creative writers endeavored to support the Literary Revolution movement and prevent it from likewise following the New Culture movement to an early demise. By that time, the Creation Society already had ascended that stage and was engaged in unremitting struggle with the wretched environment. Its writers, via their spirit of defiance, via their fresh work style, within four or five years had nurtured in the literary world a spirit of independent creation, greatly stimulating the general youth population. The Society steered the course of the Literary Revolution, taking the lead in moving forward; they swept away all false literary criticism, and they drove out a good many clumsy, inferior translations. They made the most complete negation of the old thought and the old literature; with genuine zeal and critical attitude they fought for the whole literary movement.

There are those who say that the Creation Society's characteristic features were romanticism and sentimentalism; this is merely a partial observation. My own analysis is that the Creation Society represented the revolutionary petit-bourgeois intelligentsia. Romanticism and sentimentalism are qualities peculiar to the petite bourgeoisie, but in terms of their significance vis-à-vis the bourgeoisie, these qualities still can be considered revolutionary.

It was this endeavor within the creative sphere that saved our entire Literary Revolution movement. The Creation Society, through its spirit of defiance, ardent zeal, critical attitude, and unceasing effort, on the one hand gave encouragement and comfort to awakened youth and on the other hand unceasingly worked to perfect our vernacular form. Due to the inspiration of the Creation Society, the intelligentsia of the entire country never failed to continue its struggle; the great fire of the Literary Revolution is burning to this day; the New Culture movement fortunately has preserved this one field of endeavor.

IV. The Present Stage of the Literary Revolution

To what stage, after all, has our Literary Revolution now advanced?

1. The present mainstay of our literary movement:
   Mainstay—one section of the intellectual class.
2. The present actual situation of our literary movement:
   Content—petit-bourgeois ideology;
   Medium—vernacular style, although differing quite a bit from actual speech;
   Form—fiction and poetry comprise the bulk, very little drama.

The results of practical analysis are thus, and in theory they should also be thus. This all originated from the basic nature of the petite bourgeoisie.

The Creation Society always has been extremely diligent in the perfection of our vernacular form; its writers do not forget for a single minute their work in this area. In fact, owing to great effort in this area, their success has not been inconsiderable. Formerly, they had three guidelines:

1. Strive to use correct grammar;
2. Strive to adopt common idioms, create an increased vocabulary;
3. Experiment in the use of complicated syntax.

When it came time to apply these three principles, they never dreamed that their writing would depart so far from actual speech.

Turning away from literature per se, but within literature's sphere of influence, there are several kinds of phenomena worth noting:

1. Every large bookstore at present still sells textbooks written in the classical style;
2. Many textbooks written in the vernacular style contain quite a few unclear passages;
3. Modern punctuation is still in the process of becoming prevalent, and as before there is chaotic punctuating.

As regards the investigation of the present stage of the Literary Revolution, a word must be said about a special phenomenon in Beijing. This is the little game being played by the Zhou Zuoren clique, centered around the *Thread of Words* magazine. Their motto is "taste." I have previously stated elsewhere that what they take pride in is "leisure, again leisure, and a third time leisure"; they represent the leisured capitalist class and the petite bourgeoisie who are "sleeping inside a drum." They have transcended the age. They have already lived this way for several years; perhaps if Beijing's foul and murky fog is not someday blasted through by a million tons of smokeless gunpowder, they will muddle through in this way forever.

V. The Future Progress of the Literary Revolution

Does the foregoing historical investigation enable us to determine the future progress of the Literary Revolution?

No, this we decidedly cannot do.

Literature, in the total organization of society, constitutes one part of the superstructure. We cannot comprehend each individual part when separated from the whole; we must take up the entire social structure to investigate the part that is literature. Only then can we acquire a true understanding.

If we want to research the future progress of the literary movement, it is necessary to understand clearly the current stage of our social development; if we want to understand clearly the current stage of our social development, it is necessary to engage in complete and rational criticism of modern capitalist society (critique of the economic, political, and ideological processes), grasping firmly the method of dialectical materialism, understanding the inevitable development of history.

We can set it forth simply as follows:

Capitalism has already developed to its final stage (imperialism); the reformation of all human society is now at hand. We, who are under the double oppression of capitalism and feudal power, are already dragging our lame feet in starting our national revolution, while our literary movement—one line of demarcation of the total liberation movement—still searches wide-eyed and in broad daylight for the remnants of a bygone and illusory dream.

We have fallen far behind the times. We have as our mainstay a class that is soon to be sublated [aufgehoben], using its ideology as our content. In thus creating a "middle-of-the-road" vernacular writing style, which is "neither ass nor horse," we have given free scope to the wretched qualities of the petite bourgeoisie.

If we still would bear the responsibility of revolutionary intelligentsia, we must negate ourselves once more (the negation of negation), we must endeavor to acquire class consciousness, we must make our medium approach the spoken language of the worker and peasant masses, we must take the worker-peasant masses as our target.

In other words, our literature movement henceforth should constitute a step forward and take the one step—from a Literary Revolution to a Revolutionary Literature!

VI. Revolutionary Intelligentsia Unite!

Capitalism already has reached its final hour; the world has formed in two warring camps: one side is the isolated citadel of fascism, capitalism's lingering poison; the other side is the united war front of all the world's worker-peasant masses. Each and every cell is organizing for combat, and the literary workers ought to take charge of a sector. Forward! Have you not heard the stirring battle cry?

No one is allowed to stand in the middle. You must come to this side, or go over there!

Do not merely follow, much less fall farther behind; consciously participate in the historical process of social change!

Strive to obtain an understanding of dialectical materialism, make an effort to grasp the dialectical materialist method; it will give you correct guidance, show you invincible tactics.

Overcome your own petit-bourgeois qualities; turn your back on the class that is soon to be sublated. Start walking toward the ragged mass of workers and peasants!

Persevere in your work with a clear consciousness; banish the spreading evil of capitalist ideology and its influence from among the masses. Cultivate the masses: unceasingly give them courage, maintain their confidence! Do not forget—you are standing in a sector of the battlefront!

Describe with true zeal what you see and hear on the battlefield, the acute sorrow and anger of the worker-peasant masses, heroic behavior, the joy of victory! By so doing, you can ensure final victory, you will achieve outstanding merit, and you will not be ashamed to call yourself a warrior.

Revolutionary intelligentsia unite! Don't worry about losing your chains!

—*Translated by Michael Gotz.*
Previously published in *Bulletin of
Concerned Asian Scholars* (Jan.–Mar. 1976),35–38.

Chapter 30

The Bygone Age of Ah Q

Qian Xingcun

The age depicted in Lu Xun's creative works—the Boxer Rebellion and the Revolution of 1911—transcending the age and pursuing the age—past outcries and present hesitation—treatises on cursing life and *Wild Grass*—running up against walls on all sides and unable to find a way out—the future of the grave—petit-bourgeois observers—representatives of aberrant national character—appraisal of "The True Story of Ah Q"—the bygone age of Ah Q—period literature and period technique

I

No matter how many works Lu Xun writes, no matter the extent to which he is worshipped by some of his readers, and no matter how venomously witty the language in "The True Story of Ah Q," the fact is Lu Xun is not the representative of the present age.[1] Nor can the ideas contained in his

---

1. Qian Xingcun 錢杏邨 , "Siqule de A Q shidai" 死去了的阿Q時代, *Taiyang yuekan* 太陽月刊, Mar. 1, 1928. In this essay, Qian makes repeated reference to and cites Lu Xun's two collections of short stories, *Nahan* 吶喊 (Call to arms) and *Panghuang* 傍徨 (Hesitation), and his collection of prose poems, *Yecao* 野草 (Wild grass). English translations for most of the texts referred to can be found in Lu Xun 1980, or in William Lyell, tr., *Diary of a Madman and Other Stories* (Honolulu: University of Hawaii Press, 1992), and *Wild*

works represent the main trend in Chinese literature over the past ten years!

The transformation in Chinese literary thought during the past ten years, when analyzed in detail, has been as radical as the change in politics. Time and again we have witnessed new political ideologies become obsolete. One after another we have seen central political figures fail to grasp the age and be swamped by its angry tide. The persistent political fragmentation and betrayal of the revolution by the non-revolutionary classes during the past two years proves this over and over. The phenomenon in literary circles is the same. In the view of a few old writers, the Chinese literary world still seems to be dominated by their "humor," "taste," and "individualist trend."[2] In reality, the central forces silently shifted direction long ago, taking the road of revolutionary literature.

We will start with the May Fourth movement. Ostensibly, the May Fourth movement originated with a diplomatic provocation, but it is an undeniable fact that it was propelled by the spirit of the culture movement's initial stage, which lay latent in the hearts and minds of the youth. The initial stage of the culture movement created the glorious May Fourth, and because of the agitation caused by the May Fourth the culture movement developed to its utmost potential. Thus was the foundation for the ideological tide of the first phase of the New Culture movement laid. "Individualism" had already become a term of profanity in the ideological tide of this period. The youth came to regard social responsibility as their own personal obligation, and this made them question everything: society, the family, all the forces of the old society and the old system. They all stood up, turned toward society, and took up the great task of social reform. Thus, the writer who can truly represent this period is one whose works are imbued with shades of suspicion, express a complete mistrust of society, and demonstrate the death of the individualistic spirit.

This ideological tide developed gradually, but before it could completely unfold, Sun Yat-sen died and the May Thirtieth massacre followed soon after. With the impact of these two great attacks from within and without, and the recent tide of "isms" quietly fermenting in the hearts and minds of young people, the tide erupted during the May Thirtieth period with the suddenness and violence of a great volcano and transformed once again. The ideological tide of this period made huge advances: the youth of

---

Grass (Beijing: Foreign Languages Press, 1974; translators not indicated). The translators of the present essay have borrowed occasionally from these translations. Qian's references are to the original book publications of *Nahan* (Shanghai: Xinchao, 1923); *Panghuang* (Shanghai: Beixin, 1926); and *Yecao* (Shanghai: Beixin, 1927).

2. These are terms associated with the essayist and literary critic Lin Yutang 林語堂.

the entire nation became conscious of nationality and class, they came to an understanding of imperialism and at the same time fiercely demanded revolution. The concept of the individual clan nearly died in their hearts and minds. Following the first period of literary thought, the latent call for revolutionary literature could also gradually be heard, and much progress was made in literary circles.

After the May Thirtieth massacre, there was suddenly a great change in China's class structure. The power of the working and peasant classes gradually began to manifest itself. Again and again events spurred on the youth: the Shanghai workers' struggle against the May Thirtieth massacre; the nineteen-month strike by Hong Kong workers; the support of Hunan and Hubei workers for the revolutionary army campaign during the Northern Expedition; the three insurrections of Shanghai workers to drive out the Manchurian and Shandong warlord armies; the previous massacre of Beijing-Hankou railway workers on February 7, 1923; the help the revolutionary army received from the peasants wherever they went, and the revolutionary army's reliance on the peasants and workers as their primary force. One after another, these events incited the youth and made them dissatisfied with the ideological tide of the second period.[3] They went wholeheartedly over to the side of the workers and peasants to struggle against their bourgeois oppressors. These events stimulated the intense, bloody struggle that continues today. Escaping the bonds of the nation, the ideological tide turned toward the fight for unification of all the oppressed classes of the world. Consequently, the long-fermenting call of the proletarian fourth class's literary movement gradually began its upsurge, creating the present situation of interchange between revolutionary art and literature and workers' art and literature.

The changes in Chinese literature over the past ten years have been outlined above. We can now return to examine Lu Xun's works and see, after all, which ideological period of the New Literature movement they can represent. Apart from a few doubts about Confucian ethics expressed in "Diary of a Madman," the expression of some youthful spirit in "A Happy Family," and the historical backgrounds of "The Misanthrope" and "Storm in a Teacup," the great majority lack any contemporary relevance! Not only are his novels not ideological products of the age, they also lack characters that can represent the age! After all, to what period do characters like Ah Q,

---

3. Qian sees these events (surrounding the May Thirtieth movement) as signaling the dawn of a third period in the revolutionary movement begun with the May Fourth and May Thirtieth periods. Mao Dun, in his "On Reading *Ni Huanzhi*" (see the next essay in this volume), sees 1928 as the beginning of a new period, the "fourth period." Presumably, Mao Dun's periodization begins with the 1911 Revolution.

Chen Shicheng, Siming, and Gao Erchu belong? Those who have read *Call to Arms* and *Hesitation* can probably answer this question. Lü Weifu from "In the Tavern" says, "Old people's memories are long indeed!" (*Hesitation*, 44). We feel this sentence should really be accorded to Lu Xun—*old people's memories are long indeed*. He can unflaggingly narrate events from the age of the civil service exams and the Revolution of 1911 to dress up the "modern" literary scene, as if oblivious to recent changes. This is a rare feat indeed! "Things that appear when the sun goes down can't do you any good" (*Wild Grass*) becomes an appropriate criticism of Lu Xun. His works really do little good in terms of relevance to the age. Like the narrow world of imperial concubines of the High Tang, he depicts great events of the imperial court and nothing more. From our contemporary perspective, we just don't need this kind of thing.

We can therefore honestly say that Lu Xun's creative works do not have a modern flavor and cannot represent the modern age. The period of the great majority of his works passed long ago and is, moreover, distant and remote. The background and historical settings of his works make him very appropriately discussed in conjunction with Li Boyuan and Liu E. The period of Lu Xun's works is absolutely no later than the May Fourth. Indeed, they can really and truly only represent the ideological tide of the *New Citizen Journal* period.[4] They can indeed only represent the thought of the late Qing and the Boxer Rebellion eras. His works that can really represent the May Fourth era are few. On this point I hope the reader won't be mistaken: we are not saying that historical novels should not be written, but from the standpoint of literature's social mission we feel they should have some relevance to the present age. For the most part, however, this kind of spirit can be found neither in Lu Xun nor in Lu Xun's creative works.

Regardless of what country's literature one examines, there is no true writer of an age whose works do not take that age into account and represent it. The bit of spirit that transcends the age is the only life of a writer of an age! But what about Lu Xun's works? Naturally, he hasn't transcended the age. Not only has he never transcended the age, he has never grasped it. Not only has he never grasped the age, he has never pursued it. Being unable to catch up with the times, Hu Shi immersed himself in a pile of old papers.[5] What about Lu Xun? The spirit manifested in his works is a creative spirit that sees no need to give due consideration to the age. He has

---

4. *Xinmin congbao* 新民叢報 was a very influential late Qing journal edited by Liang Qichao.

5. After the split with Chen Duxiu over the political direction of *New Youth*, Hu Shi became involved in the movement to *zhengli guogu* 整理國故 , or review of the Chinese cultural heritage.

no way of catching up with the times. The motivation for his works is probably the same as the mood of Zijun: "sitting across from each other under the lamp reminiscing, pondering the pleasure of reconciling a conflict as if being born again" ("Regret for the Past," *Hesitation*, 187). Works written under the influence of this kind of ideology—based on the so-called individualistic model of literature—don't have the kind of eternal essence of great creations. They are the wasteful and meaningless sort of literary garbage associated with the diversions of the capitalist class!

Thus, in relation to the problem of the period represented by Lu Xun's works, according to *Call to Arms*, *Hesitation*, and *Wild Grass*, we feel that his thought stagnated when he reached the late Qing period. Because of this, if his works can be said to represent an age, it is only the age from the Boxer Rebellion to the end of the Qing. In other words, with the exception of his literary technique and a small number of works that can represent the spirit of the May Fourth period, most of his creative works don't illustrate the present age!

II

The names of his two collections of creative works, *Call to Arms* and *Hesitation*, really explain Lu Xun himself. Looking at those two creative works along with *Wild Grass*, we feel that he has never found a way out: all the while he is crying out, hesitating, and like a patch of wild grass, is never able to grow into a tall tree! In fact, what we can find in Lu Xun's creative works is only the past, only the past. At best they touch upon the present, but there is no future. And how about what Lu Xun has seen? It has already been stated very clearly in *Wild Grass*: the so-called future is the grave! Because the only future he perceives is the grave ("The Passer-by," *Wild Grass*, 41), he feels "all kinds of youth dash before me in procession, but I am surrounded by dusk" ("The Awakening," *Wild Grass*, 93). So he has tossed all his hopes into the grave, not even retaining one. He means that since hope is empty, one is better off without it. We can read his confession:

> Before this my heart was full of sanguinary songs: blood and iron, fire and poison, resurgence and revenge. Then suddenly all these became empty, but at times I deliberately filled my heart with useless, self-deluding hope. Hope, hope. Using this shield of hope I defied attack in the void of the dark night, although behind the shield was also dark night amid the void. Yet, in just this way I squandered my youth.

How could I not know that my youth had passed long age? But I believed youth still existed around me: stars, moonlight, stiff-fallen butterflies, flowers in the darkness, the inauspicious hoot of the owl, the blood-cry of the cuckoo, the vagueness of laughter, the soaring dance of love. . . . Though it was a dismal apathetic youth, it was nonetheless still youth.

But why is it lonely like this now? Could it be that even the youth around me have departed, that the young of the world have all grown old? ("Hope," *Wild Grass*, 21–22)

With such a bleak view, Lu Xun comes to feel that life is too bland. Yet he does not want to die and instead says, "I have to live a little longer" ("The Misanthrope")! He is quite convinced that "the world is not entirely without a way out for the fighter" ("Regret for the Past"). Nevertheless, he lives not for the future, but for "survival" ("Regret for the Past"). Survival is what he craves even though it is meaningless. Survival means simply to live, but living, after all, is painful. On the one hand, he sees a gloomy future and, on the other, he feels dissatisfied with present reality. He cannot find a way out, but he is unwilling to sink into depravity. As a result, he can only let out a few wild cries while hesitating at a fork in the road. He has meticulously dissected such psychology himself:

If I find heaven displeasing, I won't go; if I find hell displeasing, I won't go; if I find their future golden world displeasing, I won't go. Oh, no, I'm not willing to go; I'd rather "hesitate" in limbo.

I'm nothing but a shadow. I must leave you and sink into the darkness. But the darkness will swallow me; yet the light will also make me disappear. Nevertheless, I'm not willing to wander between light and darkness, I'd rather sink into the darkness. ("The Shadow's Leave-taking," *Wild Grass*, 6)

In this passage, Lu Xun completely reveals the nature of his evil petit-bourgeois habits. We can see the self-will, suspicion, jealousy, and the obstinate refusal of the petit-bourgeois class to admit mistakes. Accordingly, although there is a very clear path right in front of him, if there is "something displeasing," then he "won't go." He is neither satisfied with reality nor maintains hope in his ideals. Consequently, he can only linger on the wrong path and hesitate in limbo! This is the psychological reason Lu Xun still hasn't found the way out: he is impaired by his petit-bourgeois temperament! Actually, we are always running into people ruined by these kinds of attributes. If they don't drive the thoughts of leadership and heroism from their minds, there won't be any hope! Going one step further, we can say that the condition in which Lu Xun is mired is completely due to the damage from so-called liberal thought. Only contradiction results from liberal thought. Only wavering results from liberal thought. In this world, so-called liberal thought is just a term that deceives people, and Lu Xun is one of those who has been deceived. . . .

Just crying out in misery without trying to find a way out is Lu Xun's suicidal elixir. He drank this elixir without regret. . . . Perhaps at this point some people would like to refute me. To be sure, Lu Xun does appear to have a way out, as he mentions in "Regret for the Past." Yet what is his way out? "Deep mountains, marshlands, Shanghai's foreign concessions, a sumptuous feast beneath electric lights, the very darkest night, the stab of a sharp blade; soundless footsteps" ("Regret for the Past," *Hesitation*, 206). What kind of way out is this? We think it does not require any explanation. Because his way out is merely the economic solution for the present without any other consideration, it is extremely superficial, and he eventually becomes dissatisfied and gloomy. In the end, even this superficial hope disappears like a long, winding snake into the darkness ("Regret for the Past," *Hesitation* 212)! To be sure, Lu Xun has already been awakened and aroused by the pounding of pale bloodstains. Thus, in "Amid Pale Bloodstains" he says,

> The fierce rebel warrior rises from humanity; he stands towering above, clearly seeing all the past and present ruins and abandoned graves; he remembers all the deep and long-felt bitterness and pain; he squarely faces the whole welter of congealed blood, he knows that everything is dead, just born, to be born, or unborn. He sees through the Creator's tricks; he's going to raise humanity from the dead, or perhaps exterminate the human race, the Creator's good people. (*Wild Grass* 88–89)

But this kind of indignation is only that of a shallow sympathizer. We certainly have never seen him towering above humanity or fighting in the avant-garde. Actually, in Lu Xun's case, even such indignation is just a momentary soap bubble! He will not stand up. The rush of pale bloodstains cannot cover up his individualistic spirit. Although filled with totalistic rebelliousness, his thought amounts to an overflow of ideas devoid of much benefit. In the end, he's still hesitating! Furthermore, not only has he not stood up, he basically isn't even excited. No matter how the young people's blood boils, at best he stands by the wayside and whistles a few tunes! Look at "The Awakening" and we will see: "The spirits of the youth tower in front of my eyes, already having committed violence, or perhaps about to do so. Yet I love these bleeding and traumatized spirits because they make me feel that I am among people—living among people" (*Wild Grass* 91). What kind of meaningless, superficial thought is this? All in all he only cries out once or twice! . . . In sum, Lu Xun's thought merely harbors doubts and offers no solutions: "Boxed in on all sides, with nails pounded in from the outside. I am completely defeated. Alas, I'm done for!" ("After Death," *Wild Grass* 74).

Because of the stagnation in Lu Xun's thought and his inability to move forward, he couldn't help but immerse himself in recollections of the past and draw upon them to write *Call to Arms* and *Hesitation*. He couldn't help but turn life into something miserable, dark, and gloomy. And because of this, he said that life is painful, abnormal, and unsound. He used a slowly melting snow Buddha to symbolize the gloom of life; he used "Tombstone Inscriptions" to explain the masochism in life; he also used "Tremors of Degradation" to explain the suffering of a person's entire life. He feels that life is devoid of even the slightest bit of light. We can see this from the examples below:

But the snow Buddha just sits there alone. The sunny days melt his skin, and the cold nights put a layer of ice on him, changing him into a kind of a translucent crystal. Successive sunny days change him into I don't know what, and the rouge on his lips also fades away. ("Snow," *Wild Grass*, 26)

I tear out my heart to eat it, because I want to know its true taste. But the wound is excruciatingly painful, so how can I know its true taste?. . . When the pain subsides, I slowly eat it. But the heart is already old, so how can I know its original taste? ("Tombstone Inscriptions," *Wild Grass*, 61)

Her bare body exposed, she stood like a stone statue in the middle of the field. Suddenly, the entire past flashed before her eyes: starvation, anguish, surprise, humiliation, elation, and as a result she began to tremble; tormented, wronged, compromised, and the ensuing convulsions; killing and its resultant tranquillity. . . . Again, everything instantaneously came together: affectionate reminiscences and the unequivocal termination of relations; loving caresses and revenge; nurturing and annihilating; giving blessings and bitterly cursing. ("Tremors of Degradation," *Wild Grass* 65)

Lu Xun sees life just like this, and so upon opening *Wild Grass* one feels assailed by a chill, a gloomy feeling, as if going down an ancient path. If it's not life's depression, it's a dark fate; if not ruthless slaughter, it's society's hostility; if not the death of hope, it's the destruction of life; if not the massacre of the spirit, it's the worship of dreams; if not the curse that all humanity should perish, it's an explanation of humanity's evil and bestial transformation. . . . All this leads the youth onto the road of death and destruction, and has dug countless graves for those who follow him. Thus, he explains the cessation of life: "Shouldering the heavy burden of the void and walking the so-called road of life under an inexorably cold gaze: how frightening a thing this is! Worse yet, at the end of this road is a tombstone without an inscription" ("Regret for the Past," *Hesitation*, 206).

Here Lu Xun is greatly mistaken. Even if humanity is "fierce like a lion, with a rabbit's timidity and the slyness of a fox" ("Diary of a Madman," *Call to Arms*, 10), what about good hopes? What about the so-called bright side of life? Humanity is not without the hope of improvement, nor does it lack a way out. Since pain and boredom have origins, there is eventually a way out, and a bright avenue emerges in front of our eyes. Yet he deliberately refuses to take it. Instead he takes a blind alley just to display the spirit of running up against a wall. What is the ultimate meaning of all this? Lu Xun's observations about life tell us only that he is a desecrater of life who doubts reality and lacks revolutionary spirit. He can do nothing but curse. When has he ever "placed a kiss on the formless, colorless, fresh bloody violence" ("The Awakening," *Wild Grass*, 91)? And when has he ever thought of the anguish of hesitation, the meaninglessness of outcry, the realization of hope and the brightness of the future? He said the following:

> Yet, I'm also unwilling that they live life out of anger, just like me, bitter and unsettled. I'm also unwilling that they should live bitter, benumbed lives like Runtu's. I'm also unwilling that they live bitter, reckless lives like other people's. They should have new lives, the kind of lives we have never lived ("My Old Home," *Call to Arms*, 110).

These words are nothing but momentary exhilaration! The lives we've lived are not as gloomy and pathetic as the ones that Lu Xun has seen!

III. The Bygone Age of Ah Q

Lu Xun, however, still has Lu Xun's good points, and Lu Xun still has Lu Xun's status. Although "The True Story of Ah Q" is not a great work, it can truly represent Lu Xun himself. We do not want to talk about the techniques of "The True Story of Ah Q" here. Hidden in "The True Story of Ah Q" is the aberrant national character of China's past—a point worthy of our attention. The necessity that a work represent the national character, following past theories, objectively prevents us from refuting the ideological tide of the age in "The True Story of Ah Q." Lu Xun was able to grasp and express the aberrant part of the national character quite succinctly. This is very difficult to accomplish and not readily found in his other creative works. After reading "The True Story of Ah Q," we are left with at least two deep impressions from which we can determine the special characteristics of Chinese of the past. The first of these so-called impressions is our recognition that from an attitude of passive fatalism the Chinese of earlier ages became pitiful and detestable beings who bore no opinions about life and merely lived and died in ignorance. The second impression is our recognition of the deceitfulness, maliciousness, snobbishness, and various other similar coldhearted characteristics, of the Chinese people, as well as their use of social class and powerful connections to bully others. These two absolutely opposed kinds of character, indeed the most significant part of the Chinese people's aberrant character, have been explicitly revealed in one of Lu Xun's short stories. We can therefore objectively say that this work may represent the bygone, aberrant national character of the Chinese people. As such, it is the one work of Lu Xun's most worthy of commemoration.

The good points of this work are that it not only represents the aberrant national character, but at the same time dissects a part of the thought of people in farming villages during the initial period of the Revolution of 1911. More generally speaking, Ah Q's thought also represents a part of the mass ideology in the cities at that time. To grasp Ah Q's life most easily, we have to analyze the thought of village peasants of the period. Of course the peasants had just awakened from the dreamworld of emperors and vassals. The emperors ruled by the principle that people could be governed as long as they remained unenlightened. This was particularly true for country folk since few could read, and even those who learned how were only trained to know their place. As such, it is natural that a vast number of people were as muddled as Ah Q. "The True Story of Ah Q" thus came into being as a response to the times! That was when the gentry class rode roughshod in the countryside, frequented government offices, and bullied and humiliated the weak. It was a natural tendency of the peasants, unenlightened as they were, not to dare to resist, but simply endure such treatment in silence. Once the revolutionary army arose and overthrew the entire ruling class, how could the ignorant, long-suffering peasants not be indignant and begin to think of revenge? Look at Ah Q's sympathy toward the revolutionary party and his idea, "So revolution it is. Revolt against this frigging bunch! They are so abominable! So hateful! . . . Even me, I'll throw in with the revolutionary party too" (*Call to Arms*, 161), Here we can imagine the psychology that caused the peasants to vent their anger at that time. Ah Q wanted to join the revolution to vent his anger and to take pleasure in the revolu-

True Story of Ah Q" has its good points and it has a status of its own, but it cannot possibly represent the age. The age of Ah Q died long ago! The death of the age of Ah Q is already very distant! If we haven't yet forgotten that age, then we had better hurry up and bury Ah Q! Courageous peasants have already given us the material for many valuable, sound, and glorious works. We will never again need the age of Ah Q.

Not only has the age of Ah Q already died, but the technique of "The True Story of Ah Q" has also died! If we use the standards of petit-bourgeois literature to examine the technique of "The True Story of Ah Q," we will of course see it has many extremely good points and many places worthy of our praise. But it is already dead. It is already dead! The present age is not one that can be grasped by the insidious and venomous writer; the present age is not one that can be represented by the pen of a subtle and witty writer; the present age is not one that can be represented by a writer without political ideology! An old bottle cannot hold new wine, an old woman will never be able to recover the beauty of her youth, and the ingenuity of "The True Story of Ah Q" died along with Ah Q. This violent, stormy age can only be represented by a writer with a violent and stormy revolutionary spirit. This age can only be represented by an author whose entire body is burning with faithful and sincere emotion, who has an intimate knowledge of politics, and who stands on the front line of the revolution! The technique of "The True Story of Ah Q" does not have the power to do this! The age of Ah Q died long ago! We need not be infatuated with skeletons. Let us bury Ah Q's body and spirit together. Let us bury Ah Q's body and spirit together! . . .

Shanghai, February 17–18, 1928

Postscript

"The Bygone Age of Ah Q" can now be considered finished, but there is something I should add here. My commentary is based entirely on Lu Xun's three works—*Call to Arms*, *Hesitation*, and *Wild Grass*. All judgments have also been based on these three works. This cannot, therefore, be considered a complete treatise on Lu Xun. In the assessment of the true value of Lu Xun, I feel his articles, random thoughts, and translations are even more important than his creative works. He had great power and status in the initial phase of China's new literature movement. At the same time, his works were also a great help in advancing new literature. This is a fact that cannot be erased. However, this article only discusses his creative works,

Chapter 31

On Reading Ni Huanzhi

Mao Dun

I

Even those most prone to forgetfulness would likely not forget that ten years ago on this very day arose the epoch-making May Fourth movement.[1] Who cannot picture in their mind or distinctly recall the energy unleashed from that initial awakening of men's minds.

Now a full ten years have gone by. The "heroes" who rose with the great May Fourth tide have passed through numerous metamorphoses. One need not dwell on those many who rose and ebbed with the tide of the May Fourth; even the fates of the prominent "pillars" of that time give one much food for thought. Some died of illness, some were martyred for the cause, some retired, some degenerated, some turned reactionary, and some stagnated. Each in his respective manner revealed his true colors before Mr. History. The wheel of an historical epoch ground down the spineless with-

---

1. Mao Dun 茅盾, "Du Ni Huanzhi" 讀倪煥之, *Wenxue zhoubao* 文學週報 8, no. 20 (1929): 591–614; reprinted in *WXYDSLX*.

out mercy! Only those who were strong of limb could keep pace with the times, but in the end most became "outcasts."

A friend once openly expressed the following opinion: "Many people consider the course from the May Fourth to the present a linear succession; that is wrong, for the May Fourth and the present are two obviously different periods." He classified the May Thirtieth as a separate, great epoch and called the present time "the eve of the fourth period." This observation strikes me as being quite correct. However, we cannot but recognize that although the activists before and after the May Thirtieth have in spirit progressed beyond the May Fourth, they belong nonetheless to the few bravest offspring of the May Fourth. Without the May Fourth, there would probably have been no May Thirtieth and, by the same token, there would probably have been no so-called eve of the fourth period today. So is history determined.

II

Let us now turn back to the past. What are the conspicuous remains back there, piled up high, of the great May Fourth? A few philosophy books in translation; a few volumes of magazines with the common heading of "new" this and "new" that, on whose pages all kinds of incompatible "new thoughts" are presented side by side and expounded with equal enthusiasm; translations of some French and Russian literary works. The promotion of a new literature was perhaps the most significant slogan of the May Fourth, yet literary works reflecting this great epoch never appeared. The short stories of Lu Xun, which had the most impact at that time and were later collected together in the volume *Call to Arms*, certainly represent the spirit of the May Fourth in their attack on traditional thought. However, they do not reflect the continuously changing consciousness of the people during and after the May Fourth. In *Call to Arms* can be heard the sound of the crumbling edifice of feudal society, the bewilderment and panic of the old and useless adherents to the feudal society in their final desperate struggle; there are also the dark backward villages of Old China, inaccessible to the impact of the wave of new thought, unaware even of the changing of dynasties; as well as the sons and daughters living in those dark secluded villages of Old China. But the cities are not there, nor are there the pounding hearts of the urban youth. Some people have criticized *Call to Arms* for this, saying that Lu Xun has not represented life in contemporary China, that the principal sentiment of *Call to Arms* is attachment to and sadness for the decline of the feudal outlook. But this view is unjust. I have written an essay to rebut this impression; to my surprise I was said to be "toadying to Lu Xun." To this day I remain firm in my former conviction; I still believe that *Call to Arms* does represent life in contemporary China, only that the life represented in the work is the life hidden in secluded dark corners of Chinese villages impervious to change; I still believe that the central theme of *Call to Arms* is an attack on traditional thought, although the method used to achieve this is a negative satire. Weighing the matter calmly, we must admit that changes in Chinese villages with the so-called underground spring peasant movement, as some critics so firmly hold, have come about only during the last two or three years. At the time when Lu Xun was writing about village life in *Call to Arms*, these villages were just like the ones Lu Xun depicted. Moreover, if we face up to the actual reality today, we must admit that there are still in China many villages and many sons and daughters of Old China like those presented in *Call to Arms*. Wang Tongzhao's recently published short story "Swirling Snow, Troubled Dreams"[2] is nothing but a realistic portrait of some Shandong villages in the year 1928. Although we do not like the nostalgic and melancholy sentiment of the characters in the piece, the facts cannot be denied. From the preface to *Call to Arms*, we can see that Lu Xun was in a rather pessimistic mood when writing some of its stories, which also explains why he specifically chose to write about these backwater villages around the time of the May Fourth. He was directing his incisive irony at the excessively optimistic and at the same time providing a sharp contrast to city life, which had been stirred by the angry wave of the May Fourth. I think we should understand the contents of *Call to Arms* in this manner, although we cannot but admit at the same time that it is unfortunate that *Call to Arms* did not capture the keynote of the May Fourth urban melody.

Just as the purpose of the title *Call to Arms* is brought out in its preface, the meaning of Lu Xun's second collection of short stories, *Wandering*, can be seen in the quotation from "Encountering Sorrow" that appears at the beginning of the book. In *Wandering* there are two pieces depicting life in the city, "Happy Family" and "Regret for the Past." On the surface these two works deal with love, but what is intimated beneath the ostensible topic covers a much broader range. Here is a clear statement of the frustrations of the young people after the May Fourth. So we have found at least two examples portraying the life of young urban intellectuals who are the keynote players of the May Fourth melody. But just as the depiction of the villages in *Call to Arms* could only represent one segment of life in contemporary China, so also these two pieces in *Wandering* represent but a segment

---

2. Wang Tongzhao 王統照 (1897–1957), "Jiao tian feng xue meng laosao" 攪天風雪夢牢騷; first published in *Haosheng* (The call of the bugle) (Shanghai: Fudan shuju, 1928).

of the life of the young people in the May Fourth epoch, leaving us still dissatisfied.

III

Authors other than Lu Xun have used the life of contemporary young people as the main subject of their work. "Sinking" by Yu Dafu, *The Sorrows of Mr. Zhao* by Xu Qinwen, *The Night of Spring Rain* by Wang Tongzhao, *Smile in a Dream* by Zhou Quanping, *Taili* by Zhang Ziping—these are all outstanding examples.[3] But the life reflected in these works remains narrow and partial; we cannot find in them the range of perturbation of the young after the "May Fourth." Recently, Luo Mei[4] wrote to me, "I feel that during this period the psychology of 'wandering' is really of a very widespread type. Another 'keynote' is the material poverty of intellectuals, expressed in many fictional works with unprecedented 'sharp' [*sic*]" (cf. the original letter in *Literature Weekly* 8, no. 10). This judgment is correct, but I still believe that works of this period have failed to express sufficiently the sentiment of wandering of the young in actual life. To pursue the point further, I believe that works of this period have not captured the broad and profound background of this "wandering": such as the confusion in the ideological realm, the basic instability of society, and the complex, deadlocked struggle between the forces of the old and the new, with no clear sign of victory or defeat. Since they depict only superficially some cases of depression, works of this period lack a strong and pervasive social significance. The portrayal of the frustrations of the young in "Sinking" can be considered of "oustanding talent and peerless beauty." Yet if we analyze the background of the hero's depression, it is surprising how little social significance there is to it. No wonder that works imitating "Sinking" are but worthless pornographic pamphlets that do not even give expression to a small part of the frustration of the epoch.

Similarly, the psychological love stories of Zhang Ziping, Xu Qinwen, and Zhou Quanping all fail to express with any force that it is the aimless and frustrated youth of the May Fourth whose psychology of love is being presented. Even though the *The Sorrows of Mr. Zhao* and *Taili* are well written, they unfortunately do not carry the distinguishing brand of the epoch.

---

3. Yu Dafu, "Chenlun" 沈淪; first published in *Chenlun* (Shanghai: Taidong shuju, 1921). Xu Qinwen 許欽文 (1897–1984), *Zhao xiansheng de fannao* 趙先生的煩惱 (Shanghai: Beixin shuju, 1928). Wang Tongzhao, *Chun yu zhi ye* 春雨之夜 (Shanghai: Shangwu yinshuguan, 1924). Zhou Quanping 周全平, *Mengli de weixiao* 夢裏的微笑 (Shanghai: Gaunghua, 1925). Zhang Ziping 張資平, *Taili* 苔莉 (Shanghai: Guanghua, 1927).

4. Luo Mei 羅美; the indentity of this person remains unknown.

When we analyze Mr. Zhao's sorrows, we sense that his spiritual world is occupied only by love and the suspicion and jealousy it engenders. Taili is a woman of the same sort. Read purely as portraits of love, we cannot say that these works are unsuccessful, but when we look for a deeper representation of the spirit of the May Fourth era, we come away feeling dissatisfied.

I do not now remember very well the content of *Night of Spring Rain*, but my general impression is that one does not sense in it any thorough characterization of the epoch. Comparatively speaking, Wang Tongzhao strives more consciously to depict the influence of the May Fourth on the thoughts of the young. But we might as well admit that he has not grasped the basic melody of the May Fourth in his portrayal.

Of course one cannot say that these few authors represent all of May Fourth literature. I have not brought books with me on my travels and can only give the above summary discussion from what I can recall, but I believe that it pretty well describes the general situation.

IV

Why is it that the great May Fourth could not produce literary works representative of the epoch? It would be wrong to say that this was because at this early stage the "new literature" was not yet ready to produce mature works. If maturity is the only consideration, we cannot say that the authors mentioned above did not produce "mature" works. The problem lies elsewhere. At that time there was a confusing hodgepodge of literary theories distracting the attention of writers! More specifically, the real reason is that at that time there emerged a school that overlooked the social character of literature, objected to literature's social significance, and loudly proclaimed the doctrine of "art for art's sake," thereby leading many writers astray. Here we should recall a few things from that time!

Today, at the mention of such a phrase as "the contemporary and social character of literature," the so-called revolutionary literary critics stand up angrily and shout "too old and gray!" Perhaps not everyone has forgotten that the selfsame revolutionary literary critics five or six years ago were doing their utmost to deny the contemporary and social character of literature. For these are none other than the erstwhile gentlemen of the Creation Society. Even the most forgetful must still remember that at that time those pillars of the Creation Society, Guo Moruo and Cheng Fangwu, forcefully attacked and labeled as utilitarianism any requirement that literature have contemporary relevance and a social dimension—the view expounded by their opponents among the members of the Literary Research Association, called by a third party the "art for life school." At that time the slogan of the Creation Society was "art for art's sake," and they made such statements as: "Poisonous mushrooms are beautiful even though poisonous. The poet is content to contemplate their beauty; only the vulgar remember the poison." Sentimentality and individualism pervade their works from that period. Nearly all the things Cheng Fangwu bitterly cursed last year are transgressions he was himself guilty of earlier; this is an interesting new form of confession. Why did the views of the Creation Society have so many followers at that time? Because it was a period of "indecision and frustration," because the May Thirtieth had not yet occurred, because the gentlemen of the Creation Society were living in their ivory tower, and because sentimentality, individualism, hedonism, and aestheticism offered a momentary intoxication for the abnormal psychology of "indecisive and frustrated" youths. That the epoch of the May Thirtieth had not yet arrived and that the members of the Creation Society were still living in their ivory tower also explains how the gentlemen of the Creation Society, propagating sentimentality, individualism, hedonism, and aestheticism, also shared the widespread sense of "indecision and frustration" at that time. Their means of escape then was to amuse themselves with that "plaything, bourgeois literature," which they curse today, and not just for their own amusement, but to use it to assert a place for themselves in the world. Just at that time, however, May Thirtieth appeared on the Chinese horizon, and in Western Europe an emergent proletarian literature had become the focus of international attention (in Japan proletarian literature remained quiescent). If at that time Mr. Guo, Mr. Cheng, and their colleagues had gotten out of their "snail's house" on Rue Joffre in the French Concession in Shanghai and tried to participate actively in underground work, they would probably have had something better to do than to amuse themselves with the plaything of bourgeois literature. To speak more explicitly and to borrow the words Cheng Fangwu used last year, if they had chosen not to be so "unrevolutionary" and so "petit bourgeois," then Cheng Fangwu's brave statement of last year would have been uttered years ago. Perhaps only "Mr. Epoch" knows why it happened as it did.

I have said all this not to settle old accounts, but to illustrate how greatly people's consciousness is influenced by historical forces. It also helps explain why six years ago Cheng Fangwu was able to defend "the palace of artistic art" with all seriousness and six years later could just as seriously defend "the palace of revolutionary literature." His actions were guided by the law of necessity and were not necessarily opportunistic or done just to attract attention, as has been crudely conjectured. Moreover, this may also explain the influence on others of their having mistakenly picked up the "plaything, bourgeois literature," for their amusement instead of participating in practical underground work. Their mistake had led some astray and now they rail at those who misled others. Therefore, it was not accidental that during the May Fourth era there were no literary works reflecting the epoch—let alone works to guide the development of events.

Consider the effect the "plaything bourgeois literature" had on the literary world. Everybody will presumably remember that the publishing world was full of works of "impromptu fiction"[5] that were sentimental, individualistic, hedonistic, and aesthetic. These works reflected only the very narrow environment of individuals, of sensual stimuli and fleeting emotions. The "non-collectivist" *Sorrows of Young Werther* became the plaything and narcotic of indecisive and frustrated youths. In this miasma, literature did not reflect the epoch, still less did it have any social character.

Up until the time of the May Thirtieth movement, the first fruit of our underground work, this miasma remained stifling. But then the wheel of progress gave a push to the aesthetes in their ivory tower. It was about a year later that the Creation Society issued a manifesto changing its direction. In the early spring of last year, as I recall, *Sun Monthly* and *Cultural Review* (of the Creation Society) even published attacks on each other, competing quite unabashedly to be the orthodox "revolutionary literature" or claiming a "patent" on its discovery. Strongly prone to forgetfulness, Cheng Fangwu not only forgot what he proposed five years ago on the "age of art for art's sake school" (of course this forgetfulness is commendable), he also forgot what he had learned only yesterday, the ABCs of the dialectical method: namely, that human thought is determined by the social environment and the social environment is determined by economic conditions. The argument about "orthodoxy" or "patents" is therefore quite senseless. Needless to say, the manifesto of the Creation Society announcing its change of attitude expressed no regret about its past, exhibiting rather a kind of attitude of foresight or "perspicacity," or being in the "vanguard"; this makes it hard for those who are less forgetful to refrain from smiling. But we can appreciate that the change from individualism, heroism, and idealism to collectivism and materialism is really not so easy as turning one's body about. I therefore feel it unnecessary to complain too much that their manifesto retains some flavor of the old dregs.

---

5. *Jiyu xiaoshuo* 即 與 小 說 seems to be a term coined by Mao Dun to refer to fiction written by members of the Creation Society. Its origins may be in Japan where the term *jiyu shi* 詩 (impromptu poetry) is common.

V

What has been said above is not meant to probe anybody's "old wounds," it is intended only as an example to show the tremendous influence of an epoch on the human mind. Even the Creation Society is no exception. Apparently they have finally awakened and cast off the "plaything of bourgeois literature," which they once so staunchly defended, to march with the May Thirtieth epoch. This is but one example we have on hand. Still there are many anonymous people who have formed no society or club, but who have as individuals kept pace with the progress of one epoch after another! The amalgamation of these nameless figures constitutes the life force of the society of an epoch. For a work to describe this life force, even though it may not point out any clear course for the future, is at least comparable in spirit to a work of collectivism. It has frequently occurred to me that May Fourth passed without leaving any literary works representing the period. If now one should describe how the May Fourth influenced one person and how that person, having experienced the May Thirtieth, arrived at the so-called eve of the fourth period—roughly the experience of the members of the Creation Society described above—then that would be a not altogether insignificant work. This opinion of mine has found a fitting resonance in the novel *Ni Huanzhi* by Ye Shaojun.[6]

Ni Huanzhi was published in *Education Magazine* under the heading of "educational literature," a category quite appropriate to the plot of that novel. The protagonist Ni Huanzhi, in the first nineteen chapters, which occupy more than half of the novel, is a primary-school teacher by profession. He and his comrade Jiang Bingru, the principal of the school, work extremely hard in a backwater village experimenting with the new education. They meet with no sympathy from the community, nor do they win the understanding or enthusiastic support of their colleagues; nonetheless, Ni Huanzhi carries on with great zeal. At this time he believes that education will be his lifelong career, and he greatly values its power, as seen in his maxim, "All hope hinges on education." But then the May Fourth comes to this village and Ni Huanzhi receives the full force of its furious tide. His ideas begin to change; meanwhile, he feels disillusioned in his career as an educator, in his hopes for a new family system, and in his ideals about marriage. He feels lonely. Wanting to search for new meanings in life and new forms of struggle, he leaves the village for the metropolis of Shanghai. Then the May Thirtieth occurs. The furious tide of May 30 pushes Ni Huanzhi

---

6.Ye Shaojun 葉 紹 鈞 , *Ni Huanzhi* 倪 煥 之 ; first published serially in *Jiaoyu zazhi* 1928.

even further: although he still works as a teacher in a girls high school, he also participates in political movements. At the time of the revolutionary high tide in 1927, he, too, is a part of the vital force of his society. And then, with the abrupt change in the state of affairs brought about by the counter-revolutionary coup, his heart breaks, he becomes disillusioned, sorrow-stricken, indignant. Typhus ends his life's journey. During his final delirious hour, he utters the following: "Not yet thirty-five years old, with nothing accomplished, how can one simply die like this? Alas! let it be, let it be. When one's strength is so feeble and fragile and one's emotions so unstable, it is useless, utterly useless . . . success, that is not a prize we are worthy of, in the future there will be people of an entirely different kind, let them get the prize."

In the past few years, there have probably been quite a number of people like Ni Huanzhi. One can hardly claim in all fairness that the character Ni Huanzhi is a heroic revolutionary of any magnitude. One need only note that after witnessing the great calamity, he can do no more than drown his grief in wine and weep profusely; it is obviously true, as he himself learns by the time of his death, that his strength is fragile and feeble, his emotions unstable, and that he is utterly useless. However, his eager yearning for goodness is still something that deserves our sympathy.

Ye Shaojun has written five collections of short stories: *Barriers, Conflagration, Under Battle Fire, In the City,* and *Beyond Saturation. Ni Huanzhi* is his first novel; it is also the first time he has undertaken to depict society at large. This is certainly the first full-length novel whose setting is the historical development of the past ten years. Moreover, it must be said that this is also the first work which consciously attempts to trace the development of one character—an intellectual from the petit-bourgeois class, full of revolutionary zeal—showing how he is influenced by the historical tide of the past ten years, how he moves from the countryside to the city, from single-minded devotion to education to mass movements, from liberalism to collectivism. On these two points, *Ni Huanzhi* is praiseworthy. What I said above about the abrupt passing of the May Fourth era and the need for novels that retrace the influence of this era on the minds of people is realized in the example of *Ni Huanzhi*. I also said above that the literary world after the May Fourth was full of "impromptu fiction" written rather casually, that many authors regarded fiction as the flash that comes with the sudden bursting forth of genius, achievable only fortuitously for a split second, requiring no cultivation or forging, no acute observations, no cool analysis, no careful thinking. They merely collected fragmentary impressions and searched their empty heads for their so-called inspiration; very few consciously attempted to depict contemporary phenomena or social life. It seems that, to date, this vogue has still not changed. I therefore feel even more strongly that novels such as *Ni Huanzhi*, which is done with a purpose, are very much deserving of praise today.

But perhaps *Education Magazine* originally asked Ye Shaojun for a piece of "educational literature" bearing upon the question of education; hence, the first half of *Ni Huanzhi* is completely devoted to depicting village education, and thereby the novel as a whole suffers from being top heavy. Artistically speaking, this must be considered a flaw in the structure. For this reason, moreover, the book may be mistaken for one that is only about education.

This book, however, does contain a clear and straightforward depiction of May Thirtieth. In the first half of Chapter 22, when Ni Huanzhi has turned into a politically active character, the writing is full of life. But in the next chapter, the author resorts to the individual reflections of Ni Huanzhi as a means of putting into relief the circumstances of the time; he has not portrayed the circumstances directly in a positive manner. It cannot be denied that this, too, is an artistic flaw. It slackens the pace of the narrative and does not suit the tense atmosphere of the times. Moreover, the flashback in the second half of Chapter 22, immediately following the fiery positive portrayal, also significantly obstructs the thrust of the first half. Ni Huanzhi by this time has probably already joined a certain political organization, but there is no description of the background to this organization in the narrative of Ni Huanzhi's activities after Chapter 22. As a consequence, the narrative inevitably drifts off into the high-flown actions of one individual. This also damages the basic theme of the novel. The author is busy making a living by his profession and must therefore have written the novel on stolen time. The chapters in the novel were likely written at odd times, one by one, and although there is some coherence in the overall structure, there are inevitably gaps in the arrangement of the parts.

In the last chapter, we are told after the death of Ni Huanzhi that his wife, Jin Peizhang, suddenly becomes brave. This turn of events reflects the author's conscious belief in the "future," but, if we look back and compare it with the portrayal of Jin Peizhang at the beginning of Chapter 24, as Ni Huanzhi sees her, we cannot help but feel that her sudden transformation at the end is somewhat abrupt. From Chapter 24 to the last chapter, more than a year elapses, and an extremely eventful year it is. It is, therefore, possible that Jin Peizhang could have undergone such a change in her outlook. But the author mentions nothing after Chapter 24 about Jin Peizhang's actions except to tell us of her abrupt turnaround in the concluding section, as if the transformation of a person's outlook could occur so "miraculously." We can infer from this that the author must have concluded the book too hastily.

Therefore, whether one thinks in terms of the development of the plot or in terms of the development of the characters, the first half of *Ni Huanzhi* is written with greater polish than the second half. In the first half, we see that Ni Huanzhi moves in a well-defined environment; in the second half, we begin to feel that Ni Huanzhi is only moving in front of a painted backdrop that seems insubstantial and unreal. Insofar as characterization is concerned, in the first half of the book Ni Huanzhi, Jiang Bingru, and Jin Peizhang all are three-dimensional characters. But in the second half even the main character, Ni Huanzhi, has become a flat, paper-thin figure, simply flitting about in front of stage backdrops. Hence, even though the plot in the second half is much more exciting, it nonetheless fails to yield as deep and solid an impression as the first half. By that time the author was likely eager to finish the novel and was no longer taking the same care or pride in his work. Moreover, the deadline for the last of the yearly twelve issues of *Education Magazine* was also drawing near, and the author as a matter of course had no chance to weigh his words. This may also account for the unsatisfactory second half of *Ni Huanzhi*.

VI

In my opinion, when criticizing a novel one must not measure it in a hairsplitting manner, arbitrarily using one's own yardstick. As far as the artistic achievements of a novel are concerned, it is best to let each reader make his own appraisal. What I have said above about the artistic dimensions of *Ni Huanzhi* is nothing more than my personal impression. It is not to be taken as my main point of emphasis. In addition to the point about "consciously depicting what influence the May Fourth has on an individual and how that person passes through the May Thirtieth and arrives at the so-called eve of the fourth period," I want to stress the "feeling of an epoch" in this novel. Let me say a few words on this latter point.

To endow a novel with the "feeling of an epoch," it is not sufficient to merely depict the atmosphere of the epoch. (A work that neglects to express even this atmosphere of the epoch, however beautifully it is written, can only be a literary plaything of the bourgeoisie.) In addition to this atmosphere, this so-called feeling of an epoch should contain, in my view, two other essential ingredients: first, the nature of the epoch's influence on people and, second, how the collective life force of the people pushes the times in new directions (in other words, how it hastens the movement of history into inevitably new eras, or how the collective activities of the people cause historical inevitability to be realized earlier). This is the meaning of "feeling of an epoch" that current literature of the new realist school insists on.

Let us now look at the novel *Ni Huanzhi* again to see whether it has the "feeling of an epoch" in this sense.

Undeniably it depicts the atmosphere of the epoch. Although during his tenure as a primary-school teacher the central character firmly believes that "all hope hinges on education," after the May Fourth his doubts about this exclusive concern with education and his feeling of loneliness come to resemble the kind of indecision and frustration that prevailed among the intellectuals after the May Fourth. Next, the influence of the epoch on people finds its clear expression in the very person of Ni Huanzhi. It is obviously the force of the tide of the epoch that leads Ni Huanzhi from education to mass movement, and from liberalism to collectivism. But Ni Huanzhi is, after all, a feeble intellectual from the petit-bourgeois class. Even though the epoch pushes him forward, he cannot make himself an inseparable part of the social life force that makes for progress. Even though he says "we should turn the wheel of history, so that it spins faster than usual," he does not really have any clear idea of either the wheel of history or how to make it spin faster. Thus, at a time when the revolutionary situation becomes extremely precarious, he is needlessly worried that "the students have gone on a strike, and there are no definite plans for resuming classes," and for this reason he experiences disillusionment. After the abrupt change in the political situation, he lapses into his old habit of more than ten years earlier of going alone to a wine shop to get thoroughly drunk. In his delirium before dying, he sees workers clenching their iron hammers, wearing blue cotton shirts with chests bared, finally crushed under a shower of rocks like a pile of burned-out cinders. He comments to himself: "You have no part in this!" So even if he has some confused hope for the future, he has eyes only for his wife and son, but not for the masses.

This is true not only of the character of Ni Huanzhi. Even in the depiction of the character Wang Leshan, who better understands the meaning of revolution, we are not shown what work he has done to advance the epoch. The portrayal of Wang Leshan is all in profile; we can only vaguely infer what his activities may be, without getting any more positive or deep impression.

VII

So much for an analysis of the "feeling of an epoch" in *Ni Huanzhi* as I see it. I suspect that there are many people who do not like this novel because of this weakness. But isn't it "expecting a grown rooster when seeing an egg" to expect a world-shattering work at such a time as the present in the backward East? When many authors now rely on a little secondhand dialectics or commonsensical social science to write (with their excessive conceit) "impromptu fiction" full of what they call revolutionary sentiment, such a serious work as *Ni Huanzhi* deserves our praise despite its many defects.

To achieve brilliant results for the new literature after the era of May Thirtieth or on the "eve of the fourth period," we must first ask for a balanced development and maturing of content and form (i.e., thought and skill). Writers should realize that a little secondhand commonsense social science is not enough and that it will not do to write fiction in the enthusiastic style of mass meeting agitation. One who prepares to devote himself to the new art and literature must first have a head for organization, judgment, observation, and analysis; it is not enough to be equipped with a trumpet that will serve to transmit one's voice. One must first be able to analyze by oneself the mixed noises of the masses and quietly listen to the dripping of the underground spring, and then structure these into the consciousnesses of fictional characters. One should painstakingly hone one's craftsmanship and choose subjects with which one is most familiar. Last year I wrote an essay, "From Guling to Tokyo,"[7] pointing out the strange phenomenon visible in the literary world of "balancing a stone plate on one's head over an empty belly." I expressed the belief that such an act would not keep the stone plate on one's head, but would injure the belly. I suggested that writers with lofty goals would do better to choose for their subject the environment most familiar to them and at the same time most suitable for the majority of potential readers, namely, the petit-bourgeois class. I simply did not approve of the proletarian literature that they were so enthusiastically advocating; it could neither express the consciousness of the proletarian class nor be understood by that class; as proletarian literature it was a kind of quack remedy sold by traveling salesmen or a commercial advertisement. My stand attracted a good many malicious attacks. Malicious attacks, of course, are nothing unusual in this China where there is no distinction between black and white, right and wrong. But I was surprised by an article by Mr. Kexing [Qian Xingcun] in *Creation Monthly* and one by Mr. Pan Zinian in *Recognition*,[8] where a number of con-

---

7. "*Cong Guling dao Dongjing*" 從牯嶺到東京, *Xiaoshuo yuebao* 19, no. 10 (1928); for an English translation, see Berninghausen and Huters 1976.

8. Kexing 克興, "Xiao zichanjieji wenyi lilun zhi miuwu: ping Mao Dun jun de 'Cong Guling dao Dongjing'" 小資產階級文藝理論之謬誤:評茅盾君的從牯嶺到東京, *Chuangzao yuekan* 創造月刊 2, no. 5 (1928); reprinted in *GMWX* 2: 747–63. Pan Zinian

crete problems about "revolutionary literature" raised in my essay were remarked upon. However, both of them avoided any real discussion of these
problems, concentrating instead on scathing attacks. I am sorry that my essay "From Guling to Tokyo" was written so informally and that its many
inconclusive statements lent themselves so readily to misunderstanding or
malicious distortion. But take a look at Mr. Kexing's statements:

> Consider his [i.e., my] *Vacillation.* In his own words he says that "what is
> depicted in *Vacillation* is precisely vacillation, the vacillation of those en-
> gaged in revolutionary work who vacillated when the revolutionary strug-
> gles became fierce." What is vacillation? According to Mr. Mao it means to
> move "from sympathy for the left to left-infantilism, from trying to rectify
> left-infantilism to a gradual rise in rightist thought, then to the great reac-
> tion."[9] This explanation is Mr. Mao's own from beginning to end and has
> nothing to do with the objective situation of last November and December.
> At that time (last November and December) the objective situation was not
> that rectifying left-infantilism led to a rise in rightist thought which finally
> yielded the great reaction, but rather that the earlier high tide reached its
> highest development. Feudal landlords conspiring with the national bour-
> geoisie to protect their own interests carried out a large-scale terrorist poli-
> cy. Although members of the petit-bourgeois class were under the oppres-
> sion of the capitalists, they could not but vacillate because, first, they them-
> selves were in conflict with the high tide of the revolution and, second,
> they were frightened by the terrorist policy.

I do not know whether Mr. Kexing has read my *Vacillation.* If he has
read it, he should have noticed that the period depicted in *Vacillation* was
January to May 1927, and that the story was set in a county of Hubei along
the upper Yangtze River. This was made extremely explicit, yet Mr. Kexing
assumed it was November and December of 1927 and made his pointless
attack on me. How ridiculous! (Since Mr. Kexing was writing in November
1928, "last November and December" in his essay must mean November
and December 1927.) This shows how the "critics" of today will go so far as
to manufacture facts and unscrupulously distort the contents of a work to
facilitate their attack, to say nothing of maliciously misinterpreting statements that were deliberately left ambiguous by the author in that work. I
have felt that replying to such malicious attacks is really a waste of paper,
and up to now I have not uttered a single sentence in response.

潘梓年 (1901–?) was one of the founding members of the League of Left-Wing Writers,
brother of Pan Hannian 潘漢年; unable to trace this article.
  9. Cited from Mao Dun's essay "From Guling to Tokyo"; see note # 7 above.

As for their self-conceited "revolutionary theory" (here Mr. Kexing is somewhat superior to Mr. Pan Zinian), it rather reminds me of the characters in the "Committee for Training Political Workers" described in my *Disillusionment*. To put it bluntly, the characters in the "Committee for Training Political Workers" long ago perfected the delivery of this sort of speech.

VIII

In my informal essay "From Guling to Tokyo," I expressed the opinion that the life of the petit-bourgeois class should be made the subject of fiction. This is not a striking assertion; it means no more than the idea proposed above that an author "should choose to portray what is most familiar to him." Put more specifically, this should make it possible from now on for art and literature to exert an influence on those of the petit-bourgeois class who can more or less keep up with the epoch. I have not said that an art and literature of the petit-bourgeois class should be created. Although I do not like to quibble over the bit of dialectics or commonsense social science which the "revolutionary writers" boast of, no matter how closely I look, I have not found anything in their writing that goes beyond the books on my own shelves. If I may speak less politely, their disquisitions fail to cover more than the lecture notes I once prepared for my teaching; so I am not impressed by their attempts to put me down with their modicum of dialectics. They begin by arbitrarily claiming that I advocate the creation of a literature of the petit-bourgeois class and then (as if they'd just discovered the new world) they explain that petit-bourgeois literature is an impossibility: all this sounds to me like the familiar trumpet of the peddler of quack medicine.

As a matter of fact, prior to their angry attack on me, they had already formed a most unjustifiable prejudice against any art or literature depicting the life of the petit-bourgeois class. Such work they most often dogmatically label as "behind the times," irrespective of the content. Naturally, a novel portraying the life of the petit-bourgeois class must contain some characters who are "behind the times," but it is the characters in the book who are "behind the times," not the work itself. If the "backwardness" of the characters in a book is equated with the "backwardness" of the book or even of the author, does this not make an author who writes about robbers a robber himself? Unfortunately, such childish absurdities make their way into print. To see what bizarre absurdities such "criticism" has led the puerile literary scene in China to, we need only look for an accurate reflection in the so-called revolutionary literature debate of the early spring of 1928.

Considering the matter calmly, we will have to admit that even a work which portrays only the "backward" petit-bourgeois class can also have its positive value as a negative example. As a potential influence and guide, such a depiction of darkness probably has a more profound effect than those unrealistically optimistic pictures that are so out of touch with reality! In contemporary China, where the reader's power of judgment is generally rather weak, depicting darkness may have a harmful side effect because irony is often misunderstood. But the duty of the critic is precisely to point out the underlying meaning of those pictures of darkness, not to blindly condemn them as "backward," much less to arrogantly revile a work before even reading it closely. For example, Mr. Kexing says: "As to *Pursuit*, it obviously exposes the author's own disorderly mixture of obsessive melancholy and frenetic agitation, the rest is even less worthy of comment." Irresponsible vilification before he had even read and understood the original work! Anybody who has read *Pursuit* carefully should be able to judge what this novel is about. Qian Xingcun has commented, "Every principal character in the book has his aspirations, but 'one after another, they are dashed against the four painted yellow walls,' and in the end, 'even those who got what they were after found the object transformed the very second they were holding it in their hands'; they all then collapse into disappointment!" Qian Xingcun is for a "literature of force," and for a literature that can create life.[10] He is therefore not satisfied that every character in *Pursuit* should end in disappointment. He says, "Sickliness is depicted everywhere in the whole book; sickly characters, sickly thoughts, sickly actions, everything is sickly, everything is unhealthy. Objectively the ideas expressed by the author do not go beyond despair and vacillation. So the standpoint of this novel is wrong." I have to admit that Qian Xingcun's observation is not incorrect; *Pursuit* was intended to expose the sickliness and confusion of the intellectuals in the early spring of 1928. But I cannot concur with his conclusion that "the standpoint of this novel is wrong." I feel I ought to explain myself here. Before writing *Pursuit*, I spent some time reflecting on what approach to use. My final decision was more or less this: I wanted to show how, after times of disillusionment, intellectuals generally still wished to pursue a goal, but on account of their class background none could follow the correct path, with the result that their efforts all led to disappointment. On the basis of this decision, I made all the characters in the book represent intellectuals of the petit-bourgeois class who were passion-

---

10. Qian sets out this theory of a literature of force in *Li de wenxue* 力 的 文 學 (Shanghai, 1929). For a discussion of Qian's writings on literature, see Gálik 1980: 182–90.

ately enthusiastic for, but had no clear understanding of the meaning of, revolution. Since they lacked an accurate understanding, they all followed wrong paths. Should one not depict such people as completely disappointed? If I had inserted among them a character who recognized the correct path and revealed a ray of hope amid all the sickliness, Qian Xingcun might have felt a little more satisfied. I am quite capable of seeing his point. But I didn't do it, because I believe that if the characters in *Pursuit* had been true revolutionaries, they would have decided their course long before the early spring of 1928 and would no longer have been engaged in fruitless pursuit. This explains why all is darkness in *Pursuit*.

IX

Let me return to *Ni Huanzhi*. Because it, too, depicts petit-bourgeois intellectuals, I do not find it blameworthy that there is not a single uplifting revolutionary character in it. To put it more explicitly: although the main character Ni Huanzhi is "useless," for just that reason he represents faithfully the "form of consciousness" of the revolutionary intellectuals in the transitional period. The appearance of such a purposeful and carefully planned novel on the current chaotic literary scene has, in any case, to be considered a meaningful event. If writers deliberately go on producing such serious works, it will be possible to say in the future: "The literary scene after the May Thirtieth was not as unproductive as the May Fourth era in creating works representative of the spirit of its epoch." Contemporary criticism is on the whole blind. Writers should have the self-confidence to calmly persist in working without any wavering or doubt.

X

Like my previous essay, "From Guling to Tokyo," this essay has also been written informally and contains a number of undeveloped statements, leaving me open to distortion and attack. I am used to being attacked, but I still hope that the attackers read my essay carefully first before making their remarks, so that I will not be put in the position of not knowing how to reply. I have never been one to try to conceal my shortcomings, but as a rule I do not change my opinions lightly either.

Perhaps I have once more "raised many real and concrete problems" in this essay. If so, I am especially anxious that the "revolutionary critics" will attempt to "criticize and analyze from every angle" these concrete problems, and not just display their clichés of the marketplace in the manner of

Chapter 32

Literature and Revolution

Liang Shiqiu

We have often heard about the nature of literature; as for revolution, not only have we heard tell of it, but it seems as though we have also witnessed it with our own eyes.[1] The question of the relationship between these two, literature and revolution, ordinarily would not greatly concern us, yet it is one to which we must give extra consideration, especially today when the cry "revolutionary literature" is reaching the clouds.

My first question is: What, in the end, is revolution all about?

All civilization is created by a minority of geniuses. Science, art, literature, religion, philosophy, writing, even political ideology and social institutions are all brought forth by a minority of men whose abilities and wisdom surpass that of others. Naturally genius does not bear the slightest mark of the divine: genius is based in human nature. What makes a genius a genius is nothing more than that his natural endowments are particularly abundant, his vision particularly far-reaching, his intellect particularly

---

1. Liang Shiqiu 梁實秋, "Wenxue yu geming" 文學與革命, *Xinyue* 1, no. 4 (June 10, 1928).

strong, his emotions particularly sensitive; everything that the average person cannot feel, comprehend, penetrate, grasp, are all within the capacity of the genius. Thus it is very natural, very fitting, that within the life of a collective, whether it be a political organization or a social grouping, it should be the case that relatively outstanding individuals are in leadership or ruling positions, and in fact this often is so. It is a normal and natural route for relatively outstanding individuals at the center of public life to achieve their position entirely as a result of their intelligence and wisdom. It is the good fortune of any country or collective to be led or ruled by such outstanding individuals. The duty of a minority of outstanding geniuses is to use their brilliant wisdom to work for the greatest happiness of the collective, and all creative effort must be of benefit to ordinary people, either by continually enhancing the provision of their material benefits or by enriching the cultivation of their spirit. The true genius is never a parasite on society but an indispensable guide for ordinary people. Thus, under normal conditions, the people praise artistic genius, esteem scientific genius, and endorse political genius.

However, human nature is not completely good, and those in positions of leadership in political groups or social organizations are often not those with leadership qualities and even more do not have the ability to be creative geniuses, but are more often than not mediocre or even unprincipled types who, through luck or inheritance, succeed in occupying ruling or leadership positions. This kind of false leader makes no contribution to non-active members of the population and is perhaps deleterious to positive members. The true genius is concealed among the people until a time comes when things can no longer be endured, and then he will lead or direct the people in a resistance movement. This resistance movement is revolution. The true meaning of revolution is to use destructive means to topple false leaders and, with a positive spirit, to uphold true leaders. There are several relevant points regarding revolution:

1. A revolutionary movement comes into being under a changing political life;

2. The aim of a revolution is to restore the normal conditions of life;

3. The spirit of revolution is the spirit of resistance and that which is resisted is falsity;

4. The process of revolution is a temporary change: it is not a permanent state;

5. The eruption of revolution is, in terms of the people, pure feeling;

6. The organization of revolution should have rules and should respect genius.

Given the above-stated meaning of revolution, let us now go on to discuss the relationship between revolution and literature.

During a period of revolution, literature very easily takes on a particular shade. We certainly cannot say, however, that within a revolutionary period all writers must create "revolutionary literature." Why should this be? Poets, indeed all literary men, are those who stand at the forefront of the times. People's suffering, society's corruption, political darkness, false virtue: none feels these things earlier, or deeper, than the writer. It is not that people living under vile conditions, rich or poor, are without perceptions or unaware of suffering, but they cannot express what they feel, and even if they can give voice to it, then what they say does not conform to the rules of art; it is only writers who, because of their inherent nature and long-standing apprenticeship, are able to be the mouthpiece of all the people, to give expression to the sufferings of all peoples, and to use different kinds of artistic methods to express their dissatisfaction with the status quo. Writers of intense feelings might launch a direct attack on contemporary hypocrisy; writers rich in imagination might evoke a golden past; writers who are optimistic and indulge in fantasies will create their ideal paradise; but they are all equally dissatisfied with the present status quo. Writers have always been the unofficial representatives of the people, unconsciously representing their intimate pains and joy, thoughts and inclinations. Particularly in times of suffering, the stimuli writers receive are exceptionally heartfelt and thus their anguished cries are exceptionally moving. Because writers are the first among people to feel, the first to be aware, we know from a historical perspective that *literature rich in revolutionary spirit always appears before the actual revolutionary movement.* Thus, "revolutionary literature" prior to revolution is the first cool drop of sweet dew in people's souls, and it is the most intense, the most sincere, the most natural. Instead of saying, "First revolution, then 'revolutionary literature,' " say rather, "First 'revolutionary literature,' then revolution." After the actual revolution has broken out, the revolutionary coloring of literature naturally becomes increasingly intense, to the point where a great quantity of literature that comes close to rhetoric or propaganda is produced. *Writers do not give expression to any spirit of the times, it is rather that the times reflect the spirit of writers.* Of course, since writers cannot exist apart from real life and since the life of an entire revolutionary period is also not without commensurate stimuli for a writer, we must therefore begin by acknowledging that, during a revolutionary period (including the periods of "fermenting and erupting"), literature easily takes on a particular kind of coloring.

So why do I say again that writers do not need to create "revolutionary literature" in times of revolution? From a literary perspective, the term "revolutionary literature" is basically untenable. *In literature there is only "literature of a revolutionary period," and certainly no so-called revolutionary literature.* From the standpoint of an actual revolutionary, that is, from a utilitarian point of view, we could say that one thing is "revolutionary literature" and another "not revolutionary literature" and furthermore, using communist theory, we could extend this to say that "non-revolutionary literature" is "counter-revolutionary literature." However, in literary theory we divide literary categories according to the most basic qualities and tendencies, and external realities such as revolutionary movements or restoration movements cannot be borrowed to be used as standards by which to measure literature. Moreover, great literature is founded on a fixed universal human nature and good literature is only that which flows forth from the depths of the human heart, for what literature finds hard to achieve is fidelity: fidelity to human nature. And it is unimportant what kind of connection results from the tide of the times; and whether it is influenced by the times or influences the times, or if it is integrated with revolutionary theory or is restricted by traditional thinking bears no relationship to literature's value. This is because human nature is the sole standard for measuring literature. The term "revolutionary literature," even if not necessarily a concoction devised by revolutionaries, at the very least serves to add confusion to the understanding of literature. Furthermore, human nature's complexity and profundity need abundant experience before a commensurate understanding can be reached, and it is not necessarily the case that everyone will have revolutionary experience in a time of revolution (spiritual and emotional aspects of life also count as experience), and we definitely cannot compel those without revolutionary experience to write "revolutionary literature." The creation of literature cannot undergo any form of coercion. Literature containing revolutionary ideology is literature, and as literature it makes public the anxieties and feelings of a period. And yet there are many different kinds of human suffering: to be oppressed by the warlords is to suffer; to incur imperialist aggression is to suffer; are not the troubles of birth, aging, illness, and death suffering? Are not the vagaries of fate suffering? Are not one's own hesitations and conflicts suffering? How can all this be limited to "revolutionary literature" alone?

Since democratic[2] ideology is flourishing today, it is very easy for us to assign too high a status to the masses. It seems as if revolution is a movement of the masses, but in fact it is also the product of the inspiration and guidance of one or two geniuses. Leadership is needed by an effective revo-

---

2. Liang uses the transliterated term *demokelaxi* 德謨克拉西.

lutionary movement even more than at ordinary times. Thus, although in the process of revolution many insurrections are inevitable, as is direct action by the masses, it is to the leaders that transformations must be looked for in terms of true revolutionary trends and revolutionary theory. *The words and actions of the leaders most fully represent the masses' consciousness.*

Writers are indeed the unofficial representatives of the masses. "Representation" here is not the same as the political representation of the popular will: that which writers represent is general human nature, all humanity's feelings and thoughts, and they certainly carry no responsibilities or duties toward the masses and even less do they bear the burden of having to improve lives. Therefore writers' creations certainly are not bound by anything extrinsic, writers' minds certainly do not hold any fixed class viewpoint and even less do they have any preconceptions about working for the interests of a certain class. Writers never lose their independence. The literary works of a revolutionary period always implicitly reveal the people's suffering or satirize the hypocrisies of the age: this certainly is not a question of a writer imparting the decrees of the masses or of a writer voluntarily wishing to fulfill his mission to the masses. A writer accepts orders from no one, only the orders of his own heart; a writer has no mission except that of his own heart's demand for truth, goodness, and beauty. Therefore, in a time of revolution just as in normal times, a writer is not merely a member of the masses, he is also a genius, a leader: he still has not lost his individuality.

Sentimental revolutionaries of recent times, and even superficial humanists, have limitless sympathy for the majority of the people. This limitless sympathy always overwhelms all due considerations toward civilization. There is a group of writers who are also tainted with this limitless sympathy and who call out loudly for "majority literature." They feel that when the masses are in dire straits those who have literary talent cannot turn a blind eye but should soak their pages with tears, crying out against injustice on behalf of the masses. It is this alone that is "revolutionary literature," only this that is "literature which does not go against the times." And if at this time there are those who write verse in praise of the moon and wind, or write love poetry or love stories, or discuss ancient arts, then charges of "aristocratic," "petit-bourgeois," "unrevolutionary," or "counterrevolutionary" are heaped upon them. Why? Because this kind of literature is individualistic literature, literature of the minority and not of the majority! In fact the term "majority literature" is itself contradictory—*the majority has no literature, literature does not belong to the majority.* As for the literatus hiding in his pavilion, no matter if he is describing the suffering of the fourth class or the life of ease and comfort of the third class, no matter if he is calling for blood or singing of the moon and wind, in the end is it not a reflection in the mirror of one's individual heart? If one depicts each and every weak nation under the iron heel of imperialist oppression, such a work is great because it is a reflection of an entire nation's spirit; yet if one painfully and profoundly describes the anguish of lost love or the emotions engendered by spring flowers and autumn winds, such a work is also great because it is a reflection of the shared human nature of all humanity. That which literature needs is truth, fidelity to human nature. All "true" literature has a common essence, and how this common essence can be understood in an appropriate and accurate fashion is a question of a writer's individual talent and long-standing apprenticeship. Thus a "true" work is the product of common humanity filtered through an individual. Such concepts as "individualistic," "minority," and "majority" simply do not constitute a problem in literature. The spirit of democracy has no place for implementation in literature. For writers in the midst of revolution, as at any other time, the sole training lies in understanding human nature, the sole art lies in how to give expression to that understanding. The materials of creation are the special experiences of an individual or the shared lives of ordinary people, it does not matter which, for all that is necessary is that you write deeply and that what you write of is human nature: then it is literature. "Majority literature" is a term without meaning.

In the past, the literature of the Romantic movement, with its relative stress on the author's internal experience and sedulous description of characters' individuality, represented a new direction, an expression of liberation, so that there is a close relationship between Romantic literature and a revolutionary movement. A Romantic movement at base is an emotional resistance, a reaction against the rules, regulations, and traditions, and so on, of an excessively feudal ethical code, and where such a spirit of resistance actually manifests itself in political or social action, it is indeed a revolutionary movement. Romantic movements and revolutionary movements are both forms of resistance to unreasonable constraints, both are destructive, both value genius, both bring about the arousal of the masses through the initiatives of a minority. Thus, ordinary people *all firmly believe that Romantic literature is revolutionary literature.* I feel this parallel is most appropriate. Romantic literature reveres individualism, but in the eyes of contemporary revolutionaries I am afraid this individualism does not count as revolutionary, because Romantic literature is not "majority literature." Yet Romantic literature, seen from the point of view of political ideology, always has a revolutionary nature. Those who promote "majority literature" not only do not have a correct understanding of literature but also are equally deficient in their cognizance of revolution. *No matter whether it be literature or revolution, without exception the focal points are individualism, the worship of heroes, and the veneration of genius, with absolutely no relation to so-called majority literature.*

If there is in literature something called revolutionary literature, then probably there are two versions: one is Romantic literature, the other is so-called proletariat literature (or majority literature). The reason why Romantic literature is richly imbued with a revolutionary nature is because it upholds individual freedom and resists cruel laws; the reason why so-called proletariat literature or majority literature is richly imbued with a revolutionary nature is because it is fraught with the implications of class struggle and resists capitalist oppression. As was stated above, "proletariat literature" and "majority literature" are untenable terms, because all literature takes humanity as its basis with absolutely no class divisions. We acknowledge that literature of the first class, if there truly is such a thing, is literature, no matter how aristocratic, for its aristocratic flavor certainly cannot reduce its value as art; we can also acknowledge that literature of the fourth class, if there truly is such a thing, is literature, for its plebeian flavor cannot raise its value as art. In fact, after a work is created, it does not belong to any one class or to any one person, for it is a precious treasure shared by all humanity, capable of being appreciated, criticized, and accepted by everyone, if everyone has the requisite literary taste and long-standing apprenticeship. If a work of art cannot be appreciated and understood by the proletariat, this is not necessarily because the work belongs to another class or has an aristocratic nature, but is perhaps because the proletariat at base lacks the capability to appreciate it. The appreciation of literature is not a basic instinct like drinking, eating, sex, etc.: it is not a capability shared by everyone. To be able to truly appreciate literature is a very rare pleasure, and this pleasure is not the monopoly of one class, *for both poor and rich classes have a small number of people of literary taste, and both have a greater number who cannot appreciate literature.* Therefore, when talking about the relationship between a work and its reader, we can see no class barriers. The production of literature bears even less relationship to class. There are many examples of ancient literature that are not the product of single authorship but instead, some suspect, collective works. We could take, for example, folk songs and the like, but even these are not the products of a particular class, nor are they produced by the united efforts of large groups of either the propertied class or the proletariat gathered together in a single hall. It is still those rich in talent within the collective who would be the first to create, and all the rest would just supplement these and cheer them on. From the time when people left the primitive state of existence, the tendency for literature has been to become increasingly individualistic in terms of authorship: in other words, literature has increasingly become the product of genius. The apportioning of genius is not something that can be controlled by economic power or social position: the proletariat class and the propertied class can equally bring forth genius, and just as equally not bring forth genius! Thus, in terms of the production of literary works, we can also see no class barriers. *Literature is without class nature.*

If literature does have revolutionary sentiment, it only exists as a spirit of resistance. Apart from this, literature and revolution do not have very much connection at base. And even in terms of this link, literature is not dependent on revolution for its production. Literature itself does not necessarily want to express a spirit of resistance, and a spirit of resistance in literature certainly does not give rise to any artistic value. At an appropriate time, however, literary works cannot avoid taking on something of the coloring of resistance. Moreover, literature with a spirit of resistance always appears before an actual revolutionary movement. A spirit of resistance can therefore often become the shared coloring of both a revolutionary movement and "literature of a revolutionary period," but from a literary point of view, one cannot admit that there is so-called revolutionary literature.

In a revolutionary period, a real activist might wish to use literature as a tool, a propaganda tool to achieve his aim. We have no reason or desire to express opposition to such a usage of literature. Nothing exists that has not been used by people. Yet is it only revolutionaries who wish to use literature? People in commerce might use literature for advertising and preachers for their sermons. We should not oppose true revolutionaries' using literature as a weapon to help achieve their ideals. Moreover, we must acknowledge that true revolutionaries' blazing enthusiasm filters into literature and often inadvertently helps form works that are exceptionally moving. However, if literature is simply and purely used as a revolutionary tool, then when the revolution is over, the effectiveness of the tool is also curtailed. If "revolutionary literature" is explained as using literature as a tool for revolution, then that is to devalue literature. A revolutionary movement is basically a temporary condition of change and to limit literature's essence to the "revolutionary" is as good as shrinking the fixed and eternal value of literature to the level of a temporary period of change. Literature is vast, but revolution is not enacted forever.

Great writers are enough to inspire a revolutionary movement, but a revolutionary movement can only influence comparatively few writers. The power of great literature does not lie in giving expression to ardent fervor but in concentrating that ardent fervor into regulated paths. Great writers always stand at the forefront of an age, and in a revolutionary period their eyes are clearly facing forward. Only a few writers within a revolutionary period are carried away by the tide of ardent fervor and are unable to exercise self restraint. Within such a tide of ardent fervor anyone might fail to keep a clear head and be overly excited by the phenomena of the time. Thus they are unable to "calmly examine life, and examine the whole of life." This can be seen in history. Very many great writers are exceptionally sincere in nature, despising hypocrisy and brutality above all, and are thus richly imbued with revolutionary sentiment. They express great sympathy for a revolutionary movement's beginnings, but after the revolution develops and on seeing its violent eruption with the annihilation of all standards, the destruction of all rules and the wrecking of genius, they come to consider all this too extreme and withdraw their sympathy. There is no top-notch writer who has sympathized with revolution his whole life through. The influence of revolutionary movements on literature is to kindle people's enthusiasm and incite people's hatred of hypocrisy. To stir up people's hatred against their fetters is not in itself bad, and even though it cannot raise the value of literature, at least it will not diminish its value either. However, such influence can easily bring about bad results and unavoidably leads to sentimentality, or even excessive romanticism.

Recently people have been promoting "revolutionary literature," but I feel that they are not taking the literary point of view into account, whereas those who oppose "revolutionary literature" seem to know only satire and mockery. On the basis of calm and quiet research, I consider the phrase "revolutionary literature" to be a meaningless and empty statement and, moreover, that the relationship between literature and revolution is not a topic deserving of advocacy with all one's energy.

Whether it be literature or revolution, what we need now is a clear head.

—Translated by Alison Bailey

Chapter 33

Dai Wangshu's Poetic Theory

Dai Wangshu

1. Poetry cannot rely on musicality and should discard its musical qualities.[1]

2. Poetry cannot rely on the strengths of painting.

3. The mere composition of beautiful words is not a characteristic of poetry.

4. Those of the Symbolist school say: "Nature is a prostitute who has been debauched a thousand times." But who knows if a new prostitute will not be debauched ten thousand times. The number of times doesn't matter, what we need are new instruments and techniques for debauchery.

5. Poetic meter lies not in the melodiousness of the characters, but in the melodiousness of the poem's emotion, the degree of the poetic mood.

6. What is most important for new poetry is the "nuance" of poetic mood and not the "nuance" of characters and phrases.

7. Rhyme and regularity of lines may obstruct poetic mood, or deform poetic mood. If the emotion behind a poem is made to conform to stagnant

---

1. Dai Wangshu 戴望舒, "Wangshu shilun" 望舒詩論, *Xiandai* 2, no. 1 (Nov. 1932): 92–94. This piece has also been translated by Harold Acton and Chen Shih-hsiang [Acton and Chen 1936: 173–75].

and superficial old rules, it is like placing your own feet in the shoes of another. A fool will trim the foot to fit the shoe, whereas a rather more intelligent man will choose for himself a better fitting shoe. A wise man, however, will make for himself a pair that fits his own feet.

8. Poetry is not a pleasure felt by a single sense alone, but something felt by all the senses, or which transcends the senses altogether.

9. New poetry should have new emotions and new forms for expressing these emotions. And this so-called form is most certainly not the superficial arrangement of characters, nor the mere compilation of new words.

10. There is no need to necessarily have new objects as thematic material (although I am not opposed to this), for new poetic moods may be found in old poetic objects.

11. Diction of the old classics cannot be opposed when it bestows on us a new poetic mood.

12. One should not simply indulge one's fancy for resplendent adornment, for this will never be eternal.

13. Poetry should have its own *originalité*, but you must also give it a *cosmopolité* [*sic*] quality; neither is dispensable.

14. Poetry is born from reality passing through the imagination; it is neither only reality nor only imagination.

15. When poetry expresses its own emotions and causes people to feel something, it seems to take on a life of its own and is not a lifeless thing.

16. Emotion is not captured as with a camera, it should be brought out through description in an ingenious style. This style must be alive and ever-changing.

17. If one uses a certain language to write poems and the people of a country feel them to be good poems, they are not really good poems but at most the magic of language. What is good in a real poem is not just the strengths of language.

—*Translated by Kirk A. Denton*

Chapter 34

Form in Poetry

Wen Yiduo

I

If we assume that the "play-instinct" theory[1] fully accounts for the origin of Art, then it is perfectly conceivable to compare writing poetry to playing chess; one can no more dispense with rules when playing chess than one can dispense with form when writing poetry. (Here I use *gelü* 格律 as the equivalent for the English "form." Although in recent days the word *gelü* has become tainted by objectionable associations, it is more appropriate than such literal translations as *xingti* 形體 ["form" in the sense of a physical object's external features] and *geshi* 格式 ["form" in the sense of a pattern or model to be copied]. When we remember that form is intimately re-

---

1. Wen Yiduo 聞一多, "Shi de gelü" 詩的格律, *Beijing chenbao*, May 13, 1926. The "play-instinct" theory, *youxi benneng shuo* 遊戲本能說, developed by and debated among European scholars through the eighteenth and nineteenth centuries, maintains that human beings have a deep-seated and instinctive need to play, and that play, far from being a trivial activity, is in fact the motivating force behind artistic expression. Spokesmen for the play-instinct theory were Friedrich von Schiller (see his *Aesthetical Letters*) and Carl Groos (*The Play of Man*). Wen Yiduo may have first encountered this concept in Bliss Perry's *A Study of Poetry* (Boston: Houghton Mifflin, 1920), 15-16.

lated to rhythm, *gelü* seems a satisfactory translation.) If one were to set one's chessmen at random on the board and play a game in complete disregard to the rules, what sort of amusement could one derive from the contest? Pleasure is derived from playing when, through some brilliant stroke, one obtains a victory within the game's prescribed limits. So it is, too, that one may derive pleasure from writing poetry. If poetry could be written without regard to form, would it not be easier to write a poem than play a game of chess, soccer, or mahjongg? Small wonder it is that in recent years New Poetry has flourished to such a degree. I realize that some do not enjoy listening to my views, but Professor Bliss Perry is even more inflexible on questions of poetic form. He writes: "Few poets will admit that they are really in bondage to form. They love to dance in fetters, and even dance in the fetters of other poets."[2]

I will go on to predict that after many budding poets read the passage quoted above, they jumped to their feet and cried: "If that is poetry, I will never write again! What do you think of that?" I must confess that I feel it would be no great loss if such poets discontinued writing, because if they refuse to dance in fetters, they will never produce respectable poetry. The poet Du Fu once made a wise remark worth considering in this regard: "The older I grow, the more care I take with poetic rules."[3]

Next the revolutionary spirits of the poetic world cry out: "Return to Nature!" What they must realize is that, although one needs to look carefully, one can still perceive subtle traces of form in the natural environment. The problem is that more often than not Nature's handiwork exists in an imperfect state, and only Art can remedy Nature's deficiencies. Seen in this light, perfectly realistic depictions of Nature impoverish Art. Oscar Wilde put the case well when he wrote, "Art takes up where Nature leaves off."[4] Nature is not always beautiful. We see beauty in Nature only where Nature happens to approximate Art. This proposition is most easily corroborated by drawing an analogy with the visual arts. Often when we admire a beautiful view existing in raw Nature, we say that it is just as beautiful as a

---

2. Perry's original statement reads differently: "And few poets, furthermore, will admit that they are really in bondage to their stanzas. They love to dance in these fetters, and even when wearing the same fetters as another poet, they nevertheless invent movements of their own, so that Mr. Masefield's 'Chaucerian' stanzas are really not so much Chaucer's as Masefield's" (*A Study of Poetry*, 202).

3. Du Fu (712–770). The line reads "*Lao qu jian yu shilü xi*" 老去漸於詩律細. *Lao qu* should read *wanjie* 晚節 : "*In my later years* I have gradually become careful with poetic rules." See Du Fu's "Qian men xi cheng Lu Shijiu caozhang" 遣悶戲呈路十九曹長.

4. This concurs with much of what Oscar Wilde had to say on the relationship between nature and art, but I have been unable to locate where he may have made this specific remark.

painting. Indeed, we Chinese tend to judge beautiful only those views that resemble traditional landscape paintings. The conception of ideal feminine beauty in pre-Renaissance Europe may be proven incompatible with the modern conception when we compare paintings of the two ages, but the modern-day conception of ideal feminine beauty does tally with that of ancient Greece, as the latter is exemplified in sculpture.[5] This is because the excavation of Greek sculpture stimulated the development of Renaissance art, and ever since the Renaissance, artistic representations of beautiful women have been patterned upon the Greek model, in this way modifying the conception of feminine loveliness in the minds of Europeans. I have run across a similar theory suggested in a poem by Zhao Yi:

> Exactly like a "potted-pond," grouping emerald crags;
> Finely-sculpted stumps of stone, filling the river's coves.
> Forces of creation, too, enjoy a novel trick;
> Oddly they dress mountains up in the guise of man-made hills.[6]

絕似盆池聚碧屏,
嵌空石笋滿江灣.
化工也愛翻新樣,
反把眞山學假山.

This poem tells of one instance in which Nature imitated Art. Our natural environment does, of course, contain beauty, but when we happen to catch a glimpse of beauty in Nature it is only by happy accident. Once in a while we hear poetic rhythms in speech, but if we were to decide on this basis to equate poetry with everyday speech, we would in actuality be doing away with poetry. (Note that I do not exclude the possibility of composing poetry in regional dialects of spoken Chinese. I believe, as I hope to show at a later date, that regional dialects are a rich area for potential development in New Poetry. Right now I would merely have the reader note

---

5. The original in this sentence reads *bu tong* 不同 (does not tally), but this does not make sense in the context. This is likely a misprint for *you* 又 (once again), as the inverse misprint occurs later in the text.

6. Zhao Yi 趙翼 (A.D. 1727–1814). This is the second of a pair of heptasyllabic quatrains entitled "A Boatride on the River Li" ("Li jiang zhou xing" 灘江舟行). See *Oubei quanji* 甌北全集, 47.6b. The *penchi* 盆池, "potted pond," is a sort of artificial landscape in miniature arranged in a basin and used as a garden ornament by Chinese gentlefolk (See E.H. Schafer's "Notes on T'ang Culture," *Monumenta Serica* 21 [1962]: 194–96). The words *shi sun* 石笋, "stumps of stone," suggest geologic formations resembling the woody root of the bamboo, whose shape is similar to the contours of the karst hills lining the River Li near Guilin. Zhao's quatrain, then, compares the natural beauty of Guilin to the domesticated beauty of a *penchi*. In places like Guilin, the forces of erosion care for the landscape with the same attention to detail that a gardener looking after a *penchi* exercises.

that poetry may be "composed" in regional dialects—the word "compose" suggesting that such informal language can be transformed into poetry only after a process of editing and selection.) Poetry's ability to excite the emotions rests solely upon rhythm, and rhythm is metrical form. When Shakespeare's plays build up to their frequent climaxes of charged emotion, the playwright naturally slips rhymes into the speech of his players. Goethe also used verse in *Faust*, as he once told Schiller in a letter. When Han Yu (768–824) "hit upon an obscure rhyme, he did not look about for alternatives, because ingenuity is best displayed under adverse conditions. The more difficult the rhyme-scheme, the more extraordinary the poetic effect."[7] In this way, the more masterful a poet is, the more gracefully he will dance in his fetters. Only those who dance poorly resent their fetters, and only poetasters feel hampered by form. Form impedes the free expression of only those who cannot write poetry; to a true poet, form is a "sharp instrument" that helps him express himself.

Now another group of young poets flourishing the colors of Romanticism prepares to attack form. I only wish to remind these poets of one fact. If they persist in touting Romanticism as their literary creed, all they will do is acknowledge the insincerity of their desire to write poetry, because when we examine what they have written we find that, far from attending to literature, they merely seek the adulation of the reading public. Each of these narcissistic youths fancies himself the most adorable man alive: he feels that all he needs to do is bare his breast to the reader and a literary work will have been created. Do we not hear their constant ranting about "self-expression"? What they have discovered are in actuality no more than the raw materials of Art. They fail to acknowledge form, the tool which transforms these raw materials into literature. The fact that they use a written language as their medium for expression is of no consequence. What concerns these poets most is exhibiting what they refer to as "the Ego," letting the world know just how talented and sensitive a young man "I" am. They gaze lovingly into the mirror their literature proffers, admiring through tear-filled eyes their rakish attitudes of easy grace. How droll it is! How romantic! Yes: the Romanticism of which they speak is romantic only in this respect—it has nothing whatsoever to do with the schools of literary thought. This sort of poet's interests do not lie with literature; so it is too much to ask them to adhere to rules of poetic form, because given such restrictions they would be unable to write poetry. If they did give consideration to poetic form, would they not be unfaithful to their code of writing

---

7. This quote comes from Ouyang Xiu, "Shihua" 詩話 , *Ouyang Wenzhong gong wenji* 歐陽文忠公文集, Sibu congkan edition, 128.11b.

poetry as they please? To state the case more bluntly: we may see this pseudo-Romantic poetry as a meaningless game, or, if we choose, a peep-show, but on no account should we mistake it for poetry. Consequently, we need not discuss whether it adheres to rules of poetic form. They may denounce poetic form if they wish, but there is no point in wasting our breath bickering with them.

I have stated above what I mean when I use the word "form." Certainly, Art cannot exist without it. I have also stated that poetic form is nothing more than rhythm. When put in such simple terms as these, the importance of form is doubly evident; casual prose essays can get by with comparatively little attention to rhythm, but poetry cannot and will never make do without rhythm. Poetry has never been divorced from formal and rhythmic considerations. No one has ever considered questioning such a basic assumption. And yet today we find that even assumptions as unassailable as this must have their merit proven. Why carry on over this issue? Do people really believe that poetry can dispense with form? Perhaps the furor is due to some anarchist spirit of the age, to a senseless love for fads, to sheer laziness, to a fear of betraying one's incompetence in technical literary discussions, or to . . . well, I give up. I don't know what the reason could be!

II

In the preceding pages we have discussed a few of the reasons poetry should not do away with form. Now let us briefly consider the essential properties of poetic form. On the surface of things, we may surmise that poetic form may be examined under two headings: the visual, and the auditory. Actually, these headings should not be considered separately, because each is closely related to the other.[8] Examples of visual form would include evenly proportioned stanzas and orderliness of individual lines. Auditory form would include such elements as format, poetic feet, deflected and inflected tone patterns, and end-rhymes. But if format is neglected, stanzas will be unevenly proportioned, poetic feet will be mismanaged, individual lines will be in disarray.

Rao Mengkan has ably discussed questions pertaining to format, poetic feet, tone patterns, and end-rhymes in his article entitled "Thoughts on Meter in New Poetry" (published in two previous issues of this literary supplement). But his comments were primarily addressed to the auditory aspects of poetry, and he neglected to deal with two of the visual aspects. Admittedly, the latter are of secondary importance. But in Chinese literature

---

8. Read *bu dang fenkai lai jiang* 不當分開來講, not *you* 又 *dang fenkai lai jiang*.

especially we must not overlook this important matter, because our written language is pictographic, and when we read literary works at least half of the impressions we receive are of a visual nature. Literature is an art that occupies both time and space. It is regrettable that, although the literatures of Europe have physical modes of existence, they lack the ability to present concrete visual images. Our written language can evoke such impressions, and it would be a sad thing indeed if we did not exploit this potential. Therefore, New Poetry's adoption of the Western convention of writing poetry in lines of a length determined by the poet is a breakthrough of considerable consequence. Whether or not the first Chinese poet to write verse in lines realized the value of his discovery need not concern us here. We still owe him a debt of gratitude, because only now can we see that the true power of poetry is derived not only from musical beauty (meter) and pictorial beauty (ornate vocabulary), but from architectural beauty as well (evenly proportioned stanzas and orderliness of individual lines). If someone were to ask what one of the characteristics of New Poetry is, we might reply that it provides poets with new possibilities for architectural beauty.

Recently more and more people have begun to express the suspicion that stanzas of even proportion and orderliness of individual lines symbolize a return to antiquated methods of versification. What a sad fate it is to belong to the past of China! Does this phenomenon not strike one as rather odd? Not only have such honorific titles as "sage" and "master" been denied Confucius, he has even been stripped of his personal name. And yet now, in an age when Confucius is pejoratively referred to as "Junior," Jesus retains his title of "Christ," and Socrates is still called Socrates. We Chinese may still write poems in sonnet form if we wish, but we must beware lest our poems resemble Regulated Verse. Why in the world has Regulated Verse fallen into disfavor? Even if one wished to write Regulated Verse in vernacular Chinese, would it be possible? If one writes a poem whose stanzas are of even proportion and whose lines are ordered, should one be condemned for writing Regulated Verse?

To be sure, Regulated Verse as a formula for composition does possess architectural beauty, but when we compare its beauty to the possibilities for architectural beauty in New Poetry, we realize just how limited Regulated Verse is. Regulated Verse will never present more than one pattern for poetic composition, whereas the number of patterns possible in New Poetry is limitless. This is the first difference between Regulated Verse and New Poetry. When writing a poem in Regulated Verse, one must fit one's theme and artistic conception into the predetermined pattern—almost as though one has been given a suit of clothes, and no matter whether one is a man or a woman, an adult or a child, one must try to wear it as best one can. New Poetry, on the other hand, tailors itself to individual needs. "Wang Zhaojun Leaves China" could no more have been composed using the format of "Lotus Picking Song" than "Railroad Ballad" could have been composed using the format of "Final Determination," or "Eighteenth of March" could have been composed using the format of "Searching."[9] If any critic should feel that there is a point in one of these poems where content is at odds with format, where mood is incompatible with construction, I would be intrigued to hear his reasoning. But I ask you: is there an instance in which mood and construction are found compatible within the cut-and-dried formats of Regulated Verse? And among all the examples of scrambled, asymmetric, slapdash free verse, can one poem be found in which mood and construction are compatible?

The second point of divergence between Regulated Verse and New Poetry is that with Regulated Verse form and content are dissociated, whereas with New Poetry form is designed according to the spirit of content. The format of Regulated Verse has been determined for us by our predecessors, whereas the format of New Poetry is decided upon spontaneously according to the artist's predilection. This is a third difference between Regulated Verse and New Poetry. Now that we understand these three points of divergence, we must consider whether the format of New Poetry constitutes a restoration of familiar archaism, or whether it is an innovation; that is, whether it is a step backward or a step forward.

Recently we have seen a certain poetic format used by many poets that divides poems into four lines per stanza, with the same number of characters in each line. Readers accustomed to asymmetrical free verse must find this particularly distracting—those lines with the same number of characters look just as though they have been trimmed with a pair of scissors. "How irritating it must be to worry over the length of every line!" they think. Then it occurs to them that, if writing poetry is made so difficult, poetic inspiration must stand in danger of perdition. "And if inspiration is lost," they fret, "where can one begin to look for poetry?" Although it is true that poetry is lost without inspiration, refining the lines of one's poems so that they are of even length is hardly an insurmountable task, and inspiration need not come to harm in the process. I have asked several poets who use this poetic format, and each has said the same thing: while they admit that flaws may be found in some of their poems, they feel that the

---

9. "Zhaojun chu sai" 昭君出塞 and "Cai lian qu" 採蓮曲 are both by Zhu Xiang 朱湘 (1904–33); "Zuihou de jianjue" 最後的堅決 and "Tiedao xing" 鐵道行 are by Liu Mengwei 劉夢葦 (1900–1926); "Xunzhao" 尋找 and "Sanyue shiba ri" 三月十八日 are by Rao Mengkan 饒夢侃 (1902–67). These were all poets of the early Crescent Moon Society, with which Wen himself was also associated.

flaws are a consequence of their imperfect technique and should not be attributed to some defect in the poetic format itself. Let us compare two
poems—one written in lines of chaotic syntax, the other in lines of well-
ordered syntax—to see for ourselves whether syntactic organization of individual lines affects a poem's metrical grace:

> Would that I might pierce the silent haze, that sheer floating gauze!
> Carefully I listen through the misty drizzle which quietly descends upon
> the eaves,
> Hearing the falling rain's murmur as it wafts from afar through the empti-
> ness,
> Dimly aware of delicate white petals falling, one by one, to the ground.

> 我願透着寂靜的朦朧, 薄淡的浮紗,
> 細聽着淅淅的細雨寂寂的在簷上,
> 激打遙對着遠遠吹來的空虛中的噓嘆的聲音,
> 意識着一片一片的墜下的輕輕的白色的落花.

> At the story's pause, the lamp outside sputtered
> And the old man's terror his eyes for him uttered;
> The children gazed in dismay at the old man's face,
> He glanced in dismay to where the red flames fluttered.

> 說到這兒, 門外忽然燈響,
> 老人的臉上也改了摸樣;
> 孩子們驚望着他的臉色,
> 他也驚望着炭火的紅光.

Which sounds better: the poem with ordered syntax, or the one whose
lines are syntactically chaotic? To get to the heart of the matter, organizing
one's syntax, far from cramping poetic meter, facilitates achieving metric
harmony. Again, some may take exception to this judgment. Let us take a
closer look at the second passage cited above to see whether or not orderly
syntax impinges upon a poem's metric harmony.

孩子們　　驚望着　　他的　臉色
haizimen / jingwangzhe / ta de / lianse
(The children gazed in dismay at the old man's face,)

他也　驚望着　　炭火的　紅光
ta ye / jingwangzhe / tanhuo de / hongguang
(He glanced in dismay to where the red flames fluttered.)

Both of these lines may be broken down into four poetic feet, two
"trisyllabic feet" and two "disyllabic feet" (my terms for feet made up of

three syllables and two syllables, respectively). The location of the components is left to the poet's discretion, but each line must be composed of a sum of two trisyllabic and two disyllabic feet. Composed in this manner, a poem can possess euphony at the same time that each of its lines bears the same number of syllables. Therefore, orderly lines are an inevitable phenomenon associated with metrically harmonized poetry. In a perfectly organized poem, each will be of the same length. (But if we turn the formula about, we realize that when the number of syllables in each line of a poem is the same, the meter of the poem will not necessarily be perfectly organized. This is because simply having lines of equal length does not ensure that the poetic feet are properly arranged. Mere syllabic uniformity among lines presents a facade of symmetry, rather than the naturally harmonious outward form created by a fine poem's rich content.)

For this reason, the importance of having the same number of syllables in each line cannot be exaggerated, because the existence or lack of rhythm as one facet of poetry's outward form can establish the nature of its inner spirit. However, if the reader feels that the examples discussed above are insufficient, we may use the same criteria to analyze my poem "Stagnant Waters."

Beginning with the first line,

這是　　一溝　　絶望的　　死水
zhe shi / *yi gou* / *juewang de* / *sishui*
This is / a fen of / hopeless, / stagnant waters,[10]

the poem employs a metrical scheme which requires that each line contain three disyllabic feet and one trisyllabic foot. Of course, each line contains an equal number of syllables. The result is a poem that, as an experiment in poetic meter, is more successful than any I have written to date. Many friends have expressed puzzlement over the formal mahjongg I play with poems like "Stagnant Waters," which divide their poetic feet into increments of two and three syllables, so I have taken the liberty of dealing with this question here. I hope the reader has noted that the metrical nature of New Poetry, as the analysis above has shown, suggests certain practical methods for poetic composition. I predict that when these methods for ma-

---

10. In Wen's 1928 essay on Du Fu, he quotes part of a sonnet by Wordsworth: "Milton! thou should'st be living at this hour: / England hath need of thee: she is a fen / Of stagnant waters . . . "; see *Selected Poems and Prefaces by William Wordsworth*, ed. Jack Stillinger (Boston: Houghton Mifflin, 1965), 172. Previous translators of Wen's *Sishui* 死水 have rendered the title literally as "Dead Water," but the similarity of Wen's line to that of Wordsworth is probably not coincidental.

nipulating meter are more fully disclosed, New Poetry will enter a new period of innovation. In any case, we should recognize that such innovation will be an event of cataclysmic significance in the history of New Poetry.

Whether the cataclysm represents progress or decline will soon cease to be a point of contention.

—*Translated by Randy Trumbull*
Previously published in
Renditions 21–22 (Spring–Autumn 1989): 127–34.
Reprinted by permission.

Chapter 35

The Divergence of Art and Politics

Lu Xun

—A talk given at Jinan University, Shanghai
December 21,1927

I'm not much for giving public lectures; that I've come today is only because I promised so often.[1] So here I am and that should settle it. The reason I don't give public lectures is, for one thing, I have no opinions to speak
of and, for another, as this gentleman has just said, many of you have read
my books, which means there's not much for me to talk about. People in
books are probably a little nicer than the genuine article: characters in *The
Dream of the Red Chamber* like Jia Baoyu and Lin Daiyu made me feel an unusual sympathy; later on, after looking into some of the facts of that era, I
saw them both, performed by the opera stars Mei Lanfang and Jiang
Miaoxiang in Beijing, and didn't find them edifying in the least.[2]

---

1. Lu Xun 鲁迅, "Wenyi yu zhengzhi de qitu" 文藝與政治的歧途, *Xinwen bao-
Xuehai* 新聞報-學海 182, 183 (Jan. 29, 30, 1928); collected in *Jiwai ji* 集外集; reprinted in
Lu Xun 1981a: 7: 113–21.
2. Lu Xun's distaste for Beijing opera is elaborated on in "On Photography," also included in this collection.

I have no grand comprehensive theory and no edifying views, so I'll just talk about something that recently came to mind. I have often felt that art and politics are in constant conflict. Art and revolution are not actually opposites, and in fact they both feel the same uneasiness with the status quo. But politics would maintain the status quo, and naturally its direction is different from art, which is uneasy with the status quo. And yet, art dissatisfied with the status quo did not arise until the nineteenth century and has only had a very short history. Politicians take very poorly to anyone who opposes their opinions, anyone who means to think or speak out. In earlier societies no one ever thought anything, or ever spoke out. Just look at the animals, at monkeys: they have their leaders, and the way their leaders want them is just the way they'll be. Similarly, tribal societies have chiefs who are followed and whose word is law. If the chief wants them dead, they have no choice but to go and die. In those days there was no art, or at best nothing more than praise of God (still not as profound as the *Domine* coined by later generations)! How could there be any free thought? Then these tribes began swallowing each other until, having devoured a vast number of small tribes, some gradually grew into "great nations." With the advent of nations, internal affairs became more complex, involving many different ideas and many different problems. This was when art arose in ceaseless conflict with politics: politics wanted to keep the status quo from falling apart, but art hastened the social evolution that caused the gradual disintegration of society; although art ruptured society, this is how society progressed. Since art is a thorn in politicians' flesh, it can't avoid being squeezed out. Many foreign writers, unable to hold their ground in their own land, make a mad dash for another country; this method is called "escape." If they don't make it, they're executed, beheaded; beheading is the best method, since they'll neither speak out nor think anymore. This is what happened to many Russian writers; many others were exiled to icebound Siberia.

There is a faction in the discussions on art that advocates casting off from real life and talking about, oh, the moon, or flowers, or birds (things are different in China where the National Essence moral code doesn't permit talk of moon and flowers, classing it as taboo discourse), or talking exclusively of "dreams," or future societies—nothing too immediate. All writers like this hide in an ivory tower; but, you know, "ivory towers" can't stand very long! Ivory towers exist in the real world where political oppression is unavoidable. When war breaks out, all you can do is escape. A literary group in Beijing has utter disdain for writers who describe society, and they think that allowing the lives of rickshawmen into fiction amounts to breaking the laws of fiction, which is supposed to tell stories of how a

poem leads to love between a genius and a beauty. Ah, but now they themselves can no longer be lofty writers and have to come south to escape, for
their daily bread wasn't being handed to them through the windows of the
"ivory tower"![3]

By the time even these writers escaped, others had long since escaped
or died. Still others had long felt dissatisfied with the status quo, had felt
compelled to protest, to speak out, and that was their undoing. Art being
an emotional engagement with contemporary life, I believe that what the
writer feels personally will leave its imprint in art. There is a writer in Nor-
way who describes hunger in a book based on his own experiences.[4] "Hunger" (to stick with this one among life's experiences) can be tried out if
that's your pleasure. It only takes a couple of days without food for its aroma to become a distinct temptation; if you find yourself walking past the
door of an eatery, you'll feel your nose is being assaulted by the aroma. We
don't think twice about spending money when we have it, but when it's
gone, a single coin takes on significance. The book describing hunger tells
how the character who goes hungry for a long time sees everyone on the
street as his enemy, and someone wearing even thin clothes strikes him as
arrogant. It reminds me that I myself wrote about such a person, didn't
have a penny on him, kept opening drawers to take a look and see if he
could find anything in the corners and along the edges; he'd search everywhere up and down the street to see what he could find; this is something
I've gone through myself.

When someone who's led a life of poverty becomes rich, one of two
things can easily develop: he can live in an ideal world where compassion
for those in the same predicament turns into humanitarianism; or, having
earned everything on his own, his former hard times make him feel everything is merciless, which sours into individualism. Our China will likely
have a majority of individualists. The advocates of humanitarianism think
of finding a way out for the poor, of changing the status quo, which strikes
the politician as a fate decidedly worse than that promised by the individualists; so there's a conflict between humanitarians and politicians. The
Russian writer Tolstoy spoke for humanitarianism, opposed war, and
wrote a thick three-volume novel, *War and Peace*; although an aristocrat

---

3. Lu Xun is referring to the Crescent Moon Society. One of its members, Liang Shiqiu,
wrote an essay, "Xiandai Zhongguo wenxue de langman de quxiang" 現代中國文學的
浪漫的趨向 (The romantic trend in modern Chinese literature) (*Chenbao-fukan*, Mar. 27,
1926) in which he attacked the fad in modern vernacular poetry of portraying the miserable lives of rickshawmen. This essay is included in Liang Shiqiu 1927.

4. The Norwegian writer Knut Hamsun (1859–1952) won the Nobel prize in 1920. His
fame began with the 1888 novel *Hunger*.

himself, he had experienced life on the battlefield and had felt the misery of war. His guilt was especially sharp when he stood before his commander's iron plate (top officers on the battlefield each had an iron plate as protection against artillery). He had witnessed the battlefield sacrifice of many of his friends. War, too, can result in the development of two attitudes: one is held by the hero who sees that others have died or been wounded, but as long as he's in one piece, he considers himself terrific and glorifies his bravery on the battlefield. The other is held by those who've turned against war and hope the world will never again take up arms. Tolstoy was the latter, advocating non-resistance as a means to eliminate war. The government couldn't stand him, of course, because he made this his cause; opposing war conflicted with the tsarist lust for aggression. His cause of non-resistance would have men in the ranks not fight for the tsar, police not enforce law for the tsar, judges not pass sentences for the tsar, the public not exalt the tsar. The tsar was all in favor of exaltation, for what sort of tsar would he be without it. All of these provoked further conflicts with the government. With the appearance of such writers, who were dissatisfied with the status quo, always criticizing this and that until everyone in society became personally aware of it and grew uneasy because of it, the only solution was for heads to roll.

But the language of the writer is the language of society. He is simply sensitive, quick to feel and quick to express (too quickly, at times, so even society opposes and excludes him). Take military drill for example: in presenting arms the regulation command is "pre-s e e e e nt ARMS," and you damn well can't present them until the word ARMS is called. Yet some people raise the rifle as soon as they hear the word "present," causing the instructor to punish them for their error. That's exactly how it is with the writer in society; he speaks a little too soon, and the public hates him for it. Politicians are convinced that the writer is an instigator of social disorder and intend to kill him off so society can have some peace. Little do they know that with the writer killed, society will still have revolution. The number of Russian writers killed or exiled isn't small, but the fires of revolution flared up everywhere, didn't they? Throughout his life a writer will likely get no sympathy from society. His life is one of frustration; then four or five decades after his death he's discovered by society, and the public really acts up. For this, politicians detest him all the more, figuring the writer had long ago sown the seeds of trouble. Politicians would like to debar the public from thinking, but the savage age for that ended long ago. I don't know the views of all of you here, but I figure they certainly wouldn't tally with those of the politicians. Since they always blame the writer for ruining their social unity, so biased are they, I've never agreed to talk to politicians.

Time passes and society eventually changes; the public gradually recalls what the artist said before, and however much he suffered the taunts of society during his lifetime, everyone now approves of and compliments his foresight. Just now as I came up to speak, you gave a sudden round of applause, but this clapping shows that I'm not all that great. Applause is a dangerous thing: being applauded might give me the idea I'm so great I can stop trying; so it's better not to clap. Now, as I've said, the writer is more sensitive, many concepts touch him first before society has any sense of them. For example, a certain gentleman is wearing a leather coat while I'm still in cotton; the gentleman's sense of the cold is more acute than mine. Another month maybe and I, too, will feel I have to put on a leather coat. If one can be a month off in his sense of the weather, he can be thirty to forty years off in his sense of ideas. When I say things like this, there are many writers now who object. In Guangdong I once criticized a revolutionary writer[5]—currently in Guangdong unrevolutionary literature doesn't count as literature, and nothing counts as *revolutionary* literature without "strike, strike, strike, kill, kill, kill, revolt, revolt, revolt"—I simply didn't think revolution could be linked with literature, although in literature there are *literary* revolutions. People in literature simply have to have the time for it; who is free to write literature in the midst of revolution? Let's just consider: life is hard enough without the inconvenience of pulling a rickshaw and turning out a fine prose style at the same time. There were some ancients who did manage to write poems while farming, but they surely didn't farm with their own hands; they hired some men to do the farming for them so they could chant their poems. If you really want to farm, there's no time to write poems. And so it is in a time of revolution when no one has time to write poems. During the fight against the warlord Chen Jiongming, several students of mine were on the battlefield.[6] As I read what they wrote to me, I could see their language getting rustier with each succeeding letter. After the Russian Revolution people got into bread lines with bread coupons in hand. In those days the nation no longer cared whether you were writer, painter, or sculptor. If getting bread took up all

---

5. Wu Zhihui 吳稚暉 was criticized in Lu Xun's 1927 essay "Geming wenxue" 革命文學 (Revolutionary literature); see Lu Xun 1981a: 3: 543–46.

6. In the early 1920's, under the aegis of Sun Yatsen, the Nationalists and the Communists jointly formed a revolutionary army with the goal of unifying China by driving out local warlords and foreign imperialists. Their defeat of Chen Jiongming 陳炯明, warlord of Guangdong, secured them a base in that southern province, from which they launched their Northern Expedition in 1926.

your time, when could you think of literature? And when literature did re-appear, the revolution had already succeeded. After its success, things re-laxed a bit, and some people flattered the revolution and others sang its praises, but by then none of this was revolutionary literature. To flatter and praise the revolution was to praise those in power, and what does that have to do with revolution?

There may well have been sensitive writers who both felt discontent with the status quo and were ready to speak out. The political revolutionar-ies had previously endorsed the writers' words, but when the revolution succeeded, its politicians began to readopt the old methods of those they originally opposed. And with artists inevitably discontent, they had to be barred or beheaded. Cutting off heads, as I have said, is the best of methods —from the nineteenth century to the present that has been the trend in world art.

Art from the nineteenth century on bears little resemblance to art prior to the eighteenth. The aim of eighteenth-century English fiction was to en-tertain wives and young women with happy, humorous stories. The last half of the nineteenth century saw a complete change, as the problems of life took on immediacy in literature. It is sheer agony to read it, yet we read on compulsively. The reason is that earlier art seems to describe a different society that we can appreciate only from a distance. Contemporary art de-scribes our own society, and even we are written into it; society can be found in fiction, and so can we. Previous art, like a fire across the river, had little to do with us. In contemporary art even we ourselves are burning; we certainly feel it deeply. And once we feel it, we certainly want to take part in society!

The nineteenth century can be called an age of revolution, "revolution" meaning uneasiness with the present, discontent with the status quo. Art that hastens the gradual elimination of the old is also revolution (the new can only emerge with the elimination of the old), but the writer's fate doesn't go through the same transformations simply because the writer joined the revolution. Instead there are brick walls at every turn. The revo-lutionary forces have already made their way north to Xuzhou. North of Xuzhou writers had never been able to hold their ground; south of Xuzhou writers still can't hold their ground; even when communized, writers still won't be able to hold their ground. Revolutionary writers and revolutionar-ies, it's fair to say, are completely different things. Revolutionary writers rant against the great irrationality of warlords; revolutionaries overthrow warlords. Sun Chuanfang was sent packing, blasted out by artillery in revo-lutionaries' hands, and not driven out by the "Hey, Sun Chuanfang, hey, we'll get rid of you" in a few essays by revolutionary writers.[7] During a revolution, writers are busy dreaming of what kind of world it will be when the revolution succeeds; after the revolution, look around, the reality is not what they had meant at all, and once again they suffer. To go by their weeping and wailing, nothing has succeeded; neither going forward nor backward leads to success, the ideal and the real don't coincide, and all is decreed by fate, just as the Lu Xun you perceived in *Call to Arms* and the Lu Xun on the rostrum don't coincide (maybe you all imagined I'd part my hair and wear a foreign suit, but I haven't worn a foreign suit and you see how close-cropped my hair is). And so, self-appointed revolutionary literature certainly isn't revolutionary literature—where in the world is there a revolutionary literature pleased with the status quo? Unless it's been etherized! There were two writers before the Russian Revolution, Esenin and Sobol,[8] who sang the praises of revolution, but later died crashing into the solid monument of the revolution they had sung of and hoped for. At that time the Soviets had been established!

And yet, society is so dreary that only such people can make it at all amusing. Humanity likes to see a little theater, writers volunteer to perform, getting bound or dispatched to the headsman or else to the nearest wall facing a firing squad, all of which liven things up. It's also like the Shanghai Concession police clubbing someone. The public gathers round, and although they themselves don't want to be clubbed, seeing someone else clubbed is mighty amusing. So writers are the ones who take the clubbing on their own hides!

It's not very much but that's today's talk, and as for a title, call it . . . "The Divergence of Art and Politics."

—*Translated by Donald Holoch and Shu-ying Tsau*

---

7. Sun Chuanfang 孫 傳 芳 , warlord of the lower Yangtze (Fujian, Zhejiang) was defeated that winter. By April 1927 the Nationalist leader Chiang Kaishek (who had taken over after the death of Sun Yatsen) would break openly with the Communists and, claiming the mantle of revolution, continue the Northern Expedition. Internal trouble was already brewing when the revolutionary army took Xuzhou on December 16, 1926. Revolutionary sympathizers north of this city were exposed to warlord hostility; to the south they were subject to purges.

8. Sergei Esenin (1895–1925) and Andrei Sobol (1888–1926) were Russian writers who became disillusioned with the revolution and committed suicide.

Chapter 36

Thoughts on Realism

Zhou Yang

I

In a recent lecture, Gide discussed the importance of the link between literature and reality and drew an intriguing analogy with the Greek myth of Antaeus the Giant.[1] As long as Antaeus made sure his feet never left his Mother Earth, his strength would continue to increase, but when Hercules lifted him up in the air, he became weak as a kitten. This is a profound analogy. All the literary giants of the past have trod firmly on the soil of reality, and the close bond between literature and reality has been the wellspring of literary power.

The efforts of writers in the past to draw close to reality have left us the legacy of literature's foremost tradition: realism. Giving realism the highest accolade requires us to analyze in concrete terms its origins and development, considering the specific historical and social characteristics of each era's literature. Only if we take the development of realism, its waxing and

---

1. Zhou Yang 周揚, "Xianshizhuyi shilun" 現實主義試論, *Wenxue* 文學 6, no. 1 (Jan. 1, 1936); reprinted in Zhou Yang 1984.

waning, together with the historical limitations of the times in which each writer lived, the fluctuations of the various social strata, and the writers' creative methods and worldviews can we draw things like inherent qualities into our explanation. The substance of realism has emerged in highly complex form.

The style, or one might even say the school, known as "realism" followed on the heels of romanticism and came to dominate European literary circles during the latter half of the nineteenth century. Prototypical forms of realism, however, began to appear in mid-eighteenth-century European literature ahead of the romanticist movement. The eighteenth century saw the flourishing of the bourgeoisie, the soil of reality being well suited at the time to its growth and development. Diderot called out for "drawing close to true reality," and Rousseau, Richardson, Fielding and others drew their themes from the domestic life, customs, and morality of the newly rising bourgeoisie in creating works of "sentimental realism."

If we delve into realism more broadly and deeply, we can see that the works of all the great writers of the past are brimming with its key elements. Goethe's writings "explored the broadest reaches of social reality during his time, analyzed countless characteristic types, and went a long way toward portraying the way the bourgeoisie actually lived" (S. [*sic*] Schiller). Even more obvious an example is Shakespeare, who, by depicting vast scenes of the struggles between capitalism and feudal forces, painted a scroll of incomparable resplendence revealing the morality and customs of Renaissance England. In the works of these two great poets can we not detect in abundance the key threads of realism, or even, as Kirpotin says, of dialectics and materialism?[2]

In the history of literature, realism has generally been understood as the opposite of romanticism. This distinction is rigid and inaccurate. In fact, these two currents often intertwine, permeate each other, even fuse together. Brandes asserts that French romanticism is thinly veiled naturalism, and that the great romanticist masters Balzac and Stendhal are in fact realism's leading practitioners. Although Russian realism had no firm foundation until Gogol's time, the lyric poets Pushkin and Lermontov laid the first cornerstones. *Evgeni Onegin* and *A Hero for Our Time* exerted great influence on Russian realism. That the works of a single author could include elements of both realism and romanticism is even more commonly recog-

---

2. Valerii Iakovlevich Kirpotin (1898–?), secretary of the Union of Writers of the USSR in 1932–34, literary historian, and critic. His criticism focuses on the aesthetic attitude and worldview of the author and often takes a psychological approach to the author's personality.

nized. Gorky went so far as to say that in great artists, romanticism and realism seem always to be mingled together. Here we need look no further than Balzac and Gogol. More than a few of Balzac's realist works are Hoffmannesque fantasies, and Gogol, as the author of *Evenings on a Farm near Dikanka* and *Taras Bulba*, is indeed an outstanding romanticist.

By what criteria, then, do we distinguish realism? There is a paragraph in Dinamov's[3] discussion of Shakespeare well worth mulling over:

> We cannot judge Shakespeare in the light of realism's outward guise; what matters is that Shakespeare did not observe reality from an idealistic stand-point. In his intentions, in the content of his works, and in their essential quality, he is a realist. Using various dramatic forms and themes, from comedy to tragedy and from tragedy to amusing tales, he has never taken objective reality for a mere reflection of the "spirit." His basic roots are in the world around him—the world as it is, not a fabrication.

Here the criteria for realism have acquired fairly precise parameters, and our understanding of realism must proceed from this newly reappraised point of view.

II

In the wake of the establishment of ruling authority by the nineteenth-century bourgeoisie, realist literature carved out its own broad domain. Most of the best realist authors were the "unworthy descendants" of the bourgeoisie, members of declining families crushed by the nouveaux riches, or sons of the petite bourgeoisie who had sprung free of the stifling atmosphere around them. They cherished no sweet affection for the realities of bourgeois society; rather, with their artistic talent and innate powers of penetration, and infected with the scientific spirit intrinsic to the bourgeois age, they courageously portrayed society's flaws and contradictions, reaching a peak in the exposure of reality's ugly side. English idiomatic usage links realism with a partiality for the ugly face of humanity, as the history of early realism verifies.

Although the realists have attacked society's ugliness and exposed its defects, they stop at criticism, contributing nothing positive. Their inborn

---

3. Soviet literary critic, editor of *Literaturnaya gazeta*, and member of the leftist faction of RAPP (Russian Association of Proletarian Writers). The article referred to is "Xuexi Shashibiya" 學習莎士比亞 (Study Shakespeare), Yiwen 2, no. 5 (1935).

detachment prevents them from coming out with their own program. In this passivity, this contemplative nature, lie the basic faults of old-style realism, bound as it was by the constraints of the time.

Since the nineteenth century, realism has drawn ever closer to pessimism. Writers have been unable to discover a way out of the loathsome and unfortunate social conditions they have exposed; thus they often resort to a warm humanistic sympathy (as does Dickens), or seek support from the comforting hand of religion (as do Tolstoy and Dostoevsky). Consider Balzac, among the greatest of realists: even his ideas and perceptions of reality still go no further than the realm of metaphysics, and his attitude toward life is intuitively materialistic.

Gorky has quite aptly pointed out that nineteenth-century realism is "critical realism." Its greatest merit lies in the critical light it has shed on the customs, traditions, and behavior of the bourgeoisie, but owing to the hindrances and deficiencies attached to the authors' worldview, it has by no means reached the point of fully reflecting the truth of life.

Now the soil of reality in which old-style realism grew is in danger of disintegrating. There remain only two reliable roads left open to writers who lean toward realism: either to part with the rapidly changing times and shrink the compass of their observations of reality, sinking intoxicated into the minutiae of "microscopic realism"; or to open wide the cage of the old world, remolding themselves with complete candor and honesty and moving toward reality's future.

III

Artistic truth is only possible when the development of the writer's subjectivity and that of objective reality proceed in unison. Subjective honesty is of course an indispensable prerequisite for realist artistic creation. However, whereas the main current of nineteenth-century literature was realism, the decadent literature of today displays escape from reality as its major trait. We cannot explain this solely on the basis of writers' honesty or dishonesty, but must seek the reasons in the foundations of the decadent era of bourgeois society. To cite another specific example, although one cannot say that Bunin[4] lacks subjective honesty, still, since leaving his native country, he not only has failed to produce works reflecting objective reality but has long been mired in a "creative impasse."

---

4. Ivan Bunin (1870–1953), Russian novelist whose early fiction before the October Revolution portrayed the hardships of rural life sympathetically. He emigrated to Paris in 1920, disenchanted with the revolution.

Su Wen holds that objective truth exists within subjective truth and further asserts that since subjectivity and objectivity are naturally united, writers need not concern themselves with the matter. This view is simply a lot of threadbare, idealistic rigmarole, the greatest danger it poses being that it imperceptibly encourages writers to be satisfied with an inferior form of reality and to abandon their persistent efforts to draw closer to objective truth.

The objective world exists and develops independently of our subjectivity. The union of subjectivity and objectivity is the recognition that the world around man must be acted upon. On the surface, all objective phenomena appear jumbled and difficult to fathom. Only by penetrating their outer layer and probing to the very heart of objective reality can we temper and substantiate our subjectivity, and only then will we acquire the ability to grasp the ordered nature of objectivity. Literary knowledge depends on perceptual images, and artists must derive living images from reality, from life itself. Therefore the relationship between literature and reality is especially direct and close.

Reality is now forging ahead by leaps and bounds. Old-style realism has long since grown powerless, and negative romanticism has also been swept away by reality's surging tide. If writers do not stay smugly bound by such notions as the "artist's soul" and do not mistake the narrow social circles in which they live for the whole of the objective world, then the first question they must deal with is how, in practical terms, to attain an organic interconnection with developing reality in order to enable their own subjectivity to merge with the current of objectivity.

Carrying on the realist line in the history of literature, adhering to the most correct modern worldview, attaining a new closeness with reality, reflecting reality in both movement and development—these arduous and formidable tasks of creative production already confront every writer and can only be accomplished if each writer trains his consciousness while thoroughly investigating and absorbing reality.

IV

New realist methods must be based on a correct modern worldview. A correct worldview can guarantee true understanding of the laws of social development as well as of human psychology and thought; it can also greatly enhance the ideological force of artistic creation.

Here we cannot avoid touching on questions of creative method and worldview that have already been widely debated. Ignoring the special nature of artistic creation and reducing the question of method all the way

down to a simple question of worldview are mistakes that have already received justifiable criticism. The great realist writers of the past have, as a result of practical observation, research, and analysis of reality, frequently
contradicted their own innate worldviews and reached conclusions that are
artistically both correct and beneficial. Critics have frequently invoked the
examples of Balzac and Gogol, and these are the most familiar to us. But if
we are bedazzled by these "wonders" of realism, we will all too easily ignore and undervalue the crucial function of worldview in artistic creation.

Meng Shijun, in a piece on realism in the journal *Essays*, writes: "Practical study is the most important pivotal point in understanding; if you examine reality closely, it will weaken and collapse your preestablished
worldview, and teach you something new." In the same journal, Xin Ren
has this to say: "If a writer has talent and life experience, his writings will
generally adhere closely to reality and reflect its development."[5] Here,
Meng Shijun views the relationship of subjectivity to objectivity as completely passive and exaggerates the power of blind objectivity. He sees only
as far as the disintegration of the writer's worldview induced by realist
methods and does not see how this disintegration has left traces in written
works, rent the warp and weft of art, and given rise to contradictions within realism. (Remember Balzac's numerous stories steeped in sympathy for
the aristocracy and also the second part of Gogol's *Dead Souls*.) Xin Ren neglects the function of the writer's subjective consciousness even further. In
fact, however, if you want to achieve a true reflection of reality, then relying on talent and experience alone is far from adequate. In Balzac's case, if
he had not possessed what one great thinker has extolled as "a profound
understanding of reality's interrelationships," he would not have been able
to portray the full panorama of French society from the weakening of the
feudal order down to the collapse of the royal court on Bastille Day.

The contradiction between a writer's worldview and his creative methods reflects that between the subjective interests of the social class to which
he belongs and the objective tendencies of reality. This contradiction is not
an eternal one; it will be resolved in the course of historical development.
In fact, we have already attained a higher-level worldview than that of early realists, one far removed in essence. One aspect of a worldview could be
at odds with another aspect in writers of the past. We see this situation not
only in Balzac and Gogol; the French materialists explained history in ide-

---

5. Meng Shijun 孟式鈞 and Chen Xinren 陳辛人 joined the Tokyo branch of the
League of Left-Wing Writers in the 1930's and were active in leftist cultural circles. The essays referred to are Meng Shijun, "Xianshizhuyi de jichu" 現實主義的基礎 (The foundation of realism), *Zawen* 2 (1935); and Xin Ren 辛人, "Cong chuangzuo fangfa jiangqi"
從創作方法講起 (Beginning with a discussion of creative method), *Zawen* 2 (1935).

alist terms, and the rigorous realist Tolstoy also lived by idealist tenets. These examples are familiar to us all. However, the worldview we have now attained is integrated, consistent, and free of internal contradictions. If we say that earlier realist artists went against the grain of their own worldviews to achieve a correct expression of reality, then our realism draws support from our worldview to render the expression of reality even more accurate.

Meticulous observation and study of reality naturally can lead a writer in the direction of a correct worldview; conversely, a correct worldview is the guiding principle for observation and study. Writers, owing to differences in their social positions and upbringing, all have their own views, biases, and partialities regarding human life. If they do not have a fairly correct worldview, then even if they are in touch with reality, they are likely to lose their bearings amid the confusion of facts and phenomena and be unable to grasp either reality's essence or its direction and future prospects. The power of a scientific worldview lies precisely in the fact that it can generate "the ability to perceive a clear sense of direction and to comprehend the intrinsic connections among events happening around us." Of course, it would not be justifiable to insist that writers regard a well-assimilated correct worldview as a precondition for writing, but to maintain and expound such a worldview is the surest way to lead writers in the correct direction.

China's present reality appears turbulent and chaotic. Intellectuals, owing to their inclination and susceptibility to detachment, have during this important era experienced unprecedented vacillation, depression, and uncertainty. However, the suffering of the people leaves everyone but one common way out, with the correct worldview as the shining beacon illuminating their forward progress. Critics must give the greatest prominence to worldview. Su Wen advocates absolute freedom for writers' subjectivity and holds that a unified worldview is tantamount to forfeiting the artist's individual soul. To say this is to argue in favor of a whole spectrum of inferior petit-bourgeois views of human life and the world at large. Xin Ren and others rightly point out Su Wen's error, but owing to their own underestimation of worldview they are unable to strike at the heart of their opponent's theoretical foundation, the more so because Su Wen certainly does not oppose in theory the expression of objective truth and has in the past called himself a humanist realist.

Without study of and immersion in reality, maturity of one's worldview in and of itself cannot produce art; this point is self-evident. For a work to become formulaic and generalized destroys realism's artistry. The worldview must form the "very core of a work that lends images concrete form"

(Yu Ding).[6] As great thinkers have indicated, the art of the future will mean precisely the union of the highest artistic forms with a worldview founded on extensive thought.

V

Realist artists must strive to give expression to types that are as true to reality as possible. "Realism, to my mind, implies, besides the truth of detail, the truthful reproduction of typical characters under typical circumstances."[7] This classic dictum not only spells out the essence of realism but also points to the source of the power manifested by all the great works of the past. A work of art is not a random display of facts but a selection from among the miscellaneous facts of human life of what is shared, characteristic, and typical; through these elements people can clearly discern the whole of life. This ability to generalize the typical is precisely the power of art.

The great artists of the past have successfully portrayed lifelike typical characters; Hamlet and Quixote are names on the tip of everyone's tongue. Creating types entails extracting from a certain social group the most characteristic traits, habits, tastes, aspirations, actions, speech, and so forth and embodying these in a character, ensuring that the character does not lose its distinctive personality. Thus a type possesses particular traits common to a specific time and a specific social group, while endowed simultaneously with an individual style and features distinguishing him from the social group he represents. In the words of one thinker: "Every character is a type, and at the same time a fully unique individual—'this one,' as Hegel said."[8]

In one of his essays, Hu Feng interprets the universality and particularity of types as follows:

> The term "universal" refers to the various individuals within the social group to which that character belongs; the term "particular" refers to other social groups or to the various individuals within those other groups. If we look at peasants around the time of the 1911 Revolution as well as those in a few backward areas today, the character Ah Q's personality is universal; but among merchant, landlord, or worker groups, among individual mer-

---

6. No information available on Yu Ding 虞丁.

7. Engels, "Letter to Margaret Harkness" (in English; April 1888), in *Literature and Art by Karl Marx and Frederick Engels: Selections from Their Writings*, 41–43.

8. Engels, "Letter to Mina Kautsky" (Nov. 26, 1885) in *Literature and Art by Karl Marx and Frederick Engels: Selections from Their Writings*, 88.

chants, landlords, or workers, and among peasants now living within a different set of social relationships, his personality is a particular one.[9]

This interpretation needs to be corrected. Ah Q's personality is universal in the context of the time around the 1911 Revolution and among backward peasants today, but his particularity definitely does not exist with respect to groups other than the peasants he represents; rather, it lies precisely in the fact that even among the peasants he represents, he is also a particularized being, having his own unique set of experiences, a unique lifestyle, and his own particular psychological makeup, habits, mannerisms, mode of speech, and so on. In short, Ah Q is truly an Ah Q, a "this one." If Ah Q's personality differed only from that of a merchant or landlord, his animated and vivid figure would not have left so deep an imprint on people's minds. After all, even under the pen of the clumsiest of artists, a peasant could never be portrayed in the same way as a merchant or a landlord.

A type is not a copy of a model, nor is it a fantasized image. Instead, the writer uses his rich imagination to take an actually extant or embryonic personality common to a certain social group, synthesize it, magnify it, and render it as accurately and truthfully as possible. Gorky puts it well: "True art operates by the rules of enlargement and exaggeration. Hercules, Prometheus, Quixote, Faust—these are by no means simply 'products of fantasy,' but are entirely normal and inevitable poetic exaggerations arising from objective facts."

VI

Only after the source material of reality has passed through the crucible of artistic imagination and fantasy can it reappear garbed as a work of art. Of course this is not what Su Wen calls "modifying" objectivity, but is instead "standing even higher than reality, by no means separating man from reality, but elevating him above it" (Gorky). In this sense, the new realism not only does not reject romanticism but in fact requires it as one of its intrinsic elements.

Casting aside what has been a rigid, one-sided interpretation of romanticism, we can gain from Gorky an explicit and penetrating understanding of it. He has pointed out two distinct tendencies embodied in romanticism. Negative romanticism is intuitive, uselessly hidden deep inside the individ-

---

9. Hu Feng 胡風, "Shenme shi dianxing he leixing" 甚麼是典型和類型 Hu Feng 1984: 1: 96–99.

ual's own inner world, inducing a return to the past. Positive romanticism, on the other hand, strives to strengthen a person's will, arousing strong feelings of resistance against reality and against everything else that inhibits the will.

The latter kind of romanticism is just what we need now. Reality has stifled us. In the darkness surrounding us, it is easy for our eyes to lose the ability to discern what lies ahead. Within a nation of people who have been "injured and insulted," there are on the other hand plenty of instances of "heroism" and "pathos" to inspire us. Is there not fertile soil here in which romanticism can flourish?

—Translated by Catherine Pease Campbell

Chapter 37

Realism: A "Correction"

Hu Feng

Discussions of Realism, Part I: A Response to Zhou Yang on the Question of the Universality and Particularity of "Types"

I

The problem of "types" is a central issue in literary theory on which many have stated their views, and I have also made some sketchy comments on it in response to the Literary Society's call for articles[1] ("What Are 'Type' and 'Stereotype'?" in *One Hundred Questions on Literature*).[2] Today, half a year later, I see that in the January issue of *Literature* Zhou Yang has touched on this question in his "Thoughts on Realism," [see previous essay] but he has by no means dealt fully with the substance of the question, only issuing a "correction" of my opinions on the universality and particularity of types. The present article is a "correction" of his "correction," because, to begin

---

1. Hu Feng 胡風, "Xianshizhuyi de 'xiuzheng' " 現實主義的修正; reprinted in Hu Feng 1984: 1: 341–52.

2. Hu Feng, "Shenme shi dianxing he leixing?" 甚麼是典型和類型; in *Wenxue baiti* 文學百題, eds. Zheng Zhenduo and Fu Donghua (Shanghai: Shenghuo shudian, 1936), 216–20; reprinted in Hu Feng 1984: 1: 96–99.

with, in his critique of others' arguments he has indicated the source of each one but, for some reason, has not done so for mine. This renders the reader unable to compare my entire essay with his, creating the same danger as showing the reader an elephant's trunk to stand for the whole elephant. Second, his arguments are not only ineffective in bringing the question closer to a fairly valid solution, but on the contrary have muddled it even more. So perhaps taking this opportunity to carry study of this question a step further will not be entirely meaningless. Let us look first at my original essay.

My view:

> The idea that it [a character] embodies both universality and particularity appears self-contradictory. However, the term "universal" refers to the various individuals within the social group to which that character belongs; the term "particular" refers to other social groups or to the various individuals within those other groups. If we look at peasants around the time of the 1911 Revolution as well as those in a few backward areas today, the character Ah Q's personality is universal; but among merchant, landlord, or worker groups, among individual landlords or workers, and among peasants now living within a different set of social relationships, his personality is a particular one. (*One Hundred Questions on Literature*, 217)[3]

Zhou Yang's "correction":

> This interpretation needs to be corrected. Ah Q's personality is universal in the context of the time around the 1911 Revolution and among backward peasants today, but his particularity *definitely does not exist* with respect to groups other than the peasants he represents; rather, it *lies precisely in the fact that even among the peasants he represents, he is also a particularized being,* having his own *unique* set of experiences, a *unique* lifestyle, and his own *particular* psychological makeup, habits, mannerisms, mode of speech, and so on. In a word, Ah Q is truly an Ah Q, a "this one." If Ah Q's personality differed only from that of a merchant or landlord, his animated and vivid figure would not have left so deep an imprint on people's minds. After all, even under the pen of the clumsiest of artists, a peasant could never be portrayed in the same way as a merchant or a landlord (January issue of *Literature*, 89; italics added—Feng).[4]

---

3. Hu Feng omitted the word "merchants" from the original passage.
4. See Zhou Yang, "Thoughts on Realism," included in this volume.

This is very clear. I say Ah Q's personality is universal in the context of a certain category of peasants, whereas Zhou Yang says Ah Q is a particularized being among the peasants he represents. These two views are diametrically opposed.

II

To begin with, what he calls a "particularized being" has one possible explanation—namely, that on the one hand a type intrinsically possesses the particular traits of a certain specific group, but on the other hand it must be a *living character in whom these traits have been individualized.* Earlier, he says that "a type possesses particular traits common to a specific time and a specific social group, while endowed simultaneously with an *individual* style and features *distinguishing* him from the social group he represents." This statement can actually stand as a premise for the above interpretation.

However, if this is the case, then his "correction" of my point fails completely, because in that essay I had already stated:

> In fact, these characters really do not exist, although they are by no means the author's fabrications. Although characters who actually exist *resemble them, they are less well-integrated, and their personalities are less distinct, less clearly contoured.* . . . A type is a *concrete, living character,* but one intrinsically possessing the particular traits of a certain group and representing that group. (*One Hundred Questions on Literature*, 216–17)

That is to say, the formation of a type requires that the group traits first be *individualized.* With group traits alone, the type cannot become art, but *an individual lacking the traits of the group is not a type.* In the words of a thinker invoked by Zhou Yang, "Every character is a type, and at the same time a fully unique individual—'this one,' as Hegel said."[5] This is just what I mean, although I have used plainer language.

Furthermore, my essay also uses real examples to explain the term "stereotype." Merely by seizing on one or two common superficial traits you cannot come up with a complex, living visage. Here only the term "stereotype" will do. "This kind of character has no *individuality*" (*One Hundred*

---

5. Author's note: I have also used the translation 'unique' [*dutede* 獨特的] here, but it should actually be translated as 'specific' [*texingde* 特性的]—Feng.

Questions on Literature, 220). I have stressed repeatedly the *individualized aspect* of types.

III

In fact, however, Zhou Yang is by no means inadvertently duplicating my argument; rather, he is denying in earnest the universality of types.

First of all, since "even among the peasants he represents" Ah Q "is also a particularized being," and since he has "his own unique set of experiences, a unique lifestyle, and his own particular psychological makeup, habits, mannerisms, mode of speech, and so on," this character's personality cannot embody universality and therefore cannot be a "type."

Second, though, Zhou Yang does use the phrase "the peasants he represents." In what way, then, does he "represent" them? If the peasants in question have drawn up a petition or something to tuck inside his bosom and have sent him off someplace as a "representative," then perhaps it doesn't matter how "unique" he is. If he were to wear a scholar's long gown, that would of course be fine, as would be Western dress; he could wear a queue, or cut it off and grow his hair out Western-style with impunity. But Ah Q has not been accorded such honor. If we say he represents a certain category of peasants, then the fulfillment of his mission as a "representative" must lie in his "experiences," "lifestyle," "mode of speech," and so on. Doing seasonal labor, being a thief, wanting to make revolution but "not allowed" to do so—his "experiences" are those that peasants of his kind can and often do have, and are certainly nothing "unique" to him. Smoking tobacco, wearing a beat-up felt hat, sleeping in the village god's temple, having no wife, husking rice for others in the evenings—his lifestyle is also one that peasants of his sort can and often do have, and is likewise not "unique" to him. If everything about Ah Q were "unique," I don't know whether he'd qualify for a mythological role, but he definitely could not be a "type."

Third, Zhou Yang says earlier that one must select "from among the miscellaneous facts of human life what is shared, characteristic, and typical," and also says that "a type possesses particular traits common to a specific time and a specific social group." What is common or shared cannot be unique, and I do not understand why he contradicts himself like this. But his preceding sentence says that "creating types entails extracting from a certain social group the most characteristic traits, habits, tastes, aspirations, actions, speech, and so forth, and embodying these in a character, ensuring that the character does not lose its distinctive personality." Since the habits and other elements constituting a personality are extracted from a specific social group, those elements must be shared by many other individuals within that specific group, and that being the case, they cannot be distinctive or unique attributes of the type being created. I do not understand why his argument is so muddled.

IV

In order to resolve these uncertainties, I have inquired into their causes. As it turns out, the problem lies in Zhou Yang's misinterpretation of the thinker he quotes earlier.

"Every character is a type, and at the same time a fully specific individual—a this one." As I have already explained, the phrase "specific individual—this one" refers to a character with group traits which *have been individualized*, thereby enabling it to be a type as well. I think this point calls for further elaboration. This statement appears in a letter to a woman writer, Mina Kautsby [sic].[6] Why did he say this? Because in her work (*Old and New*) there is a character who has definitely not become a "specific individual"; she has made him into a person of utmost goodness and beauty, "idealized" him, and deprived him of the appearance of a realistic character with its complexity and core of basic contradictions. This is what is known as "individuality dissolving into principle." His reference to a "specific individual—this one" aims *right at* this kind of character whose "individuality has dissolved into principle" and *right at* tendentiousness, which does not "flow naturally from the situation and action." My critique of "stereotypes" in my earlier essay derives from none other than this line of reasoning.

Zhou Yang, however, proceeds from this statement to attack the universality of types by saying that Ah Q's "particularity definitely does not exist with respect to groups other than the peasants he represents; rather, it lies precisely in the fact that even among the peasants he represents, he is also a particularized being." This is no small error. What the above thinker calls for is the individualization of group traits, whereas what Zhou Yang calls for (at least unconsciously) is a "distinctive personality" or a "particular being" with no group attributes. When he says that "Ah Q is truly an Ah Q, a this one," he intends not to show that Ah Q's group traits have been individualized but instead to illustrate emphatically that Ah Q is also a "par-

---

6. For political reasons, Hu Feng and Zhou Yang (see previous essay) never state openly the source of the citation to which they are both referring: Engels's "Letter to Minna Kautsky" (Nov. 26, 1885); reprinted in *Literature and Art by Karl Marx and Frederick Engels: Selections from Their Writings*, 44–46.

ticularized being" among the peasants he represents. Of course one could say this is a "correction," but I do not want to take it as a "correction" Zhou Yang consciously intends.

In another sense, a type is formed from the essential traits common to a certain group, and possesses the particular qualities shared by that group. This idea has already become widespread and is frequently mentioned by Gorky, whom Zhou Yang is so fond of citing. Although he wants to give this idea its due, he has been hampered by his misinterpretation of that thinker's statement, losing sight of one thing while attending to another, finally falling into irretrievable confusion.

V

What is the result of this confusion? It is the denial of the universality of types, and ultimately the very denial of the concept "type." This is because we can say that a type may differ from various individuals in the group he represents, but only in the sense of what I said in my other essay, that those individuals "are less well integrated than they (meaning types) are, and their personalities are less distinct, less clearly contoured." Yet we still must stress that *types all resemble to a certain extent the various individuals in the groups they represent*, because in a work portraying types, each individual character represents the characters of many individuals and embodies the universal nature of a certain social group. Therefore we can say "so-and-so-like," "Ah Q-like," or that somebody or other is an Ah Q; and we can discuss whether or not a certain type still exists in real society. To deny this aspect is to deny types themselves.

On this basis, I can sincerely point out that Zhou Yang's "unique individuals" and "distinctive personalities" are incompatible with the concept of "type," and that his argument could go so far as to result in the denial of "types." This is hardly a mere meddlesome dispute, since his views could exert unwarranted objective influence, as follows:

First, his views could muddle the meaning of the nature of art. Art and science alike are means for understanding objective truth, but they are not identical. Science uses general theoretical formulas to represent sentient individuals, whereas literature and art express universality (the content of reality's inner nature—rational ideological content) by means of concrete individuals (this one). Types in works of literature and art, therefore, must be individuals embodying the universal qualities of specific social groups.

Why art can exert such great power,[7] and why art can enable us to "expand" and "deepen" our understanding of reality—here is the underlying reason. If we deny the universality of types, can literature and art still serve life?

Second, his views could confuse our understanding of the "people" who are the central object of literary and artistic expression. In my other essay I cited the statement: "A person is the summation of social relationships,"[8] and said that "a literary type also necessarily reflects the interrelationships of the society from which that character comes." Since a type "reflects the interrelationships of the society from which he comes" and since a person is also always *part of a group*, how can he not embody universal qualities, instead being "distinctive" or "unique"? Moreover, the aim of art and literature is precisely to cast off what is accidental and to express what is innate (universal). When Zhou Yang says that "after all, even under the pen of the clumsiest of artists, a peasant could never be portrayed in the same way as a merchant or a landlord," at first glance this seems like a very sharp blow, but he has forgotten that the true task of literature and art is precisely to depict the *true differences* between peasants and merchants or landlords. For many who are not "the clumsiest of artists," although they have *not necessarily* depicted peasants resembling merchants or landlords, the defect lies in their inability to depict a peasant who resembles an *authentic* peasant or who differs *in some way* from merchants or landlords; sometimes they go so far as to portray peasants as moralists or poets who would suit the taste of merchants or landlords. Denying the universality of types can lead to an unintentional denial of people's group nature, and of the group nature of types as well.

VI

Because Zhou Yang has not grasped the concept of types firmly enough, he has not been able to explain in full the process of creating types. Although he repeatedly brings up such notions as "generalization" and extracting characteristic features from within a group, "generalization" and "extraction" are both scientific methods, and with these alone we cannot create art. When we use the term "artistic generalization," the word *artistic*

---

7. Author's note: Zhou Yang says, "The ability to generalize and typify is precisely the power of art." This is inexplicable. Generalization applies only to the creative process, to the power of the artist; how can one say it is the power of art? At the stage of "generalization" a work of art has still not succeeded, still not come face to face with the reader!

8. The subject of this sentence in the original article is *rende benzhi* 人的本質 and not *ren* 人; see Hu Feng 1984: 1: 98.

is not appended lightly. His views on creating types take up only this one paragraph:

> A type is not a copy of a model, nor is it a fantasized image. Instead the writer uses his *rich imagination* to take an actually extant or embryonic personality common to a certain social group, synthesize it, magnify it, and render it as concretely and truthfully as possible. (*Literature*, January 1936, 89)

It is true that creating types requires a "rich imagination," but the use of imagination alone is not necessarily enough, because it is also capable of creating *Journey to the West, Investiture of the Gods*, or *A Thousand and One Nights*.

I have discussed this point in my other essay as follows:

> For the task of creating "types," an artist needs to use imagination and intuition to smelt all the impressions he has gleaned from life, and also needs the ability to understand life, to analyze it, in order to ensure that what he gleans from life is essential and authentic. (*One Hundred Questions on Literature*, 219)

Although this is a sketchy way to put it, I have stressed the importance of the artist's ability to understand and analyze human life and to comprehend objective reality, because a realist artist's intuition (his artistic sensibility) bears no resemblance to that of a child coming in touch with the external world, but must have *undergone long-term training in real life and must be controlled by real-life knowledge*. Likewise, the artist's imagination is in no way unrestrained—a "heavenly horse roaming the skies" or "fantasy" without parentheses—but *must be permeated by profound thought*. Only in this way can we explain the great *ideological nature* (the formation of types) of works of art; only in this way can we find a way to resolve the problem of artists and living practice.

First of all, therefore, although artists extract the most characteristic traits common to a specific social group and from them create types, still, in You Jin's words, "an author can only reach this stage under the following conditions, namely, when the truth of our reality *fills the artist's emotions to overflowing, becoming inseparable from his individual personality*, when his study of reality is that careful, when his *use* of and '*immersion*' in his materials is that deep."[9] Only in this way can the "creative" stage take shape, the stage of subjective and objective unity. By using the word "smelt" (melt and cast), I intended to express this very idea, by no means *merely* Zhou Yang's "rich imagination" and his "crucible of fantasy."[10]

In the second place, sometimes the formation of types does not entail the artist's consciously extracting the most characteristic commonly held traits from a specific social group. Instead he simply discovers a new personality within a certain environment, feels inspired, and sets the creative process in motion, thereby still coming up with a typical personality. Creating a type out of a personality just forming within a certain social group, as Pushkin created Onegin, is even more common. Why is this possible? Because an artist's ability to understand reality and his artistic sensibility (not mere *imagination*) are guiding him, ensuring that the personality he has seized hold of is characteristic of the new nature of that social group and that his creative process operates within the context of the relationship between the character and its society. Thus the character's traits will certainly be commonly held and inherent within the social group, and the character will emerge as a type. If the character is created from the sprouts of a new sort of personality, those sprouts will grow taller and spread further day by day in the inevitable soil of society (the social interrelationships that the artist uses as a basis for creation). In such a case, the character the artist has created becomes a "pioneering" type, and the artist himself a "prophet."

Third, an artist can create *several types* from the same specific social group, each type *emphasizing a certain aspect* in its manifestation of the shared traits of that group's inherent nature, representing the many individuals in whose personalities that aspect emerges more strongly. To cite one obvious example, in *Dead Souls* Gogol has created several landlord types, but all the differences of these types rest on a common foundation, existing only in the different *ways* in which the shared traits of their inherent nature are *manifested*. They are by no means "distinctive personalities," having all grown up with the feudal landlord society as their common foundation. Moreover, those types whose ideological nature is the strongest (i.e., those with the greatest universality) are those containing the fullest range of shared traits, Ah Q being an example.

---

9. No information available on You Jin 尤錦.

10. Author's note: I have used the term "crucible" [*ronglu* 熔爐] in another essay, but I was referring to mental activity as a whole, including the function of understanding reality, certainly not simply to imagination or "fantasy" —Feng.

VII

In the above, I have given a rough analysis of Zhou Yang's arguments. These arguments arise in part from his misinterpretation of that certain thinker's statement, as I have already said, although they also stem from his failure to use the actual situation of literature as a theoretical base. But what is the actual situation of literature, in terms of creating and interpreting types?

First, the popular interpretation sees the task of creating types as no more than weaving stories or recording them, and even the more progressive views go no further than saying that writers should portray facts worth singing or sobbing over. Writing about the "facts" but neglecting people leads to "slogans." The central task of literary and artistic creation is to portray people and create types; only successful types can generate great ideological power. This idea has not yet been *universally* understood or recognized, even less so the practical task of creating types. Older writers aside, quite a few outstanding writers have appeared since the Mukden Incident of September 18, 1931,[11] and they have written a number of fine works, but concerted efforts to create types have been quite rare. When reading such works, I feel that the authors have engaged far too little in the process of synthesis, which often seems a real shame.

Second, ever since the question of creating types was raised, the wind has been shifting: today this writer says that in one of his works he portrays several typical personalities, and tomorrow that critic says that a certain story depicts several successful types—here a type, there a type, until it seems that our world of letters is moving toward a golden age. Clearly most of them are following a misinterpretation of the subtler meaning of "type." Many writers have depicted what Gorky would call relatively successful reflected images of people, so they term those fairly vivid characters "types." However, although they can be called "characters"[12] (individuals with numerous random qualities but a severe lack of inherent shared traits), they cannot be called "types" or "typical characters"[13] (individuals possessing traits common to a social group) and are no more than what Gorky calls reflected images lacking "social educational significance." This is simply due to not understanding the *universality* of types with respect to the social groups they represent.

---

11. When the Japanese began their occupation of Manchuria.
12. The original reads "character" in English.
13. Appear as "type" and "typical character" in English.

Third, another form of misinterpretation holds that a type embodies either eternal "human nature," as Hamlet represents a certain kind of human nature and Quixote another, or a "national character," as Ah Q represents the Chinese people. This is a very harmful misinterpretation, although it is the most prevalent and influential view. Still, we do often say that a certain person is a "Hamlet," or that a certain person is an "X." First, we most often mean this in the sense of an "analogy" and, second, the society that has spawned all our literary types (from feudal society down to the period of full-blown capitalism) still exists either little changed or in disguise, and therefore the individuals such types represent are still spread throughout the world, be they many or few, obvious or concealed. The misinterpretation here comes from not understanding the *particularity* of a type with respect to social groups other than that which it represents. Hence my explicit point that Ah Q typifies the backward "lumpen" Chinese poor peasant.

Under these circumstances, the intrinsic meaning of literature and art will inevitably be subject to distortion. Therefore, with reference to the first situation, we shall posit that the central object of literary and artistic creation is people, and that literary and artistic types are characters rendered as individuals; regarding the second, we must raise the question of the universality of types; and regarding the third, we shall pose the problem of their particularity. Although most writers have tended to portray people, they have merely depicted, in minute detail, photographic images of individual people as they currently exist. Here the question of the universality of types should be brought to the fore. Raising and discussing the question of types is by no means a matter of abstract theory but instead holds profound significance for practice.

January 5–6, 1936

—*Translated by Catherine Pease Campbell*

PART IV

The Debate on Literary Freedom
1932–1935

Introduction

While serving a positive purpose (at least from the perspective of the leftist writers) in attacking literary conservatives like Liang Shiqiu, the debate over revolutionary literature also stirred up deep animosities between the May Fourth old guard and the young radicals of the Creation and Sun societies. Such open conflicts among the intellectuals of the left were not, naturally, conducive to the kind of organizational unity necessary for a revolutionary movement. With the active prodding of the CCP, Chinese leftist writers and intellectuals disbanded their literary factions and formed in 1930 one umbrella cultural organization, the Chinese League of Left-Wing Writers. The League organized writers into workshops and study groups to pursue questions first raised in the debate on revolutionary literature about how to create a literature for the masses. It also founded numerous journals that promoted and published works, written for the most part by bourgeois writers, depicting the lives of workers and peasants.

In its first two years, as Wang-chi Wong has argued, the League was a fairly harmonious body that made significant steps, without an atmosphere of oppressive dogmatism, toward creating a literature of the masses (1991:

87–100). Bitter over the attacks he had suffered from young radicals like Qian Xingcun, Lu Xun had with some suasion been made the nominal head of the organization, and this seemed to appease the group of writers and intellectuals sympathetic to him. But by 1932, embarrassing rifts began to appear in the League.

The first major debate to rock the League came in two stages, referred to as the "Free Man" and the "Third Category" debates. As they are essentially about the question of the independence of the writer from political or class affiliations, they have been placed together under one heading, "literary freedom." The Free Man debate began when Hu Qiuyuan, a knowledgeable student of Plekhanov, quit the League and wrote a series of articles criticizing the overpoliticization of literature by the League leadership. In his "Do Not Encroach Upon Literary Art," Hu lamented the fact that art had become a "political gramophone"[1] and declared himself a liberal (or free man), unaligned with any political cause, and an ardent supporter of creative freedom.

Su Wen, at the time editor of the highly respected independent journal *Les contemporains* (*Xiandai*), which published modernist-inspired poetry and fiction as well as leftist writings, responded (in the essay included here) by declaring himself a writer of the "third category," neither bourgeois nor proletarian. Su supported Hu Qiuyuan's ideas on creative freedom, although in a rather backhanded way by first attacking his superficial knowledge of Marxist literary theory. In his "Freedom for Literature but Not the Writer," Qu Qiubai, a former secretary of the CCP, attacked both Hu Qiuyuan and Su Wen from a strictly determinist position. He mocked as illusory the idea that writers can stand outside politics and declare themselves independent; to assert oneself as apolitical is to oppose the revolutionary cause. Qu claimed to see through Hu Qiuyuan's veneer of false Marxism to a writer who glorifies art as a transcendent realm of noble, universal truths. Su Wen's "third category" he saw as patently absurd, since all men, even writers, are representatives of some class. Although determinist in his critique of these two apostates, Qu maintained for literature an important "agitational" role in promoting the revolutionary struggle.

Lu Xun's response to the debate is typically complex. By 1932 Lu Xun had embraced, though not without reservations, Marxist political theory. As a Marxist, especially one influenced by Plekhanov, Lu Xun could not

---

1. Hu is alluding here to Guo Moruo's call during the revolutionary literature debate for literature to become a gramophone for the revolution. See Mai Ke'ang 麥克昂 (Guo Moruo), "Liushengjiqi de huiyin" 留聲機器的回音 (Echoes of the gramophone), in *GMWX* 1: 215–227. As Gálik points out, Guo had in his earlier individualist phase opposed such uses for literature (1980: 55–57).

support Su Wen's notion of the class independence of the writer. At the same time, however, he was critical of the "theorists" who similarly believed they could transcend their own bourgeois class background and speak as the vanguard of the proletariat.

The essays by Mu Shiying and Li Jinfa, modernist writers associated with *Les contemporains*, reveal an impatience with the dictates of leftist cultural leaders for literature to conform to the ideological demands of the revolution. Both sought in their writing, so they claim, to be true to their own emotions and own visions of the world, which in emanating from deep within the self, was more real than the false visions of the world imposed by an ideological system. Mu's brief piece also says something about the very modern sense of the alienation of individuals from each other that lay behind much of his fictional work. In his emphasis on the Freudian concept of the unconscious and the idea that people are "spiritually cut off from each other," Mu and other modernists in the 1930's were out of step with the collectivist and highly politicized nature of mainstream leftist literature.

Zhu Guangqian's was the most consistent voice promoting a Kantian aesthetics through the 1930's and 1940's. His essay "Literature and Life" rejects for literature any utilitarian role (among which he would presumably include politics); it does not, however, revel in any radical aestheticism. Literature is a central human activity; it ennobles man, provides him delight and pleasure, and joins minds together in a sort of spiritual communion. The impulse behind literature is self-expression, but in expressing the self the writer necessarily expresses principles common to all humanity.

Chapter 38

Do Not Encroach Upon Literary Art

Hu Qiuyuan

Several friends have stated that in "On Literature for the Dogs"[1] I emphatically denied the value of proletarian literature while at the same time denying the value of nationalist literature.[2] However, this was not my intention: I did not devalue nationalist literature, nor did I devalue proletarian literature. As Hegel said, "All existence is rational." China's nationalist literature isn't just the rantings of a few wild dogs. It has its social basis. By the same token, the fact that proletarian literature exists in China and has developed and undergone struggle means that proletarian literature does exist, does develop, and does undergo struggle. Taking the measure of any kind of literary art can be done from many points of view, for example, from a political point of view or from an artistic point of view. Because I am an outsider

---

1. Hu Qiuyuan 胡秋原, "Wu qinlüe wenyi" 勿侵略文藝, *Wenhua pinglun* 文化評論 1, no. 4 (1932); reprinted in *WXYDSLX*. For the original text of "On Literature for the Dogs," see "Agou wenyi lun" 阿狗文藝論, *Wenhua pinglun* 1, no. 1 (1931); reprinted in Su Wen 1933.

2. In the early 1930's a group of patriotic writers promoted a literature based on the Chinese national consciousness that was openly opposed to the class-based literature of the League. This group is conventionally viewed by Marxist literary historians as fascist and in line with the GMD.

to the field of politics, I certainly do not wish to stand on the side of politics to applaud or censure nationalist literature and proletarian literature. Moreover, in regard to attitudes toward art, there is a difference between analysis according to artistic theory and acceptance or rejection according to artistic policies. As a liberal, I cannot advocate permitting only a certain type of art to exist while expelling other kinds of art.

Thus, I feel one cannot but allow the various literary schools that have arisen since the beginning of the Chinese new literature movement to exist: naturalism, popular entertainment literature, romanticism, revolutionary literature, proletarian literature, petit-bourgeois literature, nationalist literature, and, most recently, democratic literature. But I also do not advocate letting only one kind of literature dominate the literary scene. Whoever is able to use the most appropriate literary form, give expression to the most moving material, observe and write closely of events and phenomena, recognize reality, and get a finger on the pulse of the times is the era's most outstanding writer. Yet this person may not necessarily be the most celebrated writer of his or her times.

Recently a journal appeared by the name of *South China Literary Arts* [Nanhua wenyi] that exclusively advocates "democratic literature." Since the demise of nationalist literature, it seems that democratic literature will become the fashionable thing. This, of course, is to be lauded. Yet does this theory have an actual basis? The democratic literary theorists, Mr. Zeng Zhongming and Mr. Shun Min,[3] are both plagiarizing the theories of the French positivist and literary critic Taine, and their intelligence does not exceed that of the advocates of nationalist literature—especially Mr. Shun Min, who continues to spout off about nationalist literature and such laughable views as the grace of the southern character and the boldness of the northern character. Plekhanov has already critiqued in detail the failings of Taine's theories. Mr. Shun Min has himself admitted to "having read too few books" and to "having never traveled abroad." I only hope that he will not again obstinately close himself off to the opinions of others. Mr. Zeng writes effusively on literature and society and on literature and revolution. He perhaps feels that he alone knows all the answers to these questions, yet in actuality what he discusses is already out of date.

There are some persons of a certain political persuasion who often gleefully wed their political views to their artistic views. Thus there is A-ism literature, X-ism literature, even Z-ism literature—a glittering noisy array of

---

3. Zeng Zhongmin 曾仲鳴 (1901–39) and Shun Min 舜民 (?) were minor critics of the 1930's. Zeng was a teacher of French literature, a close aide of Wang Jingwei, and assassinated, some say mistakenly, as a collaborator during the Sino-Japanese war.

isms! A while ago Mr. Nie Yuntai joked about feces-ism.[4] Perhaps in the future one will come across the term "fecal literature." We certainly don't dispute the convergence of literary and political consciousness, with two provisions. First, that kind of political stance should be high-minded and match the needs of the greatest number of people. As Plekhanov said, "The responsibility of art is to describe in such a way as to arouse interest and excite people about everything." Second, that kind of political advocacy cannot be so overly subjective as to destroy artistic form, because art is not propaganda; description is not debate. If it is, then people will tire of it.

The slogan "Literature of the Three People's Principles"[5] was raised by several "comrades" last year. I recall the party regulations at the time included phrases like "must be in accordance with the spirit of the princely way" and philosophic phrases like "to know is difficult, to act is easy." At the time I felt that for creative activity to hold to these rules would really be more difficult than to eat shit! I don't know how the Three People's Principles evolved into only One People's Principle, that of nationalism. And now, in addition, here comes democratic literature. Democracy means the power of the people. This, then, must be the Literature of the Second People's Principle. In a few days, I suppose there will be people advocating the splendor of both the Literature of the People's Livelihood and the Historical Viewpoint of the People's Livelihood. The Historical Viewpoint of the People's Livelihood and the Literature of the People's Livelihood are, of course, quite delightful concepts, and I believe there will certainly be quite a few disciples for each, since the Principle of the People's Livelihood is the principle of eating one's fill. Shouldn't the Literature of Eating be this deliciously practical?

Several days ago a friend spoke of Doctor of Economics Li Quanshi's advocacy of a certain tax, which he claimed was first of all well suited to nationalism, second, well suited to democracy, and third, well suited to the people's livelihood.[6] Why must the thought of all our so-called scholars always burrow in and around the Three People's Principles? No wonder it is

---

4. Nie Yuntai 聶雲台 (1880–1953) was an industrialist who owned and managed silk factories and who seems to have dabbled in literature. The source of this reference is unknown.

5. GMD propaganda head Ye Chulun 葉楚倫 first proposed this slogan in 1929 as a counter to leftist calls for a proletarian revolutionary literature. The Three People's Principles is the fundamental ideology of the GMD: nationalism, democracy, and the people's livelihood.

6. Li Quanshi 李權時, a leading economist in the 1920's and 1930's and dean of the school of commerce at Fudan University. Among many other things, Li wrote *An Outline of the Principle of the People's Livelihood*, to which the author may be referring.

fashionable to use such names as The Three People's Hotel and The Three People's Socks.

There are still several points worth mentioning: First, Mr. Zeng Zhongmin stated that "one must certainly advocate democratic literature." Whatever this "thing" is, adding a "must certainly" to it means that this "democratic" literature is no longer democratic. Second, Mr. Zeng advocates romanticism and the proclamation of Xu Meixun.[7] Mr. Zeng, who pompously speaks of the exigencies of the age, has forgotten that the China of 1932 is already beyond the eighteenth and nineteenth centuries. Third, we recognize that at present the struggle for democracy and freedom is necessary, but truly believing we will be able to put into actual practice a democratic government is nothing less than illusory. Under the present circumstances in China and the international community, that is very improbable. What is obvious is the inherent weakness in "Democracy," and the fact that it is being married off to satisfy "Art." Literature, which has no elevated thought, and art, which has hurt itself by its vain pretensions, are seldom worth preserving. I hold to this belief always.

So, you descendents of Caesar, religious pontiffs, church elders, Pharisees and Sadducees: "Hands off Art!"

—*Translated by Jane Parish Yang*

---

7. Xu Meixun 許美勛, or Xu E 許峨 (1901–?), is perhaps best known for his cohabitation with the poetess Feng Keng in the late 1920's (which he relates in a biography of Feng). He joined the CCP in 1929, was a member of the League of Left-Wing Writers, and became a contributor to *Tuohuangzhe* 拓荒者 (Pioneers), a leading League journal. It is not clear what "proclamation" Hu is alluding to.

Chapter 39

Regarding the Literary News *and* Hu Qiuyuan's *Literary Arguments*

Su Wen

First, I would like to state that I am not writing this article with any ambitious purpose in mind.[1] That is, I'm not rolling up my sleeves to enter the fray because I see others enjoying the "battle." I have even less intention of challenging anyone on any subject, since I realize quite clearly that I am unfit to do so. However, I will speak about that which I have experienced.

I have read little recently, especially those domestic journals or newspapers that supposedly sell over seven or eight thousand copies an issue. However, I had the fortuitous opportunity recently to read two brilliant pieces, one by Mr. Hu Qiuyuan entitled "Exposing Qian Xingcun's Theory" in *Reading Magazine* (2, no. 1)[2] and the other, an anonymous piece entitled

---

1. Su Wen 蘇汶, "Guanyu *Wenxin* yu Hu Qiuyuan de wenyi lunbian" 關於文新與胡秋原的文藝論辯, *Xiandai* 1, no. 3 (July 1, 1932).

2. "Qian Xingcun lilun zhi qingsuan yu minzu wenxue lilun zhi piping" 錢杏邨理論之清算與民族文學理論之批評, *Dushu zazhi* 2, no. 1 (1932).

"Liberal Cultural Movement" in *Literary News* (5, no. 56).[3] These two pieces, which on the surface seem to have no strong connection, are, in fact, 100 percent contrary to each other, and they interested me greatly. I was especially interested that Mr. Hu added that phrase "endorsing Marxist literary theory." I recall that Mr. Qian Xingcun has also seen himself as a 100 percent Marxist.

The literary stage has now begun rehearsing a drama entitled "The New Case of the Double Judge Bao." As for myself, I of course haven't the ability to discern which Judge Bao is real and which is false. One can't tell the true from the false by sitting in the audience. One must go behind the scenes. Yet even behind the scenes one might not be able to tell.

I am, at this point, reminded of an old joke. Of course jokes by their very nature are tiresome, and an old joke is even less worthy of being repeated. However, since the words contained in the Three People's Principles, which all party members have read innumerable times, can be mentioned hundreds or thousands of times in articles written for party members to read, my repeating an old joke in this unworthy dog shit of an article is of no consequence, I'll wager:

Long ago a merchant, a candidate for the county-level civil service examination, a rich man, and a beggar took shelter from a snowstorm together in a temple. Out of boredom, they collaborated on writing a quatrain. Needless to say, their topic for the poem was "snow." The first three lines of verse were as follows:

Billowing snow falls to the earth (merchant),
Auspicious blessings from the emperor (scholar),
May it fall for another three years (rich man).

"Another three years of snow! That would be a catastrophe!" The beggar, thus angered, forgot the topic "snow" and added a curse for the final line:

Your mother farts like a dog!

I peeked behind the curtain at the rehearsal of "The New Case of the Double Judge Bao" but have come to no conclusion. I only thought of this joke. In fact, this debate over literary theory (perhaps every debate over literary theory is the same) is similar to the collaborative poem in the old tem-

3. " 'Ziyou ren' de wenhua yundong: dafu Hu Qiuyuan he 'Wenhua pinglun' " 自由人的文化運動: 答復胡秋原和文化評論, *Wenyi xinwen* 5, no. 56 (May 23, 1932).

ple: this thing called literary theory is the topic, and everyone has his say, but to get all sides to agree on the conclusion is impossible.

Confucius actually did not have very penetrating thoughts and shouldn't be pulled into the Marxist ancestral hall, yet in truth he did state a few words of wisdom. He said, "When ways of thought are dissimilar, people cannot mutually cooperate." This article of mine is very pedestrian, I just want to put into play in this literary debate what is applicable from this old saying. Thus, I also entitle this piece "On having dissimilar thought with mutual cooperation."

I now will stop writing nonsense and look at the origin of this theoretical debate.

First, of course, the origin was in Russia. Some people whose names are so long that we can't remember them clearly were debating these theories at a time when we hadn't even imagined that there were such problems to discuss. Next, the battle moved to Japan. It seems that the Japanese aren't as clever as the Russians. They discussed the issues over and over, but it had all been said by the Russians long before. These weren't Qian Xingcun's "singular creations," as Mr. Hu Qiuyuan has imputed to him. If we can use Mr. Hu's phrase borrowed from Voltaire, then the Japanese have already acted as first-rate idiots in being the second to compare women to flowers. Thus, these same words have come to Shanghai by way of Tokyo, but only now have they come written in four-cornered square Chinese characters, suddenly transforming themselves into the Chinese people's own theories.

Actually, in speaking of theories, we might well have honestly taken these goods in stock wholesale from the Russians and have avoided making fools of ourselves. Qian Xingcun certainly can't deceive anyone in calling these new "models." Neither can Mr. Hu Qiuyuan. However, Mr. Hu can still be considered to have stuck to one theory, that of Plekhanov, whereas Mr. Qian can't help but borrow haphazardly from many theories.

Those directing the activities of the left-wing literary circles are quite a bit more enlightened. They no longer refer to problems such as "artistic origins" or "artistic definitions," which now only bookworms puzzle over. They just settle on present needs, then debate, decide, and carry out their plans in a methodical and concrete manner.

Yet the left-wing literary circle's transformation into what it is today wasn't wrought overnight. Lu Xun was the first to use a public forum for literary debate. This venerable old warrior, having stated that "we need theories," gave someone the idea to translate some of Plekhanov and Lunacharsky. Although the translation was not completely comprehensible, Lu Xun was satisfied. Next, Mr. Mao Dun jumped onto the platform.

He declared, "We don't want to listen to eighteen lines of crackpot gibber-
ish, we want to see the real merchandise." Although the merchandise still
wasn't brought out, critics began to stress and discuss the question of artistic technique. Thus Mao Dun, too, was satisfied. But one couldn't have pre-
dicted that now along would come Mr. Hu Qiuyuan, leaping out of a
crowd of people, none of whom dared to show off his talent. It is said that
his fists are legitimate heirs to the Shaolin kungfu line. Of course no one
dares predict whether in the future Mr. Hu Qiuyuan will be as satisfied as
Lu Xun and Mao Dun were, but since at present he has already conspicu-
ously planted his heels onto the left-wing literary stage, it seems unlikely
that he will change his position in this present theoretical debate. Thus, according to my own lowly opinion, this debate over the written word probably won't allow either side to come to a satisfactory conclusion.

Why not? When ways of thought are dissimilar, people cannot mutually
cooperate.

Looking at Mr. Hu's writings as a whole, from his worship of
Plekhanov, his censure of the theory or proposal that literature directs life,
to his many others ideas, we can recognize that he is an absolute anti-
utilitarian. On the other hand, the leading theorists of the left-wing literary
circles will point out which kind of literature is useful and which is not,
which kind we need and which kind we don't need. The distance between
these two kinds of Marxists cannot be calculated.

In fact, merely to say that the left-wing literary arena is Marxist does not
seem appropriate. We should say that they are Marxist-Leninists. As for
this difference, at present they do not have the time to discuss what is true
or not, but only what the present needs are. It's a kind of present-ism. Seeing what they advocate as a type of scholarly theory is not as appropriate
as seeing it instead as a type of political strategy or way of action. Moreover, this strategy and action are, in fact, really their theory. When the
needs of the present change, their advocacy will follow those needs and
change, too. This, then, is a "dialectic."

Can one weigh on a scale the importance of things? How could one
weigh truth and art in pounds and ounces against the whole proletarian
liberation movement? This would be the narrow truth of a dark garret, I'll
bet. And the literary art of petit-bourgeois male and female dogs! If one
were really a progressive warrior in these debates, one would want neither
truth nor art.

For example, let's discuss this question of their advocating the popularization of literature for the masses. They view laborers now as having nothing to read but old feudal (that is to say, harmful) comic books and song
books. Thus they want writers to write some beneficial comic books and

song books to give to the laborers to read. This of course would be opposed by critics like Mr. Hu, but he wouldn't be the only one to oppose this. I'm afraid every person who clings for dear life to literature would oppose this step. Could this kind of low form produce good literature? In truth, comic books would produce neither a Tolstoy nor a Flaubert. Could left-wing theorists not know this? They naturally are not that stupid. But what would they want with a Flaubert or a Tolstoy anyway? They not only would never dream of calling on writers to become Flauberts or Tolstoys, but if one happened to appear, they still wouldn't want him—at least "for the time being." Moreover, their not wanting one is correct, dialectically. Perhaps in the future—in the future, perhaps—they would forgive one who did appear. But these are words for the future, not now.

Mr. Hu Qiuyuan has called Lunacharsky a "bureaucrat, a foppish aristocrat, an inexplicable enigma." But why does his disdain run so deep? Actually, from this we can really see that Mr. Hu will never understand Lunacharsky. Lunacharsky once vehemently criticized Tolstoy, but on the centennial of Tolstoy's birth he also praised him effusively. His words seem to have come from two different persons. How could contradiction reach this level of absurdity? How could one pay so little attention to the "truth"? Actually, it is very reasonable that Tolstoy would be "rejected" as unnecessary during a time of national difficulty but later "forgiven" during a time of national peace.

If you are a true Marxist, then you should not criticize Lunacharsky as an enigma and say he changed his mind too easily [*biangua* 變卦]. Change, after all, is the law of dialectics. Some persons have stated that dialectics can be traced to ancient China. The *Book of Changes* is one example. Unfortunately, I haven't studied either the law of dialectics or the *Book of Changes* in any depth and so don't dare develop this point, but I do know that in the *Book of Changes* are the alternating Trigrams [*biangua*], and no more.

We seem to have gotten further and further away from the point and should return to it, but the reason I bring up these last points is but to say that what the left-wing literary circle advocates is action, pure and simple. Moreover, it is living action. Yet Mr. Hu Qiuyuan doesn't understand this. The left-wing literary circle tried several times, first hinting, then directly requesting that he not emptily carry on about "truth," explaining that there *is* no truth apart from action. Yet Mr. Hu still does not understand this point. Mr. Hu would obstinately say that action without truth is incorrect action. But the left-wing literary circle would also state that truth without action is incorrect. Thus, how could this debate come to any conclusion?

Even if Mr. Hu Qiuyuan claims Marxism for his banner, actually, he is really only a scholastic Marxist. This kind of Marxist enjoys pontificating first and foremost on the most distant, most difficult-to-solve problems. They say that these are the fundamental questions. For example, as soon as they open a discussion about art, they head right to the problem of defining art, which they see as "the first question in the discussion on art," as Mr. Hu is fond of saying. Certainly Mr. Hu has inherited Plekhanov's mantle when he easily turns a difficult, enigmatic problem into a short, eight-character phrase, dismissing the question as "art is form and thought," as if it were an unalterable principle. He damns Qian Xingcun, saying that if he doesn't understand this, then he is not fit to discuss art. In truth nothing can be as simplistic as this. Can you find the definition of "capital" in Marx's *Capital*? The whole three volumes of the text is the definition of "capital." Can true Marxists assert that since Marx couldn't define capital succinctly, he was not fit to discuss economic questions? Only scholastic bookworms remain hung up on definitions.

These kinds of definitional questions end up hindering more urgent business. Enthralled with truth, some Marxist scholars would lock themselves up in a library to read books on anthropology and archaeology. "The impoverished literatus is meticulous in scholarship; so he studies another ten years." Thus it is no wonder that left-wing literary circles say this is "teaching the masses passivism."

Strictly speaking, Plekhanov couldn't help but also carry with him a bit of a bookworm's air. Note that this political theory was in the end criticized by Lenin, and now even his theory of art is said to be shaky. Scholarly bookworms are, after all, undesirable and ultimately dispensable.

I recall that formerly Zhang Taiyan boldly proclaimed "bookworm-ism,"[4] saying that all great enterprises were carried out by bookworms. Yet in politics he, too, was dispensable, a victim of his own bookwormism. Are ivory tower Marxists all of the same ilk?

This is called a scholar's rebellion: even after three years the rebellion is far from accomplished.

Thus, although we admit that every word of Mr. Hu Qiuyuan fits 120 percent with Marxism, the left-wing literary circle's "ability to act" fits even closer with Marxism. Even if they were to admit that his words fit 120 percent with Marxism, they still would certainly want to attack him, as Lenin attacked Plekhanov. This is because he hindered their acting, and this hinderance goes against Marxism. Even if Mr. Hu were to write ten vol-

---

4. Zhang Taiyan 章 太 炎 (1869-1936), classical scholar associated with the National Essence movement and anti-Qing revolutionary. Given his political activism in the late Qing period, this "bookwormism" (*shudaizi zhuyi* 書 獃 子 主 義) was likely something Zhang promoted in his later years.

umes filled with 400,000 characters on "Historical Materialism's Theory of Art," it would be useless, or at least "at present" it would be useless. Left-wing literary circles would still want to criticize him because the time has not come when Lenin can forgive Plekhanov as Lunacharsky forgave Tolstoy.

If one has never experienced standing in an "unfree, party-dominated" crowd, then one would be smart to remain silent.

From this, we can see two opposing standpoints: one emphasizes practice, the other only wants scholarly texts. One undertakes a political mission, the other wraps itself in the mantle of truth. Thus, these two kinds of Marxism grow farther and farther, almost poles, apart.

Bernard Shaw said that representatives of the proletarian class understand both the proletariat and the capitalists, but the capitalists' representatives understand neither. Let me make a first-class fool of myself. I want to copy Shaw and assert that Marxist-Leninists understand Leninism and Marxism, but academic Marxists understand neither when they analyze them to death.

However, Mr. Hu would leap to his feet if he heard that someone said that he didn't understand Leninism. He'd question me: "Well, then, do you understand Leninism?" And that would really leave me speechless.

In truth, Mr. Hu did once point out that in the arts "purposeful ideology is nothing more than a mechanical application of Lenin's political thought to art." What he said was not incorrect, but judging from phrases like "is nothing more than" and "mechanical," I see that Mr. Hu at least is hinting that Leninism is nothing but that and shouldn't be applied to the arts.

If, by misfortune, Mr. Hu really did understand Leninism, then those people saying he didn't understand Leninism would be the biggest fools on earth. I really can't discern Mr. Hu's purpose. No wonder that there are some who say that he has purposefully "liberated" Marxism from actual practice and intentionally turned it into a kind of dead Marxism, a scholastic text that retards the revolutionary movement and in reality serves the enemy of the proletariat.

Actually, it would be better if Mr. Hu let people call him a bookworm. This would be more beneficial to him. In this way, he'd still have the hope of being another Plekhanov. Perhaps a future university would even establish a Hu Qiuyuan College, just as in Russia there is a Plekhanov College.

At a time when "free intellectuals" and "bound, Party-affiliated" intellectuals vie for domination on the literary scene, the most difficult stance is that of the third type of writer. Yet the third type constitutes the great flock of writers.

In truth, writers to a greater or lesser degree all exhibit the same characteristic of strangling literature, unwilling to let go. If this weren't the case, they certainly wouldn't have chosen this least promising enterprise as their endeavor (perhaps to call it a "career" would be a bit better). You have only to watch them: forget about those who write nothing. It's those who write a little of whom I speak: they all weigh their writings on artistic scales, even to the point, as Mr. Shi Tie'er said, of subconsciously attempting to win fame with one stroke of the pen.[5] If we were to speak of it calmly, we would acknowledge that everyone shares this to some extent. After all, people aren't saints, nor can each and every one of them be a Marx or a Lenin.

But what kind of status do writers enjoy under present circumstances?

In the beginning, before any notion of class literature had entered writers' brains, writers were still dreaming that literature was a kind of pristine virgin. But soon someone informed them that not only was she not a virgin, but she was also just a common prostitute. She would sell herself one day to the capitalists, the next day to the proletariat. Writers were caught off guard when they first heard this. But having heard this was true, they had no way to deny it. But since this prostitute literature was quite comely, both the capitalist and proletarian classes wanted to possess her. Thus literature could only make the choice to be faithful to one master. And what of her future? She "becomes a stranger to her lover,"[6] the writer.

Take a look around you. Haven't a lot of writers both famous and unknown all given up their trade?

Of course some writers still hope to drag literature out from behind the heavily cloistered gates where she is ensconced. Others happily accompany her to her new marital home.

The former kind of writer has been "rejected" at the gate, it goes without saying. As for the latter kind, he has been accepted, but subject to stringent regulations that strive to remake him into another kind of person. In the end, literature is no longer literature, but a kind of comic book. Writers are no longer writers, but turned into propagandists. Writers who cling for dear life to literature can in the end only release their grip. Yet do you think they do this willingly? They still pine for artistic worth in literature.

By speaking thus I do not mean to blame the left-wing literary scene and say it shouldn't dominate literature in this way. They are correct to do

---

5. Shi Tie'er 史鐵兒 is one of Qu Qiubai's (see Glossary) many pen names.
6. An allusion to a poem by Cui Jiao 崔郊, "Zeng qu bi" 贈去婢 (To a servant girl): "Deep as the sea sinks the maid when entering the aristocrat's gate, / and from this moment on her lover becomes a stranger" 從此蕭郎是路人.

so for the revolution and for their class. But they do seem a bit devious, unwilling to state directly that they don't need literature at the present time, or at least temporarily don't need it. Sometimes they haul out "artistic worth" to let these so-called writers have a taste, so they can accompany the wedding without worries. Actually, this way of dealing with writers leaves them defenseless. Should they write for literature or for the revolution? Or for both? Or should it be sometimes for literature, other times for revolution?

I feel that the critic Li Chuli of the early period in the literary debates had a happier solution. He would first ask you seriously: Are you supporting the revolution for the sake of literature or do you write literature for the sake of the revolution? If you agreed to the former question, he would ask you to leave. If you supported the latter, he'd welcome you into his ranks.

Mr. Hu Qiuyuan appeared as the protector of art precisely because there were writers who were puzzled over which way to turn. He told people not to touch art. This kind of libertarian theory of artistic creation ought to be welcomed by writers, but unfortunately Mr. Hu isn't a total libertarian. He fiercely attacks purposeful, ideological literature. In this way one is still not permitting writers complete freedom. If Mr. Hu's attitude of not allowing persons to touch art is that "you can't touch it but I can," isn't that controlling them as others do, not letting them be free to decide?

In these times when no one is willing to give an inch, how difficult indeed it is to be a writer.

Everyone has his own way of thinking, which is not another's way of thinking. If you say things which I don't want to hear and if I say things you don't want to hear, then our composing a quatrain together will be quite a battle! Only writers have their own ways of thinking but don't dare speak up, much less dare challenge others' ways of thinking. Their sole desire is to keep a thread of life alive in literature, whether through propaganda or sleaze. But they are afraid that their omnipotent leaders will cast lots for them, deciding they are dogs of that class.

Under "present" conditions, it is a blessing to be ignorant and a wise thing to be silent.

—Translated by Jane Parish Yang

Chapter 40

Freedom for Literature but Not the Writer

Qu Qiubai

I. A "Dazzling but Befuddled" Hu Qiuyuan

Who is Mr. Hu Qiuyuan?[1] He himself says: "We are liberal intellectuals who stand completely on objective ground . . . without party or sectarian affiliation. Our methodology is historical materialism, and our attitude is that of the free man. . . . Literature should always be free and democratic."

Of course Mr. Hu's views on literature are not limited to these alone, but this is his basic stand. He says his methodology is that of historical materialism, and it is likely for this reason that he makes copious citations from various historical-materialist literary theories. Sometimes he says "art contemplates through living images," or "art only has one goal, and that is the expression, understanding, and criticism of life," or "the highest goal of art is in eliminating all the class barriers that separate humanity"; he goes so far as to say "although literature is not the highest, it certainly is not the

---

1. Yi Jia 易 嘉 (Qu Qiubai 瞿 秋 白), "Wenyi de ziyou he wenxuejia de bu ziyou" 文藝的自由和文學家的不自由, *Xiandai* 1, no. 6 (1932); reprinted in Su Wen 1933.

basest of things. . . . To lower art to the status of a gramophone is to turn our backs on art," and "an art without noble thoughts, or which is marred by intellectual hypocrisy, very seldom has any value. This I have always believed." What sort of Marxist historical materialism is this! . . .

Mr. Hu Qiuyuan's artistic theory is actually a disguised theory of the glorification of art. He says that the debate over pure art is a "vain" one. Why is it vain? Because there are both revolutionary writers and reactionary writers who support pure art; it's the same for those who oppose pure art. But this is only superficial sophistry on his part. His basic stand lies in the fact that he feels that art should only express noble thoughts and should not be a "gramophone" for politics. So he feels art has autonomy, that it has dignity and is like a palace, and that it expresses personality [*renge*]. He warns the various political factions "not to encroach upon literature" and repeatedly declares that art is not the basest of things. If Mr. Hu Qiuyuan won't recognize that he adheres to the theory of the glorification of art, then at least it could be called a theory of the nobility of art. He embraces something approaching an autonomous art of nobility, an entity that has nothing to do with Marxist literary theory.

Mr. Hu Qiuyuan's theory is, according to his own admission, inspired by Plekhanov. He cites the line from Plekhanov that "art contemplates through living images." He adds that "art is the imagistic expression of thought and feeling, and the value of art is based on a view of the excellence of the thoughts and feelings concealed within it."[2] But these few lines do not explain things adequately, and a question immediately arises: What standard does he use to determine this so-called excellence? Is it the standard of the aristocracy, the standard of the bourgeoisie, or the standard of the proletariat? On this point he offers no explanation. Likely he uses the standard of the so-called liberal. Hu Qiuyuan's theory thus smacks of false objectivism. What he has done is precisely to have cleansed Plekhanov's theory of all its finer points and exaggerated his Menshevism to its furthest degree, transforming him into a hypocritical, bourgeois sideliner. In point of fact he denies the positive function of art, denies that art can influence life at all. And yet all class literature not only reflects life, it also influences life. Literary phenomena are tied in with all social phenomena. Although literature is an expression of so-called ideology (the highest level of the superstructure), cannot determine the changes in a social system, and is by our reckoning always ruled by the conditions of the forces of production and class relations, art is still able to turn back to influence social life and, to a considerable extent, either push forward or impede the development of

---

2. From G. V. Plekhanov, *Art and Social Life* (London: Lawrence and Wishart, 1953).

class struggle, or at least alter slightly the shape of this struggle by strengthening or weakening the power of a particular class. . . .

Plekhanov's theory of art is not without an element of objectivism or disdain for class character, and also holds the seeds for an artistic pessimism. But in the hands of Hu Qiuyuan it is further tarnished with his own theories and those of Andreyev.[3] The result is that it is transformed into a liberalism that is thoroughly bourgeois. He demands "freedom" for literature so that all kinds of literary works can appear, which he can then research and critique from a "completely objective stand" in order to promote his own evaluation of the "noble sentiments" on art held by the "free man" "without party or sectarian affiliation." This is really something else! This must be his goal for demanding freedom for literature . . .

II. "How Difficult Indeed to Be a Writer" Su Wen

Fate denies you freedom,
   holds you bound;
Inflicting on me too
   a heavy wound.
In closest harmony
Our hearts resound;
In contemplation of the Ancients
Is solace to be found.
                (Cao Xueqin's Lin Daiyu).[4]

Mr. Su Wen himself claims to be one who will "cling for dear life to literature," and anyone who will do this is sure to welcome Mr. Hu Qiuyuan's liberal theory of creativity. And who is it who clings to literature for dear life? Mr. Su Wen says it is "the flock of writers." I feel that it is all right for the time being to call them a "flock," although a writer is by no means a sheep. Yet it is certainly debatable if the entire "flock" welcomes Mr. Hu Qiuyuan's theory. There are always at least a few who do not approve. So let's look at Mr. Su Wen himself.

Mr. Su Wen is a true writer indeed. His essay is written in beautiful prose—a work of art, with real "artistic value." Which is to say that his article is written ingeniously and is very moving, at least to his "flock" of writers. But precisely because of this, it also has political value, for it is a sharp

---

3. Leonid Andreyev (1871-1919). novelist and playwright, was known for the extreme pessimism of his writings, and it is likely this that is "tarnishing" Hu's ideas.

4. The translation of this poem has been taken from David Hawkes and John Minford, tr., *The Story of the Stone*, 5 vols. (London: Penguin, 1982), 4: 172.

weapon aimed at certain political goals. Of course, the sharper a weapon is, the better it is; the more moving a work of art is, the better it is. . . .

Mr. Su has said that Hu Qiuyuan's "liberal theory of creativity should be welcomed by writers." . . . And yet Mr. Su curses Mr. Hu for being a bookworm and a fool. Mr. Su says: "Under present conditions it is a blessing to be ignorant and a wise thing to be silent." Which is to say that although in his heart he welcomes Mr. Hu's theory, it is best that he not say so aloud, and even better to throw a few curses Mr. Hu's way. His curses, however, are not real curses. What he is really saying is that theory and action are essentially incompatible, just as literature and revolution are incompatible, and that Mr. Hu does not understand this fact and is therefore a bookworm [who relies too much on the theoretical writings of Plekhanov and Lenin]. . . .

First, true scientific literary theory is established by the emergent international revolutionary class. Only this class, in the course of revolutionary action, is truly able to establish and develop a scientific literary theory. China's emergent class, as well as that of Japan, England, etc. is of course still under the heavy weight of oppression. This is especially true of China's emergent class, for the cultural constraints placed on them by the vestiges of feudalism are particularly tight. They have no hope that the ruling class will "promote" of its own volition a culture of the masses, and so must with great difficulty learn from the proletariat of the world's various countries, especially that of Russia. They are not afraid of the mockery the ruling class has for any theory that "comes wholesale from Russia." They are studying hard, investigating, and using theory in the course of action. On the one hand, they are simply unwilling to say that "action is theory," and so "only want action and not truth." On the other, they are even more unable to say that theory should precede action. They cannot sense any separation or incompatibility between theory and action.

Second, the emergent class is fighting for its own liberation, fighting to liberate the broad masses of working people; they want to reform this world, and reform themselves—reform the broad masses. They want to purge the ruling class of its intellectual influence, purge it of its influence in shaping consciousness. The established class relations that exist in the current exploitative system determines the worldview and lifeview of the masses. And the conservative and backward worldviews and lifeviews among the masses are not an "innate" part of the masses, but are secured and imparted by the ruling class through various methods and instruments. Among these instruments, and one of great power, is literature. So when the emergent class revolts, it must at the same time use literature to help the revolution. It is a weapon that can be used to reform the worldview and lifeview of the masses. Certainly, not just any "progressive warrior" can do literary work. But why, then, does Su Wen say that when one is "truly a progressive fighter. . . he no longer needs literature." Why? It can only be that he himself is willing to cede an armament to the enemy. Any "warrior" willing to surrender arms is no progressive warrior. One could perhaps respond: "But you are still holding this weapon, so how can we speak of disarming." But it is precisely for this reason that we should exert ourselves to obtain the weapon. Whoever advises the emergent class not to take this weapon, naturally embraces objectively a "certain political goal"—even though he himself feels that he "has not the least bit of political stench."

Third, since the emergent class stands on the ground of the destructive and exploitative system, it is able to truly appraise the value of art and to make use of the literary heritage of the aristocracy and the bourgeoisie. They simply are not some "utilitarians living for the present." Their standing on the literary front is similarly to create a completely new social system—to fight for a completely new worldview and lifeview. The literature of all ruling classes, even that of the petite bourgeoisie, wants to critique and analyze. The content of these literatures often harbors many contradictions and cannot be evaluated as simply "very good" or "very bad"; nor can it be "useless in revolutionary times" but "useful in a time of reconstruction. . . . "

Fourth, the emergent class may certainly use literature as a tool for agitation, but not all agitators are writers. Literature, broadly speaking, is all agitation or propaganda; consciously or unconsciously, it is all propaganda. Literature is always and everywhere a political "gramophone." The problem lies in what class it is a gramophone for. And whether it does it cleverly or not. In short, literature is but one form of agitation, and not all agitation is literature. Every class uses literature for propaganda, but some classes are unwilling to openly admit this and instead hide behind the pretenses of "culture," "civilization," "nation," "people," "freedom," "elegance," etc. But the emergent class cannot use these false masks. The emergent class not only wants a common agitation, it wants the agitation that literature can provide. From around 1905 up to 1917, works like those of Gorky and Serafimovich[5] (which even Mr. Su would recognize as literature) certainly had artistic value. But these things were at the same time works of agitation. To be an agitator, then, does not necessarily mean that one cannot

---

5. Alexsandr Serafimovich (1863–1949), Russian writer who wrote short stories "exposing capitalism" before the revolution and was a war correspondent for *Pravda* during WWI; his *Iron Stream* (1924) is considered a classic of Soviet literature.

still be a writer. Writers like Gorky, although they may not cling for dear life to literature like the "flock of writers" in China, still have not necessarily sunk below the point of Chinese writers. Writers like Gorky are indeed great propagandists. The emergent class itself also criticizes works of agitation that have no literary value, which means not that it seeks to eliminate its agitational possibilities but to strengthen the artistry of works of agitation. Moreover, the reflection of life through literature is not a mechanical gramophone or camera, as these words might suggest. Vulgar gramophonism or photographism does nothing but weaken literature as a weapon. To be able to truly make use of the power of art is to strengthen its agitational power; at the same time, writers who truly serve the masses will be able to refine their artistic power even more through their agitational work. Art and agitation are by no means incompatible. Naturally, there will be those who say that something that's agitational can't be literature. This view is possible and may be even "useful." But "useful" for whom? For the classes that are unwilling to admit that they exploit literature for their own agitational purposes. . . .

Mr. Su's argument is actually very clear. Yet, after writing four thousand characters, he adds a humble: "Writers have their truths, but dare not speak them."

Why does he "dare not to speak," why is he so pitiable, so mournful? Because he sees himself as a "third man." He says that "since this prostitute literature was quite comely, both the capitalist and the proletarian classes wanted to possess her. Thus literature could only make the choice to be faithful to one master. And what of her future? She became a 'stranger to her lover,' the writer."[6] These writers, "so particular about the value of art," are the so-called "third men." Their lover, that "prostitute literature," has been stolen away by the bourgeoisie or the proletariat.

But literature is in fact not a common prostitute. Literature belongs to a certain class; each class has its own literature, and there is no need whatsoever for them to steal each other's. But a heated struggle has developed between these two literatures. The emergent class previously had no literature and is now creating its own; the old class has its own literature, which is now encircling and destroying the emergent class. How can it be stopped? With a little originality and ingenuity it can be poisoned to death, or strangled, or starved. . . . The literary movement of the emergent class is not interested in "occupying" or "monopolizing" anything; it seeks only to

---

6. An allusion to a poem by Cui Jiao 崔郊, "Zeng qu bi" 贈去婢 (To a servant girl): "Deep as the sea sinks the maid when entering the aristocrat's gate, / and from this moment on her lover becomes a stranger" 從此蕭郎是路人.

point to the true face of literature—its class nature. It seeks only to do battle on the intellectual and literary fronts with the forces of reaction.

The writer can never be any sort of "third man." The writer—the literary man—has no need to be a handmaiden for a bride, following literature as it is married off to some class. Every literary man, consciously or unconsciously, whether actively involved in writing or silent, is always a representative of the ideology of a certain class. In this intricate web that is class society, there is no escape, nor can you become any "third man." . . .

Mr. Su Wen sighs and says: "In these times when no one is willing to give an inch, how difficult indeed it is to be a writer." But why is this really necessary? A writer who is truly willing to serve the masses will only welcome the correct literary theory, will strive to understand all mistakes, and demand a criticism that progresses day by day. As for the writer who worships literature as an unencroachable god, let him be a writer even if he is brazen about it. The literary man who has true "love for literature" and can really cling for dear life to literature should fear nothing. If he is a little afraid, then this is not clinging for dear life to literature. Just look at those women in this world who would die for good looks. They prefer to sell themselves out for this. Good looks are a form of beauty, "the value of art" is also beauty (an abstract beauty that submits to no higher authority). The only way out for the "third man" is to sacrifice everything for "beauty."

July 1932

—Translated by Kirk A. Denton

Chapter 41

On the "Third Category"

Lu Xun

The last three years have seen very few polemics on art and literature.[1] Apart from those "theorists" protected by the commander's sword who call themselves "left-wingers" and find arguments for the freedom of art in Marxism and for exterminating "Communist bandits" in Leninism, practically no one else can open his mouth. The "art-for-art's-sake" writers are still "free," of course, because no one suspects them of accepting roubles. But members of the "third category," that is, those who "cling for dear life to literature," cannot escape the bitter premonition that left-wingers will call them "flunkeys of the bourgeoisie."

In Numbers 3 and 6 of the magazine *Modern Age*, Mr. Su Wen takes up the cudgels on behalf of this "third category." (I should point out here that I say "on behalf of this third category" for convenience sake, though I know that just as Mr. Su Wen's "group of writers" may well disapprove of such indefinite terms as "perhaps," "more or less" or "influenced," they do not approve of definite terms either, because once you have a definite label you

---

1. Lu Xun 魯迅, "Lun disan zhong ren" 論第三種人, *Xiandai* 1, no. 6 (Dec. 1933); reprinted in Lu Xun 1981*a*: 4: 438–44.

stop being free.) He believes that left-wing critics call authors "flunkeys of the bourgeoisie" on the least provocation, that they even consider neutrals as partisans, that once a man stops being neutral he risks being dubbed a "flunkey of the bourgeoisie," and that whereas so-called "left-wing writers" may be "left" but abstain from writing, the "third category" want to write but dare not. And so the world of letters is a blank. Still, a part at least of literature is said to transcend the class struggle, and this is the literature of the future, the true, immortal literature to which the "third category" clings. Unfortunately, though, the left-wing theorists have scared everyone off writing such literature, because the authors have a premonition of being branded before they start. People may well have such a premonition, especially those who call themselves the "third category." There may also well be writers, as Mr. Su Wen says, who understand a good deal of theory but find it hard to change emotionally. But when the feelings are unchanged, the degree of theoretical understanding is bound to differ somewhat from cases in which the feelings have changed or changed a little, and this leads to a divergence in views. And from my point of view Mr. Su Wen's view is wrong.

Of course, since left-wing literature came into being, the theorists have made mistakes, and not only do some left-wing writers simply pose as "left" but abstain from writing, as Mr. Su Wen claims; others veer from Left to Right and even join the ranks of "nationalist literature" or become owners of bookshops or spies for the enemy party. Still, the left-wing literature handed down by those writers who have tired of it remains. Not only so, the movement goes on developing and overcoming its failings as it advances upon the hallowed ground of literature.

Mr. Su Wen asks: Why haven't they succeeded in overcoming their failings after three years?

The answer is: True, we must go on overcoming them, perhaps for another thirty years. But while overcoming failings we can forge ahead. We shall not be such fools as to wait till all our failings are overcome before going forward. Mr. Su Wen says as a "joke" that left-wing writers are accepting payment from capitalist publishers. Now I would like to say in all seriousness that left-wing writers are still being oppressed, imprisoned, and slaughtered by the laws of this feudal-capitalist society. That is why all left-wing periodicals have been persecuted, and only very few are left, while even those which appear occasionally contain very few critical reviews, and those there are do not dub writers "flunkeys of the bourgeoisie" on the least provocation or reject "fellow-travelers." Left-wing writers are not angels sent down from heaven, nor foreign foes who have fought their way in from abroad. They welcome not only those "fellow-travelers" who have gone a little way with them, but even call on all the bystanders at the road-side to advance with them.

Let us ask another question, though. At present the left-wingers are too crushed to publish many critical articles, but if a day should come when they are in a position to do so, will they dub the "third category" "flunkeys of the bourgeoisie" on the least provocation? I think so long as left-wing writers have not given their word not to do this and take a gloomy view of things, it is possible—in fact worse is possible. But I believe such predictions are as unnecessary as committing suicide on the off chance that the earth may crack up some day.

But it is said that Mr. Su Wen's "third category" have "laid down their pens" for such fear of the future. But would they do such a thing because of some imagined evil that they have not yet experienced? Is the grasp of these writers who "cling for dear life to literature" so weak? Would two lovers be afraid to embrace for fear of social censure in the future?

The truth is that the "third category" have not "laid down their pens" because left-wing criticism is too harsh. The real reason is that no "third category" can exist, and if no such men exist, they cannot have "third category" pens, let alone lay them down.

To live in a class society yet to be a writer who transcends classes, to live in a time of wars yet to leave the battlefield and stand alone, to live in the present yet to write for the future—this is sheer fantasy. There are no such men in real life. To try to be such a man is like trying to raise yourself from the ground by tugging at your own hair—it can't be done. You may fume, but it is not because others shake their heads that you stop tugging.

So even this "third category" cannot overstep class. If Mr. Su Wen himself anticipates class criticism, how can any writing get away from class interests? It cannot get away from the fighting either. So, taking a step ahead, Mr. Su Wen protests in the name of the "third category," although he does not want to be accused of "protesting." Meanwhile, as it is impossible to overstep the present, before he writes a work for posterity that transcends class, he starts worrying about left-wing criticism.

This is certainly an awkward predicament. And it arises because fantasy cannot come true. Even if there were no left-wing literature to complicate matters, there could be no "third category," let alone works written by them. But Mr. Su Wen has dreamed up this specter of a despotic left-wing literature and lays at its door the crime of preventing the emergence of his illusory "third category" as well as the birth of the literature of the future.

Admittedly there is nothing wonderful about left-wing writers who produce comic books and scripts for operas. But they are not as worthless as Mr. Su Wen thinks. They want Tolstoy and Flaubert too. However, they do not want Tolstoys and Flauberts who "strive to write for the future" (because there is no need for them *today*). Tolstoy and Flaubert wrote for their contemporaries. The future is determined by the present, and only something that has meaning today can have meaning for the future. Tolstoy in particular, who wrote tales for peasants, never styled himself one of the "third category," and no amount of attacks from the bourgeoisie could make him lay down his pen. Although as Mr. Su Wen says, left-wingers are not so stupid as not to know that "comic books cannot give birth to a Tolstoy or Flaubert," they do think these may give birth to artists as great as Michelangelo or Leonardo da Vinci. And I believe that opera scripts and popular tales may produce a Tolstoy or a Flaubert. No one has a word against Michelangelo's paintings today, but were they not actually religious propaganda and comic book pictures of the Old Testament? They were done, too, for the "present" of the artist's time.

In brief, Mr. Su Wen is not wrong when he says that rather than deceive others or sail under false colors, the "third category" should do their best to write. And with even more truth he asserts, "A man must have faith in himself before he has the courage to work." Yet Mr. Su Wen alleges that the premonition that left-wing theorists will criticize them has made many lesser and greater members of the "third category" lay down their pens!

"What is to be done?"

October 10, 1932

—Based on the translation by
Gladys Yang and Yang Xianyi,
in Lu Xun: Selected Works.

Chapter 42

Preface to Public Cemetery

Mu Shiying

Some have said that the stories in *North Pole, South Pole* are works that belong to my early period and that the eight stories in this collection constitute my later period.[1] If you disregard the dates of my writings and consider only the order of publication, judging from the content and technique in these stories, this would seem to make a lot of sense. But in fact, two stories completely different in style were written at the same time—that I could have two such very different emotions and write such different pieces at the same time is something others have seen as inexplicable (I myself don't understand it) and has become a cause for many people to censure me. The source of this paradox, as Du Heng has said, is the dual nature of my personality. I am a rather straightforward and sincere person; there is nothing I won't say openly for all to hear. I am unwilling, as so many today are, to adorn my true face with some protective pigment, or to pass my days in hypocrisy shouting hypocritical slogans, or to manipulate

---

1. Mu Shiying 穆時英, "*Gongmu zixu*" 公墓自序, in *Gongmu* 公墓 (Public cemetery) (Shanghai: Xiandai shuju, 1933); reprinted—Beijing: Renmin wenxue, 1987. *Nan bei ji* 南北級 (Shanghai: Xiandai shuju, 1933).

the psychology of the masses, political maneuvering, self-propaganda, and the like to maintain a position once held in the past or raise up my personal prestige. I feel this is base and narrow-minded behavior, and I won't do it. If I am called backward, a fence sitter, a peeled radish, whatever it be, at least I can stand on top of the world and shout out loud: "I am true to myself and to others." Sincerity is something needed by all societies! I can still face those who berate me and say: "Perhaps I have committed crimes, but I bravely and sincerely shoulder responsibility for them—the question is who will be the one able to pick up a stone and throw it at me. Lie down on your beds and think it over carefully."

Enough of this. I have no need for further explanation, except to explain something about the eight stories in this collection. A most strange occurrence in this world is when someone is able to interpret your stories completely at odds with your own intention. I remember a critic who said that several of these stories were completely divorced from life, from living society, that the world was not that way, that the world was really full of workers, peasants, and the masses, loansharks, dawn, struggle . . . and the like. But I am someone who lives in the society portrayed in my fiction, everything in it is something I have personally witnessed. Perhaps I lived this life in a dream, for my critics tell me that my fictional world is fortuitous, divorced from society, that it comes from my unconscious. If it is a dream, or fortuitous, or comes from my unconscious, fine. In sum, I don't want my works to be misunderstood, distorted, or dismissed because of some political maneuvering, so this short explanation is perhaps necessary.[2]

"A Man Used as a Diversion" and "Public Cemetery" are rather early works. In the former I merely sought to write about the tragedy of someone used as a diversion, to create a kind of depressed atmosphere. In the latter, I have written part of a honeyed romance of early spring.

"Shanghai Foxtrot" is a fragment of the novel *China—1931*. It is only a technical experiment or exercise. When it was published in *Les contemporains*[3] there were some announcements telling the editors to cut it off, perhaps for the sake of the dignity of the journal; but I find I must say one thing, and that is that *China—1931* was only a technical experiment.

The remaining five stories, "Evening," "Five in a Nightclub," "Black Peony," and "Craven A," were written with just about the same design in

---

2. This authorial fear of "misinterpretation" by critics and readers reappears in Mu Shiying's story "Pierrot."

3. *Xiandai* 現代 (1932–34) was the leading journal of the so-called modernist, or neo-Perceptionist, school of writers, with which Mu was associated.

mind. At that time I simply wanted to describe something about the *pierrot* who had fallen in life and sunk into poverty. In my society there are those who have been crushed flat by life and those who have been squeezed out by life, but by no means do they necessarily, or let us say inevitably, show the face of opposition, tragic anger, or enmity; they could wear a happy mask on top of their tragic faces. Each of us, unless he be utterly without feeling, has stored within the deep recesses of his heart feelings of loneliness, a loneliness that cannot be expunged. Each of us is partially or fully incomprehensible to others and is spiritually cut off from others. Each of us can feel this. The more the bitter flavor of life is tasted and the more sensitive a man's feelings become, the more this loneliness will penetrate down deep into his very bones. The bankrupt financier Hu Jinyi, the aging socialite Daisy Huang, the cynic Li Jie, the university student Zheng Ping, the unemployed city government secretary Mu Zongdan in "Five in a Nightclub"; the wanderer in "Falls the Lotus Blossom"; the seaman and dancer in "Evening"; the "I" and Black Peony in "Black Peony"; and the absurd young woman in "Carven A" [*sic*] are all of this sort, and this is what I intended to write.

At this point I would like to extend my gratitude to Shi Zhecun and Zhao Jiabi, two who have always turned scorn and humiliation into a means of encouraging me. Du Heng [Su Wen], pulling a long and serious face, would watch over me with a critic's eye. Gao Ming and Ye Lingfeng, with whom I often discussed technical problems, offered me many suggestions. [4]

To end, I dedicate this book to the tittering *pierrot* across the ocean, Dai Wangshu. February 28, 1933

—*Translated by Kirk A. Denton*

---

4. All of the above figures were associated with the journal *Xiandai.* For more on this group of writers, see entries for Su Wen, Mu Shiying, and Li Jinfa in the Glossary.

Chapter 43

A Record of My Own Inspiration

Li Jinfa

I remember eight years ago, when my collection of poems first appeared on the Chinese literary scene, an admirer made the following critique: "When you first read his poems, they are not terribly clear; but the more you read, the more flavor [*wei* 味] they have; you can't bear to put them down, and you feel a kind of indescribable aesthetic pleasure."[1] (This was the general tenor.) The advertisement from the publishing company read: "Mr. Li's poems are very difficult to read, yet you still want to read them. . . . " When writing poems I never prepared myself to worry if people found them difficult, I simply sought to give vent to the poetic feeling [*shiyi* 詩意] in my heart of hearts. Now, indeed, there are many in the world whose heartstrings have struck a common chord with mine. My style has universal appeal. I just cannot be like others and use poetry to write about revolutionary thought, or stir people to strike out or shed blood. My poetry is a record

---

1. Li Jinfa 李金發 , "Shi geren linggan de jilubiao" 是個人靈感的記錄表 , *Wenyi dalu* 文藝大陸 2, no. 1 (Nov. 29, 1933); reprinted in *Zhongguo xiandai shi lun* 中國現代詩論 (Modern Chinese essays on poetry), 2 vols. (Guangzhou: Huacheng, 1985), 1: 250.

of my own inspiration, a song sung aloud in intoxication, I cannot hope that everyone will understand it.

Although I have written little fiction, I still have an opinion about it, which is that the joys and sorrows of any life, especially the fragments of life overlooked by people, all make for excellent material for fiction, and can all intimate life. Why must China's critics recite over and over the empty phrases "consciousness of the epoch," "point toward brightness," "revolutionary life," etc.

August 31

—*Translated by Kirk A. Denton*

Chapter 44

Literature and Life

Zhu Guangqian

Literature is the art that has language or writing as its medium.[1] As a form of art, it has things in common with music, painting, sculpture, and all the other artifacts that can be put under the name of arts: namely, that the author of the work must have some unique and fresh perceptions and observations of the various aspects of life; that these perceptions and observations must be given a unique and fresh form of expression; and that the expression and what is expressed, the form and the content, must seamlessly fuse together to become an organic and harmonious whole that will lead the audience from play to pleasure and joy. It is only when such a condition is reached that a work can be called "beautiful," which is a prerequisite for literature and all the other arts. Since it has as its medium language and writing, which are the same instrument of thinking and speaking used in our daily life, literature does not seek an external medium as painting or sculpture does in shapes and colors, or as music does in sounds. Not everyone can use shapes and colors, but whoever can speak can use language,

---

1. Zhu Guangqian 朱光潛, "Wenxue yu rensheng" 文學與人生, in *Tan wenxue* 談文學 (Discussing literature) (Shanghai: Kaiming, 1946); reprinted in Zhu Guangqian 1987: 4: 157–63.

and whoever can read can use writing. Language and writing are our wonderful inborn faculties for expression and bear a most direct relationship with our thoughts and feelings. Because of this, literature is the straight and the easiest way for the average person to come close to art; and also because of this, literature is the form of art that has the closest ties with human life.

When we speak of language and writing as a whole, we refer to the actual condition of our culture at the present stage, but in the process of evolution, the spoken language predates writing, and the two forms may be separated by a gap of thousands or even tens of thousands of years. Even today there are many nations in the world that have a spoken language but no writing. Human beings already had language long before writing was created, and once there was language, there was literature. Literature is the most primitive but also the most universal of all the arts. Among the primitive peoples everyone loved to sing, to tell stories, and to imitate other people's actions and gestures, and therein we have the origin of poetry, fiction, and drama. Many ancient classics that come down to us today, such as the Chinese *Book of Songs*, the Homeric epics, and medieval ballads and romances, were originally all transmitted orally and were written down at a later date. At the stage of oral transmission, literature was largely a collective creation by the entire nation. A song or a story was begun by a group of people and complemented by another group, and then it was passed on from one to another and to more and more people, of whom each one contributed to the original piece by adding or omitting something in the process of transmission. It can be said that a literary work does not have fixed copyrights in a primitive society, and that it is fluid, constantly changing, and cumulative. The stage of its transmission is also that of its growth, and its audiences are also its creators. Such works of literature are most representative of the whole society's outlook on life, and that is why those concerned with politics and education would try to learn about the customs of a people and the condition of a nation from songs and ballads, and indeed the collection of songs and the observation of folk music was an important political institution in the Spring and Autumn period [770–476 B.C.]. We can further argue that the literature of a primitive society almost equals its entire culture; that its history, politics, religion, and philosophy are all reflected in its poetry, mythology, and legends. We can find evidence in Greek mythology and epics, in medieval ballads and legends, and in the songs, myths, and folk tales of the ethnic minorities in modern China.

The change from oral literature to a literature fixed in writing can be seen from one perspective as a great progress, because a work now no longer depends on memory for its preservation, or on recital for its transmission, and its influence can be extended immensely in time and space. From another perspective, however, such a change can also be seen as unfortunate for literature, because written signs must be learned with a special effort, and they become a sort of obstacle to literary creation and appreciation for those who cannot read, and insofar as literature is preserved and transmitted through writing, it becomes the prerogative of a special class. Men of letters form such a special class, and the class distinction becomes increasingly intensified as society evolves, with the result of a gradual alienation of literature from the people as a whole. Many bad consequences follow from such a change: first, as literature drifts away from the people as a whole, it cannot give expression to the spirit and the ideas of the people as a whole, nor can it draw its strength and nourishment from their lives; it cannot but turn narrow and then traditionalist, formalist, and thus rigidified. Second, since it is of interest only to a special class, its influence is also limited to that class and not universal, having no close relations with the lives of average people; and as a result, average people do not consider it of any importance. At the present stage of our culture, literature has become a luxury and not a necessity in life. In the beginning, all those who could use language loved literature; and then, with the emergence of writing, only those who could read could love literature; but now even those who do read are mostly unable to love literature, and some of them despise or even hate literature, accusing it of unwholesome influence or uselessness. Under these circumstances, anyone who wants to talk about literature as something meaningful and serious is likely to feel somewhat diffident and vulnerable, and he needs at least to provide some rationale as a defense for his inopportune behavior. This preamble is intended to offer such a defense for the dozen or so articles on literature that will follow.[2]

Let us first talk about whether literature is useful or not. The average person dismisses literature for its uselessness, but those who advocate "art for art's sake" in modern times hold that the beauty of literature lies precisely in its being useless. Like other arts, it is a free activity human beings are engaged in beyond the restraints of natural needs. For instance, teapots are useful because they hold tea, and all pots can do so whether they are made of baked or unbaked clay, whether round or flat in shape, insofar as the natural need is satisfied. Human beings, however, are not satisfied by this alone; they require that pots not only hold tea but please the eye and the mind, and so they make every effort to make teapots look pretty by using the right kind of material, shape, or color. Such efforts are, from the utilitarian's narrow point of view, rather superfluous and useless, but from

---

2. This essay was originally published as the first in a volume of essays on literature.

the point of view that goes beyond utility, they are actions of man's free will. It is only by painstakingly engaging in such useless but free actions that human beings show that they are their own masters, that they have human dignity and are not mere slaves driven by natural forces, and that they have noble minds and high aspirations. They want to do better than nature, to mend nature's defects, and to make perfect what is imperfect. And such is literature. It originates in practical use, in the need to tell others what one knows and feels, but it transcends practical use and seeks to tell good things and tell them in such a good way that others will derive pleasure from both the content and the form of what is being told. That is why literature is a noble art worthy of our further discussion and explorations.

The argument of "art for art's sake" is not without its rationale, and we should not evaluate literature from the shallow and narrow-minded view of utilitarianism. But even if we concede a point in our argument, I still think that literature cannot be said to be completely useless. Human beings are what they are not because they have thoughts and emotions but because they can express their thoughts and emotions in speech and writing. If like the brute animals humankind had no language and writing, would there be such great splendors of human culture? Culture can be said to largely consist of the products of language and writing. Only through language and writing have so many noble ideas and subtle sensibilities, so many praiseworthy and tragic deeds and actions been passed down to us and disseminated abroad, issuing from one heart to touch innumerable hearts and inspire their creativity. The efficacy of the power to touch and inspire wholly depends on the proper use of language and writing. Would it have been possible for the characters and actions described in the *Zuo Commentary* and the *Records of the Grand Historian* to remain so alive before our eyes after thousands of years, had they not been described in the lively and vivid style of a Zuo Qiuming or a Sima Qian? Would it have been possible for us to feel that the ideas expressed in the Platonic dialogues are interesting and relevant to us after thousands of years, had they not been expressed in the language of Plato that makes the profound readily accessible? So many ideas and actions that deserve to be transmitted to us have simply sunk into oblivion because they were not touched and embellished by a literary hand. Do we not often feel the pain of our inability to express what we have to say? Confucius once said: "If you speak without any embellishment, your words will not go far enough."[3] Just this function to make words "go far enough" already has incredibly far-reaching implications.

---

3. From the *Zuo Commentary*, twenty-fifth year of Duke Xiang.

Plato, Rousseau, Tolstoy, and Cheng Yichuan[4] all expressed doubt about the influence of literature, which they believed to be immoral or unwholesome. We do not have to deny that some literary works are indeed so, but we cannot throw out the baby with the bathwater, that is, we cannot declare the whole of literature guilty even though we may blame some literary works for their imperfections. From a purely aesthetic point of view, the mind is self-contained when one is completely absorbed in literary creation or appreciation, and the question of morality will not arise and intrude into consciousness. Even if we determine the value of literature in real life apart from aesthetic considerations, the influence of literature and art cannot possibly be immoral; moreover, if one is properly cultivated in art and literature, the moral influence one is subjected to can be much more profound and wide-ranging than that of any other experience or teaching. "Moral" and "wholesome" are not different in meaning. The wholesome ideal in life is the harmonious development of the manifold aspects of human nature, with none of them crippled and none excessive. It is like a plant that under favorable conditions will generally be filled with vitality and grow into full bloom and luxuriance. Feelings and thoughts are the vitality in a human being that need to grow, to burst out and to flower. When feelings and thoughts cannot be expressed, one's vitality is stifled and maimed, just like a plant that is sick and in arrested development. In giving expression to feelings and thoughts, literature and art bring one's vitality to full development; and therefore the realization of life's full potential cannot do without literature and art. Many people in this world who take no interest in literature are dull and vulgar, without any sign of liveliness; they are indeed spiritually crippled. They are so either because their vitality has never been strong, or because their strong vitality has been stifled and mangled. If a moral outlook produces spiritual cripples, then it is itself immoral.

Expression is not a luxury but a necessity of life, for growth and development are possible only when expression is. Literature and art give expression to feelings and thoughts and at the same time nourish them to quicken their growth. We all know that literature and art "cultivate one's disposition." Please take note of the significance of the word "cultivate"! In being cultivated, our disposition is bound to be healthy, expanding, joyous, but it is not easy to accomplish one's "cultivation." In the hustle and bustle of this world, we spend most of our time and energy in solving practical problems of daily sustenance, running about and circling around mechanically with the fast-moving traffic, and how often do we have a moment to

---

4. Cheng Yichuan 程 伊 川 , or Cheng Yi 程 頤 (1033–1107), Sung dynasty neo-Confucian scholar of the rationalist school.

pause and reflect on our own disposition, let alone cultivate it? All art and literature create from the real world another world of images beyond the real, and so it is a reflection as well as a transcendence of the real world. When our disposition is being cultivated in the sweet spring of art, for a moment we shake off our worries and burdens, and we experience a spiritual release, a heart-felt joy like the freedom a fish enjoys in water. Or to use a different metaphor, it is like taking a bath in a clear spring and reposing oneself for a while in the shade under a lush tree after one has been exhausted from walking in a dry and scorching desert. Many people in this world are floundering in pain and sin, and become intolerably vulgar and miserable, all because they have too little chance to take such a bath or repose. The Chinese literati used to argue for the dictum that "literature is a vehicle for conveying the *Dao*." Some later thought that the dictum smacked too much of a Confucian scholasticism, so they retrieved from the ancient classics the old saying that "poetry articulates one's intention," and held that the use of literature was only to articulate the intention; they interpreted "intention" as "that to which the mind goes," and understood the articulation of intention as inclusive of all mental activities. Thus literary theorists divided literature into two schools, one considering literature as "a vehicle for the *Dao*," and the other for "articulating one's intention," as though the two schools were two mutually exclusive extremes, the first being "art for the sake of moral teaching," and the second "art for art's sake." As a matter of fact, the key to this question resides in how the word *Dao* is interpreted. If *Dao* is understood in the narrow sense of moral teaching, then the notion of literature as a vehicle for conveying the *Dao* obviously degrades literature, which has no obligation to preach the world's sermons nor a high-sounding treatise of moral perfection. If *Dao* is understood as the principle and reason of the various phenomena in the human world, then literature cannot be separated from the *Dao*, which is simply the truth of literature. As that to which the mind goes, intention must also agree with *Dao*, because the truth of feelings and thoughts is itself the *Dao*. Therefore to "articulate one's intention" is to "carry the *Dao*"; they are not two separate things. Philosophy and science are concerned with *Dao*, so are art and literature. The only difference is that the *Dao* in philosophy and science is abstract, a concept drawn from all the phenomena in the human world, like the salt extracted from saltwater. Whereas the *Dao* in art and literature is concrete, contained in the various phenomena of the human world, like the salt dissolved in water; the drinker can taste its saltiness but cannot tell the salt from the water. To use a different metaphor, the *Dao* in philosophy and science is objective, cold, having spirit but no flesh, whereas the *Dao* in art and literature is subjective, warm, with spirit and flesh fused into a com-

Not everyone engaged in art and literature can reach that level, but that may well serve as a noble ideal that is not only worthy of our pursuit but is also, if we try our best in cultivation, eventually attainable.

—*Translated by Longxi Zhang*

PART V

The Period of National Crisis
1936-1945

to accept a united front with the Communists. As they had during the revolutionary Northern Expedition (1925–27), the CCP and GMD again reluctantly joined forces to defeat a common enemy.

The second united front policy led to the disbandment in 1936 of the fractious League of Left-Wing Writers, which had become mired in factional disputes between Lu Xun (and his supporters Feng Xuefeng and Hu Feng) and Zhou Yang, who had emerged as the leading CCP spokesman within the League. The Two Slogans debate was the straw that broke the League's back. With the prospect of a united front in the imminent War of Resistance, literary figures set out to create a slogan for a literature that would reflect the demands of this new age. Supported by the CCP, Zhou Yang reaffirmed ("On National Defense Literature") the slogan "national defense literature" that he had first devised in 1934. Motivating this slogan was the united front policy, initiated by the Comintern in response to European affairs and imposed on a reluctant CCP. For Lu Xun, Zhou's slogan reversed everything the League had fought so hard to uphold. Intellectuals were expected to forget the battles waged between the leftists and the GMD and dispense with the problem of class that had been so central to the cultural program of the League. With the blessing of Lu Xun, Hu Feng ("What Do the Broad Masses Demand of Literature?") countered Zhou Yang's slogan with one that attempted, with most unfortunately awkward results, to include something of the notion of class struggle as a continuing part of the process of national liberation: "mass literature of national revolutionary struggle." Although fueled by personal animosities, the Two Slogans debate was more than simply a clash of personalities. The debate raised the important question of what part class, and class-based literature, would play during a war of resistance against imperialist aggression.

With some urging from the party, aided by the convenient death of a recalcitrant Lu Xun in October 1936, League writers were persuaded to set aside their partisan interests and form with intellectuals of the right a national cultural organization supporting resistance to Japan. Thus was the All-China Association of Literary Resistance founded. One of the mandates of this cultural organization was to create a literature that would contribute to the war effort, which meant exploiting the propaganda potential in the arts to support the military, educate the masses as to the nature of the conflict, and incite resistance. The principal slogan of the association was for "literature to the countryside, literature into the ranks of the troops"; writers were both to enhance their works by drawing from real experience with peasants and soldiers and to write for their benefit. For art to realize this latter end, it had to be comprehensible to the poorly educated and the illiterate. This could best be achieved through traditional and popular artistic forms, including regional opera, storytelling, songs, simple folk narratives, and poems. Writers and cultural figures found themselves in the position of having to abandon the literary ideals of the cosmopolitan May Fourth and return to the very traditional artistic forms that the May Fourth Movement had sought to eliminate.

The conventional Marxist view of the resulting debate on "national forms" is that it was initiated in 1938 by Mao Zedong himself in "The Role of the Communist Party in the National War," where he called for an abolition of "foreign stereotypes" in party writing and a return to the "fresh, lively style and spirit the common people of China love." Part of the process of developing a new national culture, Mao wrote in another essay, was to sift through traditional culture and extract from it the positive and the progressive ("On New Democracy"). But the issue of the popularization of literary forms had been raised well before Mao under the auspices of the League, most extensively by Qu Qiubai, to whom Mao was greatly indebted for much of his thinking on cultural issues. Qu's 1932 "The Question of Popular Literature and Art" criticized May Fourth elitism and recognized the need to develop a literature for the proletariat from the art forms familiar to them. But Qu's orientation was principally urban, whereas the demands of wartime propaganda dictated a more rural direction. The issue of popular forms, or "national" forms as they were known in the fervor of wartime patriotism, became more pressing during the war as the need for education of the masses intensified; the peasantry sometimes could not distinguish between Chinese troops of the CCP, GMD, or local warlords and those of the Japanese invaders.

Most writers and critics supported or paid lipservice to the goals of national forms, although few of the May Fourth writers (with the notable exception of Lao She) produced literary works that adhered in any way to these forms. Mao Dun's "Literature and Art for the Masses and the Use of Traditional Forms" expresses something of the ambivalence of May Fourth writers toward these forms. Mao Dun recognized the need for traditional forms in the process of creating a literature for the masses, but by no means wished to dispense with the "new literature," by which he presumably meant May Fourth cosmopolitan writing and critical realism. But his support for national forms is largely disingenuous, for he never wrote in anything like a traditional literary form, nor did he refrain from coming to the support of a beleaguered realism on several occasions during the war period.[1]

---

1. See Mao Dun, "Haishi xianshizhuyi" 還是現實主義 (It's still realism), *Zhanshi lianhe xunkan* 戰時聯合旬刊 3 (Sept. 21, 1937); reprinted in Mao Dun 1981: 2: 681–83.

The clearest voice speaking out against national forms was Hu Feng, a poet and critic who had been active in the League. Although Hu's major treatise on the subject is too long for inclusion here, we certainly sense his unswerving faith in May Fourth critical realism in his essay "Realism Today," written in 1943. Critical realism was associated with the cosmopolitan literature of the May Fourth and especially with Lu Xun, Hu Feng's literary mentor. It meant something like a literature that sought to expose, by depicting the horror of the Real, the falseness of conventional values. Returning to traditional literary forms, Hu Feng believed, would bring with it the feudal ideology that the May Fourth had sought to extirpate from the minds of Chinese. Content, in other words, could not be separated from form.

By early 1938 China was divided into three separate political entities: littoral China occupied by the Japanese, including the major urban and industrial centers of Beiping, Shanghai, Nanjing, and Wuhan; the CCP-held areas in the northwest, based in Yan'an; and the GMD southwest, with its capital in Chongqing. The political structures in each of these areas held tight control over what was written and produced artistically. Writers in occupied Shanghai generally refrained from overt criticism of the Japanese, although playwrights occasionally used historical themes allegorically for subversive purposes. On the whole, writing in Beiping and Shanghai tended toward either the entertainment style of the Butterfly school, pure aestheticism, or the portrayal of individual psychology, in each case avoiding the inherent political risks in writing overtly on the themes of nationalism and revolution. Zhang Ailing's "My Writing" disdains the grand and sweeping design of heroic literature in preference for the small and intimate, the simple and ordinary things of life. Her view is diametrically opposed to the mainstream May Fourth ideal that literature participate in the process of nation building and cultural revolution. Qian Zhongshu ("On Writers"), who wrote most of his satirical stories during the war period, lampoons the literary state of affairs during the war which had reduced the writer to self-negation and led to an epidemic of what he terms "poésophobia."

The view that literature had been impoverished by the demands of propaganda and overbearing cultural czars was shared by Shen Congwen, who spent most of the war in Kunming under GMD dominion. Shen's "Universal or Restricted?" laments the fact that literature was monopolized by a handful of "cultural figures" who imposed their vision of literature on all writers. Other writers in the GMD areas denounced the restrictions placed on writers to write only about the war. Liang Shiqiu, for example, wrote a piece (not included here) that was assailed by leftist cultural figures in Chongqing, in which he declared his wish for writing to broaden its scope beyond the narrow subject matter of the war.

Writers in Yan'an were also beginning to feel dissatisfied with the restrictions placed on them and for the failure of this Marxist mecca to live up to their utopian hopes. In the spring of 1942, in the pages of the *Liberation Daily*, writers like Ding Ling, Luo Feng, Wang Shiwei, Ai Qing, and Xiao Jun wrote satirical essays in the style that Lu Xun had made famous during the 1930's, criticizing Party abuses of privilege, the oppression of women, thought reform, and the lack of freedom of speech. Invoking the name and spirit of Lu Xun in an allegorical dialogue with the authorities in Yan'an, Ding Ling's "We Need the *Zawen* Essay" speaks of the enduring need for writers to voice their opposition to tyranny, even if the source of that tyranny is the revolution itself. Mao Zedong responded to this flurry of criticism with his famous "Talks at the Yan'an Forum on Literature and Art," originally presented as two lectures in May 1942 to Yan'an political and cultural cadres. Although Mao appears almost fair-minded in recognizing and respecting both sides of important literary issues (questions of the class stand of the writer, of audience, and of artistic standards versus popularization), the thrust of his argument is that literature should be subservient to the demands of the political sphere. Like Ding Ling (and so many others whose essays are included in this volume), Mao invoked the name of Lu Xun, but to undermine the critical autonomy of the writer that Lu Xun stood for in the minds of most writers and intellectuals. That literature should be made to serve politics in a period of national crisis is an understandable goal, one that was promoted with equal vigor by the leading GMD literary figure of the war period, Zhang Daofan.[2] But the "Talks" were established after 1949 as literary law and continued, up until the death of Mao in 1976, to direct all cultural activity in the PRC.

The final essay included here is one by Hu Feng, written from Chongqing in response, it seems clear, to the "Yan'an Talks." Hu made a lyrical plea for realism against the kind of revolutionary romanticism that the "Talks" seemed to promote. His vision of creativity was a dialectic of the writer's subjectivity with objective reality. He disdained with equal fervor literature guided by abstract ideology and literature that imitated the purely objective, neither of which was grounded in the concreteness of the writer's subjectivity. It is appropriate to end the collection with Hu Feng's

---

2. Zhang Daofan 張 道 藩 (1896–1968) was the leading cultural figure in the GMD. His best literary polemic was written not long after the "Yan'an Talks"; see "Women suo xuyao de wenyi zhengce" 我們所須要的文藝政策 (The literary policy we need), first published in *Wenyi xianfeng* 1, no. 6 (Dec. 25, 1942).

voice, for he, and his vision of a realism infused with the subjectivity of the writer, was the object of a sustained party attack (first in a series of polemics published in 1945–48 and again in 1955, when he was finally jailed as a counterrevolutionary). The case of Hu Feng carries out on the political level what is pointed to in Mao's "Talks": the writer could not be allowed to stand outside politics; he had to serve the interests of the state, or be silenced.

tions from past authorities to disguise the erroneous nature of his views, and this may confuse the perceptions of some of his readers.

We should first point out that the source of Mr. Xu Xing's error is his total misunderstanding of the theoretical rationale for the united front and of the present situation in China. He completely denies, or perhaps simply does not know, that an anti-imperialist unified front is the principal strategy at this stage of the national revolution in colonial and semicolonial countries, and at the same time he does not understand that the annexation of China by the imperialists of the Far East has stirred up a new high tide in the national revolution. Multitudes of the laboring masses have risen up to fight for the survival of their nation, and the petite bourgeoisie and intellectuals have also turned to the revolution in large numbers. There are even sectors of the national bourgeoisie and many rich peasants and small landlords in the villages who may also opt for sympathetic neutrality or even participation in the new national movement. The real-life foundation of the united front for national revolution is not something that Mr. Xu Xing can obliterate single-handedly; our proposal for a national revolutionary united front is one that stems from reality; it is a proposal for real change in accordance with the most progressive theories and strategies.

Mr. Xu Xing cites events in Paris in 1871 and the words written by past authorities as the theoretical basis for his opposition to all national defense fronts, be they political or cultural; this simply proves that he completely misunderstands the new situation of the moment and does not comprehend that correct theoretical principles can be creatively applied in special and specific circumstances. Mr. Xu Xing urges critics to consult historical sources before setting pen to paper to write their essays, and this is, to be sure, valuable advice, but I feel that if, at the time of referring to historical sources, we do not apply correct methods flexibly, then not only will the historical sources be of no use in understanding the present, but they may on the contrary give one a case of indigestion. As for those mechanical methodologists, I trust they will bear in mind the following admonition: "When materialist methodology is not used as a guideline for historical inquiry, but serves instead as a ready-made model for the promotion and dissection of historical facts, it may become its own opposite."

Because Mr. Xu Xing does not have the guidance of correct methodology and lacks any profound understanding of the present movement, he cannot grasp the rapid advances of the times or the precipitous changes that are taking place in the relations between all levels of society. In this great social transformation, the various levels of that most sensitive of classes—the artistic intelligentsia—although they may hold diverse views on life and art, are nonetheless mostly unanimous in their concern for the perilous state of the nation and their demand for national liberation. Most of the best writers since the May Fourth movement have displayed an anti-imperialist and anti-feudal spirit. National defense literature continues the revolutionary tradition of previous literature, while also being grounded in the realities of the high tide of the national revolution, and propels the anti-imperialist and anti-feudal role of literature into the literature of the new era. Of course, no one can deny the role and achievements of culture since 1927, and no one can deny that the literature which takes the standpoint of the laboring masses is the most thoroughly anti-imperialist and anti-feudal literature, that it is the fundamental force in the new literary movement. It is precisely because we have this kind of force that we wish not only to preserve this role and these achievements but also to cause them to expand. We must admit that outside revolutionary literature there still exists an abundance of neutral literature, which still commands a majority of the reading public. They are certainly not, as Mr. Xu Xing would claim, "rubbish crushed beneath the wheels of history." He should know that although the wheels of history can crush people, they can also move them forward. Many facts prove this point. In the united national front, we can find many allies among the neutral or even the backward writers, and all the literary forces for national salvation must be newly deployed. Revolutionary literature should be the main force in the arts for national salvation; it is not guild literature; rather, it is a literature for the broad laboring masses, and in its implications for national liberation, it is also a literature for the whole Chinese nation. The issue of national defense should be on the agenda for creative practice of every revolutionary writer and all other writers who are not traitors, and the movement for national defense literature is one that mobilizes all the forces for national salvation in literature. If we are to achieve this broadest mobilization of literature, we cannot but refute the following supposedly "leftist" contention of Mr. Xu Xing: "We know that the only sector of Chinese society that thoroughly opposes imperialism is the Chinese masses who sell their strength, and they alone are the vanguard; and only literature which occupies this viewpoint is literature that can save China." To believe that only the literature of the laboring masses is literature that can save China is tantamount to reducing the base and scope of the present salvation literature, pulling literature away from the forces friendly to it, and forcing it into a position of absolute isolation. We should recognize that all intermediate literature, providing it aims to oppose the enemy and save the nation, can be beneficial to the liberation of the Chinese people even if it does not adopt the standpoint of the laboring masses, as long as it reflects the national movement to some degree. We should make an appropriate evaluation of the anti-imperialist elements in literature of this kind, while pointing out how the small-producer mentality and worldview obstruct understanding and correct artistic reflection of the real nature of national revolution. Only thus can national defense literature develop broadly and go more deeply.

National defense literature is not the literature of narrow patriotism, but if it is not infused with nationalist sentiment, the force of its artistic appeal to readers will be reduced. Mr. Xu Xing finds "patriotic fervor" repugnant, and castigates the proponents of national defense literature for falling into the "slough of patriotism." Then, using a celebrated remark by a past authority,[2] he declares that patriotism is the kind of sentiment that just happens to be suited to the conditions of small-scale private ownership. But he "just happens" to forget that this same past authority also praised the Russian people and in no way disparaged nationalist sentiment. Nationalist sentiment can arouse burning hatred at the enslavement of our nation and can encourage us to struggle for the freedom and liberation of the nation. In the recent short story "Children Without a Nation,"[3] the young protagonist's passionate feelings of love for the nation's flag moves us; this is not some narrow nationalism but is naturally in harmony with the spirit of internationalism. Unconditional hatred for nationalist sentiment, if not itself the product of a traitor mentality, at least runs the risk of helping traitors by preparing people psychologically to become a conquered nation.

But what Mr. Xu Xing fears most is that the "filth of patriotism" will pollute the artistic community and destroy the purity of literature. He says: "The most important thing in literature is ideology, and the ideology expressed by artistic methods should be pure and not some hybrid that takes no account of faction, social stratum, group, individual, religion, or faith." These are generalized clichés. His "purity" is an abstract criterion, and if this criterion were used to measure the value of an artist's work, then we would be in no position to explain the greatness of Gogol, Tolstoy, or Balzac, since their thinking certainly was not all that pure; the reason that their works endure is that they reflect the objective reality of their period, its development and contradictions. Ideological content certainly has a definite role in a work of art, but as Kirpotin[4] points out, rich ideological content in art is not an abstract ideological richness that transcends history but is closely connected with the concrete artistic depiction of the essential artistic aspects of reality. The themes of artistic creation are extremely com-

---

2. This likely refers to Lu Xun, with whom Xu Xing shares many ideas about the priority of class struggle over the anti-imperialist struggle.

3. "Meiyou zuguo de haizi" 沒有祖國的孩子, a short story by Shu Qun 舒群, collected in a 1937 volume of the same name.

4. See note 2 to the translation of Zhou Yang's "Thoughts on Realism" in this volume.

plex, encompassing all kinds of different elements. The question is not one of reducing the themes—that is, limiting them to that portion that Mr. Xu Xing considers "pure"—but is, on the contrary, one of guiding all manner of component parts to participate in the movement for national liberation. In the case of a talented writer who is also faithful to reality, then no matter what stratum of society he belongs to, what belief he espouses, or what his level of understanding of the real meaning of national revolution, he can still reflect in his works some important aspects of this revolution. We do not in the least underestimate the illuminating function of a progressive world outlook, but neither do we look down on the educative power of reality itself.

National defense literature summons all writers, regardless of their social stratum or faction, to take their stand on the united national front and to join their efforts to create literary works relevant to national revolution. The theme of national defense should become the priority for all authors, other than traitors. Not only does this not reduce the field of vision for authors' creativity, but it actually expands it. All themes of significance to national defense, derived from the realities of the past or the present, must be presented concretely and extensively. The struggle for the survival of our nation exists in all spheres—politics, economics, culture, and daily life. The question of priority and the question of method cannot be separated; the creation of national defense literature must adopt a progressive realist method. Mr. Xu Xing, however, describes these two things as being opposites.

A progressive realist method means depicting reality in the development of the actual revolution truthfully, concretely, and historically, for the purpose of educating the laboring masses in the spirit of socialism. To recognize and reflect reality as it develops is an important methodological principle, because those who cannot see development certainly cannot grasp truth. If you cannot see the prospects for "tomorrow," then "today" has no future; likewise, without "today," "tomorrow" becomes vain hope. National defense literature is not utopian literature; it must first and foremost reflect the real struggle of the Chinese people for the liberation of their own nation, in all its aspects and objectives. Without this present struggle, the "new society of tomorrow" of which Mr. Xu Xing dreams cannot be achieved. "Protect all our territory" may well be, in the eyes of Mr. Xu Xing and his ilk, "patriotic fervor" of an "extremely narrow" kind, but this is precisely the common demand of those millions of people who have lost their land and of the people of the whole country who are not prepared to be the citizens of a defeated nation; it is precisely the means necessary to achieve "the new society of tomorrow." The basic duty of national defense literature is to provide the literary expression of the desire of the broad masses for national liberation. It must combine this with the duty to raise the consciousness of readers concerning the nature of national revolution, and proclaim to the reading public that "socialist revolution is the savior of the nation, and opens up for it a road to increasing prosperity" (Dimitrov).[5]

It is appropriate to demand of national defense literature the most progressive realist works, but the creators of national defense literature are not limited to those authors who are capable of using the most advanced creative methods; even those authors whose ideology and outlook are somewhat backward can still do their best with what they have in the creation of national defense literature. In this respect, national defense literary criticism has an important role to play. The national defense literature movement is a literary movement on the national united front; in order for this movement to expand and develop, it is necessary that we constantly correct and censure the "left" factional viewpoints of people like Mr. Xu Xing. "All factionalists inevitably find themselves separated from the political responsibilities of the moment," and with this quotation from Kirpotin, I conclude this modest essay.

—*Translated by Richard King*

---

5. G. M. Dimitrov (1882–1949), a native Bulgarian, was general secretary of the Comintern from 1935 to 1943, during which time he was responsible for instituting the Soviet popular front policy, which this essay reflects.

Chapter 46

What Do the Broad Masses Demand of Literature?

Hu Feng

I

Since the May Fourth, realism has been the literary mainstream, reflecting the truth about the lives of the broad masses and evoking their aspirations.[1] Of all the shackles that the colonial Chinese people must suffer, the greatest and most pervasive is imperialism; its power extends into all realms of life, spreading venom into the broad masses and sucking their blood. The beginnings of this new literature were motivated by fervor for national liberation, and the need of the broad masses of the people to oppose imperialism was transfused directly into the themes of the new literature.

However, since the Japanese encroachment of September 18, 1931, the crisis facing our nation has become even more urgent. After the problems arose in North China, the entire Chinese nation was brought to the brink of destruction. All this has wrought havoc on the lives of the broad masses,

1. Hu Feng 胡風, "Renmin dazhong xiang wenxue yaoqiu shenme" 人民大衆向文學要求甚麼, *Wenxue congbao* 文學叢報 2 (1936); reprinted in Hu Feng 1984: 1: 374–76.

bringing about new gloom, new anxiety, new anger, and new resistance, all of which have resulted in a new historical era. Naturally this new historical era demands of literature the reflection of its particular characteristics and provides the basis for a new aesthetics. What we should have is a new slogan that captures the character of this new literature—Mass literature of national revolutionary struggle!

In order to explain this new slogan, I wish first to point out the foundations in real life on which it has been built:

1. On that part of our territory that has been lost, national revolutionary struggle is widespread and erupts constantly.

2. In all salvation and liberation movements, the highest common goal is the struggle with the enemy—the movement for national revolutionary struggle.

3. The fervor, hope, and strength of the broad masses of the people are fomenting revolutionary struggle throughout our sacred nation; this revolutionary struggle has the capacity to unite and mobilize all those among the broad masses of the people who are not prepared to become either a conquered people or traitors.

4. Of all great anti-imperialist movements, from the Taiping Heavenly Kingdom to the battle for Shanghai of January 28, 1932, only those that adhered to the principle of national revolutionary struggle have been of any real value. . . .

As we can see from this analysis, "mass literature of national revolutionary struggle" relies on an actively realist method, for it is the concentrated expression in literary form of a real social need; at the same time, the slogan also includes aspects of a positive romanticism, because national revolutionary struggles also embody feats of boundless heroism and mighty aspirations.

II

Thus, "mass literature of national revolutionary struggle" combines all *socially disruptive* issues. It should however be noted that to say it *combines* all these issues is certainly not to say that it *eliminates* them.

For example:

1. Feudal consciousness and the antiquarian movement may preserve or even reinforce among the masses the notion of "Asiatic passivity."

2. The impediments to and constraints on the aspirations of the laboring masses may diminish or even extinguish their fervor and strength.

3. Dissolute enjoyment of special privilege and abuse of power are poisons contaminating the movement to mobilize and unite the broad masses.

All these things are the handmaids of imperialism, the territory of traitors; they provide the conditions that propagate treachery, and all the social disruptions that they have newly induced are embodied in the issues of "mass literature of national revolutionary struggle." Therefore the slogan "mass literature of national revolutionary struggle" should make clear that the interests of the laboring masses are identical to the interests of the nation. It should also make clear who are the organizers of the national revolutionary struggle, who are the main forces for overcoming the enemy, and who it is that would wittingly or unwittingly betray the nation.

III

One aspect of this mass literature of national revolutionary struggle, which has arisen from a real social need, is that it also continues in the tradition of the revolutionary literature of the May Fourth, particularly in its synthesis of the creative achievements made since September 18, 1931.

Since September 18, 1931, the highest form of anti-imperialist struggle has developed into the national revolutionary struggle. This has also been reflected in literature, and in recent times several successes have been recorded. In these works we observe a rather truthful portrayal of national heroes, of the heroism being newly demonstrated in national revolutionary struggle, and especially of the inseparability of national revolutionary struggle and the life of the broad masses of the people. These works are the harbingers of "mass literature of national revolutionary struggle"; they are the basis for the literature that is proposed by this slogan.

"Mass literature of national revolutionary struggle" should critically follow the path newly blazed by these works, should courageously surpass their achievements, should reflect the movement for national revolutionary struggle more truthfully and from more perspectives, and should promote the movement for national revolutionary struggle, responding to the demands of the broad masses with both great works of towering ideological force and smaller, more adroit pieces.

5 A.M., May 9, 1936

—*Translated by Richard King*

Chapter 47

The Question of Popular Literature and Art

Qu Qiubai

I. What Is the Problem?

In China the laboring people are still culturally in the Middle Ages.[1] Popular literary and artistic forms such as storytelling, romantic adventure, ditties, cinematic peep shows, comic books, and outdoor theater are used by China's merchant-gentry class as tools to impose their enslaving education on the laboring people. In both written and oral form the origins of all this reactionary popular literature and art lie several centuries in the past; in a most subtle fashion it penetrated deeply among the people and became a part of their daily lives. Consequently, their knowledge of life and their observations of social phenomena—in a word, the cosmology and new view of humankind held by the laboring masses—have been derived, for the most part, from this corpus of reactionary popular literature and art. Naturally reactionary popular literature and art of this sort give full expression

---

1. Qu Qiubai 瞿秋白, "Dazhong wenyi de wenti" 大衆文藝的問題, *Wenxue daobao* 文學導報, June 10, 1932; reprinted in *WXYDSLX*.

to the prevailing feudal consciousness of the time. In it we see the flesh-devouring principle of *li* (Confucian doctrine of propriety) flash its teeth and brandish its claws, we witness the terror of Hell, prostrations before Grand Magistrates, fantasies of knight-errantry and magic swordsmen, the propaganda of popularized Eastern culturalism, and evil, indecent, and cruel attitudes toward women. . . . As usual everything is shrouded over in a fog, and there is *no representation whatever* of the birth and growth of revolutionary class consciousness or the emergence of a determination to resist. Recently during the Japanese encroachment in Manchuria (1931) and attack on Shanghai (1932) the counterrevolutionary bourgeoisie made use of these same tools to obstruct increasingly revolutionary expressions of understanding on the part of the masses.

The May Fourth–New Culture movement was a waste of time with regard to the people! May Fourth new classical literature (the *so-called* vernacular, or *baihua*, literature) and the early revolutionary and proletarian literature, which clearly arose from the May Fourth foundation, simply provided the Europeanized gentry with yet another sumptuous banquet to satisfy their new tastes while the laboring people were still starving. How did this come about? Because under the prevailing class system, feudal remnants in China are particularly evident in cultural life. In the past the gentry used the classical language, and it had a system of writing; the common people used the vernacular language, and they simply had no system of writing, thus the only things they were able to use were the dregs of the gentry's writing system. Now, one portion of the gentry class has been Europeanized, and it has created a new Europeanized classical language, but, as usual, the inability of the common people of today to understand the so-called new artistic works is no different from the inability of common people in earlier days to understand the written language of ancient poetry and literature. In a word, there is no common language linking the new-style gentry to the common people. As a consequence, therefore, regardless of how good the contents of revolutionary literature might be, these works will have no relation whatsoever to the people so long as they continue to be written in the language of the gentry. In short, the May Fourth–New Culture movement has had almost no impact on the masses. Among the masses, for example, anti-Confucianism is a lesson derived directly from a practical revolutionary struggle to which the literary struggle has not contributed in the least.

Currently, therefore, the problem definitely is not a simple matter of popularizing literature and art; it is a question of *creating a revolutionary popular literature and art*. What is needed is a *literary renaissance movement led by the proletariat, a cultural revolution and a literary revolution led by the prole-*

tariat, *a "proletarian May Fourth movement."* Of course, from time to time this movement will have an anti-bourgeois thrust, but in the present stage this movement obviously will be performing an essentially bourgeois-democratic task.

This is where the problem lies!

Up to the present time the revolutionary struggle on the literary and artistic front has been limited to opposing the influence of the various reactionary groups upon the Europeanized intellectual youth; the struggle to go among the laboring people, to oppose all forms of reactionary landlord-capitalist literature and art has hardly begun. Proletarian revolutionary ideas point to the need to win over the laboring people, to assault and wipe out the influence of the landlord-capitalist class; in literary and artistic matters this necessarily requires an ardent struggle for a new cultural revolution. Accordingly it will be necessary to do research on what the people are reading these days, on what sort of views the people have of life and society, on the type of material the people can understand or are accustomed to reading, and finally on the type of literary and artistic works the people will need as they struggle in this society. In sum, this means it will be necessary to use the language of the laboring people themselves, to keep in mind the actual life of the laboring people while responding to all problems, and to create a revolutionary popular literature and art. In the process of doing this, the literary revolution of the working people will be completed and a literary language (*wenxue de yuyan*) of the working people will be created.

In short, *the problem of revolutionary popular literature and art concerns nothing less than the movement for both a cultural revolution and a literary revolution led by the proletariat.* The tendency to ignore this bourgeois-democratic task in the past explains why, on the one hand, there has been so much hollow chatter in the revolutionary literary world about popular literature and art and the popularization of [elite] literature and art, while, on the other hand, there has been no effective struggle.

II. What Sort of Speech Should Be Used When Writing?

After the May Fourth movement, appeals for "literary revolution" were replaced by appeals for "revolutionary literature," and this represented a step forward in the struggle.[2] But it was precisely in the revolutionary literature camp that the tendency to ignore the continuation and final com-

---

2. See Cheng Fangwu, "From Literary Revolution to Revolutionary Literature," in Part III of this volume.

pletion of the literary revolution was most noticeable. Consequently it became a common practice to thoroughly disregard the customs of spoken Chinese and to make widespread use of classical Chinese grammar, European grammar, and Japanese grammar, and to write in a so-called vernacular language that in fact cannot be understood by the listener. Without question there were some famous writers who were capable of writing in a genuinely vernacular language. But, since 1925 no one has pointed out the need to continually stress the question of literary revolution. All the creative writings and essays of the "new literature," and especially translations, make carefree use of the new-style classical writing (the so-called vernacular), but as yet this work has not received the slightest bit of criticism. Of course, it is unnecessary to point out that landlord-capitalist literature is like this, but so, too, is revolutionary literature. The reactionary groups are able to exploit this weakness among the revolutionary rank and file, and, thereby, strike a blow at the development of revolutionary literature. There is no difference between this mistake and the sort of errors made in leading revolutionary political organs, which, objectively speaking, assist the forces of counterrevolution and cause a widening of the distance separating them from the broad masses.[3]

Thus, in the first place, the problem of popular literature and art involves the need to begin work by thoroughly completing the literary revolution. Although the matter of what spoken language to use in writing popular literature and art is not the most important question, its resolution is a precondition for asking all the other questions. Just as English workers are unable to read fiction written in medieval English or Latin, so, too, are Chinese workers unable to read the various written works that use ancient Chinese or Europeanized grammar.

Today the situation regarding the written Chinese language is this: a variety of dissimilar systems are being used simultaneously—first there is the ancient classical language (used now in sending "four-six" style telegrams),[4] second is the classical style of Liang Qichao (used in legal and official papers, etc.), third is the so-called vernacular language of the May Fourth period, and fourth is the vernacular used in traditional fiction. We

---

3. This is an extremely interesting, if oblique, reference to Qu's disenchantment with the Wang Ming leadership group, which dominated the CCP in the early 1930's. It was precisely their dogmatism and subjectivism that helped widen the gap between the party and the urban masses in this period. Qu himself was expelled from the Politburo of the Central Committee by the Wang Ming group in 1931.

4. The *siliu dianbao* 四六電報 was an extremely concise and stylized method of sending telegrams in the early Republican period—a form that alternated lines of four and six characters.

are aware that the Chinese ideographs themselves are a most damnable legacy, but, in addition to this confusion, a variety of different grammars have been thrown in. Under these circumstances how are the more than 300 million Han people going to be able to acquire literacy?![5] It has virtually been decided that this task is impossible. To understand a copy of Shang-hai's paper, *Shen bao,* requires a minimum of five years' study! It is pre-cisely this state of affairs that serves to sustain the landlord-capitalist class. To revolutionize the written language is unquestionably a bourgeois-democratic task, but China's bourgeoisie is unable to complete this task—indeed, it has already opposed a deepening of the literary revolution. They took advantage (perhaps unconsciously) of the early May Fourth move-ment for literary renaissance by creating a new classical vernacular, and then bestowed this new classical gift upon their own Europeanized sons for their enjoyment. As usual, the laboring people were left with the dregs of merchant-gentry language—the vernacular of traditional fiction found in the tunes sung by the fortune-teller.

Nevertheless, when compared to May Fourth new classical, the ver-nacular used in traditional fiction has a number of things to recommend it.

The written language of the May Fourth new classical is composed of a mixture of classical Chinese, European, and Japanese grammar along with the vernacular speech of both ancient and modern times. Thus it is basically a written language that cannot be read aloud. But the vernacular used in traditional fiction is ancient vernacular, and it regulated the influx of clas-sical grammar relatively well. It was the language spoken by the people of the Ming dynasty, and although we can tell when it is read aloud that it is not the language spoken by modern Chinese people, it is, after all, the speech of traditional drama and definitely can be read aloud. For this rea-son the vernacular used in traditional fiction is relatively close to the peo-ple, and the people are accustomed to reading it. When compared to all the other so-called Chinese languages, this variety of vernacular has one im-portant special feature—it has developed from the oral literature of the people (the common speech of the Song and Yuan dynasties). Reactionary popular literature and art take this characteristic into account, thereby strengthening its hold on the literary and artistic life of the laboring people. If revolutionary literature and art do not fight this, then they are simply handing the people over to literature and art of this sort.

---

5. By using the ethnic / racial term "Han" here, Qu is suggesting that the literacy prob-lem is a Chinese problem. There is no need to impose the Han language and script (and its problems) on minority groups in China.

Therefore the new literary revolution must not only continue to clean out the remnants of the classical language and overthrow the *so-called* vernacular or new classical, but it must also *firmly oppose the vernacular used in traditional fiction*, because, in fact, it is a dead language. To oppose a dead language of this sort means that we must *all* make use of the modern vernacular spoken by living Chinese when we write, especially the language spoken by the proletariat. And the proletariat cannot be compared to the rural peasantry. The language of "rural folks" is primitive and obscure. But in the major cities, which have drawn people from all parts of China, and in the modern factories, the proletariat's language has already evolved, in fact, into a Chinese street vernacular [*putonghua*]—not to be confused with the so-called national language [*guoyu*] of the officials! It contains aspects of a variety of local dialects while having eliminated the obscure localisms of these dialects, and it has been receptive to foreign phraseology. Thus it is creating a new technical language for modern scientific, artistic, and political usage. But, on the other hand, it is clearly not the same as the new classical language of the intellectuals. New classical has *invented* a considerable amount of new phraseology, and it has stolen European and Japanese grammar, thereby not only failing to take into account the customary features of grammar found in *classical* texts, but actually violating the customs of all Chinese grammar. As it developed and grew, street vernacular was also infused with foreign phraseology and even some foreign syntax, but it was placed on the foundation of the customary grammar of spoken Chinese. In sum, each written work should adopt the following standard: "It can be understood when read aloud." Then there can be no question about its being the language of living people.

As for revolutionary popular literature and art, it is especially important that it begin by making use of the most simple proletarian street vernacular. On the surface of things, it will appear at the outset to be modeled on the vernacular of traditional fiction. But on no account should this be construed as a policy of surrender. It is a matter of the proletarian vanguard leading *all* the laboring people in the task of creating a new and rich *modern Chinese literature*. At times it will be necessary to use the various local dialects in writing, and in the future perhaps a special literature for Guangdong, Fujian, and other places will be constructed.

III. What Should Be Written?

What sort of things should revolutionary popular literature and art write? For the purposes of discussion, let us divide the question into two parts.

First, there is the question of form. At the outset, the following must be explained clearly: the revolutionary vanguard should not separate itself from the mass rank and file or engage single-handedly in "heroic and magnanimous activities." To insist the new content must necessarily be expressed in new forms and to insist that the level of the people be raised in order that they might appreciate art rather than lowering the standard of art to the level of the people is to speak with the arrogance of a "great writer"! Revolutionary popular literature and art must begin by utilizing the strong points of traditional forms—things the people are accustomed to reading or viewing such as fiction, lyrics, or drama—gradually adding new ingredients and cultivating new habits among the people, so that by working together with the people the level of art will be raised. With regard to form, there are two points to be made for traditional popular literature and art: one is its relationship to the oral literary heritage, and second is its simple and plain manner of narration and exposition. Revolutionary popular literature and art should heed these two points. Fiction of the storytelling variety can reach the illiterate, and this is exceedingly important for revolutionary literature and art. It represents sensible and straightforward narration—in contrast to the "mindless and confusing" writing method of the new literature and art—and it is the easiest thing for the people of today to understand.

Revolutionary popular literature and art, therefore, should make use of forms such as storytelling and boatman's songs. Naturally we should be ready to introduce new forms that can be readily accepted by the people. For example, it might be possible to compile current events fiction by inserting some spoken dialogue into popular folk music, or to use pure vernacular to create a new short story form. And the possibilities for handling drama in new ways are even greater. After practical work begins, our experience will teach us many new methods, and the people themselves will be able to create new forms. To rely totally on traditional forms is to walk down the path of surrender.

Second, there is the matter of content. At present the primary work slogan for revolutionary popular literature and art and for the proletarian literary movement in general should be: "*Tear off all masks and put the heroes of revolutionary war on display.*" But of special importance is the need to have a clear perception of precisely where the consciousness of the enemies of the revolution has made its impact among the people. This is a cardinal task in the revolutionary struggle on the literary and artistic front. If the enemy's strength cannot be calculated, then naturally there can be no fight. Because there was no assessment of the actual situation during the early period of revolutionary literature, only posters and slogans were yelled out. This is not attacking the enemy, nor is it assaulting reactionary consciousness, it's just yelling. To be assembled on the battlefield shouting in triumph with all eyes fixed on flags fluttering in the heavens, rather than pointing the guns of the revolutionary army in the direction of the enemy, may appear to be very "bold," but in fact it is not the same as doing battle! For this reason there are those among us who oppose ripping masks from the faces of the enemy; that is, they are not in favor of us writing about the landlord-capitalist class and the petite bourgeoisie.[6] At present it must be profoundly understood that it is the task of the revolutionary literary movement to clearly perceive what means the enemy uses *in each and every crisis* to mislead the people, to clearly perceive what sort of reactionary consciousness is inflicted upon the *daily lives* of the people, and to rip off every variety of mask. Our work must reflect the *actual revolutionary struggle* by presenting revolutionary heroism, particularly the heroism of the people. This will require exposing reactionary consciousness and the timid wavering of the petite bourgeoisie, thereby bringing to light the influence of this consciousness upon the struggle of the people and thus assisting in the growth and development of revolutionary class consciousness.

Revolutionary popular literature and art, therefore, can have a variety of dissimilar source material. In order to reflect quickly the revolutionary struggles and political crises of a given moment, there can be "instant" and "rough" popular literature and art of the reportage variety. Perhaps works of this sort have no artistic value; perhaps they will have nothing more than new, popularized current events essays. But art will be created in the process of the agitation-propaganda struggle. Content can be drawn from traditional source material, giving rise to a "New Yue Fei" or a "New Water Margin."[7] It can be "romantic adventures" or revolutionary struggles such as "The Taiping Revolution," "The Canton Commune," or "Zhu De and Mao Zedong atop Jinggang Mountain." It can be translations of international revolutionary literature. It can be work that exposes capitalist-imperialist aggression on the part of the Big Powers. It can be a new form of "social gossip," because if reactionary popular literature and art can make use of things such as the trial of Yan Shuisheng, the love affair between Huang and Lu, and the Shu Jing murder trial, then revolutionary popular literature and art should also describe the family life of the labor-

---

6. Refers to the radical Marxist writers who criticized Mao Dun and others for writing about the petite bourgeoisie in the late 1920's and early 1930's. See Qian Xingcun, "The Bygone Age of Ah Q," and Mao Dun, "On Reading *Ni Huanzhi*," in Part III of this volume.

7. Yue Fei 岳飛, a Song general, is the hero of a variety of traditional popular novels.

ing people and the question of love, while describing the landlord-capitalist class for everyone to see.[8] This last point is worthy of everyone's attention, because, up to the present time, revolutionary literature and art has been deficient in accomplishing the special tasks of this literary and artistic struggle.

IV. What Lies Ahead?

The future of revolutionary popular literature and art will depend on its ability to become a strong and powerful enemy of reactionary popular literature and art and to become the true successor of "nonpopular revolutionary literature and art."

The struggle to create a revolutionary popular literature and art will be long and difficult. It will necessitate linking up with the broad masses, tapping vast public potentialities, and establishing a cadre for the literary and artistic movement of the laboring people (It is important that it be led by workers.). At first the cadres should be concerned with oral literature, but in time they certainly will become involved in written literature. All these things will require a long and difficult period of organized and systematic work.

The situation at present is this: popular literature and art and nonpopular literature and art exist side by side. This is because the remnants of the feudal system—particularly in the area of cultural relations— still retain a dominant position: the gentry class and the people have no common language. Whoever ignores this fact will be unable to adopt an appropriate line of struggle, and consequently will either abandon the tasks of the new cultural revolution or be deluded into thinking that it will be possible to rely thoroughly upon the Europeanized intellectual youth to engage in a liberal program of "instructing" the people in the matter of cultural revolution.

At present we must popularize nonpopular revolutionary literature and art while simultaneously carrying forward the struggle against the influence of all reactionary Europeanized literature and art among the masses of petit-bourgeois intellectual youth. We must also see to it that a *revolutionary popular literature and art arises from the people*, and, working with people, ensure that the level of art is raised and that the difference between popular literature and art and nonpopular literature and art is erased. To accom-

---

8. Real murders and famous love affairs were often used for materail in the sensationalist fiction of the Mandarin Ducks and Butterfly school See Glossary for more information.

plish this, it will be necessary to get rid of nonpopular literature and art that use the new classical language while building a "modern Chinese literature" of high artistic quality, but one the people are able to use.

Rewritten on March 5, 1932

—*Translated by Paul Pickowicz*
Previously published in *Bulletin of
Concerned Asian Scholars* (Jan.–Mar. 1976): 48–52.
Reprinted with permission.

Chapter 48

Excerpts from Mao Zedong

Mao Zedong

From "The Role of the Communist Party in the National War"[1]

Generally speaking, all Communist Party members who can do so should study the theory of Marx, Engels, Lenin, and Stalin, study our national history, and study current movements and trends; moreover, they should help to educate members with less schooling. The cadres in particular should study these subjects carefully, while members of the Central Committee and senior cadres should give them even more attention. No political party can possibly lead a great revolutionary movement to victory unless it possesses revolutionary theory and knowledge of history and has a profound grasp of the practical movement.

The theory of Marx, Engels, Lenin, and Stalin is universally applicable. We should regard it not as a dogma, but as a guide to action. Studying it is not merely a matter of learning terms and phrases but of learning Marxism-

---

1. Mao Zedong 毛澤東, "Zhongguo gongchandang zai minzu zhanzheng de diwei" 中國共產黨在民族戰爭的地位; presented first as a report to the Central Committee of the Chinese Communist Party, October 1938; Chinese text in *Mao Zedong xuanji* vol. 2; translation from Mao Tse-tung 1975: 2: 208–9.

Leninism as the science of revolution. It is not just a matter of understanding the general laws derived by Marx, Engels, Lenin, and Stalin from their extensive study of real life and revolutionary experience, but of studying their standpoint and method in examining and solving problems. Our Party's mastery of Marxism-Leninism is now rather better than it used to be, but is still far from being extensive or deep. Ours is the task of leading a great nation of several hundred million in a great and unprecedented struggle. For us, therefore, the spreading and deepening of the study of Marxism-Leninism presents a big problem demanding an early solution that is possible only through concentrated effort. Following on this plenary session of the Central Committee, I hope to see an all-Party emulation in study that will show who has really learned something, and who has learned more and learned better. So far as shouldering the main responsibility of leadership is concerned, our Party's fighting capacity will be much greater and our task of defeating Japanese imperialism will be more quickly accomplished if there are one or two hundred comrades with a grasp of Marxism-Leninism that is systematic and not fragmentary, genuine and not hollow.

Another of our tasks is to study our historical heritage and use the Marxist method to sum it up critically. Our national history goes back several thousand years and has its own characteristics and innumerable treasures. But in these matters we are mere schoolboys. Contemporary China has grown out of the China of the past; we are Marxist in our historical approach and must not lop off our history. We should sum up our history from Confucius to Sun Yatsen and take over this valuable legacy. This is important for guiding the great movement of today. Being Marxists, Communists are internationalists, but we can put Marxism into practice only when it is integrated with the specific characteristics of our country and acquires a definite national form. The great strength of Marxism-Leninism lies precisely in its integration with the concrete revolutionary practice of all countries. For the Chinese Communist Party, it is a matter of learning to apply the theory of Marxism-Leninism to the specific circumstances of China. For the Chinese Communists who are part of the great Chinese nation, flesh of its flesh and blood of its blood, any talk about Marxism in isolation from China's characteristics is merely Marxism in the abstract, Marxism in a vacuum. Hence to apply Marxism concretely in China so that its every manifestation has an indubitable Chinese character, i.e., to apply Marxism in the light of China's specific characteristics, becomes a problem that is urgent for the whole Party to understand and solve. Foreign stereotypes must be abolished, there must be less singing of empty, abstract tunes, and dogmatism must be laid to rest; they must be replaced by the fresh, lively Chi-

waste matter to be discarded—before it can nourish us. To advocate "wholesale Westernization"[3] is wrong. China has suffered a great deal from the mechanical absorption of foreign material. Similarly, in applying Marxism to China, Chinese Communists must fully and properly integrate the universal truth of Marxism with the concrete practice of the Chinese revolution, or in other words, the universal truth of Marxism must be combined with specific national characteristics and acquire a definite national form if it is to be useful, and in no circumstances can it be applied subjectively as a mere formula. Marxists who make a fetish of formulas are simply playing the fool with Marxism and the Chinese revolution, and there is no room for them in the ranks of the Chinese revolution. Chinese culture should have its own form, its own national form. National in form and new-democratic in content—such is our new culture today.

New-democratic culture is scientific. Opposed as it is to all feudal and superstitious ideas, it stands for seeking truth from facts, for objective truth and for the unity of theory and practice. On this point, the possibility exists of a united front against imperialism, feudalism, and superstition between the scientific thought of the Chinese proletariat and those Chinese bourgeois materialists and natural scientists who are progressive, but in no case is there a possibility of a united front with any reactionary idealism. In the field of political action Communists may form an anti-imperialist and anti-feudal united front with some idealists and even religious people, but we can never approve of their idealism or religious doctrines. A splendid old culture was created during the long period of Chinese feudal society. To study the development of this old culture, to reject its feudal dross and assimilate its democratic essence is a necessary condition for developing our new national culture and increasing our national self-confidence, but we should never swallow anything and everything uncritically. It is imperative to separate the fine old culture of the people, which had a more or less democratic and revolutionary character, from all the decadence of the old feudal ruling class. China's present new politics and new economy have developed out of her old politics and old economy, and her present new culture, too, has developed out of her old culture; therefore, we must respect our own history and must not lop it off. However, respect for history means giving it its proper place as science, respecting its dialectical development, and not eulogizing the past at the expense of the present or praising every drop of feudal poison. As far as the masses and the young stu-

---

3. Wholesale Westernization was the view held by a number of Westernized Chinese bourgeois intellectuals who unconditionally praised the outmoded individualist-bourgeois culture of the West and advocated the servile imitation of capitalist Europe and America.

dents are concerned, the essential thing is to guide them to look forward and not backward.

New-democratic culture belongs to the broad masses and is therefore democratic. It should serve the toiling masses of workers and peasants who make up more than 90 percent of the nation's population and should gradually become their very own. There is a difference of degree, as well as a close link, between the knowledge imparted to the revolutionary cadres and the knowledge imparted to the revolutionary masses, between the raising of cultural standards and popularization. Revolutionary culture is a powerful revolutionary weapon for the broad masses of the people. It prepares the ground ideologically before the revolution comes and is an important, indeed essential, fighting front in the general revolutionary front during the revolution. People engaged in revolutionary cultural work are the commanders at various levels on this cultural front. "Without revolutionary theory there can be no revolutionary movement";[4] one can thus see how important the cultural movement is for the practical revolutionary movement. Both the cultural and practical movements must be of the masses. Therefore all progressive cultural workers in the anti-Japanese war must have their own cultural battalions, that is, the broad masses. A revolutionary cultural worker who is not close to the people is a commander without an army, whose firepower cannot bring the enemy down. To attain this objective, written Chinese must be reformed (given the requisite conditions) and our spoken language brought closer to that of the people, for the people, it must be stressed, are the inexhaustible source of our revolutionary culture.

A national, scientific, and mass culture—such is the anti-imperialist and anti-feudal culture of the people, the culture of New Democracy, the new culture of the Chinese nation.

Combine the politics, the economy, and the culture of New Democracy, and you have the new-democratic republic, the Republic of China both in name and in reality, the new China we want to create.

Behold, New China is within sight. Let us all hail her!

---

4. V. I. Lenin, "What Is to Be Done?"

Chapter 49

Literature and Art for the Masses and the Use of Traditional Forms

Mao Dun

No one opposes the popularization of literature and art for the masses.[1] Especially during our present War of Resistance against Japan, those who once opposed it no longer do.

When it comes to the question of making use of traditional literary forms, however, there are a plethora of opinions. When the call for making use of traditional forms becomes too strident, some see in this a "crisis" and wonder if reverting to the traditional forms, which had long since been repudiated by the new literature, wouldn't be inviting another "literary revolution."

This sort of concern would appear "reasonable to maintain," but what about the facts? The facts are that in the past twenty years traditional forms have been repudiated only by the writers of new literature and not by the new literature itself, much less by the masses. It is a disgrace that we writ-

---

1. Mao Dun 茅盾, "Dazhonghua yu liyong jiu xingshi" 大衆化與利用舊形式, *Wenyi zhendi* 文藝陣地 1, no. 4 (June 1, 1938).

ers of new literature are guilty of this, and we should have the courage to acknowledge it.

Since these are the facts, when the demand for the popularization of literature and art for the masses arose for the first time in the literary world seven or eight years ago, the question of making use of traditional forms was already discussed. At that time, however, the objective circumstances for acting on the question were not favorable and the discussion, as a consequence, could not evolve beyond "armchair strategy." Only since the War of Resistance began has this long-unresolved question finally been put into a large test tube for practical experimentation. But who would have expected that no sooner did the testing begin (though only a miserable few were involved in the testing) than opinions again began to diverge. There are even those who are worried that the exalted place of the new literature is in jeopardy. But how can this be?

Isn't it eminently clear that when one says "to make use of," one does not mean unconditional acceptance? Our urgent task at this moment should be to study the extent to which the traditional forms can be made use of; to study the question of, and experiment in, how to bring the new out from the old; and to make a critical evaluation of the results of these experiments from an affirmative standpoint. To act alarmed and worried over the pending doom of the new literature is no better than spinning nonsense.

It is said that there are others who want to take advantage of this state of affairs (i.e., the furor over the use of traditional forms) to threaten the new literary forms and to virtually wipe out the new literature movement with one stroke. But one need not worry about this either. The new literature has developed through a continuous process of struggle against hardships and cannot possibly be "wiped out" by external forces. If making use of the traditional forms is one of the assignments in the process of popularizing literature for the masses, we should do all we can to further that end. We should not be so afraid of others making use of this "making use" that we ourselves stop working. During this period of War of Resistance against Japan, there are quite a few evil forces that are making use of the War of Resistance to serve their own interests. Are we to stop fighting on that account?

What the writers of new literature should really guard themselves against is the new literature's continuing stagnation in a narrowly confined circle. In that sense, the most important task facing us today is the popularization of literature and art for the masses. The facts have already shown us clearly that in order to popularize literature and art, we cannot spurn, nor totally ignore, the assignment of using traditional forms. Nothing would be easier than simply spurning this assignment, but then the masses will also ignore you. "Literature to the countryside! Literature to the army rank and file!" To try to act out these slogans by wearing the usual Western clothes and brandishing the usual walking stick would be nothing more than deluding ourselves and deluding others.

—Translated by Yu-shih Chen

Chapter 50

My Writing

Zhang Ailing

Although I write fiction and essays, I don't pay much attention to theory.[1] Recently, I suddenly felt there are some things I need to say and have written them down here.

Literary theory, I believe, emerges from works of literature. It has been this way in the past, it is this way now, and in the future it will likely continue to be so. Of course a writer who wants to improve self-awareness will find it beneficial to extract some theories from her work and use them to measure future works. But in this measuring, it is necessary to remember that in the development of literature the literary work and theory are like two horses, side by side, pulling a cart: at any given time one may be ahead of the other, but they drive each other forward. Theory is not the driver seated high above with a whip in his hand.

At present, it seems that both literary works and theory are deficient. I have noticed that those involved in literature often emphasize that which is active and exciting in human life and ignore that which is stable and calm.

---

1. Zhang Ailing 張愛玲, "Ziji de wenzhang" 自己的文章, in *Liuyan* 流言 (Gossip) (Shanghai: Wuzhou shubao she, 1944).

Actually the latter is the foundation of the former. It is as if they emphasize the struggles of life but ignore the harmony. Actually people struggle so they can obtain harmony.

Emphasizing the active, exciting parts of human life gives something of a superhuman flavor. Superhumans are born only in certain eras, but the stable in human life has a flavor of eternity. Even though this calm stability is often incomplete and must be broken every now and then, it is still eternal. It exists in all eras. It is the spirit of humanity, and we can also say it is the nature of women.

In the history of literature there are few works that are simple paeans to the stable in human life, but many that emphasize its activity and excitement. But good works can describe this excitement because they are always grounded in what is stable in life. Without this basis, excitement is only floating bubbles. Many powerful works only give people excitement but cannot offer any revelation; they fail precisely because they do not know how to grasp this basis.

Struggle moves people because it is at once great and bitter. Those who are struggling have lost the harmony of life and are searching for a new harmony. Struggle for the sake of struggle loses its flavor, and when written about will not become good literature.

I have discovered that in many works there is more strength than beauty. Strength is joyful and beauty is sad; so neither can exist alone. "We have talked of life and death, union and separation; / I take your hand, and get old with you," from the *Book of Songs*, is a sad poem, but how affirmative it is in its attitude toward human life. I don't like power and force. I like sadness and, even more, desolation. Power and force have only strength but no beauty, as if they lack human nature. Sadness is like the combination of true red and true green, a powerful contrast. Yet it is better at stimulating than inspiring. Desolation leaves an even longer aftertaste because like the green of scallions and the red of peaches it is an uneven contrast.

I like writing that uses uneven contrasts because it is close to reality. In "The Love that Destroyed a City," Liusu escapes from a corrupt family, yet the baptism by war in Hong Kong does not change her into a revolutionary woman. The war in Hong Kong influences Fan Liuyuan, turning him toward an ordinary life. In the end he gets married, but marriage does not change him into a saint who completely abandons the habits and style of his previous life. Thus even though what happens to Liusu and Liuyuan can more or less be called healthy, it is still common; if you look at the facts of their lives, this is the only thing that could happen.

There aren't many people around who are either enlightened or perverse to an extreme. This is a troubled era that does not allow for any easy enlightenment. In these years people have just gone on living, and even though insanity is insanity, there are limits. So in my stories, with the exception of Cao Qiqiao in *The Golden Cangue*, none of the characters are extreme. They are not heroes; they are the ones who bear the burden of the era. But even though they are not extreme, they are serious. They have no tragedy, just desolation. Tragedy offers a kind of completion, whereas desolation offers a kind of revelation.

I know people are anxious to find completion; otherwise, they seek stimulation, even if it is just to satisfy themselves. It seems they are impatient with mere revelation. Yet this is the only way I can write. I believe writing in this way is more real. I know my works lack strength, but since I write fiction, all I can do is show the strength of fictional characters as well as I can. I can't create strength on their behalf. Furthermore, I believe that even though they are only ordinary, weak people without the strength of heroes, it is precisely these ordinary people who are better than heroes in representing the totality of this era.

In this era old things break apart and new ones emerge. But until the era reaches its apex, earth-shattering events will be the exception. People only sense, to the point of terror, that things are not quite right in all aspects of their daily lives. People live in an era, but this era sinks like a shadow and they feel they have been abandoned. In order to prove their existence and grasp a bit of something real and quite elemental, they have no choice but to draw from their ancient memories for help, memories lived by all humanity in all eras. This is clearer and more intimate than gazing toward the future. Thus a strange feeling toward surrounding reality emerges, a suspicion that this is an absurd, ancient world, dark and shadowy, and yet bright and clear. Between memory and reality an awkward disharmony frequently arises, and because of this a disruption—at once heavy and light—and a struggle—serious, yet still nameless—are produced.

"Dawn," an unfinished stone statue by Michel Angelo [*sic*], is only a crude human figure whose eyes and face are unclear, yet its vastness of spirit symbolizes a new era yet to arrive. If this kind of work were to appear in the present era, naturally it would capture our imaginations, but it has not and it cannot, because people still cannot struggle free from the nightmares of this era.

The era in which I write is precisely the kind of era for which, I believe, using the technique of uneven contrasts is quite appropriate. I use this technique to describe the memories lived by mankind in all eras and to offer a revelation to the real world. This is my intent, but I don't know if I have lived up to it. I can't write one of those works often called a "monument to the era," and I don't plan to try, because it seems that such objective, concentrated subject matter is not yet available. Things are even to the point where I only write about trivial things between men and women. There are no wars or revolutions in my works. I believe people are more free and un-adorned in love than in war or revolution. Because of the very nature of their events, war and revolution often more urgently require the support of intellect over emotion, and the reason works describing war and revolution often fail is that their technical aspects are superior to their artistic aspects. In opposition to the freedom of love, war drives one forward, and in revolution one must often more or less force oneself to act. True revolution and true wars of revolution should, I think, be emotionally similar to love, like love freely penetrating the entirety of life and harmonizing with the self.

I like simplicity, but it is only through describing the resourcefulness and ornamentation of contemporary people that I can elicit the basis of their hidden simplicity. Because of this people too readily regard my writing as overly flowery. But I don't think my goals can be accomplished by using the kind of pure narrative technique of the *Old Testament*; Tolstoy sacrificed his art this way in his later years. Nor do I condone the aesthetic school. Nonetheless, I feel that the deficiencies of the aesthetic school are not in its concept of beauty, but in failing to give beauty a foundation. The spray from a mountain stream is light and airy, but the ocean water, though it might look the same as the light ripples of a stream, contains the latent power of turbulent and mighty waves. Beautiful things are not necessarily great, but great things are always beautiful. It is just that I don't place falseness and reality into stark contrast in my writing, yet I still use the method of uneven contrast to show the reality in the emptiness, the simplicity in the ornamentation, of contemporary people. Because of this people too readily find a kind of indulgence in my work. Even so, I continue to maintain my style, ashamed only that I haven't been able to write as well as I want. I am still just practicing at literature.

When someone from the old school reads my work, they feel at ease but still not quite comfortable. Those from the new school think it interesting but still not serious enough. But I can write no other way, and I feel confident that I am not compromising myself. The only demand I place on myself is to try to write things that are more real.

Also, because I use the method of uneven contrast, I don't like adopting those classical methods that show stark conflicts between good and evil or the spirit and the flesh. Therefore, the main theme of my works sometimes isn't clear. But I feel that we should perhaps move beyond the notion that literary works should have "main themes." Fiction should involve a story, and the story should be allowed to make itself clear, which is better than concocting a story around a main theme. Things change over time, and

readers are no longer interested in the original themes of the great, enduring works; so we often just don't pay them anymore heed. Instead, we get
new inspiration from the story itself, giving the work eternal life. In *War
and Peace*, for example, Tolstoy was trying to sum up a religious, collectivist
attitude toward contemporary life, but the story's own development
emerged victorious over this predetermined main theme. This work was revised over seven times, and each time the main theme suffered. In the end
the main theme had been reduced to the status of a mere aside, and this is
the most awkward part of the book's structure. But still there was no new
theme to take its place, and when he was done writing it, Tolstoy felt something was missing. When compared with *The Resurrection*, the main theme
of *War and Peace* is indeed quite hazy, yet it is a greater work. Even now
when we read it, we feel that every inch of it is alive. It may be that the difference between modern literature and past literature lies right here: we no
longer emphasize a main theme but allow the story to give what it can and
the reader to take whatever is available.

My story "Linked Rings" was and is still being written in this way. It is
true that that work lacks attention to a main theme, but I hope there are
people who like the story itself. My original idea was very simple: since this
sort of thing occurred, I will describe it. Modern people are exhausted, and
the modern marriage system is irrational. So there is silence between husbands and wives; there are those who fear responsibility but look for momentary relief in sophisticated flirting; there are those who return to an ani-
malistic sexual desire in their visits to prostitutes (but they are still only
animal-like people, not animals, and thus more frightening than animals).
And there are couples living together out of wedlock. Living together lacks
the solemnity of the husband and wife relationship but is more responsible
than flirting and more dignified than prostitution. Since there are not in the
end many who go to extremes, today living together has become a common
phenomenon. The social status of the men who support this kind of cohabitation is middle- or lower-middle-class, men who work diligently just to get
by. They don't dare really let go, but neither are they so restrained. They
need a lively and substantial male/female relationship, something complementary to the other lively and substantial aspects of their lives. Since
they need women to take care of the home for them, they don't have such a
perverse attitude toward women. Ya Heya of "Linked Rings" is the owner
of a medium-sized textile shop and has to work behind the counter himself.
If Nixi could get along with him without conflict, it wouldn't be difficult for
them to continue on together and even become old and gray together. The
failure of their life together comes from defects in Nixi's personality. Her
other boyfriend, Dou Yaofang, is an owner of a relatively prosperous medi-

cine shop, but still without the prestige that comes with being a big capitalist. Another petty official who had previously lived with Nixi had nothing more than an aura of officialdom about him. None of them has any special feelings for Nixi, but in their relations with her there are some real emotions, something that is not all that unusual.

Women who live with men have always had a lower social status than men, but most of them have a sharp, fierce lifeforce. As far as men are concerned, these women have a kind of beguiling power, but it is the beguiling power of a healthy woman. Because if they were overly perverse, they would not be appropriate for those men's needs. They cause trouble, get jealous, and argue and fight, very wild sometimes, but they don't lose control. There is only one thing about them that is insufficient: their status is never clear. Doubt and fear cause them gradually to become selfish.

These kinds of cohabitation lifestyles are more common in China than in other countries, but no one has ever tried to write about them seriously. The literati of the Mandarin Ducks and Butterfly entertainment school of writing feel they don't have enough sentiment of the "beauty and the scholar" kind, and new-style literati feel they are relationships neither of love nor of prostitution, neither healthy nor perverse. They lack the clarity of a main theme.

What moves me about Nixi's story is her pure love for material life, something she must sometimes grasp with all her might. She wants the love of a man and at the same time wants security, but cannot get them both at once; so she ends up with neither the man nor the money. She feels that she can depend on nothing and puts all her resources into the lives of her children, saving a little human strength—the most inhuman sort of savings.

It isn't that Nixi has no feelings; she wants to love this world but can find no way to do so. She is not totally without love, but the love she receives is just the cold porridge and leftover meat of another's meal. As Du Fu's poem says, "Cold porridge and leftover meat, / hide bitterness everywhere."[2] But in the end she is still a healthy woman, and won't necessarily fall into a beggar's casket. It is like she is greedily chewing on an oil-pressed beancake: although she depends on her body and more or less gets some nutrition from the beancake, she can't help ruining her stomach when she eats it. Besides, it is a tragic thing when humans have to eat food meant for animals.

---

2. This seems to be a misquotation of a Du Fu line which should read "Leftover wine and cold meat" 殘杯與冷炙.

As for the use of words and phrases from old novels in many parts of "Linked Rings"—Cantonese and foreigners from fifty years ago sounding like characters in *The Golden Lotus*; Chinese in the fiction of Pearl Buck speaking with the flavor of British literary speech—everything is borrowed. My intent at the time was this: there is already a great distance between me and my descriptions of the romantic atmosphere Hong Kong evoked in the heart of someone from Shanghai, and in the Hong Kong of fifty years ago, the weighty distance of time is even greater. So I used a kind of outdated vocabulary to represent this immense distance. Sometimes I could not avoid artificiality, and it seems overdone. I think in the future I can alter this a bit.

—Translated by Wendy Larson

Chapter 51

On Writers

Qian Zhongshu

The writer is commendable for his modesty: while knowing how to get ahead in the world, he refrains from hankering after social position and eschews complacency with his lot.[1] In truth, the writer's own view of himself is sometimes more scornful than that of the ordinary outsider looking on. He finds it singularly annoying that he is a writer and goes to great lengths and with considerable expenditure of words, labor, time, and paper to prove how unwilling and dissatisfied he is to be a writer. In an age like the present, couldn't this be considered the mark of "a great man who fathoms the times he lives in"?

It stands to reason that the concept of "writer" ought to refer to anyone who writes books, pens articles, or submits manuscripts for publication. In actual practice, however, the use of the term "writer" is limited to authors working in such genres as poetry, the familiar essay, fiction, and playscripts. That is to say, the term refers precisely to what the ancients called a belletrist, a "useless writer," or someone who "once a writer, had

---

1. Qian Zhongshu 錢鍾書, "Lun wenren" 論文人, in *Xie zai rensheng bian shang* 寫在人生邊上 (Shanghai: Kaiming shudian, 1941). No date is given for the writing of this essay.

no prospects worth noting." As to the avoidance of such empty writing, specialists who have mastered subjects of substance in the social and natural sciences look askance at the very idea of being considered useless writers [*wenren*], even though they may have written a flood of voluminous tracts, and in spite of the fact that they can't quite measure up to the usefulness of military officers [*wuren*].[2] Perhaps this looking askance at the very idea of being considered a writer derives from a correct self-assessment on their part, since writing black characters on white paper does not necessarily make the finished product a literary composition.

We can probably divide this idea of usefulness into two categories. The first would be the utilization of waste, such as the burning of cow dung in place of firewood, or something on the order of the frugal official Tao Kan's insistence that wood chips and bamboo stubs were both too useful to be casually discarded.[3] The second would involve things that we have no choice but to use each day, such as toothbrushes and privies—things to which we feel a strong attachment akin to Wang Ziyou's regard for bamboo: "One cannot get by for even a day without this esteemed companion."[4] Although the things in this world have such a multitude of uses, it is only writers who bear the honor of the title of useless. Isn't it a pity that writers have been reduced to sighing over their inferiority to such humble things as a wood chip, a bamboo stub, a toothbrush, or a privy?

If we turn instead to useful persons [*youyong renwu*], we might as well give them a title that will serve to distinguish them from writers. We might call them "servants" [*yongren*], for example. The two characters in the term "servant" are an abbreviation of the four characters in "useful persons," making it an apt counterpart to the two-character term, "writer." A word so pithy and broad-ranging should not be monopolized by amahs, maids, and private rickshawmen. Furthermore, this term has two other advantages. First, it is replete with the revolutionary spirit of equality, in which experts

---

2. Qian Zhongshu here uses a different meaning of the word for "writer," *wenren*, than that found in the title of the essay. The second use of *wenren* refers to literati in traditional China who took the government examinations that served as the gateway to coveted postings in the civil service. The less prestigious route of advancement to wealth and power was through rising in the military, or *wu*, ranks. The suggestion seems to be that during the modern age where utility reigns supreme, the traditional respect for *wen* rather than *wu* has been inverted, since modern scientists stuck in between these two categories of the governing elite seem to aspire to the usefulness of the *wu* officials rather than to the *wen* officials' role as cultural stewards.

3. See *Jinshu* 晋書, chap. 66.

4. See *Shishuo xinyu* 世說新語, "Rendan" 任誕. For an English translation of the relevant story, see Richard Mather, tr. *Shih-shuo Hsin-yu: A New Account of Tales of the World,* (Minneapolis: University of Minnesota, 1976), 388.

and advisors carry the same title as and line up directly alongside atten-
dants and manservants. Second, it avoids running counter to the principle
of China's total Westernization. In America, there is a president who is said
to have called himself the "public servant of the citizenry," that is to say, a
servant at everybody's beck and call. In Rome, the pope calls himself the
"menial of menials," or the "servant of servants" (*servus servorum*). In
France during the Great Revolution, all the revolutionary party members
called their servants "brother" (*frères servants*). Now, the "president" is a
ruler, the "pope" is a father (*papa*), and the "frère servant" is one's elder
brother; since in Europe and America all of these terms are used in connection with "servant," it is only proper that China should follow suit.[5]

Servants look down upon writers; this has been the case since ancient
times,[6] and is not at all some news snippet gleaned from this morning's
newspaper. For example, Sima Qian's "Annals of Emperor Gaozu" record
how the Han emperor disliked literature. The "Biography of Lu Jia" explains the situation with a quote from Gaozu himself: "I have won the empire on horseback; why must I pay homage to the *Book of Songs* and the
Book of Documents?"[7] Full of candor and outspokenness, this famous dictum
can rightly be considered an imperial decree of a founding emperor.
Among the plethora of expressions and myriad words used by opponents
of literature from ancient times up to the present day, it all boils down to
these two lines. During the War of Resistance to Japan, reading these lines
about staying "on horseback" seems even more moving and lively. When
The Republic excludes poets and writers from the ideal society, Plato is dis-
gustingly long-winded; how could a fellow like him adopt a trenchant and
vigorous tone like Gaozu's? As the poem by Chen Shiyi[8] puts it, "Those
adept in literature / Will never high rank secure; / How could men in the
seat of command / Waste their time on mere words?" This explains why
Gaozu was capable of realizing his goal to become emperor, whereas Plato
could gratify his political yearnings merely by dreaming about the reign of
"philosopher-kings," devising in vain his plans (*Republic*) and blueprints
(*Laws*) for founding the nation. From this one can see not only that writers
are despicable wretches unworthy of rapid advancement in the official

---

5. The terms Qian Zhongshu employs for "ruler" (*jun* 君), "father" (*fu* 父), and "elder
brother" (*xiong* 兄) denote fundamental Confucian categories of traditional China's social
hierarchy.

6. The author is playing with Cao Pi's well-known dictum "Literary men disparage
one another; it has always been that way."

7. From *Shiji* 史記, "Lu Jia liezhuan" 陸賈列傳.

8. Chen Shiyi 陳石遺 (1856–1937) worked in the education section of the Qing government and taught at Xiamen University in the late 1920's.

world, but that even those worthies who are opposed to literature seem to come up with excessively long writings and an overabundance of discussion—they lack the dignity of someone sparing in words but high in position. Plato's writings are rich in poetical feeling, and Emperor Gaozu once experienced a spell of poetic inspiration during which he composed his "Ode to the Great Wind" in an impromptu recitation. Despite all this, a loathing for literature was shared by them both, not to mention those perfectly plebeian primates.

Théophile Gautier's *Records of Eccentrics* (*Les Grotesques*) has recounted how wealthy merchants have been susceptible to a strange sickness known as "poesophobia" (*poésophobie*).[9] This sickness manifests itself in a rather singular manner. The story goes that a man of wealth one day happened to open his son's desk drawer, there espying a sheaf of writing paper covered with words. These papers were neither account registers nor debt ledgers, and while the first letter in each line was capitalized, the last letter for some reason stopped short of the right margin. After careful investigation, the father discovered that these papers were manuscript drafts of poetry. His heart seethed with fury, and he proceeded to fly into a rage. He sorely lamented the ill-fortune that had struck his family in producing such a disobedient and unworthy son. A rapid progression toward insanity ensued.

Actually, this kind of sickness has been noted not only for its unusual origins, but also for its high degree of infectiousness. At such times, it can spread as an epidemic, just like cholera during the summertime or influenza in winter. As to a prescription, it is said that one does exist: put to the torch a diverse assemblage of literature both ancient and modern, native and foreign, then swallow the remaining ashes. According to what people say, as long as the potion is concocted properly, the upshot naturally is that the noxious humors within one's chest will be dispelled and the thorn in one's side removed; from this time on, moreover, the nation will be strong and its citizenry secure, government will be honest and its policies enlightened, and prosperity will reign with martial vigor in the ascendant! That is why the ancient Roman church father Tertullian, in his *On Idolatry* (*De idolatria*), argues that if the Great Teaching is to be manifested in all its glory and a realm of divine bliss is to be realized on earth, literature must first be uprooted. As to the magnificent theories in this mold by celebrated figures of modern times, they have long since achieved extremely broad circulation in leading periodicals of all types, and since everyone has gotten

---

9. *Les Grotesques* is a work of literary criticism in praise of "grotesques" and unpopular poets like Villon.

thoroughly acquainted with them, there is no need to belabor the point further.

Literature must be destroyed, but there is actually no harm in rewarding writers—rewarding those who turn away from the profession of writing. Pope would often speak in metrical rhythms (lisp in numbers), and Bai Juyi was able at birth to distinguish one character from another: incurable though they may be, born writers of this sort all in all amount to but a small minority in their profession. Ordinary writers, in all frankness, do not actually relish literature, nor are they particularly talented at writing it. In their diversions with literature, they resemble those daughters of good family in old novels who become prostitutes, it is said, due to circumstances beyond their control and the lack of any viable alternative. As long as there was an opportunity to escape from this fiery hell, not one of these talents in the making would hesitate to abandon his books and throw away his pens, switch professions, and turn over a new leaf. Literature is a profession of ill-fortune and gloomy spirits, where prospects are among the bleakest anywhere, hunger and cold dog one's steps, and sickness is one's constant companion. Wang Shizhen's essay "Nine Fates of Literature"[10] long ago provided an exhaustive account of how writers since ancient times have been subject to myriad calamities and misfortunes. We have all heard of "literati beggars" [*wengai*], but there has never even been a term for scholars manqués in other disciplines, such as "scientist beggar," "engineer beggar," "lawyer beggar," or "business-executive beggar." If even the most foolish and stupid of people were to find their normal avenues for securing a livelihood cut off, they would still scoff at the very idea of coming up with some poetry, fiction, and whatnot. Because of this, it is not only the casual onlooker who feels contempt for literature and writers; even writers themselves are plagued with an inferiority complex, for they are utterly deficient in either a belief in literature or a reverence for it. For example, the bona fide writer Yang Xiong once proclaimed in his *Rules of Composition*, "To the carving of insects or the engraving of seals, the stout man does not put his hand."[11] Obviously, he would rather be a stout fellow than a writer. When J. G. Lockhart wrote a biography of his father-in-law, he noted that Sir Walter Scott deeply regretted that he was able only to record the martial feats of great heroes, but was himself incapable of bringing any astounding

---

10. Wang Shizhen's 王 世 貞 (1526–90) essay "Wenzhang jiuming" 文 章 九 命 describes nine faults that plagued the writing of poetry from the pre-Qin period to the Sung dynasty.

11. From *Fayan* 法 言 , "Wuzi pian" 吾 子 篇 . Here, Yang Xiong 楊 雄 (53 B.C.–A.D. 18) belittles his own earlier aesthetic orientation with the phrase "*diaochong zhuanke, zhuangfu bu wei*" 雕 蟲 篆 刻, 壯 夫 不 爲 .

accomplishments to fruition. Hugo's poem "My Childhood Days" ("Mon enfance") articulates the same sentiment. When even persons of this sort bewail their fate and regret having become writers, one can well surmise how dim a view others take of them. Because of this, we have noticed a peculiar phenomenon: in general, scholars unanimously strike a bold pose and an imposing manner, lavishing praise upon their particular special field and declaring that they believe in it 120 percent. Writers alone, harboring sinister designs, meet rudeness with an obsequious smile and endure unending shame; even if they occasionally indulge in braggadocio during discussions of the literature of national crisis, propaganda weapons, and so on, the effect is nothing more than pounding a waterlogged leather drum, with only muffled sounds audible from the most vigorous drumming.

Goethe was once reviled for not having written patriotic poetry, and thus in his *Recorded Conversations* (*Gespraeche* [sic] *mit Eckermann*) complained bitterly that he had not been a soldier, nor ever gone to the front-lines—how could he have written war poems? Writers of modern times are far more talented than Goethe; under circumstances favorable to the creation of heroes, they are able to discourse on war and hold forth on political theory; failing that, they appoint themselves instructors of the populace, bestowing advice with largesse. So many skilled and artistic persons throng before us: they should not and cannot just bury their talents in literature. As long as there are opportunities for them to make a change, they can abandon literature and the arts without further ado and make their living some other way. In Browning's ideal world, a baker could write poetry, and a hog butcher could paint at his easel. In our ideal world, nobody would bother about literature or the arts; the poet would become a baker, and the painter would take up the trade of the hog butcher—and if there are useful occupations that offer even more fame and fortune than the trades of baker and butcher, that would naturally be all the more palatable.

In his "Defence of Poetry," Shelley argues that poets are the legislators (Legislator) of mankind. Carlisle, in his "The Worship of Heroes," claims that writers can be considered heroes. Writers nowadays are a bit different: all they desire is to assume the mantle of a hero, and they hope to become legislators or something else along those lines. If they were to go so far as to style themselves heroes or legislators, they could not avoid seeming megalomaniacal. Yet as far as the desire to be a legislator or hero goes, this is nothing other than the will to get ahead in the world. The will to get ahead in the world is something that ought to be rewarded. A person who has the will to get ahead in the world feels dissatisfaction or shame for his position in real life. In understanding shame one approaches the embodiment of courage. Courage is to be rewarded, and how much more so during an age such as this!

In brief, we should destroy literature and yet reward writers—reward them for ceasing to be writers, for having nothing to do with literature.

—Translated by Philip F. Williams

Chapter 52

Universal or Restricted?

Shen Congwen

Once humankind invented writing, the power and authority to use it were at first kept in the hands of a minority.[1] All knowledge preserved in writing was therefore restricted; a minority could use it, but the majority couldn't even take pleasure in it. That was until the invention of printing—and printing was mainly for propagating knowledge of classic texts. From then on the majority were able to enjoy the classics, but still they could not freely use writing for their own purposes. This was of course a restriction imposed from above. Once the majority can enjoy the uses of writing, universalization may be said to have been achieved. In the ideal case, when the social structure goes from the extreme authoritarianism of kings and emperors to equality in principle for all humans under democratic rule, the restricted nature of knowledge and learning is bound to lapse, in stages, and gradually be replaced by universality.

---

1. Shen Congwen 沈從文, "Yiban huo teshu" 一般或特殊, *Jinri pinglun* 今日評論 1, no. 4 (Jan. 22, 1939); reprinted in *WXYDSLX*. The word translated here as "universal" (*yiban* 一般) also has the derogatory meaning of "average" or "mediocre." The word rendered as "restricted" (*teshu* 特殊) usually has the more positive meaning of "special" or "exceptional."

And yet there's another phenomenon that must be heeded. As technology progresses and society becomes more complex, there is a division of labor in everything: all have their own preserve, their speciality, so that knowledge and learning of all types once more tend to become specialized and restricted. Universality becomes ever weaker; narrowness, ever stronger.

A nation's culture and civilization stress the narrowing of that which is universal and, at the same time, the application of this narrowing to the universality of life. With them, there is progress; without them, degeneration. This is "necessary," and also "inevitable." For example, take the transport vehicles used today in the environs of Kunming. Mostly they're still water buffalo–drawn carts. If someone could think of a way of streamlining them or even replacing them with some "wooden buffalo" or "streaming horse" contraptions [like the ones Zhuge Liang is said to have invented back in the third century A.D.], that would be taking something universal and adapting it in a restricted way. Everyone can use a labor-saving device like that. That, then, is the universalization of something restricted. In this matter of surface transportation, I speak of "wooden buffaloes" and "streaming horses," not automobiles, because even today our country is unable to make a horseless carriage.

But I draw on these horse-drawn and buffalo-drawn carts only as metaphors. The question of restrictedness and universality exists in the field of literature too, and it bears discussion.

Simply put, literature is just a bunch of words and phrases strung together. What's strange is that it seems, by turns, both useful and useless. Call it useful, and people can't agree on what its use is. Let us grant for the time being that it is useful. Whether the language is far distant from or very close to everyday speech, to use it to write a little ditty or a brief story that gives form to one's feelings or ideals, not to mention going through the labors of composing a hefty tome for some worthy purpose, one has to thoroughly understand the medium's properties. For example, in one's experiments one's writing must be "as clear as the smooth surface of a lake, or as profound as a deep pool." One needs patience and relentlessness, a willingness "to twist and wrench language to learn its malleability, to smash language down hard to test the limits of its brittleness." The more a writer understands the properties of written language, the more "proper" is it when he uses it as a tool. I say "proper," not "beautiful," because "appropriateness" is precisely what it is in great works of literature that so astonishes us about their use of language. The aspiration of every writer is to get across his precise meaning when expressing himself or society and to be able to see the kind of impression it will make on certain types of readers, and how they will react. Hence, understanding of the nature of written language can itself be called a kind of "knowledge," indeed an indispensable know-ledge—it is, to put it a little differently, technique, the technique of ordering writing.

In these times, mention of technique easily reflects a pedantic turn or views that oppose the spirit of the age. This is due to a phrase that has now become prevalent, for reasons both explicable and inexplicable: all writing is propaganda.

"All writing is propaganda" is exactly like saying that "all writing can convey the Way" [as ancient theory put it]. And yet, ever since this phrase has become so popular among writers, the only part people remember is "propaganda." People serving in organs both in and out of government [Nationalist and Communist cadres] likewise remember only "propaganda" and are unwilling to analyze its meaning. When slogans and watchwords fill the air, it's quite unclear just what effect any given slogan produces. So society has given all these items the general tag of "propaganda pieces." This term connotes "false," "overblown," "empty," "hard to pin down," "quickly dated," and so forth. And there's a word for the people who create it, "propagandists." They are of two kinds. There is a minority who are capable, and yet still never respected. But most are stupid; although they seem to be full of faith, they really don't have much knowledge. We ordinary people can't say this and aren't allowed to say it. Although our intentions might be good, we might easily dishearten the honest ones among them, and anger those who won't face up to their shortcomings. But the people who are in a position to provide guidance aren't willing to speak either. So things slowly change, until one day the meaning of the word "propaganda" becomes muddy even to them. That day isn't necessarily in the future. Maybe it has already arrived.

These days, as soon as we speak of using writing for propaganda work, it's as if the knowledge restricted to a minority of specialists had long since progressed to a universalized knowledge of the majority. It's easy enough to verify, as in the sudden increase of "cultural figures" in many places. Another thing to ponder is that every person who takes up a pen is called a "cultural figure," and they are deemed indispensable to the war for social progress. The reason is that they can make propaganda; they are fighting with their pens. If we may speak the truth, most of our friends with pens in their hands are really weak in the knowledge we've spoken of. That the phrases "eight-legged essays for the War of Resistance" [a conservative slo-gan used against ideologists] and "self-criticism" [a Communist usage] are so often seen in the journals of late is an indication of it. To elevate the knowledge of these "cultural figures," perhaps we'd better think of something outside those pamphlets written by the propagandists. Perhaps some other person should write a little something. His or her work might be a mere novel—one just about the "stupidity" and "pretense," "falsity" and "arrogance" common in ordinary society—a novel that points these out, censures them, and suggests some means of ameliorating them. It may seem to have no connection with the war, or with politics, and even less connection with propaganda, yet if such a work is written well, it may have a whole lot to do with how this nation of ours is struggling for survival—how it can reconstruct itself if we win the war, or free ourselves if we lose! It may educate only a small number of the educated, those who truly love and honor this nation, who have already been awakened, and thus very modestly seek such education. Not only might the content of this work enlighten them, the written language in it can enlighten them too.

Currently, in Chongqing, Guilin, Changsha, and Kunming, a lot of scholars have suddenly come to be called, or are calling themselves, "cultural figures." This has great implications for propaganda, because propaganda and "raising a stir" come from the same root. Wherever there are a lot of cultural figures, a stir is sure to follow. But I feel that there is another group of writers who are particularly worthy of note. They appear to be quite reserved and calm, far removed from any atmosphere of "propaganda" or status as "cultural figures," not to mention the emotions of wartime romanticism. Writing as commoners, they make their living honestly, dodging the groundfire. Or, in the name of social service, they go to the war zones—whether the frontlines or the rear areas—to learn from their fellow man. Or, even more ambitiously, they probe into history and science to analyze how our people's present has come down from our past. At first glance, the behavior of these several kinds of people may appear to lack martial glory, even heroism. But their work is no different from those involved in the war; it is truly close to the war. They have only one aim: to more deeply explore, to more closely understand from the inside, the virtues and vices of our nation, so that they may on another day use writing to explain and preserve these things. They are not the kind, on the basis of their own success and sudden changes in the fortunes of others, to become rulers or directors, ministers or officials. They only know their duty, doing all they can as Chinese citizens at a time when the nation is poised on the brink of annihilation. The strength and perseverance they need in their silence is exactly the same virtue as that needed by soldiers at the front line. These people are a "minority," compared to the "cultural figures."

Increasing the number of such people will not require "propaganda," for fire spreads easily. There appear to be few such people now, but if the war is protracted, their numbers will grow—not just writers, but other ex-

Chapter 53

We Need the Zawen Essay

Ding Ling

One day a theorist said to me, "It's very difficult to talk about the living. In the future, let's discuss only those who are dead."[1] I see his point. Talking about the living often leads to conflict. Dead people, on the other hand, can never challenge you, let alone generate the sarcasm and denunciations that come from the petty rivalries of scholars, factional viewpoints or personal feelings. To avoid trouble, it is no doubt wise to adopt a policy of prudent self-protection.

Other people, elsewhere, are saying things like, "It's best to be a good member of the group. Let's give our support to the accepted ideas—no matter what they are."

I have also heard many sullen complaints of a type that should have disappeared long ago, "Who am I anyway? Are my words even worth a fart?"

---

1. Ding Ling 丁玲, "Women xuyao zawen" 我們需要雜文, *Jiefang ribao* 解放日報, Oct. 23, 1942; reprinted in *Ding Ling wenji* 丁玲文集 (Changsha: Hunan renmin, 1983), 4: 382–84. *Zawen*, literally "miscellaneous writings," was a type of short, often satirical, essay made famous by Lu Xun in the 1930's.

What all these viewpoints show is that we still don't understand how to put democracy into practice or develop self-criticism and free discussion. Clearly, we lack tolerance and the patience to listen carefully to the opinions of others. At the same time, we lack courage and will power. We're afraid of trouble, afraid of rejection, afraid of sacrifice. The cause is sheer laziness—and we merely grumble behind each other's backs.

If someone is willing and, in fact, dares to speak out, even if the opinion is not absolutely correct, there will always be some overly sensitive people to say there's an ulterior motive behind it, that it expresses a partisan viewpoint, that it's attacking or defending this or that. They'll say it's destroying unity, it's frivolous . . . and surely no one will go along to support the person and argue to help perfect the theory. This is a disgrace in our lives.

When a person advocates an action or idea before it becomes widely understood, the first thing he is bound to encounter is criticism. Only someone who is persistent and unafraid of criticism can be successful. Lu Xun is the prime example.

Because Lu Xun wanted to cure the soul of mankind, he gave up his study of medicine for literature. And because he was able to diagnose clearly the ills of his age, he needed the sharpest scalpel, and so he turned from writing fiction to the *zawen* essay. The subjects of his essays touch upon all aspects of Chinese society. At the time they were written, his essays were not taken seriously by many envious and denigrating scholars who said he wrote them because he couldn't write fiction. But today, Lu Xun's essays have become China's greatest ideological weapon, works so splendid they are intimidating.

Obviously, if you are willing to write essays only if they're as good as Lu Xun's, you might as well decide at the outset not to write at all. But the more articles one writes, the better they become. Besides, they aren't written for fame or glory, but only for the sake of the truth.

Our era is not so different from Lu Xun's; we have corruption, tyranny, persecution, and assassination of progressive thinkers; the people aren't even freed to defend themselves in the War of Resistance. Yet all we can say is "This is the time for a united front!" We don't realize that we can build an even more solid united front through criticism. As a result, we are abdicating our responsibility.

Even in the progressive regions of the country, where the beginnings of democracy are visible, we need, more than elsewhere, determination and vigilance. The feudalistic evils deeply ingrained in China for several thousand years are very difficult to uproot. The so-called progressive regions themselves did not just drop out of the sky. They have very close links to the old Chinese society. And yet in these progressive regions we say it is inappropriate to write *zawen*, that here we ought to depict only the democratic life and glorious work of construction.

Although it is not unusual to get carried away by small successes, to ignore the disease and avoid the doctor, such behavior is no more than cowardice and laziness.

Lu Xun is dead. People keep saying we should do this and that in his memory, but we lack the courage to learn from his fearless example. I believe that the best thing we can do today is to emulate his unfailing intellectual honesty, daring to speak out for truth and being afraid of nothing. Our age still needs the *zawen*; we must not cast this weapon aside. Take it up, and the essay will not die.

—Translated by Ruth Nybakken

Chapter 54

Talks at the Yan'an Forum on Literature and Art

Mao Zedong

Introduction
May 2, 1942

Comrades![1] You have been invited to this forum today to exchange ideas and examine the relationship between work in the literary and artistic fields and revolutionary work in general. Our aim is to ensure that revolutionary literature and art follow the correct path of development and provide better help to other revolutionary work in facilitating the overthrow of our national enemy and the accomplishment of the task of national liberation.

---

1. Mao Zedong 毛澤東, "Zai Yan'an wenyi zuotanhui shang de jianghua" 在延安文藝座談會上的講話; first presented as two lectures to party cadres in Yan'an in May 1942; first published in *Jiefang ribao*, Oct. 19, 1943. This translation is based on a later edited version and was previously published in Mao Tse-tung 1975: 3: 69–98. For a detailed discussion of the differences between this text and the original 1943 version, see McDougall 1980.

In our struggle for the liberation of the Chinese people there are various fronts, among which there are the fronts of the pen and of the gun, the cultural and the military fronts. To defeat the enemy we must rely primarily on the army with guns. But this army alone is not enough; we must also have a cultural army, which is absolutely indispensable for uniting our own ranks and defeating the enemy. Since the May Fourth movement such a cultural army has taken shape in China, and it has helped the Chinese revolution, gradually reduced the domain of China's feudal culture and of the comprador culture that serves imperialist aggression, and weakened their influence. To oppose the new culture, the Chinese reactionaries can now only "pit quantity against quality." In other words, reactionaries have money, and although they can produce nothing good, they can go all out and produce in quantity. Literature and art have been an important and successful part of the cultural front since the May Fourth movement. During the ten years' civil war, the revolutionary literature and art movement grew greatly. That movement and the revolutionary war both headed in the same general direction, but these two fraternal armies were not linked together in their practical work because the reactionaries had cut them off from each other. It is very good that since the outbreak of the War of Resistance against Japan, more and more revolutionary writers and artists have been coming to Yan'an and our other anti-Japanese base areas. But it does not necessarily follow that, having come to the base areas, they have already integrated themselves completely with the masses of the people here. The two must be completely integrated if we are to push ahead with our revolutionary work. The purpose of our meeting today is precisely to ensure that literature and art fit well into the whole revolutionary machine as a component part, that they operate as powerful weapons for uniting and educating the people and for attacking and destroying the enemy, and that they help the people fight the enemy with one heart and one mind. What are the problems that must be solved to achieve this objective? I think they are the problems of the class stand of the writers and artists, their attitude, their audience, their work, and their study.

The problem of class stand. Our stand is that of the proletariat and of the masses. For members of the Communist Party, this means keeping to the stand of the Party, keeping to Party spirit and Party policy. Are there any of our literary and art workers who are still mistaken or not clear in their understanding of this problem? I think there are. Many of our comrades have frequently departed from the correct stand.

The problem of attitude. From one's stand there follow specific attitudes toward specific matters. For instance, is one to extol or to expose? This is a question of attitude. Which attitude is wanted? I would say both. The question is, whom are you dealing with? There are three kinds of persons, the enemy, our allies in the united front, and our own people; the last are the masses and their vanguard. We need to adopt a different attitude toward each of the three. With regard to the enemy, that is, Japanese imperialism and all the other enemies of the people, the task of revolutionary writers and artists is to expose their duplicity and cruelty and at the same time to point out the inevitability of their defeat, so as to encourage the anti-Japanese army and people to fight staunchly with one heart and one mind for their overthrow. With regard to our different allies in the united front, our attitude should be one of both alliance and criticism, and there should be different kinds of alliance and different kinds of criticism. We support them in their resistance to Japan and praise them for any achievement. But if they are not active in the War of Resistance, we should criticize them. If anyone opposes the Communist Party and the people and keeps moving down the path of reaction, we will firmly oppose him. As for the masses of the people, their toil and their struggle, their army and their Party, we should certainly praise them. The people, too, have their shortcomings. Among the proletariat many retain petit-bourgeois ideas, and both the peasants and the urban petite bourgeoisie have backward ideas; these are burdens hampering them in their struggle. We should be patient and spend a long time in educating them and helping them to get these loads off their backs and combat their own shortcomings and errors, so that they can advance with great strides. They have remolded themselves in struggle or are doing so, and our literature and art should depict this process. As long as they do not persist in their errors, we should not dwell on their negative side and consequently make the mistake of ridiculing them or, worse still, of being hostile to them. Our writings should help them to unite, to make progress, to press ahead with one heart and one mind, to discard what is backward and develop what is revolutionary, and should certainly not do the opposite.

The problem of audience, that is, the people for whom our works of literature and art are produced. In the Shanxi-Gansu-Ningxia Border Region and the anti-Japanese base areas of northern and central China, this problem differs from that in the Guomindang areas, and differs still more from that in Shanghai before the War of Resistance. In the Shanghai period, the audience for works of revolutionary literature and art consisted mainly of a section of the students, office workers, and shop assistants. After the outbreak of the War of Resistance, the audience in the Guomindang areas became somewhat wider, but it still consisted mainly of the same kind of people because the government there prevented the workers, peasants, and soldiers from having access to revolutionary literature and art. In our base areas the situation is entirely different. Here the audience for works of literature and art consists of workers, peasants, soldiers, and revolutionary cadres. There are students in the base areas, too, but they are different from students of the old type; they are either former or future cadres. The cadres of all types, fighters in the army, workers in the factories and peasants in the villages all want to read books and newspapers once they become literate, and those who are illiterate want to see plays and operas, look at drawings and paintings, sing songs, and hear music; they are the audience for our works of literature and art. Take the cadres alone. Do not think they are few; they far outnumber the readers of any book published in the Guomindang areas. There, an edition usually runs to only 2,000 copies, and even three editions add up to only 6,000; but as for the cadres in the base areas, in Yan'an alone there are more than 10,000 who read books. Many of them, moreover, are tempered revolutionaries of long standing, who have come from all parts of the country and will go out to work in different places; so it is very important to do educational work among them. Our literary and art workers must do a good job in this respect.

Since the audience for our literature and art consists of workers, peasants, and soldiers and of their cadres, the problem arises of understanding them and knowing them well. A great deal of work has to be done in order to understand them and know them well, to understand and know well all the different kinds of people and phenomena in the Party and government organizations, in the villages and factories and in the Eighth Route and New Fourth armies. Our writers and artists have their literary and art work to do, but their primary task is to understand people and know them well. In this regard, how have matters stood with our writers and artists? I would say they have been lacking in knowledge and understanding; they have been like "a hero with no place to display his prowess." What does lacking in knowledge mean? Not knowing people well. The writers and artists do not have a good knowledge either of those whom they describe or of their audience; indeed they may hardly know them at all. They do not know the workers or peasants or soldiers well, and do not know the cadres well either. What does lacking in understanding mean? Not understanding the language, that is, not being familiar with the rich, lively language of the masses. Since many writers and artists stand aloof from the masses and lead empty lives, naturally they are unfamiliar with the language of the people. Accordingly, their works are not only insipid in language but often contain nondescript expressions of their own coining that run counter to popular usage. Many comrades like to talk about "a mass style." But what does it really mean? It means that the thoughts and feelings of our writers and artists should be fused with those of the masses of workers, peasants, and soldiers. To achieve this fusion, they should conscientiously learn the language of the masses. How can you talk of literary and artistic creation if you find the very language of the masses largely incomprehensible? By "a hero with no place to display his prowess," we mean that your collection of great truths is not appreciated by the masses. The more you put on the airs of a veteran before the masses and play the "hero," the more you try to peddle such stuff to the masses, the less likely they are to accept it. If you want the masses to understand you, if you want to be one with the masses, you must make up your mind to undergo a long and even painful process of tempering. Here I might mention the experience of how my own feelings changed. I began life as a student and at school acquired the ways of a student; I then used to feel it undignified to do even a little manual labor, such as carrying my own luggage in the presence of my fellow students, who were incapable of carrying anything, either on their shoulders or in their hands. At that time I felt that intellectuals were the only clean people in the world, while in comparison workers and peasants were dirty. I did not mind wearing the clothes of other intellectuals, believing them clean, but I would not put on clothes belonging to a worker or peasant, believing them dirty. But after I became a revolutionary and lived with workers and peasants and with soldiers of the revolutionary army, I gradually came to know them well, and they gradually came to know me well too. It was then, and only then, that I fundamentally changed the bourgeois and petit-bourgeois feelings implanted in me in the bourgeois schools. I came to feel that compared with the workers and peasants the un-remolded intellectuals were not clean and that, in the last analysis, the workers and peasants were the cleanest people, and, even though their hands were soiled and their feet smeared with cow dung, they were really cleaner than the bourgeois and petit-bourgeois intellectuals. That is what is meant by a change in feelings, a change from one class to another. If our writers and artists who come from the intelligentsia want their works to be well received by the masses, they must change and remold their thinking and their feelings. Without such a change, without such remolding, they can do nothing well and will be misfits.

The last problem is study, by which I mean the study of Marxism-Leninism and of society. Anyone who considers himself a revolutionary Marxist writer, and especially any writer who is a member of the Communist Party, must have a knowledge of Marxism-Leninism. At present, however, some comrades are lacking in the basic concepts of Marxism. For instance, it is a basic Marxist concept that being determines consciousness, that the objective realities of class struggle and national struggle determine our thoughts and feelings. But some of our comrades turn this upside down and maintain that everything ought to start from "love." Now as for love, in a class society there can be only class love; but these comrades are seeking a love transcending classes, love in the abstract and also freedom in the abstract, truth in the abstract, human nature in the abstract, etc. This shows that they have been very deeply influenced by the bourgeoisie. They should thoroughly rid themselves of this influence and modestly study Marxism-Leninism. It is right for writers and artists to study literary and artistic creation, but the science of Marxism-Leninism must be studied by all revolutionaries, writers and artists not excepted. Writers and artists should study society, that is to say, should study the various classes in society, their mutual relations and respective conditions, their physiognomy and their psychology. Only when we grasp all this clearly can we have a literature and art that is rich in content and correct in orientation.

I am merely raising these problems today by way of introduction; I hope all of you will express your views on these and other relevant problems.

Conclusion
May 23, 1942

Comrades! Our forum has had three meetings this month. In the pursuit of truth we have carried on spirited debates in which scores of Party and non-Party comrades have spoken, laying bare the issues and making them more concrete. This, I believe, will very much benefit the whole literary and artistic movement.

In discussing a problem, we should start from reality and not from definitions. We would be following a wrong method if we first looked up definitions of literature and art in textbooks and then used them to determine the guiding principles for the present-day literary and artistic movement and to judge the different opinions and controversies that arise today. We are Marxists, and Marxism teaches that in our approach to a problem we should start from objective facts, not from abstract definitions, and that we should derive our guiding principles, policies, and measures from an analysis of these facts. We should do the same in our present discussion of literary and artistic work.

What are the facts at present? The facts are: the War of Resistance against Japan, which China has been fighting for five years; the worldwide anti-fascist war; the vacillations of China's big landlord class and big bourgeoisie in the War of Resistance and their policy of high-handed oppression of the people; the revolutionary movement in literature and art since the May Fourth movement—its great contributions to the revolution during the past twenty-three years and its many shortcomings; the anti-Japanese democratic base areas of the Eighth Route and New Fourth armies and the integration of large numbers of writers and artists with these armies and with the workers and peasants in these areas; the difference in both environment and tasks between the writers and artists in the base areas and those in the Guomindang areas; and the controversial issues concerning literature and art that have arisen in Yan'an and the other anti-Japanese base areas. These are the actual, undeniable facts in the light of which we have to consider our problems.

What, then, is the crux of the matter? In my opinion, it consists fundamentally of the problems of working for the masses and how to work for the masses. Unless these two problems are solved or solved properly, our writers and artists will be ill-adapted to their environment and their tasks and will come up against a series of difficulties from without and within. My concluding remarks will center on these two problems and also touch upon some related ones.

I

The first problem is: literature and art for whom?

This problem was solved long ago by Marxists, especially by Lenin. As far back as 1905 Lenin pointed out emphatically that our literature and art should "serve . . . the millions and tens of millions of working people."[2] For comrades engaged in literary and artistic work in the anti-Japanese base areas, it might seem that this problem is already solved and needs no further discussion. Actually, that is not the case. Many comrades have not found a clear solution. Consequently their sentiments, their works, their actions, and their views on the guiding principles for literature and art have inevitably been more or less at variance with the needs of the masses and of the practical struggle. Of course, among the numerous men of culture, writers, artists, and other literary and artistic workers engaged in the great struggle for liberation together with the Communist Party and the Eighth Route and New Fourth armies, a few may be careerists who are only with us temporarily, but the overwhelming majority are working energetically for the common cause. By relying on these comrades, we have achieved a great deal in our literature, drama, music, and fine arts. Many of these writers and artists have begun their work since the outbreak of the War of Resistance; many others did much revolutionary work before the war, endured many hardships, and influenced broad masses of the people by their

---

2. V. I. Lenin, "Party Organization and Party Literature."

activities and works. Why do we say, then, that even among these comrades there are some who have not reached a clear solution of the problem of whom literature and art are for? Is it conceivable that there are still some who maintain that revolutionary literature and art are not for the masses of the people but for the exploiters and oppressors?

Indeed literature and art exist that are for the exploiters and oppressors. Literature and art for the landlord class are feudal literature and art. Such were the literature and art of the ruling class in China's feudal era. To this day such literature and art still have considerable influence in China. Literature and art for the bourgeoisie are bourgeois literature and art. People like Liang Shiqiu, whom Lu Xun criticized, talk about literature and art as transcending classes, but in fact they uphold bourgeois literature and art and oppose proletarian literature and art. Then literature and art exist that serve the imperialists—for example, the works of Zhou Zuoren, Zhang Ziping, and their like—which we call traitor literature and art. With us, literature and art are for the people, not for any of the above groups. We have said that China's new culture at the present stage is an anti-imperialist, anti-feudal culture of the masses of the people under the leadership of the proletariat. Today, anything that is truly of the masses must necessarily be led by the proletariat. Whatever is under the leadership of the bourgeoisie cannot possibly be of the masses. Naturally, the same applies to the new literature and art that are part of the new culture. We should take over the rich legacy and the good traditions in literature and art that have been handed down from past ages in China and foreign countries, but the aim must still be to serve the masses of the people. Nor do we refuse to utilize the literary and artistic forms of the past, but in our hands these old forms, remolded and infused with new content, also become something revolutionary in the service of the people.

Who, then, are the masses of the people? The broadest sections of the people, constituting more than 90 percent of our total population, are the workers, peasants, soldiers, and urban petite bourgeoisie. Therefore, our literature and art are first for the workers, the class that leads the revolution. Second, they are for the peasants, the most numerous and most steadfast of our allies in the revolution. Third, they are for the armed workers and peasants, namely, the Eighth Route and New Fourth armies and the other armed units of the people, which are the main forces of the revolutionary war. Fourth, they are for the laboring masses of the urban petite bourgeoisie and for the petit-bourgeois intellectuals, both of whom are also our allies in the revolution and capable of long-term cooperation with us. These four kinds of people constitute the overwhelming majority of the Chinese nation, the broadest masses of the people.

Our literature and art should be for the four kinds of people we have enumerated. To serve them, we must take the class stand of the proletariat and not that of the petite bourgeoisie. Today, writers who cling to an individualist, petit-bourgeois stand cannot truly serve the masses of revolutionary workers, peasants, and soldiers. Their interest is mainly focused on the small number of petit-bourgeois intellectuals. This is the crucial reason why some of our comrades cannot correctly solve the problem of "for whom?" In saying this I am not referring to theory. In theory, or in words, no one in our ranks regards the masses of workers, peasants, and soldiers as less important than the petit-bourgeois intellectuals. I am referring to practice, to action. In practice, in action, do they regard petit-bourgeois intellectuals as more important than workers, peasants and soldiers? I think they do. Many comrades concern themselves with studying the petit-bourgeois intellectuals and analyzing their psychology, and they concentrate on portraying these intellectuals and excusing or defending their shortcomings, instead of guiding the intellectuals to join with them in getting closer to the masses of workers, peasants, and soldiers, taking part in the practical struggles of the masses, portraying and educating the masses. Coming from the petite bourgeoisie and being themselves intellectuals, many comrades seek friends only among intellectuals and concentrate on studying and describing them. Such study and description are proper if done from a proletarian position. But that is not what they do, or not what they do fully. They take the petit-bourgeois stand and produce works that are the self-expression of the petite bourgeoisie, as can be seen in quite a number of literary and artistic products. Often they show heartfelt sympathy for intellectuals of petit-bourgeois origin, to the extent of sympathizing with or even praising their shortcomings. On the other hand, these comrades seldom come into contact with the masses of workers, peasants, and soldiers, do not understand or study them, do not have intimate friends among them, and are not good at portraying them; when they do depict them, the clothes are the clothes of working people but the faces are those of petit-bourgeois intellectuals. In certain respects they are fond of the workers, peasants, and soldiers and the cadres stemming from them, but there are times when they do not like them, and there are some respects in which they do not like them: they do not like their feelings or their manner or their nascent literature and art (the wall newspapers, murals, folk songs, folk tales, etc.). At times they are fond of these things too, but that is when they are hunting for novelty, for something with which to embellish their own works, or even for certain backward features. At other times they openly despise these things and favor what belongs to the petit-bourgeois intellectuals or even to the bourgeoisie. These comrades have their feet planted on the side of the petit-bourgeois intellectuals; or, to put it more elegantly, their innermost soul is still a kingdom of the petit-bourgeois intelligentsia. Thus they have not yet solved, or not yet clearly solved, the problem of "for whom?" This applies not only to newcomers to Yan'an; even among comrades who have been to the front and worked for a number of years in our base areas and in the Eighth Route and New Fourth armies, many have not completely solved this problem. It requires a long period of time, at least eight or ten years, to solve it thoroughly. But however long it takes, solve it we must, and solve it unequivocally and thoroughly. Our literary and art workers must accomplish this task and shift their stand; they must gradually move their feet over to the side of the workers, peasants, and soldiers, to the side of the proletariat, through the process of going into their very midst and into the thick of practical struggles and through the process of studying Marxism and society. Only in this way can we have a literature and art that are truly for the workers, peasants, and soldiers, a truly proletarian literature and art.

This question of "for whom?" is fundamental; it is a question of principle. The controversies and divergences, the opposition and disunity, arising among some comrades in the past were not on this fundamental question of principle but on secondary questions, or even on issues involving no principle. On this question of principle, however, there has been hardly any divergence between the two contending sides, and they have shown almost complete agreement; to some extent, both tend to look down upon the workers, peasants, and soldiers and divorce themselves from the masses. I say "to some extent" because, generally speaking, these comrades do not look down upon the workers, peasants, and soldiers or divorce themselves from the masses in the same way as the Guomindang does. Nevertheless, the tendency is there. Unless this fundamental problem is solved, many other problems will not be easy to solve. Take, for instance, the sectarianism in literary and art circles. This too is a question of principle, but sectarianism can only be eradicated by putting forward and faithfully applying the slogans, "For the workers and peasants!" "For the Eighth Route and New Fourth armies!" and "Go among the masses!" Otherwise the problem of sectarianism can never be solved. Lu Xun once said:

> A common aim is the prerequisite for a united front. . . . The fact that our front is not united shows that we have not been able to unify our aims, and that some people are working only for small groups or indeed only for

themselves. If we all aim at serving the masses of workers and peasants, our front will of course be united.[3]

The problem existed then in Shanghai; now it exists in Chongqing too. In such places the problem can hardly be solved thoroughly, because the rulers oppress the revolutionary writers and artists and deny them the freedom to go out among the masses of workers, peasants, and soldiers. Here with us the situation is entirely different. We encourage revolutionary writers and artists to be active in forming intimate contacts with the workers, peasants, and soldiers, giving them complete freedom to go among the masses and to create a genuinely revolutionary literature and art. Therefore, here among us the problem is nearing solution. But nearing solution is not the same as a complete and thorough solution. We must study Marxism and study society, as we have been saying, precisely in order to achieve a complete and thorough solution. By Marxism we mean living Marxism that plays an effective role in the life and struggle of the masses, not Marxism in words. With Marxism in words transformed into Marxism in real life, there will be no more sectarianism. Not only will the problem of sectarianism be solved, but many other problems as well.

II

Having settled the problem of whom to serve, we come to the next problem, how to serve. To put it in the words of some of our comrades: should we devote ourselves to raising standards, or should we devote ourselves to popularization?

In the past, some comrades, to a certain or even a serious extent, belittled and neglected popularization and laid undue stress on raising standards. Stress should be laid on raising standards, but to do so one-sidedly and exclusively, to do so excessively, is a mistake. The lack of a clear solution to the problem of "for whom?," which I referred to earlier, also manifests itself in this connection. Since these comrades are not clear on the problem of "for whom?," they have no correct criteria for the "raising of standards" and the "popularization" they speak of and are naturally still less able to find the correct relationship between the two. Since our literature and art are basically for the workers, peasants, and soldiers, "popularization" means to popularize among the workers, peasants, and soldiers, and "raising standards" means to advance from their present level. What

---

3. Lu Xun, "Duiyu Zuoyi zuojia lianmeng de yijian" 對於左翼作家聯盟的意見, in Lu Xun1981*a*: 4: 233–39; 1980: 3: 103–8.

should we popularize among them? Popularize what is needed and can be readily accepted by the feudal landlord class? Popularize what is needed and can be readily accepted by the bourgeoisie? Popularize what is needed and can be readily accepted by the petit-bourgeois intellectuals? No, none of these will do. We must popularize only what is needed and can be readily accepted by the workers, peasants, and soldiers themselves. Consequently, prior to the task of educating the workers, peasants, and soldiers, there is the task of learning from them. This is even more true of raising standards. There must be a basis from which to raise. Take a bucket of water, for instance; where is it to be raised from if not from the ground? From mid-air? From what basis, then, are literature and art to be raised? From the basis of the feudal classes? From the basis of the bourgeoisie? From the basis of the petit-bourgeois intellectuals? No, not from any of these; only from the basis of the masses of workers, peasants, and soldiers. Nor does this mean raising the workers, peasants, and soldiers to the "heights" of the feudal classes, the bourgeoisie, or the petit-bourgeois intellectuals; it means raising the level of literature and art in the direction in which the workers, peasants, and soldiers are themselves advancing, in the direction in which the proletariat is advancing. Here again the task of learning from the workers, peasants, and soldiers comes in. Only by starting from the workers, peasants, and soldiers can we have a correct understanding of popularization and of the raising of standards and find the proper relationship between the two.

In the last analysis, what is the source of all literature and art? Works of literature and art, as ideological forms, are products of the reflection in the human brain of the life of a given society. Revolutionary literature and art are the products of the reflection of the life of the people in the brains of revolutionary writers and artists. The life of the people is always a mine of the raw materials for literature and art, materials in their natural form, materials that are crude, but most vital, rich, and fundamental; they make all literature and art seem pallid by comparison; they provide literature and art with an inexhaustible source, their only source. They are the only source, for there can be no other. Some may ask, is there not another source in books, in the literature and art of ancient times and of foreign countries? In fact, the literary and artistic works of the past are not a source but a stream; they were created by our predecessors and the foreigners out of the literary and artistic raw materials they found in the life of the people of their time and place. We must take over all the fine things in our literary and artistic heritage, critically assimilate whatever is beneficial, and use them as examples when we create works out of the literary and artistic raw materials in the life of the people of our own time and place. It makes a difference whether or not we have such examples, the difference between crudeness and refinement, between roughness and polish, between a low and a high level, and between slower and faster work. Therefore, we must on no account reject the legacies of the ancients and the foreigners or refuse to learn from them, even though they are the works of the feudal or bourgeois classes. But taking over legacies and using them as examples must never replace our own creative work; nothing can do that. Uncritical transplantation or copying from the ancients and the foreigners is the most sterile and harmful dogmatism in literature and art. China's revolutionary writers and artists, writers and artists of promise, must go among the masses; they must for a long period of time unreservedly and wholeheartedly go among the masses of workers, peasants, and soldiers, go into the heat of the struggle, go to the only source, the broadest and richest source, in order to observe, experience, study, and analyze all the different kinds of people, all the classes, all the masses, all the vivid patterns of life and struggle, all the raw materials of literature and art. Only then can they proceed to creative work. Otherwise, you will have nothing to work with, and you will be nothing but a phony writer or artist, the kind that Lu Xun in his will so earnestly cautioned his son never to become.[4]

Although man's social life is the only source of literature and art and is incomparably livelier and richer in content, the people are not satisfied with life alone and demand literature and art as well. Why? Because, although both are beautiful, life as reflected in works of literature and art can and ought to be on a higher plane, more intense, more concentrated, more typical, nearer the ideal, and therefore more universal than actual everyday life. Revolutionary literature and art should create a variety of characters out of real life and help the masses to propel history forward. For example, there is suffering from hunger, cold, and oppression on the one hand, and exploitation and oppression of man by man on the other. These facts exist everywhere, and people look upon them as commonplace. Writers and artists concentrate on such everyday phenomena, typify the contradictions and struggles within them, and produce works that awaken the masses, fire them with enthusiasm, and impel them to unite and struggle to transform their environment. Without such literature and art, this task could not be fulfilled, or at least not so effectively and speedily.

What is meant by popularizing and by raising standards in works of literature and art? What is the relationship between these two tasks? Popular works are simpler and plainer, and therefore more readily accepted by the broad masses of the people today. Works of a higher quality, being more

---

4. Lu Xun, "Si" 死, in Lu Xun 1981*a*: 6: 608–13; 1980: 4: 310–15.

polished, are more difficult to produce and in general do not circulate so easily and quickly among the masses at present. The problem facing the workers, peasants, and soldiers is this: they are now engaged in a bitter and bloody struggle with the enemy but are illiterate and uneducated as a result of long years of rule by the feudal and bourgeois classes, and therefore they are eagerly demanding a widespread campaign of enlightenment, education, and works of literature and art that meet their urgent needs and that are easy to absorb, in order to heighten their enthusiasm in struggle and confidence in victory, strengthen their unity, and fight the enemy with one heart and one mind. For them the prime need is not "more flowers on the brocade" but "fuel in snowy weather." In present conditions, therefore, popularization is the more pressing task. It is wrong to belittle or neglect popularization.

Nevertheless, no hard and fast line can be drawn between popularization and the raising of standards. Not only is it possible to popularize some works of higher quality even now, but the cultural level of the broad masses is steadily rising. If popularization remains at the same level forever, with the same stuff being supplied month after month and year after year, always the same "Little Cowherd"[5] and the same "man, hand, mouth, knife, cow, goat,"[6] will not the educators and those being educated be six of one and half a dozen of the other? What would be the sense of such popularization? The people demand popularization and, following that, higher standards; they demand higher standards month by month and year by year. Here popularization means popularizing for the people, and raising of standards means raising the level for the people. And such raising is not from mid-air, or behind closed doors, but is actually based on popularization. It is determined by and at the same time guides popularization. In China as a whole the development of the revolution and of revolutionary culture is uneven, and their spread is gradual. Whereas in one place there is popularization and then raising of standards on the basis of popularization, in other places popularization has not even begun. Hence good experience in popularization leading to higher standards in one locality can be applied in other localities and serve to guide popularization and the raising of standards there, saving many twists and turns along the road. Internationally, the good experience of foreign countries, and especially Soviet experience, can also serve to guide us. With us, therefore, the raising of standards is

---

5. A popular folk operetta with only two actors playing the parts of a cowherd and a village girl who sing a question-and-answer duet.

6. Characters composed of few strokes, usually included in the first lessons of writing primers.

based on popularization, and popularization is guided by the raising of standards. Precisely for this reason, so far from being an obstacle to the raising of standards, the work of popularization we are speaking of supplies the basis for the work of raising standards that we are now doing on a limited scale, and prepares the necessary conditions for us to raise standards in the future on a much broader scale.

Besides such raising of standards as meets the needs of the masses directly, there is the kind that meets their needs indirectly, that is, the kind that is needed by the cadres. The cadres are the advanced elements of the masses and generally have received more education; literature and art of a higher level are entirely necessary for them. To ignore this would be a mistake. Whatever is done for the cadres is also entirely for the masses, because it is only through the cadres that we can educate and guide the masses. If we go against this aim, if what we give the cadres cannot help them educate and guide the masses, our work of raising standards will be like shooting at random and will depart from the fundamental principle of serving the masses of the people.

To sum up: through the creative labor of revolutionary writers and artists, the raw materials found in the life of the people are shaped into the ideological form of literature and art serving the masses of the people. Included here are the more advanced literature and art as developed on the basis of elementary literature and art and as required by those sections of the masses whose level has been raised, or, more immediately, by the cadres among the masses. Also included here are elementary literature and art, which, conversely, are guided by more advanced literature and art and are needed primarily by the overwhelming majority of the masses at present. Whether more advanced or elementary, all our literature and art are for the masses of the people, and in the first place for the workers, peasants, and soldiers; they are created for the workers, peasants, and soldiers and are for their use.

Now that we have settled the problem of the relationship between the raising of standards and popularization, that of the relationship between the specialists and the popularizers can also be settled. Our specialists are not only for the cadres, but also, and indeed chiefly, for the masses. Our specialists in literature should pay attention to the wall newspapers of the masses and to the reportage written in the army and the villages. Our specialists in drama should pay attention to the small troupes in the army and the villages. Our specialists in music should pay attention to the songs of the masses. Our specialists in the fine arts should pay attention to the fine arts of the masses. All these comrades should make close contact with comrades engaged in the work of popularizing literature and art among the masses. On the one hand, they should help and guide the popularizers, and on the other, they should learn from these comrades and, through them, draw nourishment from the masses to replenish and enrich themselves so that their specialties do not become "ivory towers" detached from the masses and from reality and devoid of content or life. We should esteem the specialists, for they are very valuable to our cause. But we should tell them that no revolutionary writer or artist can do any meaningful work unless he is closely linked with the masses, gives expression to their thoughts and feelings, and serves them as a loyal spokesman. Only by speaking for the masses can he educate them, and only by being their pupil can he be their teacher. If he regards himself as their master, as an aristocrat who lords it over the "lower orders," then, no matter how talented he may be, he will not be needed by the masses, and his work will have no future.

Is this attitude of ours utilitarian? Materialists do not oppose utilitarianism in general but the utilitarianism of the feudal, bourgeois, and petit-bourgeois classes; they oppose those hypocrites who attack utilitarianism in words but in deeds embrace the most selfish and short-sighted utilitarianism. There is no "ism" in the world that transcends utilitarian considerations; in class society there can be only the utilitarianism of this or that class. We are proletarian revolutionary utilitarians and take as our point of departure the unity of the present and future interests of the broadest masses, who constitute over 90 percent of the population; hence we are revolutionary utilitarians aiming for the broadest and the most long-range objectives, not narrow utilitarians concerned only with the partial and the immediate. If, for instance, you reproach the masses for their utilitarianism and yet for your own utility, or that of a narrow clique, force on the market and propagandize among the masses a work that pleases only the few but is useless or even harmful to the majority, then you are not only insulting the masses but also revealing your own lack of self-knowledge. A thing is good only when it brings real benefit to the masses of the people. Your work may be as good as "The Spring Snow," but if for the time being it caters only to the few and the masses are still singing the "Song of the Rustic Poor,"[7] you will get nowhere by simply scolding them instead of trying to raise their level. The question now is to bring about a unity between "The Spring Snow" and the "Song of the Rustic Poor," between higher standards and popularization. Without such a unity, the highest art of any expert can-

---

7. Songs from the State of Chu in the third century. The music of "Spring Snow" was thought to be of a higher quality than that of the "Song of the Rustic Poor," but when someone sang the former in the Chu capital only a few dozen people joined in, while thousands sang the latter. This story is related in "Song Yu's Reply to the King of Chu"; *Wenxuan*.

not help being utilitarian in the narrowest sense; you may call this art "pure and lofty" but that is merely your own name for it, which the masses will not endorse.

Once we have solved the problems of fundamental policy, of serving the workers, peasants, and soldiers and of how to serve them, such other problems as whether to write about the bright or the dark side of life and the problem of unity will also be solved. If everyone agrees on the fundamental policy, it should be adhered to by all our workers, all our schools, publications, and organizations in the field of literature and art, and in all our literary and artistic activities. It is wrong to depart from this policy, and anything at variance with it must be duly corrected. Since our literature and art are for the masses of the people, we can proceed to discuss a problem of inner-Party relations, that is, the relation between the Party's work in literature and art and the Party's work as a whole, and in addition a problem of the Party's external relations, that is, the relation between the Party's work in literature and art and the work of non-Party people in this field, a problem of the united front in literary and art circles.

III

Let us consider the first problem. In the world today all culture, all literature and art, belong to definite classes and are geared to definite political lines. There is in fact no such thing as art for art's sake, art that stands above classes, art that is detached from or independent of politics. Proletarian literature and art are part of the whole proletarian revolutionary cause; they are, as Lenin said, "cogs and wheels" in the whole revolutionary machine. Therefore, Party work in literature and art occupies a definite and assigned position in Party revolutionary work as a whole and is subordinated to the revolutionary tasks set by the Party in a given revolutionary period. Opposition to this arrangement is certain to lead to dualism or pluralism, and in essence amounts to "politics: Marxist; art: bourgeois," as with Trotsky. We do not favor overstressing the importance of literature and art, but neither do we favor underestimating their importance. Literature and art are subordinate to politics, but in their turn exert a great influence on politics. Revolutionary literature and art are part of the whole revolutionary cause, they are cogs and wheels in it, and although in comparison with certain other and more important parts they may be less significant and less urgent and may occupy a secondary position, nevertheless they are indispensable cogs and wheels in the whole machine, an indispensable part of the entire revolutionary cause. If we had no literature and art, even in the broadest and most ordinary sense, we could not carry on the revolutionary movement and win victory. Failure to recognize this is wrong. Furthermore, when we say that literature and art are subordinate to politics, we mean class politics, the politics of the masses, not the politics of a few so-called statesmen. Politics, whether revolutionary or counterrevolutionary, is the struggle of class against class, not the activity of a few individuals. The revolutionary struggle on the ideological and artistic fronts must be subordinate to the political struggle because only through politics can the needs of the class and the masses find expression in concentrated form. Revolutionary statesmen, the political specialists who know the science or art of revolutionary politics, are simply the leaders of millions upon millions of statesmen—the masses. Their task is to collect the opinions of these mass statesmen, sift and refine them, and return them to the masses, who then take them and put them into practice. They are therefore not the kind of aristocratic "statesmen" who work behind closed doors and fancy they have a monopoly of wisdom. Herein lies the difference in principle between proletarian statesmen and decadent bourgeois statesmen. This is precisely why there can be complete unity between the political character of our literary and artistic works and their truthfulness. It would be wrong to fail to realize this and to debase the politics and the statesmen of the proletariat.

Let us consider next the question of the united front in the world of literature and art. Since literature and art are subordinate to politics and since the fundamental problem in China's politics today is resistance to Japan, our Party writers and artists must in the first place unite on this issue of resistance to Japan with all non-Party writers and artists (ranging from Party sympathizers and petit-bourgeois writers and artists to all those writers and artists of the bourgeois and landlord classes who are in favor of resistance to Japan). Second, we should unite with them on the issue of democracy. On this issue there is a section of anti-Japanese writers and artists who do not agree with us, so the range of unity will unavoidably be somewhat more limited. Third, we should unite with them on issues peculiar to the literary and artistic world, questions of method and style in literature and art; here again, since we are for socialist realism and some people do not agree, the range of unity will be narrower still. Whereas on one issue there is unity, on another there is struggle, there is criticism. The issues are at once separate and interrelated, so that even on the very ones that give rise to unity, such as resistance to Japan, there are at the same time struggle and criticism. In a united front, "all unity and no struggle" and "all struggle and no unity" are both wrong policies—as with the Right capitulationism and tailism, or the "Left" exclusivism and sectarianism, practiced by some comrades in the past. This is as true in literature and art as in politics.

The petit-bourgeois writers and artists constitute an important force among the forces of the united front in literary and art circles in China. There are many shortcomings in both their thinking and their works, but, comparatively speaking, they are inclined toward the revolution and are close to the working people. Therefore, it is an especially important task to help them overcome their shortcomings and to win them over to the front that serves the working people.

IV

Literary and art criticism is one of the principal methods of struggle in the world of literature and art. It should be developed, and, as comrades have rightly pointed out, our past work in this respect has been quite inadequate. Literary and art criticism is a complex question that requires a great deal of special study. Here I shall concentrate only on the basic problem of criteria in criticism. I shall also comment briefly on a few specific problems raised by some comrades and on certain incorrect views.

In literary and art criticism there are two criteria, the political and the artistic. According to the political criterion, everything is good that is helpful to unity and resistance to Japan, that encourages the masses to be of one heart and one mind, that opposes retrogression and promotes progress; on the other hand, everything is bad that is detrimental to unity and resistance to Japan, foments dissension and discord among the masses, and opposes progress and drags people back. How can we tell the good from the bad— by the motive (the subjective intention) or by the effect (social practice)? Idealists stress motive and ignore effect, whereas mechanical materialists stress effect and ignore motive. In contradistinction to both, we dialectical materialists insist on the unity of motive and effect. The motive of serving the masses is inseparably linked with the effect of winning their approval; the two must be united. The motive of serving the individual or a small clique is not good, nor is it good to have the motive of serving the masses without the effect of winning their approval and benefiting them. In examining the subjective intention of a writer or artist, that is, whether his motive is correct and good, we do not judge by his declarations but by the effect of his actions (mainly his works) on the masses in society. The criterion for judging subjective intention or motive is social practice and its effect. We want no sectarianism in our literary and art criticism, and, subject to the general principle of unity for resistance to Japan, we should tolerate literary and art works with a variety of political attitudes. But at the same time, in our criticism we must adhere firmly to principle and severely criticize and repudiate all works of literature and art expressing views in opposition to the nation, to science, to the masses, and to the Communist Party, because these so-called works of literature and art proceed from the motive and produce the effect of undermining unity for resistance to Japan. According to the artistic criterion, all works of a higher artistic quality are good or comparatively good, and those of a lower artistic quality are bad or comparatively bad. Here, too, of course, social effect must be taken into account. There is hardly a writer or artist who does not consider his own work beautiful, and our criticism ought to permit the free competition of all varieties of works of art, but it is also entirely necessary to subject these works to correct criticism according to the criteria of the science of aesthetics, so that art of a lower level can be gradually raised to a higher and art that does not meet the demands of the struggle of the broad masses can be transformed into art that does.

There is the political criterion, and there is the artistic criterion; what is the relationship between the two? Politics cannot be equated with art, nor can a general world outlook be equated with a method of artistic creation and criticism. We deny not only that there is an abstract and absolutely unchangeable political criterion but also that there is an abstract and absolutely unchangeable artistic criterion; each class in every class society has its own political and artistic criteria. But all classes in all class societies invariably put the political criterion first and the artistic criterion second. The bourgeoisie always shuts out proletarian literature and art, however great their artistic merit. The proletariat must similarly distinguish among the literary and artistic works of past ages and determine its attitude toward them only after examining their attitude to the people and whether or not they had any progressive significance historically. Some works that politically are downright reactionary may have a certain artistic quality. The more reactionary their content and the higher their artistic quality, the more poisonous they are to the people, and the more necessary it is to reject them. A common characteristic of the literature and art of all exploiting classes in their period of decline is the contradiction between their reactionary political content and their artistic form. What we demand is the unity of politics and art, the unity of content and form, the unity of revolutionary political content, and the highest possible perfection of artistic form. Works of art that lack artistic quality have no force, however progressive they are politically. Therefore, we oppose both works of art with a wrong political viewpoint and the tendency toward the "poster and slogan style," which is correct in political viewpoint but lacking in artistic power. On questions of literature and art we must carry on a struggle on two fronts.

Both these tendencies can be found in the thinking of many comrades. A good number of comrades tend to neglect artistic technique; it is therefore necessary to give attention to the raising of artistic standards. But as I see it, the political side is more of a problem at present. Some comrades lack elementary political knowledge and consequently have all sorts of muddled ideas. Let me cite a few examples from Yan'an.

"The theory of human nature." Is there such a thing as human nature? Of course there is. But there is only human nature in the concrete, no human nature in the abstract. In class society there is only human nature of a class character; there is no human nature above classes. We uphold the human nature of the proletariat and of the masses of the people, whereas the landlord and bourgeois classes uphold the human nature of their own classes, only they do not say so but make it out to be the only human nature in existence. The human nature boosted by certain petit-bourgeois intellectuals is also divorced from or opposed to the masses; what they call human nature is in essence nothing but bourgeois individualism, and so, in their eyes, proletarian human nature is contrary to human nature. "The theory of human nature," which some people in Yan'an advocate as the basis of their so-called theory of literature and art, puts the matter in just this way and is wholly wrong.

"The fundamental point of departure for literature and art is love, love of humanity." Now love may serve as a point of departure, but there is a more basic one. Love as an idea is a product of objective practice. Fundamentally, we do not start from ideas but from objective practice. Our writers and artists who come from the ranks of the intellectuals love the proletariat because society has made them feel that they and the proletariat share a common fate. We hate Japanese imperialism because Japanese imperialism oppresses us. There is absolutely no such thing in the world as love or hatred without reason or cause. As for the so-called love of humanity, there has been no such all-inclusive love since humanity was divided into classes. All the ruling classes of the past were fond of advocating it, and so were many so-called sages and wise men, but nobody has ever really practiced it, because it is impossible in class society. There will be genuine love of humanity—after classes are eliminated all over the world. Classes have split society into many antagonistic groupings; there will be love of all humanity when classes are eliminated, but not now. We cannot love enemies, we cannot love social evils, our aim is to destroy them. This is common sense; can it be that some of our writers and artists still do not understand this?

"Literary and artistic works have always laid equal stress on the bright and the dark, half and half." This statement contains many muddled ideas. It is not true that literature and art have always done this. Many petit-bourgeois writers have never discovered the bright side. Their works only expose the dark and are known as the "literature of exposure." Some of their works simply specialize in preaching pessimism and world-weariness. On the other hand, Soviet literature in the period of socialist construction portrays mainly the bright. It, too, describes shortcomings in work and portrays negative characters, but this only serves as a contrast to bring out the brightness of the whole picture and is not on a so-called half-and-half basis. The writers and artists of the bourgeoisie in its period of re-action depict the revolutionary masses as mobs and themselves as saints, thus reversing the bright and the dark. Only truly revolutionary writers and artists can correctly solve the problem of whether to extol or to expose. All the dark forces harming the masses of the people must be exposed, and all the revolutionary struggles of the masses of the people must be extolled; this is the fundamental task of revolutionary writers and artists.

"The task of literature and art has always been to expose." This asser-tion, like the previous one, arises from ignorance of the science of history. Literature and art, as we have shown, have never been devoted solely to exposure. For revolutionary writers and artists the targets for exposure can never be the masses, but only the aggressors, exploiters, and oppressors and the evil influence they have on the people. The masses, too, have short-comings, which should be overcome by criticism and self-criticism within the people's own ranks, and such criticism and self-criticism are also one of the most important tasks of literature and art. But this should not be re-garded as any sort of "exposure of the people." As for the people, the ques-tion is basically one of education and of raising their level. Only counter-revolutionary writers and artists describe the people as "born fools" and the revolutionary masses as "tyrannical mobs."

"This is still the period of the satirical essay, and Lu Xun's style of writ-ing is still needed."[8] Living under the rule of the dark forces and deprived of freedom of speech, Lu Xun used burning satire and freezing irony, cast in the form of essays, to do battle; and he was entirely right. We, too, must hold up to sharp ridicule the fascists, the Chinese reactionaries, and every-thing that harms the people; but in the Shanxi-Gansu-Ningxia Border Re-gion and the anti-Japanese base areas behind the enemy lines, where de-mocracy and freedom are granted in full to the revolutionary writers and artists and withheld only from the counterrevolutionaries, the style of the essay should not simply be like Lu Xun's. Here we can shout at the top of our voices and have no need for veiled and roundabout expressions, which

---

8. Allusion to Ding Ling's "We Need the *Zawen* Essay" (see preceding essay in this volume) and Luo Feng's 羅烽, "Haishi zawen de shidai" 還是雜文的時代 (It's still the age of the *zawen* essay), *Jiefang ribao*, Mar. 12, 1942.

are hard for the people to understand. When dealing with the people and not with their enemies, Lu Xun never ridiculed or attacked the revolutionary people and the revolutionary Party in his "satirical essay period," and these essays were entirely different in manner from those directed against the enemy. To criticize the people's shortcomings is necessary, as we have already said, but in doing so we must truly take the stand of the people and speak out of wholehearted eagerness to protect and educate them. To treat comrades like enemies is to go over to the stand of the enemy. Are we then to abolish satire? No. Satire is always necessary. But there are several kinds of satire, each with a different attitude, satire to deal with our enemies, satire to deal with our allies, and satire to deal with our own ranks. We are not opposed to satire in general; what we must abolish is the abuse of satire.

"I am not given to praise and eulogy. The works of people who eulogize what is bright are not necessarily great and the works of those who depict the dark are not necessarily paltry." If you are a bourgeois writer or artist, you will eulogize not the proletariat but the bourgeoisie, and if you are a proletarian writer or artist, you will eulogize not the bourgeoisie but the proletariat and working people: it must be one or the other. The works of the eulogists of the bourgeoisie are not necessarily great, nor are the works of those who show that the bourgeoisie is dark necessarily paltry; the works of the eulogists of the proletariat are not necessarily not great, but the works of those who depict the so-called "darkness" of the proletariat are bound to be paltry—are these not facts of history as regards literature and art? Why should we not eulogize the people, the creators of the history of mankind? Why should we not eulogize the proletariat, the Communist Party, New Democracy, and socialism? There is a type of person who has no enthusiasm for the people's cause and looks coldly from the sidelines at the struggles and victories of the proletariat and its vanguard; what he is interested in, and will never weary of eulogizing, is himself, plus perhaps a few figures in his small coterie. Of course, such petit-bourgeois individualists are unwilling to eulogize the deeds and virtues of the revolutionary people or heighten their courage in struggle and their confidence in victory. Persons of this type are merely termites in the revolutionary ranks; of course, the revolutionary people have no need for these "singers."

"It is not a question of stand; my class stand is correct, my intentions are good, and I understand all right, but I am not good at expressing myself and so the effect turns out bad." I have already spoken about the dialectical materialist view of motive and effect. Now I want to ask, is not the question of effect one of stand? A person who acts solely by motive and does not inquire what effect his action will have is like a doctor who merely writes prescriptions but does not care how many patients die of them. Or take a political party that merely makes declarations but does not care whether they are carried out. It may well be asked, is this a correct stand? And is the intention here good? Of course, mistakes may occur even though the effect has been taken into account beforehand, but is the intention good when one continues in the same old rut after facts have proved that the effect is bad? In judging a party or a doctor, we must look at practice, at the effect. The same applies in judging a writer. A person with truly good intentions must take the effect into account, sum up experience, and study the methods or, in creative work, study the technique of expression. A person with truly good intentions must criticize the shortcomings and mistakes in his own work with the utmost candor and resolve to correct them. This is precisely why Communists employ the method of self-criticism. This alone is the correct stand. Only in this process of serious and responsible practice is it possible gradually to understand what the correct stand is and gradually to obtain a good grasp of it. If one does not move in this direction in practice, if there is simply the complacent assertion that one "understands all right," then in fact one has not understood at all.

"To call on us to study Marxism is to repeat the mistake of the dialectical materialist creative method, which will harm the creative mood." To study Marxism means to apply the dialectical materialist and historical materialist viewpoint in our observation of the world, of society, and of literature and art; it does not mean writing philosophical lectures into our works of literature and art. Marxism embraces but cannot replace realism in literary and artistic creation, just as it embraces but cannot replace the atomic and electronic theories in physics. Empty, dry dogmatic formulas do indeed destroy the creative mood; not only that, they first destroy Marxism. Dogmatic "Marxism" is not Marxism, it is anti-Marxism. Then does not Marxism destroy the creative mood? Yes, it does. It definitely destroys creative moods that are feudal, bourgeois, petit-bourgeois, liberalistic, individualist, nihilist, art-for-art's sake, aristocratic, decadent, or pessimistic, and every other creative mood that is alien to the masses of the people and to the proletariat. So far as proletarian writers and artists are concerned, should not these kinds of creative moods be destroyed? I think they should; they should be utterly destroyed. And while they are being destroyed, something new can be constructed.

V

The problems discussed here exist in our literary and art circles in Yan'an. What does that show? It shows that wrong styles of work still exist to a serious extent in our literary and art circles and that there are still many defects among our comrades, such as idealism, dogmatism, empty illusions, empty talk, contempt for practice, and aloofness from the masses, all of which call for an effective and serious campaign of rectification.

We have many comrades who are still not very clear on the difference between the proletariat and the petite bourgeoisie. There are many Party members who have joined the Communist Party organizationally but have not yet joined the Party wholly or at all ideologically. Those who have not joined the Party ideologically still carry a great deal of the muck of the exploiting classes in their heads, and have no idea at all of what proletarian ideology, or communism, or the Party is. "Proletarian ideology?" they think. "The same old stuff!" Little do they know that it is no easy matter to acquire this stuff. Some will never have the slightest Communist flavor about them as long as they live and can only end up by leaving the Party. Therefore, although the majority in our Party and in our ranks are clean and honest, we must in all seriousness put things in order both ideologically and organizationally if we are to develop the revolutionary movement more effectively and bring it to speedier success. To put things in order organizationally requires our first doing so ideologically, our launching a struggle of proletarian ideology against non-proletarian ideology. An ideological struggle is already under way in literary and art circles in Yan'an, and it is most necessary. Intellectuals of petit-bourgeois origin always stubbornly try in all sorts of ways, including literary and artistic ways, to project themselves and spread their views, and they want the Party and the world to be remolded in their own image. In the circumstances it is our duty to jolt these "comrades" and tell them sharply "That won't work! The proletariat cannot accommodate itself to you; to yield to you would actually be to yield to the big landlord class and the big bourgeoisie and to run the risk of undermining our Party and our country." Whom then must we yield to? We can mold the Party and the world only in the image of the proletarian vanguard. We hope our comrades in literary and art circles will realize the seriousness of this great debate and join actively in this struggle, so that every comrade may become sound and our entire ranks may become truly united and consolidated ideologically and organizationally.

Because of confusion in their thinking, many of our comrades are not quite able to draw a real distinction between our revolutionary base areas and the Guomindang areas, and they make many mistakes as a consequence. A good number of comrades have come here from the garrets of Shanghai, and in coming from those garrets to the revolutionary base areas, they have passed not only from one kind of place to another but from one historical epoch to another. One society is semifeudal, semicolonial, under the rule of the big landlords and big bourgeoisie, the other is a revolutionary new-democratic society under the leadership of the proletariat. To come to the revolutionary bases means to enter an epoch unprecedented in the thousands of years of Chinese history, an epoch in which the masses of the people wield state power. Here the people around us and the audience for our propaganda are totally different. The past epoch is gone, never to return. Therefore, we must integrate ourselves with the new masses without any hesitation. If, living among the new masses, some comrades, as I said before, are still "lacking in knowledge and understanding" and remain "heroes with no place to display their prowess," then difficulties will arise for them, and not only when they go out to the villages; right here in Yan'an difficulties will arise for them. Some comrades may think, "Well, I had better continue writing for the readers in the 'great rear area'; it is a job I know well and has 'national significance.' " This idea is entirely wrong. The "great rear area" is also changing. Readers there expect authors in the revolutionary base areas to tell about the new people and the new world and not to bore them with the same old tales. Therefore, the more a work is written for the masses in the revolutionary base areas, the more national significance it will have. Fadeyev in *The Debacle*[9] only told the story of a small guerrilla unit and had no intention of pandering to the palate of readers in the old world; yet the book has exerted world-wide influence. At any rate in China its influence is very great, as you know. China is moving forward, not back, and it is the revolutionary base areas, not any of the backward, retrogressive areas, that are leading China forward. This is a fundamental issue that, above all, comrades must come to understand in the rectification movement.

Since integration into the new epoch of the masses is essential, it is necessary to solve thoroughly the problem of the relationship between the individual and the masses. This couplet from a poem by Lu Xun should be our motto:

Fierce-browed, I coolly defy a thousand pointing fingers,
Head-bowed, like a willing ox I serve the children.[10]

The "thousand pointing fingers" are our enemies, and we will never yield to them, no matter how ferocious. The "children" here symbolize the proletariat and the masses. All Communists, all revolutionaries, all revolution-

---

9. Alexander Fadeyev (1901-56), Soviet writer best known for his novel *The Nineteen* (1927), translated into Chinese by Lu Xun as *Huimie* 毁滅 (The debacle).

10. From "Zichao" 自潮 (Self-mockery); for a translation of the entire poem, see David Y. Chen, *Lu Hsun Complete Poems* (Tempe: University of Arizona, Center for Asian Studies, 1988), 95.

Chapter 55

Realism Today

Hu Feng

From the beginning, the new literature has been inspired by the hope that real human life can be liberated.[1] The notion that "words must have substance" reflects this basic spirit. More specifically, it means that "most of my material is *selected* from the lives of the unfortunate who live in our sick society. My motive is to *expose* the illness in order to induce people to pay attention to its cure" [Lu Xun, "How I Came to Write Fiction"].[2] It is in this way that the real content of history is given expression; the "substance" to which I refer is not something obscure. To do something "for the sake of life" means "improving life."

To do something "for humanity," one must, on the one hand, be sincere about doing it "for" humanity and, on the other hand, have profound insights into the humanity "for whom" one is doing something. The material that is *selected* and the illness that is *exposed* must deal with the truth about the human condition. The one who does the "selecting" and "exposing"

---

1. Hu Feng 胡風, "Xianshizhuyi zai jintian" 現實主義在今天, *Shishi xinbao* 時事新報, Jan. 1, 1944; reprinted in Hu Feng 1984: 2: 319–23.
2. "Wo zenyang zuo qi xiaoshuo lai" 我怎樣做起小說來, in Lu Xun 1981a: 4: 511–15; 1980: 3: 262–65.

must have a mind keenly sensitive to both the "sickness" that afflicts the "sick society" and the "misfortunes" of the unfortunate. This unity or combination of subjective spirit and objective truth has produced a militant new literature. We call it realism.

Of course during the new literature movement there have been occasions on which the element of subjective spirit has been exaggerated. The liberation of the individual is, however, a requirement of history, and the need to transcend life has long been an important aspect of creative work. Actually, realism originally embraced these ideas. It is only when subjective spirit departs from the essence of reality and drifts into emptiness that it becomes a disease that is repugnant to realism. During the new literature movement there was also the tendency to chase after the ephemeral bubbles of life. The tendency, at the beginning, had been the result of an effort to face squarely a newborn reality. But if the subjective will is frozen or consumed by the object of study, true realists will protest. In the course of the new literature movement, aestheticism, mysticism, symbolism, satanism, and other trends have appeared from time to time, but they were merely reflections in the literary realm of corrupt forces in society itself, and as such, each could have no more than a fleeting existence in the development of realism.

If one looks back upon the history of the new literature, it becomes apparent that, despite having labored under difficult circumstances and having experienced weakness, the basic spirit of the new literature has always been to reflect the demands of national and social liberation and to exert great effort in the bloody struggle for these goals. It took a stand against darkness and pursued light; it spoke on behalf of those who groaned beneath a legacy of suffering and reached out to the souls of those decent, steadfast, and industrious people who inherited this yoke of oppression. It observed with due dignity the past that was cold and dead, and sang praises to the first glimpse of dawn. . . . Because of this spirit, sparks have been scattered in the hearts of thousands upon thousands of people. These sparks have now ignited and are emitting a brilliant radiance in the sacred struggle of the present day, a struggle that finds our nation unyielding, unwilling to accept a meaningless existence, and believing firmly in victory and the bright future. What accounts for this rise in this spirit? It is the devoted will and benevolent affection of writers. It is a result of their thorough and correct understanding of real life and their total lack of self-deceiving hypocrisy. We call it realism.

This foundation of realism permits the new literature to develop further and to display its fighting qualities on those occasions when war breaks out.

this theory is exceedingly "lofty," and those writers who comply with it are able to extricate themselves from Hell and summarily ascend into Heaven. No one doubts that there is plenty of happiness in Heaven, but the writer there is limited to writing about the Jade Emperor's Golden Dragon Palace and the moon goddess's powdered face. Do the theorists want to make a rebuttal? A debate of this sort would be like demons in Hell bickering across the immense space with fairies in Heaven and would thus produce no results, but there is no harm in "talking off the top of my head" and carrying on a bit. If thought could be irrelevant or even contrary to real life, that would be the end of the argument. But if thought is for the sake of or beneficial to the liberation of the nation, or to victory in the war, how can it be divorced from real life, and how can it not be truth that flows, like blood, through real life? If thought is divorced from real life or from the life and struggle of the broad masses, how can the nation be liberated and how can the war be won? Thought that is for the sake of or beneficial to the liberation of the nation and victory in war must, of necessity, derive its flesh and blood content, its richness, and its health from real life. Great thought is always a synthesis or refinement of tendencies in the development of real life and never a burdensome fetter pressing down on the shoulders of humanity or a cloud floating in the sky. Is it not true that in the bloody struggle waged by the people, thought provides great strength and leads the way? Is this not because the new literature of the past twenty years and the literature of the War of Resistance have emerged from the depths of real life and produced the sweet aroma of the truth of life—which is thought itself?

The second theory requires writers to write about light or positive characters. Dark characters and those living in negative social environments should be ignored or, at best, be mentioned only in passing to embellish the text. Why? Because literature about light or positive characters is believed to produce virtuous people, whereas literature about dark characters and those in negative social environments is believed to cause readers to become depressed, corrupted, and even suicidal. Following such a theory could produce only one result: all writers will only daydream, with their eyes closed to reality. Think of it! If we surrender when facing violence or retreat when observing darkness, how can mankind's persistent reform movement continue to develop? How can our bitter struggle of the past six years, one in which our blood has flowed like rivers, continue to develop? Unless one is a slave by nature or through long-term practice, one need but observe the manner of the various bloodsucking brutes and unscrupulous charlatans to have one's disgust aroused. One need only see the expressions on the faces of those innocents who are killed in cold blood and the oppressed who have nowhere to file their complaints to have one's grief and indignation aroused. If this was not the case, the history of humankind would forever be subject to the reign of darkness. Think of the vast number of images contained in the new literature of the past twenty years and of the War of Resistance that portray various oppressors and brutes as well as those who have suffered and been sacrificed at their hands! Did this sort of literature lead us to depression and corruption, or did it instead lead us to sobriety and action? Why should our new literature be an exception to the great works of world literature? Some say that the people Lu Xun wrote about were all negative characters and thus conclude that there was no light in Lu Xun's heart. The fact that some "theorists" think in this manner proves that they are but cowards before the power of darkness. I approve of writing about the bright aspects of life, and I disapprove of exposing darkness just to peddle something exotic. But where does light come from, and where do we find positive characters? Light must break through the layers and layers of darkness that surround it. Positive characters are besieged by negative characters, in constant battle against them, and victimized by their barbarous slaughter. This is reality. This is truth. Only by recognizing these truths can the works written by writers be true to life and educate and encourage their readers. If readers are armed with works of this sort when they return to the battlefield of life, they will not feel that writers are insane or detestable liars.

Although a theory like this claims to promote literature that is "bright" and "lofty," in reality it does not want literature to exist at all; it wants to strangle literature. It wants literature to take leave of real life, and it wants writers to tell lies. It seeks to kill the spirit of realism. If this path is followed, literature will have to surrender its arms in the struggle for the liberation of the nation.

Of course, history will advance and realism will triumph. This sort of "theory" is nothing but a chloroformic perfume that puts you to sleep. True, the perfume may not kill you, but the enemy can more easily put you to death with one thrust of the knife when you are under its influence. We are engaged in a fierce struggle for the liberation of the nation, and our enemies are baring their fangs all around us, so we must rally all the forces latent in us.

I call the situation a crisis and I make an appeal on behalf of literature: do not force writers to tell lies, and do not malign real life!

Contrary to what some people think, this problem is not the exclusive concern of writers and literary workers. The list of those who must choose their destiny—to be enslaved by the power of darkness or to be citizens of a

Reference Matter

Glossary

All-China Association of Literary Resistance (Zhonghua quanguo wenyijie kangdi xiehui 中華全國文藝界抗敵協會; 1938–46)

An organization established in Wuhan, under the auspices of the CCP and the GMD, to foster a united cultural front for national resistance to Japan. This organization mobilized writers for the creation of anti-Japanese propaganda, encouraging the use of national forms and popular culture to foment resistance. It also organized writers' trips to the front and published the journal *Kangzhan wenyi* 抗戰文藝 (Literature and art of the War of Resistance).

Analects (Lunyu 論語; ca. 400 B.C.)

A collection of dialogues and sayings attributed to Confucius and his disciples. Made up of twenty chapters and arranged with little apparent structure, the *Analects* has at its core the concepts of benevolence, virtue, learning, righteousness, loyalty, and ritual. Praised as a repository for the moral, social, and political guidance of the "true gentleman," the *Analects* has long been one of the core books of Confucian philosophy and education, counted among the Confucian canon's Four Books, which all young students learned by heart.

Ancient-Style Prose (*guwen* 古文)

Beginning in the early Tang period (618–713), as a part of the general weakening of the aristocracy's centuries-old monopoly on literature, this was a reaction against the ornate Six Dynasties (220–589) style in prose. The Ancient-Style prose movement promoted the idea of modeling prose on both the moral themes and the straightforward, unembellished style of the Confucian classics. Important advocates included Han Yu, Chen Zi'ang, and Liu Zongyuan.

Babbitt, Irving (1865–1933)

Harvard professor and critic, promoter of a self-styled new humanism. Babbitt's literary theories included statements emphasizing the inherent cultural value of China's traditional literary canon and the foolishness of completely rejecting such treasures. His views were enthusiastically adopted by his students Wu Mi and Mei Guangdi, both critics of China's New Culture movement, and later by Liang Shiqiu.

Bai Juyi 白居易 (772–846)

One of the most popular and prolific Tang poets, known for his lucid, simple poetic language readily accessible to a broad readership. Hu Shi saw him as a spiritual precursor to the vernacular literature movement.

Ban Gu 班固 (A.D. 32–92)

Grand historian of the Later Han dynasty and noted writer of *fu* (descriptive prose-poems). With the assistance of his sister, Ban completed the *Han shu* 漢書 (History of the Former Han Dynasty), covering the period from 206 B.C. to A.D. 23, which became the prototype for official dynastic histories.

Bao Tianxiao 包天笑 (1876–1973)

One of the leading writers of the Mandarin Ducks and Butterfly school of popular literature. Edited the journals *Xiaoshuo daguan* 小說大觀 (Grand magazine, 1915–21), and *Xingqi* 星期 (Weekly, 1922–23) and wrote many works of popular fiction, particularly of the love story variety.

Bao Zhao 鮑照 (414–466)

A famous *yuefu* poet of the Six Dynasties era (220–589), noted for the rather complicated literary language he introduced to this folk song genre, elevating it to new heights of literary excellence. Bao's style is characterized by the use of evocative imagery and unique metaphors and similes.

Bianwen, see Dunhuang Transformation Texts

Bing Xin 冰心 (1900–)

One of the first woman writers to emerge in the May Fourth period. She was a member of the Literary Research Association, and was known for her poetry, short stories, and essays, as well as her writings for young readers. Important works include: *Fanxing* 繁星 (Myriad stars; 1923) and *Chunshui* 春水 (Spring waters; 1923), collections of poetry; and *Chaoren* 超人 (Ubermensch), a collection of short stories. Bing Xin remained active in literary circles until the late 1980's.

Book of Changes (*Yijing* 易經)

Also known as the *Yi* or *Zhou Yi*, the *Book of Changes* is a manual of divination, probably originating in the Eastern Zhou period (770–403 B.C.). It underwent many variations before its text was standardized into the version extant today.

Although Confucius is among the purported authors, the work is most closely associated with Daoism.

Book of History (*Shujing* 書經 or *Shangshu* 尚書)

A collection of historical documents reputedly edited and prefaced by Confucius. It consists of twenty-eight chapters containing a diverse assortment of official documents from five historical periods. Written in a terse, difficult, and elliptical classical style, the *Book of History* is one of the Five Classics of Confucianism.

Book of Songs (*Shijing* 詩經; also known as the *Book of Odes*, or the *Book of Poetry*)

The first great work of the Chinese poetic tradition, the *Book of Songs* is an anthology of 305 songs believed to have been gathered by Zhou dynasty (1122–221 B.C.) court recorders sent among the people to gauge grass-roots sentiments. Collected between 1100 and 600 B.C., these songs were classified into three general categories: *feng*, or airs, *ya* or courtly songs, and *song* or sacrificial hymns and temple songs. Often cited with reverence by Confucius (who according to legend edited the collection), it is part of the Confucian canon and has had a profound and lasting impact on the poetry of subsequent ages. Its "Daxu" 大序 (Great preface) holds an influential place in ancient Chinese literary theory, containing some of the earliest statements on the nature of poetry. The oldest extant edition of the *Book of Songs* (Han dynasty) also includes an appended commentary which began a long and hallowed tradition of "allegorical" readings of these poems, linking each poem to a specific political situation and deriving moral lessons from them.

Boxer Rebellion (Yihetuan yundong 義和團運動) (1898–1901)

A popular anti-foreign uprising led by a secret society known as the Boxers. Originally targeting the missionary presence, the Boxers received covert encouragement from the Empress Dowager Cixi and adopted the slogan "Support the Manchus, annihilate the foreigners." The Boxers grew in strength and popularity, and the Manchu court became more openly supportive, eventually declaring war on the foreign powers. In response, an eight-nation international force crushed the Boxers, and sent Cixi and the Manchu court fleeing to distant Xi'an. The Western powers then enacted the Boxer Protocol of 1901, which provided for punishments, indemnities, extraterritorial rights, and autonomous quarters for foreign legations in Beijing. This political and military fiasco helped to refocus strong domestic discontent against the Qing dynasty.

Brandes, George (1842–1927)

A Danish literary critic whose six-volume *Main Currents in Nineteenth Century Literature* (1871-1890) was perhaps the most influential introduction to Western literature among May Fourth writers and intellectuals. Brandes's particular "romantic conception of realism and naturalism" may have influenced Chinese understandings of realism.

Cai Yuanpei 蔡元培 (1868–1940)

Cai was a transitional figure between the late Qing intellectual world and the May Fourth movement. A Hanlin scholar, then a student of philosophy and aesthetics in Europe, Cai held the post of president of Peking University in 1916–26, during which time he carried out radical reforms, most notably hiring young and progressive intellectuals (such as Hu Shi, Chen Duxiu, and Lu Xun) as department heads and instructors. Under Cai's direction, Peking University was the center of iconoclast intellectual activity during the May Fourth period. He went on to found the Academica Sinica which he headed until his death.

Cao Xueqin, *see Dream of the Red Chamber*

Cao Zhi 曹植 (A.D. 192–232)

An aristocrat and talented, innovative poet of the Jian'an era (196–220), thought to be influential in the early development of regulated verse.

Chen Duxiu 陳獨秀 (1880–1942)

Founder and co-editor of *New Youth*, the most important of May Fourth progressive journals, and a contributor to the vernacular movement and the attack on Confucian ethics. Under his direction, *New Youth* took a leftist turn in 1920, and in the following year Chen became a founding member of the CCP, which he led until 1927 when he was removed from his post, blamed for the disastrous GMD coup in April of that year. His later interest in Trotsky's ideas only further alienated him from the party leardership.

Cheng Fangwu 成仿吾 (1897–1984)

One of the founding members of the Creation Society and an important essayist and literary critic of the 1920's and 1930's. He joined the CCP in 1928, did educational work in the Henan-Anhui Soviet and participated in the Long March. After 1949, Cheng devoted himself to educational work.

Cheng Yi 程頤 (1033–1108)

Cheng Yi and his brother, Cheng Hao, although they share many ideas, are often seen as precursors to the rationalist and idealist schools of neo-Confucianism, respectively. Cheng Yi's ideas on *li* 理 , or principle, were later adopted and developed by the most famous neo-Confucian, Zhu Xi (1130–1200). The rationalist school is thus often referred to as the "Cheng-Zhu school."

Chinese League of Left-Wing Writers (Zhongguo zuoyi zuojia lianmeng 中國左翼作家聯盟; 1930–36)

Writers' organization formed under the auspices of the CCP, with Lu Xun as its first head. The League's mandate was to promote the formation of a proletarian literature, establish journals to disseminate that literature, and investigate important issues such as the popularization of literature. Many of the literary debates of the 1930's involved members of the League.

Creation Society (Chuangzao she 創造社; 1921–29)

One of the most important modern literary societies, its founding members included Guo Moruo, Zhang Ziping, Yu Dafu, Tian Han, and Cheng Fangwu (who had conceived the idea of such a literary group while studying in Japan). The group was dedicated to a romantic-aesthetic view of literature, and the slogan "art for art's sake" was often pinned on them. By 1925 members of the society began to embrace Marxism, and its journals promoted Marxist-based theories of the arts. The society was banned by the GMD in 1929 and, with the blessing of the CCP, which had become dismayed at the literary infighting on the left, disbanded. Its important journals include *Chuangzao jikan* 創造季刊 (Creation quarterly; 1922–24), *Chuangzao zhoubao* 創造週報 (Creation weekly; 1923–24), and *Hongshui* 洪水 (Flood; 1924–27).

Crescent Moon Society (Xinyue she 新月社; 1923–31)

Literary society established by a group of young, Anglo-American-educated intellectuals, including Hu Shi, Xu Zhimo, Wen Yiduo, and Liang Shiqiu, who were greatly influenced by Western aesthetic and humanist theories. Through their main literary organ, *Xinyue yuekan* 新月月刊 (Crescent moon monthly; 1928–33), they promoted literary freedom, but qualified this with the demand that literature promote "healthy ideals" in a "dignified manner." The society's greatest influence was on poetry, where it demonstrated that vernacular Chinese could be successfully combined with strict rules of meter and prosody, an idea expressed in Wen Yiduo's dictum, borrowed from Bliss Perry, that good poetry be like "dancing in fetters." The society is often linked to the journal *Xiandai pinglun* 現代評論 (Contemporary review; 1924–28).

Critical Review Group (Xueheng pai 學衡派)

A group of conservative, Western-educated professors on the faculty of Nanjing Normal College. It published *Xueheng* 學衡 (Critical review; 1922–33), a literary journal aimed at promoting traditional Chinese culture in opposition to the iconoclastic agenda of the May Fourth movement. Among its members were Mei Guangdi 梅光迪 (1890–1945), Wu Mi 吳宓 (1894–1978), and Hu Xiansu 胡先驌 (1894–1968).

Dai Wangshu 戴望舒 (1905–50)

Representative of the Modernist school of poetry of the 1930's, Dai was greatly influenced by the French Symbolists, Francis Jammes and Paul Verlaine. During the War of Resistance, he became a patriot, for which he was imprisoned briefly at the end of 1941 by the Japanese army.

Ding Ling 丁玲 (1904–86)

One of modern China's leading woman writers. Her early stories, represented by "Shafei nüshi de riji" 莎菲女士的日記 (The diary of Miss Sophie; 1928), gave voice to the emotional conflicts of modern women. Ding joined the League of Left-Wing Writers in 1932. She was kidnapped by the GMD in 1933, escaped and fled to Yan'an, where she began to write more consciously leftist fiction. In 1942 she wrote essays criticizing the social and political life in Yan'an and was sent to engage in land reform as part of her rectification. She was the target of a national campaign in 1951–52 and was labeled a rightist in 1958. After the Cultural Revolution (1966–76), Ding was rehabilitated and elected vice-president of the All-China Writers Association.

Dream of the Red Chamber (*Honglou meng* 紅樓夢) (also known as *A Dream of Red Mansions*, or *The Story of the Stone*)

Universally acknowledged as the masterpiece of traditional Chinese fiction, this 120-chapter novel is believed to be the work of Cao Xueqin (ca. 1724–64), though many changes and emendations to the text were made after his death and authorship of the last forty chapters is still in dispute. The novel is beyond categorization and has been read as a love story, *Bildungsroman*, religious and political allegory.

Dunhuang Transformation Texts (Dunhuang *bianwen* 敦煌變文)

"Transformation texts" are a mixed prose-verse literary genre, the earliest extant examples of which were found in the Dunhuang caves and date back to the Tang dynasty. These texts have been shown to be closely related to a style of secular or religious storytelling accompanied by pictures and originating in the area extending from Central Asia to India.

Eight-legged essay (*Bagu wen* 八股文)

The officially prescribed essay form for the late imperial civil service examination. Written in classical Chinese and employing established rhetorical devices, these essays expounded on a given topic in a highly structured form composed of eight sections, or legs. In the May Fourth period, the term "eight-legged essay" was often used disparagingly to indicate writing that was stale and formulaic.

Feng Xuefeng 馮雪峰 (1903–76)

An important poet, translator, literary theorist, and one of Lu Xun's close associates in the 1930's. His theories of literature were expressed most cogently in his *Lun minzhu geming de wenyi yundong* 論民主革命的文藝運動 (On the literary movement in the democratic revolution; 1946). Feng was one of the leaders of the League of Left-Wing Writers and he supported Lu Xun and Hu Feng in the Two Slogans debate. He was criticized in a national campaign in 1954 and was labeled a rightist in 1957.

Feng Yuanjun 馮沅君 (1900–74)

Short-story writer and scholar of classical literature, Feng is the younger sister of the well-known philosopher Feng Youlan. She began to publish short stories in 1924; many of her works describe the psychological dimension of women's love lives. Feng has also written numerous scholarly works on the history of Chinese literature.

Free Man, *see* Third Category

Gao Yihan 高一涵 (1885–?)

One of the many young, foreign-educated thinkers brought to Peking University during the May Fourth period. Chen Duxiu's colleague in the political science department, Gao was for a time co-editor of *New Youth*, contributing many articles on democracy, nationalism, and political science. In May 1922, together with Hu Shi and Dao Menghe, Gao founded the Beijing weekly *Nuli zhoubao* 努力週報 (Endeavor; 1922–23), thus marking a definite split with the more leftist, Shanghai-based Chen Duxiu and his *New Youth*.

Great Preface, *see Book of Songs.*

Guan Hanqing 關漢卿 (ca. 1240–ca. 1320)

Guan is credited with being the inventor of the Yuan *zaju* 雜劇 drama form. With more than sixty plays attributed to him, Guan ranks as the most productive playwright of the traditional Chinese theater, although most of his works are no longer extant. His most famous play is *Dou E yuan* 竇娥冤 (The injustice done to Dou E).

Gu Yanwu 顧炎武 (1613–82)

Gu was the foremost exponent of evidential scholarship (*kaozheng* 考證), devoted to philological analysis of classical texts. Differing from the idealist school of neo-Confucianism (or "Song learning"), which emphasized moral self-cultivation, evidential scholarship is associated with the school of "Han learning," which stressed perceptive knowledge with absolute textual fidelity to authentic Confucian classics as a guideline. His works are characterized by a broad intellect, diverse subject matter, and careful documentation, earning him the title of father of "practical scholarship" (*puxue* 樸學).

Guo Moruo 郭沫若 (1892–1978)

Poet, playwright, short-story writer, literary critic, scholar, and among the founders of the Creation Society. His debut collection of poetry, *Nüshen* 女神 (The goddesses; 1921), represents the first successful use of the modern vernacular in poetic form. Guo later turned from his early romantic literary pursuits to the ardent advocacy of a socialist revolution and, after 1949, was one of the most important officials in the CCP cultural bureaucracy.

Han Yu 韓愈 (768–824)

Han is known for his attacks on Buddhist influences in the Tang court and his contribution to the Tang Confucian revival in philosophy. He also made stylistic innovations in the field of Chinese poetry, but is perhaps best known for his role in the Ancient-Style Prose movement. He is considered foremost among the Eight Great Prose Masters of the Tang and Song.

Hu Feng 胡風 (1902–85)

Poet, translator, and important literary theorist of the 1930's and 1940's, Hu was at the center of the maelstrom in some of the most vociferous literary debates of that era. He clashed with Zhou Yang in a debate on the nature of realism and in the Two Slogans polemic. Hu also edited two independent literary journals and wrote extensive literary criticism on the importance of the "subjective" to the creative act. In 1955, he and his "followers" were the object of a national campaign; Hu was jailed as a counterrevolutionary and not rehabilitated until 1979.

Hu Qiuyuan 胡秋原 (1910–)

A translator and literary critic, Hu is known largely for his 1932 debate with left-wing writers over the freedom of literature from political concerns. Together with Su Wen, he supported the argument for a Third category for writers, neither bourgeois nor proletarian. Hu traveled extensively in Europe, Russia, and America from 1934 to 1937. He entered the GMD government upon his return to China and followed it to Taiwan.

Hu Shi 胡適 (1891–1962)

Philosopher (Ph.D., Columbia), literary historian, essayist, ambassador, teacher, translator, and poet, Hu ranks among the most important cultural figures in modern China. He helped launch the New Culture movement with his article "Some Modest Proposals for the Reform of Literature," (1917). Practicing what he preached, Hu was one of the first to write poetry in the vernacular language with his collection, *Changshi ji* 嘗試集 (Experiments; 1920). Deeply committed to cultural reform, Hu had little taste for the acrimonious political debates of his time and became known as a liberal. He founded *Nuli zhoubao* (Endeavor) in 1922 and was a member of the New Crescent Society. He was ambassador to the United States from 1938 to 1942, then spent the remainder of his life teaching and doing research in America and Taiwan. Hu also made important contributions to the study of traditional vernacular literature.

Hu Yuzhi 胡愈之 (1896–1986)

Member of the Literary Research Association and the CCP, Hu spent much of his life involved in editing and publishing. He was an early proponent of language reform, the use of Esperanto, and realism in literature. Beginning in 1921, he became edior of *Dongfang zazhi* 東方雜誌 (Eastern miscellany; 1904–48), a journal that took a radical turn in editorial policy around the May Fourth movement. Hu later became involved in newspaper journalism.

Huang Tingjian 黃庭堅 (1045–1105)

Historian, master calligrapher, and art connoisseur, Huang is best known as one of the most talented poets of the Northern Song dynasty. He was the most important of the five young disciples of Su Shi and started what would later be dubbed the Jiangxi 江西 school of poetry, which used terms from alchemy and Chan (Zen) Buddhism to describe a process of studying and imitating ancient poetic masters until one attains, in a sudden enlightenment, one's own distinct style. Although later disparaged by some as little more than a plagiarist, Huang often showed creativity and originality in his poems. Late Qing imitators of the Jiangxi school were often ridiculed by May Fourth writers.

Huang Zunxian 黃遵憲 (1848–1905)

Diplomat (in the U.S. and England), historian, and political reformer, Huang is best known as the greatest poet of the late Qing "poetic revolution." His innovations in poetry included the introduction of neologisms, foreign words, and contemporary subject matter into traditional Chinese verse forms, establishing his work as transitionally important in the development of modern vernacular poetry. Huang's *Riben guozhi* 日本國志 (Chronicle of Japan; 1887), a history of Japan, influenced the late Qing reform generation. His poetry is collected in the posthumously published *Renjing lu shicao* 人境廬詩草 (Draft poems from the hut in the human world).

Jia Yi 賈誼 (220–168 B.C.)

Jia is most remembered as a writer of two famous *fu* poems, "Diao Qu Yuan" 吊屈原 (Mourning Qu Yuan) and "Funiao fu" 鵩鳥賦 (The Owl), which reflect his brooding over his political misfortunes.

Jiang Guangci 蔣光慈 (1901–31)

Jiang is considered one of the first creators of proletarian literature in China. His first poetry collection, *Xin meng* 新夢 (New dreams; 1925) exerted a great influence on many young poets. A founder of the Sun Society and a member of the CCP and the League of Left-Wing Writers, he was an enthusiastic advocate of revolutionary literature. Jiang abruptly quit the party in 1930, for which he was excoriated, and died of illness not long thereafter.

Jiang Kui 姜夔 (ca. 1155–1221)

A major poet, musician, and critic of the Southern Song period (1127–1276), Jiang is remembered as one of the greatest of *ci* 詞 (lyrical meter) poets, skilled in both the writing of lyrics and in composing new tune patterns.

Jiangxi school, *see* Huang Tingjian; Southern Society

Journey to the West (*Xiyou ji* 西遊記)

One of the most popular traditional Chinese fictional narratives, believed to have been written by Wu Cheng'en 吳承恩 (ca. 1500–82). Based loosely on popular stories and historical versions of the monk Xuan Zang's (596–664) journey to India to obtain Buddhist scriptures, the hundred-chapter narrative combines religious themes, social satire, poetry, puns, lively vernacular dialogue, and brilliant characterization.

Kang Youwei 康有為 (1858–1927)

Confucian scholar, outstanding thinker of his day, and one of the leaders of the failed Hundred Days' Reforms. Kang is best known as a scholar who radically reinterpreted the Confucian classics to paint Confucius as a progressive thinker with continuing relevance to a changing China. After the fall of the Qing, he supported an attempt to restore the emperor and was thus attacked by the progressives of the May Fourth generation. Kang's writings on Confucius and Confucian texts include *Xinxue wei jing kao* 新學偽經考 (1891) and *Kongzi gaizhi kao* 孔子改制考 (1897). His *Datong shu* 大同書 (Great harmony) may offer an important link between the Confucian tradition and Mao Zedong's Marxist utopianism.

Kong Shangren 孔尚任 (1648–1718)

Qing dramatist and author of China's greatest historical drama, *Taohua shan* 桃花扇 (The peach blossom fan), which centers around the famous love story of Hou Fangyu 侯方域 (1618–55) and his mistress Li Xiangjun 李香君.

Kong Yingda 孔穎達 (574–648)

Scholar noted for his compilation of the *Wujing zhengyi* 五經正義 (True meanings of the Five Classics), which was long employed as a standard text for the civil service examinations. Kong also wrote a commentary on the "Great Preface" to the *Book of Songs*, in which he tries to reconcile the conflict between the then-popular boudoir verse and the traditional moral function of poetry.

League of Left-Wing Writers, *see* Chinese League of Left-Wing Writers

Li Baojia 李寶嘉, or Li Boyuan 伯元 (1876–1906)

Leading writer of fiction in the late Qing period, Li's works include the well-known *Guanchang xianxing ji* 官場現形記 (The bureaucracy exposed, ca. 1905) and *Wenming xiaoshi* 文明小史 (A Brief History of Modern Times, 1903). His fiction exposed government corruption and oppression and was very popular in the reformist climate of the late Qing. Li also edited several fiction journals, including *Xiuxiang xiaoshuo* 繡像小說 (Illustrated fiction).

Li Boyuan, *see* Li Baojia

Li Chuli 李初梨 (1900-)

One of China's early experts in Marxist literary thought. As a member of the Creation Society, Li wrote numerous articles promoting proletarian literature, and Guo Moruo credited him with being the first advocate of revolutionary literature.

Li Jinfa 李金髮 (1900–1976)

One of the major symbolist poets in modern China, instrumental in introducing ideas from French symbolism into modern Chinese poetry. In the "popularization" trend of the 1930's, Li's poetry was often criticized as obscure, private, and even incomprehensible for readers.

Li sao 離騷, *see* Qu Yuan

Li Shangyin 李商隱 (813?–58)

Late Tang poet whose verse, with its highly original, fantastic imagery, often borders on the surreal. The unique, sensuous quality of some of Li's poetry has found favor with many modern readers and poets.

Liang Qichao 梁啓超 (1873–1929)

A student of Kang Youwei, Liang was one of the most important political and intellectual figures of the late Qing and early Republican periods. He was a prolific essayist on a wide range of subjects (e.g., Western culture, nationalism, constitutional monarchy, democracy, fiction). He sponsored lectures by Western intellectuals (most notably Bertrand Russell), founded and edited numerous political and literary journals, and was an excellent poet in the classical language. One of his contributions to literary theory, *Yinbingshi shihua* 飲冰室詩話 (Poetry talks from the Ice-Drinking Studio), was an important contribution to the late Qing poetic revolution. His promotion of fiction and his writings on the centrality of fiction to the renovation of society influenced both his contemporaries and later May Fourth writers. His prose style is seen as a precursor to May Fourth vernacular.

Liang Shiqiu 梁實秋 (1902–87)

Liang was a founder of the Crescent Moon Society, its leading theoretical voice, and for a time chief editor of its literary organ, *Crescent Moon Monthly*. Liang studied with Irving Babbitt at Harvard and saw himself as a "humanist"; he scorned the histrionic romanticism and radical politics of the day and was often attacked by Lu Xun in the debates over revolutionary literature. Liang also voiced classical concerns about the state of vernacular poetry in the 1930's. He went to Taiwan in 1949 and continued teaching and translating, particularly the plays of Shakespeare.

Liang Shuming 梁漱溟 (1893–1988)

An important thinker, teacher, and philosopher associated with Chinese conservatism. Liang was hired by Cai Yuanpei in 1916 to teach Indian philosophy at Peking University. After the death of his father, Liang Ji, who killed himself in 1919 to show his loyalty to the emperor, Liang became increasingly conservative in his views. He was the first person of the May Fourth era to defend the Confucian tradition in a systematic and powerfully argued manner, in his book *Dong Xi wenhua ji qi zhexue* 東西文化及其哲學 (Eastern and Western civilizations and their philosophies; 1921). In this work, Liang favorably compared certain aspects of the traditional Chinese worldview to those of the West and of India. After 1929 Liang became active involved in rural reconstruction.

Lin Shu 林紓 (1852–1924)

Poet, novelist, playwright, painter, educator, and reform advocate of the late Qing, Lin Shu's greatest impact on modern Chinese culture and literature came from his more than 200 translations of Western novels. Because he knew no foreign languages, Lin had to be assisted by bilingual friends who orally translated into colloquial Chinese as Lin simultaneously transcribed into Tongcheng-style classical prose. In the May Fourth period Lin wrote satirical essays attacking the literary revolution.

Lin Yutang 林語堂 (1895–1976)

A prominent essayist, novelist, educator, lexicographer, and linguist. From 1924 to 1930, Lin was a contributor to *Yusi* 語絲 (Spinner of words; 1924–30). He later published his own humor magazine, *Lunyu* 論語 (Analects; 1932–37), which earned him the moniker "master of humor." Lin was bitterly criticized by his more progressive contemporaries, most notably Lu Xun, for promoting humor without a strong sense of social consciousness. He also wrote essays criticizing the lack of economy and inelegance of the modern vernacular. He is perhaps best known in the West for his books in English introducing traditional Chinese culture.

Ling Shuhua 凌叔華 (1904–1990)

After graduating from Yenching University, Ling entered the literary world with the publication of her first short story "Jiu hou" 酒後 (After drinking; 1925). Her stories appeared frequently in *Xiandai pinglun* 現代評論 (Contemporary review; 1924–28) and *Crescent Moon*. She taught literature at a variety of schools in China and abroad, where she spent a good deal of her life with her husband, Chen Xiying 陳西瀅 (1896–1970), a diplomat for the GMD government who is perhaps best known for being the object of Lu Xun's bitter satire in the 1920's.

Literary Research Association (Wenxue yanjiu hui 文學研究會; 1920–1932)

One of the most important literary groups in modern China, founded by Zhou Zuoren, Zheng Zhenduo, Ye Shengtao, and Mao Dun, among others. The association advocated realism and humanism in literature, seeing writing as a form of engagement with life and society. Their manifesto criticized the stale moralizing of traditional Chinese literature as well as the "frivolous" attitude of Mandarin Ducks and Butterfly fiction. Among the literary journals edited by this group were *Xiaoshuo yuebao* 小說月報 (Fiction monthly; 1921–32), *Wenxue zhoubao* 文學週報 (Literature Weekly; 1921–29; originally entitled *Wenxue xunkan*, and then simply *Wenxue*), and the first publication devoted to the new poetry, *Shi* 詩 (Poetry; 1922–23). Many of modern China's best known writers published in these journals.

Liu E 劉鶚 (1857–1909)

A jack-of-all-trades, Liu was at various times a medical practitioner, business entrepreneur, musician, mathematician, archaeologist, poet, philologist, and novelist. He is best known for his 20-chapter novel, *Laocan youji* 老 殘 遊 記 (The travels of Laocan; serialized in 1903–4), which exposed many of the ills of the late Qing era and has since acquired the status of a prose classic, often included in secondary-school language courses. Liu was also the first scholar to take a serious interest in the collection and study of oracle-bone inscriptions.

Liu Na'ou 劉吶鷗 (1900–39)

Born in Taiwan, raised in Japan, Liu studied French at Shanghai's Zhendan Unversity where he became interested in literature and publishing. He edited several journals in the 1920's and 1930's and became one of the leading writers of the New Sensibilities school of literature.

Liu Shipei 劉師培 (1884–1919)

Liu was a follower of Zhang Binglin, with whom he shared anti-Manchu sentiments. In 1905, he established with Zhang and others the Society for the Preservation of the National Learning, which published *Guocui xuebao* 國粹學報 (Journal of the national essence). Liu was also a member of the Revolutionary Alliance. After the 1911 Revolution, he turned conservative and was one of a group of intellectuals supporting Yuan Shikai's imperial aspirations. Through Zhang's recommendation, Liu was given a teaching position at Peking University, where he wrote essays in archaic language against the New Culture movement and its literary reforms. Liu was part of the conservative group that published in the short-lived *Guo gu* 國故 (The national heritage; 1919).

Liu Xiang 劉向 (ca. 79–ca. 6 B.C.)

Historian, bibliographer, poet, and compiler of anecdotal literature in the Han dynasty, Liu is known mostly for his compilation of the *Zhanguo ce* 戰 國 策 (Intrigues of the Warring States), a collection of stories often highlighting the duplicity and subterfuge of ministers in the various courts of the Warring States period (403–221 B.C.). The emphasis on the ambitious pursuit of gain / profit (*li* 利) gave this book an unfavorable reputation among Confucian scholars. Liu also compiled the *Lienü zhuan* 列 女 傳 (Biographies of exemplary women), a handbook for women's comportment.

Liu Xie 劉勰 (ca.465–ca.520)

Literary critic of the Qi-Liang period (479–557). Liu Xie's *Wenxin diaolong* 文 心 雕 龍 (The literary mind and the carving of dragons) is the first book-length treatise on literature in the Chinese language. Still highly valued by classical scholars, poets, and literary theorists, *Wenxin diaolong* has received a great deal of attention in recent years.

Liu Yong 柳永 (987–1053)

Poet and musician of the Northern Song dynasty, Liu is famed for his mastery of the longer (*manci*) form of *ci* 詞 (lyrical poems written to music), which he helped to develop and popularize. One of Liu's great achievements was the skillful, seemingly natural combination of colloquial and literary dictions.

Lu Ji 陸機 (261–303)

A military figure, poet, and prolific author, Lu is remembered for his work of literary criticism, the *Wen fu* 文 賦 (Prose-poem on literature), which deals with the writing process from the spiritual preparation of the writer to matters of technique and genre. The *Wen fu* is one of the earliest pieces of literary criticism in Chinese and the earliest example of "poems on poetry."

Lu Xun 魯迅 (1881–1936)

Generally recognized as the greatest writer of early twentieth-century China. His literary career began in the late Qing, writing essays in the classical language, the best of which offer a cultural critique of Chinese society (i.e., "On the Power of Mara Poetry"). Lu Xun is best known for being the first practitioner of the modern short story. "Kuangren riji" 狂 人 日 記 (Diary of a madman; 1918) was in both style and content unprecedented and shocking; "Ah Q zhengzhuan" 阿 Q正 傳 (The true story of Ah Q; 1921), earned him national recognition—not all of it favorable—and became the best-known modern Chinese story abroad. Both stories are generally read as iconoclastic attacks on the Chinese cultural tradition. His stories were published in two collections, *Nahan* 吶喊 (Call to arms, or Outcry; 1923) and *Panghuang* 徬徨 (Hesitation, or Wandering; 1926). By 1927, Lu Xun began studying Marxism and Marxist literary theory and in the 1930's wrote many "satirical essays" (*zawen*) attacking GMD policies, among other things. He was appointed to head the League of Left-Wing Writers in 1930 and was involved in many of the literary debates on the left. Although Lu Xun never joined the CCP and often criticized its dogmatism, he was canonized by the Party after his death in 1936.

Lu Yin 廬隱, or Huang Luyin 黃廬隱 (1889–1934)

A teacher, novelist, and short-story writer. A member of the Literary Research Association, Lu Yin's works were published mostly in *Xiaoshuo yuebao* and have been characterized as lyrical, subjective, and romantic.

Luo Guanzhong, *see Romance of the Three Kingdoms*

Mandarin Ducks and Butterfly School (Yuanyang hudie pai 鴛鴦蝴蝶派)

Also known as the "Saturday school," after one of its principal journals, *Libai liu* 禮 拜 六 (Saturday; 1914–23), the term "mandarin ducks and butterfly" fiction was coined by progressive May Fourth intellectuals to disparage popular urban fiction, often sentimental love stories (ducks and butterflies are symbols of love), as frivolous and lacking artistic merit and social responsibility. Most of the so-called Butterfly writers were based in Shanghai. Their fiction (divisible into several types: love, scandal, detective, kung-fu, and comic) was highly popular in the 1910's and 1920's, attracting the very audience the May Fourth writers sought.

Mao Dun 茅盾 (1896–1981)

Translator, literary theorist and historian, and one of modern China's greatest novelists. Mao Dun was a founder of the Literary Research Association and

one of the most important literary critics of the May Fourth period, introducing Chinese readers to a wide range of Western literature and literary thought,
foremost among which were realism and naturalism. His famous trilogy, entitled *Shi* 蝕 (Eclipse; 1927), won him national fame, and his novel *Ziye* 子 夜
(Midnight; 1933) was lauded by leftist critics as an outstanding product of
"revolutionary realism." He held many positions in the cultural apparatus
after 1949, including that of minister of culture.

May Fourth movement (Wusi yundong 五四運動; 1915–25)

Generally understood as the nationalist movement that swept through China
after the humiliating terms of the Versailles Treaty became public in 1919.
More broadly, it may be seen to encompass the New Culture movement, a
radical anti-traditional cultural revolution that began with the founding of
New Youth in 1915. With its roots in the disappointment over the lack of societal change after the revolution of 1911, the New Culture movement adopted
an iconoclastic stance toward the very foundations of Chinese culture, namely
the Confucian ethical tradition and the classical literary heritage. Among its
many advocates were Lu Xun, Chen Duxiu, Hu Shi, Li Dazhao, Wu Yu, Yi
Baisha, and Gao Yihan. With the May Fourth incident of 1919 and the rising
tide of nationalism, the ideals of the movement spread beyond this elite group
of foreign-educated intellectuals. The movement is also seen to have spawned
the birth of the Chinese Communist Party in 1921.

May Thirtieth Movement (Wusa yundong 五卅運動; 1925)

When soldiers working for the British fired on striking Chinese workers, killing several, a nationwide anti-imperialist protest movement ensued. This
movement is often depicted as a turning point in the history of modern China,
raising the political consciousness of intellectuals and causing many of them to
turn to Marxism.

Mei Guangdi 梅光迪 (1890–1945)

Foreign-language and literature specialist, classicist, translator, and teacher.
Mei was deeply influenced by the cultural and literary theories of Harvard
professor Irving Babbitt. Together with Wu Mi and Liu Boming, he published
Critical Review, a literary journal aimed at promoting traditional Chinese culture, in opposition to the iconoclastic agenda of the New Culture movement.

Mei Lanfang 梅蘭芳 (1894–1961)

The most famous twentieth-century Beijing opera actor, noted for his perfection of the *dan*, or female, leads (traditionally played by males), as well as for
his authorship of several dramas. He is also responsible for creating an international awareness and appreciation of Beijing opera, having performed in Japan, Russia, the United States, and Europe.

Mencius 孟子 (372–289 B.C.)

After Confucius, the single most influential philosopher of the Confucian
school. Many of his dialogues with famous rulers and thinkers of his day are
preserved in the book named after him. Promoting, among other things, the
innate goodness of the human heart-mind (*xin* 心), this book exerted an im-

mense influence on Chinese philosophy, culture, political thought, and literature, especially after A.D. 1177, when it was named one of the Four Books of
the neo-Confucian canon.

Mozi 墨子 (ca. 479–381 B.C.)

Philosopher of the Warring States period (403–221 B.C.). Mozi was a "militant
preacher" whose utilitarian teachings consciously opposed the Confucians, especially in the promotion of "universal love," which rejected the Confucian
stress on rituals and hierarchies and emphasized mutual love and equality
among all humans. The Mohists were also practitioners of a sort of militant
pacifism, training themselves as invincible military strategists who would then
threaten to defend to the death any city under assault, in order to prevent an
impending conflict.

Mu Shiying 穆時英 (1912–40)

Together with Liu Na'ou and Shi Zhecun, a leading member of the New Sensibilities school (Xin ganjue pai 新感覺派), which promoted a Western-style
literary modernism and experimented with psychoanalytic themes and
stream-of-consciousness narrative. With such works as *Nanbei ji* 南 北 極
(North Pole, South Pole; 1932), Mu earned a reputation as a sophisticated writer who portrayed the dark and decadent aspects of urban life. For accepting a
position in the Japanese puppet government after the fall of Shanghai, he was
assassinated by the Chinese underground, although current scholarship has
shown that Mu may have been a GMD informant and thus killed by mistake.

National Essence, *see* Liu Shipei; Zhang Binglin

Nationalist Party (GMD, or KMT) 國民黨 (est. 1912)

Formed in 1912 from Sun Yat-sen's Revolutionary Alliance (Tong Meng Hui
同 盟 會 , 1905), the GMD dominated the elections of that year and controlled
parliament. When the militarist Yuan Shikai dissolved parliament in 1913, the
GMD was banned and forced into exile. In 1919, the party was reorganized
with a revolutionary and nationalist platform. From its base in Canton, it developed an army under the leadership of Chiang Kai-shek. During the Northern Expedition (1926–28) the GMD united with the CCP to defeat the warlords
who had divided and ruled much of Eastern China. The GMD then split with
the CCP, forcing that party into remote areas of the interior, and setting itself
up as the first government of the newly united Republic of China in 1928. Unable to maintain its political and military hold on China, the GMD fled to Taiwan in 1949, where it is still the ruling party.

New Culture movement, *see* May Fourth movement

New Poetry (*Xin shi* 新詩)

A new style of poetry that emerged from the literary reform agenda of the
New Culture movement. Inspired by their exposure to Western poetry, Chinese poets began for the first time to promote a poetics that did not demand
fixed line and stanza lengths, obligatory tone variations, rhyme positions and
categories, classical literary language, and traditional themes and allusions,
characteristics of the classical Chinese poetics that still dominated poetry writ-

ing. Instead, they promoted poetry written in the vernacular language, with a greater range of theme and fewer formal regulations. Hu Shi is considered by many to be the first practitioner of the New Poetry, with the publication of his 1920 collection, *Changshi ji* 嘗試集 (Experiments); Guo Moruo's *Nüshen* 女神 (The goddesses; 1921) also played an important role in the development of the new poetry of China. Although the May Fourth did not generally acknowledge it, the late-Qing "poetic revolution" was an important precursor to the New Poetry.

New Youth (Xin qingnian 新青年; 1915–26)

Originally entitled *Qingnian zazhi* 青年雜誌 (New youth magazine), *New Youth* was established in Shanghai by Chen Duxiu in September 1915 and quickly became the leading forum of the New Culture movement. It sought to alert young Chinese to the activities of the increasingly repressive regime of Yuan Shikai and to promote the introduction of Western literature, ideas, and cultural values, especially science and democracy. The journal published polemics against all aspects of traditional culture (with a particular emphasis on Confucianism), as well as the essays on literary reform by Hu Shi and Chen Duxiu that began the May Fourth literary revolution. With editor Chen Duxiu's growing interest in Marxism, the journal took a radical political turn in 1920.

Northern Expedition, *see* Nationalist Party

Opium Wars (Yapian zhanzheng 鴉片戰爭; 1839–42; 1856–60)

When Chinese Commissioner Lin Zexu confiscated and burned British opium shipments in an attempt to halt the opium trade that was then devastating China, Britain and China went to war. With the Treaty of Nanjing (1842), the victorious British secured, among other things, rights to five treaty ports, unrestricted trading and residence rights, Hong Kong, and a huge indemnity. In the following year, the British added the "most favored nation" clause (in the Treaty of the Bogue), which guaranteed them the same privileges granted to any other nation under any other treaties in the future. When the Qing refused to adhere to the provisions of this clause, a second Opium War resulted, ending with the destruction of the Summer Palace in Beijing.

Ouyang Xiu 歐陽修 (1007–72)

In addition to being one of the Eight Great Prose Masters of the Tang and Song, Ouyang Xiu was an outstanding poet, statesman, philosopher, archaeologist, and historian. He is well known for his revival of and leadership in the Ancient-Style Prose movement, helping to promote a prose style inspired by the then nearly forgotten essays of Han Yu. Ouyang was also a poetic innovator, establishing a new genre in Chinese poetry criticism called "talks on poetry" (*shihua* 詩話), after his famous *Liuyi shihua* 六一詩話 (Liuyi's talks on poetry).

Qian Xingcun 錢杏邨 (1900–1977)

Literary critic and literary historian (under the name Ah Ying 阿英 he wrote extensively on the late Qing novel), and one of the founding members of the

Sun Society (1928). In 1928, Qian achieved immediate notoriety for a long article criticizing Lu Xun for being a dated, anachronistic writer (see Part III). Qian was a supporter of proletarian and revolutionary literature and used the pharse "literature of power" to promote the notion of literature as a powerful form of resistance to reality.

Qian Zhongshu 錢鍾書 (1910-)

Though primarily a scholar of classical literature, Qian's novel *Weicheng* 圍城 (Fortress Besieged; 1947), is considered one of the best in the history of modern Chinese literature. Qian is known for his eclectic literary studies written in a difficult classical style: *Tan yi lu* 談藝錄 and *Guanzhui pian* 管錐篇. He is also remembered for contributing to the growth of East-West comparative literary studies in China.

Qu Qiubai 瞿秋白 (1899–1935)

Qu was perhaps the first Marxist literary critic in China and among the first to attack May Fourth writers for their elitist use of a Western influenced literary style, what he called *yang bagu* 洋八股 (foreign eight-legged essays). He was an early proponent of popularization in literature. His translations from the Russian introduced intellectuals to Marxist literary theory, and his views on literature influenced many, including Mao Zedong. Qu was appointed secretary of the CCP's Central Committee in 1927 but was removed from the post the same year, being held responsible for, among other things, the collapse of the party after the April coup by the GMD. Ill and unable to flee with his fellow CCP members on the Long March, Qu was captured and executed by the GMD in 1935.

Qu Yuan 屈原 (340?–278 B.C.)

Known as China's first great poet, Qu Yuan was a loyal and trusted high minister of the Chu king but was alienated from the court through the machinations of jealous rivals. Qu continued to contend the court's unwise policies and was soon banished to the distant south, eventually taking his own life in disappointment and protest. His heroic suicide is still celebrated as a holiday today. It is believed that Qu authored many of the poems in the *Chuci* 楚辭 (Songs of Chu), including the long, imaginative, allegorical *Li sao* 離騷 (Encountering sorrow), considered one of the greatest poems in ancient Chinese literature. Qu was revered and mythified by the moderns as a heroic voice of protest and as a nationalist.

Records of the Grand Historian (Shiji 史記)

Written by the great Han historian Sima Qian (ca. 145–ca. 85 BC), this was the first comprehensive history of China and became the structural model for most subsequent historical texts. In 130 chapters, it covers approximately three thousand years, ranging from the period of the legendary Yellow Emperor to that of Emperor Wu of Sima's day. Its lively literary style and engrossing narrative techniques aptly demonstrate the difficulty in distinguishing between belles lettres and strictly factual history in traditional Chinese literature. For this reason, it has also had a profound impact upon later Chinese fiction.

Regulated Verse (*lüshi* 律詩)

Regulated verse became an established poetic form around the beginning of the Tang dynasty. In contrast to ancient-style verse, regulated verse is characterized by complex, strict metrical rules governing line and stanza length, rhyme, parallel phrasing, and tonal pattern. (Together with the shorter quatrain, regulated verse is also known as *jinti shi* 近體詩, modern-style poetry). Having become somewhat jaded after centuries of use (mastery of it was required of all scholars and poets), regulated verse fell into disfavor and was attacked by May Fourth literary reformers as stilted, artificial, and anachronistic.

Revolutionary Alliance, *see* Nationalist Party

Romance of the Three Kingdoms (*Sanguo zhi yanyi* 三國志演義)

Ming novel allegedly written by Luo Guanzhong 羅貫中 (dates uncertain). This historical novel recounts the events of the Three Kingdoms period (220–65) in which three states fought for hegemony. It is one of the most famous of Chinese novels, and its many heroic characters are part of the Chinese cultural consciousness.

Romance of the Western Chamber (*Xixiang ji* 西廂記)

A masterpiece of northern-style *zaju* drama generally attributed to Wang Shifu 王實甫 (fl. 13th c.). The story centers around the love affair between a young student and his distant cousin, struggling against societal and familial constraints. The skillful blend of action, humor, and romance elevate it to the highest levels of theatrical achievement.

Shen Congwen 沈從文 (1902–88)

Teacher, editor, essayist, Crescent Moon Society member, and one of the most prolific and important fiction writers in modern times. Shen won fame with the publication of *Biancheng* 邊城 (Border town; 1934), a novella that depicts the life and customs of people living in his remote home of West Hunan. As much of his fiction was set in this region, Shen is often considered a "nativist" or "regionalist" writer. He shunned the political orientation of his contemporaries and during the War of Resistance even wrote an essay denouncing the unhealthy influence of political and cultural tsars on literature. Shen was criticized after 1949 and attempted suicide; he eventually took up the study of ancient Chinese clothing as a worker in the National Historical Museum.

Shi Nai'an 施耐庵, *see Water Margin*

Shihua 詩話 (Talks on poetry)

A genre of traditional Chinese literary criticism that consists of random, subjective comments on selected poems, fellow critics' views, or various other aspects of Chinese poetry. *Shihua* entries may vary from one or two lines to several pages in length but are not joined together in consistent, well-developed argument. Ouyang Xiu's famous *Liuyi shihua* 六一詩話 (Liuyi's talks on poetry) is considered the first example of this literary form.

Sikong Tu 司空圖 (837–908)

A poet of the late Tang period, Sikong Tu is remembered in literary history for his esoteric work *Ershisi shipin* 二十四詩品 (The twenty-four moods of poetry), which is usually considered one of the most important works of Tang literary criticism. A classic example of the "poems on poetry" genre (*see also* Lu Ji), it consists of twenty-four short poems in rhymed, pentasyllabic couplets, each with a terse two-word title. That these poems make few references to known poetry or other theories of poetics is tied to Sikong Tu's own belief that the essence of poetry is "a meaning beyond flavor," and "an image beyond the image." Such ideas and expressions, with their roots in Daoism and Chan Buddhism, have had a profound influence on some later critics.

Sima Qian, *see Records of the Grand Historian*

Song Yu 宋玉 (ca. 290-ca. 223 B.C.)

Warring States (403-221 B.C.) figure about whom almost nothing is known. Song's importance in the history of Chinese literature rests wholly on a handful of poems from the *Chuci* collection, the *Jiu bian* 九辯 (Nine Arguments), that are normally attributed to him.

Southern Society (Nanshe 南社)

Founded in 1909 by a group of poets from Jiangsu, among whom were Chen Qubing 陳去病 (1883-?), Gao Xu 高旭 (1887-1925), Huang Jie 黃節 (1874-1935), and Liu Yazi 劉亞子 (1887-1958), the Southern Society members had close ties to the Revolutionary Alliance and the National Essence circle. In poetry, its members generally followed the Jiangxi style of Huang Tingjian; as such they were deemed imitative, anachronistic, and flowery by May Fourth critics.

Story of the Stone, see Dream of the Red Chamber

Su Shi 蘇軾 (Su Dongpo 蘇東坡; 1037-1101)

One of the true geniuses of the Chinese cultural tradition, at the age of twenty Su had already passed the *jinshi* level of the civil service exam and would go on to excel in regulated verse, *ci, fu,* prose essays, calligraphy, and painting. Su is well known as an innovator in *ci* poetry, and for establishing the *haofang* 豪放 (heroic abandon) style of writing. Often mentioned as one of the Three Su's (along with his father and younger brother), all of whom are counted among the Eight Great Prose Masters of the Tang and Song.

Su Wen 蘇汶, or Du Heng 杜衡 (1907-64)

Novelist, translator, and literary theorist, Su is mostly remembered for his dispute with Lu Xun and other left-wing writers in the 1930's. As one of the representatives of the Third Category school, he argued for literature's independence from politics, for which he was fiercely criticized by left-wing writers.

Sun Society (Taiyang she 太陽社; 1928)

An important literary group, the first to be founded with the express purpose of propagating a Marxist literature of the working classes, challenging the Creation Society's claim to being the vanguard of the revolutionary literature movement. Eventually, these two leftist groups reconciled and together focused their energies in an attack on Lu Xun and his magazine *Yusi* (Spinner of words). Founders of the Sun Society included Jiang Guangci and Qian Xingcun, who promoted their ideas through the society's journal, *Taiyang yuekan* 太陽月刊 (Sun monthly; Jan.–July 1928). All members of the group belonged to the CCP.

Sun Yat-sen 孫逸仙 (1866–1925)

Sun is known as the father of the 1911 revolution that overthrew the Qing. After the revolution, Sun focused his efforts on establishing a unified China under a national democratic government. Sun died (1925) before he could witness the success of the Northern Expedition and the unification of China under the GMD. Sun's political theories, especially the concept of the Five-power Constitution and Three Principles of the People are still influential in Taiwan.

Taiping Rebellion 太平起義 (1851–64)

A social, political, religious, and military movement led by the charismatic Hong Xiuquan, who claimed to be the younger brother of Jesus Christ. In addition to overthrowing the Manchus (Qing dynasty), the rebel platform promised to establish a Heavenly Kingdom of Great Peace that would put an end to opium trafficking, conduct land reform, promote women's equality and rights, and establish commune-like economic communities. From their humble origins in Guangxi province, the rebels gained control of much of southeastern and south-central China, eventually establishing their capital in Nanjing. Suffering from infighting, corruption, and decadence among its leaders, combined with the assault by General Zeng Guofan's troops, the rebellion was eventually suppressed, but the total cost in lives is estimated to have exceeded twenty million. There are significant similarities between CCP policies and those of the Taipings.

Tan Sitong 譚嗣同 (1865–98)

One of the young reform-minded Confucian scholars who, with Kang Youwei, launched what came to be known as the Hundred Days' Reforms (1898). The educational, social, military, and political reforms they submitted through petition to the throne were at first enthusiastically received by the young Guangxu emperor, but were also perceived as a threat to the power of his aunt, the Empress Dowager Cixi, who promptly imprisoned Guangxu and rounded up and executed as many of the reformers as could be caught. Both Tan and Kang's brother were among the martyred. Tan is also known for his *Renxue* 仁學 (Study of benevolence; 1896), which in its attack on *li*, or ritual, may be seen as an important precursor to May Fourth iconoclasm, although Tan was working within Confucian parameters.

Tao Qian, *see* Tao Yuanming

Tao Yuanming 陶淵明 (365–427)

One of the greatest pre-Tang poets, Tao Yuanming is loved not only for his philosophical, pastoral ("fields and gardens"), and wine-drinking poems, but also for his essay "Taohua yuanji" 桃花源記 (Record of Peach Blossom Spring), a picturesque account of a hidden utopian community. His simple, direct, unembellished style, combined with the originality of his natural images, has established him as the foremost master of the traditional five-character-line ancient-style verse.

Third Category (Disanzhong ren 第三種人)

A concept proposed by Su Wen in 1932, following the lead of Hu Qiuyuan's notion of the Free Man. Both writers claimed a position for the writer between the revolutionary and the more conservative, GMD-affiliated camp. They wanted writing to come from beyond class affiliation and thus advocated the independence of literature from politics, for which they incurred fierce criticism from the League of Left-Wing Writers. Lacking both numbers and organization, the Third Category group had neither leverage nor influence in its dispute with Lu Xun and other left-wing writers.

Tongcheng school (Tongcheng pai 桐城派)

One of the leading schools of classical prose literature at the end of the Qing dynasty. The school took its name from Tongcheng county in Anhui province, home of its originators, Fang Bao 方苞 (1668-1749), Liu Dakui 劉大魁 (1698-1780), and Yao Nai 姚鼐 (1731-1815), whose prose styles—characterized by elegance and purity of language—were widely imitated by scholars throughout China. Revived by Zeng Guofan in the middle of the nineteenth century and carried on in the writings and translations of Yan Fu and Lin Shu, it dominated the Chinese literary world until the fall of the Qing. May Fourth literary reformers were particularly virulent in their attack on this school, which upheld the didactic principle that "literature" should "convey the *Dao*."

Wang Dungen 王鈍根 (no dates)

An important figure of the Mandarin Ducks and Butterfly school. Originally a writer and editor of a fiction column in one of China's earliest newspapers, *Shenbao* 申報 (est. 1872), Wang left the paper to try his hand at editing popular fiction magazines. He met with great success, founding several periodicals, including *Libai liu* 禮拜六 (Saturday; 1914-23), which became coterminous with the Mandarin Ducks and Butterfly school.

Wang Fuzhi 王夫之 (1619-92)

Philosopher, classics scholars, historian, and poet, Wang is also remembered for his work as a literary theorist and critic. One key concept of his poetic theory is his argument for poetry as a free and independent human activity that helps man in his conscious effort to attain harmony with the universe and should therefore not be forced to accord with artificial rules, *fa* 法 . Wang also argued for a more sophisticated understanding of poetic language, stating that *qing* 情 (emotion) and *jing* 景 (scene, setting) are not easily distinguishable poetic devices or concrete, separate aspects of reality, but intricately interrelated phenomena.

Wang Guowei 王國維 (1877-1927)

A prominent scholar, translator, critic and literary theorist of the late Qing, Wang was lauded by some as the greatest *ci* poet since the Song. His influential work of literary criticism, *Renjian cihua* 人間詞話 (Talks on lyric meters in the human world), the first work of Chinese literary theory to cite Western sources, expounds his belief that poetry should be a spontaneous, "unobstructed" (*buge* 不隔) expression, a fusion of the poet's feelings and the scene around him, which Wang summarized in his concept of the "poetic world" (*jingjie* 境界). He was a pioneer in the application of Western thought (particularly the ideas of Kant, Schopenhauer, and Nietzsche) to the study of Chinese literature, and his commentary on *Dream of the Red Chamber* is one of the first modern critical studies of that novel.

Wang Shiwei 王實味 (1900–1946)

A major translator of Marxist works, CCP member, and essayist, Wang was criticized during the Yan'an Rectification movement of 1942 and later executed under mysterious circumstances that have only recently come to light. His 1942 essays, "Wild Lilies" and "Politicians and Artists," were partly responsible for sparking Mao Zedong to give his "Yan'an Talks" and initiate the rectification of intellectuals.

Wang Shizhen 王士禎 (1634–1711)

Poet, anthologist, essayist, editor, and literary critic of the seventeenth century, Wang was among the more prolific writers of his day. He tried to make all his works attain to his own aesthetic-poetic standards, which involved combining traditional learning with individual creative expression. He believed that in literary texts this would reflect an intuitive, enlightened understanding of reality that is always charged with the inner spirit and mood of the poet. He defined writing that embodied such qualities as *shenyun* 神 韻 (spirit / spiritual and personal tone / mood).

Water Margin (*Shuihu zhuan* 水滸傳)

One of the greatest traditional Chinese novels, often attributed to Shi Nai'an 施耐庵 (Yuan) and sometimes to Luo Guanzhong. Originating in oral storytelling and existing in many written versions, ranging from 71 to 120 chapters, *The Water Margin* tells the story of Song Jiang and his band of outlaws who operate out of a mountain outpost. Due to its blatantly rebellious political content, in premodern times it was considered seditious and occasionally banned. The novel was a favorite of Mao Zedong. (Also translated as *All Men Are Brothers* and *Outlaws of the Marsh*.)

Wen Yiduo 聞一多 (1899–1946)

Wen belonged to what is sometimes called the New Formalist School of Poetry (Xin gelü shipai 新 格 律 詩派) which advocated careful attention to structure and meter in modern vernacular poetry. Wen's poetry collection, *Sishui* 死 水 (Stagnant waters; 1929), aptly demonstrated his poetics, proving that a vernacular poet could write good poetry while "dancing in fetters." The poems in this collection also closely follow his three-point dictum that poetry must possess "musical, pictorial, and architectural beauty." In addition to being a member of the Crescent Moon Society, Wen also made significant contributions to the study of Tang poetry, the *Book of Songs*, and the *Chuci*. Wen was assassinated by GMD agents in July 1946 for his outspoken criticism.

Wenxuan school (Wenxuan pai 文選派)

A literary group, whose members included Zhang Bingling, Wang Kaiyun 王 闓運 (1832–1916), Liu Shipei, and Huang Kan 黃 侃 (1886–1935), which promoted the imitation of the poetry and prose styles of ancient writers canonized in the highly influential *Wenxuan* anthology, compiled by Xiao Tong (A.D. 501–31), a style characterized by dense allusion and parallelism. Members of this group often saw in this literary style hope for the preservation of a traditional Chinese cultural essence. Wenxuan followers had great influence at Peking University during the 1910's and were often criticized by their radical colleagues.

Wu Woyao 吳沃堯 (1866–1910)

A journalist and well-known writer of fiction in Shanghai at the turn of the twentieth century. Wu's most famous novels include *Ershinian mudu zhi guai xianzhuang* 二十年目睹之怪現狀 (Strange events seen in the past twenty years; serialized 1905–10), and *Henhai* 恨海 (Sea of woe; 1906). The latter has been labeled a novel of sentiment and seen as a precursor of both the Mandarin Ducks and Butterfly love stories and May Fourth romanticism.

Wu Yu 吳虞 (1871–1949)

Professor at Peking University (having studied law and political science in Japan) and outspoken critic of the traditional clan structure and Confucian learning and ethics. His articles in *New Youth*, such as "Chiren yu lijiao" 吃人與禮教 (Cannibalism and Confucian ethics; 1919), established him as one of the leading voices of May Fourth anti-Confucianism.

Xie Lingyun 謝靈運 (385–443)

Scholar, painter, and calligrapher, Xie is recognized as one of the greatest lyric poets of the Six Dynasties (220–589) period. Known as China's first famous nature poet, Xie is credited with being the father of landscape ("mountains and streams") poetry.

Xin Qiji 辛棄疾 (1140–1207)

With over 600 *ci* lyrics to his name and a master of over 101 different tunes, Xin was one of the most prolific writers in the genre. His erudition also helped him to contribute to the development of the genre, as he freely borrowed from the poetic tradition, historical and philosophical works, and other sources, thereby expanding the length and scope of *ci*. Xin also earned a reputation for his mastery of poetic allusion as well as for his patriotic poetry.

Xu Zhimo 徐志摩 (1895–1931)

One of the most important modern Chinese poets. Xu was sent by his family to America to study economics, but transferred to Cambridge (England) to study literature and there became an ardent admirer of the Romantics, especially Shelley and Keats. While a professor at Peking University, he and Wen Yiduo established the Crescent Moon Society and founded *Shikan* 詩刊 (Poetry journal; 1926). Xu's first book of poems, the passionate and lyrical *Zhimo de shi* 志摩的詩 (Poems of Zhimo; 1925) was enthusiastically received by both critics and readers, and he was dubbed the most promising of the young poets. His later work became increasingly concerned with regulated forms and metrical patterns, as is reflected in the poetics he and Wen propagated under the banner of the New Formalist School of Poetry (xin gelü shipai 新格律詩派). Xu's life was cut short by a plane crash.

Yan Fu 嚴復 (1854–1921)

A publisher, translator, naval affairs expert, educator, and poet of the late Qing, Yan was the most knowledgeable scholar of Western thought in China at the turn of the century. Along with Lin Shu, he ranks as the greatest translator of his age, rendering into classical Chinese the writings of Thomas Huxley, Adam Smith, Herbert Spencer, John Stuart Mill, Edward Jenks, Montesquieu, and William S. Jevons. He possessed a mastery of classical prose style (of the Tongcheng variety) and accompanied his translations with thoughtful commentary. His ability to make useful comparisons between the Western author's ideas and those of certain Chinese thinkers made his translations very popular among educated readers. His writings and translations emphasized the need to transform China into a strong and powerful nation by unleashing the dynamic potentialities of the individual.

Ye Shengtao 葉聖陶, or Shaojun 紹鈞 (1894–1988)

One of the founding members of the Literary Research Association, Ye is conventionally thought to have written the first novel in the modern vernacular, *Ni Huanzhi* 倪煥之 (1929), about the gradual disillusionment of an intellectual from the May Fourth to the May Thirtieth movement. Ye began his literary career writing popular fiction in the classical language for the magazine *Libai liu* 禮拜六, but quit in 1917 when he fell under the influence of the the New Culture movement. He was a prolific short-story writer and was also involved in teaching throughout most of his life.

Yi Baisha 易白沙 (1886–1921)

Yi wrote the first *New Youth* article directly attacking Confucianism, entitled "Kongzi pingyi" 孔子評議 (Critique of Confucius; 1915). This theme would be picked up and elaborated on by Chen Duxiu and, most notably, in Wu Yu's acrid polemics. Frustrated by his own view of China's political future, Yi Baisha committed suicide in 1921.

Yu Dafu 郁達夫 (1896–1945)

A founder of the Creation Society, Yu gained critical attention with his story "Chenlun" 沈淪 (Sinking; 1921) and acquired a reputation as a melancholy romantic individualist. He and other Creation Society members became increasingly ardent advocates of socialism and revolutionary literature in the mid- to late-1920's. By the mid-1920's, however, Yu showed signs of a disenchantment with the Creationists' radicalization; he finally broke with them in 1927. During the Japanese occupation, he worked as an editor in Malaysia and Singapore, and was assassinated by the Japanese military police in September 1945. Yu published many short stories and autobiographical writings.

Yuan Mei 袁枚 (1716–98)

Teacher, administrator, and a prolific essayist and poet, Yuan is best known for his work as a literary critic. His advocacy of personal sentiments as the poet's most important guide and inspiration is contained in the term *xingling* 性

靈 (native sensibility). His rejection of the common practice of imitating past masters complements this concept.

Yuan Shikai 袁世凱 (1859–1916)

General of the large Beiyang army, Yuan was an opportunist who supported the Empress Dowager Cixi, but later aided the rebels in the overthrow of the Qing, after which he became one of the most powerful men in China. Owing to this fact, Sun Yat-sen offered him the presidency of China's first republic in 1912, which Yuan eagerly accepted. He then promptly abolished the parliament and began to establish an autocracy, eventually declaring himself emperor in 1915. He died the following year, but this restoration helped push many intellectuals to adopt a more pessimistic and outspoken critical stance toward traditional Chinese cultural values and those who upheld them.

Yusi 語絲 (Spinner of Words, 1924–31)

Literary society founded by Zhou Zuoren, Lu Xun, Sun Fuyuan, and others, with the object of providing a literary environment free from any dogma and accepting of any subject matter that might catch an author's fancy. The motto of the society, *quwei* 趣味 (interest, taste, or liking), was put forth in their literary journal, *Spinner of Words*, 1924–31. As the literary environment grew increasingly political and after the Zhou brothers had a falling out, the group's ideals became more difficult to uphold.

Zeng Guofan 曾國藩 (1811–72)

Although best known as the military leader who suppressed the Taiping Rebellion, Zeng was a proponent of the Tongcheng literary school in prose that was associated with Song neo-Confucianism. In spite of his traditional literary tendencies, some of his straightforward, succinct prose earned the praise of writers of vernacular literature in the May Fourth era.

Zeng Pu 曾樸 (1872–1935)

Zeng is best remembered for his novel of social criticism, *Niehai hua* 孽海花 (Flower on a sea of evil; 1905), something of a roman à clef, portraying the degenerate life of scholars and bureaucrats in late Qing society. Due to its sensational content, the book and its author earned immediate fame when it was first published in a twenty-chapter form in 1905 (it was expanded in later editions, and two other authors wrote sequels). The first five chapters of the novel were written by a friend who asked Zeng to finish it for him.

Zhang Ailing 張愛玲 (1921–)

One of the few well-known woman writers working out of occupied Shanghai in the 1940's. She was little remembered until the 1960's when the American sinologist C. T. Hsia gave his highest praise to and later anthologized an English translation of her now famous work, "Jinsuo ji" 金鎖記 (The golden cangue; 1943). There was a Zhang Ailing craze among writers and readers in Taiwan in the 1980's.

Zhang Binglin 章炳麟 (1868–1936)

Anti-Manchu revolutionary and member of the Revolutionary Alliance, classical scholar, linguist, orthographer, and educator. During the last decade of the Qing, his patriotic lectures in Japan inspired young Chinese intellectuals such as Lu Xun. Zhang was also associated with the journal *Guocui xuebao* 國粹學報 (Journal of the national essence) and wrote essays in the Wenxuan style. After the 1911 revolution, as a faculty member at Peking University, Zhang was among the older, more conservative scholars who ardently opposed the New Culture movement, and from 1924 to 1926 he served as editor-in-chief of *Huaguo yuekan* 華國月刊 (1923–), a periodical publishing articles opposed to the movement. He established his own school for the preservation of Chinese tradition in Suzhou in 1935.

Zhang Daofan 張道藩 (1896–1968)

Playwright, GMD member, educator, politician, and essayist. After studying the fine arts in England and France, Zhang returned to China and became a secretary in the GMD. He also held several administrative positions at universities around the country and promoted the GMD's cultural and literary policies. Hoping to counter the leftists' domination in the area of literary theory, in 1942 he wrote an article entitled "Women suo xuyao de wenyi zhengce" 我們所需要的文藝政策 (Our urgently needed literary policy), published in the GMD-supported *Wenyi xianfeng* 文藝先鋒 (Literary vanguard). In this article he proposed a new literature based on Sun Yat-sen's Three Principles of the People, but his ideas were confusing and uninspiring and failed to garner the kind of support Mao Zedong's "Yan'an Talks" did, although they shared many basic ideas about the relationship between art and politics.

Zhang Dongsun 張東蓀 (1886–)

Zhang was one of a group of former Qing officials who founded the Aspiration Society (Shangzhi xuehui 尚志學會 ; 1918), dedicated to introducing Western culture to China by sponsoring visits and lectures by Western thinkers. Inspired by the ideas of Russell and John Dewey, Zhang promoted a guild socialist movement in China, encouraging a period of capitalism that would lead eventually to socialism, touching off a debate with other socialists in 1920. Zhang was also involved in the 1923 debate on science and metaphysics, supporting Carsun Chang in his promotion of Chinese metaphysics over Western science. Zhang later came to support a blend of Western science with traditional Chinese spiritual culture.

Zhang Ziping 張資平 (1893–59)

Founding member of the Creation Society and writer of romantic fiction. Zhang's fiction was criticized by some critics for its unhealthy obsession with sexual matters and love affairs. Zhang was later labeled a national traitor for having accepted a position with the Japanese government in Shanghai.

Zheng Zhenduo 鄭振鐸 (1898–1958)

Zheng was one of the founding members of the Literary Research Association. In his critical essays, he promoted fictional "realism" grounded in pain and loss, a "literature of blood and tears" (*xue he lei de wenxue* 血和淚的文學). A talented writer, teacher, and devoted scholar of traditional fiction, Zheng died in a plane crash while working for the Ministry of Culture in 1958.

Zhou Shoujuan 周瘦鵑 (1895–1968)

Popular fiction writer and editor of Mandarin Ducks and Butterfly fiction. Zhou was a leading contributor to *Saturday*. He started several fiction magazines, edited others, and contributed to several popular light-fiction columns in newspapers. He also translated European and American short stories, for which he was commended by Lu Xun.

Zhou Yang 周揚 (1908–89)

CCP member who held a variety of high-level administrative positions in the League of Left-Wing Writers, Zhou Yang represented the party line in many of the literary debates of the 1930's and 1940's. He was head of the Lu Xun Academy of Arts in Yan'an during the war and in the post-1949 period held a variety of high-level cultural positions, including chair of the Writers Union and vice-minister of culture, through which he exerted a repressive control over cultural life. Zhou was attacked during the Cultural Revolution.

Zhou Zuoren 周作人 (1885–1967)

Younger brother of Lu Xun and collaborator on a collection of translations of Eastern European and Russian short fiction (1909), the first of its kind in China. Zhou was appointed to Peking University in 1917 where he taught literature and contributed essays to leading May Fourth journals. He was a founding member of the Literary Research Association and in 1924 established with his brother the journal *Yusi* (Spinner of words). While his brother's writings became gradually more political, Zhou wrote essays, in a semi-classical style, on a variety of benign subjects. During the War of Resistance, Zhou remained in Beijing where he was forced to join the collaborationist government as head of the Bureau of Education. He was tried and imprisoned after the war as a collaborator.

Zhu Guangqian 朱光潛 (1897–1986)

Zhu was the leading aesthetician of the modern period. Grounded in the prose writings of his native Tongcheng (Anhui), Zhu studied Western philosophy and aesthetics for eight years in Edinburgh and Strasbourg. His major works on aesthetics and literary criticism, *Tan mei* 談 美 (Discussions on beauty; 1932), *Shixue* 詩學 (Poetics; 1933), and *Wenyi xinli xue* 文藝心理學 (The psychology of literature and art; 1936), show the marked influence of Kant, Schopenhauer, and particularly Croce. Zhu's popularized works on aesthetics were widely read in the 1930's and 1940's. His emphasis on the aesthetic dimension of art was at odds with the prevailing views of his contemporaries for art's political utility.

Zhu Xi 朱熹 (1130–1200)

Zhu Xi is considered the central figure of the Sung revival of Confucianism known as neo-Confucianism. He compiled and commented on the Four Books (*Great Learning, Analects, Doctrine of the Mean,* and *Mencius*), which became the core of the neo-Confucian canon. His *Jinsi lu* 近思錄 (Reflections on things at hand), a collection of the sayings of four neo-Confucian masters, is generally recognized as the most important work of the rationalist Lixue 理學, or school of Principles, that dominated Chinese politics, philosophy, and culture until the late Qing period. (*See also* Cheng Yi.)

Zhu Ziqing 朱自清 (1898–1948)

Zhu's interest in the 1920's was in promoting the New Poetry, to which he contributed some verse he later described as somewhat puerile, owing to the fledgling state of vernacular poetry at that time. He edited the modern poetry volume of the 1934 collection *Zhongguo xin wenxue daxi* 中國新文學大系 (Anthology of modern Chinese literature). Zhu is also considered one of the great prose stylists of modern Chinese literature and made important contributions to the study of classical Chinese literature.

Zuo Commentary (*Zuo zhuan* 左傳)

The earliest history of the political, social, and military events of the Spring and Autumn period (722–481 B.C.) and the first sustained narrative work in early Chinese literature. In addition to its inestimable value as a genuine historical text, the *Zuo Commentary* is also one of the classics of traditional Chinese prose, possessing vivid descriptive details and at times great dramatic power. It had a tremendous influence on later histories and literature. The text as we have it was probably compiled in the Warring States period (403–221 B.C.).

Bibliography

Abbreviations:

CZSZL, see *Chuangzao she ziliao*.
GMWX, see *Geming wenxue lunzheng ziliao xuanbian*.
LGKH, see *"Liangge kouhao" lunzheng ziliao xuanbian*.
WXYDSLX, see *Wenxue yundong shiliao xuan*.
XHGM, see *Xinhai geming qian shinian jianqi lunwen ji*.
YYHDP, see *Yuanyang hudie pai wenxue ziliao*.
ZGJDLWX, see *Zhongguo jindai lunwen xuan*.
ZGXDWLX, see *Zhongguo xiandai wenlun xuan*.
ZGXDWXCKZL, see *Zhongguo xiandai wenxue cankao ziliao*.

A Ying 阿英. 1960. *Wan Qing wenxue congchao: xiaoshuo xiqu yanjiu juan* 晚清文學叢鈔:小說戲曲研究卷 (An anthology of late Qing literature: fiction and drama research). Beijing: Zhonghua shuju.
———. 1935. *Xiandai Zhongguo wenxue lun* 現代中國文學論 (On modern Chinese literature). Shanghai: Caihua shulin.
Abrams, M. H. 1953 *The Mirror and the Lamp: Romantic Theory and the Critical Tradition*. London: Oxford University Press.

Acton, Harold, and Shih-hsiang Chen, trs. and eds. 1936. *Modern Chinese Poetry*. London: Duckworth.

Ahmad, Aijiz. 1987. "Jameson's Rhetoric of Otherness and the 'National Allegory.' " *Social Text: Theory/Culture /Ideology* 17: 3–25.

Ai Xiaoming 艾曉明. 1991. *Zhongguo zuoyi wenxue sichao tanyuan* 中國左翼文學思潮探源 (In search of the roots of the Chinese leftist literary movement). Changsha: Hunan wenyi.

Anderson, Marston. 1989. "The Specular Self: Subjective and Mimetic Elements in the Fiction of Ye Shaojun." *Modern China* 15, no.1 (Jan.): 76–82.

———. 1990. *The Limits of Realism: Chinese Fiction in the Revolutionary Period*. Berkeley: University of California Press.

Auerbach, Erich. 1953. *Mimesis: The Representation of Reality in Western Literature*. Princeton: Princeton University Press.

Babbitt, I. 1919. *Rousseau and Romanticism*. Boston: Houghton Mifflin.

Barlow, Tani. 1991. "*Zhishifenzi* [Chinese Intellectuals] and Power." *Dialectical Anthropology* 16: 209–32.

Baxandall, Lee, and Stefan Morawski, eds. 1973. *Marx and Engels on Literature and Art: A Selection of Writings*. St. Louis: Telos Press.

Becker, George. 1963. *Documents of Modern Literary Realism*. Princeton: Princeton University Press.

Berninghausen, John, and Theodore Huters, eds. 1976. *Revolutionary Literature in China: An Anthology*. White Plains, N.Y.: M. E. Sharpe.

Bernstein, Richard J. 1983. *Beyond Objectivism and Relativism: Science, Hermeneutics and Praxis*. Philadelphia: University of Pennsylvania Press.

Bing Xin 冰心. 1982. *Bing Xin lun chuangzuo* 冰心論創作 (Bing Xin on creativity). Shanghai: Shanghai wenyi.

Birch, Cyril, ed. 1965. *Anthology of Chinese Literature*. 2 vols. New York: Grove Press.

Bonner, Joey. 1986. *Wang Kuo-wei: An Intellectual Biography*. Cambridge, Mass.: Harvard University Press.

Borland, Harriet. 1950. *Soviet Literary Theory and Practice during the First Five-Year Plan, 1928–32*. New York: King's Crown Press, Columbia University.

Bush, Susan, and Christian Murck, eds. 1983. *Theories of Art in China*. Princeton: Princeton University Press.

———. 1985. *Early Chinese Texts on Painting*. Cambridge, Mass.: Harvard-Yenching Institute.

Cao Shunqing 曹順慶. 1988. *ZhongXi bijiao shixue* 中西比較詩學 (Sino-Western comparative poetics). Beijing: Beijing chubanshe.

Chan, Stephen Chingkiu. 1986. "Realism as Cultural and Historical Transformation in Post-May Fourth China: Some Preliminary Analyses." *Tamkang Review* 16, no. 4 (Summer): 363–80.

———. 1993. "Split China, or, The Historical / Imaginary: Toward a Theory of Displacement of Subjectivity at the Margins of Modernity." In Liu Kang and Xiaobin Tang, eds. *Politics, Ideology, and Literary Discourse in Modern China: Theoretical Interventions and Cultural Critique.* Durham: Duke University Press, 70–101.

Chan, Sylvia. 1983. "Realism or Socialist Realism?: The 'Proletarian' Episode in Modern Chinese Literature 1927–32." *The Australian Journal of Chinese Affairs* 9 (January): 55–74.

Chang, Hao. 1976. "Neo-Confucianism and the Intellectual Crisis of Contemporary China." In Charlotte Furth, ed., *The Limits of Change: Essays on Conservative Alternatives in Republican China.* Cambridge, Mass.: Harvard University Press, 276–302.

———. 1987. *Chinese Intellectuals in Crisis: Search for Order and Meaning, 1890–1911.* Berkeley: University of California Press.

Chang Hao 張灝. 1989a. *You'an yishi yu minzhu chuantong* 幽暗意識與民主傳統 (Dark consciousness and the democratic tradition). Taibei: Lianjing.

———. 1989b. "Xingxiang yu shizhi: zai ren Wusi sixiang" 形象與實質: 再認五四思想 (Form and substance: a new understanding of May Fourth thought). In Wei Zhengtong, ed., *Ziyou minzhu de sixiang yu wenhua* 自由民主的思想與文化 (Liberal democratic thought and culture). Taibei: Zili bao, 23–57

Chaves, Jonathan. 1977. "The Legacy of Ts'ang Chieh: The Written Word as Magic." *Oriental Art* 23, no. 2 (Summer): 200–215.

———. 1982. "Not the Way of Poetry: The Poetics of Experience in the Sung Dynasty." *Chinese Literature: Essays, Articles and Reviews* 4: 199–212.

———. 1985. "The Expression of Self in the Kung-an School: Non-Romantic Individualism." In Robert E. Hegel and Richard Hessney, eds., *Expressions of Self in Chinese Literature.* New York: Columbia University Press, 123–50

Chen Jingzhi 陳敬之. 1986. *Wenxue yanjiu hui yu Chuangzao she* 文學研究會與創造社 (The Literary Research Association and the Creation Society). Taibei: Chengwen.

Chen, Xiaomei. 1992. "Occidentalism as Counterdiscourse: 'Heshang' in Post-Mao China." *Critical Inquiry* 18, no. 4 (Summer): 686–712.

Chen, Yu-shih. 1986. *Realism and Allegory in the Early Fiction of Mao Tun.* Bloomington: Indiana University Press.

Cheng, Gek Nai. 1984. "Fiction for National Salvation: The Dominant Chinese View of Fiction in the 1900s." *Chinese Culture* 25, no. 3 (Sept.): 81–92.

Cheng Jincheng. 1987. "Lun Zhongguo xiandai wenxue de keguan zaixian yu zhuguan biaoxian" 論中國現代文學的客觀再現與主觀表現 (On objective mimesis and subjective expression in modern Chinese literature). *Wenxue pinglun* 3: 4–14.

Cheng, Zhongyuan. 1984. "On Verifying 'Ge Te' as the Pseudonym of Zhang Wentian." *Social Sciences in China* 1: 36–48.

Chou Chih-p'ing. 1988. *Yuan Hung-tao and the Kung-an School*. Cambridge, Eng.: Cambridge University Press.

Chou, Min-chih. 1984. *Hu Shih and Intellectual Choice in Modern China*. Ann Arbor: University of Michigan Press.

Chow, Rey. 1986–87. "Rereading Mandarin Ducks and Butterflies: A Response to the 'Postmodern' Condition." *Cultural Critique* 5 (Winter): 69–93.

———. 1991. *Woman and Chinese Modernity*. Minneapolis: University of Minnesota Press.

———. 1993. *Writing Diaspora: Tactics of Intervention in Contemporary Cultural Studies*. Bloomington: Indiana University Press.

Chow, Tse-tsung. 1960. *The May Fourth Movement: Intellectual Revolution in Modern China*. Cambridge, Mass.: Harvard University Press.

Chuangzao she ziliao (CZSZL) 創造社資料 (Materials of the Creation Society). 1985. 2 vols. Fujian: Fujian renmin.

Craig, David, ed. 1975. *Marxists on Literature*. London: Penguin Books.

Dangdai Zhongguo wenyi lunji 當代中國文藝論集 (Collection of essays on contemporary Chinese literature). 1933. Shanghai: Lehua.

Dazhong wenyi congkan piping lunwen xuanji 大衆文藝叢刊批評論文選集 (Selected critical articles from *Mass Literature*). 1949. Beijing: Xin Zhongguo.

de Bary, Wm. Theodore. 1975. "Neo-Confucian Cultivation and the Seventeenth Century 'Enlightenment.' " In de Bary, ed., *The Unfolding of Neo-Confucianism*. New York: Columbia University Press, 141–216.

Deeney, John, ed. 1980. *Chinese and Western Comparative Literature Theory and Strategy*. Hong Kong: Hongkong University Press.

de Man, Paul. 1983. *Blindness and Insight: Essays in the Rhetoric of Contemporary Criticism*. Minneapolis: University of Minnesota Press.

Demetz, Peter. 1967. *Marx, Engels, and the Poets: Origins of Marxist Literary Criticism*. Chicago: University of Chicago Press.

Denton, Kirk A. 1992. "The Distant Shore: Nationalism in Yu Dafu's 'Sinking.' " *Chinese Literature: Essays, Articles and Reviews* 14 (Dec.): 107–23.

Dirlik, Arif. 1978. *Revolution and History: Origins of Marxist Historiography in China, 1919–1937*. Berkeley: University of California Press.

—————.1989. *The Origins of Chinese Communism*. New York: Oxford University Press.

Doleželová-Velingerová, Milena. 1977. "The Origins of Modern Chinese Literature." In Merle Goldman, ed., *Modern Chinese Literature in the May Fourth Era*. Cambridge, Mass.: Harvard University Press, 17–35.

—————, ed. 1980. *The Chinese Novel at the Turn of the Century*. Toronto: University of Toronto Press.

Duara, Prasenjit. 1993. "De-constructing the Chinese Nation." *The Australian Journal of Chinese Affairs* 30 (July): 1–26.

Eagleton, Terry. 1976. *Criticism and Ideology: A Study of Marxist Literary Theory*. London: Verso.

—————. 1990. *The Ideology of the Aesthetic*. Oxford: Basil Blackwell.

Eber, Irene, ed. 1986. *Confucianism: The Dynamics of Tradition*. New York: Macmillan.

Eide, Elisabeth. 1987. *China's Ibsen*. London: Curzon.

Ellmann, Richard, ed. 1965. *The Modern Tradition: Backgrounds of Modern Literature*. New York: Oxford University Press.

Elvin, Mark. 1978. *Self-Liberation and Self-Immolation in Modern Chinese Thought*. 39th Morrison Lecture. Canberra: Australian National University.

—————. 1986. "The Double Disavowal: The Attitudes of Radical Thinkers to the Chinese Tradition." In Shaw Yu-ming, ed., *China and Europe in the Twentieth Century*. Taipei: Institute of International Relations, National Cheng-chih University, 112–37.

—————. 1990. "The Collapse of Scriptural Confucianism." *Papers on Far Eastern History* 41 (Mar.): 45–76.

Erlich, Victor, ed. 1975. *Twentieth-Century Russian Literary Criticism*. New Haven: Yale University Press.

Ermolaev, Herman. 1963. *Soviet Literary Theory: 1917–1934*. Berkeley: University of California Press.

Ershi shiji Zhongguo xiaoshuo lilun ziliao 二十世紀中國小說理論資料 (Materials on twentieth-century Chinese fiction theory). 1989– . Chen Pingyuan and Xia Xiaohong, eds. 7 vols. Beijing: Beijing daxue.

Feigon, Lee. 1983. *Chen Duxiu: Founder of the Chinese Communist Party*. Princeton: Princeton University Press.

Furth, Charlotte, ed. 1976. *The Limits of Change: Essays on Conservative Alternatives in Republican China*. Cambridge, Mass.: Harvard University Press.

Gálik, Marián. 1969. *Mao Dun and Modern Chinese Literary Criticism*. Weisbaden: Verner Steiner.

———. 1980. *The Genesis of Modern Chinese Literary Criticism, 1917–1930*. London: Curzon Press.

———. 1986*a*. "The Comparative Aspects of the Genesis of Modern Chinese Literary Criticism." In Ying-hsiung Chou, ed., *The Chinese Text: Studies in Comparative Literature*. Hongkong: Chinese University Press, 177–90.

———. 1986*b*. *Milestones in Sino-Western Literary Confrontation (1891–1979)*. Weisbaden: Otto Harrassowitz.

———. 1990. "Interliterary and Intraliterary Aspects of the Study of Post–1918 Chinese Literature." In H. Goldblatt, ed., *Worlds Apart: Recent Chinese Writing and its Audiences*. Armonk: M. E. Sharpe, 231–45.

Geming wenxue lunzheng ziliao xuanbian (GMWX) 革命文學論爭資料選編 (Selected materials from the Revolutionary Literature debate). 1981. 2 vols. Beijing: Renmin wenxue.

Goldman, Merle. 1971. *Literary Dissent in Communist China*. New York: Antheneum.

———, ed. 1977. *Modern Chinese Literature in the May Fourth Era*. Cambridge, Mass.: Harvard University Press.

Grieder, Jerome. 1970. *Hu Shih and the Chinese Renaissance: Liberalism in the Chinese Revolution, 1913–1937*. Cambridge: Harvard University Press.

Gunn, Edward. 1980. *The Unwelcome Muse*. New York: Columbia University Press.

———. 1991. *Rewriting Chinese: Style and Innovation in Twentieth-Century Chinese Prose*. Stanford: Stanford University Press.

Guo Moruo 郭沫若. 1979. *Wenyi lunji* 文藝論集 (Essays on literature). Beijing: Renmin wenxue.

Guo Shaoyu 郭紹虞. 1955. *Zhongguo wenxue piping shi* 中國文學批評史 (History of Chinese literary criticism). Shanghai: Xin wenyi.

———, ed. 1979. *Zhongguo lidai wenlun xuan* 中國歷代文論選 (Selections of Chinese writings on literature). 2 vols. Shanghai: Shanghai guji.

Guofang wenxue lunzhan 國防文學論爭 (Polemics on national defense literature). 1936. Shanghai: Xinchao.

Hall, David L., and Roger Ames. 1987. *Thinking Through Confucius*. Albany: State University of New York Press.

Holm, David. 1982. "The Literary Rectification in Yan'an." In W. Kubin and R. Wagner, eds., *Essays in Modern Chinese Literature and Literary Criticism*. Bochum: Brockmeyer, 272–308.

———. 1991. *Art and Ideology in Revolutionary China*. Oxford: Clarendon Press.

Holzman, Donald. 1974. "Literary Criticism in China in the Third Century A.D." *Asiatische Studien / Etudes Asiatiques* 28, no. 2: 113–49.

Hsia, C. T. 1971. *A History of Modern Chinese Fiction*. New York: Columbia University Press.

———. 1978. "Yen Fu and Liang Ch'i-ch'ao as Advocates of New Fiction." In Adele Rickett, ed., *Chinese Approaches to Literature from Confucius to Liang Ch'i-ch'ao*. Princeton: Princeton University Press, 221–57.

Hsia, T. A. 1968. *The Gate of Darkness: Studies on the Leftist Literary Movement in China*. Seattle: University of Washington Press.

Hsu, Kai-yu, ed. 1980. *Literature of the People's Republic of China*. Bloomington: Indiana University Press.

Hu Feng 胡風. 1984. *Hu Feng pinglun ji* 胡風評論集 (Hu Feng's literary criticism). 3 vols. Beijing: Renmin wenxue.

Hu Shi (Hu Shih) 胡適. 1933. *The Chinese Renaissance*. The Haskell Lectures. Chicago: University of Chicago Press.

———. 1953. *Hu Shi wencun* 胡適文存 (Collected works of Hu Shi). 4 vols. Taibei: no publisher.

———, ed. 1976. *Wusi xin wenxue lunzhan ji huibian* 五四新文學論戰集彙編 (A compendium of writings from the debates of May Fourth new literature). 3 vols. Taibei: Changge.

———. 1984. *Changshi ji* 嘗試集 (Experiments). Beijing: Renmin wenxue; reprint of 1934 ed.

Huters, Theodore. 1982. *Qian Zhongshu*. Boston: Twayne Publishers.

———. 1984a. "Critical Ground: The Transformation of the May Fourth Era." In Bonnie S. McDougall, ed., *Popular Chinese Literature and Performing Arts in the People's Republic of China 1949–1979*. Berkeley: University of California Press, 54–80.

———. 1984b. "Blossoms in the Snow: Lu Xun and the Dilemma of Modern Chinese Literature." *Modern China* 10, no. 1 (Jan.): 49–77.

———. 1987. "From Writing to Literature: The Development of Late Qing Theories of Prose." *Harvard Journal of Asiatic Studies* 47, no. 1 (June): 50–96.

———. 1988. "A New Way of Writing: The Possibility for Literature in Late Qing China, 1895–1908." *Modern China* 14, no. 3 (July): 243–76.

———. 1993. "Ideologies of Realism in Modern China: The Hard Imperatives of Imported Theory." In Liu Kang and Xiaobing Tang, eds., *Politics, Ideology, and Literary Discourse in Modern China: Theoretical Interventions and Cultural Critique*. Durham: Duke University Press, 147–73.

Jameson, Fredric. 1986. "Third World Literature in the Era of Multinational Capitalism." *Social Text: Theory/Culture/Ideology* 15 (Fall): 65–88.

————. 1991. *Postmodernism, or, The Cultural Logic of Late Capitalism*. Durham: Duke University Press.

Jiu Ge 九歌. 1989. *Zhuti lun wenyixue* 主體論文藝學 (Subjective literary studies). Beijing: Zhongguo shehui kexue.

Judd, Ellen. 1985. "Prelude to the 'Yan'an Talks': Problems in Transforming a Literary Intelligentsia." *Modern China* 11, no. 4 (July): 377–408.

Jullien, François. 1985. *La valeur allusive: des catégories originales de l'interprétation poétique dans la tradition chinoise (Contribution à une refléxion sur l'altérité interculturelle)*. Paris: Ecole Française d'Extrême Orient.

Jusdanis, Gregory. 1991. *Belated Modernity and Aesthetic Culture: Inventing National Literature*. Minneapolis: University of Minnesota Press.

Keene, Donald. 1984. *Dawn to the West: Japanese Literature in the Modern Era: Poetry, Drama, Criticism*. New York: Henry Holt.

Kockum, Keiko. 1990. *Japanese Achievement, Chinese Inspiration: A Study of the Japanese Influence on the Modernisation of the Late Qing Novel*. Stockholm: Orientaliska Studier.

Kubin, Wolfgang, and Rudolf Wagner, eds. 1982. *Essays in Modern Chinese Literature and Literary Criticism*. Bochum: Brockmeyer.

Lan Hai 藍海. 1981. *Zhongguo kangzhan wenyi shi* 中國抗戰文藝史 (The history of literature and the arts of the Chinese War of Resistance). Ji'nan: Shandong wenyi.

Larson, Wendy. 1991. *Literary Authority and the Modern Chinese Writer :Ambivalence and Autobiography*. Durham: Duke University Press.

Lee, Leo Ou-fan. 1973. *The Romantic Generation of Modern Chinese Writers*. Cambridge, Mass.: Harvard University Press.

————, ed. 1985a. *Lu Xun and His Legacy*. Berkeley: University of California Press.

————. 1985b. "Romantic Individualism in Modern Chinese Literature: Some General Explanations." In Donald Munro, ed., *Individualism and Holism: Studies in Confucian and Taoist Values*. Ann Arbor: Center for Chinese Studies, University of Michigan.

————. 1987. *Voices from the Iron House*. Bloomington: Indiana University Press.

————. 1990. "In Search of Modernity: Some Reflections on a New Mode of Consciousness in Twentieth-Century Chinese History and Literature." In P. Cohen and M. Goldman, eds., *Ideas Across Cultures: Essays on Chinese Thought in Honor of Benjamin I. Schwartz*. Cambridge, Mass.: Council on East Asian Studies, 109–35.

Lee, Mabel. 1974. "Liang Ch'i-ch'ao (1873–1929) and the Literary Revolution of Late Ch'ing." In A. R. Davis, ed., *Search for Identity: Modern Literature and Creative Arts in Asia*. Sydney: Angus and Robertson.

Legge, James, tr. 1979. *The Four Books*. Taibei: Culture Book Co.; reprint.

Lenin, V. I. 1970. *On Literature and Art*. Moscow: Progress Publishers.

Levenson, Joseph R. 1965. *Confucian China and Its Modern Fate: A Trilogy*. Berkeley: University of California Press.

Li Helin 李何林. 1947. *Jin ershi nian Zhongguo wenyi sichao lun* 近二十年中國文藝思潮論 (Chinese literary trends of the past twenty years). Dalian: Guanghua shudian.

———. 1984. *Zhongguo wenyi lunzhan* 中國文藝論戰 (Chinese literary debates). Shanghai: Shanghai shudian.

Liang Shiqiu 梁實秋. 1927. *Langmande yu gudiande* 浪漫的與古典的 (The romantic and the classical). Shanghai.

"Liangge kouhao" lunzheng ziliao xuanbian (LGKH) 兩個口號論爭選編 (Selected materials from the Two Slogans debate). 1982. Beijing: Renmin wenxue.

Lidai shihua cihua xuan 歷代詩話詞話選 (Selections from critical comments on poetry and lyrics). Wuhan: Wuhan daxue, 1984.

Lin, Yü-sheng. 1973. "Radical Iconoclasm in the May Fourth Period and the Future of Chinese Liberalism." In Benjamin I. Schwartz, ed., *Reflections on the May Fourth Movement: A Symposium*. Cambridge, Mass.: East Asian Research Center, Harvard University, 23–58.

———. 1979. *The Crisis of Chinese Consciousness: Radical Anti-traditionalism in the May Fourth Era*. Madison: University of Wisconsin Press.

———. 1989. "Maichu Wusi yi guangda Wusi—jianda Wang Yuanhua xiansheng" 邁出五四以廣大五四：簡答王元化先生 (Stepping beyond the May Fourth to enhance the May Fourth: a brief response to Mr. Wang Yuanhua). In *Wusi: duoyuan de fansi* 五四：多源的反思. Hongkong: Sanlian, 28–45.

Lin, Yutang. 1967. *The Chinese Theory of Art*. New York: Putnam.

Link, Perry. 1981. *Mandarin Ducks and Butterflies: Popular Fiction in Early Twentieth Century Chinese Cities*. Berkeley: University of California Press.

Literature and Art by Karl Marx and Frederick Engels: Selections from Their Writings. 1947. New York: International Publishers.

Liu, James J. Y. 1962. *The Art of Chinese Poetry*. Chicago: University of Chicago Press.

———. 1975. *Chinese Theories of Literature*. Chicago: University of Chicago Press.

———. 1977. "Toward a Synthesis of Chinese and Western Theories of Literature." *Journal of Chinese Philosophy* 4: 1–24.

———. 1982. *The Interlingual Critic: Interpreting Chinese Poetry*. Bloomington: Indiana University Press.

———. 1988. *Language–Paradox–Poetics: A Chinese Perspective.* Princeton: Princeton University Press.

Liu, Lydia H. 1993. "Translingual Practice: The Discourse of Individualism Between China and the West." *Positions* 1, no. 1: 160–93.

Liu Xie (Hsieh). 1983. *The Literary Mind and the Carving of the Dragon,* bilingual ed. Tr. Vincent Yu-chung Shih. Hongkong: Chinese University Press.

Lovejoy, Arthur O. 1955. *The Revolt Against Dualism: An Inquiry Concerning the Existence of Ideas.* La Salle: Open Court.

Lu Xun 魯迅. 1980. *Lu Xun: Selected Works.* 4 vols. Beijing: Foreign Languages Press.

———. 1981*a. Lu Xun quanji* 魯迅全集 (Complete works of Lu Xun). 16 vols. Beijing: Renmin wenxue.

———. 1981*b. La Tombe.* Tr. Michelle Loi. Paris: Acropole.

Lukács, Georg. 1973. *Marxism and Human Liberation: Essays on History, Culture and Revolution.* New York: Delta Publishing.

———. 1979. *The Meaning of Contemporary Realism.* London: Merlin Press.

Luo Genze 羅根澤. n.d. *Zhongguo wenxue piping shi* 中國文學批評史 (The history of Chinese literary criticism). Dianwen.

Lynn, Richard. 1975. "Orthodoxy and Enlightenment: Wang Shih-chen's Theory of Poetry and Its Antecedents." In Wm. Theodore de Bary, ed., *The Unfolding of Neo-Confucianism.* New York: Columbia University Press, 217–70.

Lyotard, Jean-François. 1984. *The Postmodern Condition: A Report on Knowledge.* Minneapolis: University of Minnesota Press.

Malmqvist, Goran, ed. 1975. *Modern Chinese Literature and Its Social Context.* Stockholm: Nobel Symposium.

Mao Dun 茅盾. 1981. *Mao Dun wenyi zalun ji* 茅盾文藝雜論集 (A collection of Mao Dun's miscellaneous essays on literature and the arts). 2 vols. Shanghai: Shanghai wenyi.

———. 1983. *Mao Dun zhuanji* 茅盾專集 (Collection of writings by and about Mao Dun). 4 vols. Fuzhou: Fujian renmin.

Mao Tse-tung. 1975. *Selected Works of Mao Tse-tung.* 5 vols. Beijing: Foreign Languages Press.

Martin, Helmut, and Jeffrey Kinkley, eds. 1992. *Modern Chinese Writers: Self-Portrayals.* Armonk: M. E. Sharpe.

Matlaw, Ralph E., ed. 1976. *Belinsky, Chernyshevsky, and Dobrolyubov: Selected Criticism.* Bloomington: Indiana University Press.

McDougall, Bonnie. 1971. *The Introduction of Western Literary Theories into Modern China.* Tokyo: Center for East Asian Cultural Studies.

———. 1975. "On the Social Implications of the Aesthetic Theories of Zhu

Guangqian." In Goran Malmqvist, ed., *Modern Chinese Literature in Its Social Context*. Stockholm: Nobel Symposium, 76–122.

———, tr. 1980. *Mao Zedong's "Talks at the Yan'an Conference on Literature and Art": A Translation of the 1943 Text with Commentary*. Ann Arbor: Center for Chinese Studies.

Meisner, Maurice. 1970. *Li Ta-chao and the Origins of Chinese Communism*. New York: Antheneum.

Metzger, Thomas A. 1977. *Escape from Predicament: Neo-Confucianism and China's Evolving Political Culture*. New York: Columbia University Press.

Miller, Lucien. 1979. "Allegory and Personality in Modern Chinese Literary Criticism: Chou Tso-jen and Wang Kuo-wei." *Tamkang Review* 9, no. 4 (Summer): 379–406.

Miner, Earl. 1983. "The Grounds of Mimetic and Nonmimetic Art: The Western Sister Arts in a Japanese Mirror." In Richard Wendorf, ed., *Articulate Images: The Sister Arts from Hogarth to Tennyson*. Minneapolis: University of Minnesota Press.

———, ed. 1985. *Principles of Japanese Classical Literature*. Princeton: Princeton University Press.

Murck, Christian, ed. 1976. *Artists and Traditions: Uses of the Past in Chinese Culture*. Princeton: Princeton University Press.

Norbu, Dawa. 1992. *Culture and the Politics of Third World Nationalism*. London: Routledge.

Owen, Stephen. 1985. *Traditional Chinese Poetry and Poetics: Omen of the World*. Madison: University of Wisconsin Press.

———. 1992. *Readings in Chinese Literary Thought*. Cambridge, Mass.: Harvard Council on East Asian Studies.

Parkes, Graham, ed. 1991. *Nietzsche and Asian Thought*. Chicago: University of Chicago Press.

Pickowicz, Paul. 1981. *Marxist Literary Thought in China: The Influence of Ch'u Ch'iu-pai*. Berkeley: University of California Press.

Plaks, Andrew. 1977. "Towards a Critical Theory of Chinese Narrative." In idem, ed., *Chinese Narrative: Critical and Theoretical Essays*. Princeton: Princeton University Press.

———. 1987. *The Four Masterworks of the Ming: Ssu ta ch'i-shu*. Princeton: Princeton University Press.

Plekhanov, Georg. 1953. *Art and Social Life*. London: Lawrence and Wishart.

Pollard, D. E. 1973. *A Chinese Look at Literature: The Literary Values of Chou Tso-jen in Relation to Tradition*. London: C. Hurst.

Prušek, Jaroslav. 1970. *Chinese History and Literature*. Dordrecht, Holland: D. Reidel.

———. 1980. *The Lyrical and the Epic.* Ed. Leo Ou-fan Lee. Bloomington: Indiana University Press.

Qian, Liqun. 1984. "Lu Xun and Zhou Zuoren: A Comparative Study of the Evolution of Their Literary Views." *Social Sciences in China* 3: 123–46.

Qu Qiubai 瞿秋白. 1986. *Qu Qiubai wenji* 瞿秋白文集 (Collected works of Qu Qiubai). 5 vols. Beijing: Renmin wenxue.

Rickett, Adele. 1967. *Wang Kuo-wei's "Jen-chien tz'u-hua": a Study in Chinese Literary Criticism.* Ph. D dissertation. University of Pennsylvania.

———. 1977. *Wang Kuo-wei's "Jen-chien tz'u-hua": a Study in Chinese Literary Criticism.* Hongkong: Hongkong University Press.

———, ed. 1978. *Chinese Approaches to Literature from Confucius to Liang Ch'i-ch'ao.* Princeton: Princeton University Press.

Rolston, David, ed. 1990. *How to Read the Chinese Novel.* Princeton: Princeton University Press.

Roy, David. 1971. *Kuo Mo-jo: The Early Years.* Cambridge: Harvard University Press.

Said, Edward W. 1994. *Culture and Imperialism.* New York: Vintage Books.

Sanshi niandai zuoyi wenyi ziliao xuanbian 三十年代左翼文藝資料選編 (Selected research materials on leftist literature and arts of the 1930s). 1980. Chengdu: Sichuan remin.

Schwarcz, Vera. 1986. *The Chinese Enlightenment: Intellectuals and the Legacy of the May Fourth Movement of 1919.* Berkeley: University of California Press.

Schwartz, Benjamin. 1964. *In Search of Wealth and Power: Yen Fu and the West.* Cambridge, Mass.: Harvard University Press.

Shea, G.T. 1964. *Leftwing Literature in Japan: A Brief History of the Proletarian Literature Movement.* Tokyo: Hosei University Press.

Shih, Vincent Y. C. 1977. "Literature and Art in *The Analects.*" *Renditions* 8 (Autumn): 5–38.

Spence, Jonathan D. 1990. *The Search for Modern China.* New York: Norton.

Su Guangwen 蘇光文. 1985. *Kangzhan wenxue gaiguan* 抗戰文藝概觀 (An overview of War of Resistance literature). Chongqing: Xi'nan shifan daxue.

———. 1986. *Kangzhan wenyi jicheng* 抗戰文藝記程 (A chronology of literature and arts during the War of Resistance). Chongqing: Xi'nan shifan daxue.

Su Wen 蘇汶, ed. 1933. *Wenyi ziyou lunbian ji* 文藝自由論辯集 (Collection of essays from the Literary Freedom debate). Shanghai: Shanghai shudian.

Sun, Lung-kee. 1986–87. "Chinese Intellectuals' Notion of 'Epoch' (*Shidai*) in the Post-May Fourth Era." *Chinese Studies in History* 20, no. 2 (Winter): 44–74.

Tagore, Amitendranath. 1967. *Literary Debates in Modern China, 1918–1937.* Tokyo: Centre for East Asian Cultural Studies.

Tan Bi'an 譚彼岸. 1956. *Wan Qing de baihuawen yundong* 晚清的白話文運動 (The vernacular movement in the late Qing). Wuhan: Hubei renmin.

Tolstoy, Leo. 1929. *What is Art? and Essays on Art.* London: Humphrey Milford.

Touponce, William. 1981. "Straw Dogs: A Deconstructive Reading of the Problem of Mimesis in James Liu's *Chinese Theories of Literature.*" *Tamkang Review* 1 (Summer): 359–90.

Trotsky, Leon. 1966. *Literature and Revolution.* Ann Arbor: University of Michigan Press.

Tsubouchi, Shōyō. 1981. *The Essence of the Novel.* Tr. N. R. Twine. Queensland: Department of Japanese, University of Queensland.

Tu, Wei-ming. 1976. " 'Inner Experience': The Basis of Creativity in Neo-Confucian Thinking." In Christian Murck, ed., *Artists and Tradition: Uses of the Past in Chinese Culture.* Princeton: Princeton University Press, 9–15.

———. 1989. *Centrality and Commonality: An Essay on Confucian Religiousness.* Albany: State University of New York Press.

Walker, Janet. 1988. "On the Applications of the Term 'Novel' to Modern Non-Western Lengthy Fictions." *Yearbook of Comparative and General Literature* 37: 47–68.

Wang Yao 王瑤. 1953. *Zhongguo xin wenxue shigao* 中國新文學史搞 (A draft history of modern Chinese literature). Shanghai: Xin wenyi.

Wen Tianxing 文天行. 1985. *Guotongqu kangzhan wenyi yundong da shiji* 國統區抗戰文藝運動大史紀 (Chronicle of the literary movements in the Guomindang area during the War of Resistance). Chengdu: Sichuan sheng shehui kexueyuan.

———. 1988. *Guotongqu kangzhan wenyi yundong shigao* 國統區抗戰文藝運動史稿 (A draft history of the literary movements in the Guomindang area during the War of Resistance). Chengdu: Sichuan jiaoyu.

Wen Yiduo 聞一多. 1948. *Wen Yiduo quanji* 聞一多全集 (Complete works of Wen Yiduo). 4 vols. Shanghai: Kaiming.

Wenxue de 'Minzu xingshi' taolun ziliao 文學的民族形式討論資料 (Materials on the discussion of popular forms in literature). 1986. Ed. Xu Naixiang. Nanning: Guangxi renmin.

Wenxue yundong shiliao xuan (WXYDSLX) 文學運動史料選 (Selections of historical materials of literary movements). 1979. 5 vols. Shanghai: Shanghai jiaoyu.

Williams, Raymond. 1977. *Marxism and Literature*. Oxford: Oxford University Press.

Wimsatt, William K., and Cleanth Brooks. 1983. *Literary Criticism: A Short History*. 2 vols. Chicago: University of Chicago Press, reprint.

Wolff, Ernst. 1971. *Chou Tso-jen*. New York: Twayne.

Wong, Siu-kit. 1983. *Early Chinese Literary Criticism*. Hongkong: Joint Publishing.

Wong, Wang-chi. 1991. *Politics and Literature in Shanghai: the Chinese League of Left-Wing Writers, 1930–1936*. Manchester: Manchester University Press.

Wu Mi 吳密. 1922. "Xieshizhuyi liubi" 寫實主義流弊 (Deficiencies of realism) *Zhonghua xinbao*, Oct. 22.

Wusi yundong wenxuan 五四運動文選 (Selected documents of the May Fourth movement).1979. Beijing: Sanlian.

Xian jieduan de Zhongguo wenyi wenti 先階段的中國文藝問題 (Issues in the literature of China's first stage). 1937. Ed. Yang Jinhao. Shanghai: Beixin.

Xinhai geming qian shinian jianqi lunwen ji (XHGM) 辛亥革命前十年間期論文集 (Essays from the period of the ten years preceding the 1911 revolution). 1977. 3 vols. Beijing: Sanlian.

Xu Huaizhong 許懷中. 1990. *Zhongguo xiandai xiaoshuo lilun piping de bianqian* 中國現代小說理論批評的變遷 (The development of modern Chinese fiction theory and criticism). Shanghai: Shanghai wenyi.

Yan Jiayan 嚴家炎. 1987. *Lun xiandai xiaoshuo yu wenyi sixiang* 論現代小說與文藝思想 (On modern fiction and literary thought). Changsha: Hunan renmin.

———. 1989. *Zhongguo xiandai xiaoshuo shi liupai* 中國現代小說史流派 (History of the schools of modern Chinese fiction). Beijing: Renmin wenxue.

Yang Yi 楊義. 1986. *Zhongguo xiandai xiaoshuo shi* 中國現代小說史 (History of modern Chinese fiction). Beijing: Renmin wenxue.

Yang, Zhou-han. 1983. "The Mirror and the Jig-saw: A Major Difference Between Current Chinese and Western Critical Attitudes." *Representations* 3 (Fall): 101–7.

Ye Shengtao 葉聖陶. 1982. *Ye Shengtao lun chuangzuo* 葉聖陶論創作 (Ye Shengtao on creativity). Shanghai: Shanghai wenyi.

Yeh, Michelle. 1987. "Metaphor and *Bi*: Western and Chinese Poetics." *Comparative Literature*. 39, no. 5 (Summer): 237–54.

———. 1988. "Taoism and Modern Chinese Poetry." *Journal of Chinese Philosophy* 15: 173–97.

———. 1991. *Modern Chinese Poetry: Theory and Practice Since 1917*. New Haven: Yale University Press.

Bibliography 535

Yip, Wai-lim. 1976. *Chinese Poetry: Major Modes and Genres*. Berkeley: University of California Press.

———. 1993. *Diffusion of Differences: Dialogues between Chinese and Western Poetics*. Berkeley: University of California Press.

Yu Dafu 郁達夫. 1982. *Yu Dafu wenji* 郁達夫文集 (Collected writings of Yu Dafu). 12 vols. Guangzhou: Huacheng.

Yu, Pauline. 1983. "Allegory, Allegoresis, and the *Classic of Poetry*." *Harvard Journal of Asiatic Studies* 43, no. 2 (Dec): 377–412.

———. 1987. *The Reading of Imagery in the Chinese Poetic Tradition*. Princeton: Princeton University Press.

———. 1988. "Alienation Effects: Comparative Literature and the Chinese Tradition." In Clayton Koelb and Susan Noakes, eds., *The Comparative Perspective on Literature: Approaches to Theory and Practice*. Ithaca: Cornell University Press, 162–75.

Yü, Ying-shih, et al. 1994. "Roundtable Discussion: Wm. Theodore de Bary. *The Trouble with Confucianism*." *China Review International* 1, no. 1 (Spring): 9–47.

Yuanyang hudie pai wenxue ziliao (YYHDP) 鴛鴦蝴蝶派文學資料 (Literary materials of the Mandarin Ducks and Butterfly school). 1984. 2 vols. Fuzhou: Fujian renmin.

Yuwen lunzhan de xian jieduan 語文論戰的先階段 (The first stage in the polemics on language). 1934. Ed. Wen Yi. Shanghai: Tianma.

Zhang, Jingyuan. 1992. *Psychoanalysis in China: Literary Transformations, 1919–1949*. Ithaca: Cornell University, East Asia Program.

Zhang, Longxi. 1992. *The Tao and the Logos: Literary Hermeneutics, East and West*. Durham: Duke University Press.

———. 1993. "Out of the Cultural Ghetto: Theory, Politics, and the Study of Chinese Literature." *Modern China* 19, no. 1: 71–101.

Zhongguo jindai wenlun xuan (ZGJDWLX) 中國近代文論選 (Selected writings on literature from modern China). 1962. 2 vols. Beijing: Renmin wenxue.

Zhongguo xiandai shi lun 中國現代詩論 (Essays on modern Chinese poetry). 1986. 2 vols. Ed. Yang Kuanghan and Lui Fuchun. Guangzhou: Huacheng.

Zhongguo xiandai wenlun xuan (ZGXDWLX) 中國現代文論選 (Selections of modern Chinese literary essays). 1984. 2 vols. Guizhou: Guizhou renmin.

Zhongguo xiandai wenxue cankao ziliao (ZGXDWXCKZL) 中國現代文學史參考資料 (Research materials on the history of modern Chinese literature). 1959. 3 vols. Beijing: Gaodeng jiaoyu.

Zhongguo xiandai wenxue qikan mulu 中國現代文學期刊目錄 (Catalogue of modern Chinese literary periodicals). 1961. Shanghai: Shanghai wenyi.

Zhongguo xiandai wenxue shetuan liupai 中國現代文學社團流派 (Societies and schools of modern Chinese literature). 2 vols. Ed. Jia Zhifang. Jiangsu: Jiangsu jiaoyu.

Zhongguo xin wenxue daxi 中國新文學大系 (Compendium of modern Chinese literature). 1935. 10 vols. Ed. Zhao Jiabi. Hongkong: Xianggang wenxue yanjiu; Shanghai: Liangyou, 1980 reprint.

Zhongguo xin wenxue daxi xubian 中國新文學大系續編 (Supplement to the compendium of modern Chinese literature). 1968. 10 vols. Hongkong: Xianggang wenxue yanjiu.

Zhongguo xin wenxue daxi, 1927–37 中國新文學大系 (Compendium of modern Chinese literature). 1987. 20 vols. Shanghai: Shanghai wenyi.

Zhongguo xin wenxue daxi, 1937–1949 中國新文學大系 (Compendium of modern Chinese literature). 1990. 20 vols. Shanghai: Shanghai wenyi.

Zhou Yang 周揚. 1984. *Zhou Yang wenji* 周揚文集 (Collected writings of Zhou Yang). 2 vols. Bejing: Renmin wenxue.

Zhou Zuoren 周作人. 1932. *Zhongguo xin wenxue de yuanliu* 中國新文學的源流 (The origins of new Chinese literature). Shanghai: Shanghai shudian; 1988 reprint.

———. 1972. *Zhou Zuoren lunwen ji* 周作人論文集 (Collected essays of Zhou Zuoren). Hongkong: Huiwen ge shudian.

———. 1984. *Zhou Zuoren zaoqi sanwen xuan* 周作人早期散文選 (Selected essays from Zhou Zuoren's early period). Shanghai: Shanghai wenyi.

Zhu Guangqian 朱光潛. 1987. *Zhu Guangqian quanji* 朱光潛全集 (Complete works of Zhu Guangqian). 5 vols. Anhui: Anhui jiaoyu.

———. 1982. *Zhu Guangqian meixue wenji* 朱光潛美學文集 (Zhu Guangqian's collection writings on aesthetics). 3 vols. Shanghai: Shanghai wenyi.

———. (Chu Kuang-tsien). 1987. *The Psychology of Tragedy*. Hongkong: Joint Publishing.

Zhu Ziqing 朱自清. 1942. *Zhu Ziqing wenji* 朱自清文集 (Collected writings of Zhu Ziqing). 4 vols. Shanghai: Kaiming shudian.

Translators

Julia F. Andrews (The Ohio State University)
Alison Bailey (School of Oriental and African Studies, University of London)
John Berninghausen (Middlebury College)
Catherine Pease Campbell (Western Washington University)
David Y. Ch'en (The Ohio State University)
Yu-shih Chen (University of Minnesota)
Gek Nai Cheng (University of Malaya)
Kirk A. Denton (The Ohio State University)
Gilbert C. F. Fong (The Chinese University of Hongkong)
Paul Foster (The Ohio State University)
Howard Goldblatt (University of Colorado, Boulder)
Michael Gotz
Donald Holoch (York University, Toronto)
Theodore Huters (University of California, Los Angeles)
Nicholas A. Kaldis (The Ohio State University)
Richard King (University of Victoria, British Columbia)

Jeffrey C. Kinkley (St. John's University)
Haili Kong (University of Colorado, Boulder)
Wendy Larson (University of Oregon)
Sherry Mou (Wellesley College)
Ruth Nybakken (Ohio University)
Paul Pickowicz (University of California, Los Angeles)
Randy Trumbull (Wellesley College)
Shu-ying Tsau (York University, Toronto)
Philip F. Williams (Arizona State University)
Ernst Wolff
Kam-ming Wong (University of Georgia, Athens)
Timothy Wong (The Ohio State University)
Yenna Wu (Univeristy of California, Riverside)
Jane Parish Yang (Lawrence University, Appleton)
Michelle Yeh (University of California, Davis)
Longxi Zhang (University of California, Riverside)

Index

In this index an "f" after a number indicates a separate reference on the next page, and an "ff" indicates separate references on the next two pages. A continuous discussion over two or more pages is indicated by a span of page numbers, e.g., "57-59." *Passim* is used for a cluster of references in a close but not consecutive sequence. Numbers in bold indicate entries in the Glossary.

Library of Congress Cataloging-in-Publication Data

Modern Chinese literary thought : writings on literature,
1893–1945 / edited by Kirk A. Denton
      p. cm.
Translated from various Chinese sources.
Includes bibliographical references and index.
ISBN 0-8047-2558-6. —ISBN 0-8047-2559-4 (pbk.)
1. Chinese literature—20th century—History and
criticism—Theory, etc. I. Denton, Kirk A., 1955–
PL2302.M63   1995
895.1'509—dc20
95-1269   CIP

This book is printed on acid-free paper

Original printing 1996